# THE OAK AND THE CALF

*Also by Aleksandr I. Solzhenitsyn*

*Aleksandr I. Solzhenitsyn*

# THE OAK
# AND THE CALF

## SKETCHES OF LITERARY LIFE
## IN THE SOVIET UNION

*Translated from the Russian by* HARRY WILLETTS

HARPER & ROW, PUBLISHERS

NEW YORK

Cambridge
Hagerstown
Philadelphia
San Francisco

London
Mexico City
São Paulo
Sydney

1817

# ACKNOWLEDGMENT

The translator wishes to express his warmest gratitude to Alexis Klimoff of Vassar College, who read the translation with minute care and whose suggestions were invariably helpful and frequently invaluable.

A limited first edition of this book has been privately printed by The Franklin Library.

This book was first published in Russian under the title Бодался Теленок с Дубом.

Portions of this work originally appeared in *Life* magazine, *The Kenyon Review*, and *The New York Times Book Review*..

FIRST HARPER & ROW EDITION

*Designer: Sidney Feinberg*

Library of Congress Cataloging in Publication Data

Solzhenitsyn, Aleksandr Isaevich, 1918-
  The oak and the calf.
  Translation of Bodalsia telenok s dubom.
  Includes index.
  1. Solzhenitsyn, Aleksandr Isaevich, 1918-
—Biography. 2. Authors, Russian—20th century—
Biography. 3. Solzhenitsyn, Aleksandr Isaevich,
1918-    —Contemporary Russia. I. Title.
PG3488.O4Z49513     891.73'44 [B]     79-1685
ISBN 0-06-014014-3

80 81 82 83 84 10 9 8 7 6 5 4 3 2 1

# Contents

# By Way of Explanation

There exists a large body of so-called *secondary* literature: literature *on* literature, literature apropos of literature, literature begotten by literature (new works which would never have been born if something similar had not existed beforehand). As a professional writer, I myself like reading such things. But I rate them considerably lower than works of primary literature. Besides, so much has been written, and people have less and less time for reading: should we, in all conscience, be writing memoirs, and literary memoirs at that?

I had indeed never expected that I myself, in the forty-ninth year of my life, would dare to piece together these scrappy memoirs. But two circumstances have combined to set me on this course.

One is the crippling and cowardly secretiveness from which all our country's misfortunes come. We are afraid not only to say openly, in speech or in writing or even in conversation with friends, what we think and how things really were; we are afraid even to confide it privately to paper, for the headsman's ax hangs still over the neck of every one of us, and may descend at any moment. How much longer this secretiveness will last there is no knowing: many of us may be decapitated before it ends, and what we have kept to ourselves will perish with us.

The second circumstance is that a noose was draped around my neck two years ago, but not drawn tight, and I want to see what will happen next spring if I jerk my head slightly. Whether the noose will break or I shall be strangled cannot with any certainty be foreseen.

Besides, I am at this moment between two great boulders: one of them I have rolled out of my way; the second daunts me, so that I find myself with a short breathing space.

I have decided that perhaps it is time to explain a few things just in case.

*April 1967*

# The Writer Underground

Underground is where you expect to find revolutionaries. But not writers.

For the writer intent on truth, life never was, never is (and never will be!), easy: his like have suffered every imaginable harassment—defamation, duels, a shattered family life, financial ruin or lifelong unrelieved poverty, the madhouse, jail. While those who wanted for nothing, like Lev Tolstoy, have suffered worse torments in the claws of conscience.

All the same, to plunge underground, to make it your concern not to win the world's recognition—Heaven forbid!—but on the contrary to shun it: this variant of the writer's lot is peculiarly our own, purely Russian, Russian and Soviet! It is now certain that Radishchev* was writing something important in the last years of his life, and that he prudently kept it well hidden—hidden so well that we won't find it now and will never know what it was. Pushkin, too, cleverly enciphered the tenth chapter of *Eugene Onegin,* as everyone knows. That Chaadayev practiced cryptography for years is not so generally known. He distributed his manuscript sheet by sheet among a number of books in his large library. Of course, this is no way of hiding things if the Lubyanka comes looking; however many books there may be, it can always muster enough operatives to take every book by its spine and patiently worry it. (Never hide things in books, my friends!) But the Tsar's gendarmes had no eyes for such things. Chaadayev died, but his library remained intact into the postrevolutionary era, and the disjoined pages which no

---

*Asterisks refer to Publisher's Notes, which start on page 539.

one knew of languished within it. In the twenties they were discovered, assembled and studied, and in the thirties prepared at last for publication, by D. I. Shakhovskoy. But then Shakhovskoy was *put inside* (never to emerge) and Chaadayev's manuscripts are to this day kept secret in Pushkin House: publication is now forbidden because of their *reactionary character!*

And so Chaadayev holds an unbeaten record—110 years after his death!—as the longest-suppressed Russian writer! What a piece of writing this must have been!

Much freer times followed. Russian writers no longer wrote "for the desk drawer" but could publish whatever they liked (and only critics and publicists used carefully chosen Aesopian language). So freely did they write, so free were they to rock the framework of the state, that Russian literature, no other, nurtured all those young people who conceived a hatred for the Tsar and the gendarmes, took up revolution, and carried it through.

But once across the threshold of the revolutions it had summoned into being, literature stopped short; it found itself not in the sparkling daylight beneath the open sky, but under a sloping ceiling, in the narrowing space between converging walls. Soviet writers very quickly discovered that not every book can *get through.* Ten years or so later, they had discovered that royalties may take the form of barred windows and barbed wire. Once more writers started concealing what they had written, although they did not utterly despair of seeing their books in print before they died.

Before I was arrested, I knew very little about such things. I drifted into literature unthinkingly, without really knowing what I needed from it, or what I could do for it. I just felt depressed because it was so difficult, I thought, to find fresh subjects for stories. I hate to think what sort of writer I would have become (for I would have gone on writing) if I had not been *put inside.*

Once arrested, once I had spent two years in prisons and camps, depressed now by the mountainous overabundance of subjects, I accepted as effortlessly as the air I breathed, accepted with all the other unchallengeable realities before my eyes, the knowledge that not only would no one ever publish me, but a single line could cost me my life. Without hesitation, without inner debate, I entered into the inheritance of every modern Russian writer intent on the truth: I must write simply to ensure that it was not all forgotten, that posterity might someday come to know of it. Publication in my own lifetime I must shut out of my mind, out of my dreams.

I put away my idle dream. And in its place there was only the surety that my work would not be in vain, that it would someday smite the heads I had in my sights, and that those who received its invisible emanations would understand. I no more rebelled against lifelong silence than against the lifelong impossibility of freeing my feet from the pull of gravity. As I finished one piece after another, at first in the camps, then in exile, then after rehabilitation, first verses, then plays, and later prose works too, I had only one desire: to keep all these things out of sight and myself with them.

In the camp this meant committing my verse—many thousands of lines—to memory. To help me with this I improvised decimal counting beads and, in transit prisons, broke up matchsticks and used the fragments as tallies. As I approached the end of my sentence I grew more confident of my powers of memory, and began writing down and memorizing prose—dialogue at first, but then, bit by bit, whole densely written passages. My memory found room for them! It worked. But more and more of my time—in the end as much as one week every month—went into the regular repetition of all I had memorized.

Then came exile, and right at the beginning of my exile, cancer. In autumn 1953 it looked very much as though I had only a few months to live. In December the doctors—comrades in exile—confirmed that I had at most three weeks left.

All that I had memorized in the camps ran the risk of extinction together with the head that held it.

This was a dreadful moment in my life: to die on the threshold of freedom, to see all I had written, all that gave meaning to my life thus far, about to perish with me. The peculiarities of the Soviet postal censorship made it impossible for me to cry out for help: Come quickly, take what I have written, save it! You can't very well appeal to strangers anyway. My friends were all in camps themselves. My mother was dead. My wife had married again. All the same, I sent for her to say goodbye, thinking that she might take my manuscripts away with her, but she did not come.

In those last few weeks that the doctors had promised me I could not escape from my work in school, but in the evening and at night, kept awake by pain, I hurriedly copied things out in tiny handwriting, rolled them, several pages at a time, into tight cylinders and squeezed these into a champagne bottle. I buried the bottle in my garden—and set off for Tashkent to meet the new year (1954) and to die.

I did not die, however. (With a hopelessly neglected and acutely malignant tumor, this was a divine miracle; I could see no other explanation. Since then, all the life that has been given back to me has not been mine in the full sense: it is built around a purpose.) That spring as I deliriously took possession of the life restored to me (perhaps only for two or three years?), in the first flush of my happiness I wrote *The Republic of Labor*. This I did not try to memorize: for the first time I knew the joy of not having to burn a work piecemeal as I learned it by heart; the joy of writing *Finis* with the beginning still undestroyed, of being able to survey the play as a whole, of making a fair copy of each successive draft, correcting it and copying it again.

But when I had destroyed the rough copies, how was I to preserve the final draft? A fortuitous suggestion, and some timely help from outside, took me along a new path: it appeared that I must master a new trade, must learn to make *hidey holes,* some farther away, some near to hand, where my papers, finished or in production, would be safe not only from a casual thief but from the perfunctory inspections to which exiles were subjected. As though I had too little to do, with my thirty hours of teaching, and my administrative duties at school, and my bachelor cookery (my secret life as a writer made it impossible for me to marry)—as though writing underground were not difficult enough in itself, I must now learn a new skill: that of hiding what I had written.

One new skill led to another: that of microfilming my manuscripts for myself (without a single electric light bulb and under a sun that hardly ever retired behind the clouds). The microfilms were then fitted into the covers of a book, in two envelopes addressed to Aleksandra Lvovna Tolstoy, at her farm in the U.S.A. I knew nobody else in the West, not a single publisher, but I felt sure that Tolstoy's daughter would not deny me her help.

You read about the front line, or about the underground, when you are a boy and you wonder where people found such desperate courage. You cannot imagine yourself enduring so much. That was what I thought as I read Remarque *(All Quiet on the Western Front)* in the thirties, but when I got to the front myself I came to the conclusion that it is all much less difficult, that you gradually begin to feel at home even there, and that writers make it seem much more frightening than it really is.

It is the same with the underground. If you are plunged into it suddenly and find yourself wearing a black mask and taking a solemn oath or signing your name in blood by the light of a red lantern, it is no doubt very frightening. But a man whom family life has long ago rejected, who lacks foundations on which to build a solid existence (even if he still wanted to), who has only his inner life, can learn one new shift after another, find hiding place after hiding place, make contacts which lead to new contacts, get used to code words in letters or at rendezvous, know some people only by nicknames and communicate with others through a chain of intermediaries, until he wakes up one morning and thinks: Well, I'll be damned! I've been underground all this time without realizing it!

It is mortifying, of course, to have to go underground not for the revolution but merely for the sake of literature.

The years went by, I was released from my place of exile, I moved to Central Russia, married, was rehabilitated and permitted to lead a life of modest comfort and degrading conformity—but I was by now just as accustomed to the cryptoliterary underworld as to the smooth surface of my life as a teacher. Whatever problems arose—which draft to consider final, what completion date to aim at, how many copies to type, what size paper to choose, how to squeeze more lines on the page, what typewriter to use, where to put the copies afterward—I could not breathe freely while they answered themselves, like the writer who has only to complete his work, feast his eyes on it, and move on. No, for the underground writer all these problems meant hard and anxious calculation: where and how the work is to be kept, under what cover it will be transported, what new hiding places must be devised as the volume of writings and of copies steadily grows.

Volume indeed was the most important thing—not creative output measured in thousands of words, but bulk in cubic centimeters.

My still unimpaired eyesight, my naturally minute "onion seed" handwriting, and the especially thin paper which I sometimes managed to bring back from Moscow were all a great help. I made things still easier for myself by destroying outright all rough drafts, outlines and superseded versions; by typing as tightly as possible, leaving no space between lines and using both sides of the paper; and by burning the fair copy of the manuscript as soon as the copying was finished (since I first began writing in jail, I had put my trust in fire alone). This method was followed for my novel *The First Circle,* my story *Shch-854,** and my film script *Tanks Know the Truth,* to mention nothing earlier.[1]

Some of these precautions, of course, proved not to have been strictly necessary, but God helps those who help themselves. It was statistically almost unthinkable that the Cheka-KGB might suddenly come crashing into my apartment for no better reason than that I was an ex-zek; there were millions of ex-zeks around, after all.[2] But I was guided by the proverb "The woodpecker could hide in the forest but for his beak."

I had to adapt my whole life to the need for tight security; make no friends or acquaintances at all in Ryazan, where I had recently gone to live; invite nobody to my home and accept no invitations—because if I did, it would be impossible to claim later on that I never had a single hour free, not one in a month or even in a year, not even on public holidays, or when I was on vacation. I could not afford to let any scrap of what I had hidden escape from the apartment, or allow an observant eye inside for a moment. My wife observed my rules strictly, and I greatly appreciated this. Among my colleagues at work I took care never to reveal any broader interests, and always to make a show of indifference to literature ("hostile" literary activity had been one of the charges brought against me at the time of my arrest in 1945, and KGB agents might be keeping me under observation to see whether or not I had cooled off in this respect). And finally, though at every step in my daily life I collided with conceited, rude, stupid and greedy bureaucrats of every degree and in every institution, and though I sometimes saw a chance to crash through a barrier and sweep away the rubbish with a well-aimed complaint or a determined protest, I could never allow myself to do so, never take half a step out of line in the direction of rebellion, of resistance, but had always to be a model Soviet citizen, always to submit to every bully and acquiesce in any stupidity.

The pig that keeps its head down grubs up the deepest root.

It was not at all easy! I might as well be in exile still, or back in the

---

1. I could have wept when I destroyed the original of my film script. It had been written in very special circumstances. But one anxious evening I had to burn it. The job was made much easier by the fact that my Ryazan apartment was heated by a stove. With central heating, burning a manuscript would have given me much more trouble.

2. But if they had descended, death, and nothing less, is what I could have expected, unknown and defenseless as I then was. The reader will be able to convince himself of this when, someday, he reads the complete original text of *The First Circle* (in ninety-six chapters).

camp wearing the same old number patches, still unable to hold my head up or straighten my back, owing obedience to every pair of epaulets.

My indignation could safely boil over in the book I was writing at the time—but I would not allow that either, because the laws of poetry command us to rise above our anger and try to see the present in the light of eternity.

But all this tribute I paid without a murmur: even under these conditions I was working solidly and well, though I had little enough spare time and no genuine peace and quiet. It was a strange experience for me to hear prosperous, leisured, famous writers on the radio, instructing listeners on methods of achieving concentration at the beginning of a working day, telling them that it is most important to eliminate all distractions, and especially important to surround yourself with congenial objects. I myself had learned long ago in the camp to compose and to write as I marched in a column under escort; out on the frozen steppe; in an iron foundry; in the hubbub of a prison hut. A soldier can squat on the ground and fall asleep immediately, a dog in freezing weather is as snug in his own shaggy coat as he would be by a stove, and I was equipped by nature to write anywhere.

Now that I was free I had become fussier (the human spirit is subject to the law of compression and decompression). I was disturbed by the radio and by people talking, but even so, even to the accompaniment of the constant roar of lorries hurtling toward my window in Ryazan, I acquired the knack of writing a screenplay. All I needed was an hour or two of continuous free time! God had spared me creative crises, fits of despair and impotence.

Throughout these years as an underground writer—five years in the camp before my illness, seven years of exile and then of freedom, my "second life" after my astounding recovery—my mood, my state of mind, which I would almost call one of exultant happiness, hardly varied. The shrill, vainglorious literature of the establishment—with its dozen fat magazines, its two literary newspapers, its innumerable anthologies, its novels between hard covers, its collected works, its annual prizes, its adaptations for radio of impossibly tedious originals—I had once and for all recognized as unreal, and I did not waste my time or exasperate myself by trying to keep up with it. I knew without looking that there could be nothing of merit in all this. Not because no talent could emerge there—no doubt it sometimes did, but there it perished too. For it was a barren field, that which they sowed. I knew that in such a field nothing could grow to maturity. When they first came to literature they had, all of them—the social novelists, the bombastic playwrights, the civic poets, and needless to say the journalists and critics—joined in an undertaking never, whatever the subject, whatever the issue, to mention the essential truth, the truth that leaps to the eye with no help from literature. This solemn pledge to abstain from truth was called socialist realism. Even writers of love poems, even those lyric poets who had sought sanctuary in nature or in elegant romanticism, were all fatally flawed because they dared not touch the important truths.

Moreover, I lived through those years as an underground writer in the conviction that I was not the only aloof and cunning one. That there were dozens of stubborn, self-contained individuals like me—each of us writing, with honor and conscience as his guides, all that he knew about our age, the essential truth about it, which is not entirely made up of prisons, executions, camps and places of exile, but which cannot be told in full if you overlook them. Yes, dozens and dozens of us, all suffering from lack of air—but for the present it was impossible for us to come out into the open and reveal ourselves even to each other. When the time came we should all emerge simultaneously from the depths of the sea, like the Three and Thirty Heroes of Pushkin's tale *Tsar Saltan*—and this was how the great literature that we had scuttled at the time of the Great Break, or earlier, would rise again.

A third belief of mine was that we, the host in gleaming casques, would rise from the sea only posthumously and figuratively. Our books, preserved by faithful and ingenious friends, would rise and not our bodies: we ourselves should be long dead. I had not as yet come to believe that an upheaval in our society might be caused by literature, might begin in literature (though this was surely the very lesson that Russian literature should have taught us). I thought that society would be shaken and even renewed for other reasons, that when a fissure appeared, a breach opening onto freedom, our underground literature would at once push its way through to explain to perplexed and troubled minds why things could not have been otherwise, to trace the tangled threads back to 1917.

The years went by, and it began to look as though I had been mistaken in all three of my beliefs.

The field of literature proved not quite so barren as I had thought. Try as they might to leach all nutriment out of the soil, all moisture, everything that sustains life—life still broke through. Who can deny the vitality of Tvardovsky's "Tyorkin in the Next World" or of the peasants in Zalygin's "Krutye Luchiny"? How can we deny that there is life in the names of Shukshin, Mozhayev, Yevgeny Nosov, Tendryakov, Belov, Maksimov and even Soloukhin? Or that Yuri Kazakov would be a powerful writer of lasting worth if he would look the great truths in the face? There are other names I could list, but this is not the place. And there are bold young poets besides. But in my too general view, the Writers' Union, which in its day had refused membership to Tsvetayeva, anathematized Zamyatin, treated Bulgakov with contempt, ostracized Akhmatova and Pasternak, seen from the underground was a veritable Sodom and Gomorrah, or a rabble of hucksters and moneychangers littering and defiling the temple, whose stalls must be overturned and they themselves scourged and driven into the outer porch. I was surprised and overjoyed to find myself mistaken.

I was mistaken in my second prophecy too, but this time to my sorrow. We were after all rather few—secret and stubborn, yes, and fortunate men. We should never add up to a whole literature. The Cheka had swept with a stiffer broom than I had thought. How many fine minds, perhaps even geniuses, had been ground into the earth, as though they had never been, with nothing to show for their lives? (Or are there some still more obstinate and cunning than we were? Are they still, today, writing away in silence, keeping their heads down, because they know that the hour of freedom is not yet at hand? It may be so. If my story had been told in the Prose Section a year or two earlier, who would have believed it?)

Varlam Shalamov put out his leaves at the very first sign of spring: he believed in the promise of the Twentieth Congress and dispatched his verses along the pioneer trails that samizdat was blazing. I read them in summer 1956, trembling as I recognized a brother! One of the secret brothers of whose existence I knew beyond doubt. I had a chance, through some intermediaries, to confide in him there and then, but I was less trusting than he was, and besides, I had still a great deal to get on paper and my health and my age allowed me to be patient —so I kept silent and went on writing.

I was mistaken in my third belief too. We began to emerge from the black, bottomless waters much sooner than I had expected, to emerge in our own lifetime. I lived to enjoy the happiness of peeping out and shying the first pebbles at Goliath's stupid brow. The brow was undamaged, the pebbles bounced off, but as they fell to the ground they blossomed into break-herb,* and people greeted them with joy or hatred; none passed by heedlessly.

Later, by contrast, the pace slackened. Life dragged on like a lingering cold spring. History began to cast loop after nooselike loop of complications, hoping to lasso every one of us, and strangle as many as possible. Things moved so sluggishly (just as we should have expected) that we no longer had any choice: there was nothing for it but to hurl a few last stones, with our last remaining strength, at that impenetrable brow.

Yes, yes, of course—we all know that you cannot poke a stick through the walls of a concrete tower, but here's something to think about: what if those walls are only a painted backdrop?

Looking back, even a fool would be able to predict it today: the Soviet regime could certainly have been breached only by literature. The regime has been reinforced with concrete to such an extent that neither a military coup nor a political organization nor a picket line of strikers can knock it over or run it through. Only the solitary writer would be able to do this. And the Russian younger generation would move on into the breach.

Obvious? Yet no one foresaw it, either in the thirties or in the fifties. That's the trouble with the future: it slips away and eludes us.

*          *

*

For twelve years I quietly wrote and wrote. Only in the thirteenth did I falter. This was in spring 1960. I had written so many things, all quite unpublishable, all doomed to complete obscurity, that I felt clogged and supersaturated, and began to lose my buoyancy of mind and movement. I was beginning to suffer from lack of air in the literary underground.

The underground writer's enormous advantage is freedom to write as he likes: he needs to keep neither censors nor editors in his mind's eye, nothing confronts him except his material, nothing hovers anxiously over him except the truth. But there is in his position one inevitable drawback: lack of readers, and above all exacting readers of refined literary sensitivity. The underground writer chooses his readers (I had about a dozen of them, mostly former zeks, and I did not manage to show all my work to any one of them: we lived in different towns, none of us had time or money to spend on travel, nor spare rooms to put up visitors) by quite different criteria: political reliability and ability to keep quiet. These two qualities rarely keep company with refined artistic taste. So that the underground writer hears no rigorous criticism based on a knowledge of the best in contemporary literature. It seems, however, that every writer sorely needs such criticism, needs sober assistance in plotting the position of his work in the universe of art, even if it is only at intervals of five or even ten years. Pushkin's advice to the "exacting artist"—to be content if he himself is satisfied with his work —is very sound, but not the last word on the subject. When you have been writing for ten or twelve years in impenetrable solitude, you begin without realizing it to let yourself go, to indulge yourself, or simply to lose your eye for jarring invective, for bombast, for banal conventional joins where you should have found a firmer fastening.

Later, when I popped up from underground and began *lightening* my works for the outside world, lightening them of all that my fellow countrymen could hardly be expected to accept at once, I discovered to my surprise that a piece only gained, that its effect was heightened, as the harsher tones were softened; and I began to discover the places where I had let myself off too easily, putting in a chipped and crumbling brick instead of an intact and fireproof one. From my first contact with the professional literary milieu I knew that I must pull myself together!

In my complete ignorance I had fallen particularly short of the mark in my plays. When I took to writing plays in the camp, then in exile, I had in mind the only theatrical productions I had ever seen—in provincial Rostov in the thirties—which even then were on a level that world theater had long left behind. Convinced as I was that what matters most in creative art is truthfulness and experience of life, I did not appreciate that *forms* become obsolete, that tastes in the twentieth century change abruptly and cannot be ignored by any author. Now, after visiting Moscow theaters in the sixties (no longer, alas, theaters for actors or even playwrights, but theaters in which directors are almost the sole creators of the performance), I regret having written plays.[3]

---

3. Shalamov's prose has also, in my opinion, suffered from the fact that he worked for many years in seclusion. It could have been much improved, with no change in the range of material or the author's viewpoint.

In 1960 I could not have diagnosed or explained all this precisely, but I felt myself growing stale while my already sizable bundle of writing was going to waste—and I began to feel a sort of fidgety need to stretch and move around. Since there could be no movement, since I dared not stir an inch in any direction, I began to pine: my cleverly planned, soundless and invisible literary enterprise had fetched up in a blind alley.

Shortly before his death Tolstoy wrote that it is always immoral for a writer to publish in his own lifetime. We should, he thinks, write only for the future, and let our works be published "posthumously." Tolstoy reached his pious conclusions on this as on all else only after making the full round of sins and passions, but in any case, what he says is untrue even for slower epochs, and still more so for our swift-moving times. He is right that the thirst for repeated successes with the public spoils a writer's work. But it is even more damaging to be denied readers for years on end—demanding readers, hostile readers, delighted readers—to be denied all opportunity to influence the world about you, to influence the rising generation, with your pen. Quiescence means purity—but also irresponsibility. Tolstoy's judgment is ill-considered.

The new works being printed, which till then had merely amused me, now began to irritate me. It was just then that Ehrenburg's and Paustovsky's memoirs appeared, and I sent a sharp review to various journals—rejected, of course, by all of them, because nobody had ever heard of me. In form, my article looked like an attack on memoir literature generally, but its real purpose was to express my exasperation with writers who had seen the great dark epoch, and yet were forever trying to sidle round it, ignoring the things that mattered most, telling us nothing but trivialities, sealing our eyes with emollients till we no longer saw the truth. Why should they be so afraid, these established writers whom nothing threatens?

That autumn, pacing my den, with the strength going out of me, I applied my mind to the problem of writing something that, even if it could not be published, could at least be shown to people! at least not be hidden! So I had the idea of writing *Candle in the Wind,* a play about today, but set in no particular country: a play about any prosperous society, East or West, in our decade.

This play, the least successful thing I ever wrote, was also the most difficult. More precisely, I realized for the first time how a piece of work may stubbornly refuse to come right, even after four or five rewritings:

you can throw out whole scenes and replace them with others—and it still looks hopelessly artificial. I spent a great deal of labor on it and thought I had finished—but no, it was still no good. I had based it on the true story of a particular Moscow family; I had not cheated once; I had expressed only ideas I sincerely held, many of which I had long cherished, refusing right from the first act to humor the censors—why, then, was it such a failure? Could it possibly be because I had avoided a specifically Russian setting—not at all for purposes of camouflage, and not merely to ensure that it need not be hidden, but to give it a more general significance: it was even more relevant to the fat, complacent West than to us—and that off Russian ground I am doomed to lose my feel for the Russian language? But others write easily in this faceless, tongueless style and it comes off, so why can't I? Obviously, some writers have no gift for generalization, just as others have no talent for the specific. You can't take abstraction just so far, and from then on write concretely. (But perhaps the main reason for failure was the insubstantiality of the female character.)

I made another attempt in 1961, without clearly realizing what I was doing. For no particular reason, I simply took *Shch-854* and copied it out in a "lightened" version, leaving out the roughest episodes and expressions of opinion, and also the long story that the captain second class tells Tsezar about the way Americans were taken in by our faked prosperity at Sebastopol in 1945. I did it for no clear reason—and put it aside. But I let it lie without concealment. What a happy state to be in, what a feeling of freedom it gave me—not racking my brains to find a hiding place for a newly finished work, but simply keeping it in my desk drawer: a reason for happiness that writers do not sufficiently appreciate. I had never once gone to bed without making sure that everything was hidden, and rehearsing my behavior in case there was a knock in the night.

All my secrecy was beginning to wear me out, and it created problems more head-splitting than any that arose from my writing. But there was no relief in sight from any quarter, and the Western radio, which I always listened to in spite of jamming, as yet knew nothing of the deep subterranean shifts and fissures which were soon to produce a quake on the surface. No one knew anything, and I had nothing good to look forward to, when I began polishing and revising *The First Circle*. After the drab Twenty-first Congress, which damped and muted the splendid promise of the Twentieth, there was no way of foreseeing the sudden fury, the reckless eloquence of the attack on Stalin which Khrushchev would decide upon for the Twenty-second! Nor, try as we might, could we, the uninitiated, ever explain it! But there it was—and not even a secret attack, as at the Twentieth Congress, but a public one! I could not remember when I had read anything as interesting as the speeches at the Twenty-second Congress. In my little room in a decaying wooden house where one unlucky match might send all my manuscripts, years and years of work, up in smoke, I read and reread those speeches, and the walls of my secret world swayed like curtains in the theater, wavered, expanded and carried me queasily with them: had it arrived, then, the long-awaited moment of terrible joy, the moment when my head must break water?

I must make no mistake! I must not thrust out my head too soon. But equally, I must not let this rare moment pass me by!

There was also a good speech at the Twenty-second Congress from Tvardovsky, and one theme he touched on was that although it had long since been possible to publish more freely and boldly, "we do not take advantage of the opportunity." *Novy Mir,* he hinted, might publish bolder and more polemical things, if only it had them.

I did not distinguish the Tvardovsky who had written *Muravia* from the general run of poets who swung the censers of falsehood. And I knew none of his memorable individual poems: I had discovered none when I looked through his 1954 two-volume collected works in my place of exile. But long ago, at the front, I had taken note of *Vasily Tyorkin* as a remarkable feat: long before the appearance of the first truthful books about the war (since Nekrasov's *In the Trenches of Stalingrad,* not so many of them have succeeded—perhaps half a dozen in all), amid the fume and crackle of gibbering propaganda which always accompanied our bombardments, Tvardovsky had succeeded in writing something timeless, courageous and unsullied, helped by a rare sense of proportion, all his own, or perhaps by a sensitive tact not uncommon among peasants. (This sensitivity beneath the coarsened and uncouth peasant exterior, and in spite of the hardships of peasant life, never ceases to astonish me.) Though he was not free to tell the whole truth about the war, Tvardovsky nevertheless always stopped just one millimeter short of falsehood, and nowhere did he ever overstep the one-millimeter mark. The result was a miracle. I am not speaking only for myself; I had excellent opportunities to observe its effects on soldiers in my battery during the war. It was the peculiarity of our job as a sound-ranging unit that they had a great deal of time, even in combat conditions, to listen to readings (at night, at field signal posts, while someone would read from the communications center). Of the many things offered them, they obviously had a special preference for *War and Peace* and *Vasily Tyorkin.*

But lack of leisure in the camp, in exile, as a teacher and underground had prevented me from reading "The House by the Roadside" or any of his other work. (I did read "Tyorkin in the Next World," in manuscript copies, in 1956. Samizdat always had first claim on my attention.) I did not even know that a chapter of *New Horizons* had been published in *Pravda,* and that the poem had received a Lenin Prize that year. I read the poem as a whole much later, the chapter "Thus It Was" when I came across it in *Novy Mir.* As things then were, in the atmosphere of general timidity, it looked daring: Auntie Darya's night work; "Hurrah, he'll get it right again"; and even "Like some strange fairground fantasy, skyscraping Moscow rose before me . . ." As long ago as that I had felt my first impulse to show some of my writing to Tvardovsky. Should I risk it? But leafing through the same chapter and reflecting on it, I also encountered the "stern father," who was "unjust" yet "just," and found that to him, too, we "owed our victory"; learned of Stalin's affinity with "martial steel," and that

> In history's golden book of fame
> No doubtful comma, not a crooked line
> Shall cast a shadow on our name.
> What's done is done. . . .

This was a little too bland: had forty shameful years of camps cast no shadow on our honor? A little too smooth: "What's done is done"; "there's nothing we can do, or undo." The same could be said about fascism in all its forms. Perhaps Nuremberg was unnecessary? What's done is done . . . ? An impotent philosophy, that does not venture to pronounce judgment on history.[4] The poet's foot cautiously explored

---

4. Lydia Chukovskaya, in her *Notes on Anna Akhmatova,* recalls how angry Tvardovsky's chapter "Childhood Friend" had made Akhmatova five years earlier: "New lies for old!" she had exclaimed.

the ground beside the paved highway, but he dared not step off it.

What would he do if I struggled out of the quagmire, hand out-stretched: Step down and help me! Would he come—or would he hang back?

Nor was *Novy Mir* clearly distinguished in my mind from other journals: judging by the content of its main pages, I saw little difference between it and them. (The contrasts among the magazines that they themselves discerned were trivial in my eyes and are still more so in historical perspective—whether you look backward or forward.) All these magazines used the same terminology, the same oaths and adjurations, and none of this could I take even by the teaspoonful.

But the muffled rumble of subterranean strata, which broke through into the Twenty-second Congress, must have had some meaning. I made up my mind to it. I had never known what prompted me to "lighten" *Shch-854,* or what purpose it could serve, but this was where it proved useful. I decided to submit it to *Novy Mir.* (But for this, something worse would have happened. A whole year of claustrophobic nausea had worn me down to the point at which I must break out.)

I did not go to *Novy Mir* myself: my legs simply would not carry me, since I foresaw no success. I was already forty-three, and I had knocked about the world too much to call on an editor like a boy with his first story. My prison friend Lev Kopelev undertook to hand the manuscript in. Although there were six author's sheets of it, it made quite a slim packet: typed, of course, on both sides, with no margins, and no spaces at all between lines.

I handed it over—and was gripped by the agitation, not of an ambitious young author, but of a hard-bitten camp veteran who has been incautious enough to leave a trail.

This was at the beginning of November 1961. I had never been near

---

"Our country? Why bring the country into it?
The people? The people had no part in it."

Ah, but the poet was one with the zek—

"Had sampled it all, and eaten the same bread"—

while the zek

"With an invitation card like mine
Was the Kremlin's no less welcome guest!"

Yes, a useful escape ladder of lies for 1956.

a Moscow hotel, but on this occasion I took advantage of the slack season just before the holiday and obtained a bed. There I lived through days of last-minute waverings and indecision—and I still had time to stop the story, to ask for it back. (I stayed on not because of my indecision, but to read a samizdat copy of *For Whom the Bell Tolls,* lent to me for three days. Until then I had not read a single line of Hemingway.)

The hotel, as it happened, was in Ostankino, right next to the *sharashka* in which the action of *The First Circle* takes place, and where, with my first experience of prison, I began writing seriously. In the intervals of reading Hemingway I went out and strolled along the fence around my old *sharashka*. It stood just as it had then, its unchanged perimeter enclosing the same tiny space in which so many outstandingly able people were once squeezed together, and which had seethed with our debates and our ingenious schemes.

I strolled about now some ten meters from the bishop's arklike house, and those old linden trees, those immortal lindens under which I had paced back and forth, back and forth, back and forth, morning, noon and night, for three years on end, dreaming of freedom's bright distant dawn in other and brighter years, and in a brighter Russia.

Now, on a clammy overcast day, in the sloppy November snow, I walked on the other side of the fence, along a path by which only guards on their way to relieve comrades on the watchtower had trudged in the old days, and I thought: What have I done? I have put myself in their hands again.

How could I, with no one forcing me, have come to inform against myself? . . .

# Out of Hiding

There followed a whole month of misery in Ryazan: somewhere in the invisible distance my future was being decided, and I looked forward with growing certainty to the worst. Belief in change for the better is almost too much to ask of a veteran zek, one of Gulag's sons. Besides, after years of camp life you lose the habit of making your own decisions (in almost all important matters you drift helplessly with the tide of destiny), and get used to the idea that it is safer never to decide, never to take the initiative: you're alive—be satisfied with that.

Now I had broken the camp law, and I felt frightened. Besides, a new work was in progress, and all that I had done of it was in my apartment, which made the *Novy Mir* stunt seem even more obviously suicidal frivolity.

For all the fulminations at the Twenty-second Congress, for all the solemn promises to erect a monument to fallen zeks, or rather to the Communists among them—it has not been erected to this day—to believe that the time had come to tell the truth was simply impossible; our heads, our hearts, our tongues, have for too long been trained to avoid it. We meekly accept that we shall never speak the truth, nor shall we ever hear it.

However, a telegram arrived from Lev Kopelev at the beginning of December: "Aleksandr Trifonovich delighted with article." ("Article" was our code word for the story: an article might be about anything—methods of teaching mathematics, for instance.) Like a bird flying smack into a pane of glass that telegram came. And my long years of immobility were over. A day later (on my birthday, as it happened), another telegram arrived, from Tvardovsky himself, summoning me to his office. And the day after that I went to Moscow, and superstitiously paused by Pushkin's statue as I crossed Strastnaya Square on my way to *Novy Mir*—partly to beg for his support, and partly to promise that I knew the path I must follow and would not stray from it. It was a sort of prayer.

Together, Kopelev and I climbed *Novy Mir*'s broad, aristocratic staircase—the very place to shoot ballroom scenes for a film. It was midday, but Tvardovsky had not yet arrived, and the rest of the staff had only just come in; they didn't believe in starting too early. We introduced ourselves to the prose department. One of the editorial staff, Anna Samoilovna Berzer, had played the key role in bringing my story to Tvardovsky's exalted hands.

It was a year or so later that I was told how this had come about. The manuscript which I had preserved in deepest secrecy for so long had been left lying openly on A. Berzer's desk for a whole week, without so much as a folder for cover, exposed to the first informer or sneak thief who came along. Anna Samoilovna had not been warned about the nature of the work. One day she began clearing her desk, read a few sentences, and saw that this was no way to keep such a manuscript, and indeed no place to read it. She took it home to read in the evening. She was shaken. She compared her reactions with those of her friend Kaleria Ozerova, an editor in the criticism section. They were identical. Knowing the ways of *Novy Mir* as she did, Anna Samoilovna reasoned that any member of the editorial board obedient to his conception of the magazine's best interests would block the manuscript, sit on it, swallow it—anything to keep it out of Tvardovsky's hands. So she had to use her ingenuity to toss it clear of all the heads between, lob it over the bog of caution and cowardice, and land it in Tvardovsky's hands first of all. Even then he might be put off by the manuscript's beggarly, dense and clotted appearance. Anna Samoilovna therefore asked to have it recopied at the magazine's expense. This took time. It took time, too, waiting for Tvardovsky to return from his latest binge (one of those wretched drinking bouts which, as I gradually came to see, were perhaps also his salvation). But the most difficult part was outmaneuvering the other editors and breaking through to Tvardovsky, who usually did not want to see her and, quite unfairly, disliked her. (He somehow failed to appreciate her aesthetic judgment, her diligence, her selfless devotion to the magazine. All his authors were her friends, and forever hanging about the prose department.) Still, she knew very well the characters and weaknesses of all her superiors, and she began with the nearest of them, Y. Gerasimov, head of the prose department. "There's a story about the camps. Will you read it?" The complacent Gerasimov, a voluminous prose writer himself, waved her away: "I don't want to hear any of that stuff about camps!" She tried the same question on the chief editor's second deputy, A. Kondratovich, a little fellow so mauled and terrorized by censors that his ears seemed permanently pricked up and his nose permanently atwitch for the scent of danger. Kondratovich's reply was that he knew all there was to know about the camps, and didn't need any more telling. And anyway, he said, the thing couldn't be published. Next, A. Berzer laid the manuscript before B. G. Zaks, the managing secretary of the editorial board, and shyly asked him to "take a look and see if you'd like to read it." She could not have phrased it more adroitly. For many years, B. G. Zaks, a desiccated and tedious prig, had asked only one thing of literature—that it not interfere with the comforts of his declining years: his sunny Octobers in Koktebel and his enjoyment of the best Moscow concerts in winter. He read the first paragraph of my story, put it down without a word and walked away.

A. Berzer now had every right to turn to Tvardovsky: the rest had all said no! She waited her chance—true, Kondratovich was present; she couldn't catch Tvardovsky alone—and told the chief that there were two unusual manuscripts which must be read by him personally: Lydia Chukovskaya's *Sofya Petrovna,* and another one, about "a prison camp as seen through the eyes of a peasant, a work in which you could hear the voice of the Russian people." She had done it again; she could not have aimed more accurately at Tvardovsky's heart than she did in those few words. "I'll take a look at that one," he said immediately.[1] But Kondratovich woke up and jumped in. "Let me have it overnight. I'll read it first." He could not fall down on his job as protective filter for his chief.

He took it away, and realized from the first few lines that the mysterious nameless author (not putting my name to it seemed to me a way of slowing down any menacing turn of events) did not even know how to arrange the clauses of a sentence in proper order, and also used

---

1. Whereas *Sofya Petrovna,* known as *The Deserted House* in the West, had to wait several years longer—until it was a quarter of a century old, and was published abroad. It is very easy for us to understand, but incomprehensible in the West, why the same magazine would never dare publish a second story on the prison theme. It might, of course, have begun to look like a fixed policy.

bizarre words. He had to take his pencil and scrawl all over the first page, the second . . . the fifth . . . the eighth, restoring subject, predicate and attributes to their rightful places. But the story proved to be illiterate from start to finish, and after several pages of this work Kondratovich gave up. What opinion he had formed by the following morning I do not know, but I think that it could equally well have been positive or negative. Tvardovsky, however, took the story away to read himself without asking what Kondratovich thought. Later, when I discovered what life at *Novy Mir* was like, I felt sure that *Ivan Denisovich* would never have seen the light if A. Berzer had not shouldered her way through to Tvardovsky and hooked him with her remark that it was "seen through the eyes of a peasant." The chief's three guardian angels —Dementyev, Zaks and Kondratovich—would have gobbled up my Ivan Denisovich alive.

I cannot say that I had precisely planned it, but I did accurately foresee that the muzhik Ivan Denisovich was bound to arouse the sympathy of the superior muzhik Tvardovsky and the supreme muzhik Nikita Khrushchev. And that was just what happened: it was not poetry and not politics that decided the fate of my story, but that unchanging peasant nature, so much ridiculed, trampled underfoot and vilified in our country since the Great Break, and indeed earlier.

As Tvardovsky later told the story, he had gone to bed and picked up the manuscript. But after two or three pages he had decided that he couldn't read it lying down. He had got up and dressed. While his household slept, he had read through the night, with breaks for tea in the kitchen—read the story once, then reread it. (He never read any subsequent work of mine twice, and indeed he never reread anything, even to check changes he had asked an author to make, although this sometimes landed him in difficulties.) So the night passed, and what for peasants are the early morning hours arrived—but for literary persons it was still night, and Tvardovsky had to wait a little longer. He had no thought of going back to bed. After a while he telephoned Kondratovich and ordered him to ask Berzer (why didn't he ask her himself? protocol forbade it) who and where the author was.

This led Tvardovsky to the next link in the chain, Kopelev, whom he now telephoned. He was particularly pleased to find that it was no hoax on the part of some well-known writer (though he had been quite confident about this) and that the author was neither a professional nor a Muscovite.

For Tvardovsky the days that followed were full of the joy of discovery. He rushed from friend to friend with the manuscript, calling for a bottle to celebrate the appearance of a new writer. That is Tvardovsky for you: what makes him a true editor, an editor unlike others, is that he yearns to discover new authors, as feverishly, passionately, as any prospector longs to find gold.

He rushed to see his friends—but here was something strange: at the age of fifty-one, a famous poet, the editor of the best magazine in the country, an important figure in the Writers' Union, and not unimportant in the Communist Party, Tvardovsky had few, hardly any friends. There was his chief deputy, Dementyev (a dark spirit); his drinking companion, the bleary I. A. Sats; and M. A. Lifshitz, a dogmatic Marxist fossil. He had, so they say, made many attempts in the course of a lifetime to find himself a friend. There were periods of tender friendship with Viktor Nekrasov, with Kazakevich, and others, but sooner or later each of these friendships ran into a bumpy patch, struck a snag and was wrecked. None of them prospered. Obviously, there was something about Tvardovsky that doomed him to stand alone. For one thing, his talent. For another, his *awkward* character. Also his peasant origins. And on top of all this, the unnatural life a Soviet grandee leads: he had once prided himself on enjoying Fadeyev's favor, and he was capable of looking down on people.

While all those bottles were being split and my original manuscript fetched in to be marveled at, with its letters huddled together like penned sheep and never a blank space for an editorial pencil to take exercise—back in the office they were, as they always did on important occasions, putting their considered opinions of the manuscript in writing. Kondratovich wrote as follows: "We shall pretty certainly not be able to publish it. . . . The author should be advised above all to bring in one missing theme—the prisoners' expectation of an end to their sufferings. . . . The language needs cleaning up." Dementyev: "Seen from this angle, it is horrible inside the camp, and just as horrible beyond the camp boundaries. A difficult case: if we don't publish, it will look as though we are afraid of the truth . . . but publication is impossible, because it does after all give a one-sided picture of reality." (The reader should not deduce from this that Dementyev was really of two minds. He knew very well that to publish was impossible, that it would be damaging, and that they weren't going to do it—but since the boss had fallen and was so infatuated with the thing, it could not be too abruptly dumped.)

All this I learned or worked out for myself later, over the years. On this first visit, Kondratovich, trying to look imposing (although a fleeting glance told me that he was a lightweight with no mind of his own), solemnly asked me—the bashful author whom fortune had smiled upon —"What else have you got?"

An easy question! A natural question: they had to have some idea whether or not my success was a flash in the pan. But this, of all my secrets, was the greatest. I had not spent five years outwitting camp searches, three years devising hidey holes in exile, and another five lying low after my release, just so that I could now keep my end up in polite conversation. I answered Kondratovich curtly: "I should prefer to leave that question to a later stage in our acquaintance."

Tvardovsky arrived, and I was called into the big staff room. (*Novy Mir* had very cramped quarters in those days, and what passed for Tvardovsky's office was a corner of that same room.) I knew him only from bad photographs in newspapers, and with my poor eye for faces I might not have recognized him. He was large, and of ample girth, but the other man who rolled toward me was also large and of ample girth, and the nicest fellow you ever did see, bursting with good humor. This second person turned out to be Dementyev. Tvardovsky behaved with dignified politeness, as the occasion demanded, but even so I was immediately struck by the childish expression of his face—childish in its candor, even vulnerable in its childishness—not in the least spoiled, I thought, by long years at the highest levels of society, nor even by favors from the throne.

All the top people of *Novy Mir* seated themselves around a big, antique, elongated oval table, with me facing Aleksandr Trifonovich. He was trying hard to control himself and to look businesslike, but with little success: his smile grew brighter and brighter. This was one of his happiest moments: it was his birthday party, not mine. He looked at me with a benevolence that was already on its way to becoming love. Unhurriedly he ran over various details of the story, some more, some less important, as they occurred to him, handling them with the pleasure, the pride, the happiness, not of a discoverer, not of a patron, but of a creator: he could not have quoted more affectionately, more tenderly, if he had suffered the birth pangs himself and this had been his best-loved creation. (The other members of the editorial board nodded and murmured approval of their chief's praise, except, if I remember rightly, Dementyev, who sat there aloof and noncommittal. In fact, he did not speak up at all on this occasion.)

Of all those at the table, none was less demonstrative than I, none wore a look so nearly grim. I had chosen to play this part in the expectation that any moment now they would begin pitching into me, demanding amendments and excisions, and I had no intention at all of making any. They did not know, of course, that what they had in their hands was the "lightened" version with all the wrinkles ironed out. I supposed that they were just letting me down gently but would shortly set to work with their shears, snipping off the prickly details of camp life, the ragged bits, and the flowers. My grim looks were intended to show them in advance that my head was not turned and that I did not set too much store by my new association.

But, miraculously, they did not put the thumbscrews on me. Miraculously, they did not drag out their wide-mouthed shears. Had I gone mad? Surely the editorial board could not seriously believe that the thing was publishable?

Tvardovsky's only observations took the form of courteous requests, uttered in the most tentative manner—just two of them: Ivan Denisovich should not covet the less than legal occupation described in his wife's letter, dyeing carpets; and he must not altogether reject the idea that he would someday be free. This seemed fair enough, and I readily promised to do something about it. Then Zaks delivered his opinion that Ivan Denisovich could not seriously believe that God breaks bits off the moon to make stars. And Maryamov drew my attention to two or three incorrect Ukrainian words.

So we were all bosom pals, and at this rate we would be able to work together! This was not what I had imagined our editorial boards to be like. . . .

They suggested that I make my short story "weightier" by calling it a "tale"; right then, a tale it is.[2] Then Tvardovsky said, in a manner

---

2. I was wrong to give way. The dividing lines between genres are becoming more and more blurred in our country, and the result is a devaluation of forms. *Ivan Denisovich* is of course a short story [*rasskaz*], though it is a large and dense one. Less substantial than the story is the novella—it is light in construction and clear-cut in subject and ideas. A tale [*povest*] is what many of us too readily call a "novel." There are several story lines, and the action almost inevitably extends over a fairly long time. A novel [*roman*] (odious word! surely we could find a better one?) differs from a tale not so much in size, nor in the duration of the action (compression and a rapid tempo can indeed be virtues in a

that precluded argument, that the tale could never be published with a title like *Shch-854*. I did not know their passion for anodyne, watered-down surrogate titles, and once again put up no resistance. Suggestions were tossed back and forth over the table, with Kopelev joining in, and our collective creative effort produced *One Day in the Life of Ivan Denisovich.*

Tvardovsky warned me that he could give no firm promise of publication (Heaven help us! I was only too glad that they hadn't forwarded it to the Cheka-KGB!) and could say nothing about dates, but that he would spare no effort.

Out of mere curiosity they asked me a number of closely related questions. How long had it taken me to write the tale? (Handle with care! Dynamite! Tell them two months and they will want to know what I've been doing all the rest of my life.) Well, you know, it's difficult to estimate. I did it at odd moments, after school. How many years ago had I begun, when had I finished, how long had I been holding on to it? (All the dates glowed in my memory in letters of fire. But naming them would make it clear at once how little of my time the tale had filled.) Somehow or other, I couldn't remember in which year I had started or finished. . . . Why did I type so closely, with no line spacing or margins, and on both sides? (Have you never heard of cubic centimeters, you donkeys?) Well, you know, it's simply that you can't buy paper in Ryazan (which was true).

They interrogated me about my way of life, past and present, and all fell silent in embarrassment when I cheerfully replied that I earned sixty rubles a month by teaching, and that this was enough for me (I had not wanted a full-time job, which would have left me less time of my own, and my wife earned so much that there was no need for me to contribute to household expenses). Figures of this sort are below the threshold of comprehensibility for writers who are paid as much for a review a few lines long. My dress was consistent with income. Rejoicing in his sovereign power, Tvardovsky gave instructions that I should there and then be put under contract, on the best terms *Novy Mir* could offer. (The advance alone was as much as I earned in two years.) I sat in a stupor, trying hard to concentrate on telling them no more about myself than they needed to know.

---

novel), but in the number of destinies it embraces, the breadth of its horizon and the depth of its ideas.

The question to which Tvardovsky and his colleagues most persistently returned was: "What else have you to offer? Ah, yes—and besides that? Isn't there anything further?" Mentally running through the layers secreted over the years since 1948, I selected things I could mention to them. On my way there, I had meant to reveal nothing else, but I couldn't keep it up: it would have been difficult to convince them that *Ivan Denisovich* was a beginner's exercise.

Said the fox to the peasant: "Just let me put my paw on your cart; I'll jump up all by myself."

It was the same with me.

I promised to do a little digging for next time, said that I thought I could put my hands on another story, and a few little prose poems and some verses. (Here Kondratovich looked happier, and announced that this was all to the good: after *Ivan Denisovich* the camps were exhausted as a subject, and I should do well to take the war as my theme. A fife band thousands of mouths strong had been monotonously tootling its martial airs for twenty years, and still the army at war was an inexhaustible subject! Whereas the fifty millions who had perished in exile and in the camps could make do with one little grave mound—my story!)

That December I had to make two more trips to Moscow. They had toned down a dozen expressions in my tale, but Berzer—she and I had soon become firm friends—gave me a cautionary hint which proved accurate: there was no knowing what would pass and what would get stuck, so that it was best to put off corrections as long as possible. In any case, I was in no mood for concessions. I would take the tale away from them rather than mutilate it.

On these visits I took Tvardovsky a few of my camp poems, a few of the more innocuous "Miniatures,"* and the story "Without one righteous person, no village can stand," "lightened" of its least acceptable sentences. He took the "Miniatures" to be "jottings on your scribbling pad, for future use"; the genre meant nothing to him. As for the verse, "Some of it is publishable, but we want something to make a bang, and this isn't it." (The rebellious spirit called for the storm! No, he hadn't gone moldy, this Tvardovsky!) The story was discussed at an editorial conference on 2 January 1962.

(At this point I realized that a record of these literary meetings might someday come in handy, and I began making notes while they were fresh in my mind, or even during the discussion. This was how I recorded all that I have to say about Tvardovsky. It would be a pity not to give a comprehensive and accurate account of these meetings here, although it may overstrain the structure of these sketches, and rob them of the brevity and lightness that I should like to see in them.)

We were at the elongated oval table around which so many of them had sat just the other day, but this time Tvardovsky had failed to gather a quorum; some said they hadn't had time to read the story, others were not in the office. Dementyev arrived. (He was a full-time member of the staff of the Institute of World Literature; he put in brief appearances at *Novy Mir,* not to earn money but to perform an important mission.) "Sasha, come and sit down!" Tvardovsky invited him. But Dementyev dismissed this as pointless. "What's the good of talking?" He tried to sound heartbroken (We can never print it anyway), but I detected a different note—of anger because the stories I brought them were getting more and more impudent, and because I was seducing Tvardovsky from the familiar well-paved path. I sensed right away the real meaning of their brief wrangle, and when I got to know them both better I was confirmed in my suspicions.

Dementyev had already read it at home and had tried to persuade Tvardovsky (they lived in the same building) that publication was out of the question. But Tvardovsky was enchanted and would not be moved.

They were on intimate terms—"Sasha" and "Sasha"—and never minced words with each other. Nobody else on the magazine dared to contradict Tvardovsky, but Dementyev had set himself up as an independent thinker and haggled to his heart's content. Indeed, it was the established rule that Tvardovsky considered no decision final until he had persuaded Dementyev; if he could not, he himself would back down. It was particularly easy for Dementyev to get the upper hand when he and the chief were at home. Tvardovsky might shout and hammer the table, but more often than not he would agree in the end. Sasha No. 1 was at the wheel of *Novy Mir,* Sasha No. 2 its back-seat driver. Dementyev is said to have used his influence tactfully and sparingly. Tvardovsky would scarcely have tolerated it if Dementyev had always tried to hold him back. It was not all that unusual for Dementyev to egg the chief on, tell him that there was "nothing to be scared of." (This happened with V. Grossman's stories, for instance.) When Tvardovsky proved stubborn for reasons of personal prejudice, as sometimes happened, Dementyev would nearly always speak out: "You're wrong, Sasha! This is something we must publish!" Dementyev would argue, but he had a sense of proportion and knew when to back down and acknowledge defeat. He was never pompous or arrogant, and this made life easier for him and for the editorial staff. No editor was ever afraid to turn to him, and it made no difference, as it did with Tvardovsky, whether he was in a gracious or a bad mood. Dementyev was always businesslike, he was quick to grasp essentials, and where the chances of pushing a sentence or a paragraph through could be improved by careful shading or by rearranging words, he would always give a helping hand. He was not indifferent, as Zaks was, to quality; he did his best to make each issue fresh, lively, even challenging—but always within reason! Everything must be nipped in by dependable ideological hoops, held down by a dependable ideological lid.

He talked to authors easily and effectively too: free from self-infatuation, he had eyes to see what they were like and how to deal with them. He had a very pleasant northern accent, a pleasant smile, and was conscious of his charm: a likable fat-faced muzhik, not quite sixty, with the gentlest of curls in his rapidly thinning hair. He could squint quizzically too, and drop whispered hints. He was everybody's friend; you knew just where you were with him. See how eagerly he accepts your manuscript: "We shall have to *work on it* a bit, of course." (Mangle it, in fact!) And who better to put in a word for you with the chief, who makes you so nervous: "You're right, Sasha, it *is* crap, but we can't put your head on this writer's shoulders. Let's give him a lift, touch the stuff up a bit and publish it."

But when the hoop was in danger of bursting, when the lid was being forced off, Dementyev saw no need for debate. This was where Tvardovsky's heart and his vision came into their own. This was why Dementyev had failed with *Ivan Denisovich.* The impressions left by that sleepless night and those two successive readings were so strong that Dementyev dared not oppose the headlong enthusiasm that united the poet and the peasant in Tvardovsky.

Once again, it was some years before I heard and understood these things. At the time, I only knew instinctively that Dementyev was my enemy. I did not realize that the crucial discussion of "Matryona" had already taken place between the two of them, at home and out of earshot, and that this time Sasha No. 2 had prevailed over Sasha No. 1. He had prevailed over the editor but could not shout down the feelings

of the poet. So that Tvardovsky, fated to reject me, was suffering torments, which was why he had summoned Sasha No. 2 to sit in on a
discussion that could not affect the decision—to help him overcome his
own confusion and explain to me why my story about Matryona could
never, no, not under any circumstances whatever, be published. (Although I was suggesting nothing of the kind! I had only brought them
the story to buy myself immunity from their interrogations.) But
Dementyev walked out, and Tvardovsky had to conduct the "discussion" unaided, with three of his staff sitting silently by, and me making
occasional feeble rejoinders. This discussion, or rather Tvardovsky's
monologue, went on for almost three hours. His speech was rambling,
confused and full of genuine emotion. (Berzer, who was sitting among
us, told me afterward that in all her years at *Novy Mir* she had never
heard Tvardovsky speak like that.)

He went around in circles, first talking about the story, then making
some general observations, then returning to the story, then going over
his general observations again. . . . A true artist himself, he could not
reproach me with not telling the truth. But to admit that it was the
whole truth would have undermined his political and social beliefs at
their foundations.

It was not, of course, the first time that he experienced a destructive
collision within his soul, though never before, perhaps, had the two sides
of his nature come together in such a tight impasse. Ever since he had
first memorized verses by Nekrasov as a barefooted boy, ever since he
had written his own first poem at the age of thirteen, Russian literature
alone had sustained him. His first loyalty was to Russian literature, with
its devout belief in the moral duty of a writer. He had wanted only to be
like them—like Pushkin and those who came after him. Repeating
Yesenin's words, he could have readily died of happiness if he had been
granted a fate like Pushkin's. But this was another age, and another,
more powerful truth had been implanted in all of us, especially in chief
editors, and had been everywhere acknowledged: the Party's truth. In
our time he could not set the course of Russian literature, could be of no
help to it, without a Party card. Nor could he carry a Party card without
believing in it. It was vitally important to him that these two truths
should not diverge but merge. (He would shortly make a close friend and
adviser of Lakshin, who knew how to mediate between the two truths, to
glide so smoothly from one to the other that the fissure became invisible.)
Whenever Tvardovsky's first (poetic) self felt strongly attracted to a

manuscript, he had to test the feelings of his second (political) self before he could publish it as a work of *Soviet* literature.

All the rest of us sat motionless, while he rose from time to time and made use of the space behind his chair to pace a few steps to left and right. "You are so determined," he said, "to show the village at its worst. You might have given us one little glimpse of the sunny side. Everybody in sight is a degenerate or a vampire—yet when you think of it, generals and factory managers come from villages, where else, and go home there on leave." But here he changed his tack: "I'm not saying you should have made Kira a member of the Komsomol; oh, no." One minute he was finding the narrator's attitude to life "too Christian"; the next, he was riveted by the thought that in our time "goods" [*dobro*] had come to mean only "property." This brought Tolstoy to his mind: "Children, the old man has told you a great good [*dobro*]!" First he praised my story for its resemblance to Tolstoy's moral tales. Then he found fault with it because it was "aesthetically less compact" than *Ivan Denisovich*. (If so, this of course was reason enough not to publish it.) But almost in the same breath he was praising it again, either for its use of peasant speech or for its observation of village life.

He went so far as to praise the story's "realism—I use the word without an adjective" and to admit that "critical realism" was every bit as much to his liking as the "socialist" variety.

Then there was a great deal about the economic and technological base; and how both America and Sweden were so much more highly developed that we would not reach their level in twenty years, yet we were already "shocked and repelled by it." Here he recalled how Stalin, contradicting Trotsky, had promised "not to plunder the village to pay for the building of socialism." He paused suddenly, as though a shaft of light had taken him by surprise, looked at each of us in turn and asked, "How, then, was it paid for?" But we said nothing, held out no straw for him to clutch, and he began pacing the sticky parquet floor again and holding forth about the gap between our economic-technological and our moral development. He insisted, however, that "religion had exercised only a slight restraining influence on bad instincts." (What, then, I wondered, had held them in check?)

So he went on, in an almost unbroken monologue. One moment radiating nobility. The next, afraid of bumping his head on the ceiling of dogma. Sometimes shuddering as he felt the promptings of a truth that the poet's fingers could not yet grasp or his eyes discern. Sometimes like a bulldozer doggedly pushing Augean muck heaps before him to form a barricade.

The rest of us neither argued nor agreed; we kept silent. His opponent was the story about the poor old woman Matryona, the mute manuscript he had promised Dementyev to reject. And when, without hearing a word of disagreement, he nonetheless felt defeated on every point, the conscience-stricken Aleksandr Trifonovich groaned out his last and weightiest argument: "How could anyone possibly say that the October Revolution was in vain!"

No one there had said anything of the sort! Or written it! But the embarrassing thing was that not one of us hastened to assent, or smiled, or even nodded. Our silence was indecent. What? Did we, then, not understand this simplest of facts? Blinking wildly, as though still dazzled by headlights, Aleksandr Trifonovich rounded on us like a bull ready to charge and bellowed in anguish: "But for the Revolution, Isakovsky would never have been discovered! . . . And what would have become of me without the Revolution? . . ."

These secondary poetic events were all that sprang to his lips at that moment! (What of Yesenin, what of Klyuyev—did they owe their existence to the Revolution?)

The upshot of this "discussion" was that the piece obviously could not, emphatically could not be published. That being so, the manuscript would normally have been returned to the author, but Tvardovsky hemmed and hawed apologetically. "But still, leave it here in the office for a while. Other people may want to read it. . . ." Now that I had revealed its existence, I had nothing to lose by leaving it.

Aleksandr Trifonovich had yet another request to make of me (and after all that he had said, it sounded quite astonishing). "Only please don't become *ideologically stalwart!* Don't write anything that my staff could pass without my having to know about it."

In other words, he could publish nothing of what I had brought him —and he asked me to go on writing in exactly the same way! That much I could easily promise him.

Trying even harder to soften the blow for me, Aleksandr Trifonovich began talking about ways and means of publishing *Ivan Denisovich* —all for the time being purely imaginary—and got stuck. He himself really did not know how to set about it, from which angle to tackle it, and when. His words were conciliatory. "Don't try to hurry us, though. Don't ask which issue it will be in." I wasn't intending to; I had been spared the Lubyanka, and asked no more. I had lost only by abandoning secrecy in the first place, so that now I should have to be trebly careful to conceal my finished manuscripts and current work.

"It's when you're young," I answered, "that you can't wait to see yourself in print. I've had time to get my second wind."

After this we parted for quite a long time. I did not try to hurry Tvardovsky, and that was a year in which his slowness seemed to me quite justified. In any case, what standard of comparison was there, in what units could it be measured? Had there been any precedent in Soviet literature?

It is easy to find fault with the past. If a hen's egg is placed upright on one slightly dented end, everybody sees that it can stand. Before this was first done, nobody could prevent its rolling over. If Tvardovsky had not done it first, which of the mandarins of Soviet literature would ever have wanted, let alone dared, to present such a pernicious piece as *Ivan Denisovich* to those on high? At the beginning of 1962 it was impossible to guess what course of action he might think up, or how good his chances of success were.

But the years have gone by, we know that Tvardovsky held up publication for eleven months, and it is only too easy now to accuse him of taking his time, of improper delay. For a little while after my tale reached *Novy Mir,* Nikita was still pelting and lambasting Stalin, looking around for more stones to cast at him. This tale by one of his victims would have come very conveniently to Nikita's hand! If it had been published right then, before the impetus of the Twenty-second Congress was spent, the anti-Stalinist hue and cry that greeted it later would have been even more easily raised, and I believe that in the heat of the moment Nikita would have cheerfully splashed those chapters of *The First Circle* called "One Night in the Life of Stalin" over the pages of *Pravda.* I had a clear, a vivid picture of my work published in *Pravda* (circulation a tidy five million). I could almost see it with my eyes open.

Even now I do not know how to judge his behavior. Left to myself, I would never have taken it to Nikita, never have got it through to him. Without Tvardovsky's assistance, any number of Twenty-second Congresses would not have helped. At the same time, how can I refrain from saying now that Tvardovsky let slip a golden opportunity, missed the flood tide that would have carried our small keg beyond the Stalinist reefs to safe inner waters and only there disclosed its contents? If we had published the Stalin chapters there and then, two or three months after the congress, we should have stripped him down much more thoroughly, made it much more difficult to touch him up again in glowing colors. Literature could have accelerated history. It failed to do so.

Viktor Nekrasov said to me fretfully in July 1962: "I can't understand these complicated roundabout routes of his. He collects a lot of readers' reports so that he can base a letter on them. Yet he can get straight through to *the* number! Just take the phone off the hook and ring Nikita directly! Only he's afraid. . . ."

Tvardovsky's character was indeed such that the thought of incurring a rebuff made him feel sick. He was said to suffer torments when he was asked to put in a good word for somebody, help somebody get an apartment: What if they said no to him, a Deputy of the Supreme Soviet and a Candidate Member of the Central Committee? Just think of the humiliation. . . .

He may also have feared that a too direct, a too abrupt approach to Khrushchev might damage the story's chances. But in my view, the main thing was the habitual leisureliness of the high official circles in which he had moved for so long: they live idle lives, and hurrying after history to impose a shape on it as it glides away is not among their habits. They may think it can never leave them behind. They may even think it is they themselves who shape it. Then again, Tvardovsky's appetite abated for some months after his discovery; even unpublished, the story was sustenance enough for him. Taking his time, he had let Chukovsky read it, then Marshak—not merely because their names would give the manuscript greater momentum, but because he wanted to enjoy their reactions himself, to read them out to his editorial staff and to take them around for his friends to see (though he did not show them to me for fear of spoiling me). He even gave the manuscript to Fedin (who did not react at all), and did not withhold it from Paustovsky and Ehrenburg (though he didn't like them enough to offer it to them himself). He spent a long time trying to write a fitting preface to the story (though strictly speaking there was no need for it: why make excuses?). Month after month he conducted his leisurely preparations, with no definite plan for taking the matter *higher*. Simply to have the story set in type and send it to the censors would, he thought, be disastrous (and so it would have been): the censorship would not only forbid publication but immediately report to the "Cultural Department" of the Central Committee, which would not be slow to mount a preemptive attack.

The months went by, the excitement generated by the Twenty-second Congress cooled and was no more. The erratic Nikita, who was always even quicker to drop things than to take them up, and never in the same mood for long at a time, now had to support Nasser, equip Castro with rockets, and discover the definitive (better than best!) scheme for saving Soviet agriculture and bringing it into full bloom, besides jollying along the space program and tightening up the camps, which had grown slack since Beria's fall.

There was another and to Tvardovsky quite unforeseen danger in his practice of passing the manuscript around, collecting positive reports, systematically preparing the ground: in our age of typewriters and photocopying, copies were soon leaking in all directions (some people needed a day to make a copy, for others twenty minutes was enough). While the master copies were kept in *Novy Mir*'s safe, and their movements strictly accounted for, dozens if not hundreds of typed or photographed copies had seeped all over Moscow and Leningrad, and percolated to Kiev, Odessa, Sverdlovsk, Nizhni Novgorod. Its circulation was speeded up by the universal assumption that such a work would never get into print. Tvardovsky was angry, and looked for "traitors" in the office, not realizing, in his ignorance of the techniques and tempo of our age, that he himself, with his habit of collecting oral encomiums and written reports, was mainly responsible for spreading it around. While he was shilly-shallying, the months went by, and a new danger loomed—that the story would leak to the West, where people are quicker off the mark. Once in print there, it would never be published at home. (The logic of this is readily understood by any Soviet citizen, though quite incomprehensible to the Westerner. To us, peace means, not peace, but constant struggle between opposing camps. We are trained to see it like that.) It may have been this danger that forced Tvardovsky to bestir himself. In July he passed the manuscript, festooned with recommendations, to Khrushchev's adviser on cultural matters, Vladimir Semyonovich Lebedev. All this time Tvardovsky had not summoned me once, and it was only from Berzer's accounts that I got to know what was happening at *Novy Mir*. I also started meeting people who had read my story. After the unbroken silence of my underground existence, two dozen such readers made me feel that the eyes of the crowd were on me, and my fame was growing dizzily.

I made hasty preparations for a new and dangerous stage in my life. It was one thing to hide manuscripts when I was one grain of sand among millions, quite another now that I had shown myself: the Lubyanka might be more persistently inquisitive than *Novy Mir* and send some of its hangers-on to make an unhurried search for anything else I might have written. I began reviewing my hiding places, and they now seemed too obvious, too easily guessable by expert housebreakers. So I myself broke into some of them and destroyed their contents, eliminating every trace. I burned all superfluous drafts and rough copies. The rest I decided not to keep at home, and on the eve of 1962 my wife and I took all that I had spared of my archive to her friend Teush in Moscow. (It was this archive that the *oprichniki* would seize three and a half years later.) I have a particularly vivid memory of this removal, by local train on New Year's Eve, because a drunken hooligan burst into the compartment and began abusing the passengers. It so happened that none of the men present tried to stop him: those who were not too old were too cautious. It would have been natural for me to jump up: I was sitting quite close, and I had the right sort of mug for the job. But the precious suitcase containing all my manuscripts stood at our feet, and I dared not move: if it came to a fight, I would inevitably have to tag along to the militia station, if only as a witness, either taking my suitcase with me or—just as bad—leaving it behind. It would be a truly Russian happening if all my cunningly woven threads were snapped by this hooligan. So in order to fulfill my duty as a Russian, I had to exercise a quite un-Russian self-restraint. I sat there, feeling ashamed and cowardly, staring at the floor while the women scolded us for our unmanliness.

This was one of many times when my secret life as a writer robbed me—not always in such a humiliating way, but just as aggravatingly—of my freedom of action, my freedom to speak my mind, my freedom to stand up straight. We all had heavy loads on our backs, but I was also dragged down, and my spiritual energies diverted from literature, by unwieldy burdens hidden beneath the surface. My bones would ache with longing: Straighten up! Straighten up if you die for it!

I had transferred my archive, but I learned from a visit to *Novy Mir* in January that nothing was actually on its way to the printers. In my new, vulnerable position I had to go on writing at odd moments, and combining this with my work as a teacher. I felt the need to make one last revised copy of *The First Circle,* and I risked beginning it in January 1962. For four months, till the end of April, I had no time for anything else, and I felt no concern for the fate of *Ivan Denisovich* except to hope that nothing would start moving, that nothing would change: it didn't matter if he got nowhere as long as I could finish the novel in peace.

There was no need for me to say my prayers: Ivan Denisovich stayed just where he was. On the May Day holiday I took the copies of the retyped novel to their several destinations without trouble, then by the time I had tidied up a few loose ends, summer was approaching and I thought I would spend it enjoyably, on the move. The whole business with *Novy Mir* seemed to have run into the sands—so much the better, I thought; I shall gradually find my way back to safety!—and my wife and I had the idea of going to the Yenisei and Lake Baikal. (I had been in Siberia, but only by prisoner transport, and only as far as Novosibirsk.) As the proverb has it: "A poor man may marry; but his wedding night is short." In Irkutsk, and not a mile nearer home, a copy of an urgent telegram from Tvardovsky awaited me, inviting me to look in 'briefly' at the office. Since four days' travel lay between me and the brief look-in, Baikal remained unviewed.

Once again they had arranged a general editorial conference. I was apprised that my story had found favor at some unspecified high level (which, translated, meant V. S. Lebedev). But a wish to see certain *improvements* made had been expressed. In Tvardovsky's opinion, the changes requested were not at all numerous, and he would urge me to carry them out and not let slip the opportunity that had presented itself.

It was costing him a great effort not to betray his jubilation. His childlike spontaneity made it impossible for him to hide the happiness in his eyes. He was very pleased that the campaign on which he had spent so many months was beginning to succeed. Because editorial protocol demanded it, he made a show of adding some observations of his own, but all that mattered to him was that I should accept Lebedev's. He did not, however, say so outright, but kept the conference formal, and invited all the other editors to state frankly what amendments they thought necessary.

Things were said, but nothing of moment, because their only object was to please the chief editor, and views of their own, distinct from his, were the last thing any of them wanted. Some day historians of literature will look into it and discover to their surprise that in the years when the Stalin cult was under violent attack, the Soviet editorial board best known for its love of freedom and its liberalism conducted its internal affairs on the basis of a personality cult of its own. Nor was it Tvardovsky who had created this situation; it had created itself, quite naturally, as it did in every institution, every echelon in the Soviet system, so that every part is an epitome of the whole—but at *Novy Mir* of all places it looked outrageous. Tvardovsky's vision and his sense of humor were impaired, or he would have noticed the lingering frosts and dispelled them.

But then Dementyev, too, was sitting by, and he at least could see the hoop about to burst and the lid about to fly open. Aleksandr Grigoryevich Dementyev, who had never once wavered in his post as Party organizer of the Leningrad Writers' Organization in the grim days of 1949, and who in Khrushchev's time had become commissar of the most liberal magazine (someone must have had good reason to send him there—in part no doubt to recover his freshness, in part to purge his crimes, but also to see that they didn't get away with anything!). With his mind on those who had sent him here on half salary but with dual responsibilities, he could not now recognize the authority even of Khrushchev's expert, could not succumb to the euphoria of the editorial board as a whole. He was too hard-headed to think it worth arguing in December 1961, when everyone was praising me and making a fuss over me; he at least knew that the story would never be published. But events had taken such a perverse and irregular course that the story seemed likely to break through to the light—and he must do all he could to correct it.

Where now was the alternation of coyly friendly and boldly friendly looks, the ingratiating tilt of the graying head? How harsh the endearing, the irresistible northern brogue had become! How flushed he was, on fire from ear to ear! At least he was not hurling thunderbolts from Olympus, but was arguing with us—excitedly, nervously, afraid that he might not win, might not carry his point. The thunder rolled only in the terminology—communism, patriotism, materialism, socialist realism. If Dementyev could have had his way, he would have planed down my story till the surface was perfectly smooth. But as things were, he had to stick to essentials. So he accused me of insulting the banner and symbol of Soviet art, *Battleship Potemkin,* and said that the whole conversation about it should be cut. So also should Shukhov's conversation with Alyoshka about God, because it was artistically ineffectual, it was ideologically incorrect, it was too long, and it only spoiled a good story. Further, the author should not avoid giving a precise political assessment of the Bandera-ites, even as found in the camps, because they were bespattered with the blood of our Soviet people. Then again . . . He had, it appeared, made a lot of notes on the manuscript, and could show them to me in detail, but he had left it at home.

By the end of his monologue Dementyev looked like a wild boar inflamed with rage, and if someone had put the 150 pages of my story before him just then he might easily have scattered it to the winds with his tusks.

Tvardovsky meanwhile was silent. No good saying it wasn't true! The political commissar's reasoning was very sound: he wanted to fashion my shapeless story into a weapon of socialist realism, and what could the chief editor say against that? He could not argue—but for some reason he was silent. He did not so much as nod or raise an eyebrow in support of Dementyev. Instead he looked expectantly at me. If I had given way, that would have been that.

However, Dementyev had gone too far! Clever and quick he certainly was, but he knew nothing of the species zek and what a hardened breed it is. If he had chosen his words more carefully, if he had demanded concessions which though small were nonetheless unpalatable and enough to ruin the thing, I would have written it all down. I would have thought it over, together with the demands of Khrushchev's expert, and might have made some ruinous changes. But faced with that malevolent glare, I answered easily and unhesitatingly, without pausing to think what I stood to lose. I thought of my zeks, my brothers, the hunger strike in Ekibastuz, the Kengir rising, and I felt ashamed and disgusted with myself for arguing at all with these people, for seriously thinking, even after the Twenty-second Congress, that writers who carried those little red Party cards had it in them to publish a word of truth.

"I've waited ten years," I answered, throwing off all restraint, "and I can wait another ten. I'm in no hurry. My life doesn't depend on literature. Give me back my manuscript and I'll be on my way."

Here Tvardovsky intervened in alarm. "You don't *have to* do anything. Everything we've said today you can take or leave as you think fit. It's just that we all very much want the manuscript to get through."

Dementyev argued no more. He fell silent. He went limp. He had reached the point at which his influence on the chief stopped abruptly. He could not risk going further.

It then proved necessary for me to go home with—yes—Dementyev, to pick up the top copy. How changed he was, how friendly he had suddenly become. Could this be the man who just half an hour earlier had advanced on me furiously, stamping his hoofs? To my surprise, he offered to let me work in his apartment, completely forgot his glossary of thunderous "isms," and began appealing to me in a vague and roundabout way to try and understand him. No chunk of solid iron, then, this commissar—oh, dear, no! He had been in so many discreet inner offices—and every one of them had depressed him more than the last. Incidentally, I heard later that he came of a rich merchant family —and he was old enough for the old way of life to have retained some hold on him. Perhaps it was nervousness about his curriculum vitae that made him so ostentatiously orthodox? It can happen; Sofronov is apparently just the same. . . .

So I was left face to face with my story again. I knew something the *Novy Mir* staff did not know: that what we had was by no means an authentic version, that it had been tinkered with and trimmed before they saw it, that my tale was not the brand-new article, untouched by any hand. Having once begun, I could continue. I could reduce the explosive charge, and there would still be plenty left. But this seemed to me a bad beginning to a literary career: to compromise as all the rest did. I remember clearly that at the time I would have liked nothing better than to leave it uncorrected—and if they wouldn't publish it, to hell with them. All the same, it would have been stupid not to try my luck at all. Reduced in strength by one half or three quarters of one percent (and the concessions that I had decided to make to Lebedev and *Novy Mir* were no bigger or more significant than that), it would still be quite potent in print. No, it was worth a trial.

Looked at closely, Lebedev's demands were in fact startling in their triviality. They affected nothing of major importance in the story. The most desperate passages, which I might have given up with a heavy heart, had been ignored, almost as though he had not noticed them. Who was this cryptoliberal up above there, so close to the First Secretary of the Central Committee? How had he worked his way to the top? How did he hold on? What was his program? Obviously he must be helped!

The main thing Lebedev demanded was that I should remove all passages in which Captain Buynovsky was shown as a comic figure (by Ivan Denisovich's yardstick)—as he was intended to be—and that I should put more emphasis on his Party membership (there must, after all, be a "positive hero"!). This seemed to me the lightest of sacrifices. I removed the comedy, and all that was left could be seen as "heroic"

—though, as critics subsequently found, it was not always "sufficiently explicit." The protest Buynovsky made on work parade now looked a little overdone (I had intended it to be comic), but this did not perhaps mar the picture of the camp. Then I was required to use the word "screws" more sparingly; so I reduced the number of its appearances from seven to three. The camp officers were to be called "vermin" less frequently (my version was rather well seasoned with the word); and if not the author himself, then Buynovsky must condemn the Bandera-ites. (I did put a sentence to that effect in the captain's mouth, but cut it out when the story appeared in a separate edition. It was natural enough for the captain, but Bandera-ites had been far too freely reviled elsewhere.) I was further asked to credit the zeks with some hope of freedom (but that I could not do). And—most comic of all for one who hated Stalin as I did—I must mention him just once, as responsible for all these miseries. (In fact, he was never once mentioned in the story and this was hardly an accident.) I gave way on this, and mentioned "old Whiskers" just once. . . .

I made the alterations, left Moscow and found myself in yet another period of unbroken silence and darkness. Once again, all was still and dead. The story might never have been set in motion. It might all have been a dream. It was the end of September before I learned from Berzer, in great secrecy, how things were developing. Lebedev had started reading the story to Khrushchev at his dacha in Pitsunda. (Nikita did not read himself if he could help it, but tried to extract an education from films.) He had listened carefully to this entertaining tale, laughed in the right places, groaned and grunted in the right places, and sent for Mikoyan halfway through so that they could listen together. They gave the whole thing their approval and of course liked particularly the "labor" scene, in which Ivan Denisovich was "so careful with the mortar." (Khrushchev mentioned this again at a Kremlin meeting.) Mikoyan did not disagree with Khrushchev, and the story's fate was decided by this fireside reading. Khrushchev, however, wanted the arrangement to appear democratic.

Two weeks later, when he returned to Moscow from leave, *Novy Mir* received at midday an order from the Central Committee: submit no fewer than twenty-three copies by the following morning. The office had only three. If typed, they couldn't possibly be ready in time! The only thing to do was to set up the story for printing. They took over some typesetting machines in the *Izvestia* printing shops, and distributed parts of the story to different compositors, who set it up in complete bewilderment. In the same way, *Novy Mir*'s proofreaders read it piecemeal in the middle of the night, reduced to despair by the strange words and the strange layout, and marveling at the subject matter. Then, in the shift before dawn, all twenty-five copies were bound in *Novy Mir*'s dark-blue cardboard, and next morning, twenty-three copies were delivered to the offices of the Central Committee, as though it had needed no additional effort from anyone, and the plates were hidden away in the strongroom under lock and key. Khrushchev ordered the distribution of copies to the senior Party leaders, while he himself left for Central Asia to put its agriculture to rights.

He returned two weeks later, beneath what were for him the baleful stars of mid-October. At a regular meeting of the Politburo (or Presidium, as it then was) Nikita sought agreement to the publication of the story. I do not know for sure, but I am inclined to think that members of the Politburo showed reluctance. Several made no comment ("Why don't you say something?" Nikita demanded), and someone ventured to ask "whose mill would it be grist to?" But Nikita in those days was the Great-I-Am, and I daresay he remembered to praise Ivan Denisovich for his conscientious bricklaying. So that it was decided to publish the story. Or at any rate, no one spoke unambiguously against it.

This was how a miracle befell the Soviet censorship—or more precisely, it was an example of what was described three years later as "voluntarism in the field of literature."

On Saturday 20 October, Khrushchev received Tvardovsky to announce the decision. I don't know whether it was their first, but it was their last unhurried tête-à-tête. The longing to believe was very strong in Tvardovsky's heart, as no doubt it is in that of every Russian, indeed every human being. That was why in the past, for all that the ruin of the peasantry was plain to see, for all the sufferings of his own family, he had become a slave to his faith in Stalin, and years later sincerely mourned his death. Afterward he had just as sincerely recoiled from the unmasked Stalin and tried to believe in the new, refurbished truth and the new man from whom the light of that truth emanated. This was how he saw Khrushchev during their two- or three-hour meeting. A month later, when we were more intimate than we would ever be again, Tvardovsky said to me: "What a warm-hearted and clever man he is! How lucky we are to have such a man over us!"

At that meeting with Tvardovsky, Khrushchev was soft-spoken, pensive, indeed quite philosophical. It is easy to believe this. A hostile constellation was already pointing like a dagger at his heart. He must already have received the telegram in which Gromyko reported a conversation the day before in the White House: "Tell me honestly, Mr. Gromyko, have you any rockets in Cuba?" With his usual honesty and assurance, Gromyko had answered "No." Khrushchev did not, of course, know, as he chatted peacefully with Tvardovsky about literature, that blown-up photographs of Soviet rockets in Cuba were being mounted on display boards in Washington, to be shown to delegates at an O.A.S. meeting on Monday, at which Kennedy would obtain consent to his unprecedentedly bold step: inspecting Soviet ships. Only Sunday stood between Khrushchev and his week of humiliation, fear and surrender. And it was on that very last Saturday that he issued *Ivan Denisovich*'s visa.

"I even found myself interrupting him!" Tvardovsky recalled, in surprise. "Babies aren't made by kisses," I told him. "Why don't you abolish the censorship of imaginative literature? Books are circulating in illegal copies—what could be worse than that?" And Nikita had heard him out pacifically and behaved as though he was no stranger to this idea, or so it seemed to Tvardovsky. (Comparison of the various accounts he gave in the office suggested that Tvardovsky had, without realizing it, ascribed statements of his own to a silent Khrushchev.)

Khrushchev had told Tvardovsky that three volumes of documents on Stalin's crimes had now been collected, but that they were not being published for the present.[3] "History will pronounce judgment on what we have tried to do." (Khrushchev always became solemn and subdued when he spoke of our common mortality, and of man's limited span. This note could be heard in his public speeches too. It was a Christian trait in him, of which he was unconscious. No Communist leader before or after him, to east or west of him, has ever spoken like that. Nikita was a tsar who completely failed to understand his own true nature and his historical mission, who was forever cutting the ground from under the feet of those social groups which would and could have supported him, who had never had and never felt the need to seek a wise counselor.

---

3. Khrushchev never carried anything through to completion, and the deposition of Stalin was no exception. He had only to go a little further, and no one would ever again have unclenched his teeth to bay about the murderer's "great services."

His nimble, go-getting son-in-law was not very clever either, but he was an adventurer into the bargain, and hastened his father-in-law's downfall.) Khrushchev was quite sure that Stalin had murdered Kirov, but realized that Kirov was not a person of any importance in his own right.

It looked as though no further decision on the story was needed, and Tvardovsky gave orders for it to be included in issue No. 11. But this was when the curtain went up on the confrontation with America. There was a possibility that the storm blowing along the corridors of the Kremlin all the way from the Caribbean might whisk my story into oblivion. But no, the storm died down! On the eve of the November holiday, exactly a year since I had first let the story out of my hands, I was called in to read the galleys. When I had sat over typewritten pages it had all been pure fantasy, and I had felt no particular emotion. But now that the uncut magazine pages lay before me, I imagined the truth about the way we had lived in the camps emerging like some hideously cruel monster into the light of day, where the ill-informed millions could see it—and in the luxury of my hotel room I wept, for the first time, as I read the story.[4]

At this point, a request from Lebedev was passed on to me—that I should also omit these words spoken by Tyurin: "I crossed myself, and said to God: 'Thou art there in heaven after all, O Creator. Thy patience is long, but thy blows are heavy.' " They had finally seen it. . . . They had seen it, but too late, that key passage in the story in which I had stood on its head and turned inside out the whole legend of the destruction of the leading cadres in 1937! The editors tried to bend me: Lebedev, after all, had been so sympathetic! It was he who had crashed through all barriers and arranged the whole thing! It was my turn to make a concession to him. They were right, and I would have done so —at my own cost, or at that of literary effect. But what they were suggesting was that I should make concessions at the expense of God

---

4. *Novy Mir* played a neat joke on the censors, submitting the first make-up of *Ivan Denisovich* without explanation. The censors in their deep dungeons knew nothing of the Central Committee's decision; it had been taken *sub rosa*, as always in our country. When they received the story, the censors were appalled by this act of "ideological sabotage," and made a menacing telephone call to the magazine. *"Who* sent this manuscript?" "Why, we did, of course," N. P. Bianki, the office manager, innocently replied. "But which one of you authorized it?" "Oh, we all liked it," chirped Bianki. Threatening noises from the other end, receiver put down. Half an hour later, they phoned up quite cheerfully: "Send us a few more copies" (they wanted to read it themselves). Khrushchev was all very well, but every page must still bear the censor's stamp of approval.

and of the peasant, and this I had vowed never to do. And so I said no to my still unknown, still mythical benefactor.

The boulder, once dislodged, bounded downhill with such momentum that even Khrushchev's adviser could not put things right and stop it!

It was Adzhubei who made an attempt, not to stop it in its downward rush, but at least to divert it: perhaps under pressure from the righteous and orthodox, who were eager to give their own version of the history of the camps for the first time (with themselves as principal martyrs and heroes), or more probably with pettier motives, merely to seize the initiative from Tvardovsky, put a spoke in his wheel, outgallop him now that he had made the running, and snatch the prize. Adzhubei vented his wrath on the assembled editorial staff of *Izvestia* because his paper had not been the first to "open up" an important theme. Somebody recalled that a story along those lines had come in from the district of Chita, but that it was "unviable" and had been rejected. They rushed to the wastepaper baskets, but the story had been destroyed. They got through to G. Shelest, and he booked an emergency call from Chita and dictated his "Rough Diamond." It was in fact published in the holiday number of *Izvestia*—published in a shamelessly offhand way, without so much as an exclamation point, as though stories about camp life had been appearing in newspapers for forty years and were boringly familiar to everyone. Tvardovsky was very upset at the time, and very annoyed with Adzhubei. As I see it, "Rough Diamond" did them no good: our stone sped on with unchecked impetus, and it was in our presentation that Russian readers were destined to see the contours of a camp for the first time.

Already assured of victory, Tvardovsky, like the prudent and skillful editor he was, took a look into the future and before the November holiday was over, sent me a long letter.

> I want to use the right which my age and literary experience give me to say certain things. We have already had so many people trying to get your address out of us, showing an interest in you which is sometimes heightened by other than literary stimuli. What will happen when the piece appears in print? . . . What will happen is all the things which we call fame. . . . My purpose in saying all this is to stress my hope that you will keep your head, not be carried away by it all, preserve a lofty sense of your own dignity. . . . You have undergone a number of ordeals, and I can hardly imagine you failing to stand up to this new test. . . . On the contrary, I have sometimes

thought that your unconcern is perhaps excessive, amounting almost to apathy. . . . Together with my colleagues on the magazine, I felt as though I was celebrating a victory, a great triumph, on the day when I heard that "all was well"—and I found myself just a little hurt by your guarded response to my telegram of congratulations, by that feeble word "pleasant," which—forgive me for saying so—was simply insulting to me in the circumstances. . . . But now it is to your self-restraint and your good sense that I am appealing—may they be strengthened and confirmed in you, may they remain the constant companions of your future labors. . . . You will be pestered with tiresome requests to "let us have something," an excerpt, a fragment; you will be offered contracts and money. . . . I implore you . . . to hold out. . . . Don't put yourself in anyone's hands, plead your prior commitment to *Novy Mir* (we have some right to hope that you will do so), say that it takes everything that comes from your pen.

They had had a "victory celebration"! In reply I explained my position to him:

Do you know what my thoughts were when I opened your envelope? My wife brought it to me and said anxiously, "A fat letter from *Novy Mir*. Why is it so fat?" I felt it and said, "It's perfectly obvious. Somebody wants me to make further concessions, but I can't do it. I've done with publishing for the time being. . . ." My life in Ryazan goes on just as before (early in the morning, in my camp jerkin, I go to split logs for the stove, then I prepare for my lessons, then I go to school, where I am scolded for skipping political instruction or for neglect of extracurricular activities)—so much so that Moscow conversations and telegrams seem nothing but a dream. Your telegram made only one thing clear to me: that *so far* my work had not been banned. So please, dear Aleksandr Tvardovsky, do not hold it against me that I used the feeble word "pleasant." I should have been insincere if I had expressed myself more strongly. I felt no wild joy at the time. I may say that my whole life has trained me to expect the worst much more often than not, and I am always readier, more willing to believe, the worst. In the camp I took to heart the Russian proverb: "Don't let good luck fool you or bad luck frighten you." I have learned to live by this rule, and I hope never to depart from it. . . . The greatest happiness which "recognition" has given me I experienced in December last year, when you found *Denisovich* worth a sleepless night.

But it would have been strange if his exhortations to "hold out" and "not to put myself in anyone's hands" had not awakened sympathetic echoes in me.

Fame "will not devour me. . . . But I foresee that its duration will be brief, and I want to use it as sensibly as possible (for the sake of the works I have already written)."[5]

We were already on terms of such warm friendship, although we had never once met tête-à-tête, with none of his colleagues present. . . . Shortly afterward I was at his home, at the very moment when a messenger from his office (later spotted as an informer) brought us the advance copy of No. 11. We embraced, and Aleksandr Tvardovsky was as happy as a schoolboy, flitting about the room for all his bearlike bulk. "The bird is free! . . . The bird is free! . . . They can't very well hold it back now! It's almost impossible now!" (Almost . . . He was not quite certain himself until the very last minute. Had there not been occasions when every copy of an issue had been destroyed? Who cares if work and money are wasted? Ideology is what we care about.) I congratulated him: "The victory is more yours than mine."

"Come right over—on the double!" These were his extraordinary words over the telephone when I next arrived in Moscow. Immediately after the publication of No. 11 there had been a plenary meeting of the Central Committee—to discuss industry, I think. Several thousand copies of the magazine, originally intended for Moscow retailers, had been transferred to the bookstalls provided for the delegates. Khrushchev had announced from the platform that this was an important and much needed book. (My name eluded him, and he called the author "Ivan Denisovich" too.) He even complained to the plenum about his Politburo: "Shall we publish it or not? I ask them. And they don't say a word." So the delegates had "come home from market" with two books —one red (materials for discussion at the plenary meeting), one blue (*Novy Mir*, No. 11). Yes, said Tvardovsky, laughing, there they were, each with one red volume tucked underneath his arm and one blue. Before Khrushchev's closing speech the secretary of the Novosibirsk obkom had said to Tvardovsky: "Worse things have happened. . . . There are establishments like that in my oblast to this day, I know very well. But why write about it?" But after Nikita's speech he had sought out Tvardovsky, to shake hands and qualify his ill-judged words.

So potent was the effect of general praise, of universal rapture, that Tvardovsky said to me: "Now let's launch 'Matryona' "—the story *Novy Mir* had refused to touch at the beginning of the year, the story that

---

5. *Novy Mir* as yet knew nothing of them.

"could never appear in print." He had now quite forgotten that he had previously rejected it, and was for sending it to the printers without further ado.

"The second step is the most dangerous," Tvardovsky often warned me. "Any fool can write one thing, they say: It's the next one that counts."

And he would look at me anxiously. By my "next one" he did not mean "Matryona" but whatever I might write now. And when I looked them over I could not decide which of my writings to bring into the open: they were all too hot to handle. Fortunately, that very month I was able to write "An Incident at Krechetovka Station"—with so little effort that it seemed to write itself—especially for the magazine, the first time I had done such a thing in my life. A.T. was very agitated when he took it from me, and still more so as he read; he could not have dreaded failure more if the work had been his own. Tveritinov's arrival on the scene added to his apprehensions: he made up his mind that this was going to be a patriotic detective story, and that it would all end with the capture of a genuine spy.

When he had reassured himself, he immediately sent me a joyful telegram. As he worked on "Matryona" and "Krechetovka," which, if he had his way, would consolidate my reputation, he refrained for the first and last time from "political" calculations about what would or would not "get through," and instead sat with me in a cloud of cigarette smoke doing an honest job of editing.[6]

In his observations and recommendations, particularly those on rural matters, he made points of great subtlety, useful correctives to my overconfidence: you cannot talk about "village carpenters" because in a village everybody is a carpenter; "deal laths" makes no sense; if a piglet is fat he will not be greedy; berrying or mushrooming in the forest is not work but pleasure (here, however, he conceded that for country people today it has become work, because it pays better than laboring in the kolkhoz fields); furthermore, aspens do not grow around station buildings, because all the trees there are planted, and nobody

---

6. Consideration of what would or would not "get by" so clouded the brains of *Novy Mir*'s editors (and still more the editors of other magazines) that they were left with little vision, taste or energy to make substantive remarks on aesthetic quality. Works of mine that aroused no aesthetic objections in *Novy Mir* were most effectively and searchingly criticized in private—and not, as a rule, by people officially concerned with literature.

would ever plant an aspen; a "youth" is older than a "kid." He was also very insistent that gerunds are out of place in the speech of ordinary people, and that sentences like "Having mixed and kneaded the dough, I shall bake it" were impossible. Here I did not agree: Russian proverbs sometimes do sound like that.

We met frequently in the autumn of 1962 and were, I would say, both very frank and very friendly. In those months A.T. could not make enough of me and took as much pride in my successes as if they were his own. What particularly pleased him was that I behaved as he would have wished any author discovered by him to behave: I chased away reporters, gave no interviews, dodged photographers and newsreel cameramen. He felt as though he had created me, molded me from clay, and would now always prescribe the best solutions for all my problems and lead me along the glittering path of fame. His assumption (though I had never made any such promise) was that henceforth I would never take any important step without seeking his advice and approval. He took it on himself, for instance, to decide which photographer I could consent to sit for. (The photographer, as it turned out, was a bad one, but all that mattered to me was my expression—one of exhaustion and deep sorrow—and this we managed to convey.) The time had come to issue some sort of brief biography, and A.T. personally took up his pen to compose it. I thought that it should indicate the reason for my imprisonment—disapproving remarks about Stalin—but Tvardovsky peremptorily resisted this, simply would not hear of it. (He could not know that it might have proved very useful later on, when the Party alleged at briefing sessions that I had committed treason.) He had a broad view of the present, but hardly ever looked into the future. Moreover, there was more than one layer of hidden reasons for his overt behavior. He had, for instance, gone on believing in Stalin for a long time, and anyone who had not believed *even then* was an insult to the Tvardovsky of today. For the same sort of reason he rejected my explanation that natural fastidiousness was cause enough for Tveritinov to dislike Stalin. What *could* have made such a man *dislike* Stalin? It was obvious: either he himself or relatives of his had been inside. A.T. would have it no other way.

I was in no hurry to rebel against his patronage; I was not anxious to demonstrate that at forty-four I had set firm and could not be re-molded. But there can be no genuine friendship without at least some acknowledgment of equality. Tvardovsky exaggerated the similarity of our range of interests, our aims, our experience of life. He had a good knowledge of the political pecking order, of the moves to be made at meetings, by telephone or behind the scenes, and considered this a very important part of his experience. But he was too ready to believe that this system was all-embracing and durable. He could not imagine anyone rejecting the system from the outset. He could not imagine my discerning or knowing things about literature or politics that he himself could not see or did not know. He took pleasure in patronizing the young, but was incapable of close association with his peers.

The hope that at last he had found a friend flared up again when I appeared. But I did not let myself be misled. I loved the peasant core of the man; the way in which the childlike poet showed through the veneer of grandee mannerisms; that peculiar natural dignity with which he met his enemies (sometimes persons in high places)—met them face to face, I mean: on the telephone he usually became flustered —and which kept him out of ridiculous or demeaning situations. But his past and mine were too unlike, and what we had carried away from it too incongruous. I could never be so candid with him, so much at ease with him, as I could with dozens of people on whom the groves of Gulag had cast their indelible shadow. A bump or two, a certain amount of friction, a little adjustment, and our characters might have become a better fit; but there can be no friendship between men where there is no similarity of outlook, no mutual appreciation and consideration. We were like two mathematical curves, each illustrating its own equation. They may approximate at certain points, may meet, may even have a common tangent, a common derivative, but their archetypal peculiarity will quickly and inevitably carry them in different directions.

# On the Surface

If a deep-sea fish used to a constant pressure of many atmospheres rises to the surface, it perishes because it cannot adjust to excessively low pressures, and in much the same way I, who for fifteen years had lurked discreetly in the depths—the camps, exile, underground—never showing myself, never making a single noticeable mistake about a person or a situation, now that I had risen to the surface and to sudden fame, inordinately resounding fame (for in our country abuse and praise alike are always carried to extremes), began making blunder after blunder, completely failing to understand my new position and my new possibilities.

I did not realize the extent of my newly won strength or, therefore, the degree of audacity with which I could now behave. The force of inertia kept me cautious and secretive. Caution and secrecy were both necessary, it is true, because my chance breakthrough with *Ivan Denisovich* had done nothing to reconcile the System to me and promised no easy road ahead.

Nonetheless, for the time being—for a couple of months, or for a month at least—I could have pressed steadily forward: for that one month, obsequiously extravagant publicity had opened the doors of all theaters and all editorial offices to me.

But I didn't realize it. I was in a hurry to stop before I was stopped, to take cover again and pretend that I had nothing to offer and nothing further in mind. As though the way back were still open! As though they would ever let me out of their sight again!

Moreover, I could not help feeling triumphant now that my story was in print, and so failed to appreciate that Tvardovsky and I were losers rather than winners: we had lost a whole year, missed the tide-

50

race loosed by the Twenty-second Congress, and ridden ashore only on the last expiring wave. I allowed myself, at a modest estimate, at least half a year, perhaps as much as two years, before openings were boarded up and all gates barred to me. In fact, I had a single month—from the first favorable review on 18 November to the Kremlin meeting on 17 December. Or rather, less—until the first counterattack by the reactionaries on 1 December (when Khrushchev was sicked onto the modernist artists in the Manège—which was intended to be the beginning of a much broader campaign). But even two weeks should have given me time to occupy a few bridgeheads, to make the titles of a few other works known to the public.

I did nothing of the sort, because I had adopted a false policy. My intention was to use my short run of fame "to the best effect," but that was precisely what I did not do—out of a mistaken sense of obligation to *Novy Mir* and Tvardovsky.

Let me make myself clear. I did, of course, owe something to Tvardovsky, but the debt was purely personal. I had, however, no right to look at things from a personal point of view and to worry about what *Novy Mir* would think of me. My point of departure should always have been that I did not belong to myself alone, that my literary destiny was not just my own, but that of the millions who had not lived to scrawl or gasp or croak the truth about their lot as jailbirds and their later discoveries in the camps. Troy, after all, does not owe its existence to Schliemann, and our many-layered camp culture makes solemn demands of its own, so that I, who had returned from the world that never gives up its dead, had no right to swear loyalty either to *Novy Mir* or to Tvardovsky, to stop and ask myself whether they would believe that my head was not in the least turned by fame, but that I was coolly and systematically digging myself in.

Yet, although my anxieties about *Novy Mir* fettered me less than my excessive caution, I nonetheless felt them holding me back. As A.T. had prophesied, I was always being asked for "a little piece—anything will do" for literary newspapers, or for the radio, and I ought to have given them without delay something from *The First Circle,* which was ready for publication, or from the plays I had by me, so that by making their titles known I should have staked claims from which it would not have been easy to dislodge me later on. In the four weeks while everyone was stunned by the blast from my tale, I would have run into no obstacles. But I said no. I imagined that by doing so I was safeguarding my work.

I took pride in resisting the temptations of fame so easily.

Newspapermen tried to force the doors of my home and of the Moscow hotel rooms in which I stayed; there were telephone calls from embassies in Moscow to my school in Ryazan; written questionnaires were sent from press agencies with such stupid requests as "Could you tell the Western reader just how brilliant you consider Khrushchev's 'resolution' of the Cuban crisis to be?" I said not a single word to any of them, although there was nothing to stop me from saying a very great deal, very boldly, and the thunderstruck newsmen would have splashed it to the ends of the earth. I was afraid that if I once started answering Western correspondents, I would be asked questions by Soviet newsmen too, questions that would predetermine my response: either an immediate act of rebellion or a life of cheerless conformity. Not wishing to lie, and not daring to rebel, I preferred silence.

At the end of November, ten days or so after the story appeared, the artistic council of the "Sovremennik" Theater auditioned my play *(The Love Girl and the Innocent,* a toned-down version of part of *The Republic of Labor)* and urged me to let them put it on *immediately;* they would stage the play in a month's time if it meant dining and sleeping in the theater! They would have kept their promise—I know the "Sovremennik." And yet I refused.

You may well ask why! To begin with, I felt that one more revision was necessary before it reached the public, and this would take seven clear days or—what with my work at school, and the spate of enthusiastic letters from people with nothing better to do—perhaps even a month. "Sovremennik" seemed ready to accept even that, and to let me make further changes to the text as we went along—but then I could not simply abandon my school! Why not? Well—can a man ever become free quite so suddenly? Suddenly be without burdensome daily obligations? And again, how could I refuse to take the kids to the end of their semester? Who could award their marks? Then again, an inspection party chose this worst possible moment to descend on us, for the whole month left to me. How could I let the headmaster down, when he had been so kind to me for so many years, and slip the leash? I could have given "Sovremennik" a text ready for performance within a week; I could have issued "lightened" versions of excerpts from my novel at the rate of two a week; I could have been giving readings and interviews on the radio—and instead I was messing about in the school lab, setting up silly little experiments in physics, compiling lesson-by-lesson study plans, marking exercise books. I was a worm in orbit in space. . . .

Then again, what if "top people" happened to see it before its premiere, got angry and put the lid not only on the play but on the stories that should be appearing in *Novy Mir* anytime now? The circulation of *Novy Mir,* remember, was 100,000, whereas "Sovremennik"'s auditorium seats only seven hundred people.

Yet again: I had after all promised Tvardovsky first refusal of all my work. How could I hand the play over to "Sovremennik" before *Novy Mir* had taken a look at it? So I kept the brisk and energetic "Sovremennik" dangling, and handed over my play to a sleepy magazine. One member of its staff, however, was not at all sleepy—Dementyev—and the play never reached *Novy Mir* itself, went no farther than the two apartments on Kotelnicheskaya Embankment, and the two Sashas. They decided between them, and Tvardovsky informed me, that "it doesn't come off artistically," "it isn't theater," "it's Ivan Denisovich again—you're plowing the same old field instead of breaking new ground." How could I defend my work? Perhaps it wasn't theater. But it certainly wasn't "plowing the same old field": as yet, no one had seriously begun breaking that ground. This was not about a Special Camp, but about a Corrective Labor Camp, in which both sexes, and criminals of various sorts, were mixed up together; the professional criminals and their psychology reigned supreme; the camp authorities ran a fraudulent enterprise.

All right—it looked a bit feeble after *Ivan Denisovich.* I can easily believe that Tvardovsky genuinely did not like the piece. There the matter should have ended—with *Novy Mir* rejecting the play and leaving me free to do what I liked with it. Nothing of the kind! That was not how Tvardovsky understood my promise and saw our collaboration now, in days to come, and to the end of time. I had been his forty-three-year-old discovery, and but for him I should never—or so he supposed —have been a writer at all. I did not even know the value of my work (bringing him one piece, and keeping a dozen up my sleeve). From now on Tvardovsky (and Dementyev) must sit in judgment on each piece: should it be printed in *Novy Mir,* or hidden away and shown to no one? There was no third possibility.

This was precisely their verdict on *The Love Girl and the Innocent* —not to publish it or to show it to anyone else. "I must warn you against those theatrical gangsters!" Tvardovsky would say in all seriousness. This was how the editor of the country's most liberal journal spoke of the country's youngest and most daring theater! What made him so sure of his judgment? Had he seen many of "Sovremennik"'s productions? He had not seen a single one, he had never crossed its threshold (for fear of lowering himself). His high position compelled him to obtain information at second hand and from not very clean sources. In the Government Rest Home at Barvikha, at some Kremlin banquet or other, and also from a few obliging people in his own office, he had heard that the "Sovremennik" was impertinent, subversive, not a Party theater—a den of "gangsters," in fact.

As it was only two weeks since I had appeared in print and the honeymoon with Tvardovsky was not yet over, I thought it neither proper nor useful to rebel openly, and so found myself a supplicant—pleading for permission to show people my own work, with Tvardovsky digging in his heels, dissuading me, contradicting me, and in the end exasperated by my disobedience. He very reluctantly *consented to let me* show the play to a theater—not to "Sovremennik," though, but to Zavadsky's moribund playhouse (simply because it had staged *Tyorkin*). His consent came too late. Relying on A.T.'s difficulty in obtaining information (he was so remote from, so much above, the ordinary literary public and the livelier Moscow circles), I had kept in touch with "Sovremennik." I had, however, held back my play for a month—a whole irrecoverable month!—waiting for the censors to pass "Matryona" and "Krechetovka." Now I handed over the play to "Sovremennik," but it was too late: the theaters were already feeling the pressure after the December "meeting" in the Kremlin. "Sovremennik" could not even bring itself to start rehearsals, and the play was stuck fast for several years. Tvardovsky was late in learning about my breach of discipline, but when he did, it rankled, and in subsequent years he rebuked me more than once: how could I have approached "Sovremennik" when he had asked me not to?

In a letter A.T. once called me "the man in all literature I hold most dear," and he did sincerely love me, selflessly yet tyrannically: as a sculptor loves the work of his hands, or perhaps as a suzerain loves a favorite vassal. It never, of course, occurred to him to inquire whether I had opinions, advice, suggestions of my own to offer, to the magazine or to him personally. It never occurred to him that my experience of life outside literature might provide a fresh viewpoint.

Even in the tempo of our everyday lives we were incompatible. After our great victory, why couldn't we now sit comfortably around the big editorial table, drink tea and nibble bubliki, chat about matters great or trivial? A.T. urged me to try it. "All writers do it—Simonov, for instance," he said jokingly. "They sit down for a quiet smoke like respectable people. Why are you always in such a hurry?" I was in such a hurry because in my fifth decade I was bursting with all that remained to be written, and because falsehood stood only too firmly on its feet of clay—or rather its feet of reinforced concrete.

Triumphantly A.T. laid before me Simonov's long review of my book in *Izvestia* (the first, just out, and I had not yet seen it), but from the very first paragraph it seemed to me like a boring official communiqué, and I put it aside unread and asked him to carry on with our editorial discussion of "Krechetovka." A.T. was exasperated, and probably put it down to affectation. He could not see how very long and dangerous was the road ahead, and how short in the leg were these unsolicited reviews.

We were even further apart in our ideas about what literature should do next and what *Novy Mir* should now be. A.T. thought his magazine extremely daring and progressive—witness its great success with the Soviet intelligentsia and the close attention paid it by the Western press.

Well, there was some truth in that. But the devotees of *Novy Mir* measured it in the first place against the general ruck of uninspired journals, with their emetic subject matter and their deadening indifference to artistic quality. (If anything of interest, anything "to whet the reader's appetite," ever appeared in those magazines—I am leaving *Yunost* out of it—it was either by some dead writer, baited in his time by curs like those who now exploited his name— *Moskva* was notorious for this—or else it was in an article that had nothing to do with literature.) Tvardovsky's native dignity and nobility, which never let him down even in his most painfully myopic moments, helped him to keep the most shameless bilge out of the magazine (though, to be truthful, it percolated even into *Novy Mir*, particularly in the memoirs of persons of rank, such as Konev and Yemelyanov, but only in a modest trickle) and to sustain that tone of high seriousness which made it appear an enlightened journal, superior to the times. There might be thin or worthless things in the first half of a number, but the second—commentary, criticism, bibliography—was always solid and informative, there was always much of interest in it.

There was, however, another criterion. Could the journal have made itself a platform on which our literature might rise from its knees? To this end, *Novy Mir* should have stiffened the dose of daring in each of its sections. Every number should have been put together without reference to the mood of the day among top people, the shifting pattern of rumors and fears—not just to fit within the confines of what was permitted yesterday, but so as to push out the boundaries at some point with every number. This, of course, would have meant charging headfirst into a brick wall rather frequently.

I shall be told that this is stuff and nonsense, that such a magazine would not have lasted a year in our country. I shall be informed that *Novy Mir* never left out half a paragraph if there was the slightest possibility of sneaking it in. That however streamlined, however Aesopian, however guarded its language, it made up for this by its circulation and its fame, that it tirelessly levered away at loose stones in the crumbling wall. Editors simply cannot rush into one fatal, shattering collision, and then terminate their magazine's existence. A magazine—and the same is true of a theater or a cinema studio—is a sort of industry, and should not be at the mercy of a single individual. All three involve the labor of many people, and in times of persecution they inevitably tack and trim their sails.

Perhaps there is more truth in this argument than in what I was saying. But I still cannot help feeling that whatever *Novy Mir* did, it came nowhere near the limits of the possible. Did it, for instance, take advantage of those first few months after the Twenty-second Congress, months of unrepeatable freedom? Did not issue upon issue barely scrape by? How many were there with two or three pages worth publishing, and the rest characterless and unfit for consumption? So that the ratio between good pages and bad gave a lower coefficient of efficiency than the most ineffectual heat engine? All this because the active forces on the editorial staff were kept down and the wooden dolls who were on the board for camouflage (Zaks and Kondratovich) were only too ready to sacrifice anything for a quiet life and a firm seat in their editorial chairs.

Year by year our liberal magazine became more and more enamored of freedom not because its editors were, but because it was buoyed up by the constant inrush of manuscripts from freedom-loving authors for whom it was the only magazine. This supporting pressure was so great that however many manuscripts were thrown out, however savagely they were mutilated, there was still much of value in what remained. Nonetheless, the journal was settling into a hierarchical and conservative mold. Only favorable and fulsome reports were sent "upward," and anything untoward was smothered on sight just as effectively, if with less preliminary discussion, as at *Moskva* or *Znamya*. Tvardovsky had only a garbled secondhand knowledge of these manuscripts that were rejected for their excessive daring. He told me that "somebody keeps trying to foist provocateurs and anti-Soviet propaganda on *Novy Mir*. You are the only free magazine, they tell us; where else can we get published?"

He thought that his editorial staff performed a great service in seeing through these approaches and promptly snubbing them. Whereas in reality the workings of freedom could be seen in these "provocations," and the "provocateurs" were "set on" *Novy Mir* by that respectable matron called Russian literature.

All that I have said describes the general situation at *Novy Mir* but does not apply to my own case at all. On the contrary, Tvardovsky did his utmost to promote my work even when there was no hope for it. I am writing about dozens of works which came much closer to legitimacy, and for which *Novy Mir* could have done more if Tvardovsky's entourage had not clung so frantically to their elbow rests, if they had not been paralyzed by their constant nagging fears: "This happens to be a particularly awkward moment . . ." "Just at this moment, things are . . ." The moment had already lasted half a century.

I once asked A.T. whether I, with the interests of the magazine at heart, could recommend to him things that particularly pleased me. A.T. very warmly invited me to do so. Yet my two attempts to use the right conferred on me not only were unsuccessful, but put a strain on my relations with the magazine.

The first occasion was during our honeymoon, in December 1962. I had persuaded V. T. Shalamov to get together those verses from his *Kolyma Stories* and *Shorter Poems* which seemed to me incontestably good, and handed them in a sealed packet to *Novy Mir*'s secretary for transmission to A.T.

*Novy Mir* had a poet at its head, yet its verse section was weak; it had never discovered a single notable poet, though it had sometimes made minor reputations, which were soon forgotten. It carefully observed the "inter-republican" diplomatic code and published in translation[1] verse from the non-Russian national areas, or else it published poems, two or three at a time, by some already well-known poet. But it never gave us an extended sequence of poems that could have set a "trend," either by their ideas or by their form. The verses published by *Novy Mir* were never an artistic event.

Shalamov's selection included "Homer" and "Avvakum in Pustozersk" from the *Shorter Poems,* and about twenty other pieces, among them "In the Hours of Icebound Night," "Archimedes" and "Funeral." For me, of course, neither the man Shalamov nor his verse could be accommodated in the realm of "mere poetry"; they were the product of burning memory and heartache. Shalamov was my far-off and unknown brother from the camps; he had written these poems as I had written mine, when he could scarcely drag himself along, committing them to memory because his main concern was to avoid discovery by the searchers. When everything that looked like a writer had been totally destroyed in the camps, those of us who had wriggled through to safety could easily be counted on one hand.

I do not consider myself a judge of poetry. I did, on the other hand, acknowledge that Tvardovsky had a refined poetic taste. Perhaps I was badly mistaken about Shalamov, but given the dullness of *Novy Mir*'s verse section, should it have rejected him so peremptorily? By the time these jottings of mine can be published the reader will have read Shalamov's banned poems. He will have learned to appreciate their courage, their anguish, qualities that elude younger poets of limited experience, and he will be able to judge for himself whether they deserved the treatment Tvardovsky gave them.

He told me that he was put off not only by the poems themselves —"too much like Pasternak"—but by the trivial fact that he had opened the envelope expecting to find something new from me. To Shalamov he wrote that he emphatically did not like the poems from the *Kolyma Stories,* which were not the sort of poetry to touch our readers' hearts.

I tried to explain that this was no "intrigue" on the part of Shalamov,

---

1. There is the literature of particular peoples, and there is world literature. But there can be no intermediate "multinational" literature (with balanced representation as in the Council of Nationalities). This hollow concept, together with socialist realism, has done its share to hamper the development of our literature in past decades.

that I myself had suggested that he make a selection and submit it through me, but Tvardovsky wouldn't believe a word of it! He was extraordinarily unreceptive to simple explanations. He remained convinced that Shalamov was a schemer who had tried to use me.

On the second occasion (in the autumn of 1964), I found myself pressing the editorial board to print Zhores Medvedev's *Essays on the History of Genetics.* They contained a popular exposition of the gist of the genetics controversy—of which the public at large knew nothing— but there was more to them than that: a white-hot protest against injustice based on material now completely legal yet calculated to make society's heart beat furiously. This book was "unanimously liked," as they put it, by the editorial board (meaning that only Dementyev opposed it).

At the editorial conference Tvardovsky asked me to curb my eloquence because they were "all convinced" beforehand. They would like the author to make some "small cuts," that was all—and later on, some rather bigger cuts—and later still, "to be patient for a month or two," which was where the whole business ran into the ground. The book carried a heavier charge of heresy than was yet permissible. Nor would Tvardovsky forgive me for daring to approach "Sovremennik" with *The Love Girl and the Innocent.* His resentment would not lie quiet in his breast; it did not fade, it rankled. He quite unnecessarily reverted to this episode on a number of occasions, and not only condemned the play, not only spoke of it with hostility, but *prophesied* that it would never see the light of day, or in other words, declared his faith in the stoutness of the censor's defenses. More than this, on 16 February 1963 (three months after the climactic success of our collaboration), he told me that "I wouldn't exactly ban your play if it depended on me. . . . I would write an article against it . . . or perhaps I might even ban it after all."

When he was saying unkind things his eyes looked cold, turned white even, and it was quite a different face, not in the least childlike. (Why, though, would he ban it? With the best of intentions—to protect my good name.)

"But you yourself," I reminded him, "advised Nikita Sergeyevich to abolish the censorship of the arts."

He made no reply. But not because he agreed with me at heart. Oh, no—he had no secret awareness of any contradiction. If something didn't suit him, why shouldn't he fall back on the government's authority to obstruct it? Exchanges of this sort with Tvardovsky stunted our friendship in its first growth.

It was no mere threat: he succeeded in putting obstacles in the path of my play. Just at that time, at the beginning of March 1963, I was looking for some way of obtaining permission to produce the play, and I myself sent it on to Ivan Denisovich's benefactor, V. S. Lebedev. His first question was "Has Tvardovsky read it? What did he say?" I told him (toning it down a bit). They had some further discussion about it, and on 21 March Lebedev turned me down flat.

"It is my profound conviction that the play in its present form is not suitable for production. The people at 'Sovremennik'—I'm not blaming them, I'm not accusing them of anything—want to put on your play to attract an audience with your name and a theme that would certainly create a furor if presented on the stage. [What more does any theater want?] I do not doubt that theatergoers would break the doors down, as the saying goes, in their eagerness to find out . . . what sort of thing went on in the camps. However . . . 'Sovremennik' will ultimately have to give up the idea of staging the play because those 'huge fat flies' of which N. S. Khrushchev spoke in his recent speech would swarm over it in clouds. In this case the fat flies would be the correspondents of foreign newspapers and agencies, the whole collection of home-grown philistines and . . . others of the same kind."

"Philistines" and "others of the same kind"! Putting it simply—the people? The theater itself will "give up the idea"? Of course, when it gets a telephone call from the Central Committee, reminding it of the times we live in, of the theater's duties—and of the speaker's official standing . . .

The relationship between Tvardovsky and Lebedev was not simply that between a dependent editor and an adviser to the monarch. They both, I believe, called it friendship, and Lebedev felt flattered by his friendship with the country's leading poet (officially recognized as such at a particular date and according to the Table of Ranks). He treasured Tvardovsky's manuscripts (and later on mine). (In his usual methodical way he kept them, I believe, in a special file.) When Tvardovsky took *Ivan Denisovich* to him, garnished with the recommendations of hoary-headed writers, Lebedev was at pains to show that he, too, was a connoisseur, that he had an excellent insight into the virtues of the piece, and that he would never be tempted to lay a coarse meddling finger on its delicate fabric.

How he found his way into Khrushchev's entourage and what his previous occupation had been were things I never found out. This mysterious liberal in chief regarded himself as a journalist by profession. Perhaps he was moved by personal rivalry with Ilyichev, whom he could outgallop only on the liberal nag? . . . He and I were introduced to each other at the first "Kremlin meeting of party and government leaders with the creative intelligentsia," on 17 December 1962.

I could give a very detailed description of these meetings from my notes, but that would be a digression, and in any case, others have probably done it already, or will do it. The summons to the first meeting took me aback. An order from the obkom of the Party arrived at my school on Saturday evening; I was to report to Comrade Polikarpov (the chief suppressor of literature and art) at the Central Committee's offices on Monday, and one of the obkom's cars would take me there. With my underground habit of mind, I indulged in gloomy conjectures. I decided that Polikarpov, having failed to hold back my story, would now try to make the best of things by forcing me into the Party. And I deliberately went in the suit I had bought at "Clothes for the Workingman" and wore to school; in my much-mended shoes with patches of brown leather on black; and badly in need of a haircut. This would make it easier for me to balk and feign stupidity. Thus disguised as a yokel, I was carried to the marbled and silky Palace of Meetings, where strapping fellows in smart livery took charge of my tattered overcoat, frock-coated waiters prepared to serve a seven-course banquet fit for kings, and a pack of newspaper, cinema and television cameramen caught the notables in a dazzling crossfire (the lenses were draped while we took refreshment).

Then it was, during one of the intermissions, that people began walking past the end of the table at which Tvardovsky and I were sitting (they tried to look casual, but in fact there was nothing accidental about it): first Adzhubei, red-faced and haughty, then the obsequious nonentity Satyukov (editor of *Pravda*), then a short man, very much the intellectual, and very unassuming in appearance and manner, to whom Tvardovsky introduced me. This was Lebedev. I was struck by his lack of resemblance to the Party bosses, his quiet manner and unmistakably intellectual cut. (He wore rimless glasses; you saw only the flash of the lenses and were left with the impression that they were pince-nez.) Perhaps it was because he was my main benefactor and looked at me kindly that I perceived him in this fashion. We talked about nothing in particular. He assured me that I was now in an orbit from which I could not be shot down, approved of my refusal to give interviews, and asked for a signed copy of *Ivan Denisovich*. He was a Chekhov-type angel, sent from heaven to guide the errant Khrushchev.

At that first Kremlin meeting I was still praised to the skies, still the target of applause and cameras—but nonetheless *Ivan Denisovich* proved to be the last gasp of the enthusiasm generated by the Twenty-second Congress. The Stalinists were already mounting their all-out counterattack, with the short-sighted Khrushchev complacently supporting them. We heard from him that the press is a long-range weapon and that the Party must check its performance; that he was not in favor of the rule "live and let live"; that ideological coexistence was an obscenity; and that the struggle admitted of no compromise.

The second Kremlin meeting, on 7–8 March 1963, was one of the most shameful pages in the history of Khrushchev's rule. It was rigged so that the Stalinists had a preponderance of five to one (obkom officials and other apparatchiki were invited), and the air was filled with harsh invective and destructive hostility to anything that gave off the faintest whiff of freedom. (Only I remained untouched for the time being. Sholokhov and Kochetov were forced to substitute speeches for those they had ready, out of respect for Khrushchev's "personal artistic taste.") It took only a short time, a matter of hours (oh, how easy it was), to recreate the atmosphere of intolerance we had known in the thirties, the atmosphere of the "unanimous" meetings where savage beasts were trained and the doomed and flayed had only till nightfall to live. At long last Nikita had identified the major enemies of all his agricultural, administrative and international initiatives—abstract artists and liberal intellectuals—and he pitched into them with the savagery of a man who feels his fists and shoulder muscles throbbing and his eyes misting over with hatred. "You over there," he yelled, "you in the red sweater near the pillar—why aren't you clapping? Let's have you up here! Right—let him speak next!" And the chorus of inflamed Stalinists bayed at the artist Golitsyn: "Let him explain why he is not clapping!" The completely loyal Rozhdestvensky and Voznesensky were rashly abused as apostates. "I can't keep calm when I hear people truckling to our enemies!" he said, banging the table, though not on this occasion with his shoe. And—yelling at the top of his voice—"Keep your hands off the younger generation or you'll find yourself under the Party's grinders."

These meetings of Khrushchev's carried us all the way back to where we had been—not before the Twenty-second but before the Twentieth Congress. He had sent his billiard ball of a head rolling toward the Stalinist pocket. Just one more little push was needed.

Lebedev made no attempt to see me at this meeting. He was preoccupied, and hurried through one door, into the Sovnarkom corridor, and out another. He wore a more official look than before. Two weeks later he gave me my answer about the play.

Meanwhile the ideological merry-go-round went on turning. Stopping it would have been harder than stopping the sun itself. The echoes of the two conferences had not yet died down when something even more important was thought up: The June 1963 plenary meeting of the Central Committee was entirely devoted to "cultural questions." (Apparently Nikita could find no greater cause for concern in his neglected topsy-turvy empire.) And because Khrushchev did things on the grand scale, thousands of "workers" from this sector were invited to the plenum. I could look forward to a week of coming and going and of stupefyingly boring sessions in the June heat, just as though I had been a "member of the Party since 19——" instead of a benighted zek, a writer in the first months of newly won freedom. My luckless fame was beginning to draw me into the Party's court circles. This was in itself a blot on my record.

I had to ask Lebedev for an interview in the hope of getting him to relieve me of the high honor of an invitation to the plenum and to leave me alone. This was how we met for the third and last time, in the Central Committee offices, on the fifth floor, main entry (Khrushchev's staircase).

My request came as a very great surprise to him. Tickets for these meetings and plenums were much sought after, people phoned in to beg for them, and to obtain or fail to obtain one was an indication of status. Was I able to be frank with him? Of course not. I muttered something about family circumstances.[2]

Lebedev explained to me all over again what was wrong with my

---

2. And Tvardovsky reprimanded me later on: The *Oktyabr* crowd will think you've been passed over, that your stock is going down. I had no right, whatever the circumstances—said he—to refuse. After all, I was no longer just myself. My demotion reflected upon *Novy Mir* too. . . . For decades, politicking of this sort was what literature meant in our country.

play: people were sometimes *successfully reeducated* in the camps, people *did* leave the camps—and this did not appear in what I had written. Further (and this was very important), the play would *offend the intelligentsia:* it emerged from the play that some people had compromised, some had fought for privileges . . . and our public had grown used to revering the memory of those who had perished in the camps. (Since when?) It was an unnatural feature of my work that the dishonest triumphed and the honest were doomed to destruction. (Rumors about the play had already got around, and even Nikita was asking what it was like. "If it's a dramatization of *Ivan Denisovich* let them put it on." But Lebedev had told him, "No, we mustn't." It was of course time for Lebedev to slam on the brakes in his dealings with me.) Lebedev vaguely tried to convince me that "if Tolstoy were living now and wrote as he did then"—meaning, of course, against the government—"he would not be Tolstoy."

And this was the liberal friend of Khrushchev's bosom, his highbrow good angel, who all alone had brought about the miracle of *Ivan Denisovich.* I sat in his office observing him closely, and the longer I sat there, the more insignificant, the more lacking in distinction, he seemed to me. It was impossible to imagine that smooth little head holding a single thought distinct from the thoughts of the Party, let alone a political program of its own.

It was just that the frying pan had been so hot after the Twenty-second Congress that my pancake had tossed itself, browned nicely and found its way to the sour cream. But now the pan had cooled and anyone could see how undercooked the pancake was, how heavy it would be on the stomach. The cook would be lucky not to be dragged off to the stables for a flogging.

Every now and then he picked up the receiver to chat with some Central Committee big shot (always about something trivial: it was all silly jokes, or talk about soccer, or how they'd put it over on somebody with an article in *Komsomolskaya Pravda*), and as he talked he laughed unpleasantly, affectedly, making short barking noises. He took photograph after photograph until my head ached, boasted of the new West German Leica that had cost him 550 rubles ("Well, we received a prize for a book"—a Lenin Prize for his coverage of Nikita's American travels). He proudly and eagerly showed me the heavy velvet-bound albums, one for each of Nikita's rallies abroad, in which he kept his big colored snapshots under celluloid covers: Ilyichev dressed as Neptune,

Ilyichev again, balancing a dish on his head; Adzhubei and Satyukov hugging the statue of a goddess, with idiotic looks on their faces; Khrushchev kissing a delightful Burmese girl; Gromyko reclining blissfully in an airplane seat. They did indeed live in the happiest society on earth. (Furthermore, the processing of Lebedev's snapshots was carried out entirely by the photographic laboratory of the Central Committee, and he himself had only to look them over, classify them and arrange negatives and prints, all during office hours.)

In one of the albums, with those very bookshelves against which he had just snapped me for background, Sholokhov and Mikhalkov smiled and smiled. There were empty spaces for me too. . . . Lebedev really had no idea how mistaken he was about me.

But I was mistaken too, in thinking that I had two years, or at any rate half a year, before all loopholes were blocked. My publication period flashed by, and was over before it had really begun. The oleaginous V. Kozhevnikov was commissioned to test how staunchly the throne would defend me. In a neatly turned article, he set out to discover whether "Matryona's Home" might be discreetly rapped. The answer was that it might, that neither I nor even Tvardovsky had any protection "up above." (Lebedev was getting cold feet, wishing he hadn't yoked himself so closely to us.) Then they unleashed a second and a third assailant, tearing the short stories to pieces first, then the tale that had won favor with the All Highest—and still no one intervened.

Schooled as I was in the camps, I was not really hurt or vexed by these attacks. "Sticks and stones may break my bones, but words will never hurt me." On the contrary, I had been much more surprised and humiliated by inordinate praise in the same papers earlier on. I was now quite willing to call it a draw: If you bark quietly and don't bite, I'll keep quiet too. Considered realistically, my position was splendid. I had been admitted to the Writers' Union with rocketlike speed, and thus released from the teaching that had absorbed so much of my time; for the first time in my life I could go and live by a river during the spring floods or in the woods in autumn, and write; and at last I could get a permit to work in the restricted-access section of the public library—and I flung myself lustfully upon those forbidden books. It would have been nothing less than a sin to resent not being published. No one was trying to stop me from writing; what more did I want? I was free, and I was writing; what more could I ask?

My days and my months had expanded, and I began to write an

inordinate number of things all at once: four large works. I was collecting material for *The Gulag Archipelago* (my name had been advertised to zeks throughout the country, and they had begun bringing me material and stories), as well as the major novel on the 1917 Revolution (provisionally entitled *R-17*), which was my most cherished ambition; I had started *Cancer Ward,* and I had decided to screen certain chapters of *The First Circle* in case an opportunity to publish them suddenly arose.

Keep quiet! That seemed the best bet in my position. But it is not so easy to keep quiet when you are tied to an editorial board that has your interests at heart. I did take them things from time to time, to salve my conscience—and so as not to miss any opportunity. On one occasion I took in a few chapters of my old novel in verse (*Highway of Enthusiasts,* also modified and toned down), which Tvardovsky quite rightly rejected. "I realize," he said, "that in the camps you had to keep writing if you didn't want to go moldy. But still . . ." He was anxious not to upset me. I reassured him.

"Aleksandr Trifonich! You can reject ten of my things in a row and I shall still bring the eleventh to you."

He brightened up and was sincerely pleased. My promise proved prophetic. I had to lug along not quite but very nearly ten things before it was clearly established that he had forfeited all rights over me.

In the spring of 1963 I wrote a story for *Novy Mir* which I felt no inner compulsion at all to write: "For the Good of the Cause." It seemed reasonably hard-hitting, yet viable in the overcharged atmosphere after the Kremlin meetings. But I found it pretty hard to write (a sure sign of failure) and it didn't go very deep. Nonetheless, it was greeted by *Novy Mir* with great, indeed this time unanimous, approval (another bad sign!), simply because it would put the magazine in a stronger position, show that they had not made an ideological mistake in sponsoring my entry into literature.

The magazine was so sure of its rights over me that while I was away on a trip during the summer, Zaks let the censors remove one or two loaded expressions from the story without my knowledge (the word "strike," describing the protest that the students wanted to make, was one of them). This was something they often did to many other authors. The issue must be saved! The magazine must live! And if the author's ideas suffer as a result, no great harm is done. . . . When I got back I reproached them bitterly. Tvardovsky sided with Zaks. They simply couldn't understand me—why all this flaunting of principles? All right, they'd pruned my story. But we who wrote for *Novy Mir* had been brought into the world by it and must make sacrifices for it.

The publication of this story left a nasty taste in my mouth. True, when almost everything was banned, even this provoked a great deal of lively comment. But in "For the Good of the Cause" I was beginning to slip: a telltale trickle underfoot showed that I was slithering toward conformity.

It was some time before I learned my lesson and realized that *Novy Mir* must be handled with the defensive cunning necessary in all dealings with authority: it often pays to keep out of sight; it's best to reconnoiter first and find what's in the wind. During this visit, in July 1963, while I was so worked up about the censor's distortions, A.T. tried in vain to make me share his own happiness.

"Speak of the devil—we've just been talking about you *over there!*"

I say happiness, but he had more than one way of looking happy. In the intervals between his lapses, his was a pure, radiant happiness. But this time he was half dead, a pitiful sight, with bloodshot eyes (only the day before he had been jerked out of a drinking jag by drug therapy, for delivery to Ilyichev at the Central Committee). Besides this, he smoked incessantly, recklessly. A.T. was happy this time because he had "scented something new on the breeze"—felt some "warming rays" at his conference with Ilyichev. (It was just one of Agitprop's little wiggles, just a maneuver. But life as editor in chief of a suspect journal brought him so few privileges and so many humiliations, and his heart thumped against the little red book in his left breast pocket with such genuine devotion, that Tvardovsky was doomed to despair and to seek oblivion in drink whenever he received an unfriendly telephone call from some minor official in the Central Committee, and to blossom whenever the head of the "Cultural Department" bestowed a crooked smile upon him.)

What had happened *over there,* on Staraya Ploshchad,* was this: They had been trying to "get right" the composition of the Soviet delegation to a COMES (European Community of Writers) symposium in Leningrad on the future of the novel, and A.T. had managed to achieve my inclusion. (Ilyichev had given way because the symposium would be the better for a little window dressing.)

Before he had finished speaking, my mind was made up. Nothing on earth would make me go! The life of a writer "on the surface" is made up of such merry-go-round rides. This was an inexpensive way they had found of exhibiting me to Europe (if a gathering under Vigorelli's wing could be called Europe!): as a member of a delegation, *unanimous,* of course, in its opinions, any departure from the collective view being not only betrayal of my country but treachery to my nearest and dearest —to *Novy Mir.* It was quite impossible to say what I really thought. And too soon. But to go there like a pet monkey would be shameful. After turning down so many Western newspapermen, I had to stick to my line.

"You shouldn't have gone to such trouble, Aleksandr Trifonich. I have no desire at all to go, and anyway it isn't convenient: I've only just come back from Leningrad, and I'm not used to all this rushing around."

Once again we had reached the dividing line which we never managed to cross in all the years of our literary intimacy: neither of us could really understand and accept what the other was thinking. (It was particularly difficult for *him* to understand *me,* because I had to keep my work and my aims hidden.)

A.T. was offended. (It was his habit not to vent his resentment all at once, but to live with it and come back to it time and again. But then, I am just the same.)

"I made it my business to see justice done. You can refuse if you like, but it's your duty to be there *in the interests of Soviet literature.*"

Ah, but I had taken no oath of loyalty to Soviet literature.

There with us, as it happened, was Viktor Nekrasov, who had recently been vilified at the March "meeting" and had been under investigation by the Party in Kiev for some months past. Yet he, too, even he tried to persuade me to go! There was so much that even he still did not understand, and that could not be explained to him. . . .

Simultaneously, they both felt drawn to a place of refreshment. I would sooner have dropped dead than cross its threshold, but with nothing decided, we drifted first toward Strastnoy Boulevard. It was then that I noticed how timorously and awkwardly A.T. crossed the street. ("These Moscow intersections are so dangerous.") He had of course lost the habit of moving about the streets, except by car. A man used to riding in a car cannot understand a pedestrian—even in a symposium. A.T. was now saying that the symposium would obviously be pointless: there were no novels worth arguing about; in fact, there were no novels at all nowadays; *"it is doubtful whether a novel can be written* in our time." (*Cancer Ward* was already begun, *The First Circle* had been finished a year before, but I didn't know in what form I dared offer it to Tvardovsky.) And I was supposed to sit in a symposium, bound and gagged, listening to forty mouths chorusing: "The novel is dead!" "The novel is obsolete!" "There can be no more novels!"

A.T. also said sadly that he was well known in the West as a progressive editor, but unknown as a poet. "Of course, I write metrical verse and it always has a subject. . . ." (He had missed the point. It didn't matter that he was not a modernist. But how could any translator reproduce the Russianness of his idiom, the earthiness, the peasant homespun quality of A.T.'s best verses?) "Mind you, my 'Stove-Setters' has gone all around Europe," he said, cheering himself up.

They had swallowed one bitter pill too many—what with the inquiry in Kiev and my obstinacy—and they tore themselves away from me and went off to drink *lemonade*. I said goodbye to them as to two lost souls. In an age when things moved at such speed, they did not know what to do with their time.

This was not the end of it. To escape that symposium I yet had to flee from home on my bicycle, without leaving an address. Just like my headmaster in earlier days summoning me to school, the board of the Writers' Union insisted in telegrams and by special messengers that I should stop arguing and go. But they failed to find me. (Tvardovsky, however, used this symposium to quite good purpose. The participants were taken afterward to Khrushchev's dacha at Pitsunda, and there Lebedev performed another public service. He arranged a reading of "Tyorkin in the Next World." The foreigners looked blank, but Khrushchev laughed—which was as good as an imprimatur. They had smuggled it through.)[3]

"Tyorkin in the Next World" had lain around awaiting publication for too long (nine years), and for nine years it had tied Tvardovsky's hands—but now they were untied, and he could afford to take risks. So in the autumn of 1963 I selected chapters from *The First Circle* and tried them on *Novy Mir*, calling them "a fragment."

*Novy Mir* rejected them. Because they were only a fragment? Not only that. This was "that prison theme again." (And the prison theme

3. The rascally Adzhubei was in fact the first to publish it, but with an introductory note saying *how beautifully Sholokhov had listened* (!) to the poem. That's Adzhubei all over—running with the hare and hunting with the hounds. It also tells you what you do when you've produced nothing of your own for thirty years: you *listen beautifully.*

was exhausted, wasn't it? Already overdone?) This was just at the time when they had to print a summary of next year's publishing plans. I offered them my long tale *Cancer Ward,* which I was already writing. The title was quite unsuitable! To begin with, it smacked of allegory, and anyway, "It's too frightening in itself; it'll never get through."

Tvardovsky, who insisted on renaming everything submitted to *Novy Mir,* immediately decided on the new title: *"Patients and Doctors.* We'll put it in the prospectus."

Like a smear of porridge on a plate! *Patients and Doctors . . .* I wouldn't hear of it. If you have found the right title for a book, or even a short story, it isn't a mere label, it is part of the soul and essence of the thing, organically linked with it, and changing the title means mutilating the work itself. When Zalygin's tale is given the nebulous title *On the Irtysh,* when Mozhayev's *Alive!* (how profound! how grand!) is twisted into *Scenes from the Life of Fyodor Kuzkin,* they are irreparably injured. But A.T. would have none of that; he considered titles a trivial matter, and the sycophants on his staff and his fulsome friends encouraged his belief that he had a remarkable gift for renaming things at first squint. The titles he gave were less eye-catching, less expressive, on the calculation that he would be able to get them through the censorship more easily—as indeed he often did.

We couldn't come to an agreement, and *Cancer Ward* was left out of the list of works promised by *Novy Mir* for 1964. On the other hand, the magazine involved itself in the campaign to get a Lenin Prize for me. A year earlier the red carpet had been rolled out everywhere, but now things were more complicated. (In another three years it would be clear to everybody that this was a gross political error, an insult to Lenin's name and to the institution of the Lenin Prize itself.)

A.T. took the struggle very much to heart and eagerly followed every foxy move, every ambivalent statement by Adzhubei. True, Tvardovsky was not on his feet for the first round, and the victory was won without him. But in the second round he set to doggedly, carefully judging the fine shades of opinion within the committee (he meant to cast his vote so as to win for himself as many supporters as he could). In the literary section the vote was split in a way that was not at all accidental but quite prophetic: Tvardovsky and all the non-Russians voted for *Ivan Denisovich;* all the Russians except Tvardovsky voted against it. The nays had the majority. But according to the rules, voting in the film and drama section had to be taken into account, and there the majority were for it. As a result *Ivan Denisovich* was entered on the secret ballot, but *against* the votes of the "Russian" writers. This success made my enemies very uneasy, and at a plenary meeting of the Central Committee of the Komsomol, its First Secretary, Pavlov, made a speech in which he slandered me. This was the first, relatively innocuous, calumny in a long series: he asserted that I had been in the camps not as a political offender but as a common criminal. Tvardovsky shouted, "Not true," but he was stunned. What if it was a fact? His reaction is significant. For more than two years we had embraced whenever we met or said goodbye at his office, yet there was such an unbridgeable gulf between us that he had never felt the urge to ask me, and I had had no occasion to tell him, how I had come to be imprisoned. (In fact, I had never told him a single story about my life in prison and the camps, of the sort that I told anyone and everyone at the drop of a hat, nor even about my days at the front.) For his part, he had told me nothing about the banishment of his family, which greatly interested me—though I was always leading up to it—but only anecdotes about his life as a literary bureaucrat and courtier: about Khrushchev commissioning five poets and five composers to write a new anthem; about incidents in the Barvikha sanatorium; about moves made by the editors of *Pravda, Izvestia* and *Oktyabr,* and his own countermoves—which were usually pretty feeble but as dignified as could be. On my advice, he now requested from the Military Panel of the Supreme Court, and obtained within a day, a copy of the court ruling rehabilitating me. (In that age of rapidly growing freedom, collections of such documents should obviously have been published for reference, but they were not even divulged to the rehabilitated themselves. I discovered how to get at them only by accident, through my interview with the Military Panel.) Tvardovsky was able to make an impression on the Lenin Prize Committee the next day by reading out the court's ruling before the secret vote was taken. The message was clear—that I had been an opponent of the "personality cult" and of our lying literature during the war and ever since. The Secretary of the Central Committee of the Komsomol had to stand up and apologize. However, the machinery had been set in motion. That morning's *Pravda,* two hours before the vote was taken, declared that in view of the high standards set (it now appeared) by previous awards, a story about one day in a camp was obviously unworthy of a prize. Immediately before the secret ballot, the Party members on the committee were told that it was their duty to vote against my candidacy. (Nonetheless, Tvardovsky told me, no one else had collected enough votes. The committee was reconvened. Ilyichev arrived, and ordered them to vote again, in his presence, for Gonchar's *Tronka*. Gonchar, who had won more than one Lenin Prize already and was a member of the committee itself, sat right there by the urn, shamelessly observing the secret ballot.)

Even then, in April 1964, people in Moscow were saying that this business of the secret ballot was a "rehearsal for the putsch" against Nikita: would the apparat succeed, or wouldn't it, in turning down a book sanctioned by The Man himself? In forty years they had never mustered the courage to try such a thing. But they had suddenly grown bolder, and succeed they did. This gave grounds for hope that The Man was not all that secure.

That morning, before the final ballot, Tvardovsky sat in his new office (in the building where the cells of the Strastnoy Monastery used to be) a broken man, staring at the *Pravda* article as though it were a telegram announcing his father's death. He greeted me for some reason in German: *"Das ist alles,"* which reminded me painfully of Chekhov's dying words: *"Ich sterbe."* I never heard a single foreign word from Tvardovsky before or after. The Lenin Prize for which Tvardovsky had fought without sparing himself (and, surprisingly, he did not hit the bottle even when he was defeated) would have meant prestige for his magazine, it would have been like a medal pinned to that blue cover.[4] When they turned me down, he was eager to resign in protest (this was not the first or the last time)—though on this occasion only from the Lenin Prize Committee—but his coeditor and his family persuaded him that his job was to run the magazine and safeguard its interests. They were of course right: this was not an issue on which to resign.

I myself simply didn't know what I wanted. Winning a prize would have its advantages: it would consolidate my position. But there were more disadvantages: it would consolidate my position—for what? It would not help me to get my work published. An "established position" carried obligations—to be loyal and to be grateful: in other words, not to take out of my desk drawer the ungrateful pieces with which it was exclusively stuffed.

---

4. Results bore out his anticipations. After I had been denied the prize, A.T. complained that the magazine's position had become quite intolerable, that the censors caviled at the most trivial details. And to prevent hopeless delays in the publication of each issue, he had no choice but to give in to them.

I spent the whole of that winter finishing a new version of *The First Circle* (I called it *Circle 87* for the number of chapters), "lightened" for the publishers and for the public. "Lightened" or not, there was almost as big a risk in showing it to people as there had been in the case of *Ivan Denisovich* two years earlier. It overstepped a line that had never been crossed before. It would knock the wind out of Tvardovsky: would it be a heavy enough blow to make him my enemy?

Anyway, all through those winter months while he was battling for the prize, I had done nothing to hinder him in his fight and, although I had promised to do so, had not shown him *Circle*. Now it was spring, and time for Tvardovsky to read my novel. But how was I to tear him from the clutches of all his nay-saying advisers, and especially Dementyev, for long enough to read it? I had to make sure that A.T. would form his own unaided opinion of the novel.

"Aleksandr Trifonich," I said to him, "the novel is ready. But do you know what it's like, surrendering a novel to a publisher when you intend to write only two in a lifetime? It's like marrying off a son. Pretend it's a wedding and come and stay with us in Ryazan."

He agreed, with genuine pleasure. I don't think anything like this had happened to him in all his time as an editor.

In Ryazan, on Easter Saturday evening (though A.T. would hardly be aware of that), we welcomed him as stylishly as we could—in our own Moskvich. But he looked somewhat subdued as he squeezed into the little car (it really was small for one of his figure): in his position he was unused to riding in anything humbler than a Volga. He had, moreover, traveled as an ordinary passenger on the local train, buying his ticket himself at the Round Tower, not through the deputies' room of the Supreme Soviet. He probably hadn't traveled like that since his early days in Smolensk.

As we ate our first supper together, A.T. tactfully warned me that every writer has his disappointments and must take them in his stride. Next morning he began reading, with little sign of excitement at first, but from lunch until dinnertime he was swept helplessly along; he forgot to smoke, he bobbed up and down in his chair as he read. I wandered into the room from time to time to check his reactions against the number of the chapter he was reading. "Great stuff!" he would say, getting up from the table—and immediately correct himself: "I'm saying nothing, mind you." (In other words, he could not promise that his final judgment would be the same.) My ideas about work being what they are, I thought that he should stay sober until he had reached the end, but hospitality demanded that both cognac and vodka should be served at dinner. As a result he quickly lost control of himself, his eyes became wild, all whites, and the need to speak his mind loudly was too much for him. He suddenly wanted to walk down to the post office and phone Moscow (he and his wife were discussing the purchase of a new dacha). The post office was four hundred meters away, but it took us two hours to get there and back. A.T. stopped every minute, blocking the footpath, and however much I urged him to walk on and lower his voice, he went on loudly airing his views. No man, I learned, should feel indebted to another. He talked about the "touching affection of our bosses for themselves." Marshal Konev, he recollected, had said, by way of praise, that he would like to promote A.T. from colonel on the reserve list to major general.[5] He commented on the mysterious ways of the Moscow Registration Commission, which decided who could and who could not live in the capital. He revealed that there were secret places of exile (islands in the Arctic Ocean) for war cripples. (Tvardovsky was the first to tell me of this, and I do not doubt its authenticity, though it is beyond the understanding of anyone but a Soviet citizen how these ex-heroes, these sacrificial victims who brought us victory, could be cast out so that they would not mar the carefully arranged tableau of Soviet life with their stumps of limbs, nor too noisily demand their rights.) And had I heard how Brezhnev had become a "victim of the cult"? (Stalin had made him suffer for taking over the municipal park in Kishinev as his viceregal headquarters.) Payment for volumes of collected verse was unfair, he continued; big imprints earned proportionally less than the small ones. (I had had occasion to notice that he went carefully into payments and deductions in connection with his own published work, that he would praise a well-produced volume and add, "The money isn't bad either." This was not greed but the hearty pride of an honest toiler—he was like a peasant returning from market.) He had something to say about Bulgakov ("brilliant, a light touch"), and about Leonov ("Gorky inflated his reputation, built him up out of all proportion"), and about Mayakovsky ("his wit falls flat—he is not a national poet, although he skillfully manipulated Church Slavonic mannerisms—he does not deserve a Square next to Pushkin's").

---

5. I once saw Konev in the editorial office in mufti. He looked like an ordinary, fairly obtuse kolkhoz foreman.

That evening I tried to make him see that one of his deputy chief editors was a nonentity and the other hostile to his efforts, a creature from quite a different camp. A.T. couldn't agree with any of this. "Dementyev has developed a lot in the last ten years." "How can you say that when he fought tooth and nail against *Ivan Denisovich?*" "He has been badly mauled. . . ." But still, A.T. confessed that his dream was to have as "number one" in the office a deputy who knew his job and could make decisions, someone who could if necessary manage the magazine himself without putting a foot wrong. (This future "number one" already existed in the office, and was already on his way up—Lakshin.)

The second day's reading was accompanied by cognac throughout, and whenever we tried to restrain him, A.T. insisted that he must have his "tot." Once more he ended the day with crazily rolling eyes.

"No, no—I don't believe you'd go and spoil it in the second half!" he kept saying, hopefully and apprehensively.

After Chapter 64: "You'd have a job to spoil it now, right at the very end!"

Some chapters later: "You are a terrible man. If I ever came to power, *I'd put you away.*"

"Don't worry, Aleksandr Trifonich. I have that to look forward to, whatever happens."

"Well, if I'm on the outside myself, I'll bring you parcels. You'll live better than Tsezar Markovich.* You'll even get the odd bottle of cognac."

"They won't allow it in. . . ."

"Don't worry. I'll give one bottle to Volkovoy and one to you."

He meant it as a joke, of course, but the tainted prison air was entering more and more deeply into his lungs.

After Chapter 72: "Tomorrow we shall have a talk—and it won't be at all on the plane you imagine. We shall be talking mostly not about you, but about me."

(About his limited opportunities? . . . about the debts of conscience? . . . about his awareness of changes within himself? . . . No such conversation ever took place, and I still don't know what Tvardovsky had in mind.)

This gloomy thought, that he himself would not escape *a spell inside* —or perhaps it was more like the spiritual uneasiness, the stirring of regret, that Tolstoy experienced in old age: Why was I never inside? I'm the one who needed to be!—came over him several times during his visit. He had brought Yakubovich-Melshin's book *In the World of Outcasts* to read on the train, and it had put him in the right frame of mind. He showed a great interest in the details of life behind bars, and eagerly questioned me: "Why do they shave people's pubic areas?" "Why don't they allow any glassware inside?" One line in the novel made him say: "Go to the stake if you must, but make it worthwhile!" No longer meaning or feeling it to be funny, now that the cognac fumes were mounting, he reverted time and again to his promise to bring me parcels when I went to jail, but now made it a condition that I should do the same for him while I was outside. Toward the evening of the second day his reading had brought him to the point at which Innokenti's arrest had become inevitable ("You lose the feeling that you are protected"), and after three tumblerfuls of *starka* he became very drunk and asked me to "play MGB lieutenants" with him; I was supposed to yell accusations at him, while he stood at attention.

To my annoyance, the reading of my novel was merging with the beginning of one of A.T.'s regular drinking bouts—and that in the house of a writer who did not drink! However, the feeling that we were in real danger was nourished not by the drink but by the novel.

I had to help him undress and put him to bed. But before long we were awakened by a loud noise: A.T. shouting and talking to himself—what is more, in different voices, acting several different parts. He had lit all the lamps (he always liked plenty of light in a room—"it makes it more cheerful") and was sitting in his underpants at the table, now devoid of bottles. He kept saying plaintively, "I shall go away and die soon." Then he would roar: "Silence! On your feet!" and jump up at his own command, with his thumbs along his seams. Then came histrionics: "Come what may, I can do no other." (Here he was resolving to go to the stake for my lethal novel!) Then he fell to musing: "Smoktunovsky! What a name! Still, he made a better Hamlet than I do!"

At this point I went in to him, and we sat up together for another hour. He had a smoke, his face gradually softened, and after a time he even began laughing. I took him back to bed soon after, and he caused no further disturbance.

He had only a few chapters left on the third day, but he started the morning with a request: "Your novel can't be read without vodka!" When he was coming to the end of the chapter called "Not You!" he twice wiped away his tears. "I'm sorry for Simochka. She went there as though she was going to communion. . . . I would have given her some comfort. . . ." Most of the time he reacted to particular passages as an ordinary reader rather than as an editor. He laughed at Pryanchikov, put himself in Abakumov's shoes ("I ask you, what can you do with somebody like Bobynin?"). On the subject of writers with refrigerators, and country homes near Moscow: "Yes, but there were some honest writers among them too. After all, I had a dacha myself."

When he had finished reading we went off together to view the Ryazan Kremlin and talk about the novel. The promised conversation about Tvardovsky himself had obviously oozed away in his nocturnal soliloquy.

He: "Having just finished a novel like this, how could you travel around collecting material for the next?"

I: "There has to be a quick follow-up. You can't stop at the river—you must seize the bridgehead for your next advance."

He: "True. Otherwise you finish one, take a rest, then sit down to the next—and hell, there's nothing there."

Tvardovsky praised my novel from various points of view and in emphatic terms. The opinions he expressed as a fellow artist were most complimentary. ("Your narrative energy comes from Dostoyevsky. . . . It's firmly constructed, a real novel. . . . A great novel . . . Not a superfluous page, not a line too much . . . I like the irony in your self-portrait—a self-infatuated writer can't describe himself." "You lean only on the greatest [i.e., the classics] and you don't cling too closely even to them, you go your own way. . . . A novel like this is a whole world, with forty to seventy people. We can absorb ourselves completely in their lives . . . and what people they are." He praised the descriptions of nature and the weather for their brevity and restraint. But the editor's official verdict was also heard. "Essential optimism . . . defends basic moral values . . . Most important, the novel's standpoint is that of the Party—it contains no condemnation of the October Revolution. . . . Though some people in the position of these prisoners might have reached that point. . . ."

The remark about the Party standpoint (of my novel!) calls for comment. This was not the cynical formula of an editor planning to bulldoze a novel through. He was a poet, but also a Communist, and if he had not been able to feel with deep sincerity that the viewpoint of the novel coincided with that of the Party, he could never have set himself the goal of publishing it. That this was his ambition he now told me.

True, he asked me to make some changes—but very small ones, mostly to do with Stalin: he wanted me to remove the chapter called "Study of a Great Life" (in which I tried by psychological and factual arguments to prove the hypothesis that Stalin had collaborated with the tsarist secret police); and he didn't want me to be so confident and precise about the details of the monarch's private life, since I could not be sure of them. (My view was that Stalin should reap the harvest of his secretiveness. He had lived mysteriously—so now anyone was entitled to write about him as he thought fit. The author's right, the author's duty, is to give his own picture and stimulate the reader's imagination.)

His general remarks about the Stalin chapters were sound, though: they could be left out, but their absence might be seen as proof that the author had "taken fright," that he had "been afraid he couldn't manage the theme." It might even be possible to allow a little overweight in these chapters—a little more than the minimum required by the structure of the novel.

Spiridon he found too crafty, too tricky—"a bit of a city slicker." I was surprised at first. I felt sure that I had done a good job of writing there. Then I understood. From the twenties onward, so many bad things had been said about the peasant that anything except unmixed praise for him hurt Tvardovsky's feelings. It was a conditioned reflex, an unthinking idealization.

On the morning of the fourth day we made a clumsy attempt to check A.T.'s lapse by denying him a hair of the dog. However, he was quite incapable of taking a single crumb into his mouth without a drink. He smiled like a child begging not to be hurt. "Of course, the Cheremis never take a livener the morning after. But who wants to live like they do? What a low level of civilization!" He grudgingly agreed to have beer with his breakfast. But at the station he hurried upstairs to the restaurant, drank half a liter with hardly a bite to follow, and waited for his train in a blissful condition. All he could say—over and over again—was "don't think badly of me."

Perhaps out of consideration for Tvardovsky it would have been better not to bring all these details under the spotlight. But if I didn't, the reader would not understand how unsteady, and how helplessly limp at times, were the hands that managed *Novy Mir*—nor how very big and how receptive the heart.

So my plan to captivate Tvardovsky with my novel in Dementyev's absence seemed to have succeeded. He had not only praised it; he was preparing to suffer for it. His very last words as we parted were that I should hurry with the revision of the Stalin chapters and bring him the final draft soon.

This went beyond the limits of my expectation! I could never have believed that *The First Circle* might slip into print in 1964. But why, then, had I given it to Tvardovsky? What had I been hoping for? Perhaps it had been *Ivan Denisovich* all over again: I had wanted to shift responsibility for the thing from myself to him. I had wanted him to know that such a thing existed. And not to have to reproach myself with doing nothing to further its cause. But now I seemed to have involved myself in a lot of superfluous and unavailing fuss and bother, which only distracted me from my real work.

Two weeks later I took Tvardovsky the revised version of the novel. Like all the manuscripts from my cave-dwelling days, it was typed on both sides of the paper, with no breaks between paragraphs, and with narrow margins. It still had to be completely retyped before anything could be done with it.

The A.T. who welcomed me to his home was so spruce and cherubic in his little velvet jacket that it was impossible to suspect him of ever taking a drop too much, or to imagine him in his underpants bellowing like a wild bull. He was alone. His wife had gone to take a closer look at the dacha they had just bought at Pakhra. (He had made a gift of the old one to his married older daughter.)

A.T. had recovered not only from his drinking bout, but from his rapturous intoxication with the novel as well, and he was by now in a much more cautious frame of mind. He had already started cutting down the list of those who would be asked to read it. "Al. Grig." (Dementyev) was, of course, to be the first.

I took the opportunity to warn him again: "Dementyev will be against it, of course. It's extraordinary—he's a man of sixty and he's known what it is to be persecuted; how long can he go on sitting on the fence?"

"I can see him developing all the time," Tvardovsky repeated.

Lakshin, however, was rapidly gaining the chief editor's confidence, and his influence in those years was exerted in opposition to that of Dementyev, with whom he frequently came to grips. During one of their set-tos Lakshin said: "Aleksandr Grigoryevich and I are both historians of literature and should realize that nowadays real literary history is what goes on right here at *Novy Mir,* not at the Institute of World Literature."

That was well said (and there were months when it was true). Lakshin supported *The First Circle*.

While the novel was being retyped, Tvardovsky would collect all the copies and put them in the safe, to make sure that only members of the board read it. (He wouldn't even let those invaluable and ever-faithful workhorses, the editorial assistants in the prose department, read it.) What he now dreaded above all was that like *Ivan Denisovich* in its day, the novel would be passed from hand to hand.

Tvardovsky had spent the three days of Easter reading the novel at my home, and as it happened the editorial board met to discuss it on Ascension Day, 11 June. The session went on for nearly four hours, and A.T. began by declaring it to be "a swearing-in ceremony." He said that never for a moment in the past forty days had the novel been out of his thoughts. He had been trying not just to see it in the light of eternity but as it might be read by those on whom the decision would depend. Tvardovsky declared that only my detailed account of Stalin's private life invited attack; he would also like me to modify the "harsher anti-Stalinist touches," and he would leave out the "Trial of Prince Igor" as "too literary." He concluded his introductory remarks on a solemn note: "By the normal standards of Soviet criticism, not only should this novel be scuttled, but the author should be prosecuted. But what sort of people are we? Can we evade this responsibility? Who would like to give us a lead? Who is willing to take the plunge for once?"

Forcibly detaching the novel read by Tvardovsky from his deputies had then been worthwhile! "The very first discussion" would take place as A.T. had said it would, there and then, in my presence, and the chief editor had begun it with this awesome invitation. As I came into the conference room I had made a point of greeting all the others before Dementyev. I was expecting him to charge head on this time. Instead of lolling comfortably in an armchair, he had begun for some reason by perching on the ledge of an open window. The roar of traffic could be heard from the street outside. Tvardovsky did not fail to remark on it.

"What's the idea—are you going to tell us later on that you couldn't hear what people were talking about?"

Dementyev stayed where he was, uncomfortably dangling his legs. "It's hot," he said.

Tvardovsky wouldn't let it go. "So that's the plan—to catch pneumonia? And take to your bed till it's all clear?"

Dementyev had to leave his perch and sit with the rest of us. He was too down in the mouth to make a joke of it. He had long ago foreseen exactly where these games with the unassuming writer from Ryazan would get them.

But it fell to Kondratovich to open the debate. Kondratovich's face might have been made for the earnest expression of opinions already current and defined. In such circumstances he can speak effusively, breathless with ingenuous zeal for the truth, ready, you might think, to die should duty demand it for the opinion he is defending. But I cannot imagine his face lighting up as belief ripens spontaneously within him. Opening the discussion would have been an unbearable ordeal to Kondratovich if long association with the censors had not adjusted his sense of smell to theirs. Putting it differently: just as the angle gauge set in military binoculars can be superimposed on anything within the field of vision, so Kondratovich's eyes were forever taking readings from a base line drawn red for danger.

Kondratovich was glad to note that "the novel as a genre was not dying" but was evidently "on the move." This was immediately followed by a little tummy-rumbling about "sapping the foundations": "The greater the artistic power of the writing," he said, "the more surely do the critical revelations turn into symbols." ("It's all right," A.T. reassured him. "The idea of communism is not called in question.") Yes, but a full-time secretary wasn't just an individual who happened to be a party organizer like Stepanov; he was a symbolic figure! Kondratovich suggested that some of the caustic digs should be removed—there were too many such passages. He even found "unnecessary" things in the chapters about the Great Lubyanka. It perturbed him that the steps of the Lubyanka had been worn away by thirty years of traffic. Was "the shadow meant to fall on Dzerzhinsky too?" His final opinion, like that he had once given on *Ivan Denisovich,* was conveniently open-ended. "It's impossible to publish. And morally impossible not to. How can we keep a thing like this lying around, where no one can read it?"

The chief had set them a problem, all right! The tender tips of their feelers told them that there was no way ahead, but the chief would keep egging them on. You can do it! Just follow the trail!

The next to speak was dim, slow, circumspect Zaks. He was so scared that his normal submissiveness to Tvardovsky abandoned him. He began by saying that they should give it a second reading (i.e., play for time). He was glad, he said, that everybody understood (but Tvardovsky didn't understand! that was the trouble—and that was what Zaks was so heavily hinting at) the exceptional difficulty of the case. He didn't really have any suggestion to make, he only had a *feeling*. And what he felt was that the chapters set outside the prison were neither necessary nor interesting, that there was no need to extend the story to society at large. Nor was it right to say that soldiers had a harder time of it at the front than war correspondents: a lot of correspondents had been killed too (Zaks himself had worked on a newspaper where this had happened). Then again, he was worried about the business of the secret telephone. (His censorial nose had served him well! But Tvardovsky innocently retorted: "Oh, come on—that's all complete fantasy! A very felicitous invention, though!") Another thing he didn't like was the scene with Agnia, and all that Christianity. The passages in which the heroes philosophize were just as bad. And the author did find an extraordinarily wide range of subjects to cavil at, as though he had made a special effort to leave nothing out. (Roitman's night was another thing he didn't like at all, but he told me this on a later occasion.)

At this point I couldn't help interrupting: "That's second nature with me. I can't by-pass any important question. Take the Jewish problem: you might wonder why I had to mention it. It would have been less bother to avoid it. But there you are—I can't."

The literature they were used to was too timid to broach problems at all, while a literature afraid to overlook a single problem irked and galled them.

Zaks's proposal was formulated in very diplomatic terms: "If we rush in too soon we shall ruin whatever chance the thing may have!" (He was for "the thing," of course—which was why he wanted it snuffed out, right there, in *Novy Mir*'s offices.)

But A.T.'s knowledge of editorial prevarications was up to this. "You mustn't let your fears get out of hand," he admonished Zaks.

Lakshin's statement was full of good will, but when I now look through my notes on the discussion (my fingers were moving at great speed throughout the meeting: I had no thought for anything else), with these sketches of mine already so inflated, I cannot see anything worth quoting. Lakshin took Tvardovsky's line—about the novel as a whole and about the Stalin chapters, which he said were essential. He did, however, say in the same helpful spirit that the didactic passages were like jagged rocks breaking the smooth surface of the novel—and Tvardovsky immediately interrupted him: "Steady there! That's a feature of his style." That's the kind of editor he could be!

Maryamov contributed a few friendly words: associated himself with the last speaker, praised the book, failed to see any undermining of foundations.

"And what does our commissar think?" Tvardovsky anxiously inquired. He had consulted his commissar so often in the past, on so many manuscripts, before forming his own opinion, had waited until they could form an opinion together! But today his tone of voice was a warning that Dementyev would find dispute difficult.

Dementyev did not in fact rush into single combat as I had expected. He was so depressed that he hardly knew how to begin.

"I am not going to talk about specific details. . . . I find it difficult to collect my thoughts. . . ." (He, with experience enough for ten!) "If you start giving advice to an artist of such caliber you run the risk of looking foolish. . . . The propaganda passages sometimes border on pamphleteering. . . ."

Tvardovsky: "Isn't the same sometimes true of Tolstoy?"

Dementyev: ". . . But the writing is tremendous, of course. . . . The Stalin chapters should be compressed into one. . . . If we live in the real world and have not given up thinking and feeling, the novel plunges us into doubt and dismay. . . . Bitter, grievous, dreadful truths . . . if you have a Party card in your pocket. . . ."

Tvardovsky: "And not only in your pocket . . ."

Dementyev: "You become one with it. . . . Truths like these cut so deep that intentionally or unintentionally they go beyond the bounds of the personality cult. . . . Literature and art are precious things, but *not the most precious of all."* (My emphasis—A.S. Obviously, the dictatorship of the proletariat must be dearer than these things to the editors of a literary magazine?) "It becomes hard to see *why the revolution was ever made."* (Now he had himself under control! Now he was standing up tall! Ready to take the offensive!) "On the philosophical side the author has no answers to the question 'What must be done?' Behave decently—is that all he can tell me?" (He was inviting me to stick my neck right out!)

Tvardovsky: "Camus says that much. But this is a thoroughly Russian novel."

Dementyev: "Dostoyevsky and Tolstoy give answers to the questions they ask; Solzhenitsyn doesn't tell us. . . ."

Tvardovsky: "Tell us what? How to improve meat and milk supplies?"

Dementyev: "I must think about it. . . . I still don't know what to say." Even he didn't know! He subsided again. The chief had put them on the spot! Here Maryamov and Zaks started whispering to each other, which brought an indignant outburst from A.T. "What are you whispering about there? I suppose you think we ought to find some way of dodging the problem?" Dementyev was so much on edge that he thought this was meant for him. "I'm not whispering," he said, and added incomprehensibly, "Can't the author think a bit more kindly of people and of life?"

This rebuke would be hurled at me over and over again. You must be an unkind person because you are unkind toward the Rusanovs, the Makarygins, the Volkovoys; the *mistakes* of our past, the faults of our system. (*They,* of course, had all been so kind to us!) "He simply does not *love the people!*" This was the indignant cry at all those closed seminars in which agitators were unleashed upon me in 1966.

Yet there had been a time when I, and Ivan Denisovich, and especially my hapless Matryona, were publicly castigated for being too kind, "indiscriminately kind," whereas you should not "be kind to everybody" (they were certainly practicing what they preached on me!), because if you return good for evil you only increase the amount of evil in the world. (*Oktyabr* in its stupidity flogged away at this dead horse for a long time, imagining that in attacking "nonresistance to evil" it was aiming its blows at me.)

What did it all add up to? To what they call dialectics.

After the members of the board, I was invited to speak and I noted with surprise that in the minds of some of them my novel related not to the personality cult, a luxuriant growth not completely eradicated, but to our society as a whole, which was growing healthier all the time, or even to Communist ideas in general. Still, it was undoubtedly a difficult matter. It was for the editorial board to choose, not me; as far as I was concerned, the novel was written and I had no more choices to make. But if the magazine made two or three wrong decisions in such matters it would—forgive my bluntness—turn into something like *Znamya* or *Moskva.*

I permitted myself this impudence. But Tvardovsky was so generously inclined toward me that he did not take offense even then, nor did he allow any of the others to do so. Instead he observed that I was paying them the compliment of putting them above those other magazines.

He had conducted the whole discussion so as to wring their consent to publication of my novel out of his fellow editors, and he ended by saying with great satisfaction, "It is extremely gratifying that for the very first time [?] no one has held back, as much as to say, I'm the clever one here, and I'm just going to sit still and keep my mouth shut." (Which was exactly what they had all been trying to do!) "Nowadays Sholokhov's rank makes people forget that his hero Melekhov is not the Soviet type of hero, and that in his novel the Party is represented only by unpleasant people. The question that *Quiet Flows the Don* asks is: What is the cost of revolution? The question in the novel we are discussing is: What does socialism cost, and is the price within our means? In the contents of the novel there is nothing contrary to socialism; it is simply that it lacks the clarity we should like to see. Its 'war' is dealt with exhaustively, but its 'peace'—all that was best in those years—is not shown at all. Where is the historic creativity of the masses? My one humble wish as a reader is that this brighter side of our lives could be seen, at least as a gleam on the horizon. That the horizon should be lit up at least to the extent that the artist thinks this possible. . . ."

Alas, there was nothing I could do to make it look brighter. I considered my horizon sufficiently well lit as it was. (The novel I had given them was already a much "lightened" version.)

Tvardovsky, however, in what was one of his supreme moments as an editor, did not insist. "Still," he said, "if Tolstoy had been a supporter of the Russian Social Democratic Workers Party, I wonder whether he would have given us any more than he did?"

In a matter of days a contract for the novel was drawn up, on Lakshin's insistence. (The cautious Zaks looked black, withdrew into his shell, and somehow succeeded in evading what was normally his duty: he pushed the task of signing the contract onto Tvardovsky.)[6]

In any normal country there would have been no further cause for delay. The novel would have been sent to the printers, and that would have been that. But in *our* country the editorial decision in itself meant nothing. Except that the time had now come to cudgel our brains and think of a plan.

But apart from sending the novel to be butchered by the censors in

---

6. At about the same time, the rigorist M. A. Lifshitz, who for many years had an extraordinarily strong influence on Tvardovsky, submitted a written opinion of my novel. It anticipated the critical storm clouds that would have gathered over the novel had it been published, and it may partly account for Tvardovsky's hesitations. I had to defend myself in writing.

the usual way, what could Tvardovsky do? Should he show this as well to Lebedev? "To my mind," said A.T., "even if Lebedev fancies that he sees something odd in it, he won't be the one to run and report. . . . He stands to lose too much himself."

Lebedev, of course, ran nowhere, but the novel wasn't going anywhere either. I naïvely imagined that any weapon would be welcome in the tussle with the Chinese, and that my Stalin chapters would be very useful, especially as responsibility for reviling Stalin would be assumed not by the Central Committee but by a mere writer. But this was August 1964 and Lebedev could no doubt feel how treacherous the ground was becoming under his patron's feet. He had often, no doubt, regretted blotting his record by supporting me.

A.T. gave him only a quarter of the novel as a sample, telling him, "This is Part One. He's working on the rest."

It so happened that A.T. and Lebedev had just clashed over Ehrenburg. Polikarpov (of the Central Committee's "Cultural Department") and Lebedev wanted Tvardovsky to take the lead in rejecting the last part of Ehrenburg's memoirs, wanted them not to be "forbidden by the censor" but "rejected by the editors." A.T. replied with dignity: "It is not I who made him a laureate, a member of the Supreme Soviet and a fighter for peace. I am not, in fact, one of his admirers. But since he is a laureate, a deputy, *and* world famous, *and* over seventy, we ought to print anything he writes."

Their annoyance with one another was intensified by the chapters from my novel. Lebedev declared them to be a libel on the Soviet system. A.T. asked him to explain himself. Lebedev answered with a single example: "Do we really believe that officials in Soviet ministries worked nights? And—according to this author—spent their time playing checkers? . . ."[7] His advice: "Keep this novel well hidden. Don't let anybody see it." A.T. answered firmly: "This is not a bit like you, Vladimir Semyonovich! Do you remember how you and I felt not so long ago about reviewers who said that sort of thing?" Lebedev: "If only you knew *who* has now taken a dislike to *Ivan Denisovich* and regrets that it was ever published!"

(We were reliably informed by other sources that Khrushchev's

---

7. I was told just recently that Lebedev had once been a Chekist. A little thought about dates tells us that this was in Stalin's day, when, of course, *their* little game was something different from checkers.

wife, Nina Petrovna, had complained to a retired general: "Oh, if only you knew *what we've had to put up with* because of Solzhenitsyn. We shan't be meddling anymore, that's for sure!")

Anyway, miracles don't come down the same path twice. Why chide Lebedev for backing away? Shouldn't we rather be surprised that he found the courage the first time around?[8]

This was the end of *Circle*'s progress for a while. True, Tvardovsky in his publication plan for 1965 made so bold as to announce that I was "working on a long novel for *Novy Mir.*"

I wanted to keep silent and write. I wanted to refrain from anxiously peddling my wares, but I couldn't keep it up. It was difficult to determine the true meaning of the situation, and the best line to take—I might so easily miss a chance. And so I hawked *The Light That Is in You (Candle in the Wind)* around several theaters, but this play proved unattractive to producers. Then, in spring 1964, forgetting my usual cautious tactics, I impulsively gave copies of my "Miniatures" to a number of readers, stipulating that they need not be hidden but should only "be shown to good people."

Unlike the play, these "Miniatures" had a great success. They were very soon circulating in hundreds of copies and reached the provinces. The most unexpected thing for me was the warm response of intellectuals to my outspoken defense of religion (which until recently would have been thought so disgraceful in Russia that no writer's reputation could have survived it). Samizdat did its job of disseminating the "Miniatures" beautifully, and seemed likely to offer a reasonable alternative for a writer whom the authorities had decided to ban. The

---

8. After Khrushchev's overthrow, Lebedev lost his post, but because of the new mutual aid system among the top people he was not cast down from his eminence, nor did he fall into poverty. K. I. Chukovsky met him in 1965 in the Barvikha sanatorium. The former "privy councilor" was writing his memoirs, or something of the sort, and told Chukovsky that he was refuting all my inaccuracies about Stalin's private life. (Those chapters of mine had really got under his skin.) As late as 1966 he sent me New Year's greetings—which astonished me because I was on the brink of arrest. (Perhaps he didn't know?) Rumors had reached him that Tvardovsky and I had quarreled, and he urged me to make it up. I was too sick of them all at the time to appreciate what was perhaps the most disinterested gesture he had ever made. Then there was a period of nearly a year in which I had no contact with Tvardovsky, either. It was during that year, as I learned recently, that Lebedev died, though he was scarcely fifty. At the funeral of the once all-powerful councilor there was no one from the Central Committee, no representative of the Party at all, and no one from the literary establishment—except Tvardovsky. In my mind's eye I can see that sturdy, broad-backed figure bending sadly over little Lebedev's coffin.

"Miniatures" circulated so briskly that only six months later, in autumn 1964, they were published in *Grani,* as *Novy Mir* and I were informed in a letter from a Russian lady living abroad.

The illicit circulation even of my smaller things (which he had in any case already rejected!) caused Tvardovsky acute displeasure: a mixture of jealousy when he saw something of mine by-passing his editorial approval, and of fear that all this might "spoil things" for the novel and for my legitimate work as a whole. (But what further damage remained to be done?) Either he was changing or he was showing another of his many facets. How long was it since he had excelled himself in his efforts to promote my luckless novel? But now, after reluctantly reading one of the "Miniatures" (he had been forced into it at a gathering in Pakhra and had read it with something like disgust—apart from anything else, it was not being circulated by him!), he squeamishly asked: " 'The Creator'—and with a capital *C?* What is all this?"

He was thunderstruck by the news that the "Miniatures" had been published abroad. They looked up *Grani* in the censor's handbook and were terrified to read what a horrid anti-Soviet magazine it was. (There was no mention of its articles on such subjects as Dostoyevsky and Lossky.) However, if it had taken the "Miniatures" six months to reach Europe, it took another eight for a report on this event to make its way upward through the various levels of our dilatory bureaucracy.

In the meantime, the "Little October Revolution" had taken place: Khrushchev had been thrown overboard. Those were anxious days. I had not expected a "simple coup" in this form, though I had prepared myself against the eventuality of Khrushchev's death. I owed my rise to this one man: perhaps my survival also depended on him alone? With his fall, must I come crashing down too? These apprehensions were natural in an eternally persecuted ex-convict—for I was incapable of imagining the true strength of my position. I had been dumb and still before Khrushchev's removal, and I intended to be dumber and stiller now. My first reflex action was an urgent visit to Tvardovsky at his new dacha. He was as cheerful as I was anxious. For him any decision taken by a plenum of the Central Committee had moral and not just executive force. If a plenum of the Central Committee had seen fit to remove Khrushchev, it meant that his experiments were indeed no longer to be tolerated. Two years earlier Tvardovsky had been in ecstasies at the thought that we had "a man like that" over us. Now he found the new leadership very reassuring, seen from certain angles. (He had "liked the way they talked" to him *"up top."*) And it must be admitted that Tvardovsky's life had been made unbearable in the last months of Khrushchev's reign. There had been moments when he simply could not see how the journal could survive. *Moskva,* that carrion crow among magazines, could publish Bunin (savagely cut) and Mandelstam and Vertinsky—and *Novy Mir* could publish no one, publish nothing: even Bulgakov's *Theatrical Novel* was held up for two years: "because it might give offense to the Moscow Art Theater." "What we need is a loyalist story from you," he would say sadly, without for a moment expecting me to treat it as a request.

I had come to him with a pretty panicky scheme: *to substitute one novel for another.* In other words, I would remove *The First Circle* from the safe—no one except Lebedev, who had now lost his power, had seen it—and in its place I would very shortly hand over *Cancer Ward,* which would pass for "the same novel," renamed by the author. I was afraid that any day now they would come to inspect the *Novy Mir* safe, confiscate my novel—and Tvardovsky and I would be cast down into the depths of hell. By now I felt that I had committed a foolish blunder in dragging my novel out from underground and submitting it to the *Novy Mir* editors. By now I was desperately anxious to escape observation by hugging the ground and melting once again into its gray surface. If only I could say goodbye to publishers, and sit quietly writing, as I used to.

But I still didn't understand Tvardovsky very well or I wouldn't have suggested a dubious prison-camp stunt of that sort. He had too much respect for his magazine and his position to go in for "hidey holes" or switching manuscripts. And anyway, what was there to hide if the novel contained "nothing against the Communist idea," as we had agreed at the meeting of the editorial board? . . . I could hardly backtrack now and say, "You've missed the point! It's much more dangerous than you think!"

A.T.'s fears were quite different. That summer he had begun asking menacingly whether the novel was going the rounds. "I hear rumors that people are reading it," he said, trying to frighten me just in case. If it had been so, he would have regarded it as black treachery on my part. All roads were closed to the novel; it might be years before it got any further; but I, the author, must not dare to let anyone read it. This was how A.T. interpreted my understanding with his editorial board.

Still, now that I was expecting reprisals any moment, I myself was not particularly anxious for *Circle* to be spread around.

When Nikita was toppled I lost a complete set of my writings: one of two sets in safekeeping at a distance from Moscow. Its custodian had my permission to burn everything in the event of danger. Out in the backwoods it is difficult to keep things in perspective, and he saw the fall of Khrushchev as the sort of danger I had in mind: after the coup an orgy of house searches and arrests would follow. So he burned it. Luckily, there were three or four copies of everything, except *The Feast of the Victors,* of which there were two, only one of them now in Moscow.

It was Khrushchev's fall that drove me into action to safeguard my writings; every scrap of my work was in the Soviet Union, and could be suppressed. That same October, with my heart in my boots, I sent *The First Circle* to the West—and it arrived safely. I felt a lot easier. They could shoot me now if they liked!

All the same, Khrushchev's overthrow was for me something of a relief—a slight, almost a spectral relief. I would not feel the benefit of it till much later, but it was nonetheless real: Khrushchev's departure released me from a debt of honor. I, who had been raised up by Khrushchev, would never have enjoyed real freedom of action while he was there: I would have had to go on showing my gratitude to him and to Lebedev—ridiculous as this may sound to any ex-zek—that ordinary human gratitude which no self-righteous political orthodoxy can abolish. Released from patronage (had I ever enjoyed it, though?), I was also excused from gratitude.

I believed that there would be better times and even that I was destined to see them, believed that an age of complete freedom of the press would someday dawn. In the meantime I had chosen for many years ahead the way of silence and clandestine labor. As far as possible, I would not take a single public step. I would let people forget me (how I longed to be forgotten!). Make no attempt to publish. Just write and write. What was wrong with that? . . . I thought it was the wise course to take. In fact, it meant self-destruction.

For six months after this I didn't even visit *Novy Mir;* I had no business there. Throughout the winter of 1964–1965 my work went well. I was writing *The Gulag Archipelago* at top speed, and there was by now an abundance of material from zeks. Jollying fate along, trying to make up for half a century of neglect, I rushed off to Tambov oblast to collect scraps of information about the peasant insurrectionaries, whom even their descendants and relatives had been trained to call *bandits.*

I did not feel any more harassed than before. I had been gagged in Khrushchev's time, and there was no need to tighten the gag now.

So I let myself go again, and lived as though no threat hung over me. I took it into my head to move to Obninsk, and bought a marvelous summer dacha there on the Istya near the village of Rozhdestvo. I was tearing myself apart, trying to write *Gulag* and begin *R-17* at the same time.

However, the new leadership was very cautious, very slow to take decisions or make changes. It was only in April 1965 that "Agitprop," or whatever it was now called, acquired a new boss—Demichev. Just as Tvardovsky went into a long relapse, and was sent to a hospital and then to a sanatorium. (A purely Russian way of doing things! He could escape from the dimmest of blind alleys, from all the strains and humiliations of his work as editor, for two or three weeks, or on this occasion for two months, along some baffling alcoholic parabola into a world that did not exist for his colleagues and his staff but was quite real to him, and return from it physically sick, it's true, but spiritually more fit.) It was July before Tvardovsky went to see Demichev for the first time. He was received cordially, and Demichev let it be known that he would like to meet "that Solzhenitsyn" too. Tvardovsky did not know where to look for me, and promised nothing, but that very day I felt irresistibly drawn to the *Novy Mir* office: let who will say that thoughts and wishes cannot be projected. A.T. immediately phoned Demichev and an interview was arranged for the following day, 17 July.

Almost the whole editorial staff was sitting in Tvardovsky's private office. It had been a long time since I had seen them all, and I felt out of place and bored in their presence. My head was full of *Gulag,* and of Tambov in 1921, and there they were, demanding from me in unison a "viable little story," trying to convince me that after a break of two years (and as a token of loyalty to the new leadership) it was now "very important" that "something or other" by me be published.

Of course it was—for them and for the loyalist *Novy Mir.* But for me, a "viable little story" would mean ruining my reputation; would be an empty shell, a hollow space. The strength of my position was that my reputation was unstained by compromise, and I must keep it so, if I had to keep silent for another ten years.

They all joined, too (following Tvardovsky's lead, it is true: they always let it be clearly seen that they unanimously supported their boss, even on the most trivial matters), in pressing me to prepare for the next day's visit by shaving off the beard I had recently grown. I was an independent, non-Party Russian writer about to present myself to the head of Agitprop (why, exactly? to what purpose?), but it was imperative for me to assume the faceless appearance to which the Party apparat was accustomed. So earnestly did they try to persuade me, that you might have thought the magazine had no more serious concerns. Three times, four times I declined (without of course mentioning the apparat in so many words), and then they started begging me not to go in a frivolous open-necked shirt worn outside my trousers, but in a dark suit and a tie—this in the heat of July!

I tried to have a private talk with A.T., but it was no good, a waste of time. He was excited, indeed exhilarated, because they had spoken kindly to him, and he had high hopes for my interview the following day, which should, he thought, reinforce my position and that of *Novy Mir.*

My object in going to see Demichev was different: to prolong my existence as a nobody indefinitely. I am not the least bit dangerous to you, so leave me in peace. I work very slowly, I have practically nothing written except what has already been published or is with the editors. And anyway, I am really a mathematician, and quite prepared to go back to that work if literature will not provide me with a living.

This was the age-old, familiar style of the camp—"putting up a smoke screen"—and it worked beautifully. Demichev was very much on his guard, very suspicious to begin with, but in the course of our two-hour conversation he warmed to me, and ended by believing everything I said. His quiet voice was normally devoid of emotion, but a trace of feeling finally began to show itself—and the feeling was relief. He was extremely unprepossessing and he spoke in threadbare clichés.

By this time the technique of "slander from the platform" had made its appearance; a technique that cannot possibly be applied in an open society, because the accused can always answer back, but that in our closed society is an unerring and murderous weapon: the press preserves its silence (for the benefit of the West—why draw attention to the witch hunt?), while speakers at public meetings and closed briefing sessions, obeying a single command, authoritatively and confidently utter any lie they please about the undesirable in question. And he not only has no access to their meetings and briefing sessions for purposes of reply, but does not even know for some time what has been said about him and where, knows only that he is trapped inside blank walls of slander.

This slander campaign was still in its infancy, the forms it would take were still discernible only in outline, but they had already announced that I was a traitor, that I had been a German prisoner of war, that I had been in the *Polizei.* Should I sue someone? There were too many slanderers, and they held official posts.

Demichev looked at me with one stern yet sympathetic—sympathetic yet accusing—eye (the other one did not work properly).

I steered the conversation myself and contrived to answer the newspaper criticisms of "Matryona's Home." What a stupid journalistic complaint—that I had not traveled twenty kilometers farther and shown my readers a champion kolkhoz: after all, I wasn't a journalist but a schoolteacher and I worked where I was sent.[9] Besides, how could my picture of a kolkhoz be called gloomy when *Izvestia* itself, in its attack on me, had confirmed that not just Matryona's village but the entire cluster of collective farms in the region *still did not harvest as much grain as they sowed*—and this not in 1953, but ten years later! A splendid agricultural system—if you want the grain to rot in the ground. As for the Matryona type—the selfless woman who worked without pay whether it was for the kolkhoz or her neighbors—wouldn't we like to see everyone behaving unselfishly?

He still said nothing, and I asked the question that is not supposed to be directed *upward.* "Do you agree with me? Or do you wish to make some objection?"

The challenge was too abrupt; he had still not made up his mind (and could not make it up unaided!). My arguments did not fit into the fixed pattern of phrases with which his kind are familiar, and he tossed the question a safe distance: "Do you always understand what you are writing, and why?"

Steady now! . . . I cannot, of course, help understanding, corrupted as I am by the Russian literary tradition. But it is too early to declare myself. I tread cautiously along the slippery path. "Depends which of

---

9. The critics simply did not notice that I had mentioned the chairman of the neighboring collective farm who had put it on its feet by blackmarket deals in timber.

my things you're thinking of. In 'For the Good of the Cause'—yes, I did know: I wanted to affirm that faith is a precious thing for young people: to remind people that communism must be built within themselves first and in stones afterward. In 'An Incident at Krechetovka Station' my conscious aim was to show that evil deeds were committed not only by a limited number of inveterate evildoers but that the purest and best of men can commit them and one must struggle with the evil in one-self." (Demichev, however, said later that he had read neither "For the Good of the Cause" nor "Krechetovka," so that he was *not prepared* for a discussion with me.) Whereas in "Matryona" and *Ivan Denisovich* I had simply followed where my heroes led. I had set myself no specific aim.

For him this would prove to be the key passage in our conversation. In a number of public speeches he would relate, always in the very same words, how he had pinned me to the wall by asking *why* I wrote, and I had been lost for an answer, and could only repeat the hoary old argument, which had no place at all in socialist realist literature, that I had "followed where my heroes led." The writer should lead and his heroes follow.

Defending *Ivan Denisovich*, I hit out simultaneously at Dyakov's book (why couldn't that lofty intellectual lay bricks for socialism, how was it that in five years he managed to do just half an hour of women's work—lopping branches from felled trees?) and at G. Shelest's stories (how could his favorite hero accept bread and other food stolen from the working prisoners, all the while writing out synopses of Lenin's works?). But Demichev saw nothing culpable in the behavior of Shel-est's old Communist, and was ready with his retort.

"Well, didn't Ivan Denisovich wangle himself an extra portion of gruel?"

"Yes, but that's Ivan Denisovich! Intellectually he is not fully grown —he doesn't write summaries of Lenin! He is corrupted by the camp! We feel sorry for him because all he does is fight for a bigger ration."

"Yes," said Demichev solemnly. "I can't help wishing that he had listened more to the politically conscious people there who could have explained to him what was going on. . . ."

(And where were you, with your explanation, while it was all going on? What would you have done with my poor story if I had tried to explain everything?)

I: "If we wanted to take in the whole problem of the camps, yet another book would have to be written. But"—expressively—*"should it be, I wonder?"*

He: "It should not! We need no more about the camps! It is a painful and unpleasant subject."

While insisting that I regretted nothing I had written, and would do exactly the same again, I deliberately tried to impress upon him that I was a very slow worker and was therefore thinking of going back to mathematics (this obviously inspired in him no anxiety for the future of our national literature), that I was usually dissatisfied with my work and often destroyed what I had written.

"However immodest it sounds, I want my things to live for twenty or thirty or even fifty years."

He forgave me for my lack of modesty, and referred warmly to Gogol, who had burned Part Two of *Dead Souls.*

"That's right! I do just the same!" (This made him very happy.)

"How long did it take you to write *Ivan Denisovich?"*

"Several years," I sighed. "I couldn't say how many."

All this time I was waiting to be asked about *The First Circle*, which had been high and dry in the safe at the *Novy Mir* office for a whole year. And about the "Miniatures," which had been published in the West. But the head of Agitprop, needless to say, *knew nothing* of all this.

Warmed by these candid exchanges, I betrayed my most cherished literary ambition—the writing of *Cancer Ward.*

"Isn't the title too morbid?"

"It's only a provisional title. It will show doctors at work. The human spirit defying death. Kazaks and Uzbeks."

He was still not reassured. "But won't it be too pessimistic?"

"Oh, no!"

"Generally speaking, which are you—a pessimist or an optimist?"

"I am an unshakable optimist—can't you tell from *Ivan Denisovich?"*

Then he enumerated for me the things that should not be done and that the Party did not wish to see in works of literature (this was all very precise—memorized and ready for use):

1. Pessimism.
2. Denigration.
3. Surreptitious sniping.

(I was struck by the careful choice of words under Point 3, which seemed to be aimed straight at me. I wondered which of them had formulated it.)

I passed over "surreptitious sniping" and sought a closer definition of the term "denigration." Take, for instance, the peasants who won't let Princess Mary evacuate Bogucharovo (and are themselves probably looking forward to Napoleon's arrival). Is this a denigration of the war of 1812 or not?

But Demichev had evidently not read the novel in question, and no discussion resulted. Still, our conversation was settling down nicely.

"I'm glad you aren't distressed or offended by criticism," he said in almost friendly tones. "I was afraid you might be embittered."

"In my most difficult moments I've never been bitter."

In the course of conversation he paid me more compliments than mere politeness demanded. "You are a strong personality"; "You are a strong man"; "The attention of the whole world is fixed on you. . . ."

"What do you mean!" I said in amazement. "You are exaggerating!" (And so he was: at that time I was politically fashionable in the West, but not many saw anything more in me.)

"Yes, their attention is fixed on you." He himself seemed at a loss to understand it. "Fate has played a little joke on you, if I may put it like that."

He was warming to me more and more, and even felt called upon to comfort me.

"Not every writer wins recognition in his lifetime, *not even* in the Soviet epoch. Think of Mayakovsky."

(Ah, but that's just what I want! You let me alone, I'll let you alone! Leave it to eternity to decide.)

"I can see you really are an honest, straightforward Russian," he said happily.

I nodded shamelessly. That's what I should have been, all right, if you hadn't marooned us in the Gulag Archipelago. If for one single day in the whole forty-five years since you abolished secret diplomacy and secret appointments you had been honest and open with us.

"I can see that you really are a very modest man. You have nothing in common with Remarque."

So that was what they were afraid of—that I might be another Remarque! They had lost the habit of fearing Russian literature. Shall we ever succeed in retraining them?

I cheerfully assented. "No, nothing in common with Remarque."

All this frankness on my part finally earned me a frank admission from him.

"In spite of our successes, we are in a difficult situation. We have to carry on an internal as well as an external struggle. Some of our young people are prone to nihilism and criticism for criticism's sake, and some public figures [?] do nothing but push them in that direction."

Not I, though! I cried out in all sincerity that I was perturbed by the obstinate indifference of young people to life's broadest and most important questions.

It now emerged that we had been born in the same year, and he invited me to remember the ardors and the sacrifices of our own younger days.

(Yes, comrades, that's just how I remember it. . . . But history will surely not repeat itself quite so drearily. History shows some taste, after all.)

We were both well pleased with our talk.

I had not asked him either to publish a collection of my stories or to help me with my plays. The main result of our meeting was that quite unexpectedly, without any trouble or preliminary effort, I had reinforced my position with the new leaders and could now go on writing in peace and quiet for a certain number of years.

"*They* have not been given a second Pasternak," said the Secretary for Agitation by way of farewell.

No, the average twentieth-century engineer or mathematician could never get used to the tortoise pace at which Staraya Ploshchad shuffles into position to pick up information from its own apparatus! It was a mere nine months since the "Miniatures" had been printed in *Grani;* how could Demichev know about them? . . . It was only a month ago that Polikarpov had found out, shown them to Tvardovsky, and asked whether they were mine. Tvardovsky had replied that he was sure that most of them were not mine.

Now, Tvardovsky had never seen them, yet there he was, certain that they were not mine! So sure that when he was sending me off to see Demichev, he hadn't even mentioned this conversation, hadn't warned me. I would certainly have told him that they were all mine! That is the logic of the officeholding hierarchy: a subordinate (I) must not know all that his superior (Tvardovsky) knows. And the subordinate (I) could not have written anything of which his superior (Tvardovsky) had not been notified.

Then, suddenly, A.T. happened to discover that the journal *Semya i shkola* was about to print part of the series here at home. He was almost panic-stricken: he had given his word to the bosses that the "Miniatures" were not mine! Moreover, he was stung by jealousy: no one (not even I myself!) had the right to publish my works, no one but *Novy Mir*. Besides, he had classified the "Miniatures" three years ago as raw material: how could they possibly be published? And finally, now that the frightful disaster had occurred and they had been published in the West, they would obviously *never* be published at home! (This idea, that work published abroad was irretrievably lost, and its author disgraced, stayed with Tvardovsky through all the years I knew him. He was at first just as squeamish about samizdat. He recognized only open state-approved publication, which was less easily available to those who wrote for his magazine than to anyone else.)

He immediately set about *summoning* me. It is just the same, I daresay, with other publishing houses, but I can speak only for *Novy Mir*, and it has never ceased to surprise me: an author makes a slip and is *summoned* to see his editors! The author is obviously regarded as a servant of the state attached to his magazine, and just as in any other branch of state service, he may be required to present himself to his senior officer.

That August, however, Tvardovsky found no one to help in tracking me down before he went off to Novosibirsk (where, incidentally, a written question was handed in at a readers' conference: "Is it true that Solzhenitsyn was employed by the Gestapo?").

I can only try to guess at the nature of the change of course that some were planning in our country in August–September 1965. If we live to see our history brought into the public domain, we shall be told what precisely happened. But we can say with near certainty that what was planned was an abrupt return to Stalinism, with "Iron Shurik" Shelepin in the lead: he wanted, so they say, to tighten up the economy and the administration, Stalin fashion, and on this he is supposed to have been at odds with Kosygin; but on the need for a tighter ideological line not one of them disagreed. Shelepin proposed that they should bow down to Mao Tse-tung, and acknowledge that he was right: this would be no skin off their noses, and the two countries would combine their strength. What, the Stalinists inquired, had been the point of overthrowing Khrushchev if not to revert to Stalinism? When were they going to try it out? That August, an important ideological conference took place, at which it was explained that though the struggle for peace went on, the Soviet people *must not be disarmed* (that is to say, their minds must continually be poisoned against the West); we must reinforce the martial spirit, must combat pacifism; our general line was emphatically not mere *coexistence;* Stalin was guilty *only* of abolishing collective leadership and illegally repressing Party and state cadres, and of nothing more; there was no need to fear the words "administration by decree"; it was time to *resurrect the useful concept "enemy of the people";* the spirit of Zhdanov's decrees on literature was sound; *Novy Mir* must be *looked at more closely* to see why the bourgeois praised it so much. (There was something about me too: I had distorted the true picture of the camp world, where only Communists suffered, and our enemies were imprisoned with good reason.)

No one knows all the steps that the Shelepinites had in mind. But one step they took successfully: the arrest of Sinyavsky and Daniel at the beginning of September 1965. (Semichastny's henchmen were calling for the arrest of "a thousand intellectuals" in Moscow.)

In those anxious early September days I made plans to remove my novel from *Novy Mir:* they might come along and open the safe, and . . . I had been clever too soon. I must quickly vanish into the underground and camouflage myself as a mathematician.

On 6 September I went to see Tvardovsky at his dacha, although he was in the early stages of a drinking bout. He came downstairs with heavy steps, in his undershirt, with muddied eyes. Even if he had been sober it would have been difficult for me to say what had to be said, but with Tvardovsky in this state it was so much harder. He could only trot out his own grievances, and had neither eyes nor ears nor understanding for anything else.

"I put my head on the block for you, and what do you do? . . ."

It was understandable enough: I had not been open with him; the intricate pattern of my plans, calculations, moves, had been concealed from him and had come to light only accidentally.

In a confused conversation, with no connecting thread, A.T. made the following points:

That I had no right to act independently, "without consultation" (meaning without asking permission).

That I should not have let *Semya i shkola* have the "Miniatures."

And then—that beard! that beard, now . . . It was extraordinary how that beard preyed on his mind. Kingdoms were tottering, heads were rolling, and he . . . talked about my beard. This time, however, in a fit of drunken candor, he explained himself.

"They say you're doing it because you want to escape. . . ."

"Who says? Who have you been talking to?"

"I don't have to answer that. . . . People say, 'He must have some reason for growing a beard.'. . . It's very convenient for crossing the frontier."

"How on earth can a beard help anyone across the frontier?"

"You could shave it off, of course, and go across unrecognized."

He tried to look triumphantly knowing, but a drunken squinting leer was the best he could manage. . . . In the same breath A.T. reported what they were saying in the "Cultural Department" of the Central Committee: that I had pretty certainly given the "Miniatures" to *Grani* myself.

I felt bitter. Not because things like that were being said about me in the Central Committee, but because Tvardovsky himself had been weak enough to let this nonsense get a grip on him.

Still, I somehow managed to bring it home to him that I wanted to remove *The First Circle* "to alter the grammar."

He wouldn't believe it.

I confessed that I did not trust the *Novy Mir* safe.

This seemed absurd to him: what could be more secure than a safe in the offices of a Soviet institution! Although I was the author, I was enslaved by my contract and the magazine had the right not to let me have the novel. Especially as I was insisting on making a clean sweep of all four copies.

But A.T. was feeling kind, and took me at my word. With great regret, he promised to call his office next day and tell them to hand the book over.

So far, so good. All I had to do was outlast "Iron Shurik"! I had stuck my neck out too soon. Much too soon . . .

On 7 September I rang Tvardovsky's dacha from the *Novy Mir* office and with some difficulty got him to the phone. His voice was weak but businesslike, not as it had been the day before. He begged me in the friendliest way not to take the book. No need for it! Quite safe with us! No point in it! Oh, all right then, take three copies and leave us one.

He might have been a mother clinging to her sons. Please, please let one of them stay at home with me!

But I was a man possessed. I had to have all of them. (I could see more clearly and farther than A.T.! My mind was made up! I remembered how Grossman's novel had been taken from that very safe at *Novy Mir.*)

This restless anxiety of mine! Forever prodding and pricking me into thinking twenty moves ahead.

I took all four. These were wide-spaced editor's copies and they made such a bulge in my suitcase that I could hardly shut it.

If I had been carrying something different, something secret, I would have taken immediate precautions, looked carefully about me, covered my traces. But this was copy ready for the printer, and for all the world to see. I was only taking it away because *Novy Mir* itself was in danger. It was not my immediate purpose to hide the thing.

True, I was taking it to an apartment that was both important to me and quite unsafe. Until recently I had kept most of my archives there —those that had been brought in from Ryazan on New Year's Eve. But I had removed most of what was hidden there—a whole treasure chest —a little while ago, leaving only semi-overt things of secondary importance, and, before going away for the summer, the tenant of the apartment, V. L. Teush, a retired professor of mathematics and an anthroposophist, had handed over all these remnants to his disciple, the young anthroposophist I. Silberberg.

There are moments when reason flags and falters. When excessive foresight turns into grossest blindness, cool calculation into helpless confusion, firmness of purpose into feeble apathy. (But for such lapses, we should not know our own limitations.) Teush was a thoroughly decent man, but alas, careless, a muddler, a happy-go-lucky conspirator. I knew what he was like—but still, we had somehow got away with it for more than three years, although he was garrulous on the telephone and had written a "criminal" work of his own on *Ivan Denisovich;* indeed, we had heard a rumor that his work had already been deposited with the Central Committee. None of this worried us! Although my custodian was what he was, I had, not long before, removed the portable hidey hole containing my archives without checking its contents, and without a "warder's inspection" to make sure that only less important things were stored for all to see in Teush's flat. He had, however, broken our rules and occasionally taken things out to read or reread: it might be *The Feast of the Victors* (the one surviving copy!), or *The Republic of Labor*, or the camp verses, and it would be a miracle if he did not look at some of the rest. *In his carelessness he had put none of it back where it belonged!* He had come across it again in my absence and coolly dispatched it for safekeeping during the summer to Silberberg, whom I did not know and had not checked on.

It was to Teush's flat—imagining that it was a safer place than the *Novy Mir* offices—that I now lugged my suitcase with four copies of *The First Circle*. (As I heaved it along I felt like a panting beast hunted through the streets of Moscow, no doubt because owl eyes held my back in their searchlight beam.)

It was ridiculous, this sudden loss of reasoning power. I had resolved like a man to vanish into the depths, then like a child put my faith in Y. Karyakin and his specious assurances that his oh, so very liberal boss, Rumyantsev, now editor of *Pravda*, was thinking of publishing one or two innocuous chapters of *The First Circle*. So I left three copies at Teush's place and took the fourth with me for *Pravda*. I was out of my mind.

On the evening of 11 September—in the narrow interval between the arrests of Sinyavsky and Daniel—the KGB boys simultaneously visited the Teushes (where they took *The First Circle*) and, alone among the Teushes' friends, Silberberg, to pick up my archive.

In that very last moment before I could dive into the depths, my very last moment on the surface, I had been winged!

Winged.
Winged . . .

# The Wounded Beast

That was less than two years ago, and it is twenty-two years since I was arrested, but although my feelings about that have faded, I know that the later disaster was harder for me to bear. The blow of my arrest was easier to bear because I was at the front, in the battle line, when they took me; I was twenty-six years old; no finished works of mine would perish with me (they simply did not exist); I found myself involved in an interesting, indeed an exciting game; and I had a vague yet clairvoyant presentiment that my arrest would enable me as nothing else could to influence the destiny of my country. (In my naïve imaginings I saw the men in Moscow suddenly wanting to hear my ideas on straightening out all that Stalin had made crooked.)

But the catastrophe of September 1965 was the greatest misfortune in all my forty-seven years. For some months I felt it as though it were a real, unhealing physical wound—a javelin wound right through the breast, with the tip so firmly lodged that it could not be pulled out. The slightest stirring within me (perhaps the memory of some line or other from my impounded archive) caused a stab of pain.

The hardest blow was to find that after going through the full course in the camps, I was still so stupid and vulnerable. I had been an underground writer for eighteen years, weaving my secret web and making sure that every thread would hold. A mistake about one single person could have plunged me into a wolf pit with all I had written—but I had made no mistake and had not fallen. So much effort had gone into keeping it all safe, so many sacrifices into writing it. My plan was an immensely ambitious one; in another ten years' time I should be ready to face the world with all that I had written, and I should not mind if I perished in the flames of that literary explosion—but now, just one slip of the foot, one careless move, and my whole plan, my whole life's work had come to grief. And it was not only my life's work but the dying wishes of the millions whose last whisper, last moan, had been cut short on some hut floor in some prison camp. I had not carried out their behests, I had betrayed them, had shown myself unworthy of them. It had been given to me, almost alone, to crawl to safety; the hopes once held in all those skulls buried now in common graves in the camps had been set on me—and I had collapsed, and their hopes had slipped from my hands.

Throughout this period I felt a constriction in my chest. There was a sickening tug somewhere near my solar plexus, and I could not decide whether it was a spiritual sickness or a foreboding of some new grief. There was an unbearable burning sensation inside me. I was on fire, and nothing helped. My throat was always dry. I felt a tension that nothing would relax. You seek salvation in sleep (as you once did in prison); let me sleep and sleep and never get up again! Switch off and dream untroubled dreams! But within a few hours the shutter of the soul falls away and a red-hot drill whirls you back to reality. Every day you must find in yourself the will to put one foot in front of the other, to study, to work, to pretend that the soul can and must do these things, although in reality your mind wanders every five minutes: Why bother? What does it matter now? . . . In your daily life you seem to be acting a part; you know that in reality it's all gone pfft. It is as though the world's clock has stopped. Thoughts of suicide—for the first time, and I hope the last. (One thing helped me to bear up: my microfilms were already in the West! Not all my previous work was lost!)

I spent three months in this condition—though there were brisker and more cheerful intervals. On impulse, I took certain defensive steps; only the most urgent and obvious (though I sometimes made mistakes), but I could not accurately assess my general position and decide on the right course of action. Almost every night I fully expected to be arrested. I had a new firm policy in case of arrest: I would refuse to make any depositions; I would declare *them* unfit to act as prosecutors and judges of Russian literature; I would demand a sheet of paper for "testimony in my own hand" (the Criminal Procedural Code gave me that right) and I would write as follows: "Conscious of my responsibility to my predecessors in the great literature of Russia, I cannot recognize and accept the supervisory right of gendarmes over it. I will answer no questions under interrogation or in court. This is my first and last statement." (Like it or not, they would have to include this in the record.) So I was ready for anything—if need be, for death or for indefinite imprisonment. But in either event, my work would come to an abrupt end. The interruption had in fact already occurred. The disaster had caught me working furiously on *Gulag*. My precious notes and part of the completed first draft existed only in single copies, and were as dangerous as atom bombs. All this had to be transferred, with the help of reliable friends and with great precautions against being followed, to the distant Hiding Place, and there was no knowing when I might return to that book.

My work was at a standstill, even though I had not yet been arrested.

News of the disaster reached me in two installments, not all at once. First I learned only that *The First Circle* had been seized—but even this stung me to the quick. What had I done! Instead of listening to Tvardovsky, I had taken the novel away. I myself was its destroyer. Then I was told about Sinyavsky's arrest. Didn't my novel give them just as good reason for arresting me? Perhaps the only reason I hadn't been taken in during the last two days was that they hadn't yet tracked me to Rozhdestvo. What might have happened at my Ryazan apartment I just did not know—my life was so fragmented. Perhaps they had already *called* there?

It was late afternoon. We hurriedly threw some personal belongings and such manuscripts as I had by me into the car (they might turn up and search the place before we had been gone an hour), and skirting Moscow, we traveled by suburban roads to Tvardovsky's dacha. I was in a hurry to give him the news before I was grabbed.

I just cannot understand now why the discovery of the novel then seemed such a catastrophe. I did not yet know about the more important catastrophe, and if the novel had ended up in the Lubyanka—well, books have their own destiny, as the Latin proverb says: this was the starting point of its peculiar literary career. (I don't think that the novel was what they had come for. It was an unexpected bonus. No doubt somebody got a medal for it, no doubt departments high and low exulted. Whether or not they were rejoicing in their own misfortune, time will tell. Like a glacier in the mountains, the novel might have been less dangerous to them had it not been set in motion.)

More trouble. I ran out of petrol with a kilometer still to go, and had to walk through the writers' colony at Pakhra with an empty jerry can. Tvardovsky was at home, in conference with the workmen who were reinforcing the fence around his new dacha and moving the main gate. They were asking for a hefty advance. I butted in on this discussion and, motioning him aside, said quietly:

"Bad news. They've grabbed the novel."

It took the wind out of his sails.

"What—from where *you* put it?"

He still had the workmen to deal with, while I had to go to Tendryakov's place for petrol and then fetch the car—all of which gave A.T. time to get used to this new thought.

His self-control that evening was perfect, which is much more than I can say for myself. A week before, in those very rooms, with much less cause, he had been so annoyed, so upset, so reproachful, but now it was quite the contrary: although he had been proved right, he uttered not a word of reproach. This time he took it bravely, he thought before he spoke, he was not even in a hurry to question me as to where and how the thing had happened, or to offer his views on it. In his gloomy castle of a dacha he put a match to some brushwood in the ceremonial fireplace and for a while we just sat there.

His first impulse was to complain in person to Demichev next morning. An hour later, on reflection, he decided it would be better for me to do it.

I immediately began drafting a letter, and the first faint crack of what would later be a yawning gulf became discernible. A.T. insisted on language so very mild that it was almost apologetic. In particular he would not allow me to write *"unlawful* removal." A.T. absolutely insisted that the adjective must go because nothing *they* did could be "unlawful." I half-heartedly resisted. Next day in Moscow, he phoned to make doubly sure that I had reworded it. To my shame, I gave in, and substituted the servile word "unwarranted." No more appropriate word beginning with the same letter—and so requiring a minimal change—came into my darkened mind.

After a sleepless, feverish night we drove early to Moscow. There, a few hours later, I heard of a still worse disaster: on the same evening, 11 September, *The Feast of the Victors, The Republic of Labor* and my camp verses had all been seized! This was the real thing, and all that had come before a mere foretaste of disaster! Bridges were breaking and collapsing beneath my feet—prematurely and ingloriously.

Still, I wrote my statement to Demichev as though I knew only about the novel. I cut through the sunlit, crowded, quite unreal Moscow day, passed the hawk-eyed security controls again, entered the resplendent building of the Central Committee, where I had so recently been such a success at a reception, went along broad, deserted corridors furnished like drawing rooms, where the doors of offices displayed not their occupants' functions—we were supposed to know them all anyway—but their names, their unknown, undistinguished, fast-fading names, and handed my statement to the courteous secretary, whom I had met before.

From there, I went on to *Novy Mir*. A.T. was still worrying about the "unlawful" actions, and needed reassurance from my own lips that I had removed that word. He had another very important request to make: I *must tell no one* that the novel had been taken from me! Otherwise, *undesirable publicity* would make the situation much more difficult.

The crack was widening. Make whose situation more difficult? That of the *top people*—or my own? *Undesirable* publicity? . . . But that was the one thing that could save me! I would tell anybody and everybody! I would seek out and hunt down the listeners likeliest to shout my story from the housetops! (It was a help, not a hindrance, that *The First Circle* had been taken as well as the treasonable *Feast:* I could speak more loudly about the confiscation.)

But if I revealed all this to Tvardovsky right away, he would have a heart attack! How could such unthinkable impertinences worm their way into the head of an author discovered by a sound Party journal like *Novy Mir?* . . . And what would happen to *Novy Mir* if I did all that? No, A.T. was not ready yet to hear such horrors. I would prepare him for a lesser one. "Apparently it isn't only the novel they've taken. There was also an old version of *The Love Girl and the Innocent* and my camp verses."

A.T.'s gloom deepened. "And I don't suppose the poems are all about mummy and daddy?"

He was turning sour. But he was glad that one typed copy of the novel had survived—in *Pravda*'s safe, no less! (I had been planning to publish chapters in *Pravda*, of course!)

There was, however, a general upheaval in the next few days. Rumyantsev was dismissed, and my well-wisher Karyakin had his work cut out to spirit the *Pravda* copy away.

That was on 20 September. In the week that had passed since the arrest of Sinyavsky and Daniel, "all Moscow," as they call it, had been running around in a panic, transferring samizdat and illicit émigré books from one hiding place to another, carrying bundles of them from house to house and hoping that they were doing the right thing.

Just two or three police raids—and suddenly there was such a commotion, such a change of hearts—yes, and so much apostasy! So fragile and precarious were the freedoms—to talk, to possess manuscripts—that had been bestowed under Khrushchev and had expired with him.

I asked Karyakin to bring the novel straight from *Pravda* to *Novy Mir*. Exaggerating the watchfulness of the Cheka-KGB and the swiftness of their pounce, we were not sure that he would get there with it. But he brought it in safely, and I put it on the little couch in A.T.'s office and awaited The Man himself. I did not doubt that when he saw the rescued copy A.T.'s heart would leap up, and that he would happily restore the novel to his safe. I could picture his delight! Then A.T. arrived and we started talking, while the familiar fat folder lay slantwise across the couch. A.T. spotted it, went closer, and taking care not to touch it, nervously inquired: "What's that?"

I told him. And at once he was sullen, remote, unrecognizable.

"Yes, but why did you bring it here? Now that the other things have been confiscated." (He'd said it at last! Confiscated—*legally confiscated!*) "We cannot have it in the office. You mustn't hide behind our backs *now!*"

It was like a smack in the face! Not because I was afraid for that particular copy. I had others (and there was one in the West), but he thought, remember, that it was one of only two surviving! A little scene that deserves to be engraved in the annals of Russian literature! . . . A.T. liked to hear his magazine compared with Pushkin's *Sovremennik*. But if Benckendorff had been stalking a novel, and someone had brought it to Pushkin for safekeeping, we can be sure that he would have eagerly seized the folder, instead of murmuring evasively, "I come of a good landed family. I'm a gentleman of the bedchamber. What *would* they say at court!"

The poet's standing in the nation has changed, and so have the poets themselves.

Worse still, A.T. refused to publish in *Novy Mir* my rebuttal of slanderous allegations about my past ("worked for the Germans"; "in the *Polizei*"; "Gestapo agent": Komsomol and Party agitators were by now carrying these tales throughout the land). Two weeks earlier A.T. himself had advised me to write such a letter (beginning enigmatically:

"I have been advised to . . ."). But something unfortunate had happened: I had sent *Pravda* the top copy of my letter, since I was counting on Rumyantsev—now a burst balloon—and what had gone to Tvardovsky was the second copy. I now heard him saying: "It is not my practice to do anything about letters sent to me in second copy."

How poets have changed. . . .

"And what's the use of denials while your novel is under arrest? . . . People will say there's obviously *something* in it!"

He spoke with the assurance of those who are ex-officio right. It was only logical! If a novel was confiscated in 1965, how could anyone maintain that its author had not been in the *Polizei* in 1943? (This, of course, was not the real point. He was too weak to print my denial, but he had to make his refusal more palatable to himself by pretending that he thought it right.)

I sat there helpless, half-heartedly answering Tvardovsky's tedious reproaches.

1. How could I, without consulting him(!), have sent three more complaints to three more Central Committee secretaries in the past few days? In doing so I had insulted Pyotr Nilych Demichev, and must have dampened said Pyotr Nilych's desire to help me.

He offered an illustration: "Suppose somebody asks me—just me— to help him get an apartment. I do all I can for him, but if he writes: 'To Fedin and Tvardovsky,' I think: Right—let Fedin help him."

Did he really see an analogy? Did an event of such dimensions leave room for speculation about possible insults, about the personal feelings if any, of Central Committee secretaries? If Demichev had been my own father he could still have altered nothing. This was a clash between the state and literature—and Tvardovsky saw only a client petitioning his patron. . . . I had hastened to send three more letters (to Brezhnev, Suslov and Andropov—little thinking what the last would someday become), simply because I was afraid: Demichev was a dark horse, he might be a Shelepin man, he might suppress my letter and say that if I had not complained, it was obviously because I felt guilty.

A.T. was now ready to forgive the human weakness that had resulted in so much unwanted publicity. I had not resisted the urge to tell somebody about the novel. (Not resisted the urge! I had gone to a Shostakovich concert at the Conservatory for the express purpose of broadcasting the news of my misfortune.)

On the other hand:

2. Had I consulted him about further complaints, he would have recommended me to appeal immediately and directly to Semichastny (head of the KGB). Why try to *go over his head?*

I flinched as though he had struck me. That was something I would never do. Appealing to Semichastny would mean acknowledging the suzerainty of the security organs over literature!

Yet again—and again and again—Tvardovsky failed to understand:

3. How I could, some time ago, have given my play to the "Sovremennik" *against his advice.*

He could think of nothing more important than settling accounts there and then with those theatrical "gangsters," And upbraiding me in my time of trouble.

And further, (4) how I could bring myself to keep my "sacred" *Ivan Denisovich* and those embittered plays about the camps in the same place (thus casting a shadow not only on the "sacred *Ivan Denisovich*" but on *Novy Mir* too).

And another thing, (5) why I hadn't taken a Moscow apartment although at one time I "could have got a whole house."

And yet again, (6) how I could have given *Semya i shkola* permission to publish my "Miniatures."

And lastly (from a Tvardovsky morose, unsmiling and perfectly sober), a new and exceedingly important point: (7) Why had I started wearing a beard? Was it perhaps so that I could, when opportunity offered, shave it off and slip across the frontier? (He did not omit to report the suspicious inquiry of some *higher-up:* Why had I been so keen to move to Obninsk, which was a center of nuclear research?)

The repetitiousness and pettiness of these reproaches were somehow unmanly.

I did not fight back. I had misjudged the rope, and taken a tumble. I had myself to blame for my pitiful situation.

A.T.'s only friendly gesture in that whole hour was to offer me money. But it was not lack of money that seemed likely to destroy me!

I tucked my orphaned and unwanted novel under my arm and took it to the *Novy Mir* messenger (and resident informer) to get the folder sealed (another bit of servile cunning: when the KGB came, let them see that I had not been asking people to read it). However, another day went by and I realized that the best thing I could do was to deposit it in an official archive—the TsGALI.

For the past week ("Mourn if you must, but don't stop fighting") I had been busy rescuing my main manuscripts, and everything else that had escaped detection, then warning people not to write me any more letters. When I had shed the burdens, when the most immediate and essential work was done, I was gripped again by that searing, rending grief with which I began this chapter. I did not know, I could not see, how I was to live or what I was to do, and only with great difficulty could I concentrate on my work for two or three hours a day.

At this juncture K. I. Chukovsky offered me the shelter of his roof (which took great courage), and this greatly helped and cheered me. I was afraid to live in Ryazan: it would be easy to cut off my way out, and possible to seize me without fuss or fear of consequences (if need be, the blame for any "mistake" could be shifted onto overzealous local KGB men). At Chukovsky's dacha in Peredelkino no such "mistake" on the part of the operatives was possible. I strolled for hours through dark cloisters of pine trees in K. I.'s grounds with a heart empty of hope, vainly trying to comprehend my situation and, more important, to discover some higher sense in the disaster that had fallen upon me.

An acquaintance with Russian history might long ago have discouraged any inclination to look for the hand of justice, or for some higher cosmic meaning, in the tale of Russia's woes, but I had learned in my years of imprisonment to sense that guiding hand, to glimpse that bright meaning beyond and above my self and my wishes. I had not always been quick to understand the sudden upsets in my life, and often, out of bodily and spiritual weakness, had seen in them the very opposite of their true meaning and their far-off purpose. Later the true significance of what had happened would inevitably become clear to me, and I would be numb with surprise. I have done many things in my life that conflicted with the great aims I had set myself—and something has always set me on the true path again. I have become so used to this, come to rely on it so much, that the only task I need set myself is to interpret as clearly and quickly as I can each major event in my life.

(V. V. Ivanov came to the same conclusion, though life supplied him with quite different material to think about. He puts it like this: "Many lives have a mystical sense, but not everyone reads it aright. More often than not it is given to us in cryptic form, and when we fail to decipher it, we despair because our lives seem meaningless. The secret of a great life is often a man's success in deciphering the mysterious symbols vouchsafed to him, understanding them and so learning to walk in the true path.")

But now I had come to grief, and I did not understand. I seethed, I rebelled, I did not understand: *Why* must this work be brought to nothing? It was not just that it was *my* work; it was almost the only work that had survived as a monument to the truth. Why was it apparently necessary for our posterity to know less of the truth, indeed hardly anything of it (for anyone coming after me would find it still harder to dig out the truth, while those who had lived earlier had either not survived or had not preserved what they had written, or had written anything except what Russia would soon be longing for)? I had long ago come to understand the meaning of my arrest, my deathly illness and many personal misfortunes, but this disaster I could make no sense of! It rendered meaningless all that had gone before.

(That was how I saw it, so infirm was my faith! Two autumns have gone and only in this present winter have I begun to think that I understand it all. That is why I have started on these notes.)

Two by no means small political reasons for rejoicing came to me at the end of September while I was Chukovsky's guest: they arrived within a few days of each other, and under the same heavenly signs. One of them was the failure of the coup in Indonesia, the other the defeat of Shelepin's schemes. That China to which Shelepin would have us bow down had covered itself with shame, and "Iron Shurik" himself, who had begun his campaign through the apparat in August, had not succeeded in toppling a single one of Khrushchev's successors. The main speakers at the Twenty-third Congress were named six months in advance and Shelepin was not among them.

Shelepin in power would have meant a speedy end for me. Now I was promised six months' grace. There was, of course, no assurance of safety in this, only the hope of it, and that dimly glimpsed. I would have thought my safety assured if Western broadcasts had reported the arrest of my novel. It differed, certainly, from the arrest of live people like Sinyavsky and Daniel, but if a Russian writer's work, ten years of it, is confiscated, surely to God the zealous champions of Greek democracy and of North Vietnam could devote just one little line to the event? Is it a matter of complete indifference to them? Or don't they know?

I had been given a reprieve—but what ought I to do next? I had no idea. And I mistakenly decided that now was the time to publish! Anything—it didn't matter what.

So I sent off my play *Candle in the Wind* (previously unknown to them) to *Novy Mir.* When they had all read it, I went to the office.

In the month since we had last met, Tvardovsky had become still gloomier; he was subdued; he felt that he was hemmed in, helpless, ruined even: all because they had talked roughly to him *up top.* (Demichev had harshly reprimanded him for not being up and about when he was needed: he was supposed to go to Rome and be elected vice-president of the European Community of Writers; they didn't want either Surkov or Simonov.)

All the same, A.T. had twice asked Demichev about my novel. Only by telephone, it is true, but considering how painful it was to him, his efforts deserve high marks. The first time, Demichev's answer was: "Yes, I've given instructions for it to be returned." (He was lying, of course.) The second time: "Yes, I've ordered them to *look into it.*"

Tvardovsky had no idea what to do, and I wasn't much better. So I agreed to the ludicrous suggestion that I should ask for an audience with Demichev.

A.T.'s reception of the play gave me no pleasure. I knew that it was feeble and long-winded, but he found it "very stageable." (Poor A.T. His status did not permit him to visit Moscow theaters and keep up with modern drama.) Why not publish it, then?

"You've disguised it as God knows where, but it's only too obviously about our country, and the message of the play is unambiguous."

I said, quite honestly: "I was writing about the vices of modern man generally—and especially the more prosperous part of mankind. Do you grant that there may be modern vices common to different countries?"

He: "No, I can't accept that point of view without drawing a line between capitalism and socialism. Nor can I share your views on life and death. Shall I tell you what I would do if it depended *entirely* on me? I would write not a foreword but an *afterword*"—this mark of disparagement was too subtle for me—"saying that we cannot withhold an author's work from his readers"— the hell you can't! after fifty years of doing just that!—"but that we do not share the views he expresses and must protest."

I: "That would be just fine! I ask for nothing more."

He: "But it doesn't depend on me."

I: "Listen, A.T.—what if it had been written by a Western author? We would have leaped at it, we would have staged it immediately. People would have said, 'Look how he pitches into modern bourgeois society.'"

He: "Yes, if it had been written by Arthur Miller or somebody
. . . But even he would put the anti-Communist sentiments into the
mouth of a negative character."

But it wasn't just the play! A.T.'s attitude to me personally had
become cooler, warier: I was not, after all, the flawless, crystalline figure
he had hoped to present to Staraya Ploshchad and to all progressive
mankind.

Still, I had nothing to lose, and I now offered him "Right Hand,"
which I had not felt able to show him earlier.

He received it with hands almost trembling with joy. Prose was a
genre in which I had proved myself, and who knows? This might be
*viable*.

He telephoned next day: "The descriptive passages are very good,
but all in all this is the most terrifying thing you have ever written."
Then he added: "I've never guaranteed you anything, you know."

Oh, no; of course not! Of course the magazine had never committed itself! The only commitments were those I had made—to
bring everything I wrote to *Novy Mir* and nowhere else. But how
many rebuffs must I encounter before I stopped considering myself
a *Novy Mir* man? . . .

I derived much comfort at this time from reading daily, as I might
read my prayerbook, collections of Russian proverbial sayings. First, I
learned that:

"Grief won't kill you, but it will knock you off your feet."

"Some troubles you can't sleep off."

"When fate is ready, it will tie you hand and foot."

"If you miss your chance, you miss your footing on a mountain—it's
too late to look back." (This described the mistakes I had made when
I was raised to the heights, only to dawdle and hesitate and let slip my
opportunities.) But then:

"Whatever your troubles, don't put your head in a noose."

"Man is full of grief, but God is ever merciful."

"All else will pass, but the truth will remain!" This last was particularly comforting, except that it was not clear to me how I could help the
truth to prevail. After all:

"Misery won't get you over the water."

Then there was one that might have been made for me:

"One man dies of fear, another is brought to life by it."

There is also the enigmatic saying:

"If trouble comes, make use of *it* too."

What it came to was that I must be "frightened alive." I must turn my troubles into blessings. Perhaps even into a triumph? But how? How? Heaven's cipher remained unsolved.

On 20 October there was a party in honor of S. S. Smirnov (his fiftieth birthday) at the Central Writers' Club and the Kopelevs persuaded me to put in an appearance—for the first time in the three years that I had been a member of the Union—to show the world that I was alive and kicking and full of smiles. In fact, this was the very first time that I had attended a jubilee meeting and heard how they sing each other's praises. I did not know that Smirnov had been in the chair when Pasternak was expelled, or I would not have gone. In his pieces on the Brest fortress he had, as far as I could judge, done a good job.* Still, I couldn't help wondering how he would ever have managed that little job if he had not been allowed to visit the ruins of the fortress, nor to speak to the whole Soviet Union over the radio, nor to write a single line in a newspaper or magazine, nor to address public meetings, nor even to discuss the matter openly in letters; if when he met a former member of the Brest garrison they had been able to converse only in secret, fleeing from eavesdroppers and eluding spies; if he had had to travel in search of materials without official facilities; if he had had to keep his materials and the manuscript itself somewhere other than at home. *How would he have managed then?* Would he have written about the Brest fortress, and how much of the story would he have told? These were not imaginary conditions. They were the conditions under which I had collected 227 firsthand accounts for *The Gulag Archipelago.* [1]

After the ceremony, word went around in the vestibule of the Writers' Club that I was there. And a dozen or so Moscow writers, followed by members of the staff, came over to meet me—as though I were not the threatened author of a confiscated novel but a pampered and all-powerful laureate. All around, people exchanged whispers and looked

1. Incidentally, the guest most enthusiastically feted on this occasion was for some reason Marshal Zhukov, who was sitting on the platform. Every time his name was mentioned—and this happened five or six times—there was a burst of genuine applause in the hall. The Moscow writers demonstratively hailed the fallen marshal! There was a fresh breeze in the social atmosphere. But would it blow us any good? Our de Gaulle manqué sat there in a dark civilian suit, smiling pleasantly. Ever so pleasantly—but he was a lackey like all our marshals and generals. How low our nation has sunk: even among the military command there is not a single real personality.

sideways at me. What did it mean? Was it the usual magnetic attraction of fame—even fame overtaken by disgrace? Or was it an encouraging sign of the times?

Tvardovsky was also at the jubilee meeting. He screwed up his eyes as the camera bulbs flashed. Quite early on, he left the presidium (where he never felt at home), and vanished behind the scenes, perhaps to the restaurant, but he surfaced again in the vestibule. He was plagued by jealousy because *he* had not been the first to bring me to the club (and besides, I hadn't *consulted him* about this visit!). He immediately dragged me aside, away from my friends and from those who wanted to meet me, and his henchmen Dementyev and Kondratovich rallied round. Where now was the sourness A.T. had shown only two days ago! "Your beard is beginning to look less Hemingwayesque," he announced. "There's a soupçon of Dobrolyubov about it." The other two, of course, hastened to confirm this. In two days even my beard had changed! The reason? I had been promised an interview with Demichev on the following day.

"Victory! Victory!" crowed the rejuvenated Tvardovsky. He already scented the fragrant balm which any moment now would pour down from *on high*—on me first, but if on me, then on him and on the magazine. "It doesn't matter what is said there, or whether they give it back or not; the mere fact that he's *receiving* you is a victory! Call me tomorrow without fail. I shall be waiting by the telephone all day."

Poor A.T.! He had never really broken with me. In his heart he had always been for me—but I for my part must come to my senses, stop being impertinent to the bosses, regain their favor.

Next day, however, to Tvardovsky's chagrin, I was denied access to Demichev. I was not completely snubbed; I was received by his assistant, or to be more precise, his adviser on cultural matters, I. T. Frolov, but this was hardly an "audience." This adviser was a man of thirty-six.[2] His face had not yet coarsened into stupidity; he was moderately clever; and he very carefully and skillfully toed a thin line: on one side of it his private (but of course!) democratic inclinations and his extreme politeness toward a much respected writer, on the other his constant deferential awareness of his proximity to a highly placed politician.

---

2. It turned out that he had been friends with Karyakin in his younger days. They had graduated from the Faculty of Philosophy together, but while Karyakin had taken to the path of rebellion, this other had chosen that of the time server.

All I could do was to repeat to Frolov the contents of my latest letter to Demichev, in which I mentioned the sequestrated archive and also wrote that many of the Party's leaders would not wish to repeat some of their statements from before the Twentieth Congress and to take responsibility for them. The impudent thing about my letter was that I chose the very time when accommodations were being prepared for me in Lubyanka to declare that my quarters in Ryazan were impossibly bad and to ask for an apartment in Moscow![3]

For lack of any real business, Demichev's adviser and I conversed on literature at large. This is what he said: that the whole of modern Soviet literature was very dull. (They were its only begetters! *They and their censors!* He, however, explained it by a temporary dearth of talent among the people. "My view is more optimistic," I chided him. "The talent is there, but you do not give it free rein.") As a result, there was absolutely *no one* to act as a counterbalance to me, not even Sholokhov, alas; my work would be obligatory reading and the "counterweights" would not be. That was why they couldn't publish me, with my tragic themes. He said something else, something very interesting: he saw it as a form of *egoism* on the part of those who had suffered too much in prison that we were so eager to *force* our own reactions to the past on the younger generation.

This simply astonished me. It was the morality of Big Hugh in Wilde's fairy tale! Those pearls of wisdom about the egoism of those who want to speak the truth! Obviously, this idea had been purged of dross and newly minted in the leading circles, and now passed for honest ringing coin! It was nice for them, and important to them, to know that *they* were the kind ones—they who were doing their best to rear the young on lies, on ignorance of the past, and on sports.

Ten days after I had handed in my letter, it was answered via the Ryazan obkom: my complaint had been "referred to the Procurator General of the U.S.S.R."

A pretty little twist! The Procurator General is seized of a complaint from the insignificant ex-zek Solzhenitsyn (obviously prematurely "ex"!)

---

3. During the month of my brief acceptance by the whole Soviet world, an apartment in Moscow was mine for the asking, but I didn't take it because I was afraid of wearing myself to a frazzle in the Moscow literary whirl. Later on, they wouldn't give me one even in Ryazan. But now, at this moment of utmost danger and despair, they offered me my pick of apartments in Ryazan—anything rather than have me in Moscow!

against the personnel of the all-powerful state security organs! In a state ruled by law, this would be the only correct procedure: who, if not the procurators, can defend the citizen against unjust actions on the part of the police? But in Soviet circumstances it wore a different complexion: it meant that the Central Committee had refused to make a political decision—or at least to make one in my favor. There was only one course the case could follow in the Procurator's office: my complaint would be turned against me. I imagined them timidly phoning the KGB, and those gentlemen answering, "Come and read it for yourselves!" A trio of procurators goes along (two of them dyed-in-the-wool Stalinists, one a seedy nonentity) and their hair stands on end: Why, in the good old days of Stalin the only possible reply to filth like this would have been a bullet! And the insolent wretch dares to complain? . . . On the other hand, if the Central Committee had wanted to *put me inside,* there was no need to burden the procurators with such work: it would have been enough to authorize Semichastny to arrest me. However, the CC had evaded a decision. What could the Procurator General's office do now? Shirk responsibility in its turn. (And this was just what it did. A year later I learned that my novel had been put in the safe of Procurator General Rudenko and that even department heads with their tongues hanging out were not allowed to read it.) It all sounded quite frightening—"Your case has been passed to the office of the Procurator General"—but the prognosis that suggested itself to me even then was heartening.

We were nearing the end of the second month since my novel and my archive had been impounded—and they had not followed through by taking me. They had not merely an adequate but an embarrassingly abundant collection of material on which to base charges against me, ten times more than they had had against Sinyavsky and Daniel—and yet for some reason they didn't take me. Strange times had come upon us!

"Dare is halfway there!" the book of proverbs whispered in my ear. All the circumstances told me that I must be bold and even insolent! But what exactly must I do? "If trouble comes, make use of it." Yes, but how?

If only I had seen how that autumn! It all seems so simple, once you understand and act. But at the time I could think of nothing.

If only someone in the West had raised an outcry, if the whole world had been told that my novel had been impounded, I should have been in clover, I could have gone on working without a care in the world. But they were silent! The antifascists and the existentialists, the pacifists, the hearts that bleed for Africa, had nothing to say about the destruction of *our* culture, about the destruction of *our* nation, because if they stopped dressing left with us as markers, they would be weak and ineffectual. And because in the last analysis the destruction of Russia was an internal affair which concerned only us Russians. Your neighbor's toothache won't hurt you. Preparations for the trial of Sinyavsky and Daniel were complete, the claws of the gendarmes were rending my archive and my heart, and that very autumn a Nobel Prize was thrust into the hangman's hands of M. A. Sholokhov.

I put no hopes in the West—indeed, no Russian ever should. If we ever become free it will only be by our own efforts. If the twentieth century has any lesson for mankind, it is we who will teach the West, not the West us. Excessive ease and prosperity have weakened their will and their reason.[4]

All the same, I began to act. Incorrectly, as it now appears. I did not act in conformity with my usual style and my normal preferences. I was in a hurry to make my voice heard and so I took issue with Academician Vinogradov's muddled article in *Literaturnaya Gazeta*. As it happens, I had long been collecting material on the language of fiction, but here I made a hash of it, presented it in a hastily written, superficial, unconvincing and, what was worse, harshly polemic form, and, worse again,

---

4. Six months later the man whose canvassing obtained the prize for Sholokhov (and inflicted the most hurtful insult imaginable on Russian literature)—Jean Paul Sartre—was in Moscow, and through his interpreter expressed a wish to see me. I met the interpreter on Mayakovsky Square, and she told me that "the Sartres were expecting me to dine with them at the Peking Hotel." At first sight it might seem well worth my while to meet Sartre: here was a "master of men's minds" in France and throughout Europe, an independent writer with a worldwide reputation. There was no reason why we should not be sitting together around a table in ten minutes' time: I could complain about all the things that had been done to me, and this wandering minstrel of humanism would alert all Europe.

If only it had been someone other than Sartre. Sartre needed me partly to satisfy his curiosity, partly so that he would have the right later on to talk about our meeting, perhaps to criticize me—and I would have no means of defending myself. I said to the interpreter: "What's the good of two writers meeting if one of them is gagged and has his hands tied behind his back?"

"Aren't you interested in meeting him?"

"It would be unbearably painful. My head is barely above water. Let him help us to get published first."

I drew an analogy between Russian literature and the deformed boy in *Cancer Ward*. It seemed to me just as twisted and one-sided when viewed from Europe. The undeveloped potential of our great literature has remained completely unrecognized there.

I wonder whether Sartre discerned in my refusal the depth of our aversion to him?

in a newspaper article—a genre I had so uncompromisingly abjured. (Moreover, I had to suppress my most important idea—that no one had done more to ruin the Russian language than the socialists with their slovenly pamphlets, and Lenin in particular.) All I succeeded in doing in this miserable article was to yell defiance at the KGB: "Here I am—alive and in print—and not afraid of you!"

The editor of *Literaturnaya Gazeta,* the nimble and keen-scented Chakovsky, ran to "consult" Demichev. Could my name appear in print? Demichev evidently gave him permission at once.

He was right.

And I was quite wrong, I had got into a mess. I had given one more unnecessary proof that left to ourselves, with only the help of the spherical object pivoted on the neckbone, we are more likely than not to take the wrong road.

Because it was just about then that the clever *Neue Zürcher Zeitung* (God bless it!) reported that my apartment had been searched and my works taken away. For two months I had been longing for just this! Now the news could spread and win confirmation. But at that very moment *Litgazeta* arrived in the West, and it looked as though in my ridiculous article I was refuting the reports, crying out to the West: "Look, I'm alive, I'm in print, I'm just fine!" I had yelled defiance not at the KGB but at the *Zürcher Zeitung,* and made fools of its accurate informants. Still, the few lines that the newspaper had published about me greatly cheered and encouraged me. I did not immediately realize that I had made a mistake. At the time I supposed that the article in *Litgazeta* had also strengthened my position.

I regained the mental balance necessary for work, and managed to finish a few stories I had begun earlier—"What a Pity," "Zakhar Kalita" and one other—and decided to hitch them up with my dangerous "Right Hand" and submit them to someone as a set of four. To someone, but not to *Novy Mir.* Tvardovsky had by now rejected half a dozen pieces of mine—more than he had published. Besides, he had just recently been so frightened by "Right Hand" that he hadn't even shown it to members of the board. (He had, moreover, told me this as though he had done me a service—by protecting me and my "good name." But surely there were worse things than lying in the Lubyanka! Consciously or unconsciously, he was protecting himself and his own reputation, making it appear that *his* discovery of *me* had not been a mistake.)

L. Kopelev said jokingly that I had "repeated Hadji Murad's defection"* with those four stories, making the rounds of various journals in the camp hostile to *Novy Mir.* From the point of view of *Novy Mir,* and more particularly of Tvardovsky himself, I had indeed committed heinous treason. (Ill-informed as always about nonofficial happenings, A.T. somehow never got to know the full dimensions of my betrayal: that after he had hidden "Right Hand" even from his trusted aides, I had light-heartedly passed it around to his enemies, and had done nothing to prevent messengers and typists from copying it.)

I did not and still do not see any betrayal in it, because the struggle between *Novy Mir* on the one hand and *Oktyabr* and the whole "conservative wing" on the other reminds me of nothing so much as the surface tension between contending forces, together creating a film through which the livelier molecules down below cannot break out. An editor in chief who will not publish a play simply because it does not carefully distinguish between capitalism and socialism; who recoils in disgust from my prose poems *for no other reason* than that an émigré journal was the first to print them; for whom Russian literature in exile does not exist or else is little better than a refuse dump, while our own samizdat writers are as bad as drug pushers; who is frightened by a story in which the author did not hesitate to pass moral judgment on someone who carried out execution in the Civil War—in what way, except in his good intentions, does that chief editor differ from his "deadly enemies," Kochetov, Alekseyev and Sofronov? This is where you see the leveling effect of those little red books! As for the members of the other boards, Kruzhkov and Ivanov at *Ogonyok,* for instance, they really are indistinguishable from Kondratovich and Zaks, except that in the privacy of their offices they are franker and bolder (because they have not been taught to tremble). To give one example, such people seemed to speak more openly and far more naturally about the destruction of the peasantry by collectivization. Even M. Alekseyev, who had no thought for anything but his career, remarked to me that autumn (when we were alone, it is true) that "we have been building on lies for many years now —it's time we gave it up."[5]

Here I shall be stopped and told not to blaspheme, not to dare take these comparisons any further. I shall be told that for many years *Novy*

---

5. Alekseyev, of course, in his public performance builds only on lies. His own *parents* starved to death during collectivization, but in his autobiographical *The Cherry Pool* he *conceals* this as an unimportant detail.

*Mir* was the window through which the Russian reading public saw the pure light of day. Yes, it was. It was a window. But a warped window, crudely hacked in a rotten wall, and blocked not only by the censors' mesh but by an ideological screen of its own choosing—something like the opaque wire-glass in the Butyrki prison. . . . (I must qualify what I have said: in the talk of these "Oktyabrists" I sensed not only their hatred of *Novy Mir,* but their dread of its critical section, and their secret respect for it. If you think of those rolling expanses of print, those countless columns, that cozy mutual admiration club, you may wonder why they should worry about criticism from one lonely, eternally over-due, barely audible journal. But no, the scoundrels never stopped think-ing about it; it touched chords deep within them. They could not shut out the knowledge that only *Novy Mir*'s brand would take and would last, while their own stamp of approval would be washed away by the first shower. *Novy Mir* was the only judge in Soviet literature whose artistic and moral verdict on a work commanded assent, and indelibly marked its author. One who would have been the subject of such an assessment, greatly to his advantage, was Yevtushenko, had not Si-nyavksy's arrest prevented the appearance of an article already set up in type, which tore to shreds Yevtushenko's smug poem about the "Bratsk Hydroelectric Station.")

All I wanted was to eliminate an untried possibility—who knows, it might produce something—by offering my stories, and especially "Right Hand," to the notorious "conservative wing" (as though that wounded bird the Soviet press had any other!), and seeing whether it would swallow them. What if their differences with *Novy Mir* had become so irksome to them that they would set ideological loyalty at naught and carefully steer my stories between the horns of their own beloved censorship—simply in order to "kidnap" me for their side? There wasn't much of a chance, but even this "degree of freedom" should, I thought, be utilized—if only so that I would not blame myself later. If I saw "Right Hand" published even by the gendarmes' press, I would not feel ashamed.

There was also a historical test I wanted to carry out, a bench mark I wanted to make. For years now public figures of this kind had been bragging that they were *Russians.* I was giving them the first opportu-nity in their lives to prove it. (And within three days their guts turned to water, and they proved that they were just *Communists,* and not Russians at all.)

In its early hours "Hadji Murad's defection" did indeed cause a commotion among them. I wasn't allowed to take a step on foot, but was carried in and around and home again by car every time. In *Ogonyok*'s offices the whole board had assembled to meet me. Sofronov came up to town specially, happily reminded me that we were both from Rostov, and hastened to fish out of the forgotten past a laudatory review of *Ivan Denisovich* he had once written (when the whole herd was doing the same). Stadnyuk, with my as yet unread manuscripts in his hand, was moved to prayer: "I hope to Heaven this is something we can use!" Alekseyev spoke a few kind words: "Yes, you really must come and live in Moscow and make yourself at home in literary society." Pozdnyayev, the editor in chief of *Literaturnaya Rossia,* also talked with push-button affability, also reminded me of a forgotten occasion when he had had the honor to write to me, and anticipated matters by telling me how quickly they could print, and how they could remake an issue two days before it went on sale.

In this eager reception I saw yet another sign of the times: neither their loyalty to the Party nor their dread of the police was any longer absolute, as they had been in Bulgakov's time; a literary reputation had acquired an independent force.

However, their happiness did not last beyond the first reading. At *Literaturnaya Rossia* they had finished reading, and Pozdnyayev was on the phone, within two hours: "You will understand that at such short notice we haven't been able to *consult anybody.*" (They even thought it important to prove that they had not run off to denounce me!) "Let's be frank: all the things we have been hearing at recent Party meetings are still ringing in our ears. Our unanimous opinion is that only 'Zakhar Kalita' can be published."

He went on immediately to name the day of publication, and even the honorarium. He had a sharp eye to the main chance, even though party discussions were buzzing in his ears! . . . I asked him to return all four stories. He tried for a while to get around me.

*Ogonyok* had such an itch to publish me that at first they turned down only "Right Hand," and were for taking the rest. Later on they phoned to say that "What a Pity" was also out. At that point it was my turn to decline.

It is easier to write a new novel than to place a story already written with editors fresh from an ideological conference! Three days was time enough for me to get sick of this whole scheme of mine, all this fuss and bother with the stories—and I didn't call on the moribund *Moskva,* didn't telephone them, but sent the stories along through friends. *Moskva* kept them for four days with never a word, and I started fretting in case editor in chief Popovkin had trudged off to the Lubyanka to show them "Right Hand"—a weighty addition to what they had previously confiscated.

I went to *Novy Mir* on 2 December—a day when A.T. was not in—for a frank talk with the other editors, because A.T. no longer let them read my work or discuss things with me. I explained to Dementyev and Lakshin that Tvardovsky, by rejecting one thing after another, had driven me to act independently and even to approach *the others* (I had no right, you see, even to publish an article in *Litgazeta without consultation*). Dementyev, my constant enemy on *Novy Mir,* suddenly seemed to understand and approve of all I had done: my independent steps, my approaches to *the others,* the idea that I might do very well to publish somewhere other than in *Novy Mir,* to show, as he put it, that there was no cliquism, that we took the broad view.

I didn't see through him at first, but his motives were these: the "liberal" Dementyev understood more than Alekseyev, or Sofronov, or Pozdnyayev, or than any of those "conservatives"; he understood that the time was fast approaching when it would be impossible to print anything of mine at all, "viable" or not; that a ban was about to descend on my very name and that *Novy Mir* would do well to shed this burden. I gave them "Zakhar Kalita"—if only this was to be printed, let it be in *Novy Mir*—and Dementyev and Lakshin both jumped at it, strangely enough with the idea of publishing it not in *Novy Mir* but elsewhere. Lakshin suggested *Izvestia,* but Dementyev set his sights higher—on *Pravda.* In the course of that instructive evening (instructive because Tvardovsky had no part in it), this opponent of mine showed a rare concern for my interests; he spent a long time on the telephone, trying to track down the head of *Pravda*'s "cultural department," the eminent obscurantist Abalkin; in a honeyed voice, and a caressing brogue, he imparted the information that Solzhenitsyn had a fine patriotic story, topical too, and very suitable for the paper, and "we will be glad to let you have it." The junior prose editor, who had reached the end of his working day, was dispatched on his own two feet to *Pravda*'s offices, with the story in an envelope. (At all other journals even the messengers rode in Volgas. This was a perquisite that Tvardovsky had never sought for his staff. He thought it beneath him to try to obtain the most ordinary facilities for subordinates. The *Novy Mir* staff tried to put a brave face on it: "Chekhov was a pedestrian too." Tvardovsky himself, however, always found a long black limousine at the door.)

Swing high, swing low! All the next day my story was with *Pravda*, struggling uphill from desk to desk. I could locate in my mind the anti-Chinese mine I had laid and on which I mainly relied. Perhaps they didn't even notice it (or didn't want to know about it). They only noticed the word "Mongols." And, Abalkin explained to me by telephone, "the view had taken shape" (and shaped this pretty phrase to match!) that the publication of "Zakhar Kalita" would be interpreted abroad as "marking a change in our policy toward Asia. Between Mongolia and the Soviet Union a special relationship has taken shape. It could, of course, be published in a magazine—but not by us."

I believed it: that's the way they thought, they could rise no higher. But at *Novy Mir* they all laughed, and said that it was just a ploy, an evasive formula.

That day it occurred to me for the first time that because he was out of action so frequently and for such long periods, A.T. was beginning to lose his firm grip on the magazine. A magazine, after all, cannot freeze and go to ground for two or three weeks, like its chief! The day before, his colleagues had successfully stood out against A.T. for the publication of Nekrasov's stories, and now they hadn't even given him "Zakhar" to read, because there was only one copy and they had other plans for it.[6] Tvardovsky sat there like a helpless outsider.

We greeted each other coldly. Dementyev had already run through my statements of the day before and my grievances against *Novy Mir*, which shocked and puzzled A.T., because it had never occurred to him that the calf might complain of the cow. I had no intention of bandying recriminations with him in the presence of the others, but that is just what happened—and more of them joined us when they heard the noise. What I wanted was not to reproach Tvardovsky (for turning down so many of my things, for refusing to take the last surviving copy of my novel into safekeeping, for refusing to publish my defense against my slanderers); I only wanted to show that my obligations to *Novy Mir* were not unlimited. A.T., however, was keyed up to rebut my arguments

---

6. Lakshin would manage to palm it off on *Izvestia*, where it was actually set up. Only when the type was broken up would *Novy Mir* feel forced to take on publication itself.

point by point. He began irascibly to interrupt me, and I him—and our conversation became chaotic, and hurtful to both of us. He was hurt by my ingratitude, and I by his insensitive assumption of the right to patronize me, which only superior understanding would have justified.

All through the autumn he had been nagging and needling me and far from backing down now, he heaped reproach upon reproach:

• How could I, without consulting him, have taken my things to that "turd of an anthroposophist" for safekeeping? (A.T. had never seen the man, and knew nothing of him, but considered him a "turd" on the strength of his beliefs alone. Does that remind you more of Pushkin? Or of Kochetov?)

• How had I dared to keep in the same place as the "sainted" *Ivan Denisovich* ... etc., etc., etc. (Any mention of the disaster on 11 September, or of what I had kept where, touched an abscess in my memory so sore that I choked with pain—but he prodded it unmercifully.)

• How could I have disobeyed him and taken my novel out of the office?

• How could I have *slipped* the "Miniatures" to *Semya i shkola?*

• Again—a very important point, this—how could I have written complaining to four secretaries of the Central Committee, instead of to Pyotr Nilovich alone? (The iron clang of history in the making could be heard, but he had eyes only for the hierarchy of desks!)

• And yet again, why had I grown that beard? Was it perhaps to ... ?

In this boring, repetitious catalogue of complaints, new notes, like moans of pain, could also be heard: "I *discovered* you!" "Why, when they took the novel from him I was the first one he turned to! I comforted him, I gave him warmth and shelter!" (In other words, he had not turned me out of doors late at night.)

The whole office was listening to all this!

Finally, following a fresh scent, he asked:

• How could I have gone to "pay homage" to Alekseyev, who would be disemboweled in a forthcoming *Novy Mir?*

I could have made a wounding reply. But upsetting as the conversation was, I felt not the least bit angry with him. I realized that this was no personal quarrel, no mere personal disagreement: we had simply found how short was the stretch of road we could tread together as literary allies before the scratches inflicted by the sharp edges of ideology drove us apart. The divergence was between Russian literature and Soviet literature, and not at all a personal one.

My replies were therefore matter-of-fact.

"When could I have consulted you? I come to Moscow for a day or two at a time, and you're permanently missing."

It was a tragic conversation, a life-and-death conversation, yet Tvardovsky self-importantly exclaimed:

"I was away for two weeks on the banks of the Seine."

He couldn't just say "in Paris."

If that had been the only false note! But the worst falsity was in what he had been saying about me on the banks of the Seine and was now keeping from me. A true son of his Party, he sought safety in the muffling and muting of information! But *Le Monde*'s accounts of its interview with him had already been translated for me. Once the *Zürcher Zeitung* had raised the alarm, it was natural for them to ask him about me. If the fate of a writer who had already gulped salt water, whose mouth was barely above the surface, had come first with him, and "imperialism as the final stage of capitalism" second, he could, with his gentlemanly tact, have given incomplete, evasive answers, could have hesitated here and there and, with no danger to himself, let the world know that things really were going badly with me, that I really was in danger. Instead Tvardovsky had told the reporters that my extraordinary modesty (which he so greatly admired!), my truly monastic behavior, precluded him, my editor and my friend, from saying anything about my literary plans or about me personally. But he could assure the reporters that they would read many "beautiful pages" from my hand in the future.

In other words, he had reassured them that I was working and thriving, and that nothing stood in my way except my inordinate monkish modesty. He had given the lie to the *Neue Zürcher Zeitung.* The salt water in my mouth would not allow me to call out for help—and he was using the boat hook to help push me under.

Because he wished me ill? No! Because that is what the Party makes of poets. (He wished me *well:* he wanted to make me appear so docile that Pyotr Nilovich would take mercy on me!)

All the same, this hard-hitting discussion grew so heated, and A.T. so exasperated by my obstinate disagreement with him at all points, that he jumped up and shouted angrily: "If you piss in his eye he'll say it's dew from Heaven!"

I had done my best to remember all along that he was an erring and enfeebled creature. But now I lost my self-control and answered angrily myself: "Don't try to insult me! I've heard ruder things than that from my former *overseers!*" He made a helpless gesture: "Well, if that's how it is . . ." We were within an inch of a personal quarrel. That would have been quite pointless; it would only have obscured the picture that mattered—that of the schism between two literatures. But none of those present (except, I suppose, Dementyev) wanted an explosion, and they hastened to prevent it.

It ended with a perfunctory handshake.

I had only an hour left before my train and I still had—yes!—*to shave my beard off.* What a shock Tvardovsky would have had if he had found out. An hour before my train left—not for Ryazan, nor yet "to cross the frontier," but to the back of beyond, to my Hiding Place, for several months without correspondence—to the spot where my rescued and secreted *Gulag Archipelago* was waiting for me. That autumn I had been as noisy, as active, as conspicuous as I possibly could, but now it was time to break off this round of senseless exertions. I was going to a place where no one knew about me and no one would arrest me. Once again I was returning, with a feeling of liberation, to the work that the KGB had interrupted and muddled.

All went well. In my Hiding Place I followed the Sinyavsky-Daniel trial on my transistor radio. Outrages a hundred times worse, mass outrages affecting millions more, had happened in our country over the past fifty years, but in the West it had all been water off a duck's back. If they had noticed some small part of it, they had forgiven us in gratitude for Stalingrad. But now—another sign of the times—the "progressive West" was disturbed.

As far as I was concerned, I reckoned that all this uproar would make the KGB look for some other way of dealing with me. They were of two minds. In late December and early January, as I was subsequently told, their top brass declared at a number of meetings that my archive had been seized while I was "assembling it for dispatch abroad." They abandoned this version not because there were no routes leading to foreign parts from Teush's apartment (those master fakers could have rigged this without even trying), but because a second trial of the same kind would *not have gone down well* so soon after the first.

As Pasternak had done by sending his novel to Italy, and repenting under harassment, so now Sinyavsky and Daniel, by unrepentantly paying the price for their literary schizophrenia, helped to clear new paths for literature and put obstacles in the way of its enemies. The obscurantists had less and less room to move in, literature more and more.

At a meeting of writers and KGB men in Leningrad (allied trades, these: the writer and the Chekist are both engineers of souls) Granin asked: "Is it true that Solzhenitsyn has had a novel taken away from him?" The answer, delivered with that winsome ingenuousness which the Chekists have practiced to perfection, was: "Novel? No, no novel has been taken from him. *Nor indeed has he lodged any complaint with us.* There *was* a novel of some sort there called *The First Circle*, but we don't know whose it is." (My name was on the title page.)

They simply hadn't yet decided what to do.

When they finally reached a decision, it was a bizarre one: they made up their minds to *publish* my confiscated works in a restricted edition! Apparently the assumption was that they could arouse only disgust and indignation in any honest man.

When I came out into the open again in March 1966 and heard the first of many similar stories, about someone from the Central Committee offices giving my novel to Mezhelaitis *for a quick read*, handing it over not in a secure room, and not against a signed receipt, but quite casually, in a car—I just couldn't believe it. This was playing with fire; surely God had not so completely robbed them of their senses? There would soon be no holding this fire back with heatproof mittens; it would run wild, for sure! And wherever it was read, it would not serve *their* purposes: it would rob my enemies, even the rock-hard loyalist dolts, of some portion of their certainty, shed a glimmer of light in some corner of those foggy brains. Before you knew it, a growing handful would be converted by their reading.

However, in the spring of 1966, the stories multiplied, from one informant after another, from one month to the next: they had published both the novel and *The Feast of the Victors!* And were *lending them to readers!* Who were "they"? Obviously the Central Committee, which had taken over the whole thing from the KGB. To whom were they lending the books? To the more important Party bosses (though they are no bookworms as a rule, but lazy and incurious), and to the more important officeholders in the writers', artists' and musicians' unions. Khrennikov, for instance, read one and baffled a composers' conference with menacing allusions. "Do you know what sort of plays he writes? At one time he'd have been shot for writing plays like that!"

Surkov read one and spread the news that I was a "class enemy" (enemy of which class?). One who sat down to study my novel carefully was Kochetov—to see what he could steal. The chief editors of publishing houses were all shown my work—so that a cordon sanitaire around my name, and every line I might write in the future, would come into operation automatically.

No, he was not lacking in acuteness, whoever had thought this up: in a land denied freedom of information, they could smother and silence an individual without direct use of the secret police, simply by exploiting the "public opinion" of a controlled and circumscribed public—the "public," so to speak, of Party appointees. The same results could be expected, without the scandal of an arrest: they would smother me, but gradually.

All the same, they had, they really had made a blunder! A plagiarist's gamble—publishing my books without my approval and to damage me. Even in a land like ours, without laws and rights (where printing for a restricted circulation within the bureaucracy does not count as publication, and it is impossible even to sue for breach of copyright!), there was a nascent public opinion, there were far, faint echoes of world opinion too. They had sunk their talons too deep and too defiantly. Look out, you'll get stuck! Someday these methods would rebound upon them.

This restricted edition was also intended to push me into . . . into . . . Once again, in my slow-thinking way, I could not see into what. I could only see that there was no danger in this stunt. In fact, I liked it. They would turn the regime's clientele against me, was that it? Those people all hated me anyway. And on the other hand, it meant that they were not about to *arrest* me just yet.

History moves in unexpected twists and turns. At one time we, the unlucky ones, were put inside for nothing, for half a word or a quarter of a seditious thought. Now the KGB had a whole bouquet of criminal charges to pin on me (according to their legal code, of course), yet this had only untied my hands, given me ideological extraterritoriality! Half a year after the event, it had become clear that the unhappy loss of my archives had brought me complete freedom of thought and of belief. I was free not merely to believe in God, although I was a member of the Marxist and atheist Writers' Union, but to profess any political view I chose. For nothing I might think now could be worse and harsher than the angry words in the play I had written in camp. If they weren't going to *put me inside* for that, they obviously wouldn't put me in for any of the beliefs I might come to hold. I could reply to my correspondents as frankly as I pleased, say whatever I liked in conversation, and none of it could be worse than my play! I could make whatever entries I pleased in my diaries: no more need to use code and subterfuge. I was approaching an invisible divide beyond which there was no more need for hypocrisy—about anything, or to anyone!

I concluded then, in spring 1966, that I had been given a lengthy reprieve, but I also realized the need for an *overt* and generally accessible work to proclaim in the meantime that I was alive and working, to occupy in the public mind the space that my confiscated works had not been able to invade.

*Cancer Ward*, which I had begun three years earlier, would be very suitable for this purpose. I set to work completing it.

The Cheka-KGB would not wait, it was not dozing, and haste was a tactical necessity. But how can you step up the pace of your writing? Then I had the idea of publishing Part One to start with, without waiting to finish Part Two. The tale[7] itself did not call for this, but tactical necessity left me no room for maneuver.

How I should have liked to work at my own speed! How I should have liked at least to take some time off from writing daily for unhurried and disinterested language exercises. How I longed to rewrite my text a dozen times, to put it aside and come back to it years later, and to examine rival candidates at length before inserting missing words. But my life always was, and still is, a race against time, my timetable impossibly tight; I am only too happy if I manage to sketch out the most urgent things! Sometimes I can't even do that. . . .

Many writers have had to write in a hurry—usually to fulfill their contracts, to meet deadlines. But you might think that I had no need to hurry, that I could polish and polish again. No. There were always powerful, compelling reasons—the need to hide, to disperse copies, to take advantage of someone's help, to set myself free for other tasks—so that I never released anything without undue haste, I never had time to look for the precise, the definitive words.

When I was finishing off Part One of *Cancer Ward* I could see, of

---

7. I called it a "tale" at first only to avoid confusion with the confiscated novel—to prevent people from exclaiming in surprise: "Ah, so they've given it back to him!" Only later did it dawn on me that "tale" was in reality the more appropriate designation.

course, that it would not be accepted for publication. My hopes were set mainly on samizdat—but then friends advised me to submit it to the Moscow Prose Section and to Mosfilm, and so establish my right to disseminate it freely. To do this I would have needed an unassailable right to dispose of my own work, whereas I was of course supposed to take it to *Novy Mir* first. After Tvardovsky had rejected so many things of mine, I could have no hope at all that he would publish this. But there was no way of avoiding a wasted month.

We had not met once since our quarrel. I warned A.T. in a polite letter (written as though all were well between us) that I would shortly offer him half a tale, and would be greatly obliged if he did not keep me waiting too long for an editorial decision.

A.T.'s heart—needless to say—beat a little faster. He had probably never stopped hoping that we would be reunited as literary allies. He had put down our tiff to my bad temper, my impetuosity, my incorrigible wrong-headedness, but all these sins and more he was magnanimously prepared to forgive me.

But it made little difference whether one or the other of us could or could not forgive. One of us needed a fresh wind to clear his mind. My mind had been cleared by my first years of imprisonment. For A.T. the same process had begun with Khrushchev's speech at the Twentieth Congress. But for him as for the Party at large, it was soon slowed down, tangled in contradictions, and even put into reverse. Tvardovsky, like Khrushchev, was eternally, inescapably in thrall to the official ideology. In each of them, native intelligence unconsciously rebelled against ideology, and the moments when it prevailed were their highest and finest. One of these high points for the peasant Khrushchev had been his rejection of war as the road to world revolution.

As soon as the manuscript of *Cancer Ward* arrived at *Novy Mir*, it became a secret document, on Tvardovsky's instructions. In their fear that it would slip its leash and "go the rounds," they carried their precautions to ridiculous lengths: they wouldn't even show it to the staff of their own prose department! But I had already let it leak all over Moscow. The battalions of samizdat were on the march!

On 18 June, two years after what had once looked like a very encouraging discussion of my novel, we met to discuss Part One of *Cancer Ward*. Opinions were divided; sharply divided, in fact. Only their professional habit of conciliatory understatement partly concealed the rift.

It can be said that the "younger" section of the staff, and those who were "junior" in rank, were vehemently in favor of publication, while the "older" and "superior" members (Dementyev, Zaks, Kondratovich) were just as emphatically against it. The very candid Vinogradov, who had just joined the magazine, said: "If we don't print this, I see no reason for our existence." Berzer: "Cancer is a taboo subject, but here it is made a legitimate subject for art." Maryamov: "It is our moral duty to bring it to the reader." Lakshin: "It is a long time since I came across such a gallery of positive heroes in our literature. To lock this story away from the reader is a sin I wouldn't want on my conscience." Zaks tried to blur and befog what otherwise was plain: "The author lets himself be swept away by feelings of hatred. . . . It's very crude, the way he brings in Tolstoyism. . . . There's too much explosive material as it is, yet he brings in the painful subject of the special settlers as well.* *What is the ulterior motive?* . . . The whole thing has a very unfinished look." Kondratovich unhesitatingly supported him: "It's very far from finished! . . . Look at the conversation about the Leningrad blockade, and other bad-tempered blotches. . . ." Dementyev began in an indolent tone of voice: "I should of course"—wouldn't he just!—"like to see Solzhenitsyn's tale published. . . . As an exhibition of the artist's powers it is inferior to the novel. . . ." (But the novel was just what he would not accept! Now that there was no danger of the novel's being published, he could even afford to praise it.) "Objective writing suddenly gives way to naked tendentiousness. . . ." Then, becoming excited and angry as he went on: "Tolstoy or Dostoyevsky always had an inner vision for the sake of which each work was written, but here there is nothing of the sort, the underlying motivation is imperfectly thought out." (It was always the same: he was tempting me to explain my intentions fully, so that he could the more easily thrash me. Not a hope!) " 'Just take a look at yourselves and your lives, good people' is not much of a message. . . . It is not a rounded whole . . . and cannot therefore be published in this form." (As though every book in the torrent of rubbish that got into print was a more successful "whole"!) And, getting angrier all the time: "What does he mean by saying that no forethought was given to the defense of Leningrad. How could we possibly have shown greater foresight than by pushing back the Finnish frontier!"

So much for literary comradeship! See where friendship with *Novy Mir* had got me! What an extraordinary argument: they'd pushed back the Finnish frontier, so there! So I—I was beaten, I was guilty of calumny in my story. I obviously could not reveal my "inner vision" fully, could not say, "Well, what was the attack on Finland if not an act of aggression!" It wasn't just Dementyev. Later in the conversation Tvardovsky also interrupted me: "No one is asking you to make concessions on matters of principle. You are, needless to say, not against Soviet rule, *or else we should not even be talking to you!*"

So much for the liberal magazine, the torchbearer of intellectual freedom! "Soviet rule!" They had worn the phrase threadbare, yet you would never get a single one of them to understand that the *Soviets* had not ruled since 1918.

On one thing they were all agreed: they condemned Avieta, the pamphleteering style of that chapter, and indeed all the pronouncements on Soviet literature in the story: "This is not the place for them." (What, then, was the right place? Surely someone, somewhere, just once should reply to all those reams of raucous lies.) This time I was surprised to find the whole *Novy Mir* staff so lacking in courage (cowed? servile?). As a detached historian might see it, I was avenging them for the rough patch they had gone through in 1954, when Tvardovsky was removed for publishing Pomerantsev's article "On Sincerity"—but here they were urging me in unison, with Tvardovsky in the lead, not to do it, not to mention the "light-blue cover," not to defend them.

I had thought that their act of penitence all that long ago had been meant for the newspapers, for the Central Committee, to earn a good mark. But obviously their repentance had been heartfelt: writing *about sincerity* was wrong.

There was also some discussion of the "important" question (important in Soviet circumstances, at least) of what to do about the fact that the story was unfinished, and only Part One to hand. Some said, Never mind, we'll just say that it *is* Part One. But Tvardovsky, knowing his official guardians, would not even let us discuss it. "We must not even think of announcing it as Part One. They'll say, Let him write and submit Part Two as well, then we'll decide. We are obliged to publish it as complete in itself."

But it is not complete; every theme in it is left dangling! . . . Too bad; those are the conditions.

So then, the "juniors" and their "superiors" split on the question of publishing my tale, and the deciding vote lay with Tvardovsky. How changeable he was: he could be two different people on two different days, or even at different hours of the same day. He spoke now as an artist, making observations and suggestions that had nothing to do with editorial strategy, and that were quite impermissible in a candidate member of the Central Committee.

"Art does not exist in this world to be a weapon in the class struggle. Once it knows that it is a weapon, it loses its fire power. We are quite free in our judgments of this piece of yours: we are no more concerned with whether it will get by or not than if we were discussing it in the next world. . . . We are looking at it with a reader's, not an editor's eye. It gladdens an editor's heart when he finds himself hoping that he will have time to read something right through. . . . The work is topical in that it presents a moral reckoning on behalf of a newly awakened people. . . . Unfinished? Great works always bear the marks of incompleteness. *Resurrection, The Possessed*—try to think of a single exception. . . . This is something we want to publish. If the author will *work on it* a little more, we will launch it and fight for it *to the limit of our powers—and beyond!"*

So, quite unexpectedly, he had tipped the scales in favor of the "juniors" (whose fervent speeches had moved him) and against his deputies (although he had evidently promised them otherwise).

And at this very same meeting he also said quite different things—about "Soviet rule," for instance, or his statement (made without inquiring whether anyone was of the opposite opinion) that "we shall scrap the title." These, then, were the regal rejoinders with which he interrupted my reply, and his patronizing tone both on political and on literary matters. He was absolutely certain that his judgment on all the questions under discussion was better than that of anyone else present, that only he understood the paths along which literature was evolving. (He could rise to a lofty plane in discussion, yet even today he could not refrain from nagging: "You've grown that beard because you . . ." He did not know that this was my second beard. . . . He wasn't nagging for its own sake, but obediently reproducing the views of the *competent organs.*)

I answered them all in great detail, but only because I had managed to note each contribution carefully, and the sheet of paper lay in front of my eyes. There was only one place at which I showed animation: What concessions were they asking me to make? There were millions of Rusanovs, and they would never be tried in court, so that it was all the more important for them to be tried by literature and public opinion. If this could not be done, I had no use for literature and did not wish to write.

I was not going to give an inch on Rusanov's delirium, nor on the way people became mere file fodder—helpless raw material to be processed by registry clerks—nor on the habits of the "new class."

For the rest, I observed a strange detachment in myself throughout this discussion, as though it were not my book we were talking about, as though their decision did not concern me.

The reason for this was that the samizdat battalions were already on the march! . . . And I had lost my faith in legal publication. But until the tramp of marching battalions made itself heard in Tvardovsky's office, I had to *keep trying*. Especially since I foresaw that Part Two would be even less "viable."

No, they didn't demand that I take out the files, or the characterization of the new class, or the purge commission, or the deportation of national minorities. As for the Leningrad blockade, Hitler and Stalin could share the blame. The Avieta chapter I must regretfully (and temporarily!) amputate. Most senseless and vexatious of all was the need to change the title. No suitable substitute suggested itself.

All the same, I submitted, and a week later returned my manuscript, duly shorn, to *Novy Mir,* calling Tvardovsky's attention to an alternative title in brackets, just in case (*The Ward at the End of the Avenue,* or something like that—the sort of neutral splotch they were used to).

A week after this, another editorial conference was held. Whether accidentally or not, neither Lakshin, who would think it a sin against his conscience to lock the manuscript away, nor Maryamov, who acknowledged a moral duty to bring it to the reader, was present. Whereas my opponents were all there. This time they were very restrained, and did not get the least bit angry: because, of course, they had already broken Tvardovsky's back behind the scenes.

A.T.'s opening remarks on this occasion were embarrassed and ambiguous. He started by hesitantly accusing me of failure to make all the necessary "cosmetic" improvements (this time Dementyev—the fox!—calmly came to my rescue: the improvements I had made, he said, were quite substantial, and the piece had become a perfect whole . . . with the amputation of that chapter!). A.T. now demanded that the conversation about the Leningrad blockade, even in its toned-down version, and also the discussion on sincerity, should be taken out altogether. But at this point he abruptly stopped hedging, and said: "Circumstances could not be less favorable to publication than they are at present. It would probably be impossible, and it would certainly be dangerous, to try bringing it out this year." (As though next year, jubilee year, would be any easier!) "We have to have the sort of manuscript in which we can defend any passage whatsoever because we share the ideas expressed in it." (A very burdensome requirement, this: can the author never differ at all from his publishers? must he always carefully cater to their tastes?) "But Solzhenitsyn, alas, is the same as he always has been. . . ."

Even the way the camp theme cast its shadow over *Cancer Ward,* which he had previously declared to be quite natural, he now called too "literary": "It's like Grossman writing about the camps from hearsay!" (Writing from hearsay?! Me?!) Then there were "things caught in the logjam," which the magazine had to "drag through somehow." (He meant Bek's novel about Tevosyan and Simonov's *Diaries.* Dementyev and Zaks held out hopes that the *Diaries* would get through, but they, too, were butchered.) Contradicting all that had been said, A.T. then announced that the editors considered the manuscript "acceptable, by and large," and was for signing immediately a contract with a 25 percent advance, which he would raise to 60 percent later on if I found myself hard up. "Write Part Two! We'll wait a bit and see how things go."

I *was* writing Part Two, and needed no encouragement from them. In the meantime, I was being offered money to entomb Part One in their safe, and of course, in deference to *Novy Mir*'s rules and A.T.'s claims on me, to show not a line or a word to anyone, to deny *Cancer Ward* the right to live until some dirty day a KGB colonel drove over to take charge of it.

The magazine's decision was a genuine relief to me: I could cancel all the corrections immediately, restore the work to the form in which it was already being tapped out and passed from hand to hand. Gone were all my anxieties about Tvardovsky's next explosion when he learned that the piece was *going the rounds.* We were free of one another!

But I did not put all this in a dramatic announcement, because my camp training forbids declarations of intent, bids me act suddenly and silently. All that I said, then, was that I would not sign a contract just yet, and would take the manuscript with me.

You might think that from these two actions in combination the editors would have understood how things were. But they understood nothing. As they saw it, I had submitted, accepted that I was wrong, and would carry on working, feeling myself unworthy of a contract for the present. As far as they were concerned, I was once more *Novy Mir*'s harmless pet!

However, less than a month later Tvardovsky urgently *sent for me* again, through my wife's relatives the Turkins. As usual, nobody could find me, but on 3 August I happened to be in Moscow and heard the news: It had reached A.T.'s ears that *Cancer Ward* was *going the rounds* and he was enraged beyond all measure. He only wanted to make absolutely certain that I hadn't—he knew I hadn't—let it out myself (as if I would dare!), and then he would know which member of his staff to dismiss. (Suspicion had fallen on the industrious Berzer, *Novy Mir*'s faithful workhorse, who pulled her load with never a stumble.)

This poet was also a member of the Central Committee, and thought like a statesman: a book that it was impossible to publish, and "risky" even to show to the censors, but that had been written under Soviet skies, was ipso facto the property of the state. It could not be casually handed around for people to read at the whim of the simpleton who had written it!

I, however, thought just the opposite. A whole year had passed since my mishap, and slow as I am to adapt to new ideas, I had begun to see their position and mine more clearly: I had nothing, nothing, nothing to lose! *Cancer Ward,* distributed openly, right and left, without concealment or disavowal, was no whit more dangerous to me than my play about the camps which had been rotting in the Lubyanka for the past year. "You are distributing it yourself?" "Yes, I am! I wrote it myself and I distribute it myself! Your publishers can all go to hell as far as I'm concerned! People are fighting over my book, they read it and sit up at night typing copies. It will be a literary event before you can turn around. Let your Lenin Prize winners try it, and see if they'll reach a public like mine!"

So that was what the old saying meant: "If trouble comes, make use of it." Misfortune can open the door to freedom, if we have the wit to read it aright.

I had once been told how strong I was by Demichev, but had not fully understood. Now *they* had given me palpable proof of it by their year of inaction.

I did not, of course, obey Tvardovsky's summons, but I did write to him, as follows:

"If I thought that you were upset because the tale has become known to others besides the editors of *Novy Mir* . . . I should be bound to express surprise. . . . Every author has this right, and it would be strange if you had ever intended to deprive me of it. What is more, I cannot allow *Cancer Ward* to repeat the dismal career of my novel: first there was an indefinite period of waiting, during which the author was repeatedly requested by the editors not to show it to anyone else; and then the novel was lost both to me and to those who should have read it, but it is being distributed to a few select persons on a secret list. . . ."

I wrote with no thought that I was being cruel. But the effect on A.T. was very cruel. I have been told that he wept over this letter. For the loss of his childlike faith? For our lost friendship? Or for the lost tale, which would now fall into the hands of gangster editors abroad?

After that I neither set foot in *Novy Mir* nor telephoned. I was a free agent, and I cast around desperately for some other way of combating the foes who had sunk their insolent talons so deep into my novel and my archive. A protest to the courts would be hopeless. A protest addressed to the public seemed best.

At one time, when I looked at the Writers' Union from a distance, I had seen a rabble of sacrilegious hucksters in the temple of literature, worthy only of the scourge. But young grass will spring soundlessly, skirting a pile of steel girders, and if no one tramples it, someday it will even screen them from view. Healthy and unsullied stalks were noiselessly overgrowing that diseased and rotting body. Their growth had become even more rapid after Khrushchev's denunciations. When I found myself in the Union I was overjoyed to discover many live and freedom-loving people there—whether they had been so of old, or had not had time to become corrupt, or were trying to rid themselves of the pollution. (Yet another proof that we should never risk wholesale condemnations.)

It would have been easy for me now to find one hundred or two hundred honest writers and send them letters. But such people did not as a rule occupy the higher posts in the Writers' Union. If I had let myself be guided in my selection by character and not by rank, I would have put them at risk without getting any nearer to my objective—which was to publicize my resistance. Sending protests to the overmanned and undertalented boards of the U.S.S.R. and the R.S.F.S.R. Writers' Unions would have been depressingly unproductive. But I saw looming in the near distance the Writers' Congress, which had recently been postponed from June until December 1966—the first and possibly the last during my membership in the Union. Here was my chance! At the time of the congress the old leaders would have outlived their authority, and the new ones would not yet have been elected, so that I would be free to single out the decent delegates according to my own criteria. Wasn't I adopting Lenin's own tactics in appealing to the congress? This was one of the lessons he used to teach: seize the moment between "no longer" and "not yet."

But December and the congress were not so close, and I felt impelled to protest in some form against what was being done with my works. I decided for the present to address myself, once more and for the last time, to the Central Committee. I am not a Party member, but every toiler is at liberty to supplicate that semi-divine institution. Reports were reaching me that they were in fact expecting a letter from me—a "sincere," or in other words penitent, letter, of course, pleading for a chance to trounce my former self and prove that I was first and last a Soviet citizen.

At first I thought of writing to them in a quite insolent tone, saying that *they themselves* would not now wish to repeat, indeed would shamefacedly disown, things they used to say before the Twentieth Congress. But E. Henry dissuaded me; such a letter would bring no practical advantage—neither a respite nor coexistence—but could only overheat relations. I modified it so that the reproach was aimed at the men of letters and not the Party leaders. For the rest, I tried to be factual while avoiding any hint of subservience. I am not sure that I was entirely successful. This tone of voice is not traditional in Russia, and such traditions are not easily established.

The letter, addressed to Brezhnev personally, was posted at the end of July 1966. There was never any answer or acknowledgment. Restricted circulation of my work did not stop, and the insidious campaign against me through the Party propaganda network continued at full strength after what may have been a brief slackening. All the same, this letter helped me to slow down the course of events for a few months, during which I finished *Gulag.* It also, I think, made it easier for me to get permission for a discussion of Part One of *Cancer Ward* at the Central Writers' Club. (Before this, it had been under arrest for two months in the office of V. N. Ilyin, secretary of the Moscow branch of the Writers' Union, and a lieutenant general in the KGB.)

The discussion was announced in a program card put out by the

Central Writers' Club—and so, in spite of *Novy Mir,* the title *Cancer Ward* was set up in type for the first time, and was henceforth immutable. When, however, it was found that too many people wanted to attend the discussion, the officers of the Writers' Union took fright, changed the date, moved the meeting to the middle of the day, announcing the arrangements privately this time, and fiercely scrutinized the writers' invitation cards at the entrance.

This was on 16 November. In the preceding three months my readers had included many enemies, who had not only pulled my threadbare philosophy and my poverty-stricken technique to pieces in articles, but had even (V. Pankov is an example) devoted whole chapters of their textbooks to such devastating criticism. Yet, marvelous to relate, not one of this whole gang, except Z. Kedrina, the "lay prosecutor" in the Sinyavsky-Daniel trial, and Asanov, who had gone through the camps a true believer (and an informer?), dared to put in an appearance. This was an ambivalent sign: it showed the power of a newly adult public opinion (those with no arguments avoided debate, and no one feared mere denunciations any longer), but it also showed the power of a still confident bureaucracy (why come along to bark their heads off and make a spectacle of themselves, when they could block the story and suppress it on the sly?).

So the discussion did not turn into a battle, as was expected, but into a triumphant proclamation of the new literature: no one could define it, no one could analyze it, but all were eagerly awaiting its birth. It would, so Kaverin declared in a fine, bold speech (yes, but they could have started being bolder years ago; why had they waited so long?), supersede the *venal* literature of the past. Kedrina was not even allowed to speak: when she rose, a mass walkout began, with Viktor Nekrasov leading the way.[8]

A series of coincidences, and not deliberate planning on my part, made that November a very hectic month for me. There are such extraordinary periods in everyone's life, when a variety of external forces unexpectedly come into play at the same time. It was only this interplay of forces, when I was already in its grip, that taught me to conduct myself as provocatively as I could, throwing off all voluntary

---

8. What of the *Novy Mir* group? A.T. *forbade* them to attend the discussion! If the cow's gone, smash your milking pail too.

restraints. I had previously declined to make public appearances? Very well; I would now accept all invitations. I had always refused to grant interviews? Very well; I would now see anybody and everybody.

Because I had nothing to lose. They could not possibly think any worse of me than they already did.

I had not been the first to disturb my sleeping archives, to dislodge them from their peaceful niche: the KGB had clawed them out. But even the KGB had no insight into the hidden meaning of things, the secret springs of events. The KGB and I were only agents helping the pattern to unfold.

My first public appearance was arranged on the spur of the moment: I happened to meet somebody who asked me, as we were walking along, whether I would be willing to go and speak at what he called a "box number" (a classified institute). Why not? The arrangement was put into effect quickly, before the security organs could get to hear of it, and the physicists at the Kurchatov Institute held a meeting attended by six hundred people. (True, over a hundred of these were unknown outsiders "invited by the Party Committee.") The security boys were of course present in considerable strength, and there were people from the regional and the city Party Committees.

I went to this first meeting equipped not to *speak* but simply to *read* —and this I did for three and a half hours, answering very few questions, and those only cursorily. I read some of the key chapters from *Cancer Ward,* one act of *Candle in the Wind* (about the aims of science, to engage the imagination of this scientific audience), and then I grew reckless and announced that I would read some chapters (those about the visit to Lefortovo) from *First Circle*—that very same *First Circle* which had been taken into custody by the Lubyanka: if *they* could let the bureaucratic underworld read it, why should not the author read it to the general public? (I had not been the first to start untying the knot of prohibitions: with my prison-camp fatalism, I found reassurance in this.)

No, times had changed and so had we! I was not shouted down, not interrupted, my wrists were not handcuffed behind my back, I was not even called in by the KGB to explain myself or be reprimanded. Would you believe it—the head of the KGB, Semichastny himself, started replying to me! Publicly, not tête-à-tête. As security chief, he saw his spy rings and subversive networks in Europe and Asia collapse one after another while he concentrated all his forces on the ideological struggle, especially against the writers, in whom he saw the main danger to the regime. He spoke frequently at ideological conferences and in seminars for agitators. In his speeches that November he expressed indignation at my impudence: I was giving readings from a confiscated novel. And that was all the response I got from the KGB!

Every step they took showed me that my last step had not gone far enough.

I now began looking for a chance to reply to Semichastny. The news that I had appeared at the Kurchatov Institute got around, and invitations began to arrive in large numbers—some tentative, some precise and pressing, and I accepted them all as they came, provided the dates did not clash. These institutions seemed to have everything arranged —directors had given their permission, notices had been put up, invitation cards were printed and distributed—but it was not to be! *They* were not to be caught napping. An hour or two, or even a few minutes beforehand, there would be a call from the Moscow City Party Committee: "Go through with this Solzhenitsyn meeting, and you'll be handing in your Party card!" The organizing bodies (the Nesmeyanov and Karpov Research Institutes, the Semyonov Chernogolovka, the Mechanics and Mathematics Faculty of Moscow University, the Bauman Institute, TsAGI, the Great Soviet Encyclopedia) were not exactly homes for rural idiots, yet they lacked the power—and the presiding academicians lacked the courage—to protest. The meeting at the Karpov Institute was called off at the last minute, after they themselves had sent a car for me. We arrived to find a notice pinned up: "Canceled owing to the author's indisposition." The director of the FBON panicked and canceled the meeting himself: he had received a telephone call to say that a place should be kept for a KGB general, who would come to the meeting incognito and in civilian dress.

I realized, too late, that I had been too restrained at the Kurchatov Institute, and I now sought a platform from which to answer Semichastny—but all doors were slammed in my face: You've missed your chance, old chap! I wanted to make just one little speech, no more, to give a blunt answer just for once—but I was too late! Never in my life have I felt so keenly what it means to be denied freedom of speech.

Then suddenly, from the Lazarev Institute of Oriental Studies, where a previous meeting had been canceled (all the local Party brass disclaimed responsibility afterward: it wasn't they who had done it), I received a pressing invitation: it won't be canceled this time! I went straight from the Ryazan train to the meeting (on 30 November). And sure enough, it was not canceled.

This time I was there to *speak!* This time I had come with a prepared speech, and all I needed was a peg to hang it on. I read two chapters from *Cancer Ward,* and a few dozen written questions were passed to me. Taking my cue from one of these, I rapped out all that I had been forbidden to say in the past nine months, rushing through it in case I was chased off the platform. Sitting beside me were certain gentlemen from the Party Committee—there perhaps to switch off the microphone, and me, too, if things went awry? But they had no occasion to act. Those sitting in the hall were sophisticated humanists and for them things would be sufficiently clear if I trod close to the brink without overstepping it. Certain vibrations told me that someone important from the KGB was sitting there—probably with a tape recorder. I fancied that I could see the features of the Chief of Gendarmes standing out in bold relief among the moldings on the Lazarev Institute's ancient walls. But he was in no position to answer back just then—and I could object to him as much as I liked. In a loud voice, and with a feeling of triumph and simple joy, I explained myself to the public, and *paid him back.* An insignificant zek in the past, and perhaps in the future too, I might face another trial in camera, and another round of solitary confinement cells, but first I had been granted an audience of half a thousand, and freedom to speak!

"I must explain why, although I used to refuse to talk to reporters or to make public appearances, I have now started giving interviews and am standing here before you. I believe, as before, that the writer's business is to write, not to haunt public platforms, not to keep explaining himself to newspapers. But I have been taught a lesson: the writer exists not to write but to defend himself. That is why I stand before you here—to defend myself! There is a certain *organization* which has no obvious claim to tutelage over the arts, which you may think has no business at all supervising literature—but which does these things. This organization took away my novel and my archive, which was never intended for publication. Even so, I said nothing but went on working quietly. However, they then made use of excerpts from my records taken out of context to launch a campaign of defamation against me, defamation in a new form—from the platform at closed briefing sessions. What can I do about it? Only defend myself! So here I am! Look:

I'm still alive. Look: this head"—turning it from side to side—"is still on my shoulders. Yet, without my knowledge and contrary to my wishes, my novel has been published in a restricted edition and is being circulated among the chosen—people like the chief editor of *Oktyabr*, Vsevolod Kochetov. Tell me, then, why should I deny myself similar privileges? Why should not I, the author, read you chapters from *the same novel here*, today?" (Shouts of "Yes!")

You would have to live through a long life of slavery, bowing and scraping to authority from childhood up, springing to your feet to join with the rest in hypocritical applause, nodding assent to patent lies, never entitled to answer back—all this as slave and citizen, then later as slave and zek: hands behind your back! don't look around! don't break ranks!—to appreciate that hour of free speech from a platform with an audience of five hundred people, also intoxicated with freedom.

This was perhaps the first time, the very first time in my life, that I felt myself, saw myself, making history. I chose the chapters on the exposure of informers ("Our native land must know who its informers are") and about those puffed-up nonentities the mysterious operations officers. Almost every sally scorched the air like gunpowder! How these people must have yearned for truth! Oh, God, how badly they wanted to hear the truth! A written question: Explain your sentence in the chapter you have just read about "Stalin not allowing the Red Cross to contact Soviet prisoners of war." They had lived through and some of them had taken part in that unhappiest of wars, that all-devouring war, and even about that they had not been allowed to know all that they should. The dullest blockhead in the dimmest cell was familiar with it —but here sat half a thousand highly educated humanists and they had not been allowed to know. By all means, comrades, I'll be glad to explain; it's a story that is unfortunately too little known. Acting on Stalin's orders, Foreign Minister Molotov refused to sign the Hague Convention on prisoners of war or to pay contributions to the International Red Cross on behalf of the Soviet Union. So our prisoners of war were the only ones in the world who were abandoned by their native land, the only ones doomed to perish of hunger on a diet of German pig swill. . . .[9]

---

9. In one of his subsequent "replies" Semichastny accused me of slanderously asserting that *we* had starved German prisoners of war to death.

Yes, I was beginning to enjoy the new position in which the loss of my records had left me! To enjoy my proud and open defiance, my acknowledged right to think for myself! It would, I daresay, have been painful, perhaps impossible, to return to my previous quiet life. At last I was beginning to see revealed the higher and hidden meaning of that suffering for which I had been unable to find a justification, that sharp reminder from the Supreme Reason which no mere mortal can at first understand. This was why my murderous misfortunes had been sent to me—to deny me all possibility, snatch from me any chance of lying low and keeping quiet, to make me desperate enough to speak and act.

For the time was at hand. . . .

I began these notes by recalling how a perfectly ordinary person can sink underground by scarcely perceptible degrees until he awakes one morning and thinks: Lord, I'm there already. . . . In the same way, thanks to the galling mishap that had brought me to the brink of arrest or suicide, bit by bit, quantum by quantum, growing, growing, growing in awareness from week to week and month to month—happy the man who deciphers more quickly the writing in Heaven, but I am slow, I need time—yet I, too, awoke one morning a free man in a free country!!!

\*　　　　　　　\*

\*

Thus my second public appearance was a bang on the gong, challenging my enemies to fight, letting it appear that henceforth I would do nothing but make speeches—but almost immediately I submerged again, this time without shaving off my beard, and was lost from view in my remote Hiding Place in the backwoods. To work! to work! because the hour was near and I was not prepared for it, I had still not done my duty.

I calculated that all the confusion I had created had ensured me three months of peace and quiet, until spring. And so it was. Between December and February I produced my final draft of *The Gulag Archipelago*, revising and retyping over 1500 pages in seventy-three days, with time off for illness, stoking the stoves and cooking. It was not I who did it—mine was merely the hand that moved across the page!

I had also timed the explosion of another bombshell for the New Year of 1967: my first interview, with the Japanese reporter Komoto Sedze. He had taken my statement in mid-November, and was to have published it at the New Year, but now January was going by, and there was no reference to this interview on the transistor radio in my snow-bound lair, whether I tuned in to Japan itself or to Western stations, or even to Radio Liberty.

The interview in November had been impromptu and, by official standards, a piece of impudence. There existed carefully worked out procedures, which even foreign journalists were obliged to follow if they did not want to lose their accreditation in Moscow, and which were of course even more strictly binding on Soviet citizens. Writers had to have the consent of the Foreign Commission of the Writers' Union (all "foreign departments" in Soviet institutions are branches of the KGB). I had not learned these procedures when I might have needed them, and now did not want to know anything about them. My new role was that of a man with extraterritorial rights and diplomatic immunity.

Komoto had sent his request for an interview in the normal way—to me with a copy to the Foreign Commission. They did not give it a thought: they knew that I had long ago decided against giving interviews. They did not know that for more than a year now, ever since the disaster, I had been wanting just this: an interview in which I could tell the whole story of what was being done to me. And here it was—help when it was least expected: a Japanese correspondent (a Westerner to all intents and purposes, yet somehow not criminally Western) asked me for written answers to five questions, if I was unwilling to meet him in person. He gave his Moscow address and telephone number. Even those five little questions suited me fine: they included one about *Cancer Ward* (which meant that the news had got around satisfactorily), and one about my "literary plans." I drafted a written answer [Document 1].[10] Still, I could not bring myself to risk a final explosion and announce to the world at large that my novel and my archive had been confiscated. Instead I listed some of my works and wrote that I *could not find a publisher for them*. If an author whose work had been eagerly seized upon and published in all languages three years ago could not now find a publisher in his own country, surely the inference was obvious.

But how should I get my answer to the reporter? By post? They would be sure to intercept it, and I would not even know that it hadn't reached him. Should I ask one of my friends to go and put it in the mailbox on his staircase? The staircase of the special purposes building in which he lived would certainly be under observation, and photo-

---

10. Documents appear in the Appendixes, beginning on page 457.

graphs might be taken. (I did not then know that there were militiamen at the entrance who allowed no one in.) So that we obviously had to meet, and that being so, why not make it a live interview? But where could we meet? He would not be allowed to visit Ryazan, and I could not endanger anyone by borrowing a Moscow apartment. I had therefore chosen the cheekiest possibility: the Central Writers' Club. On the day when *Cancer Ward* was discussed there, I had first examined the premises carefully, then called the Japanese from a public telephone and suggested an interview in the club at noon the following day. My invitation must have sounded quite official, and he probably thought that I had consulted the proper authority. He had telephoned his interpreter (KGB tested, of course) and she had booked a photographer from the Novosti press agency to take shots of an interview at the Central Writers' Club. This again sounded all very official and could arouse no suspicions at Novosti.

I had arrived at the Central Writers' Club half an hour before the agreed time. It was an ordinary working day and there was not a trace of the bustle and the strict controls of the day before, not a writer to be seen, only workmen carrying chairs through the wide-open outer doors. Instead of a black-haired Japanese, a fair-headed Russian girl came in and made for the reception desk. I heard my name, approached and asked her to fetch the Japanese. (There were two of them, I discovered, waiting outside in a car.) The doorkeepers were the same ones who had seen me at the center of attention in the entrance hall the day before, and they did not question my authority when I said, "These people are here to see me." (I learned later that foreigners can enter the Writers' Club only with the express permission of the administration on each occasion.) I invited them into the quiet foyer with its thick carpets and comfortable furniture and expressed the hope that these modest surroundings would not prevent us from discussing our business freely. At this point the photographer from Novosti trotted in, out of breath, and lugged over the huge flash lamps belonging to the club, so that our twenty-minute interview was lit by sheet lightning. The administration saw an unscheduled event in progress, but there could be no doubt about its respectability, its importance, and therefore its official character.

Komoto spoke Russian fairly well, so that the interpreter was there only to earn her salary and had nothing to do. At the end of our meeting I had learned something further: Komoto told me that he himself had spent three years in our Siberian camps! If he had been a zek himself he probably knew very well that I had rigged our meeting. And he should have still less difficulty in understanding the things I had left unsaid. We had parted on cordial terms.

But now we were one week, two weeks into the new year, and my transistor set had brought into my seclusion not the slightest mention, not half a sentence about the interview. Had it all come to nothing? What had happened? Had Komoto himself been headed off, intimidated? Or perhaps the editor of his newspaper had not wanted to spoil the general easing of tensions in Soviet-Japanese relations? (Their Russian-language broadcasts were cast in sickeningly obsequious language.) The one possibility I tried to ignore was that the interview might have been published in full and on time, taking up four pages in each of four newspapers with a total circulation of five million (in Japanese characters, it is true, but still . . .), and not been noticed *by a single person* in the West! Every radio station in the world quoted Japanese reporters daily in connection with the cultural revolution in China, so obviously their newspapers were monitored, yet no one had noticed my interview. Could this be because fame in this world is short-lived, and the West had long ago got bored with What's-his-name, that Russian writer, who had tickled its fancy for two whole weeks with a badly translated best seller about life in Stalin's concentration camps? That was no doubt part of it. Still, if in some out-of-the-way spot, in Polynesia or New Guinea, let's say, the most fugitive report had appeared that some Greek leftist had failed to find a publisher in Greece for one single paragraph of his work, we should have had Bertrand Russell and Jean Paul Sartre and the Labor left screaming bloody murder, expressing their lack of confidence in the British Prime Minister, hurling imprecations at the American President, and promptly convening an international congress to anathematize the Greek butchers. Whereas if the process of smothering a Russian writer not quite extinguished under Stalin continued under the collective leadership, and if the end could be expected pretty soon, this did not insult their leftist creed: if people were stifled in the land of communism, that must be what progress demanded!

In those long months of complete seclusion, how easy it was for me to work and to think! Subjects and problems so easily assumed their true proportions, their true importance, their true position in relation to each other. Working feverishly and without a pause that winter, I discovered that at about fifty years of age I should reach the term "$n$ minus 1" in my work, that is, complete all that I intended ever to write except for the last and most important thing—my novel *R-17*. For thirty years now, ever since I had left school, I had been meditating on this novel, turning it this way and that, putting it aside to grow quietly, accumulating ideas and material, and all that time it had been the main object of my life. But in practice it was still not even begun; there had always been something to hinder and divert me. Only in the spring of 1967 could I expect to reach at last the work that was so dear to me I felt my hands burning if I so much as sorted through *the* books and *the* papers.

But now, surrounded by a silence almost incredible in our age, and gazing out at fir trees burdened with their stiff Epiphany mantle of snow, I was about to make one of the most important decisions in my life. One possible course was to put my trust in what appeared to be a happy state of recognized neutrality (nobody was touching me) and for as many precarious years as I was granted, to continue sitting as quietly as possible, writing and writing the history—my most important work —that no one had ever been allowed to write, and that for all I knew no one else ever would write. For this work I should need from seven to ten years.

The alternative was to recognize that I might be able to struggle on like that for a year or two, but not for seven. That I ought instead to go on blowing holes in the fraudulent façade of normality. To withdraw my ostrich head from the sand. "Iron Shurik" Shelepin was surely not nodding; somewhere out there he was creeping by dark alleys to power, and one of his first moves would be to tear off this head of mine. So perhaps on the eve of the work dearest to me I should lay down my pen and take more risks. Risk losing pen, hand, voice and head together. Or ruining my relations with the regime so irreparably and so resoundingly that my position would be stronger as a result? Surely this was the direction in which fate was pushing me? I must not force it to repeat its warning. For many decades it was because of personal considerations, because our private concerns were more important to us, that we had used our vocal cords so sparingly and let ourselves be bundled into the sack before we could raise a shout.

Some time back, in spring 1966, I had been delighted to read the protest written by two priests, Eshliman and Yakunin, a courageous, pure and honest voice in defense of a church which of old had lacked and lacks now both the skill and the will to defend itself. I read, and was envious. Why had I not done something like this myself, why was I so unenterprising? The thought must have remained and silently matured in my unconscious. And now it reemerged with the sudden vividness of an unquestionable decision: I must do something similar!

I learned from the radio that the Writers' Congress had been postponed till May. Very convenient! If the interview had not helped, all that was left to me was a letter to the congress. But this time I must *call things by their names* and shout louder.

It is infinitely difficult to begin when mere words must move a great block of inert matter. But there is no other way if none of the material strength is on your side. And a shout in the mountains has been known to start an avalanche.

Perhaps I would be badly shaken. But perhaps it was only with the world tumbling about me that I would understand those concussed souls of 1917.

Fate was not seeking its victim: the victim had set out to meet his fate.

My immediate plan, however, was to strengthen my position further by finishing and distributing Part Two of *Cancer Ward*. When I had come away for the winter I had left it nearly completed. I would finish it on my return to the noisy world.

But honor demanded that in spite of everything I should show this second part also to Tvardovsky before disseminating it through samizdat, although it was obvious in advance that this would only mean a wasted month, and as it was there were too few of them before the congress. To gain time I asked my close friends to take Tvardovsky a provisional, not quite finished, draft a month earlier, together with the following letter, ostensibly written from the woods of Ryazan.

Dear Aleksandr Trifonovich:

It seems only right to ask you to be the first [hardly the first, of course] reader of Part Two, if you so wish. . . . The text will undergo further polishing, and for the time being I am not submitting the story to your editorial board as a whole. . . . Let me take this opportunity to assure you that our inability to work together on Part One has in no way affected my attitude to *Novy Mir*. I continue to follow the activities and the policy of your magazine with complete approval. [This, of course, was stretching it a bit.] But the general literary situation is so hard for me to take that I can no longer permit myself the passive posture in which I have spent the past four years. . . .

In other words, I was not even asking him to consider publication. After our quarrel and our six-month estrangement, I was only offering Tvardovsky a chance to read it.

It could not have been better timed. By the time I got back in March 1967 to finish work on Part Two, not only A.T. but everybody at *Novy Mir* had read the book, and all that remained was for me to receive their refusal, their renunciation of any further claims on the story. Over the year I had received letters of rejection from five Soviet magazines, which declined to publish even the most inoffensive chapters of Part One, "The Right to Heal" (a Tashkent magazine would not even publish it without payment in a special charity issue). Further, the whole of Part One had been rejected by *Prostor* (whose method was cowardly procrastination) and *Zvezda:* "More hatred than artistry has gone into the creation of Rusanov"—and that, of course, was something that had never been allowed in Soviet books! "The flashbacks leave the reader feeling that the personality cult completely canceled out all the good things that the Soviet people had done"—whereas, of course, blast furnaces fully compensate for the destruction of millions and the corruption of all. Then again, they would "have liked to see the author's views more clearly distinguished from those of Tolstoy"—so that obviously they would have been still less willing to publish a single line by Tolstoy!

Each such refusal snapped one more strand of the moorings that held *Cancer Ward* like a captive balloon. It only needed Tvardovsky to snap the last of them, and there would be no irksome tether to restrain my impatient story.

We met on 16 March. I entered the room looking cheerful and pleased with life, and was met by a subdued and dubious Tvardovsky. We were there to discuss Part Two, but in the hour and a half we spent alone together we talked mainly about other things.

My path was already secretly determined; I was advancing to meet my destiny, and with a high heart. When I saw how downcast A.T. was, I wanted to cheer him up too. Since I had seen him last, he had suffered a number of political and professional setbacks He had not been re-elected to the Central Committee at the Twenty-third Congress. More recently, he had not been elected to the Supreme Soviet either ("The people have rejected him," as Demichev put it). With the loss of these posts he was more helpless than ever in face of the brazen censors who savaged *Novy Mir*'s galley proofs at will. The noose was tightening also about the stage version of "Tyorkin in the Next World" at the "Satira": the play was performed at ever longer intervals, and they were getting ready to take it off altogether. Then again, the Central Committee had recently taken an unexpected and unfathomable decision, without consulting Tvardovsky or informing him in advance, to remove his two most faithful deputies, Dementyev and Zaks. Just as in the past people failed to return from a visit to the secret police, these two had failed to return to their former work from a call on the Central Committee.[11] Formally, and in intention, this was of course spitting in the face of Tvardovsky and the whole *Novy Mir* staff, but in a more important sense mooring cables were snapping here too, setting them free to soar, because those removed were the trustiest of resident policemen, the two who had always sapped Tvardovsky's energy. But Tvardovsky was so used to confiding in Dementyev, and had such faith in Zaks's skills as businessman and diplomat, he was so attached to them by habit, and the manner of their removal was such an affront to the whole staff, that it almost came to a collective resignation in protest, and A.T. himself was never so close to giving up his editorship. (Obviously, his enemies had planned it all quite cleverly. They may well have had this, too, in mind: that without their built-in safety catches, all the firing pieces of *Novy Mir* would go crazy, blaze away too hard and often, and destroy themselves.)

I saw the retirement of Dementyev and Zaks differently: it merely made the magazine cleaner. But it proved pointless trying to convince Tvardovsky or his collaborators of this. I did my best to make him take a more cheerful view of all the rest: to see his removal from the Central Committee and the Supreme Soviet not as social demotion but as emancipation—he and *Novy Mir* were steadily moving toward the position that Pushkin and his journal had occupied, that of a free poet at the head of an independent journal. (A.T. still had a long way to go to deserve this comparison.) A.T.'s unhesitating response was that he *did not in the least regret* his dismissal, in fact he was glad of it. (It was something even to be able to say it. Within a few days of this, walking along Stoleshnikov Lane in a drunken state, he stopped a colonel whom

---

11. Dementyev, however, went on paying commiserating and lachrymose visits to the *Novy Mir* office for some time. He had never worked there just for his salary, he had always been performing a *public service*, and would probably have taken it on again with no payment at all.

he had never seen before and—poor wretch—confessed to him how badly his feelings had been hurt.)

I: "So much the better! I'm glad you see it that way—that now you're free to be yourself." (If only it were so!)

He (without any prompting on my part): ". . . nor do I care that they haven't given me a *tin badge!*" (A month earlier they had given golden stars to Sholokhov, Fedin, Leonov and Tychina, but not to him, not to Russia's number one poet—a position granted in accordance with the Table of Ranks. They had committed a breach of protocol, and all because he had shown civic courage.) "Sobolev is crying his heart out, but I'm glad they haven't given me one. It would have been a disgrace." (This was insincere.)

I: "Of course it would have been a disgrace, in such company!"

So although we had not seen each other for eight months, and it had looked as though our friendship had broken down, although he had let me see when I arrived that he felt aggrieved, and we were both afraid of giving fresh offense, of rubbing each other the wrong way, we now found ourselves conversing freely on matters of interest to both of us. It had always been my aim to make them take off at least the muzzles they had voluntarily assumed.

A.T. started telling me in detail why he had not resigned over Dementyev and Zaks; how they themselves had worked to dissuade him; how he had been told *up top* that his resignation would be an anti-Party act. He also complacently told me how cleverly and effectively he had reconstructed the editorial board, how Dorosh, Aitmatov and Khitrov had all accepted his invitation to join in identical (?) terms: "I shall consider it an honor." He further told me how the discussion of *Novy Mir* had gone only the day before in the secretariat of the Writers' Union (after an abusive article in *Pravda*): contrary to all expectations, it had been courteous and positive.

Such a survey left no cause for sorrow, but only for joy. Yet again the magazine had shown its unsinkability! How could it not be so? Had it been otherwise, the waves would have closed over it long ago, and its beacon light would have been extinguished.

But there was one thing in that rosy sky that worried A.T.: G. Markov had said in the secretariat yesterday that *Cancer Ward* had already been published in the West. Here the chief editor turned a menacing eye on me. (I had grown a beard. . . . Had I dispatched the "Miniatures" abroad myself? . . . Everything was against me.) At this point A.T. took advantage of his seniority to mention that even a certain (nameless) bourgeois publication (choosing an authority that my non-Communist intellect would understand more easily) had written that conduct like that of Sinyavsky and Daniel would of course be unworthy of Solzhenitsyn. I replied that I myself had no intention of sending anything abroad. "But I will not conceal my books from my fellow countrymen. I have handed out copies, I am still doing it, and I shall go on doing it!" A.T. sighed, but reasonably admitted that "when all is said, an author has that right." (No—before anything else is said!)

Where, then, had the rumor come from? I tried to explain to him. One chapter of *Cancer Ward*, rejected by several Soviet magazines, had indeed been published abroad—in the central organ of the Slovak Communist Party, to be exact. "That reminds me—I was interviewed the other day by some Slovak reporters: would you like me to tell you about it? Of course, I haven't told you yet about the interview I gave to a Japanese in November. . . ." ("I've heard about it." Tvardovsky nodded glumly. "You passed something illegal to the Japanese Embassy.") Yes, of course! We hadn't seen each other for eight months, and Tvardovsky was going to Italy next day, so obviously he had to be briefed on my new way of life: I was behaving quite differently nowadays! I'd better tell him all about it.

But A.T. had lost all interest in our conversation. He began ringing for his secretary, making calls to Surkov, to Bazhan, to all those of whom he had wittily remarked half an hour back that he "wouldn't sit in the same field with them." For they were the very people with whom he had to set out next day to save COMES. I remembered A.T. reassuring his interviewers in Paris about my fate in autumn 1965, and so of course helping to smother me. I now told him as eloquently as I could how much I hated Vigorelli for his lying statement in the West that he had just recently had a friendly chat with me and learned that my novel and my archive had been returned. He was helping to smother me. (Meaning: Don't *you* help them tomorrow!)

"What I do nowadays is submit my manuscripts to the Prose Section for discussion. . . ."

A.T. shook his head. "Well, you shouldn't."

"Then I make a public statement. . . ."

A.T. frowned. "That's very bad. You shouldn't. Your provocative statements put *Novy Mir* on the firing line. We get the blame: 'This is one of your alumni'; 'This is one you dragged into the daylight.'"

(Heaven help us! Not just I but all Russian literature can close its mouth and make a hole in the water, just so long as *Novy Mir* is not censured and pushed under!)

"I defend you too! I stand up and tell them out loud why some numbers of *Novy Mir* are held up for two or three months, tell them about the censors."

Tvardovsky scowled even more heavily. "Well, you shouldn't explain! I've been told that you're always saying things against me. . . ."

*"Against* you? And you *believed* it?"

"I said, 'Let him; I shan't say a thing against *him.' "*

(He had believed it, believed it instantly, had poor A.T.! But he himself would be nobler! . . . That's what friendship means.)

And what had become of *Cancer Ward* in the midst of all this talk? It was remembered, all right, intermittently—two sentences here, two paragraphs there.

For Part Two he had the highest praise. It was *three times* better than Part One. (Is there a gadget for measuring such things?) Only . . .

(Yes, I know: *Just now,* at this particular moment, the way things are, the situation being what it is . . . My dear Aleksandr Trifonich! I know all that! I'm *not asking you to publish it!* You have your journal to think of! I only gave you my story so that you wouldn't feel snubbed! I wasn't submitting it to the board, remember!)

"But let me tell you: *Even if publication depended entirely on me, I wouldn't publish it."*

"It pains me to hear that, Aleksandr Trifonovich. Why, may I ask?"

"Because of your nonacceptance of the Soviet regime. You refuse to forgive the Soviet regime anything."

"A.T.! The term 'Soviet regime' has come to be used imprecisely. It should mean government by the soviets, by representatives of the toilers and by no one else, freely elected by the toilers and freely controlled by them. I am a hundred percent in favor of such a government! . . . But as things are . . . The secretariat of the Writers' Union, with whom you wouldn't sit in the same field, is also part of the Soviet regime, isn't it?"

"Yes," he said with mournful dignity. "In a certain sense they, too, are the Soviet regime, and that is why we must try to get on with them, and support them. . . . You refuse to forget anything! *You have much too good a memory!"*

"But, A.T.! All creative work relies on the artist's memory! Without it, books disintegrate and become mere lies!"

*"You* have *no genuine concern* for the people!" (Well, let's say I am *unkind* to the *top people!*) "You give the impression that you don't want conditions in the collective farms to improve."

"But, A.T.! Not a single kolkhoz is mentioned anywhere in the book!" (Anyway, I didn't invent them. Why should I show any consideration for them?) "What really casts its shadow over the whole book is the prison-camp system. No country can be healthy while it carries such a tumor inside it! Do you know that this system, which was almost cleaned up in 1954–1955, was reinforced again by Khrushchev, and in the years around the Twentieth and Twenty-second Congresses, at that? Why, when Nikita Sergeyevich was shedding tears over our *Ivan Denisovich,* he had just authorized the establishment of camps every bit as tough as Stalin's."

I told him about them.

He listened attentively. But still . . .

"What do you suggest in place of the kolkhoz?" (Hadn't that been the point of our discussion of "Matryona"?) "A man must believe in something. *But you hold nothing sacred.* Say what you like, you must make some concessions to the Soviet regime. In the long run you can't afford *not* to—you can't fight a howitzer with a peashooter."

"We have a howitzer of our own, A.T."

"There's no public opinion in our country!"

"You're wrong, A.T. It exists. And it's growing."

"I'm afraid your *Cancer Ward* may be confiscated, like the novel."

"It's too late, A.T.! The bird has flown! It's on the wing already!"

(Not quite yet. I had to be meek and patient for two more months before Part Two would be ready. But that was just how long I had to wait for the Writers' Congress.)

"Your embitterment is beginning to damage your writing." (Strange, then, that Part Two had turned out "three times as good" as the part he had been willing to publish.)

"Where do you think help will come from? Nobody will ever publish you."

(Quite. In spite of my "behaving with greater dignity than Sinyavsky and Daniel." A neat little trap, that!)

"My books can wait, A.T.! I shall die, and every word will be accepted, just as it is. Nobody will want to correct them!"

At last I had seriously offended him.

"That's just self-infatuation. There's nothing easier than telling yourself that you're the only brave one, and all the rest are poltroons, always ready to compromise."

"Why do you put words into my mouth? There can be no comparison. I'm just a private person, and my own master, whereas you are the editor of an important magazine."

Safeguard your magazine! Take good care of it! . . . Literature will somehow get along without you.

These were not the last words of our conversation, and there would be no quarreling, no name-calling. Our parting was undemonstrative (in Tvardovsky's case absent-minded), each of us regretting that the outlook and upbringing of the other was past mending. This was the most dignified way for it to end, and I was glad of it: our differences were not personal or temperamental. The Soviet editor and the Russian prose writer could no longer march side by side because his literature and mine had sharply and irrevocably diverged.

Next day he left for Italy, and was shortly making a statement to a packed press conference (hoping once again, perhaps, that I should not find out). He was asked about me: Was it true that some of my things were circulating but were not being published? Was it true that there were things that I did not dare take out of my drawer?

"I haven't poked about in his drawer," the popular editor answered. (Of course not—that was the KGB's job.) "But in general, *all is well with him.* I saw him the very day before I left to come here"—thus assuring them of our intimacy and his trustworthiness. "He has finished Part One of a new large-scale work"—how long ago, A.T.?—"which has been very well received by Moscow writers"—"You shouldn't have let them have it"—"and is continuing his work." Have you lost Part Two, A.T.? What about my "remembering too much" and "holding nothing sacred"? Why not tell this nation of Catholics that "Solzhenitsyn holds nothing sacred"?)

Gasping for breath himself in those few months, he still gave a hand to those who were suffocating me.

A poet cannot be a Party member for so many years without paying the price.

\*                    \*
            \*

I thought that I would squeeze myself into a third of the space. I am ashamed of this sprawl.

I have only been writing this because in another few days my letter to the congress [Document 2] will go off like a bomb, and I do not know what will happen, not even whether I shall survive. Either my neck will break or the noose will snap.

It is painful to think that there will be no one to unravel and explain this story afterward.

The course I am following was not plotted or chosen by me; others plotted and chose it for me.

I am defending myself.

Hunters know that a wounded beast can be dangerous.

*Rozhdestvo-on-the-Istya*
*7 April–7 May 1967*

# FIRST SUPPLEMENT

( November 1967 )

# The Noose Snaps

What sticky dough the writer of memoirs has his hands in. He will turn his toes up and still not have finished. Something new is happening all the time—and fresh supplements are necessary. Here I am, cursing myself for writing with such tedious particularity, yet continuing to waste the reader's time and my own.

I can find nothing with which to compare the relief I feel after speaking out. You have to spend almost half a century in endless compliance, endless silence, then suddenly stand erect and bellow—not just from the rooftops, not just to the marketplace, but for the whole world to hear—to feel, as I do, the soul readmitting a universe made calm and orderly again. No more doubts, no more floundering, no remorse—just the pure light of happiness! This was the way to do it! This was what I should have done long ago! As I look at the world in this bright new glow, something like complacency floods my being, although nothing has yet been achieved.

But why do I say that nothing has been achieved? After all, *about a hundred writers* have supported me, eighty-four in a joint letter to the congress, and fifteen or so in personal telegrams and letters. (I am only counting those of which I have copies.) Isn't that amazing? I had never dared to hope for so much! A writers' rebellion! In our country! After Stalin's steamroller has lumbered backward and forward, backward and forward over and over again. Unhappy writers, artists, scholars, unhappy intelligentsia: You are the most dangerous, the hydra-headed monster they have worked to destroy ever since 1918—to ax and scythe and hound and starve and burn out of existence. Surely they've done a thorough job by now, with their basilisk glare and their swift, cruel brooms? But no—you live again! Once again, vulnerable, selfless, desperate, you are raising yourself to your full stature—you, and not your comfortable brethren the rocketeers, the atom men, the physicists, the chemists, with their safe salaries, their ultramodern apartments and their soporific way of life. They, who are so well preserved, should now take over your harsh destiny, inherit your desperate lot—but no! The rider cannot understand the man without a mount. *They* will prepare our destruction by fire, but to make the earth flower it is *you* who must perish!

Among the letters of support, some were merely formal, some cautiously noncommittal, some timid and inhibited, some full of quibbles—but still, there they were! And there were the hundred signatures! And to crown all, there was a valiant, an uncompromising letter from Georgi Vladimov, who went much further than I had in his hymn to samizdat.

Once again the spherical container on my shoulders let me down, and I did not foresee the most immediate consequences! I had written and disseminated my letter like a man voluntarily mounting the scaffold. I was attacking *their* ideology, but advanced to meet it with my severed head tucked under my arm. As I saw it, that life of which some parts were still not razed and rolled flat was over; the last brief phase of that ordered existence without which we are all waifs and strays would end abruptly. I was offering myself for sacrifice because I must, but my action was neither joyous nor reasonable. But then a few days later V. A. Kaverin said to me:

"What a brilliant move that letter of yours was!" And I saw with amazement something I had never expected! My action had not been a sacrifice at all, but a move, a stratagem, which after two years of persecution had established me on a rock-hard footing.

A blissful state! At last I had assumed my natural, my rightful position! At last I need woo and wheedle and fawn and lie no more: I need only enjoy my independence!

Who would think that I could fail to understand our literary and ideological bosses? Yet I had underestimated their insignificance and their faint-heartedness: I had been afraid of sending my letter too soon and giving them a chance to prepare a counterstroke. I had distributed copies only in the last five days before the congress,[1] when I might have

---

1. I spent a long time working out the list of recipients, examining every name minutely. I thought it necessary to send copies to all the Soviet republics, and as far as possible to none of the greatest villains (my gamble on help from the non-Russian borderlands came to nothing, however: not a hand or a voice was raised to help me); to all

done it a month before, and so obtuse were they, they would still not have thought of a reply, still have been at a loss. As it was, many decent people had received the letter too late, or had left home before it arrived (and anyway, the censorship intercepted one third of the copies posted),[2] so that fewer signatures were collected than might have been, and the blaze did not leap up to the ceiling of the hall.

In Moscow, though, the letter spread like wildfire. In the West, too, publication was remarkably well timed: it appeared in *Le Monde* on 31 May, immediately after the end of the congress, before the memory of that scandalous event had time to fade. There was an uproar—again surpassing my expectations—in other Western countries also. (All very different from my abortive interview with the Japanese. Because no interview is worth much, as I now realize. Whereas the letter to the congress was an event in our national life.) Even that part of the letter in which I questioned Western ways was taken up here and there, while the passages about our country were seized upon and heavily underlined. For a whole fortnight—the first two weeks in June—in between white-hot broadcasts on the six-day Arab-Israeli war—radio stations around the world were busy quoting, expounding, reading verbatim and (sometimes very short-sightedly) commenting on my letter.

But the bosses were silent as the grave. I began to feel that I had, surprisingly, not merely defeated but utterly routed my enemies!

Just then a message reached me that Tvardovsky urgently wanted to see me. This was on 8 June, at the Kiev Station, just a few minutes before the local train left for Naro-Fominsk. There I was with shopping bags in both hands, taking home five dozen cheap eggs, and there was the familiar voice which I had not heard for so long, booming away over the telephone, hinting at great things and great benefits to me: it was very important for me to drop everything and make for *Novy Mir* at once. It would have been a nuisance to change my plans, miss the train, lug my groceries along to the office. (How can those to whom everything is brought on a platter understand the lives of ordinary mortals?) But my mind leaped first to a less banal thought. Why would he be looking for me? If it was only so that I could make some act of contrition

---

*genuine* writers; to all members of the Writers' Union prominent in public life. And lastly, so that it would not look as though I were laying information against these people, I had to dust the list lightly with the names of some of the bosses and informers themselves.

2. We had taken this possibility into account and the letters were posted in various districts of Moscow, never more than two in any one box. I had several people helping me.

for the sake of *Novy Mir,* there was no point in discussing it. If, however, now that summer had passed them by, they were mushrooming in snow and ice, if they had decided to publish me after all these years, they could wait till Monday, wait those few days during which the BBC (according to the advertised program) would be hitting our bosses on the head three times over with my letter. It would make them all the more eager!

So my answer to A.T. was that it was absolutely impossible, and I would come to see him on the twelfth. He was very upset. His voice almost failed him. I have heard that after our conversation he wandered from room to room, looking hurt and disconsolate. It was always the same with him: if he set his heart on something, it was "Come on, let's have it!" He couldn't bear to wait. A.T. would humbly submit if his superiors raised obstacles, but he could never resign himself to obstruction from subordinates. Besides, he had had a kind thought, he'd been thinking of my good and I myself had pushed away the hand outstretched to help.

So dissimilar were our orbits, we could never move in harmony.

However, that very day I half heard something that amazed me. Here was another complete surprise. Tvardovsky was not the least bit indignant about my letter to the congress; indeed, he was pleased with it! No, I still haven't fathomed the man! I've devoted four chapters of my reminiscences to him, but I still can't make him out. I had imagined him roaring with anger and damning me till the end of time for my disobedience. (But when I thought a bit, I understood it all. I wasn't complaining to the West, I wasn't looking to the West for protection; I was keeping the quarrel in the family—punching my enemies here in the kisser. To A.T.'s way of thinking, this was quite permissible. He saw it simply as a bout of fisticuffs. *Novy Mir* is on the ropes—after a year of defeats—but now *we're* hitting *them* where it hurts!)

I saw him at his office on 12 June, for the first time since our conversation in March, the last we would ever have, I had thought. Nothing of the sort! A.T. showed a certain reserve when we shook hands, but there was a twinkle in his eye.

"I am very glad, Aleksandr Trifonovich, that you did not disapprove of my action."

Tvardovsky (unsuccessfully trying to look severe): "Who told you that I didn't? I don't approve of your action. But it's an ill wind. If you get away with this, you must have been born under a lucky star. There is a chance."

But his tone changed to one of reproachful adjuration, and I saw no hope of resuming our old friendly relationship.

"You must behave so as not to extinguish the light *in the place from which you came—the only place where any flame now burns.*"

The most awkward of arguments for me to deal with, the most serious reproach he could bring against me. But was it you who gave me my start, friends? And can it be true that no light burns elsewhere? ... And now that I have set the bells ringing, how can I retreat a single step? Why do you refuse to understand?

"How did it come about," he asked, with the same forced serious-ness, "that your letter is known in the West and has caused such a sensation?"

"What do you expect in an age when news travels so quickly; how can you have a functioning democracy, and ensure that nothing becomes known abroad? The English don't reprimand Bertrand Russell if his articles are published in the U.S.S.R.!"

A.T. waved his big arms, his big plump hands.

"Please don't start talking that sort of rot in the secretariat of the Writers' Union! Just tell me this: Were you really appealing to the congress, or was it your intention to create this uproar in the West?"

"Really, A.T.! Of course I meant it only for the congress."

"Right. Let's go along to the secretariat and you can confirm that for their benefit. Tell them that you yourself are annoyed by all this West-ern hoo-ha."

(Annoyed? It was my salvation; I reveled in it!)

"A.T.! I will not retract or modify a single word in my letter. If they ask me *to put anything in writing,* to apologize . . ."

"Of course not!" He was waving his arms again. "Nobody is asking you to write anything! You'll just confirm what you told me a moment ago, that's all. Only don't let on that you are fighting against the Soviet regime!" It was time for laughter, and this was one of his favorite jokes.

The background to all this was as follows. The high-ups in the Writ-ers' Union had thought my letter "a blow below the belt" (they wrote the rulebook, so they knew), and there had been eloquent exhortations to "return blow for blow." But their resolution had soon flagged, as had that of the still-higher-ups: because I had the support of a hundred writers, yes, but mainly because of the warning din from belfries abroad. (They had never expected anything like it.) Tvardovsky had been brisk and efficient—unusual in him—diplomatic but firm. He had managed to give Shaura (Polikarpov's replacement in the "Cultural Department") a piece of his mind ("Who do you think is the leading Russian writer? Mikhail Aleksandrovich [Sholokhov]? You're wrong!") and to put it to the secretariat of the Union that what they wanted to do was impossible, that they would be damaging themselves: if they tried to sink me they would drown with me. He had persuaded them to draft a quite different communiqué: confirming that there was no blemish on my war record, admitting that there were things in my letter that deserved examination, and "sternly" condemning my "sensational" manner of behaving. As no one in the secretariat had anything wiser to suggest, as this course gave some hope of salvation, and as they could not simply go on saying nothing (with trips abroad and questions from foreigners in prospect), they were now gradually coming around to the idea of presenting just such a proposal *up top*. And at a time like this I had failed Tvardovsky by not turning up, thus preventing him from triumphantly completing one of his best operations! (Not that it could have been carried through in any case: the *top people* were preoccupied with the disgraceful defeat of the Arabs, and their heads have houseroom for only one problem at a time.)

Why hadn't the secretariat of the Writers' Union simply *sent for me?* Because after my letter they were not sure that I would consent to come. What if I didn't, and what if they had no orders from *up top* to expel me: how would they get out of a fix like that? . . . Step by step I arrived at the truth of it: The reason they had to take a look at me was to make sure that I was still talking to them. Otherwise their communiqué would lose all meaning.

My "nimble move" had been a leap to the safety of this high crag!

We arrived at the famous house with the portico on Povarskaya Street, and Tvardovsky conducted me to the secretaries. Those present were the desk ornaments K. Voronkov (that jaw!), G. Markov (the sleek fox!) and S. Sartakov (as ugly as they come, but comic too), not one of them in any sense a writer, yet to them and no one else the six thousand members of the Writers' Union had "entrusted" all matters of pith and moment. I went in stiff as a ramrod, carrying my head like a robot, with nothing human in my movements or my expression. Voronkov respectfully heaved his figure—that of a chunky bouncer—up from his chair and lit up his underhung mug with a smile: apparently this was the beginning of one of the happiest days of his life. He was obviously overjoyed even to have the opportunity to let me go first through two doors. In a room like half a hall, with caryatids and moldings, Markov, of the sly, soft, almost womanish face, dashed down the telephone receiver as he saw at last this dearest, this most welcome of guests beneath the Union's vaulted ceilings. Sartakov emerged from a discreetly inconspicuous door. He, however, was not at all pleased to see me and sat through the next few hours in a state of glum apathy. They were also expecting Sobolev, who was flapping about in his apartment on the Sofiiskaya Embankment because there was no car free to bring him in and he knew no other means of travel. I asked for a carafe of tap water, whereupon the same discreet door opened and a maidservant appeared from some secret inner office to load the enormous polished table with fruit juices and mineral waters, followed by strong tea and expensive crumbly cakes, cigarettes and chocolate truffles (all bought with the people's pennies). Time for small talk, and I heard that this was the Rostov house, and how it was kept up, and how Countess Olsufyeva, on a visit from abroad, had asked to see it (Voronkov pronounced the word "countess" with relish and I could imagine him dancing attendance on her—or slipping into her cell to shoot her in 1917); and all about the tapestries portraying Tolstoy (in eighteen million stitches), Pushkin and Gorky which adorned the walls of this state chamber. Between my back and the window, wide open on this hot, airless day, there was a space of six meters or so. But the preservation of my precious life was of such anxious concern to Voronkov that he ingratiatingly inquired whether I felt a draft, because this room of theirs was "so treacherous."

While all this idle talk was going on, I placed two or three earlier letters of mine—to Brezhnev and to *Pravda*—in front of me on the table. The white sheets with their mysterious typewritten text lay innocently on the brown table, but Markov, sitting opposite, was horribly teased by them. He probably thought this was some new bombshell I had got ready, that I was about to deliver, and his impatience would not let him await the blow calmly. He simply must read them! He quite ruined the decorum of our conversation by craning his neck and straining his eyes to look over.

Sobolev arrived, and Markov began as follows: My letter could not be debated at the congress, because it already had a "very tight program." Unfortunately, the letter had become a matter not of merely national but of international significance, and adversely affected the interests of our state. *We must give it careful consideration and find a way out.* (As he went on, this became more and more clearly the dominant motif: how were *we* to get out of this situation? help *us* to find *a way out!*)

He spoke briefly and looked anxiously at me. In the same drawing room tone in which we had talked about the Rostovs' mansion, I inquired whether it would interest them to "hear the letter's history." It would, I found, interest them greatly. Then I began telling them at length the story of all the slanders against me, my protests, the letters I had sent (here I flourished them, to Markov's relief). Next there was the raid that had cost me my novel and my archive. . . .

Guard dog Sobolev: "What raid?"

I (sweetly): "The raid by the security police."

After this had come my various complaints to the Central Committee, all of them unanswered. Then my works had begun to appear in the "secret edition," which had all the marks of literary piracy. While the slander campaign steadily escalated. To whom, I asked emotionally, should I appeal? To whom if not to the highest organ of our Union, its congress? Could that be illegal? (Markov and Voronkov in unison: Perfectly legal. Sartakov and Sobolev sulk.) The congress was due to take place in June 1966, so I got my letter ready. (This was a fib. I hadn't even thought of it then.) But, as all of you here know, the congress was put back to December 1966. (A nodding of heads.) What was I to do? This was when I had decided to appeal directly to Leonid Ilyich Brezhnev. In my appeal I had spoken both of the position of the writer in our society and of how the Stalin cult could have been stopped in time. And what happened? There was no answer to my letter. (As quickly as though they had concerted it, like actors in a well-rehearsed scene, they told each other that "Leonid Ilyich never received it . . . it never reached Leonid Ilyich . . . of course Leonid Ilyich never received it.") I had settled down to wait till December, when I would write to the congress. (Another fib: I had gone off to the Hiding Place to finish writing the *The Gulag Archipelago.*) But the congress had been postponed again, till May. (More head-nodding.) Never mind! I had decided to wait till May. If it had been put off yet again, I would still have gone on waiting. (Perhaps they now secretly regretted not postponing it till much later.)

Sartakov: "But why four hundred copies?" (A figure taken from the BBC.)

I: "What do you mean, four hundred? It was two hundred and fifty. And the reason is precisely that letters sent in one or two copies had been pigeonholed. I was compelled to send it in hundreds."

The others: "But that's not a very nice way to behave!"

I: "What about a sneak edition of a novel by a living writer—is that nice?"

Sobolev (barking): "But where's your logic? Why send it to the delegates when it's already on its way to the Presidium?"

I: "It was important for me to get the support of writers of standing. I did get support from a hundred of them and I am perfectly satisfied."

Markov: "But why send it to a paper like *Literaturnaya Gruzia?*"

I: "Why shouldn't an official journal in a fraternal republic know about my letter?"

Markov: "People are sending us copies of your letter from all over the place. *And don't think they're all on your side.* Many are decidedly against you."

I: "Well, that's all I ask—open discussion."

Markov (plaintively): "That would be just fine—if only our *enemies* hadn't got to know about it." (That's the only term they know for those with whom we "coexist." We are surrounded by nothing but enemies.)

I: "It's very unfortunate. But it's your fault, not mine. Why did it happen? Because you went for three weeks without answering my letter! Why was so much time wasted? I was expecting the Presidium to call me on the first day of the congress and either give me an opportunity to read my letter into the record or at least arrange a discussion."

Markov (pained): "Well, never mind the recriminations; the main thing is what do we do next?" (The others echo him faintly: "What do we do next?") "You're in the thick of politics—what's your advice?"

I (astonished): "What do you mean, politics? I'm an artist!"

Voronkov: "Those broadcasts! They read it twice on every program!" (Not true, but I can't contradict him: what, me listen to Western radio?) "Israel is broadcasting it! Your letter! Israel, mind you! And the way they declaim it! What expert performers!"

Markov (sarcastically): "There is one slight inaccuracy in your letter, you know."

One *slight inaccuracy?* In a letter in which I had neatly decapitated the lot of them? And reduced the decades of Soviet rule to a heap of rubble?

I: "What, exactly?"

Markov: "I'll tell you. You say that *Novy Mir* refused to publish *Cancer Ward*. It did not refuse."

This was the answer Tvardovsky had given them. This was how he remembered it. He honestly and sincerely remembered it that way. We had been talking about it in the office earlier that morning: "Aleksandr Isayevich, when did I ever turn you down?" "Aleksandr Trifonovich! You took hold of Part Two, held it up in the air, and said, "Even if it depended on me alone . . .' " No, he didn't remember! Nor that I "was unwilling to let bygones be bygones," nor that I "held nothing sacred." He'd forgotten it all. "Maybe we were talking about some particular page? I never turned down Part Two as a whole. . . ."

Tvardovsky was now sitting in the background, smoking and watching the show with grave attention. At this point everybody looked at him.

Tvardovsky: "We both got excited and said all sorts of things. It was just talk. The magazine itself didn't refuse you."

Just "talk"—but nearly the end of all relations between us. . . .

Tvardovsky: "The whole editorial board is now willing to publish *Cancer Ward* in full. Our difference of opinion with the author is over a couple of pages; it's hardly worth talking about."

A couple of pages? I remembered them blue-penciling whole chapters, whole characters. . . . But everything had changed. . . . The victors are not judged: for the first time in my life I could apply this proverb to myself.

A.T. hastened to fill an awkward pause and—splendid fellow! who would ever think he could be so alert and resourceful—suddenly said in grave, paternally stern tones:

"But I forgot to ask you one important question while we were in the office, A.I. Give us your opinion: Could *Cancer Ward* and *The First Circle* reach Western Europe and be published there?"

Right up my alley! Ask a few more like that!

I: "Yes, *Cancer Ward* has had an extremely wide circulation. I shouldn't be surprised if it appeared abroad."

Someone (sympathetically): "They'll garble it, they'll twist it inside out!"

(No more than your censors would!)

Sobolev (horrified to find himself in such a helpless situation): "And what a way of doing things! They've announced that they'll accept for publication any manuscript that reaches them, even at third hand, and credit the royalties to the authors!"

Someone: "But how did *Cancer Ward* come to be so widely circulated?"

I: "I gave it to a few writers to get their opinion. Then I showed it to a number of publishing houses, and in general to anybody who asked. Why shouldn't I show my own works to my fellow countrymen?"

They didn't dare argue! Yes, times had changed. . . . Tvardovsky (as though he had just remembered it): "Oh, yes! Vigorelli has sent me a desperate telegram: 'COMES in danger of collapse.' His members are demanding a statement from him about Solzhenitsyn's letter. I've cabled a vague reply for the time being."

Voronkov: "A holding telegram." (Laughs cynically.)

Tvardovsky: "Of course, the European Community of Writers can't exist without us."

Markov: "Of course; it was set up especially for us."

(I learned later from A.T. that he was to have attended a meeting of the presidium of the Community at Rome in June to discuss the difficult position of writers . . . in Greece and Spain. It had all fallen through.)

I: "As for *The First Circle*, it was a long time before I let it out of my hands. But when I learned that it was being passed around behind my back, I decided that an author's rights in respect of his novel are no less than anyone else's. I stopped refusing people who asked to see it. So that this book is also circulating, though much less widely than *Cancer Ward.*"

Tvardovsky (rising in agitation and pacing the floor): "That's just why I say that *Cancer Ward* must be published immediately! That will immediately put a stop to all the hullabaloo in the West, and prevent its publication there. We must put excerpts in *Litgazeta* two days from now, with a note that the story will be published in full in"—he coyly hesitates—"well, in whichever magazine the author chooses, wherever he feels most at home."

And nobody demurred! The only matter for debate was whether two days would give *Litgazeta* sufficient time—the issue was already set up in type. Maybe *Literaturnaya Rossia* could do it?

To say that they were at their wits' end that morning would be an understatement. They had been knocked flat—not by our discussion, but by the radio bombardment beforehand. And the worst of it was that this time it had apparently been left to *them* to find a way out of the situation (the Central Committee had shirked the issue: the letter was not addressed to them!), and *that* was just the sort of thing they couldn't do; they had never solved a problem for themselves in all their lives. Taking advantage of their paralysis, the usually slow-moving Tvardovsky had seized the initiative from these dim persons.

Markov and Voronkov fell over each other to *thank* me—for what, do you think? For coming to see them! (Here I unbent a little and thanked them for dealing at last with my letter.)

That day I experienced for the first time in my life something of which I had previously had only secondhand knowledge—what it feels like to make a successful show of strength. And how well they understand that language! *That language alone! That and no other,* from the day they are born!

Tvardovsky and I went back in a big black car belonging to *Izvestia.* He was very satisfied with the way things had gone and assumed that the secretaries must have consulted somebody beforehand, otherwise how could they have been so accommodating? What had become of the "blow for blow" threat? . . . A.T. decided on the spot the chapter from which the *Literaturnaya Gazeta* excerpt should be taken, and wrote the heading "Extract from *Cancer Ward,* a Novel" in his own hand.

His honest but capricious memory had let slip completely his declaration just a year back that this very title was unacceptable, impossible. Not a word of it had yet been published, but everyone now took the title *Cancer Ward* for granted.

The problem had solved itself.

But this was too good to last. We were soon stuck fast, of course: the same *top people,* Demichev especially, were now calling for delay. There had been a KGB microphone in one of the flats, no doubt that of the Teushes, in which I had humorously described how I had pulled Demichev's leg at our interview. He had been supplied with a tape. And although anyone who listens at keyholes and gets bumped on the nose has only himself to blame, he was furious with me and became my sworn enemy. (For years to come the whole conflict would be further aggravated by his personal vengefulness. In his person the Collective Leadership had made its one and only attempt to get to know me—and look at the result.)

Needless to say, no communiqué from the secretariat, and no excerpt in *Literaturnaya Gazeta,* ever appeared. The radio bombardment from the West came to an end, and the bosses decided that life would go on if they did nothing. A.T. received reports that the problem I had created had been discussed *up top* on 30 June. Once more no decision was taken. But Demichev had thought of a plan: before the secretariat could form a judgment, all forty-two secretaries (Tvardovsky: "Pushkin had only Thirty-Three Heroes, but there are forty-two secretaries") must read both my volumes, *The First Circle* and *Cancer Ward*, but first and most important, *The Feast of the Victors* (they were very reluctant to dismount from this ever-willing hobbyhorse!). Bearing in mind that some of the secretaries not only could not handle a pen but even read haltingly, we can see that the drag chains were to be on for six months, which bade fair to slow things down until the jubilee was over and a rather tougher tone could be taken.

All this I learned from A.T. when I called at his office at the beginning of July. He was sour and gloomy. Every month he ran up against the same blank wall of mindless power, but even after a hundred and fifty months he had still not got used to it. The censors had now started forbidding him to publish the most unctuous of stories (Y. Gerasimov's). Voronkov, whom I had seen so eager to oblige not long before, was now one of those who would not always take a phone call, and if he did he answered haughtily. In honor of my visit, however, A.T. braced himself and telephoned again. Voronkov had the grace to take the call and tell him that the secretaries had started reading, but did not know where to get *Cancer Ward* (because, of course, the KGB had not confiscated it, and there was no copy with the Central Committee). A.T. came to life and said, "I'll send it along."

What it is to hope! He had decided to send the office's one and only copy—the unsoiled, unscuffed and corrected copy that I had recently given them. I was indignant. "I won't let the wretches have it! It'll come back all dog-eared and dirty!" A.T., too, was immediately up in arms. "It's a matter of life and death, and you worry about dirtying a manuscript!"

All he wanted me to do was to "chuck out the bit about secondary growths"—obviously, then, this was the "couple of pages" we could not agree about. He seemed to remember (someone on the board had put it into his head, probably Dementyev before he left) that there was a long dissertation about the camps proliferating all over the country like cancerous growths (as if I would have padded this out to fill a whole page!). It was very difficult to release A.T. from an initial misapprehension. I assured him that there was no such page, but he wouldn't believe me. I showed him the paragraph where there was a sentence roughly to the same effect, and said that I didn't mind crossing it out. No, there was a whole page somewhere! Here little Kondratovich filtered into the room and started busily nosing through the pages: it must be in one of the Shulubin passages, that was it! I started running through the Shulubin pages while they watched, and let Kondratovich look over my shoulder like a friend, never suspecting that he might snap at my flanks. But his eyes lit up—well, they weren't his eyes, of course, but replacements installed by the censorship; nor could he call his nostrils his own, since the censorship had equipped them with olfactory hairs—and suddenly, with joyful certainty, he bit off a piece.

"There you are! That's it!"

"Where?"

" 'For man in every element/Is tyrant, traitor or in chains . . .' "

"You mean that's the cancerous growths bit?"

"It might as well be! It's even worse!"

I am not, of course, concerned with Kondratovich but with Tvardovsky and *Novy Mir.* Tvardovsky was so exhausted and scared by it all that he lent an ear to Kondratovich's warning.

"So what is said there about Nicholas's Russia is meant to apply to us too?"

"That isn't about Nicholas's Russia; it's about England, when it was thinking of handing over Turgenev the Decembrist."*

Whether he was ashamed of not knowing the subject matter of a Pushkin poem, or of raising his hand against Pushkin at all, A.T. let himself be pacified.

"Well, just take out the phrase about Kostoglotov agreeing."

They were always abjectly apprehensive. It wasn't only "what will they say" about the thing as a whole. It was also necessary to foresee from which strip "they" could cut a strap, how they would tie it into a knout, and how they would spell out quotations on someone's mug.

For A.T.'s spiritual comfort I took that phrase out too. He cheered up and tried to "console" me with the thought that Yegorychev[3] had been removed but *I hadn't;* and that I had behaved well at the secretariat—neither provocatively nor in the least apologetically.

He was not a bit anxious for me to repent now. My idea of writing the letter had his emphatic approval. For the first time in all the years

---

3. Secretary of the Moscow City Committee of the CPSU, who had threatened Brezhnev.

we had known each other, he had brought himself to believe that I was capable of walking without leading strings.

We started talking about *The Feast of the Victors*: how to get it withdrawn from discussion in the secretariat, and how Simonov, following Tvardovsky's lead, had refused to read it.

"You might have given me a copy," he said.

"Honestly, A.T., I had just one and they raked that in with the other things. I haven't one for myself."

"After all," he reflected, making himself agreeable, "Bunin has his *Accursed Days*. Your play is surely no more anti-Soviet! And yet we do publish everything else of his. . . ."*

Tvardovsky was changing, all right! And not at all slowly. Was it so very long since he had asked how I dared "put all those playlets about the camps on the same level as the sacred *Ivan Denisovich*"? Since he had refused to accept whole chapters of *Cancer Ward*? It was quite reassuring to find him writing:

> Leave me to find, to call to mind
> My blunders, each and all.

All he asked was

> Don't try to see into my soul.
> Don't whisper in my ear.

He also said, good-humoredly, "I, too, allow myself to make remarks against the Soviet regime, but only in the most intimate circle." (I should explain Tvardovsky's genially smiling reference to remarks against the Soviet regime. He didn't use these words in their harsh newspaper sense; he didn't mean anything that affected fundamentals or the Party's intentions—but damn it, a man can't agree with every single detail; he has to have his own point of view occasionally!) "But say I go abroad—that's quite different: I'd sooner bite my tongue out."

Very right and proper. Breeding tells.

Another month and a half went by, and nothing had changed. Not a sound, not a sigh. Strictly speaking, I myself neither expected nor needed anything more—I had my rock to stand on! But anxiety that I might be letting some other opportunity slip made me suggest to Tvardovsky that we ought to sign a contract for *Cancer Ward* now that we seemed to have *kissed and made up*. In that treacherous state of unstable equilibrium, when they were saying neither yes nor no but refusing to give an answer, perhaps one little nudge was all that was needed? Why not give them one? At worst the contract might be vetoed. If it was not, we could go on to plug the manuscript! We ought at least to try it.

This sweet little plan put Tvardovsky in a quandary. He hadn't expected me to mention the contract first, and to try pushing him into rebellion—for that was what it would be: willfully defying authority. My belief is that his mind was made up automatically: he could not do it, he dared not do it, and he would not do it. But whereas tougher people will promptly put an instantaneous reaction into words, the soft-centered cannot bring themselves to say no abruptly. He promised in principle, but said that the details needed consideration—and ten days of detailed consideration, two superfluous visits by me to his office (he failed to turn up because his dacha was being connected to the gas mains) and finally a telephone call from his dacha together made his meaning clear: "I can't sign a contract for *Cancer Ward* until I get permission."

Since when had an editorial board needed permission before it could even make a contract? Tvardovsky had lapsed into pusillanimity again. Lapses and recoveries, blackouts and illuminations, the struggle between his dossier and his soul, made up his tormented life. He was not one of those who fear everything, nor yet one of those who crash boldly through all obstacles. His was the hardest path of all.

For me, however, his refusal was a liberation. A new plan had already formed in my mind—to administer a hefty push, not a small one, and a contract would only have tied my hands.

Rumors (which later proved false) had reached me that *Cancer Ward* was being prepared for publication in Italy. While we went on shilly-shallying! So I had thought of a precautionary step, for the record: "I've told you, and from now on you will have to answer for it!" The time was coming to break their judicial stranglehold on literature. Given our censorship, our lack of civil rights, the state's refusal to recognize the international copyright convention—who should answer for the publication of books in the West, if not our bosses? Why should it be the authors? [Document 3]

Following the pattern I had established with my first letters, I thought once again of sending out 150 copies, omitting only the non-Russian republics. However, I was persuaded for the present not to make my complaint public, not to rend my garments loudly, but only to threaten to do these things. At the time this seemed sensible. So I decided to send copies of my letter only to the "forty-two secretaries" and one to the secretariat as such, and to let no one else handle it, in case it found its way into samizdat and abroad.

I still had to choose the best time. Although there was nothing to hurry me, and I had oceans of time, it would give me more chance of success if I thumbed my nose at them before the pomp and ceremony of the Revolution jubilee began. The date I chose, therefore, was not the semi-anniversary of my letter to the congress but three months after the discussion with the secretariat of the Writers' Union at Povarskaya Street.

There was another snag, though: I should have to "consult" A.T., since we were friends once more. Could he conceivably approve of such a step? . . . And could I conceivably go back on my plan? . . .

I named a day when I would visit the office. A.T. promised to be there—and never arrived. The thought that I might ask him about my contract was too tiresome, and he avoided meeting me. So this superfluous and nonsensical notion of a contract also helped to thicken the plot. I was all eagerness to consult him! Only he was missing! So by late afternoon of 12 September, the forty-three letters were in the mail boxes of Moscow! It turned out for the best, both for Tvardovsky and for me, that we had not met.

But what would he do now? Would he hit the ceiling when he heard of this new impertinence? The recipients rose in the air as though someone had trodden on their tails, Mikhalkov raved and roared at *Novy Mir* over the telephone, and as early as the fifteenth a preliminary meeting of the secretaries was convened to rehearse their barking, off the record for the time being. Before the day was out I had received a summons to attend on the twenty-second. And before the day was done Tvardovsky had his scouts out after me.

I went to see him on the eighteenth, wondering by now whether I wasn't giving myself unnecessary trouble. Why bear down so hard on this wasps' nest? After all, I had a firm footing. I had time at my disposal —why not just work away quietly? Surely my work meant more to me than this brawl.

I confided my doubts to Tvardovsky that day—and what did he say? "You *had to do it*. Now that you've begun, you must go through with it!"

Once again he had surprised me; once again the other, the unpredictable Tvardovsky had surfaced. Gone were his dejection, his prevarications, his lassitude. He was swift and sure of himself again; my second letter had roused him like a bugle call—and he had already sustained one battle, or preliminary skirmish, his Shevardino,* at the meeting of the secretariat on the fifteenth. He told me that he had been supported (in his call for the publication of *Cancer Ward*) by Salynsky and Bazhan, and that others had shown signs of wavering. "Things aren't altogether hopeless!" he kept saying, to encourage himself as much as me.

Even one solitary meeting seemed likely to ruin both my work rhythm and my creative mood, and I was beginning to feel bored and unhopeful. How many such meetings had he endured in his long years as a poet, on that long trek through dark woods? Three hundred? Four hundred? What ought to surprise me more? That he had put up with all those efforts to twist his brain askew? Or that his spiritual soundness had enabled him to endure it all and survive?

I grumbled about his calling me in for a talk, which only took time away from my work. "You may have no time at all soon!" he retorted angrily. That was what he was afraid of, that was why he had summoned the clever and discreet Lakshin and why they had concerted their plans to coax me into the right frame of mind, so that I should behave discreetly *over there,* rein myself in, not bandy insults, not explode with rage—because if I did I was done for. The others were all blooded gamecocks and would peck me to death.

A.T. and I had known each other so long—and still knew nothing about each other!

"I'll let you in on a secret," I told him. "I never lose my self-control; it's impossible for anyone trained in the camps to do so. If I blow up, it will only be according to plan—if we arrange, say, that I should explode in the nineteenth minute, or so many times in the course of the meeting. If you don't want me to—very well, I won't."

That was all well and good. But A.T. didn't believe me. He knew what excruciating torments people were made to suffer at these meetings, how they tripped you up, stuck pins in your behind, nipped your ankles. We were at a disadvantage in that they had read *The Feast of the Victors,* were discussing *Feast,* meant to talk only about *Feast,* to attack *Feast,* and to attack me with *Feast.* We must make them stop talking about *Feast* and talk instead about *Cancer Ward.*

We somehow worked out a plan for me to steer the discussion away from *Feast* without interrupting other speakers.

I still had two days of peace and quiet left, but mentally I was already in battle. Things they might say, questions they might deluge me with,

pressed in on me from every side, exhausting me prematurely, demanding answers. I jotted down possible retorts, and from them a whole
speech began to compose itself. I had never in my life prepared a
speech in writing, word for word, and always despised the use of such
cribs, but this one I did write out. I could not, of course, foresee precisely every dig they might make, but at meetings in our country people
are used to the idea that speeches need not be relevant to each other.
More often than not, they are beside the point; everybody talks about
whatever he thinks important, and no one is surprised.

Preparing for this tussle (my first—but I had been marching toward
it for thirty years!) gave me no difficulty: for one thing, because I had
very clear-cut views on everything that could possibly stir beneath their
skulls, and for another, because as far as I was concerned, the impend-
ing meeting of the secretariat would not decide the fate of my story.
Whether or not they let *Cancer Ward* through, they had lost just the
same. Nor had I any use for the secretariat as an audience: it was
hopeless trying to bring about a genuine change of heart in them. All
I wanted to do was to meet my enemies face to face, to display my
inflexibility, and to put it all on record. When all was said, how could
they fail to hate me? For I was the one who said no, not only to their
lies, but to their whole false existence, past, present and future.

Nonetheless, toward the end of my preparations for this joust I was
getting tired, and wanted to rid myself of excessive, quite useless, un-
creative tension. But how? By medicines? Why not simply a little vodka
toward evening? At once the harsh outlines were softened, and nothing
nagged me into snarling back. I slept peacefully. This was when I
understood something else about Tvardovsky: in thirty-five years, what
means had he ever had of relieving that galling, smarting, degrading
and unproductive tension—except vodka? Who dare cast the first stone
at him? (He greatly disliked talking about his drinking bouts. If you said,
"You ought to take better care of yourself, A.T.!" he would irritably
dismiss the subject. I tried talking to him about his incessant smoking
too, tried to frighten him with *Cancer Ward,* but he brushed it aside.)

My plan was as follows. The one thing I wanted to achieve at the
meeting was to take careful notes of it. This would make it possible for
me to keep my head down when they began brandishing their fists at
me: "Tell us straight, are you *for* socialism or *against* it?" "Come on,
now. Do you accept the principles of the Writers' Union?" Besides, it
would certainly scare them: they would wonder why I was scribbling
away. For whom was it all meant? They would choose their expressions

more carefully; they were not used to seeing the dirty suds of their eloquence splashed out in the sunshine of publicity.

I prepared some clean sheets of paper, numbered them and ruled margins, and at the appointed time of 1300 hours on 22 September entered the familiar audience chamber with the caryatids. The air was already thick with stale breath and cigarette smoke; the lights were on in the middle of the day; there were dirty tea glasses and ash scattered over the polished table—they had been in session for two hours before my arrival. Not all of the 42 were present. Sholokhov would have thought it beneath him to come. Leonov, intent on immortality, walked gingerly in the eyes of posterity. The venomous Chakovsky was absent (perhaps also out of discretion), as was the furious Gribachev. But more than thirty secretaries had packed themselves into the room, and three stenographers sat at their own little table. I gave a restrained "Good day" to each side of the room and looked around for a seat. There was just one free. Beside Tvardovsky, as it happened.

Having listened patiently to Fedin's pained introduction ("Record of a Meeting of the Secretariat" [Document 4]), I seized the one short break of five seconds when he paused to swallow before calling on another speaker, and asked in my most syrupy voice:

"Konstantin Aleksandrovich! Will you permit me to say a couple of words on the subject of our discussion?"

Not a prepared statement! Not a manifesto! Just a couple of harmless little words, and on the subject of our discussion. . . . It was essential to wrest the initiative from them. My request sounded so innocent that Fedin chivalrously granted it.

Whereupon I solemnly rose, opened my folder, took out a typed sheet, and with an inscrutable face, in the voice of one intoning truths for the ears of history, I hurled at them my first statement, dismissing *The Feast of the Victors*—not apologetically, though, but accusingly: accusing them all of betraying the people for many years past!!!

I learned afterward that they had had it all planned—how and in what order they would sink their beaks in me. They were lined up in battle array, but before they could sound the charge I gave them a hundred-and-forty-four-gun salvo, and meekly resumed my seat in the hanging smoke (after passing a copy of my statement back to the stenographers).

I sat with my pen at the ready, but for some reason no one came forward. I had dashed their main weapon—*The Feast of the Victors*—

out of their hands. There was an antlike rustling, a touching of antennae —and Korneichuk popped up with a question.

"I'm not a schoolboy and I won't jump to answer every question," I answered primly. "I shall speak when my turn comes."

But then came a second question, and a third! They had hit on a scheme. They would entangle me and trip me up with questions, put me in the dock. They are good at that sort of thing, those crooks.

But I refused to join in. I would wait my turn.

They thought their beaks had found the spot! They fused into a noisy, heckling, howling mob: "The secretariat cannot begin its discussion unless you answer!" "You can refuse to talk to us altogether, but if that's your intention, say so!"

Now our neat line of battle crumples, and my tactical plans are confounded. How can I sit imperturbably taking notes? But oh, you poor feeble creatures: how is it that I knew all these questions of yours beforehand? How is it that I have ready detailed *written* answers to all your *oral* questions? There's only one casualty: I must tear my speech into strips, and use them to beat you off.

I rise and take out my sheets, and, this time not with the detached voice of history personified but in the swelling tones of an actor, I read them the answers I have ready.

And hand them to the stenographers.

They are all thunderstruck. It is probably the first time such a thing has happened in all the thirty-five years of their foul union's existence. However, the reserves press forward, the relief column moves in, the forces of darkness return to the charge. I am asked three more questions.

Blast you, I say! How can I get it all down? It's lucky I have all the answers ready. I rise and draw out the next sheets. Deploying my forces ever more boldly, steadily broadening the front, setting the bounds of battle to suit myself, no longer merely answering their questions but following my own plan, I drive them headlong over the field of Borodino to their remotest defense works.

And—there is silence, embarrassment, dismay, confusion, all around me. But whose column now comes wheeling on our flank? Not quite enemies, these, but half-friends. Salynsky and Simonov take the floor, and though they are not altogether for *me,* they are at least for *Cancer Ward.* The enemy is at a loss, no one wants to speak, there are no more questions. What can it mean? What is this if not victory? Bringing up the dragoons, Tvardovsky curvets and caracoles over the field. We're ready to decide then, right? We publish *Cancer Ward*. And put an extract in *Literaturnaya Gazeta* immediately! We were going to issue a communiqué. Where is the communiqué, Voronkov?

But nimble Voronkov takes his time. Or rather, he searches for the communiqué, cannot immediately find it and goes on searching. (Yet when I had needed to consult my letter just now he had been quicker off the mark than I, and tendered—"Allow me!"—the version put out in leaflet form by *Posev*, which I had had the sense to decline.) If only they can hold out just a little bit longer! Where, then, are the imperial reserves? . . . Here and there, men rise from under our hoofs, crying, "What do you mean, vote? We haven't made up our minds yet! Some of us are against it!"

Here they come, the Black Guard! Korneichuk, rearing up like an enraged scorpion! Kozhevnikov! And there on the white horses, Surkov's turncoat cavalry. Wave after wave, from the deep rear, the diehards pour onward: Ozerov, Ryurikov, Baruzdin, who looks like a hockey star.

(Baruzdin was sitting by me, and I asked him the name of each speaker. "Who's he? What about that one?" He names the speaker's neighbor. "No, I mean that one there!" He names the speaker's other neighbor. "No, no, the one in between—the one with a face like a well-toweled plump backside with flashing spectacles perched on it." "Oh, you mean Comrade Melentyev from the Cultural Department of the Central Committee." So that's who is secretly calling the tune. Just sits there scribbling. Scribble away! I'll show you what old zeks are made of!)

Then all the non-Russian formations: Abdumonunov, Kerbabayev, Yashen, Sharipov. In their republics virgin lands are being tamed, dams are being built. What is this *Cancer Ward?* Who is this Solzhenitsyn? Why does he write about suffering, when we write only of happy things?

Oh, how many of them there are! There is no end to their muster roll! Only the Balts sit silently, with lowered heads. They see the fate that might have been theirs. Will it never die away, the tramp of regimented feet; will there never be a break in the parroted verbiage?

The enemy forces have flooded the whole plain, the whole earth, the whole air! . . . The battlefield is in their hands! We seemed the braver, we were attacking throughout. But they remain in possession of the field. . . .

Borodino. Time must pass before either side can tell who won the day.

On Fedin's face his every compromise, every betrayal, every base act, has superimposed its print in a dense crosshatching. (It was he who set the hounds on Pasternak, he who suggested the Sinyavsky trial.) Dorian Gray's sins all showed in the coarsening lines of his portrait. It was Fedin's lot to receive the marks on his face. With his depraved wolf's features he presides over our meeting and makes the absurd suggestion that I should bark angrily at the West, while suffering the harassment and insults of the East with a smile. The face is bloodless under its patina of vice, a death's head smiling and nodding approval of the orators. Can he really believe that I will yield to them?

I had long ago got into the swing of it—I just wrote and wrote my record, wearing a meek expression. You wolves still have everything to learn about zeks! You will live to regret your rash speeches!

In my fourth, and last, statement I even permitted myself a threatening gesture in the direction of the Cultural Department of the Central Committee ("responsibility for *The Feast of the Victors* belongs to that organization which . . .") and—to tease Fedin—why, of course I welcomed his proposal! (Smiles all around! I had cracked!) Why, of course I was in favor of publicity! There had been too much hiding of stenographic reports and speeches. . . . Publish my letter, and let's see what happens! . . .

Disgruntled muttering. Howls of rage. Ryurikov rises and lugubriously wrinkles his dogmatic brow.

"Aleksandr Isayevich? You simply have no idea what horrible things the Western press is writing about you. They would make your hair stand on end. Come and see us at *Inostrannaya Literatura* tomorrow, and we'll give you some clippings and summaries."

I look at my watch.

"May I remind you that I do not live in Moscow. I am now going to catch my train, and I shall be unable to take advantage of your kindness."

More muttering. More howls. Fedin, disappointed and angry, closes the discussion, which has gone on for five hours. I mutter formal goodbyes, one over each shoulder, and take my leave.

The field of battle is in their hands. Nowhere, not an inch of ground, have they yielded.

But whose is the victory?

I was in too much of a hurry to see A.T. again that day. He wrote
to me:

"I really admired you, I was delighted for your sake and for ours.
. . . The manifest superiority of truth to any and every dirty trick and
to 'politics' . . . On the face of it things are no further forward . . . but
in reality there has most certainly been a shift in our favor. . . . The
practical conclusion I draw is that we are prepared to sign a contract
with you, and see what happens."

But even Tvardovsky gave me less of a surprise than the BBC. The
meeting had ended on Friday evening. The English "weekend" went
by, and on Monday afternoon the BBC was telling listeners—pretty
accurately too—how I had been summoned by the secretariat, and how
the meeting had gone.

I was no longer a needle in a haystack. I would never get lost now!

The Central Writers' Club was abuzz with rumors. Writers who had
supported me at the congress now demanded explanations from the
secretariat.

A few days later a letter from Sholokhov was read out at a meeting
of the board of the Writers' Union. He demanded that I should be
*prevented from writing!* (Denied the use not just of printing presses,
but of my pen! As Taras Shevchenko once was!) He could not remain
in the same Writers' Union with an "anti-Soviet type" like me! My
Russian brother-writers set the board room roaring: "Nor can we! Let's
vote on it!" Sobolev took fright (Hey—I've had no instructions!): "Comrades, it would not be in order to put this to the vote! Will those who
*can't* stay in the Union if Solzhenitsyn does please make individual
written statements. . . ."

But my right-Russian brothers funked it. Not one of them wrote in.

Some of the Moscow writers said, "Maybe *we* don't want to be in it
with *them?*"

Can we then bore holes in granite? Do the drills for it exist? Who
could have foreseen that it would ever be possible under our regime to
shout the truth aloud—and stand firm?

But isn't that just what is happening?

Memory, a prisoner's memory, tugs at the rein till the bit sinks
painfully into my gums, and pulls me up short. Call no day happy till
it is done; call no man happy till he is dead.

*Ryazan*
*November 1967*

# SECOND SUPPLEMENT

( February 1971 )

This is a strange thing I seem to be producing. One not foreseen in my early plans and not essential to them. I can write it or leave it alone. For three years I have let it rest, well hidden. I didn't know whether I would ever care enough to come back to it. A few close friends read it and said there was life in it, that I should certainly go on. So, while I take a breather between the "Knots" [volumes] of my main book, I am immersing myself in this one again.

The first thing I see is that I ought not just to carry on where I left off, but to bring out more clearly, to explain more fully, this miracle: that I walk at my ease through marshes, stand firm upon the quaking bog, go dry-shod over whirlpools, hover in midair without support. From outside it is not obvious how a man with the state's curse upon him and the KGB's hoops about him can fail to crack. How he can hold out single-handed, yes, and fork over mountains of work, find time now and then to root in archives and in libraries, to write around for information, to check quotations, to interview elderly people, to write, to type, to collate and bind copy after copy, as book after book goes into samizdat (and there is always another in reserve): Where do I get the strength? From what miraculous source?

To shirk the task of explaining is impossible, to find the right words still more so. Safer times will come, God grant, and then I shall fill the gaps. For the present I am afraid even to put the outline of an explanation on paper as an aid to memory, afraid that the scrap of paper may find its way to the Cheka-GB.

But as I read over what I have written, I see that in the last few years I have grown stronger and braver, that I dare to put out my horns more and more often, that today I can bring myself to write things that three years ago seemed deadly dangerous. I see more and more clearly where my chosen trail is leading: to victory or destruction.

What makes this piece so strange is that for any other you draw up an architectural plan, you see the unwritten parts implicit in the whole, you try to make each part subserve the whole. But this book is an agglomeration of lean-tos and annexes, and there is no knowing how big the next addition will be, or where it will be put. At any point I can call the book finished or unfinished. I can abandon it or I can continue it as long as life goes on, or until the calf breaks its neck butting the oak, or until the oak cracks and comes crashing down.

An unlikely happening, but one in which I am very ready to believe.

# Breakthrough

Yes, the analogy with Borodino held: for two months after the battle, not a shot was fired on either side—no allusions in the press, no more than routine rudenesses from the platform. But of course they were cruising their way through the Fiftieth Anniversary, and for their own convenience the occasion must pass as smoothly, with as little in the way of embarrassing incidents, as possible. I, too, was not averse to a truce, and I did not launch my "Record" of the hostilities [Document 4], rightly or wrongly keeping it in reserve for a combined assault at some other time. There had been no perceptible redeployment of literary forces—the battlefield, remember, had remained in the enemy's possession, Moscow was in his hands—but it was just because of the lull that I could sense an inaudible and invisible shifting and slippage. And did not the bloodied ground invite us to return without so much as a skirmish?

With this feeling I let the great jubilee go by, then went to Moscow, to make a show of *action* before plunging into the silent depths for the whole winter. To *act* I needed Tvardovsky, but found that he had been missing for some time; incapacitated by his old weakness for a whole month, he had not even noticed the drum rolls and fanfares of the jubilee (from which the incurably naïve West had expected an amnesty at least for Sinyavsky and Daniel, as well as for its faint-hearted Gerald Brooke; but of course no crust was cast from the festive table). This was how it always was with A.T. and myself. When he needed me, he could never get through. When I needed him, he was always out of reach.

Day after day I waited for him at his office, tried to phone him at his dacha. It was finally decided that I should go to Pakhra on 24 November, and Lakshin invited himself along with me. We set off in the morning, in one of *Izvestia*'s black Volgas, with what was still light snow falling. I had something urgent to read on the way, but it couldn't be done: my companion *would* entertain me with his conversation. Some people may think it absurd, but once I have started a piece of work, the force of inertia impels me to complete it as planned, even if what may be a unique opportunity comes along—like this chance to talk to Lakshin, with whom for some reason I had never got around to it. But with an informer at the wheel, what sort of conversation could we have? Much of it was trivial, but still, there in the back seat, keeping his voice down, he told me the following interesting story. In 1954, when Tvardovsky's replacement as chief editor of *Novy Mir* was under discussion, it might never have happened if he could have snapped out of his drinking bout in time. They had almost brought him around, but on the very day of the meeting he had given Marshak, his watchdog, the slip and got drunk. The meeting in the Central Committee offices was going well for *Novy Mir:* Pospelov was put to shame, Khrushchev said that the intelligentsia had simply *been given no guidance* on problems connected with the personality cult, the editorial board as a whole was not dismissed—but if a chief editor won't even turn up at a meeting of the Central Committee, what can they do but dismiss him?

This habit of A.T.'s was sometimes a salutary way of unwinding, and sometimes his undoing.

A harlequin Great Dane met us inside the gate. We entered the house unchallenged, and called out to the occupants. A.T. slowly descended the stairs. At that moment he looked sicker, more helpless, more horrible than I had ever seen him (later on, in the course of conversation, he pulled himself together and improved quite a lot). He had dark pouches under his pale-blue eyes, which looked more vulnerable than ever. In a strange voice, he said very sadly to neither of us in particular, "You see, friend Mack,* to what I have come."

And tears came into his eyes. Lakshin put a reassuring arm around him.

In that same hall, darkened this time by heavy snow falling beyond the picture window, we sat by the fireplace, in which brushwood had once been kindled in memory of a lost novel, while A.T. strode restlessly around us. For a short while we said nothing, giving A.T. time to come to himself, but he found the silence oppressive, and asked whether anything had happened. His hands were trembling violently, dancing, you might say, no longer just from weakness but with fear.

My reply was quick and loud. "Of course not; absolutely nothing. Remember how black everything looked last time I came? It's quite the opposite now!"

He calmed down a little and his hands almost stopped shaking. He played with a cigarette but did not light it. He sat down on the sofa and asked only half as anxiously, "Well, then, what's going on in the world?"

It gave me a pang. I remembered how as a boy I had sometimes missed two or three days' school, and felt as deeply depressed as if I had committed some crime: how had things been going on there without me? It was as though in those few days, the precarious world outside must inevitably have slid into some grave danger. Tvardovsky evidently had the same feeling after cutting himself off completely, as he had just now for a whole month, not only from the magazine but from the outside world at large.

I answered with a pun: "In the *New World* [*Novy Mir*] or in the rest of it?"

"Anywhere," he begged meekly.

The version Lakshin gave him was as follows: There had been no change for the better since the jubilee, but no change for the worse either. I myself even tried to persuade him that things were better: British television had shown a dramatized version of the Sinyavsky-Daniel trial, and the tide of support for them was rising, so that things were not too bad. . . . But this argument was wasted on both of them. As far as they were concerned, Sinyavsky and Daniel did not exist.

To keep it brief, I began summarizing my own business. Something told me that the enemy had a weak spot. The best way to feel it out would be to send several chapters of *Cancer Ward* to the printers without asking anyone's permission. Even if it didn't get through, I would be entitled to vent my indignation on the Writers' Union when *Cancer Ward* was published abroad. Look what will happen otherwise, I warned them: *Cancer Ward* will appear abroad, that's inevitable, and the blame will be put on you and me. They'll say that we didn't make the slightest effort, that we couldn't come to an agreement.

A.T.: "It needs thinking about. I can't say anything at such short notice."

I knew that tone of voice by now. He was refusing. I tried to persuade him that in either case—whether they rejected it or let it through—we would be the winners!

A.T.: "It would be too impertinent, after all that has happened, just to send it to press as though there were no problem. Somebody has to go along and *talk to them* first, but I simply *can't anymore.* You must try to understand that."

(Lakshin would explain to me later that when Tvardovsky had last visited the "Cultural Department," Shaura had again pressed him to read *The Feast of the Victors,* and he had honorably refused to yield: he would not take into his hands something that had been stolen and was being circulated against the author's will! But he had abused Shaura too roundly, and could not go there anymore.)

I: "But there's no need to go and ask. Just send it to the printer in the ordinary way; and wait. Why not?"

Lakshin (smoothly, persuasively): "I didn't tell Aleksandr Isayevich on the way here . . ."

(And why not? Hadn't there been time enough? What he was about to say was his only reason for coming, I could see that now, but it had to be said in the presence of his chief.)

". . . but there is another way. Khitrov was in Shaura's department, discussing this and that, and the conversation got around to Solzhenitsyn. One thing surprises them: when twenty-four writers have told him to write an anti-Western statement, how dare he not write it? If only he would, all would be well. It needn't necessarily be in *Pravda* or *Litgazeta* It can be in *Novy Mir,* if you like. . . ."

(Hmmm . . . So now they were backtracking, changing their tune. They were not used to firm opposition.)

This, then, was Lakshin's proposal: that we should, indeed, set up some chapters of *Cancer Ward* . . . and in the same issue, "perhaps in the letters to the editor section," there would be "some sort of statement from A.I. to say how surprised he is by all the fuss in the West."

When this prudent (thirty-five-year-old!) schoolboy and I had sat swaying together on the back seat, he had been carrying the deed of surrender—but had not shown it to me. Very prudent tactics, to be sure, on this one little square—but there were sixty-four of them on the board, and it ought by now to be clear that the adversary was *crushed!*

However, I did not even have time to answer Lakshin. A.T. moved in; his dander was up.

"*What* can he write?" he growled angrily. "What is there to write about when they've hushed it all up? He *has* written a letter—to the congress—and he can't go back on that!"

And Lakshin fell silent, made no attempt to argue. A.T.'s opinion was more important to him than that of the Central Committee. He held his peace, although privately he disagreed.

Nor did I insist any further. We talked about various things. We drank stupefyingly strong tea. A.T. got up, walked about, sat down again a time or two—and steadily became more human as he emerged from his sickness. Then Lakshin put on the table a bundle of slim new volumes by Tvardovsky, and I made the blunder of offering my pen: "Come on—pay your library dues."

He didn't even try to take the pen; his poor hands were too shaky! "I couldn't sign them now," he said apologetically. "I'll do it later."

Not wanting A.T. to lose interest in publishing *Cancer Ward,* I had not intended to tell him prematurely about *August 1914.* But his condition was so distressing that I decided to cheer him up by telling him that I was just writing about the Samsonov catastrophe and might finish it by next summer.

A.T. (by now recovering his powers of irony): "There was no *catastrophe,* and could not be. It is now an *established fact* that Russia before the Revolution was not a backward country at all. I read an article by an economist not long ago, in which even the position of the peasantry before 1861 is shown in quite a rosy light: it practically says that the landlords fed them, that they enjoyed security in old age and sickness. . . ."

(The funniest thing is that the new official stereotype is much closer to the truth than the earlier "revolutionary" versions!)

We stayed for less than an hour, because the car was waiting. (*Izvestia*'s drivers always made difficulties with the *Novy Mir* staff and tried to hurry them.) When we were getting ready to leave, A.T. took it into his head to go for a stroll. He put on a very ordinary-looking duffle coat and a peaked cap, picked up a walking stick for support—not a very stout one, it is true—and escorted us through slowly falling snow and out the gate, looking for all the world like a peasant with perhaps a year or two of school behind him. He took off his cap, and the snow fell on his big, sparsely covered, fair peasant head. But his face was pale and sickly. My heart sank. Without waiting for him to make the first move, I embraced him as we said goodbye: this was a ritual long suspended by our quarrels and explosions. The car moved off, and he just stood there in the snow, a peasant with a stick.

In the office I myself toned down Kostoglotov's conversation with

Zoya about the Leningrad blockade, so as to leave them no serious excuse for rejection.

And away I went. But I had scarcely arrived in Ryazan when a letter came from Voronkov [Document 5], an exploratory note: when, he wondered, would I finally decide to dissociate myself from Western propaganda? Were they beginning to stir? Without pausing to think, I fired a dozen questions back at him. Would *they* ever mend *their* ways? I, too, was waiting for an answer, remember! [Document 6]

With that off my mind, I went on into the backwoods near Solotcha, to stay in the cold, dark cottage of Agafya (a second Matryona), where on frost-free days they heated to fifteen degrees Centigrade, and when it was freezing I woke up more often than not to a temperature of two to three degrees. According to my work plan, which looked many months ahead, I was supposed to spend the whole winter there. I surrounded myself with pictures of Samsonov's generals and tried to steel myself to begin the most important book in my life. But I was paralyzed by awe of the subject. I hesitated fearfully on the brink. The lines flagged and petered out, my hand slipped feebly from the page. I then discovered that I had left a great deal undone in *The Gulag Archipelago* too, that I still had to study and write up the story of the show trials, and that this must come before anything else: work unfinished is as good as unstarted; it is vulnerable to every blow. Then an alarming letter reached me, saying that *Cancer Ward* was being offered for sale in England, *in my name,* which was quite impossible, which was something I had tried to guard against with every means of self-defense I had. So my work was disrupted—and then came another disturbing jangle: Tvardovsky had recovered and was tugging at his long-distance bell rope back in Moscow. Report for orders immediately! You are urgently needed! What the urgency was he did not say, and of course it was quite imaginary. You'd run a man off his feet, blast you! Slowly, grudgingly, grumbling and groaning, I got myself ready. I can't bear it when events not of my making wreck my plans.

Tvardovsky, though, was amazed that I didn't come running: he and I had been summoned to the secretariat of the Writers' Union of the U.S.S.R. for an *informal chat.* Voronkov had telephoned him; Voronkov was *worried:* had *Novy Mir* at least paid Solzhenitsyn an advance for *Cancer Ward?* After all, *a man needs a bite of something now and then!* ("A bite of something" is their workaday term for an author's needs.)

So that's your game, you parasites! But I'm not a bit surprised. If I stand firm you can't help wobbling. What does surprise me is something different. For half a century the whole world has failed to see this very simple fact: that strength and steadfastness are the only things these people fear; those who smile and bow to them they crush.

On 18 December I found Tvardovsky in his office, floating in high heaven on cushions of soft cloud. Though he himself had received no precise information, he had deduced with absolute certainty from minute and indirect indications that someone *up there,* possibly The Man (Brezhnev) himself, had—well, not exactly ordered the publication of *Cancer Ward,* not in so many words, certainly not (otherwise the signs would have been different), but had let fall something to the effect that whether it need be banned was questionable. And those few words, launched upon the air and left hanging, nowhere recorded, had nonetheless been picked up and stealthily passed on, touching hands, shoulders, ears, till Demichev's apparat and all the literary puppets were paralyzed by it, except the nimbler and more responsive, who, like Voronkov, rushed to clear a path with their wagging tails. So although nothing decisive had yet happened, there had been such a sharp change since September that there on the back seat of *Izvestia*'s Volga, as it carried us to Vorovsky Street, Tvardovsky started dreaming, as he had six months earlier, not only of publishing *Cancer Ward* in *Novy Mir,* but of sending a chapter to *Litgazeta* right away, to consolidate our advantage—and off he went again, running over the chapters to decide which should be sent, which would make the "most mouth-watering portion." He was feeling magnanimous, and at first almost settled on the next-to-last chapter (Kostoglotov walking about the city and visiting the zoo), but quickly retracted his generous concession:

"No, I won't let Chakovsky have the *jus primae noctis.*"

Were we on the threshold of a new miracle in the history of the censorship? The extraordinary thing about the world of bureaucracy is that it can for a short time suspend the operation of all physical laws within its own confines, so that heavy objects float upward and electrons stream toward the cathode. But this time I expected no miracle and, as I remember, I did not particularly want one: they would only start all over again, pinching out a line here and a paragraph there, whereas in samizdat *Cancer Ward* was circulating quite freely and quite unmutilated. By now I preferred this independent path I had discovered. Still, not wanting to interfere with Tvardovsky's brief moment of happiness, I raised no objections.

Voronkov, a chunky chameleon with broad mandibles, was once again attentive and polite—not so effusively polite, to be sure, as he had been after my letter to the congress, but equally unlike the lout who had tried to foist the *Posev* leaflet on me. We sat down in a foursome, like cardplayers, Tvardovsky and I facing each other, Sartakov opposite Voronkov; the difference was that three of us were at a little table of our own, while Voronkov was cut off from us by the great inert block of his desk, and he himself was a sedentary block, though a fairly mobile one, in a massive armchair. I spoke as sparingly as I could and refused to exert myself, since the whole game seemed so unreal. Waspish, pedantic Sartakov also intervened only rarely and the duel, implicit rather than explicit in the words they uttered, was between Voronkov and Tvardovsky, who took the offensive. Voronkov wanted to get through the conversation without really saying or promising anything, while nonetheless earning credit for affability. Tvardovsky, who knew all these dodges well enough after knocking about the Soviet literary world for thirty-five years, wanted to pin Voronkov down and extract from him at least his verbal consent to the publication of *Cancer Ward*.

"But it's up to the magazine," Voronkov kept repeating, with surprise in his voice. "Just do whatever you wish."

"At least you have no *objections?*"

"What has it got to do with the Union of Writers?" said Voronkov in tones of growing amazement.

(Surely you can't think that anybody around here would put pressure on a publisher?)

"Don't give me that—I never board a tram without a ticket!" Tvardovsky countered, in a metaphor drawn from the Writers' Union's cliché workshop, not from his own experience.

Whenever Voronkov, taking the offensive, insisted that a disclaimer was necessary (from me: I must dissociate myself from the West and from my letter), that we couldn't just ignore the whole affair, I simply let it pass because I was sick of pointless nattering; but Tvardovsky answered confidently:

"Oh, but we can. If we just keep quiet, everything will be fine."

"But how can we possibly hush it up?" Voronkov, champion of the public's right to know, was startled.

"I'll tell you how." Tvardovsky spoke emphatically and unfalteringly, as though relaying a message from the upper wall. "When Khrushchev was dismissed, the whole thing was hushed up—and nothing happened! Now, that was a rather bigger event than Solzhenitsyn's letter."

Anyway, how had Voronkov got where he was? Why, I wondered, was he in charge of six thousand Soviet writers? Because he was the finest writer of them all? As I heard it, Fadeyev had once picked a mistress from among the female office staff of the Union, which automatically disqualified her for simple clerking, and the ever-obliging Kostya Voronkov had been taken on in her place. From such beginnings he had wound and wormed his way to the top. But what had he ever *written?* The wags used to say that his most important works were the directories of the Writers' Union. Yet just a little while back (hoping, perhaps, to make life a little easier for *Novy Mir?*), Tvardovsky, of all people, had entrusted Voronkov, of all people, with the task of dramatizing "Tyorkin." Some nameless helot, no doubt, had done the work for him—and Voronkov had become a playwright overnight.

They talked for an hour and a half, but still Voronkov's slippery bulk eluded Tvardovsky's puffy paws: he led his opponent on, but he made no promises and gave no authorization. Off we went, A.T. and I, by back streets to Nikitskie Gates, and from there by way of Tverskoy Boulevard to *Novy Mir.* In that half hour of light frost under a modest winter sun, holding A.T.'s arm and taking particular care of him at the crossings, to which he was unused, I saw the happiness with which he had started the day peep out and grow and ripen again, drawing its strength this time not from a dream but from his own sturdy determination. We went into *Novy Mir,* where he ordered his secretary to call a meeting of the editorial board, and quietly triumphant, said to me:

"We'll put *Cancer Ward* into production! How many chapters?"

We settled for eight. A.T. was "boarding the tram without a ticket"!

Ah, the power of that faceless Somebody's opinion! Further exercising his firmness (the firmness of which his very name* gave a pledge—if only he had always lived up to it!), Tvardovsky did not think it beneath him to visit *Izvestia*'s printing shops in person, and convey to some manager or other that he was not exceeding his authority in the matter of *Cancer Ward,* but that Somebody was of the same opinion, and that haste was therefore necessary. One important Party appointee could not suspect another of brazen usurpation, and he did indeed work fast, not so fast that the story was set up in the course of a few night hours, as *Ivan Denisovich* had been, but by dusk of the following day a bundle of proof sheets was brought to the *Novy Mir* office, and since I had not yet gone to earth again, I corrected them then and there. (And then and there emerged victorious from a furious tussle with Tvardovsky: he *forbade* me and went on forbidding me till his eyes were blank with rage to put my own table of contents in front—the idea itself, the lettering, the suggested layout, all disgusted him. "Nobody does it like that!" But I wouldn't budge—even if it meant quarreling and parting and breaking up the type. That was Tvardovsky for you: he inhabited a number of planes simultaneously.)

The deed was done, the type was set—and the Western press would long chide our supreme villains for breaking it up again: the deed was done because of the Central Committee's momentary weakness and my editor's sudden surge of determination. This meant that my funds would last almost two years longer, two very important years in my life. But the Central Committee soon woke up to its mistake and set about rectifying it. Who had spoken those incautious words nobody ever knew; perhaps nobody had spoken them, or perhaps whoever had caught them on the wing had misheard and twisted them. Nobody knew, either, who had banned the work (Brezhnev again, perhaps), but the whole enterprise withered on the vine.

God had utterly denied them that elasticity which is the distinctive mark of living creatures.

For me it was a relief: once more the path that lay before me was straight though untrodden and, my instinct told me, was the true one. I did not let myself be distracted by regret that *Cancer Ward* had not in the end been published.

But for A.T. it was all quite different. This failure affected him like a great bereavement. He had believed! He had been so carried away by his own reckless bravery! But the dull, stodgy dough had absorbed his impetus. He felt that he had to be doing something at this time, he yearned to share his thoughts with me and he sent telegram after telegram to me in Ryazan, to say that I was urgently needed (to make some precautionary modifications, I think). But I had no wish to modify anything, and above all no wish to make the journey—two hours to Ryazan and another three to Moscow—but how could I explain to this forgetful ex-rustic that just before the New Year the ten hungry provinces around Moscow go into town to buy groceries, that there are queues for tickets, that travel is uncomfortable . . . and that I would not make a journey just to suffer excruciating discomfort. I wired my refusal. The message then changed to "Come immediately after New

Year's Day!" No, I wouldn't go then either. When was I supposed to work? If I went whenever I was called, I would soon be exhausted. He just wouldn't understand, though: it was my fight as much as his; why was I so apathetic? "Where is he? Shall I send a helicopter for him?" Lakshin and Kondratovich saw fit to express particular indignation: "When a work is going through the press, it is the author's duty to spend at least two weeks here!"

But I was right not to go. The "Cultural Department" was putting pressure on A.T. again, to make me write a recantation, even if it was greatly toned down. "We met him halfway when we published *Ivan Denisovich,* and how does he show his gratitude? With *The Feast of the Victors.* . . ." "There's nobody there worth talking to," Tvardovsky told my wife with the saddest of sighs. "They can't even get the name right; they call it *Cancer Fort.*" And, dreaming again, "If we could publish *Cancer Ward* now it would change the whole literary scene! Just think of the works we could get published after that. . . ."

Two more days went by, and our ultra-loyal A.T. also had recourse to a letter! (This was the age of letters!) True, it was not an *open* letter, it was for Fedin's eyes alone, but nonetheless there were nearly twenty-four pages of it, and A.T. spent three whole weeks over it, writing at his dacha during his best working hours, garnering thoughts and phrases while he cleared away the snow.

Meanwhile I was in Solotcha, working fast to put the finishing touches on *The Gulag Archipelago,* and indulging myself by listening to Western radio stations in the evening. In February I was astounded to hear my November letter to Voronkov—astounded because I had never released it. It made no sense by itself. It proved that keeping documents back can also have its disadvantages. (It had of course slipped through at Voronkov's end—the date had been cut off, as though it had been photocopied in a hurry—but I would be reproached with it for years to come.)

By March I had begun to have very bad headaches, and rushes of blood to the head—my first attacks of hypertension, the first intimation of approaching old age. Merely to get *The Gulag Archipelago* finished would mean working without an hour's relaxation all through April and May. Just so long as nothing broke in on these two months to hinder me! . . . I had high hopes that I should recover my strength in my beloved Rozhdestvo-on-the-Istya—from contact with the soil, from the sun, from the green fields and woods.

This was the first patch of ground I had ever been able to call my own. I had a hundred meters of stream to myself, and an extraordinary feeling of intimacy with the natural world about me. Almost every year the little house was partly under water for a while, but I always hurried there as soon as the floods began to recede, although the floorboards would still be wet and a tongue of water from the gulley crept up to my porch in the evenings. On cold nights all the water is drawn back into the river, leaving a covering of glassy white ice over the sloping water meadows and in the gulley. It hangs, a brittle film, over a vacuum, and in the morning falls away in big pieces as though someone is walking over it. On warm nights, though, the river does not sink, the floodwater does not withdraw but laps and babbles all night long. Even in daytime the roar of lorries from the highroad cannot drown the sounds of the river in spate, and I can sit for hours listening to its mysterious gurglings, feeling my health returning hour by hour. At one minute I hear a heavy gulping, at the next a sharp crack (a loose branch, lodged in a willow tree when the water was higher, has fallen), and then the even murmur of many voices begins again. The sun, blanched by the clouds, is reflected faintly in the racing water. Then the higher ground begins to dry out, and you can caress the warm earth with your rake, clearing it of withered grass to let the new green blades through. Day by day the water falls, and now you can take your fork and clear the banks of the rubbish and driftwood cast up by the river. Or simply sit thoughtlessly sunning yourself on the old workbench or the oak seat. There are alders growing on my patch, and nearby there is a birch wood, and every spring the weather signs are there to be read: if the alders come into leaf before the birches it will be a wet summer; if the birches are earlier than the alders, a dry one. (And every year it proved correct! And when birch and alder leafed at the same time, the summer was neither one thing nor the other.)

Beautiful! In just such a spring a year ago the greater part of these sketches was written here. In a month's time, when the world is warm and green, we shall type the final draft of *Gulag*, putting on a spurt in May, while there are still no summer residents about to notice.

The way from Ryazan to Rozhdestvo lies through Moscow. I could not be in Moscow without looking in on *Novy Mir*. "Good day, Aleksandr Trifonovich!" Good day, indeed. The past was over and done with. We had other things to think about. Three months had gone by since A.T. had written to Fedin; the Gorky centennial celebrations had come and gone—what had Fedin to say for himself? He had *embraced* Tvardovsky: "Thank you, thank you, my dear A.T.! I have such a load on my mind...." "Is it true, K.A., that you have been to see Brezhnev?" "Yes; comrades close to me decided we ought to see each other." "And that something was said about Solzhenitsyn?" Fedin (with a sigh): "Yes." "And what did you say?" "Well, I don't have to tell you that I couldn't say anything good." Then, realizing how it sounded: "But I didn't say anything bad either." (What, then, did he say?)

As always at *Novy Mir,* I listened mainly out of politeness, and didn't answer back. It was no bad thing, of course, that Tvardovsky had written such a letter (though to my mind it was four times too long), and still better that it had been made public. . . .

Oh, yes! He had a fresh wound to show. Why was it that some new work of mine was "going the rounds" in Moscow, and he, A.T., had been by-passed? Why? Why hadn't I brought it to him, why had I said nothing? A bunch of writers in Pakhra had *had the nerve* to offer to lend it to him, "but I refused, of course!"

But how can I explain it all? Explain that if I bring you anything you are sure to hold it up and say it isn't wanted. But I think it is wanted: let it make its way in the world. The piece in question was "Readers on *Ivan Denisovich,*" once a chapter of *Gulag,* which had dropped out at the last revision . . . but I didn't like seeing it go to waste, and so I had released it.

"Well, A.T., it isn't really *mine;* that's why I didn't bring it in. I'm not the author but merely the collector; 85 percent of it is quotations from readers. I never thought that it would circulate widely, and even enjoy a certain success. I only lent it to two old women, former zeks, to read."

"Where are these old women?" he blustered. "We'll take a car right now and go and retrieve it from them. How could it have *leaked?*"

"Well, how did your letter to Fedin leak? You didn't show it to anybody!"

This staggered him. He knew for sure that he hadn't let anyone see it.

"You'd better sit still and keep quiet for the present," he warned me.

For the present, yes, I agree. But I give you fair warning: If *Cancer Ward* is published abroad, I shall send letters of explanation to other writers. (What sort of explanation is another thing I can't tell him. If I show him my "Record" too soon, he will drop his paw on it and I can say goodbye. Thus do those who are quick to silence others doom themselves never to know the truth in time!)

With that I went away—to sit still and keep quiet. This was on 8 April. And on the ninth *Grani*'s dynamite-packed telegram was being put together in Frankfurt am Main. . . . That year I was not left for long to sip the sweets of early spring on my "country estate." It was, as it happened, Palm Sunday, but still cold. Indeed, on Saturday the thirteenth snow had started falling, quite thick snow, and it was not melting. On the BBC's evening program I heard that "lengthy excerpts" from *Cancer Ward* had been published in the *Times Literary Supplement!* A shock! Stunning but joyful! It had started! As the spring snow fell, I paced and paced the path along which I took my walks. It had started! I had expected it—and I hadn't. However anxious you are for them to happen, such events always burst upon you before you expect them.

*Cancer Ward* was precisely the book I had never tried to pass to the West. I had had offers, there were ways, but somehow I had always refused without really knowing why. But if it had found its own way there—that was how it should be; God's appointed time had come. What trick would they try now? A year after the Sinyavsky-Daniel trial, such impudence? But I had a presentiment that I was being carried along a path where none could withstand me: you'll see, nothing will happen!

My wife, fresh from Moscow, found me taking my walk in the April snow. She looked agitated. She couldn't have heard: they had only just broadcast it. No, she had brought another piece of news. Tvardovsky had been trying to find me for four days, and was ranting and raving because he didn't know where to look. I wasn't in Ryazan, my Moscow relatives "didn't know." (I kept my hideout at Rozhdestvo a secret, especially from *Novy Mir.* Only this gave me some security; otherwise, they would have yanked me out of it a dozen times by now.) We had seen each other only last Monday, and here he was on Wednesday, "ranting and raving"! "It has never been so important as it is now." With them (with *us*) it's always "never before," always "a very special occasion, so important!" You're supposed to swallow it every time. Let them wait. Don't cry wolf too often if you want to be believed. I can't twitch in sympathy with every twist in the course of events. I will go in three days' time; Tvardovsky will last till then. Am I being unkind to them? Well, they've shown me no more consideration. If I had answered every summons in the past few years I would have stopped being a writer altogether.

They couldn't have any later news than mine—that *Cancer Ward* was coming out in the West! And what I had to worry about was not that it was coming out, but how it would be received there. This was my first real test as a writer! What I had to reflect on was not why *Novy Mir* was so worked up, but whether or not the time had come for me to strike my blow. My documents had lain languishing too long, no one knew about our battle of Borodino; perhaps it was time to show these things. I wanted peace—but I must act! Not wait for them to rally for the attack, but attack them now!

I had no bird's-eye view to guide me, only a tunneler's intuition.

And this it was that sent me off on Tuesday 16 April to *launch* my "Record." There were many pages: half a hundred copies had been made and put in storage during the winter. (Litvinov and Bogoraz handed their material directly to newspaper correspondents, but I was still playing safe. I was a hunted beast, and I hid behind the backs of fifty writers.) All I had to do now was quickly finish copying out the covering note [Document 7], to bind my bombshell so that all its separate parts would go off at once and at a time that would now be generally understood.

"I have urgently warned the secretariat of the danger of my works finding their way abroad, since they have had a wide hand-to-hand circulation for a long time past. . . . A year has passed and the inevitable has happened . . . the . . . responsibility of the secretariat . . . will be clear."

Till the very last moment my Moscow friends tried to stay my hand: You must wait a bit! *At this particular moment . . . the way things are* . . . with reaction all along the line . . . they are breaking the will to resist . . . you mustn't exasperate the *high-ups*. . . .

Well, that's why now is the very time to *move!*

I had come to Moscow to do just that. And, incidentally, to look in at *Novy Mir* and see what all the uproar was about.

Their excitement was extreme! Lakshin's and Kondratovich's faces were dark with grief and anger. But they couldn't speak to me in a civilized way: protocol and discipline above all things—in A.T.'s absence they mustn't say a word! And he simply couldn't get in from his dacha: they'd had a puncture on the way in and the pampered *Izvestia* driver hadn't so much as a wrench to remove the wheel with. A.T. came in three hours later, tense but also deeply depressed—reduced to despair by me! The senior members of the staff now assembled in his office like an investigating commission, stern and inquisitorial. And they laid before me—squeamishly, as though it were loathsome to the touch—a nasty, dirty telegram from the base and treacherous *Grani* (what a splendid name for thinking people, though!):*

> Frankfurt am Main. April 9. *Novy Mir.*
> We hereby inform you that the Committee for State Security through the medium of Victor Louis has sent a further copy of *Cancer Ward* to the West, so as to block its publication in *Novy Mir.* We have therefore decided to publish this work immediately.
>
> The Editors of *Grani*

It was so unexpected and there were so many contradictions here, so many mysteries even, that I could not take it in. But I was not required to understand it. It was a *provocation!* And it was my duty as a Soviet citizen . . . Hardly anything in it was clear to them either, but they lacked the ordinary adult civic courage to begin by seeking clarification. What—and what alone—do Soviet people always do? Administer a rebuff! Don't look into it, don't investigate, don't stop to think! Administer a rebuff! The effect of many decades of intimidation. But even the young, critical, quick-witted Lakshin unthinkingly clings to the wall bars with the others! Administer a rebuff!

Oh, *Novy Mir!* You are my main weakness! My most vulnerable spot! With no one else do I find it difficult to speak, only with you. It is a long time since I owed anything to any Soviet institution except you—and it is through you that the whole slimy system clutches at me and seeks to engulf me: It's your duty! Your duty! You are one of us! You belong to us!

Tvardovsky (with heavy, not to say awesome, emphasis): "The moment is now at hand for you to prove that you are a Soviet citizen. That the man *whom we discovered* is one of us, that *Novy Mir* has made no mistake. You must think of Soviet literature as a whole, you must think of your *comrades.* If you behave badly, our magazine may be closed down. . . ."

The constant threat: *they may close us down.* . . . I am not just I, but either a millstone or a balloon around *Novy Mir*'s neck.

After Borodino I had deluded myself that I was a free man. Oh, no, not a bit of it! My feet were so firmly stuck in the mud, it was so difficult to pull them out! I tried to evade the issue:

"*Grani* is too late. The *Times* has already published . . ."

The *Times* doesn't matter; what matters is *Grani*. What matters is a smart rebuff and a show of Soviet principle!

I slipped my little covering note to A.T., and a copy to Lakshin. (I didn't give Kondratovich one; he could read it over Lakshin's shoulder.) But no, it made no impression on A.T. Nor on the others (after they had glanced at him).

"The *Times* isn't in Russian. . . ."

Lakshin: "It's very important, Aleksandr Isayevich, for the historical record. Reference books always show where a work was first published in the original language. Think of the disgrace if they say *Grani!*"

Suddenly A.T. woke up to the covering note too:

"And you mean to distribute this? It isn't the right time for it! You *know what the mood is like* at present. . . . You could lose your head. . . . They're adding a new clause to the Criminal Code. . . ."

I: "It's been a long, long time since anything in *that* whole ragbag concerned me. I'm not afraid."

A.T.: "And you've already begun sending it out?"

I hadn't, but I lied. (So that nothing could be done to prevent it.)

He did not, he certainly did not approve. He wouldn't even give drawer space to such a rash and wrong-headed piece of paper. But other things were more important just then. Grimly and of one accord they closed in on me again. And Tvardovsky without more ado dictated this to me:

" 'I categorically forbid your neo-émigré and openly hostile journal. . . . I shall take all possible measures. . . .' "

What measures? The government does not defend our rights, but does require us to defend ourselves! That's the Soviet way, all right.

"Otherwise, Aleksandr Isayevich, *we shall no longer be your comrades!*"

On the faces of Lakshin-Khitrov-Kondratovich the identical stony stare: No, we are your comrades no longer! We are patriots and Communists.

Oh, how hard it is not to give in to your *friends!* . . . And anyway, I don't want *Grani* to publish *Cancer Ward*—they'll only spoil everything—and I want it less than ever now that publication in Europe has already begun. Well, then. All right, then. I will send a telegram, then. (Has my strength failed me? And so soon?) I try to draft one, but the words won't fall into place. Give me time to think! They show me into Lakshin's private office. But it is like being under arrest: Write a telegram prohibiting publication—or you won't be let out of the office.

Always take time to think! Always look around you first! Here's something penciled on the back of the telegram: what can it be? A rough draft.

Dear Pyotr Nilovich [Demichev]:

In my opinion, Solzhenitsyn must send this neo-émigré journal [they seem to find the prefix "neo" particularly opprobrious] which is undisguisedly hostile to our country . . . I am trying as a matter of urgency to bring Solzhenitsyn, whose present whereabouts are unknown to me, back to Moscow. I await your instructions.

Tvardovsky, 11 April

(Tvardovsky had received no *instructions* in reply to this, and next day he had phoned Demichev himself in a state of despondency. Demichev said:

"Er . . . let him do just what he likes." Meaning: And you can clean up the mess. So that Tvardovsky had started looking for me even more anxiously.) Still the words wouldn't fit together in my telegram. I scrawled something, without a word of abuse in it, and took it to show A.T.—who got angry: too feeble, no good at all! I patted him gently on the back, and he was even more furious:

"I'm not the nervous one! You are!"

Well, maybe so. Anyway, I can't write it. Let's sleep on it. Give me time to think. I'll send it in tomorrow morning, I promise.

They released me reluctantly.

I felt sick at heart.

Lydia Chukovskaya was puzzled.

"I don't understand you. Why play tag with tigers? It's best to keep your distance."

True enough. What had come over me? How could I have made promises to them? Still, I ought perhaps to get to the bottom of it? There was a whole series of puzzles:

1. How did such a telegram come to be *delivered* at all? This was either a blunder on the part of the apparat or a KGB provocation.

2. Who was Victor Louis?

3. A "*further* copy"? To whom, then, and by whom, had the first been delivered?

(Neither of them, of course, would have been provided gratis! So that the proceeds of my *Cancer Ward* had already gone to reinforce the KGB.)

While the preparations for my volley (the fifty copies of my "Record") took their inexorable course, I decided to find out about Louis. I immediately came across a former zek, a woman, who brought me a wonderful bouquet of information about him. He wasn't called Louis at all, but Vitaly Levin; he had been put inside while he was still a student (something to do with foreign tourists, so they said) and had been a notorious informer in the camps. After his release he had not only not been banned from Moscow, but had become a correspondent for rather "right-wing" English newspapers. He was married to the daughter of a wealthy Englishman, traveled abroad freely, had any amount of foreign currency and a fabulous country house in the "generals' village" at Bakovka, with Furtseva for a neighbor. It was he who had taken Alliluyeva's manuscript out to the West.

Everything was now clear. The telegram was genuine (delivered by mistake or by some miracle); the KGB was peddling my *Cancer Ward; Grani* was giving Tvardovsky an honest warning; and in return it was my duty, Soviet style, to cover it with mud and let the KGB go on treating my soul as an exportable commodity—because the KGB is the Soviet power, it is *ours,* and it has the right to do so.

Half a dozen lamebrained *Novy Mir* editors had sat huffily in their offices for half a dozen days, volubly complaining to each other that I was a scoundrel to hide from them, and obsequiously yes-sirring the chief, while he stamped his feet at me, truckled to Demichev, and felt sick with anxiety for *Novy Mir*—yet not one of them had troubled to read the telegram carefully, or call up the Central Post Office to ask if it was genuine; not one of them had inquired whether anyone called Louis existed or not, which country he lived in, who and what he was.

In this you see the results of a Soviet upbringing—mutton-headed conformism, a combination of cowardice and sycophancy: all that matters is to *rebuff* the enemy, without running into danger! . . . It was simply laughable to think how unsure of myself, how ready to delude myself, I had been only yesterday.

God had preserved me from disgracing myself in their company. I had been whisked on horseback out of the eye of the whirlwind. My "Record" was on the wing, and hard behind it fluttered another letter of mine—about Louis! [Document 8] If Victor Louis hadn't existed, I should have done well to invent him, he had turned up so opportunely!

Everything to do with the publication of *Cancer Ward* was henceforth the KGB's responsibility, not mine! To make A.T. feel ashamed of himself, I left two notes for him at the office on two successive days, and went off with a lighter heart to my Rozhdestvo. All my blows had been struck, and at the best possible time. Let him thunder away without me while I got on with my work.

First, though, I must celebrate this quiet, warm Easter. There was no place of worship nearby, except the decapitated church I could see from my little balcony, the Church of the Nativity in the village of Rozhdestvo (Nativity). Someday, if I live that long, or even after my death, I must do what I can to restore it. For the present, a late-night broadcast by the BBC must replace the midnight service. On Easter Saturday, a peaceful sunny day, quite hot because the branches were still bare, I enjoyed myself raking together the tangled brushwood swept down by the floods. I was steeped in peace. How wise and powerful is thy guiding hand, O Lord!

Suddenly, I hear a firm masculine tread. It is my excellent friend A.E., always so generous with his help. He has come as fast as he could with more bad news. (But what it was all about must wait till later.)

No, you never know where to put the safety net.

There is no peace. The sun shines tranquilly as before on the same bare woods, the stream hurries by with the same mysterious murmur —but peace has abandoned me, all is changed. A day ago, even an hour ago, nothing could stop my steed in his victorious career; now he has broken a leg, and we are plunging into the abyss.

What am I to do? Nip this new threat in the bud too. Fight to keep my precarious balance on the crest, the sharp peak of danger to which the past few days have abruptly thrust me. I have written too many *letters* in a very few days, but the days are such that I must write one more! Perhaps every evil brings some good: while defending myself against *my own side* I shall have a good opportunity to tear a strip off the jackals in Western publishing houses who vulgarized my *Ivan Denisovich* beyond recognition, turned it into crude propaganda.*

It is man's way to hit his fellows when they are down, to vent his rage on the defenseless. How many Soviet writers (even when there was no need for it) have taken pleasure in railing at the Russian church, the Russian priesthood (think of Father Fyodor in Ilf and Petrov's *The Twelve Chairs,* for instance), or at the whole Western world, knowing that they can do so safely and with impunity, and that it will stand them in good stead with their government. I, too, almost succumbed to this ignoble inclination. I was tilting my letter (addressed to *Le Monde, Unità* and *Litgazeta*) too sharply against the Western publishers—as though I had any others! But friends corrected me in time. . . .

On 25 April I strolled to the offices of *Literaturnaya Gazeta* with a typewritten letter [Document 9]. A meeting with Chakovsky would have been repugnant to me, but luckily he wasn't there. His two deputies (every bit as bad as himself, of course) were flabbergasted by my appearance and met me with guarded politeness. As though it were the most natural thing in the world, as though I were one of their regular clients, I laid my little letter on a desk before them. They jumped on it, read it aloud, interrupting each other, and shuddered.

"Have you sent it to *Le Monde* yet?"

"I'm just on my way to do so."

"Wait a bit! Maybe . . . It doesn't depend on *us,* you understand"—eyebrows raised ceilingward—"but maybe if . . ."

"I quite understand. Right, I'll give you two days to phone me."

I also went to *Literaturnaya Rossia,* gave bald, wily, shameless, circumspect Pozdnyayev a scare with a similar bit of paper—and took my leave.

The hours went by—and suddenly a dismal thought began to trouble me. Perhaps I had done something dishonorable? Perhaps I had been too hard on the West? Might it not look as though I were knuckling under, crawling to our bosses?

I was disgusted with myself. The most terrible danger of all is that you may do violence to your conscience, sully your honor. No threat of physical destruction can compare with it. Although my friends assured me that there was nothing to be ashamed of in the letter, I waited with my heart in my boots for a call from *Litgazeta.* I didn't want the phone to ring!

It didn't. God has deprived them of reasoning power in order to destroy them—deprived them long ago (but still they will not perish). In their foreign policy they manage fairly well—because the West is practically on its knees before them, because all the *progressives* fall over themselves to curry favor—but in domestic policy our leaders nearly always choose the solution least advantageous to themselves. Since there is no one with whom they can discuss things freely, it cannot be otherwise.

I sent *Le Monde* a registered letter with a prepaid acknowledgment slip. (I might as well have dropped it down the drain. It would not be forwarded.) And *L'Unità?* I heard that Vittorio Strada, the Communist literary critic, was in Moscow and going home in a day or two. There was my man.

But Vittorio Strada is what they would call in the camps a sucker born and bred. It would be hard to think of anything more stupid than what he did. He put the scrap of paper, not in his pocket, but in his case, together with heavy bundles of samizdat. Evidently somebody *grassed* on him—he had too much baggage—and they took the liberty of checking. Can you believe it! Where is the pride of the "free and independent Communists"? They shook him down and stripped him bare, as if he had been the merest bourgeois tourist. And what did he do when he got home to Italy? Write to his *Rinascita?* Complain to his Central Committee? Did the Italian Central Committee complain to ours? Nothing of the kind. They held their tongues. Their independence doesn't stretch quite so far: if they come to power they will be doing the same sort of thing themselves.

At Rozhdestvo the tender green leaves were out, the first nightingales were singing, there was mist from the Istya in the early morning. From dawn to dusk the correction and copying of *Gulag* went forward; I could scarcely keep the pages moving fast enough. Then the typewriter started breaking down every day, and I had either to solder it myself or take it to be repaired. This was the most frightening moment of all: we had the only original manuscript and all the typed copies of *Gulag* there with us. If the KGB suddenly descended, the many-throated groan, the dying whisper of millions, the unspoken testament of those who had perished, would all be in their hands, and I would never be able to reconstruct it all, my brain would never be capable of it again.

*They* had been so lucky for so many decades. Every time the tidal waters had retreated before them. Surely God would not let them off again. Was justice never to be done in the Russian land?

But though birds were twittering and trilling, though frogs were croaking, though leaves grew bigger every day and the trees gave broader shade, yet there were still no people; the summer residents had not yet arrived, there were no spies on the prowl. No, *they* knew nothing, they could not see us, they would miss their chance!

True, the news reached me that V. Strada had been picked clean by the customs. A mishap at the frontier is no doubt a terrible thing to befall a Soviet citizen, but I had grown so brazen that I was no longer afraid: I was beginning to feel my strength, to feel that I had risen above all that. Anyway, it was an innocent little letter, to a Communist newspaper—so to hell with it all. Let's get on with our work! Until suddenly —addressed to me at my dacha, where there was never any mail for me (no one was allowed either to write or to call)—a letter from the customs!

". . . in connection with the need which has arisen . . . on a matter concerning you personally . . ." they invited me to the custom house at Sheremetyevo to meet somebody called Zhizhin. (Where has the Russian nation vanished to? We know where—it has seeped into the soil of the Archipelago. And they are what has oozed up to the surface—all these Zhizhins, Chechevs, Shkayevs. . . . )

So that what we thought was an untroubled sky overhead was the enormous observation dome of the KGB, and now it had *winked* at us like the severed head in *Ruslan.* * "It's our turn now! You're finished!" . . . They can see it all—all our antlike scurryings—and we are in their hands.

Our blood turned to ice. Keep calm! Take yourself in hand, think it over for an hour or two. But for your training in the camps, you, a free citizen, might go hurrying off just because a customs officer calls you. Isn't it time, rather, to put them in their place? Let's write as follows:

"In spite of what you say, I see no need for us to meet. Imaginative literature and the customs normally have no business with each other. If, however, you find it imperative, your representative may call on me at . . ."

I then mentioned the Turkins' apartment in Moscow, a date ten days after that for which they had summoned me, and the three hours during which I would await their convenience.

With that in the mail, we continue working all out for two more weeks. We're holding on; no one has snapped back at us, no one has descended upon us. Now my part of the work is finished, and all that remains is a few more days of typing. I go to Moscow. We wait in the apartment. An hour passes. My relatives laugh at me: Did you really believe they would come? They're not such fools as you think. The windows look down on a public garden, and I go out for a stroll with a friend, asking the occupant of the apartment to let me know, by opening a particular window, if they come. But we are so absorbed in our conversation that I forget to keep an eye on it, until suddenly there is a bandit whistle that could be heard a block away. (What must the poor customs officers have thought? That they had walked into an ambush . . . with all their documents . . .) I hurried back.

"I'm sorry I've kept you waiting."

They were all politeness. They had taken off their raincoats but remained standing; they were scared after that whistle. Any minute now they themselves might be tied up!

There was a major, a man of sixty or so, with a slim, apparently empty briefcase, who may well have been a genuine customs officer. And a youngish lieutenant, who was undoubtedly a KGB man.

We sat down and conversed for half an hour—and no one seemed to notice the glaring item of contraband carelessly left lying on the couch beside me—the Mondadori edition of *Cancer Ward,* which had just been brought to me.

The younger man: "Let's shut the door; we may be disturbing somebody."

(Two of my henchmen are listening at the door, of course!)

I: "What do you mean? Whom could we disturb? There are no strangers here."

The older man: "There are, after all, exceptional cases in which literature and the customs have business with each other."

He opens his slender briefcase, extracts from it a slender folder and hands me with malicious eagerness my "Record," but I realize at first squint that it has not been typed on my machine, or on any we have ever used.

I: "The contents of this are mine, but the format is not; how did it come into your hands?"

"It was intercepted at the frontier."

I (very reproachfully): "At the frontier?" (Shaking my head) "It was intended for home consumption."

He: "Just so!"

A pause. Both parties dismayed. I know nothing at all, about Strada or anyone else. I mustn't make a false move. Mustn't touch a piece unless I mean to move it.

This time, the older man deftly picks his own pocket and with exquisite courtesy hands me an envelope.

"And this?"

Four eyes bore into me. But I am not blind: the writing on the envelope is mine, and the return address is mine in Ryazan. So much the better: it shows that I have made no attempt at concealment. But now I must make my move quickly. It will look unnatural if I don't mention the name myself.

"You mean you took this from Vittorio Strada? Good heavens, you've done it now! What made you do a thing like that?"

The older man (with dignity): "We were observing normal regulations. The envelope was unsealed, you see. Now, *had it been sealed*, under no circumstances would we have opened it."

"What would you have done then?"

"We would have told the passenger to mail it in our presence."

(And of course, letters go down a chute from the mailbox to their room at the back.)

". . . But since it's unsealed we take a look, and when we see what sort of thing it is, and that it's from you . . . we think we'd better ask about it. . . ."

I flourish the "Record" at them.

"Tell me, have you studied this document?"

The older man (less confidently): "Er—yes."

"Are there many people working there with you? I should like as many people as possible to know about it. So that you will be aware of what is going on in literature."

The major tries to reassure me. "We-e-ell, not all of us have read it . . ." and succeeds, though not in the way he had intended. Obviously, eager hands have reached for it.

"Right, then." I move squarely in to the attack. "Do you realize now what is going on? Dirty work of some sort. A bunch of shady characters have sold a book of mine abroad. I am now trying to put a stop to this prostitution of Soviet literature."

"Why do you call it prostitution?"

"What would you call it? A Soviet work is sold, and appears over there in a garbled form—what other word is there for it? And I am not allowed to protest! I write to one paper, then to another; they promise to publish my letters, but they don't! So then I protest to *Le Monde,* and send my letter registered, with a prepaid acknowledgment slip, but it is intercepted. . . ."

"How do you know that it was intercepted?"

"If the acknowledgment slip doesn't come back after a month, what else can I think? . . . I put my hopes in *Unità*—but for some reason it doesn't appear in *Unità.* I can see why now! I can see the whole thing!

What have you done? . . . Whose game are you playing? . . . You must try and set things straight immediately, and send this letter on to Vittorio Strada with apologies, so that they can publish it while there's still time."

He holds his ground. "No, I'm sorry. We have our regulations. . . ."

I (smoothly and sympathetically, as though this were an ordinary conversation between Soviet citizens and fellow Party members):

"Comrades! I don't want to have to call you bureaucrats—I'm sure you know what I mean. I shouldn't like to think so badly of you. Yes, you have your duty to do, but you are also citizens, members of our society! Surely you don't take that attitude—minding your own business and ignoring what goes on next door. You have *your* regulations, well and good; but what about the *postal regulations?* Are they binding, or not? If so, why does a letter dispatched in accordance with post office regulations fail to arrive? All right—I won't invoke the Constitution. . . . But where's the sense in it? If the letter could benefit our country and our literature in some way, what was the point of holding it up? Nothing could be more stupid. . . ."

"How the post office works is no concern of ours."

"Not as *citizens?* You must concern yourself with all that goes on around you. A letter attacking pirate publishers was on its way to an Italian Communist newspaper. It would have been useful to the Italian Communist Party! Why did you hold it up? Merely because of the general revulsion which my name inspires?"

The elderly customs officer suddenly smiles as though apologizing for his epaulets, as though he has taken them off for a moment. (The expression he will wear when he tells his family all about it this evening?)

"Not in everyone. Not in everyone."

To avoid getting him into trouble with his young companion, I ignore the amendment.

"And now three weeks have been wasted!"

"Because you wouldn't come when we sent for you."

"Come on, now—was that the way to do it?" I find their summons and shove it at them. " 'You will report to . . .' Who uses that sort of language? The police, of course, when they order someone to report. I know of one old woman who got a notice like that and very nearly died —then it turned out that it was about her husband's rehabilitation: a bit of good news for her!"

The major is embarrassed. "Well, we couldn't come right out with it in a letter. . . ."

I burst out laughing. "In case it was intercepted? In case somebody read it? But if *you* weren't going to intercept it, who else would?"

The customs officer makes one last effort to return to his brief, and asks, as though by the way, as though it doesn't really matter:

"Did you hand it to Vittorio Strada yourself?"

"No, I myself didn't see him." (I had never seen him in my life.)

Still more casually and unemphatically, he asks:

"Who passed it on for you, then?"

This most innocent of questions is just the one I was waiting for!

Running my finger over the form they had sent me, I ask with a sarcastically sweet smile:

"Tell me, please, is it true what it says here—that you are from the Ministry of Foreign Trade?"

"Of course," they say, puzzled.

I loll back on the sofa, to show how much at my ease I am with these nice people.

"Well, then—isn't this *rather a lot of questions* for the Ministry of Foreign Trade to be asking?"

They are both quick to catch on.

"We're not Committee men! Don't imagine we're Committee men!"

Heavens, what a name for it! They couldn't say "KGB men."

Let's spell it out fully, then: "That being so, *the rest* cannot be of any interest to you."

Our conversation is coming to an end. In perfect mutual comprehension. But I must just insist . . .

"I must insist . . . I beg you to send the letter on to Vittorio Strada, as soon as possible! . . . At this very time our representatives are on the way to a meeting of COMES in Rome, and if this letter had been published it would have been so much easier for them to answer questions."

"We'll put a report in, of course. . . . We can't do anything ourselves."

And finally, in my most offhand manner:

"The letter isn't stamped. Should it be? I can stick one on now, if you like."

And they leave rejoicing, apparently well satisfied with our heart-to-heart talk, and without inviting me to sign a formal *statement*, or uttering any threats.

That's the way to talk to them! My witnesses were most amused.

A few days later, *Gulag* was finished and photographed, the film was rolled up into a capsule, and *on the same day* (2 June) I got some startling news.

*The First Circle* had come out in the West! Only in a small Russian-language edition for a start, to establish copyright, but the English version might appear in a month or two. And I was also offered an opportunity to send off *Gulag* in a few days' time.

We stretched luxuriously because our work was done! And at once the bell rang out. That very day, and almost at the same hour! No human planning could have brought these events so close together! The bell was tolling. The bell of fate and of history, tolling deafeningly—though as yet none but I could hear it in the tender green woods of June.

Sending *Gulag* would be a rash, a very risky, business, but opportunities were few, and there was no other in prospect. Right, I would send it. The heart had surfaced from one anxiety only to plunge into another. There was no rest.

But—two novels of mine appearing simultaneously in the West? A *double?* I felt like the Hawaiian surf riders described by Jack London, standing upright on a smooth board, with nothing to hold on to, nothing to hamper me, on the crest of the ninth wave, my lungs bursting from the rush of air. I divined, I sensed, that it would work! It would come off! And *our masters* would have to *lump* it!

All the same, a week of gloom and depression followed. A week of unlucky accidents that delayed the sending of *Gulag.* Everything would come to a boil toward June 9, the Feast of the Trinity in the Orthodox Church. The circumstances were such that I would not know whether we had failed or succeeded until several days later. I was already working on my next book—the final version of the authentic *First Circle—Circle 96* (because it has ninety-six chapters), which no one knows in its undistorted form. (What was published in the West was the eighty-seven-chapter version.*) But it kept slipping from my fingers; I could not work. In moments of weakness and distress it is good to tread closely in God's footsteps; to break off twigs in a young birch wood and adorn your beloved wooden dacha.* Where would I be in a few days' time—in jail or happily working on my novel? God alone knew. I prayed. I could have enjoyed myself so much, breathing the fresh air, resting, stretching my cramped limbs, but my duty to the dead permitted no such self-indulgence. They are dead. You are alive: Do your duty. The world must know *all about it!*

If we failed, I could still make sure of a few days, weeks, or even months, could go on working for a while, do one last thing—provided I vanished from the home in which I was beleaguered, and to which they would come for me. So on the eve of the Feast of the Trinity, I fled from my dacha. (I packed in a hurry; my brain was not working very well. This was not the first time I had known the misery of fleeing from my own home: how many must have done just this during the Civil War?) I slept in a safe apartment without a telephone.

A whole day—another day—and another. The whole Feast of the Trinity went by without news. My work was going to pieces. I was short of air, short of room to move. I couldn't even go near the windows, in case someone spotted a stranger. I had put myself in jail, except that the windows had no "muzzles" and I was not on short rations. But oh, how reluctant I was to go to the Lubyanka! Those who *know* what it is like . . . On the whole, I was on a firm footing. I had been allowed to get away with a lot. But I would not get away with *Gulag!* If they caught it on the way out, before anyone knew about it, they would smother it and me with it.

Not till the third day of the Feast of the Trinity did I learn that we had succeeded. I was free! Oh, the relief! The whole world was mine to embrace. Who says that I am in chains, a suppressed writer? On every side, wherever I turn, roads open up before me! I am freer than any officially encouraged socialist realist! Now I can finish *Circle 96* in the next three months, discharge a few small obligations—and the burden which has grown as I rolled it along year by year will be heaved over the hill, and nothing but open country will lie between me and the most important thing in my life: *R-17.*

*Litgazeta's* lengthy article against me (26 June 1968) was almost a moment of comic relief, a plump but unalarming summer cloud. I glanced through it quickly, looking for shrewd knocks, and found not a single one! How uninventive they are, how underendowed with thinking power, how loose their ancient teeth have become! I couldn't work up enough of a temperature to feel angry with the article. By way of self-flagellation they even quoted—after a delay of nine weeks—the letter I had written in April forbidding publication of *Cancer Ward.* How much time and effort must have gone into discussing and correcting this article in the secretariat of the Writers' Union and in the Agit-prop Department of the Central Committee, yet no one had perceived my most vulnerable spot: I had not protested against the publication of *The First Circle*. Why? . . .

He who fights and runs away lives to fight another day.

So that as autumn drew on, my two novels were due to appear in the major languages of the world. After the howls of rage over Pasternak, after the trial of Sinyavsky and Daniel, should I not have been cowering and screwing up my eyes in anticipation of a blow twice as hard to punish me for this insolent *double?* But no, the river of time had changed its course; after all they had done to curb it, to cage it, it flowed ever freer and fuller. All the paths I had chosen, all the moves I had made with my books and my letters, seemed now to have been devised not by my poor human brain, and sheltered by a shield which was certainly not mine.

For once the waters of Sivash Bay had not retreated. There had to be a first time.*

You cannot imagine a happier time than that summer would have been for me, as I so light-heartedly put the finishing touches to my novel. Would have been—but for Czechoslovakia.

Since I did not regard *our masters* as out-and-out lunatics, I had thought that they would not go to the lengths of occupying the country. For days and nights on end, tanks, trucks and service vehicles poured southward along the highroad a hundred meters from my dacha, but still I supposed that our leaders were doing it only to frighten the Czechs, that these were just maneuvers. But they "entered" the country and successfully crushed it. Which means, to twentieth-century minds, that they were *right*.

Those days, 21 and 22 August, were of crucial importance to me. No, we must not hide behind fate's petticoats; the most important decisions in our lives, when all is said, we make for ourselves.

In those two days I was once again choosing a destiny for myself.

My heart wanted one thing: to write something brief, a variation on Herzen's famous phrase: *I am ashamed to be Soviet!** Those few words sum up all that needs to be said about Czechoslovakia, or indeed about a half century of Soviet history! A few lines were quickly put together. My feet itched to be off, at a run. Before I knew it, I was cranking up the car.

What I had in mind was this: A number of notables, like Academician Kapitsa, and Shostakovich, had been wanting to meet me, had invited me to their homes, paid court to me. I am sickened rather than flattered by small talk in drawing rooms—which is always so shallow and pointless, the idlest of pastimes. But now—let me get in my car and quickly visit them all in turn, taking in Leontovich too—he is close to Sakharov (whom I had not yet met)—then Rostropovich (who had rushed upon me like a whirlwind in Ryazan the year before, just to make my acquaintance, and invited me to go and live with him at our second meeting)—and yes, I'll round it off by calling on Tvardovsky, and I'll lay before each of them my three-sentence text and my terse summary: *I am ashamed to be Soviet!* Come on—stop groveling! This is the most important choice you will ever have to make! Will you sign or won't you?

Well, then—with seven such signatures we would feed it to samizdat! In a couple of days it would go out from the BBC! And *our masters,* for all their tanks, would be dumbstruck, unable even to gnash their teeth.

But as I frantically turned the starting handle of my temperamental Moskvich, I felt in my bones that I would never lug the seven of them onto their feet. They wouldn't sign: their upbringing and their outlook were all wrong. The shackled genius Shostakovich would thrash about like a wounded thing, clasp himself with tightly folded arms so that his fingers could not hold a pen. The dialectical pragmatist Kapitsa would wriggle out of it by saying something to the effect that we could only harm Czechoslovakia and of course our Fatherland. At the very most, after a hundred emendations, and a month to think about it, we might write four pages saying that "in spite of our successes in building socialism . . . there are still some shadows . . . while acknowledging the genuineness of our fraternal Party's aspiration to socialism . . ." or, in other words, it's all right stifling people in a general way, but preferably not brother socialists. The other four would think much the same and contrive to warp my text in one way or another. And the result would be something that I couldn't sign myself.

The engine roared—but I went nowhere.

If any such message was to be signed, it would be by me alone. That would be the honorable and satisfactory thing to do.

If I wanted to lose my head, this was the best possible time: while the tanks were rumbling, no one would notice if they cut it off. This was their first real chance since the publication of *Ivan Denisovich*. They could polish me off under cover of the general uproar.

And I had the unfinished *Circle 96* on my hands, not to mention *R-17*, which was not even begun.

No, I understand these ecstasies of despair, and I experience them myself. At such moments I am capable of crying out! But this is the question to ask: Am I crying out against the greatest evil? Cry out just once and perish for it—yes, if you have never seen anything so horrible in all your life. But I have seen and known many worse things—*Gulag* is entirely made up of them. Why do I not cry out about that? Our past fifty years consists of nothing else. Yet we are silent. To cry out now would be to deny the whole history of our country, to help in prettifying it. I must preserve my vocal cords for the *great* outcry! It will not be long now. Wait until they begin translating *Gulag* into English. . . .

A rationalization of cowardice? or a sensible argument?

I held my peace. From that moment I bore an additional weight on my back. At the time of Hungary I was nobody, and it didn't matter whether I cried out or not. Now it was Czechoslovakia—and I held my tongue. It was all the more shameful because I bore a special personal responsibility for Czechoslovakia. It is generally admitted that the whole thing *began* there with the Writers' Congress, and the congress began with Kohout reading my letter aloud.

There is only one way I shall ever be able to rid myself of this stain: and that is if my words someday start something else, this time in our own country. . . .

I hurried to finish *Circle 96*. And by another of those coincidences that can never be planned in a human mind: in September I completed —that is, saved—*Circle 96*, and in those very same weeks the ersatz, truncated *Circle 87* began to come out in Western European languages.

It was the third anniversary of the seizure of my archive by the KGB. Two novels of mine were going around Europe, apparently enjoying success. The iron curtain had been breached. And I roamed at will through the woods by the Istya, without guards or leg irons. With my head between his jaws, the devil had missed his chance to bite it off. The wounded creature was whole again and firm on its feet.

There are a number of funny stories I could tell here: How the effete Victor Louis took to visiting my little dacha on the Istya with a squad of assistants to see where I stood, and how I crawled out from under my car, a ragged and disreputable workingman, to receive him. How he surreptitiously photographed me with a long-distance lens and sold the photographs to the West with frankly anti-Soviet commentaries, simultaneously, of course, informing on me in his capacity as a Soviet Chekist, and, I believe, planting eavesdropping devices about my property. How my neighbors, with their suspicious Soviet minds, came to think that I had a radio transmitter buried in the woods: why otherwise would I go walking there so often, accompanied, moreover, by visitors who were clearly the resident officers of foreign intelligence services? How, in the fulfillment of the contract so generously foisted on me by Mosfilm some eighteen months earlier, I made great efforts to get the screenplay of a comedy called *The Idler* (about our "elections") into their hands and how it was immediately passed "upstairs" to Demichev, and vetoed outright. How Tvardovsky, lusting for editorial conquests, begged the same screenplay from me, secretly hoping that it just might be publishable, and returned it with a genial smile, saying: "No, *inside's* the place for you, and the sooner the better!"

I was treading paths forbidden to writers on pain of anathema, while behaving with the brazen self-assurance of an accepted literary figure. And somehow getting away with it. The secretariat of the Writers' Unions of the Russian Federation tried to find out from the secretary of our Ryazan branch, E. Safonov, how I had *replied to the criticism* of my work in *Litgazeta* and in *Pravda:* they would like to take a look at the relevant document, it had somehow eluded them—and they could not believe that I had not replied at all. Soviet minds cannot accommodate such behavior, and it's been the same for the past fifty years. If you are *criticized,* you must repent and acknowledge your errors. And suddenly, there was I, refusing to play.

I was fifty that December. How often had my predecessors in the muted years watched in muffled silence as such anniversaries went by; even close friends had feared to visit them or to write. But the cordon sanitaire had broken down, the impassable barrier had been breached! To greet the outlaw, the pariah, telegrams began winging their way to Ryazan a week ahead of the date, followed by letters, most of them sent through the open mails, not clandestinely, a few of them anonymous, most of them signed. In the last few days the post office had been sending fifty or even seventy telegrams at a time, and on the day itself there were several such deliveries! Altogether there were more than five hundred telegrams and perhaps two hundred letters signed by some fifteen hundred fearless individuals, who had only occasionally camouflaged themselves (as "Shulubin," "the Nerzhins," "Ida Lubyanskaya," "Sim's children").

"May God help you to keep on just as you are."

"When things are hard, remember the debate in the Writers' Union."

"We hope to be your readers for many years to come, without having to be your publishers as well. . . ."

"Each man chooses his way through life, and I believe that you will not depart from your chosen path. . . . I rejoice that our generation's sufferings have at least produced such sons."

"Live as long again, just to spite the swine. . . . May every word you write give them hiccups."

"Please do not lay down your pen . . . please believe that not all of us are capable of loving only the dead."

"In the future as in the past, may you be the author only of works which no one need be ashamed to sign."

"You are my conscience."

"Everything that you have done gives hope of an escape from the terror-stricken trance which has paralyzed the whole country."

"To live at the same time as you is both pain and happiness."

"Praise God, you will not have to hear an insincere, hypocritical syllable on this day. . . ."

"We read your books on cigarette papers, which makes them all the more precious to us. If Russia is paying dearly for her great sins, it is surely for her great sufferings, and so that shame may not utterly demoralize us, that you have been sent to her. . . ."

"When I am not sure how to behave at work, I think about your deeds . . . in moments of despondency, I think about your life."

"Face to face with my conscience, it is a bitter thing to confess that I am silent though silence is no longer possible. . . ."

"I do not like traitors. You have just celebrated your birthday—well, in ten days we shall be celebrating Comrade Stalin's birthday. We shall raise brimming glasses in honor of that day. History will put all things and all men in their rightful places. In winning recognition in the West you have incurred the contempt of your own people. Say hello to your friend Nikita." (An unsigned typewritten letter popped into my letter box.)

"In you the dumbstruck have found their voice. I can think of no writer so long awaited and so sorely needed as you. Where the word has not perished, the future is safe. Your bitter books both wound and heal the soul. You have restored to Russian literature its thunderous power. . . . Lydia Chukovskaya."

"May you live another fifty years and may your talent lose none of its splendid strength. All else passes; only the truth will remain. . . . Ever yours, Tvardovsky."[1]

Let me scorn mock modesty and admit that I held my head high that week. Gratitude had caught up with me in my own lifetime, and I was conscious that it had not been lightly earned. On the eleventh, while reading telegrams in bundles of a hundred or so, I found a reply phrasing itself and gradually taking definitive shape, though there was nowhere to send it, except to samizdat, my usual standby, but addressed to *Litgazeta* just in case [Document 10].

". . . My sole dream is to justify the hopes of the Russian reading public."

I did not know that the day was at hand when this vow would hobble me.

---

1. I also, through samizdat, received such birthday greetings as these:

"Greatly impressed by your capacity to write the truth at the ripe age of 50. Beg you to share the secret with us in the pages of our newspaper. The Editors of *Pravda*"

"In your fiftieth year we have taken first place in the world for quantity and quality of output. We hope to continue collaborating with you for the next 50 years. Samizdat"

"Griddings! Dear man! Gret thangs for clerifying cerdain details my remargable biogravy. Not bed, not bed at all. Congradulations! Iosif Dzhugashvili"

# Asphyxiation

Carried away by my own story line, by my own plans and actions, I suddenly notice that I have neglected Tvardovsky's story, which is woven into the living fabric of this book, although I can say nothing about it except what I deduced from our meetings.

Nineteen sixty-eight, which began with his three-week letter to Fedin, was throughout a year of rapid development for Tvardovsky; his views and even his principles, which you might think had set firm long ago, unexpectedly broadened and deepened—this although he was in his fifty-eighth year. The course of this evolution was neither straight nor smooth (think of the *Grani* telegram), but still it went stubbornly forward!

When I saw Tvardovsky in summer 1968 I was startled by the change that had taken place in him over the past four months. Once again he had *summoned* me—with a shout into the black void, for the poor fellow had not the least idea of my whereabouts (though my Rozhdestvo was less than an hour by car from his dacha; if only he had known, he would have rolled down the road to see me a time or two!), or when, if ever, I would appear. "When will all this cloak-and-dagger stuff end?" he would ask, stamping the office floor. His exasperation, his desperation rather, need not surprise us. How were he and I ever to reach an understanding, to concert our actions? He had probably vowed more than once to bind me with tighter ties of obligation, but when I appeared, my willingness and amiability so disarmed him that he would relent and exact no rigid undertakings for the future.

I would probably not have turned up on this occasion either, but someone in the office gave me the news in confidence: Lakshin and Kondratovich had been told in the "Cultural Department" of the Central Committee that "Solzhenitsyn is as good as finished—Mondadori are publishing *The Feast of the Victors!*" Belyaev: "He will be torn limb from limb!" (By enraged patriots, he meant.) Melentyev: "Well, not torn limb from limb. We have *laws!* But he will go to jail." Tvardovsky had been very frightened, particularly by the thought that I myself might have let the play out. He still couldn't quite believe that I had no copy of it, and that only *they* could release it. (How they had yearned to see *Feast* in the West! How often the itch had come upon them to send it out themselves—but they could not bring themselves to do it, the wretches, because *Feast* might snap back in their faces and leave them aching and smarting more than I would be.)

I rushed off and reached Tvardovsky's dacha without delay—much sooner than he had expected me. He was delighted by this surprise, and received me with open arms. We sat down again in the gloomy hall where three years ago my peace of mind and my irresolution had perished together on a pyre of brushwood. I pretended, of course, that I did not know why he had sent for me, so A.T. told me the whole story in detail, and I, to his great relief, reaffirmed for the tenth time that I had no copy of *Feast,* and that it was an Agitprop provocation. (At this, A.T. asked: "Yes, but how can I read it myself?" and I answered: "Get it from *them,* damn them; say you have my consent." But no; he wouldn't.) I put some thoughts of my own to him: instead of turning tail and running home tearfully to A.T. (who had done an angry dance and put out a call for me), his "boys" Lakshin and Kondratovich, *Novy Mir*'s oh-so-nimble defenders, could have bent their brows sternly and given their answer right there in the "Cultural Department":

"Excuse me, but this is very serious news. Before it can take action, our editorial board must know its source and how reliable it is." In other words, if it is from a Western newspaper, give us the date; and if your information comes via secret channels, how do we know that you sweet people didn't sell the thing yourselves? . . . It wouldn't have been hard to think of something. Wouldn't have been, for men who breathed freely. But they had been reared in the service of the Soviet state, and Soviet fashion, as the *Grani* (V. Louis) episode had showed, they knew how to do one thing only: deftly field rebukes from above and sling them at others lower down. On this occasion, too, A.T. chose not to hear what seemed to him my utterly unimportant views.

All the same, everything else he said greatly pleased me. I had found him reading Zhores Medvedev's *Foreign Relations.* It was a surprise to him: "Smart lads, those two brothers!" Clutching his head in his hands, he told me how delighted he was with samizdat generally. "It's a literature in itself!" he said. "And there are critical studies and scientific monographs as well as fiction and poetry!" Was it so very long ago that anything printed *illegally*, without obtaining the approval of some editorial board and the imprimatur of Glavlit (little as he respected that body), had set his teeth on edge? In so many of my works that had taken the samizdat trail he had seen only dangerous contraband; and all at once, he had turned right around. I found that he had eagerly followed the samizdat replies to *Literaturnaya Gazeta*'s yelping attack on me. "Have you read Chukovskaya?" he asked enthusiastically. "She's done a good job there!"* And A.T. had decided to have nothing to do with Ryurikov and Ozerov (believed to be the authors of the *Litgazeta* article against me), and to travel to Lausanne by himself, not in their company as he was supposed to.

I'd heard nothing yet! As we sat there chatting, a sudden thought brought him smartly to his feet, in spite of his bulk, and he did not conceal it. "We've missed three minutes! Let's go and listen to the BBC!" Could this be Tvardovsky? The BBC! . . . It rocked me on my feet. He trotted to his "Spidola" on those big hoofs just as eagerly and impatiently as I had rushed to my set, punctually to the minute, for so many years past. This uncontrolled impulse, more than anything, made me feel closer to him, much closer, than ever before. If we could have gone another few versts together side by side, a frank friendship, without concealments, might have grown up between us.

"What, have you started listening? Did you hear what they said about your letter to Fedin?"

Eagerly, yet somewhat apprehensively: "They didn't broadcast the text in full, did they?"

That must have been when he started listening—when his letter was broadcast. Natural enough. But he had found the courage and the will power to cross his first frontier when he had sent the letter itself! Remember that this had been in the spring of 1968, just when the powers that be had recovered from their momentary uncertainty and had begun to tighten the screws on a public grown too bold, to tighten them in a very primitive yet very effective way: by "talking things over"—five to one—with all the "signatories" in Party committees and directorial offices, by expelling individuals from the Party or from their institutes; and the protest movement had petered out with astonishing rapidity as people who had learned to take fright easily resumed their servile crouch. Tvardovsky, on the contrary, had chosen *that very time* to dig in his heels when he might well have given way, and not only where *Novy Mir* was concerned (that was nothing new): for the sake of certain paragraphs about me he now sacrificed his article on Marshak, and held up a whole volume of his own collected works.

After the BBC news, he said, "There's a radio station you can take seriously—absolutely without bias."

Setting off for Rome a little while earlier, Tvardovsky had warned Demichev that "if they ask me about Solzhenitsyn I shall say just what I think." "You'll wriggle out of it somehow," said Demichev, cynically confident. But, A.T. now told me, while he was abroad people had treated him like an invalid, taking care not to mention his health and avoiding questions about *Novy Mir* and Solzhenitsyn. . . .

On this occasion I taught him how to duplicate letters with a ball-point pen. He was very pleased—"because there are things you can't give to typists."

We said goodbye more cordially than ever before.

This was on 16 August. On the twenty-first, like a bolt out of the blue, came the occupation of Czechoslovakia.

And I did not take my piece of paper to Tvardovsky. He would not have signed it in *that* form anyway, and he would probably have upbraided me. But note how he did behave. The big wheels in the CPSU, who wanted to bespatter as wide a circle of writers as indelibly as they could, had just sent two letters for A.T.'s signature: the first called for liberation of some Greek writer or other (their favorite diversionary tactic), the second told the Czechoslovak writers that they should be ashamed to support counterrevolution. Tvardovsky had replied that the first was inappropriate and that he would not sign the second.

Turn back a hundred pages: was this the old Tvardovsky?

I asked him in September: "If that vile letter appears with the impersonal signature 'Secretariat of the Writer's Union,' can I tell other people that you had no part in it?"

Tvardovsky (bridling): "I don't intend to make a secret of it."

(Three years ago it would have been "undesirable publicity"!)

"I am profoundly happy, Aleksandr Trifonich, that you have adopted this position."

Tvardovsky (regally): "Well, what other could I have adopted?"

What other, he asks! Why, the same position . . . the position that

*Novy Mir* was, at that very time, quite unforgivably and senselessly endorsing: "We warmly approve of the occupation." Adjacent columns of *Litgazeta* carried identical statements, in the same foul officialese, from *Oktyabr* and from *Novy Mir!*

In Czech eyes, the Russians were obviously murderers to a man if their one and only progressive magazine also approved. . . .

Let me remind you that in spite of everything, rebels were to be found in several Moscow research institutes at the time. At *Novy Mir* there were none. True, at a preliminary meeting of the magazine's Party group Vinogradov would not agree to sign their filthy statement, but his prudent colleagues, Lakshin, Khitrov, Kondratovich, sent him off home—so that a unanimous decision was obtained, and carried to the general meeting of the editorial staff. Still, even "Sovremennik" voted unanimously. How many *anywhere* voted against it? How many thought of anything except saving their skins? Had not I myself chosen silence rather than to cast a stone?

All the same, this is the day from which I date *Novy Mir*'s spiritual death.

Yes, of course, they were under pressure: there were telephone calls every other hour demanding that *Novy Mir* adopt a resolution, and not from the same old secretariat of the Writers' Union—they were used to that—but from the District Committee of the Party (this was a matter of vital concern *to the Party itself*)! No wonder they panicked! And Tvardovsky was not in the office; officially, he was on leave. So Lakshin and Kondratovich went to his dacha to get his agreement.

Tvardovsky was beginning to straighten his sturdy back, preparing —for the first time in his life! on a question of such importance!—for undeclared tacit resistance to those *upstairs*. How did his deputies see their mission, as they sped along the highway to him? What arguments did they take with them? If they had come to the new Tvardovsky with an ardent call to action—"Even death can be beautiful with the eyes of our brothers upon us, and maybe we shall survive with our pride intact!" (they would have survived—I feel it, I see it!)—a resolution could have been drafted in a few moments, and it is obvious what it would have been: plus multiplied by plus can only give plus. But given that Tvardovsky's position was positive, and that the product of multiplication was negative, Lakshin's position can be determined algebraically. Clearly, what he said when he got to Tvardovsky was: "We must save the magazine!"

Save the magazine! Give its cachet to a disgraceful public declaration—and the chief editor can pinch off his proud and lonely will to resist like a dewdrop from his nose. His feet were sliding apart—one on land, one on a floating raft. Resistance in his heart—surrender in public! Could that really save the magazine for long? Would the *top people,* with their vengeful memories, ever forget that he personally had said no to the occupation, but had lacked the finesse to publicize his views?

Save the magazine! The cry to which Tvardovsky could not but respond! Since, for some years now, poems and occasional verse had begun to flow more and more sluggishly from his pen, he had loved his magazine more and more passionately—and indeed it stood out among its contemporaries, those cabbage-patch scarecrows, as a marvel of good taste. This was a humane voice, a voice of moderation amid the barking of dogs. The honest face of a freedom-lover among that throng of fairground grotesques. The magazine gradually became not just Tvardovsky's main concern, but his whole life; he sheltered this cherished child with his own broad back and his own stout sides, he took all the brickbats, the kicks, the spittle; for the magazine's sake he accepted humiliation, the loss of a seat in the Central Committee and another in the Supreme Soviet, the loss of ex officio membership in delegations, omission from various honors lists (something that grieved him to the end of his days!); he broke off friendships, let slip contacts of which he had been proud, rose to ever lonelier and ever more enigmatic heights, parting company with the inert *top people,* but still not merging with the new dynamic breed. And lo and behold: his young deputy, so full of vigor and brilliance and knowledge—surely one of that new breed himself?—comes to Tvardovsky and tells him: You must give way; a straw must break in a strong hand.

A straw, yes! But only a straw. Well, brushwood too, perhaps. But no more—no, not even a healthy sapling.

Lakshin and I had met many times, but all our meetings had been brief and perfunctory (because I was always in a hurry), and we had never once been left to decide anything between us—Tvardovsky always made the decisions on my affairs. Lakshin and I kept ourselves to ourselves, and our conversation had never risen above tame generalities. I have, therefore, no firm evidence as to his beliefs and his motivation. All the same, I can't leave him out of my story. Relying on conspicuous facts, I shall venture to give, if not an altogether faithful portrait, at least a preliminary sketch.

I regard Lakshin as a very gifted literary critic, one who can stand comparison with our best nineteenth-century critics, and I have told him so on a number of occasions. He himself felt his kinship with this tradition and greatly valued it: he would pronounce Dobrolyubov's name with deep-throated relish: "Do-bro-lyu-bov." Like many among us, he was probably insensitive to the aesthetic limitations of all critical writing that cannot detach itself from a particular *trend* in social thought, and so never rises to the highest plane of intuitive understanding, that on which one great artist judges another, as Akhmatova, say, judges Pushkin. For a great critic must have a very rare gift: he must have an artist's feeling for art, without, for some reason, being an artist himself.

Lakshin follows closely in the footsteps of the nineteenth-century Russian critics. Like theirs, his articles usually contain no aesthetic analysis as such; they consist of social analysis, they elicit the hidden implications of the theme, they round out the moral portraits of the characters (all of which is very useful and necessary for the uncultivated Soviet reader). Like them, he has a solid grounding in the works of his predecessors, and quotes them often and aptly. Like them, he has his ways of involving the reader in a live conversation, and a predilection for leisurely, lip-smacking exposition, so that reading his articles is enjoyable in itself, and this is always a great merit in a literary work—although his deliberate and densely written text moves too slowly for the times we live in.

Again, Lakshin writes excellent Russian at times, and this has become a rarity in our day: many writers of articles, and for that matter of books, have no real understanding of the Russian language, and particularly of Russian syntax. One example (it amuses me to think that there need be no end to this literature about literature: here am I, the author, critically analyzing criticism of my own work) is his article on *Ivan Denisovich.* As he retells and interprets the story, the critic tries to remain within the lexical register appropriate to it. Thus, we have "to be on nodding terms with trouble"; "he was shamefaced"; "fresh as fresh." This is an artist's device, not a critic's. And here is another of them: Lakshin introduces himself into his article—sometimes as a representative of his own generation ("with green lights ahead of them, they pass life by"), sometimes as what can only be called a political accuser, expressing himself, however, with an artist's restraint and subtlety: thus, in the days when Ivan Denisovich was reporting for work in midwinter, young Lakshin "liked looking at the Kremlin walls—red, unapproachable, touched with white frost," and was busy cramming for a course on "Stalin's teaching on language." Such effects are never obtained by applying a formula: they were born of sincere heart-searching in the few months of Khrushchev's uncertain thaw, when it was possible to be lured into honestly believing that "it will never happen again."

If we give our critic credit for the diligence with which he obviously reads his materials over and over again, this way and that; if, further, we remember how magnificently skillful he is at deliberate ambiguity for the benefit of the censor, and at polemical irony when the censor is with the opposition, and he himself apparently bound and gagged— we shall be bound to admit that this is a critic of great natural gifts. Moreover, his abilities have been happily developed by long periods of sickness in his youth, which gave time for copious reading and leisurely reflection.

But the impress of our political life, those "green lights" and unapproachable battlements of the Kremlin, had also gone to form our critic's personality, his talent and his destiny. The university brought not only the systematic study of Russian language and literature, but an extensive course in Marxism-Leninism, and to obtain a good degree he had to push his beloved nineteenth-century critics into a corner and make room for the classics of the double-barreled-ism. (Not that this encroachment was so very painful: at many points the critics and the "classics" do not contradict each other, and in some respects—their utilitarianism, their social fanaticism, and particularly their uncompromising atheism—they are very close. Where they differ, a supple mind can always discern a bridging formula. The whole Vanguard Doctrine is then felt to be not a dead thing, but a spring at which the soul's thirst can be quenched.) Again, to do well at the university, to study for a higher degree, it was necessary to be a member of the Komsomol, and not an ordinary member, but one who made his mark in his academic area. This was a requirement that many of us kept before our eyes, even —don't laugh—the author of these lines, though not because I wanted to be a graduate student: from the thirties to the fifties it was the rule for young Soviet people who wanted to get on in the world.

But what next, after all this education? A literary critic is even more vulnerable to any rap over the knuckles from politicians than a creative artist. Is it possible to possess outstanding abilities and *nevertheless* find scope for their application? Nature herself protects her creatures, and equips them with the qualities they need for survival. The generation that left high school around the time of Great Stalin's seventieth birth-day saw no dichotomy between service and sincerity. In their minds the two concepts were intertwined. They could fill their lungs where there was no air. We see that Lakshin, at any rate, did not choke: he con-ducted seminars at the university, became a critic of some merit, was even in charge of book reviews in *Litgazeta,* and through his work on the commission to produce a memorial edition of Shcheglov—who had been lost to *Novy Mir*—he had drawn closer and closer to that maga-zine, had made friends with its editors, and had been noticed and liked by Tvardovsky, who decided that he would make a literary star of this boy.

Jealously, impatiently—as always with his best discoveries—Tvar-dovsky took possession of him and acquired a pen that added luster to his magazine. Lakshin, too, had made the right choice: he had avoided ninety-nine impossible situations and found the one place in which his talent could blossom in that country and in those years—under Tvar-dovsky's strong, sure, sheltering wing. Their mutual understanding rap-idly gained strength—and it was twofold: both artistic and political. Tvardovsky had always found great difficulty in harmonizing art and politics—it was as though he perceived them with different sense or-gans—whereas Lakshin always contrived to reconcile them neatly, al-ways had a quotation from Lenin on the tip of his tongue, to bridge the unbridgeable gaps. I made a note in April 1964 that "Vl. Yakov. [Vladi-mir Yakovlevich Lakshin] is more readily received by Tvardovsky than are the other editors," that he had easy access to the chief's office. Though Dementyev had been a close friend from of old, A.T. knew, with an artist's instinct, that Dementyev's formulas were nothing but dry bones, and that the magazine's destiny must be tied to the more flexible and responsive young generation. On the other hand, insofar as I can compare them from memory, the opinions of the observant, wide-awake and shrewd Lakshin always coincided with those of Tvar-dovsky, so that Lakshin often took the words out of his chief's mouth and neatly argued his point for him. (True, the workings of Tvar-dovsky's mind often showed in his ingenuous face.) I cannot recall so much as a hint of disagreement, let alone a real dispute, between them. Thus Tvardovsky was emotionally prepared for the replacement of his first deputy before the organizational thunderbolt *from on high,* and the blow was softened and easily borne. Very conveniently, 1966 was also the year in which Lakshin became a member of the CPSU—without, I daresay, doing violence to his general view of the world (although by then many intellectuals would have been only too glad to pull out of the Party), and only the hostility of the secretariat of the Writers' Union prevented him from becoming first deputy editor officially. Nominally, the post went to Kondratovich, mediator in chief between *Novy Mir* and the censors, and literary eunuch (though A.T. had not thought so when he himself had created the man), but the real first deputy was Lakshin.

We never know beforehand how new posts or new work will change us. It is not just a question of externals: the way you hold yourself, the look on your face, the shoelace mustache, the new walk, the formality with people whom you once addressed familiarly. Your critical talent itself undergoes a transformation, becoming in its second flowering a talent for administration, for circumspection, for assessing risks; in brief, if yours is a liberal magazine, that funambulistic talent without which such a thing could never appear. The *chief* is a poet and a child, and can afford to be artless alike in his anger, in his favors and in his lavish promises—whereas the first deputy editor cannot give way to impulses, but must be cautious for his chief, repair his mistakes, forestall dangers. Previously this noble work was performed by your predecessor, while you could permit yourself greater freedom, but now the hoops of Monomakh's crown pinch *your* scalp and you cannot ignore them:* should you find in your hands manuscripts by the two sisters, the late Marina Tsvetayeva's fiery "Pushkin and Pugachev" and the long-winded, anodyne, utterly inoffensive memoirs of her surviving sister, Anastasia, you will, after judicious consideration—"Yes, both sisters had talent"—lay aside the brilliant and dangerous manuscript, and the smooth one you will smooth down still further, telling yourself that to publish even this is progress. *Novy Mir* is the only guiding light in the darkness of our lives, and you must not let it be extinguished. For such a magazine, is there any sacrifice you will not make? Any lengths to which you will not go? *Here* and *here only* are literature and thought evolving, and Marxist-Leninist ideology, *intelligently interpreted,* is no hindrance at all— while samizdat, all those cliques of young people, those petitioners and demonstrators, are the stirrings of a putrescent mass. What makes your task extraordinarily difficult is precisely this: that rebels incapable of self-restraint are not allowed to air their views publicly in 140,000 copies. Which is why it is better if *you yourself* curb, convert, cut excessively hard-hitting and trenchant contributors. It is no longer just "our" magazine but in some sense *your own;* there is, there will be, no higher position for a critic writing in Russian, and you have attained it earlier in life than Pushkin, so be circumspect beyond your years, and for the sake of literature at large save this magazine from the blundering haste of the ordinary editor who thinks only of "pushing" his copy and will chance sending absolutely anything to the censors, even if it has an anti-Soviet whiff about it, thus exposing the magazine to mortal danger.

Remembering what I wrote earlier about Dementyev, you would expect the other editors to feel much freer after his replacement! But as Dorosh says, "No sooner do you settle down to a heart-to-heart talk with Aleksandr Trifonich than Lakshin comes into his office, the atmospheric pressure changes immediately, and you don't feel like talking at all."

A new generation does not always bring renewal of life's forms. (Just look at our country's leaders.) On the contrary: if you have to plan for many years ahead, you may feel compelled to seek stability.

What of our critic himself? Has he changed? Yes, as the man has changed, the critic has changed with him, though, of course, the One True Faith remains unchangeably the axis of his beliefs. What were merely regrettable patches of shadow in the early Lakshin (a Baptist's faith is "naïve and impotent" in comparison with muzhik common sense; but even Shukhov is "not up to" understanding the general situation in the countryside) now stand out like black stripes.

Here he is assessing the role of violence. He naturally asserts that violence, not self-improvement, leads to the historical heights. Noble personages, of course, do not always find violence easy: gentle, warmhearted people like Uritsky,* pensively murmuring Lermontov's words between two executions:

> No breeze stirs the dust on the drowsy road,
> No breeze stirs the leaf on the tree.
> Wait a while, dearest, the world is at rest
> And rest from the world awaits thee.

So unquestioningly does our critic accept the whole lying mythology about our recent history. The history of the past two centuries is seen in the same perspective. If Alexander II emancipated the serfs, after a fashion, and enacted certain other truncated reforms (the greatest in our history), it was because he was a "reluctant liberal," whereas his repression of the Polish rising (no reluctance there) and the jailing of Chernyshevsky and a few hundred (!) revolutionaries make him a murderer who deserved to be killed by a bomb. On the other hand, Nikita Khrushchev, who did *not* liberate the peasants, who did *not* grant a single thoroughgoing, liberating reform, who *did* (reluctantly?) suppress the Hungarian rising and the Novocherkassk revolt,* who *did* condemn *tens of thousands* to prison camps no milder than Stalin's, who *did* renew the savage persecution of religion—Khrushchev lit the beacon of the Twentieth Congress and so initiated the great progressive movement of our day with which *Novy Mir* merges its own unsparing efforts.

A man himself never notices how the movements of his soul leave their mark on his appearance. Nor does he notice how his writing changes. You spend so long preparing yourself, struggling up to the point at which you can write your long-dreamed-of article about some fine novel. At last you are there, your discoveries are made, you can write it—but your pen takes over and will do nothing but trace arabesques of discreet equivocation. Much of the interest in Bulgakov and his novel *The Master and Margarita* is "of course attributable to sensationalism." "Would you have me speak of his weaknesses . . . ?" (This "would you have me" will serve to convey the buttonholing heartiness of his manner.) You really want to know about this Bulgakov? Well, "the subjective nature of his social criteria and his emotions perceptibly narrowed his artistic range." "The portrayal of concrete social situations is *the most vulnerable aspect of his talent.*" (My italics.) Exceedingly feeble and faint, his picture of Moscow in the early Soviet years, wouldn't you say?) Then, from the aesthetic point of view, "perhaps not everything [in his novel] is smoothly and fully finished." Then again, from the philosophical point of view: "the Christian *legend*" is treated "just as if it were a real historical episode." Now, *everyone knows* that Lermontov's "Last Judgment" also "expresses no religious feeling whatsoever." Oh, well, perhaps an occasional "superstitious reader" will "cross himself." (A coy grimace to win the reader's good will and confidence.) Anyway, we are "true to the old Marxist tradition" . . . "communism not only does not despise morality—morality is the necessary condition of its final victory."

Does the article measure up to this novel, with its pirouettes of fantasy, its bursts of wild laughter, its tragic history of thirty years' concealment, during which it was almost trodden into the ground forever? Once again we see the imitative, old-fashioned, leisurely, roundabout way of retelling a story, the affected use of epigraphs (I've built up quite a stock of them: where can I put them all?), but are there any thoughts here that gallop like Woland's cavalcade? is there any attempt to read the riddle of the novel? There are none, and there is not. The perverse obsession with the forces of evil (and this is not the first book in which it appears: it is there ad nauseam in his *Diavoliada* collection), the affinity with Gogol seen in so many features and foibles of Bulgakov's talent—where do they come from? what do they mean? And how do we explain the extraordinary interpretation of the gospel story, presented so as to degrade Christ, as though it were all seen through the eyes of Satan: what is the purpose of this, how can we adjust to it?

"Steady on now," I hear Lakshin retorting. "Even for this article, with all its bowing and scraping, they nearly chewed my head off." True enough, true enough . . . but this is what worries me: It's not too bad if you only *write* that way, with your head meekly inclined, but what if your *thoughts* are no higher, no broader? In November 1968 I made all these points about his article to Lakshin, and this was his answer:

"I won't offer the excuse that I wasn't allowed to say certain things because of the censorship. I know how to say all I want to, censors or no censors."

And that was it? All he wanted to say?

So, now: the article is signed for the press on 19 August, the Czechoslovak horror begins on the night of the twentieth, and on the twenty-third, before the first copy of the current issue is off the press, and while the whole imprint can so easily be scrapped, a call comes from the District Committee of the Party asking for a formal gesture, a resolution, which commits you to nothing further, in support of the occupation, which has in any case already been concluded victoriously. Why not let them have their resolution? In which direction would you hope to sway Tvardovsky, as you drive to his dacha?

Perhaps Lakshin's thoughts were not exactly like this, but his actions were.

While Tvardovsky, who not long ago had thought and believed just these things, had begun to waver as the flame of faith flickered in him, begun to feel something of a misfit.

In those months in 1968, in which I was finishing *Gulag,* while Tvardovsky was so evidently acquiring a deeper understanding, seeking something new, I was first tempted to let him read it. He needed it—as an iron support. It would have saved him long, circuitous rambles through our modern history. But there were obstacles.

The lesser difficulty: I would have to take *Gulag* out of deep concealment, deliver it to him and live with him for the five days he would be reading it, never letting the book out of my sight.

The greater difficulty: The very first time he got drunk he would lose control of himself and share his impressions with someone, and my carefully guarded secret would leak far and wide. (Suspecting her for some reason of the same human weakness—inability to keep a secret —I felt unable to let Akhmatova read my secret works, even *The First Circle.* Such a great poet! My contemporary! Surely it was unthinkable not to show her my work? Yet I did not dare. She died without having read any of it.[1]

All the same, A.T. and I agreed that I should bring *Gulag* along sometime in November. When I arrived, however, he was out of action. He looked in, but went off again to swig cognac at someone's anniversary party, and suffered a relapse. Then he failed to turn up at the office because he was having some sort of storeroom for books fitted up in his dacha.

So I hid *Gulag* again.

A few days later, on 24 November, A.T. emerged from a meeting of the *Novy Mir* Party group in a warm alcoholic glow, full of benevolence, and rushed to embrace me.

"Is it all right for you to leave the meeting?"

"Oh, I'm not in the chair. I've put in an appearance, and that's all that matters."

Needless to say, he went on at some length about my beard. He also said, self-critically:

"When you are rich and famous, don't go in for bookrooms. . . . Still, what can you do with complimentary copies? People keep sending

---

1. I was wrong. I made a gross mistake. Lydia Chukovskaya has since explained to me that "A.A. was always on her guard against informers, and sometimes saw them where they did not exist. She was always aware of it when she was being spied on. She believed in the existence of eavesdropping devices when no one else did. She kept her 'Requiem' in her head for twenty-four years before she wrote it down! She did not keep her manuscripts at home. Political caution was a mania with her."

them, inundating me with them, every one of them hoping for a review in *Novy Mir*. My answer to them is: 'Do you know how *Ivan Denisovich* reached us? Through the hatch in the front office. And what's more, the author had absent-mindedly omitted his address, and I had to get the Criminal Investigation Department to help in the search.' "

A new legend, and not necessarily a harmless one.

Elections to the Academy of Sciences were held at about this time. Among the candidates in the Russian Language Section was Tvardovsky, but his election was prevented by pressure from above. He was greatly aggrieved. However:

"Seeing my candidacy in the papers is honor enough for me."

He learned from me that Leonov, too, had been sent packing—by the votes of physicists and mathematicians in a joint ballot. This pleased him.

But here was another cause for anxiety: a "provocative broadcast" by the BBC the day before yesterday had "changed the whole picture." What was it about? They had broadcast excerpts from his letter to Fedin, "and with absolute accuracy! How could it have trickled out?"

This ten months after it was written!

"How, indeed! You even made me read it under house arrest in this very office; you wouldn't let me take it away!"

A.T. (complacently, proud of this inspiration): "I knew you couldn't copy all seventeen pages!"

(He was right. At the time I had only managed to copy a four-page excerpt from the letter.)

He still hoped that "maybe they don't have all seventeen pages."

I: "The whole letter is in samizdat! It reached us in Ryazan—not from literary circles either; it was brought by some doctors."

"And have they got it all right?"

"Absolutely right!"

A.T. was amazed by the inscrutable ways of samizdat, but pleasurably rather than fearfully. In general, he approved of the BBC, and of the fact that they were broadcasting *Cancer Ward:* "Good, let them read it." He sighed, but without a trace of envy, as he told me:

"You're more famous in Europe than I am now."

I offered him a different thought. "In the army nowadays, if a man is seen with a blue-covered *Novy Mir* brought in from civvy street he's dragged off to the political officer, as though it were underground literature. Now, that's fame for you."

"Still," he said suddenly, "it's a beautiful bookroom, although it's made out of the cheapest wood, out of ash! Next time you come to see me, when you aren't in such a hurry . . ."

Had I ever not been in a hurry . . . would I ever not be?

He offered me money again.

"A thousand? Two thousand? Three thousand? . . . At one time they used to say, 'My purse is your purse.' Well, my savings book is your savings book."

I declined the offer. Now, what I *would* like is a 60 percent advance, instead of 25 percent, on *Cancer Ward.* I needed an officially guaranteed annual revenue; I had to know what I was going to live on.

He was embarrassed. This was more difficult for him. He would have to get it past his overlords, past the *Izvestia* accountants and, before any of that, past his young colleague the cool and cautious Khitrov.

"When Khitrov comes, he may think of something."

(This final payment, too, A.T. would arrange for me—"May as well hang for a sheep as for a lamb"—ignoring objections from Lakshin and Kondratovich that it might damage the magazine.)

Hearing that I had given Mosfilm a screenplay, he began tipsily wheedling me to let him have the thing, and without delay! Rather as though it were the forbidden extra dram.

I went to fetch it from my briefcase, and immediately roused A.T.'s jealousy:

"Are you on more intimate terms with the first floor than with the second?"

(The more important members of the staff were on the second floor, and all the lesser lights, together with the prose department, on the first, where I always left my briefcase, thus exciting A.T.'s constant jealousy.)

I removed the (separately numbered) seditious pages and took the rest to A.T. (Poor A.T.! He was always open with me, and I never had the right to be open with him.) An hour later, after the Party meeting, the whole editorial board assembled to discuss my *Idler* and A.T. immediately demanded:

"The *jus primae noctis!* It belongs to us! Warn Mosfilm that *Novy Mir* has the right of initial publication!"

This was before they had read it thoroughly.

But here's an interesting entry in my journal: although *Pravda* had chosen this very time to walk all over me, Tvardovsky and I *did not so much as mention* it in our conversation. Even to him, abuse from *Pravda* no longer meant a thing! Ah me, how times had changed!

After this, the next date that A.T. and I set for his reading of *Gulag* was the four-day holiday in May 1969. (Victory Day fell on a Friday, and was followed by three nonworking days.) I was to take him to my "hunting lodge," as he playfully called my dacha on the Istya without ever having seen it. But immediately before that A.T. had another "relapse," though this time he didn't sink all that deeply, not beyond recall. Hearing that Lakshin was going out to Pakhra, I rushed to his apartment, gave him a note intended to brace A.T., and implored him to use his influence: He must persuade A.T. to come and see me; it was important for his morale and to protect the magazine.

(Absorbed as always in my own affairs, I had no leisure for observation and reflection, or I would have seen that Lakshin, with his discreetly limited aims, must think my influence on A.T. ruinous. Ever since *Ivan Denisovich* I had been used to thinking of Lakshin as my natural ally. But this had long ceased to be so.) Lakshin's nod was polite and friendly but perhaps somewhat absent-minded. I saw at once that he would not try to persuade A.T. What made this more sure was that Tvardovsky might be stuck at my place on Monday—the Monday on which Voronkov would be making an *important* call to *Novy Mir*—and diplomatic expediency demanded that the chief should be at his post in the office when the call came through. (Tvardovsky was under silent siege. A new tactic was being tried: they were putting pressure on him, man to man, to resign voluntarily.)

Diplomacy, at home in meandering labyrinths, shuns the light of day. For that sort of subterranean resistance Tvardovsky needed the fireproof firmness to which zeks on the Archipelago are trained, and no one else.

No, A.T. did not come. I had smuggled out the book in vain. I hid it again—forever, as far as he was concerned.

This was the way we lived: we were neighbors in the struggle for existence, yet he could not read my work.

Patiently, deviously twisting and turning, Tvardovsky was trying to escape from the maze in which decades of officeholding, service as a deputy and laureateship had ensnared him. And naturally enough, he endeavored first of all to make the journey on that well-tried plow horse —his poetry. In the airless months after the suppression of the Czechoslovak rising, he wrote what was at first a number of detached pieces

("In the Hayloft"), which he then expanded to form a single long poem, "Memory Claims Its Due." He was finishing it in those spring months of 1969 when I kept vainly inviting him to come and read *Gulag*. Poor man, he sincerely thought that he was saying something new and important, breaking through a barrier that had halted all other minds: bringing mental liberation not just to himself but to millions of eager readers (who had in fact long ago stridden miles ahead of him!). Lovingly, hopefully, he went on correcting this poem in proof after it had already been rejected by the censors, and in summer 1969 he was preparing to *submit* it once again to someone or other *up top*. (What a strange fate for a chief editor: not to have the right to publish his own, his best-loved poem in his own journal!) In July he presented the proofs to me and *begged* me to write and tell him how I liked them. I read them—and my hands went limp, my lips shut tight. What could I write? What was I to tell him? Well, yes, here was Stalin again (as though he, poor lamb, mattered anymore!), and "no son shall answer for his father's crime," and later on, "the title—son of an enemy of the people."

> And still our country seemed to find
> Too few of her sons wore the convict's brand.

And, for the first time in thirty years, something about his own father, and his own filial loyalty. That's more like it! Keep it up! But no, he lacked the stamina, and collapsed almost immediately, telling us that his father, on his way into exile in a van with kulaks,

> . . . held himself proudly, stood aloof
> From those whose lot he was fated to share . . .
> . . . . . . . . . . . . . . . . . . .
> [and] . . . Amid the foes of the Soviet power
> Raised his lonely voice to praise it.

In short, a private, family rehabilitation. As for the rest of the fifteen million—let them rot into the tundra and the taiga? Tvardovsky no longer sought to make his peace with Stalin, but . . .

> Always he felt a presence beside him . . .
> *The one* who had no love of ovations . . .
> Whose image lives on to the end of time . . .
> He whom my Father humbly called
> His Teacher . . .

What comment could I possibly make on this poem? For 1969, Aleksandr Trifonich, it's just not enough! Too tame! Too timid!

In general, Tvardovsky and the editorial board over which he presided had an exaggerated idea that the pulse of progressive thought beat only in them, that they were the guides and leaders of public opinion not only in Moscow but throughout the country. (Yet what did they know, for instance, about the nationalists in the Ukraine and the Baltic States? About the affairs of the church? About the sects?) In the editorial offices, with several of them sitting in the same room for several hours at a time, they complemented each other so neatly, found each other so convincing, that in their minds they, the editors of *Novy Mir,* were the spiritual center, the source of energy, self-sufficiently in sole possession of the truth, while their authors were so many nursery plants from which no stimulating rays would be picked up.

In winter 1968–1969, back in my dark cottage at Solotcha, I spent several months timidly hesitating to make a start on *R-17.* By now the jump had begun to look alarmingly high, and besides, it was too cold to unwrap myself and sit around comfortably; so I strolled for hours at a time in the woods, reading *Novy Mir* as I walked. I went very thoroughly through a whole pile of them, more than twenty successive issues that I had missed while I was working so intensively, and I was able to form a balanced impression of the magazine. There was, of course, no more intelligent and agreeable reading to be had in the Soviet Union. It was refreshing, it toned up the thoughts. It was light gymnastics for the intellect. It was always noble, honest, painstaking (provided you leafed indulgently through hundreds upon hundreds of null or noisome pages by bone-headed hack-revolutionary, hack-internationalist, hack-patriotic hack journalists).

But this, of course, was to compare it with all other official printed matter. Where there was a choice between *Novy Mir* and something from samizdat, what hand would not reach first for samizdat's offering? With the development of unauthorized copy-typing in the sixties, all that was truly alive had moved steadily in that direction, but the editorial board of *Novy Mir* had tragically failed to understand this, so that Tvardovsky's deputies would forgather in his office and in all seriousness draw up strategic plans for the whole intellectual life of the nation. The least successful of all such attempts was probably Dementyev's article in *Novy Mir* No. 4, 1969 (which, however, appeared only in June). Though he had long ceased to be a member of the board, he was still an ideological soul mate, still a zealot for the cause and a bosom friend.

I must either omit the history of this unfortunate article or examine it in some detail. At first sight, it takes us away from the central theme of this book, but somehow it refuses to be passed over.

Nineteen sixty-eight had seen the publication in *Molodaya Gvardia* of two articles by the obscure and mediocre journalist Chalmayev (probably with someone cleverer looking over his shoulder) which gave rise to a protracted controversy in magazines and newspapers. The articles were a jumble of heterogeneous material thrown together just as it came to hand, barely literate in style, heavily bombastic in manner, larded with irrelevant quotations, and ludicrous in their pretensions: they would draw for us a "true contour map of the spiritual process," "give us our bearings in world culture," show us a "coherent perspective of the movement of artistic thought." These articles nonetheless, and rightly, attracted a great deal of anger from various quarters: the sound that had erupted from this mouth blocked by the false teeth of dogmatism could not be called speech—it was the bellowing of one who had lost the power of speech, but a bellow of longing for a dimly remembered national ideal. Of course, the ideal was wrenched into an officially acceptable form, and repulsively inflated with inordinate praise of the Russian character (it is characteristic of us alone to seek the truth, to have a conscience, to deal justly . . . ours alone is the "sacred spring" and the "light-bringing stream of ideas"); with slander of the West ("contemptible," "choking on a surfeit of hate"—while we, I suppose, have plenty of love!); with abuse of the West for its "early parliamentarianism" (even Dostoyevsky was pressed into service: his invective against socialism was redirected against the "bourgeois West"). Of course, the idea is decked in Commie-patriotic motley, with the author now and again rehearsing the Communist oath of loyalty, kowtowing to the official ideology, exalting the bloodstained Revolution as "a joyous sacramental act," thereby falling into a self-destructive contradiction, for Communist thinking seeks to eradicate all idea of nationhood (and indeed did so in our land in the 1920s). It is impossible to be both a Communist *and* a Russian, a Communist *and* a Frenchman: you must choose.

But the surprising thing is this: that in the midst of these inarticulate bellowings, words of praise ring out for "the saints and the just men born of a yearning for miracles and for loving-kindness." Some of them are even named, though not without inaccuracies: Sergius of Radonezh,

the Patriarch Hermogen, John of Kronstadt, Serafim of Sarov. Korin's
pictorial series, "Vanishing Russia," is also mentioned ("devoid of religious feeling," of course). So is "the people's longing for moral power."
There are approving quotations from Dostoyevsky, of a clearly theologi-
cal character—and there is even one cryptic reference to *Iz Glubiny**
and indeed one direct mention of Christ: how he "shook out his garments over the clearing." There is even (this is the best passage!) an
astute warning about answering violence with violence. The articles are
against cruelty, against the *estrangement of man from man*—how very
un-Leninist! Nor is it from a Leninist point of view that they take issue
with Gorky, and defend the *language of the spirit* against that of the
bazaar. There is even a hint that, seen in the millennial time scale of
Russia's history, socioeconomic "formations" merge, so that there is
room for several of them (the author is too cowardly to mention socialism by name). There is even a passing allusion to the destruction of the
Russian nation—not, apparently, at the hands of the Cheka and the
CHON but as a result of "bourgeois" development: at the hands of the
Russian merchant class, perhaps? He points to the impoverishment of
the contemporary Soviet village—its *spiritual* impoverishment, with
folk flocking in from surrounding villages to the cinema as once they
flocked to late-night services on the eve of a holiday. He takes pot shots
as well at "aluminum palaces"* and at Turgenev's Bazarov. . . . We can
pick out, list and evaluate certain thoughts in this and other, related
articles in *Molodaya Gvardia* that we should hardly expect to see in a
Soviet publication. We find:

1. A moral preference for "desert fathers," "spiritual warriors" and
the Old Believers as against the revolutionary democrats (the whole
carnival procession from Chernyshevsky to Kerensky). (I must say that
I agree.)

2. That in *Sovremennik*'s discussions the cultural values of the 1830s
were trivialized and obscured by a coating of propaganda. (Measured
against the "eternal" values, they are of course trivial.)

3. That the Peredvizhniki* failed to express the people's longing for
an ideal beauty and for moral power, but that Nesterov and Vrubel
regenerated it. (There can be no argument here.)

4. That in the second decade of the twentieth century, Russian
culture made significant contributions to the artistic development of
mankind—and Gorky (!) is rebuked for maligning this decade. (Who can
possibly doubt it?)

5. A people wants not only a full belly, but immortality. (If we do not, we are worthless.)

6. The land is eternal, and vitally necessary: a life divorced from the land is no life. (Yes, I feel this, I am convinced of it. As Dostoyevsky put it in *Diary of a Writer*, July–August 1876: "If you want man to be reborn and changed for the better, endow him with land! There is something sacramental about the land. . . . A nation can only be born and rise to maturity on the land, on the soil in which grain and trees grow.")

7. The village is the stronghold of our native traditions. (Outdated. Nowadays, alas, it is not so, for the village has been murdered. It used to be so. You would hardly say as much for Tsarist St. Petersburg. Or Moscow under the Five-Year Plans.)

8. The merchant class, too, was a vivid manifestation of the Russian national spirit. (Yes, no less so than the peasantry. And there was no higher concentration of the nation's energies.)

9. It is from popular speech that poetry draws its nourishment. (This is my belief too.)

10. An educated petite bourgeoisie has grown up in Soviet Russia. (Yes, indeed! And a horrible class it is, this immense stratum of shoddily educated mediocrities, this *educated rabble* which has usurped the title of the intelligentsia—of the genuine creative elite, which is always very small in number, and individualistic through and through. This educated rabble includes the whole Party apparat.)

11. Young people in our country are smothered by emasculated language, which lays waste all thought and feeling; by the time-wasting frivolities of television; by the hullabaloo of the cinema. (*And* by sport. *And* by political indoctrination.)

In short, during the twenties or thirties, the authors of such articles would have been bundled straight into the cells of the OGPU and shot without delay. Until 1933, wherever there was a breath of Russia in the air ("White Guard" Russia, as they put it, or "stick-in-the-mud Russia," as they called it when they were abusing muzhiks), people were executed, persecuted, exiled. (Remember, for instance, O. Beskin's articles denouncing the peasant poets Klyuyev and Klychkov for their "kulak sympathies.") Gradually they came to tolerate patriotic sentiments, bedaubed with red, swathed in red bunting, and above all, bearing the brand of fire-eating atheism. Nonetheless, if the peasant's (the merchant's? perhaps even the priest's?) children survived into manhood, however besmirched they were, however shamelessly they had perjured and sold themselves for the sake of their little red books, they were sometimes visited by an indestructible, a genuine feeling of national identity, a yearning for paradise lost. This it was that had prompted one of them to compose these articles, steer them past the editors and the censor, and publish them.

Understandably, in the months during which these articles appeared, the Soviet press, from *Kommunist* downward, blazed away at *Molodaya Gvardia*. "They were unanimously censured," writes Dementyev, "and there seemed to be no point in further discussion." But our Commie-patriots at *Molodaya Gvardia* even after the Chalmayev debacle tried to prolong the life of their hybrid of "Russianness" and "redness," that cross between a mongrel and a pig, which has the same validity as the "dialogue" between Communists and Christians (timed to end when the Communists come to power).

Perhaps nothing would ever have been heard, no mention would ever have been made of all this, and my sketches would have been several crowded pages shorter, if the editorial board of *Novy Mir* had not unluckily taken it into their heads to join in the hue and cry and commission the desiccated Dementyev to write an article.

Think back over the decades of Soviet literature—the spate of orthodox critical hogwash from all those Napostovtsy, Litfrontovtsy, Rappovtsy, the Literary Encyclopedia of 1929–1933, followed by the bureaucratic banalities of the Writers' Union—and I assure you that Chalmayev's articles will not seem the worst of specimens. Why, then, did they arouse such anger, such a lust to kill, in the editors of *Novy Mir?*

The emotional stimulus was an urge to settle scores with some of those who were forever harassing them: one of the dogs that were constantly biting *Novy Mir* had misbehaved, strayed from the pack— and its fellows were biting it. *Novy Mir* sized up the situation: Here's a chance for us to get a blow in! What weapon should they use? Why, Marxism, of course, the Vanguard Doctrine pure and unalloyed. This was very much in Dementyev's line. But at least one person on *Novy Mir*—Tvardovsky—should have remembered and understood the proverb: Don't call in a wolf when dogs attack you.

However viciously hostile the dogs, don't look to the Marxist wolf for help. Beat them with an honest stick, but don't call in the wolf. Because the wolf will end by gobbling up *your* liver.

But there we have it. To *Novy Mir*, Marxism was not compulsory ballast required by the censors. It really was thought of as the One True

Doctrine—so long as it was in its "pure and original form." Atheism, too, which was of the utmost importance in this context, was a sincerely held belief congenial to everyone on the *Novy Mir* editorial board, including, alas, Tvardovsky. So that the tone and the arguments of this disgraceful pronouncement (so shortly before the magazine came to an end) were not fortuitous, and did not seem misconceived to them.

*Novy Mir*'s original thinking, while they were still debating in the inner office and nothing had yet been put on paper, included some perfectly valid points: that "gang of crooks" was hysterically abusing the West—not just the capitalist West (Marxists, Dementyev included, did not mind that); "the West" here was a deliberate misnomer for every stirring of freedom in our country (Marxism or no Marxism, it was from the doomed West that support for these progressive trends was seen to come), a surrogate for the intelligentsia and *Novy Mir* itself. In the *Molodaya Gvardia* articles, the "foundations of the people's life"— churches, the village, the land—stood out in suspiciously bold relief. And in our country, things are at once so tense and so confused that if you use the word "people" approvingly, it is understood to mean "Bash the intelligentsia!" (80 percent of them, alas, *educated riffraff;* as for *the people,* no one has the least idea what it consists of); if you utter the word "village" approvingly, you are threatening the town; if you mention "the land," you are objecting to the "asphalt." Against this insidious, unspoken menace, with your specious internationalism for protective covering, deploying all the ingenious tricks of Marxist dialectics— into battle you go, Aleksandr Grigoryevich!

So then, easily detecting, with his professorial erudition, all that was illiterate and comic in the articles of *Molodaya Gvardia*'s ignoramuses (all very well, but heads lopped off among our people tower twenty-five stories high: should you wonder at this lilliputian gibbering?), *Novy Mir*'s critic charged with his battering ram into an old established breach, guaranteed safe and clear of mines: attacks on it have been risk-free since the twenties, and are welcomed by our rulers even now.

The critic keeps in mind the orders with which he was sent into action—to strike and to smash, never inquiring whether anything inside there deserves to live, concerning himself not with truth but with tactical advantage. He begins with older history, and cannot help shaking with rage when he hears of such people as "hermits and patriarchs," cannot suffer a word of praise for the second decade of the century, since it has been so sternly condemned by Comrade Lenin and Comrade Gorky. Although it has nothing to do with the debate, he twice pours abuse on *Vekhi** ("the renegade's Encyclopedia," "that symposium of shame"), because it is a habit with him, and because his brakes are poor. While he is at it, he snipes at Leontiev, Aksakov, and even Klyuchevsky, the *pochvenniki* group, the Slavophiles. What can we set up in opposition to them? Why, our science. (You and your science! Enough to make a cat laugh! Twice two is—whatever the Central Committee determines from time to time.) Still, the Party teaches us (though only since 1934) not to disown our heritage, and Dementyev's ample embrace takes in "both Chernyshevsky and Dostoyevsky" (one of whom summoned men to the ax, the other to repentance: he really should choose) and even Rublev's Trinity (also admissible since 1943).

Anything connected with the church sets *Novy Mir*'s critic more violently atremble than ever: whether it is corrupt "ecclesiastical rhetoric" (actually the highest poetry!) or merely a mention of "friendly shrines" and "melancholy churches" by the poets of *Molodaya Gvardia*. Think what you like of their verse, the pain it expresses is unmistakable, the regret sincere. A church is disappearing under water, and the poet vows:

> I will wrest you, I will save you
> From the surging water's hold
> Or clasp your wall and perish with you
> In the foaming deluge rolled.

"Not," says Dementyev, coldly and jarringly, "the jolliest of occurrences," but there is no need for "this state of exaltation"; "the religious theme demands a more carefully thought out and soberer approach." (More carefully thought out, you mean, than the demolition of churches in our country? In Khrushchev's time they even used bulldozers. Whatever you say about *Molodaya Gvardia*, it had, if only obliquely, put up a defense of religion. Whereas liberal, sincerely atheistic *Novy Mir* took pleasure in supporting the onslaught on the church in the post-Stalin era.)

The nature of patriotism is something else on which Dementyev leaves us in no doubt: it is not a matter of love for antiquities or for monasteries, but a sentiment to be awakened by "labor productivity" and "the brigade method." What an ugly thing is affection for your "little homeland" (your native place, the locality in which you grew up), when both Dobrolyubov and the CPSU have made it clear that your attachment must be to your "greater homeland" (the frontiers of your love precisely coinciding with those of the state, which among other things simplifies the organization of military service). And why should anyone say that picturesque Russian speech had been preserved only in the countryside (when Dementyev has been writing socialist jargon all his life—and managing very well)? Bah—the muzhik-fanciers even dare to prophesy that

> With outstretched hand, we shall seek again
> The fountainhead from which we sprang.

Will we, though? Dementyev knows we won't! If you must extol the village, let it be the *new* village, and "the great changes it has known"; show the "spiritual significance and the poetry of agricultural labor in the kolkhoz, and of the socialist transformation of the countryside." (Right, red professor, show us how you can work, twisted into a Morlock.*)

Continuing his tactical defense of Europe, why, Dementyev wonders, should *Molodaya Gvardia* object to the yowling of tape recorders in city backyards? Or the "insane ravings" of jazz in a Voronezh hamlet where no one reads Koltsov? In what way is pop music inferior to Russian songs? Soviet prosperity "leads to the enrichment of culture" (witness the domino players, card fiends and drunks we meet at every turn!). He needs no lessons in the art of turning things inside out. If *Molodaya Gvardia* assures us that Yesenin was persecuted, driven to his death—Dementyev shamelessly "remembers" how Yesenin was *loved!* (not by him, of course, as a Komsomol activist, not by Party and trade union committees, not by the newspapers, not by the critics, not by Bukharin—but loved he was!).

The really important thing is that "the Great Revolution has been accomplished," "a socialist order has come into being," "the moral potential of the Russian people is embodied in the Bolsheviks," so "let us look forward with confidence!" "The wind of the epoch is filling *our* sails. . . ."

And so on, ad nauseam; my hand gets tired of copying it. The inevitable quotations from Gorky, the inevitable quotations from Mayakovsky, all of it stuff we have read a thousand times. . . . Does he see a threat to the Soviet regime? Yes, of course—and this is it: "the infiltration of idealistic"—then, swinging with the right to confuse the opposition—"*and* vulgar materialistic . . . *and* 'revisionist' " *and* (to restore the balance) "dogmatic . . . perversions of Marxism-Leninism!" There you are—that's what threatens us! It is not the spirit of the nation, our environment, our souls, our morals, that are in danger, but Marxism-Leninism, in the considered opinion of our most avant-garde magazine!

Can this journalistic pig swill, this cold and heartless pauper's fare, be the offering not of *Pravda* but of our beloved *Novy Mir*, our one and only torchbearer—and in lieu of a policy?

You see how in our country and in our time there is not a single problem (and there are thousands of them pressed together in a twisted mass) of which we can speak lucidly, simply, without confusion. Neither of the disputant journals had set out its thoughts clearly, both had slicked over them with Communist spit and verbiage. And then the nimblest of the ghouls came on the scene: *Ogonyok* fired a two-million-copy salvo at *Novy Mir* with the "letter of the eleven"—eleven writers of whom no one had ever heard. Not—oh, no—in defense of the "land of their fathers," or of the "language of the spirit," but to drown whatever was left of the debate in political hysteria and denunciatory clichés: "bridge-building—the tactics of the provocateur!" "the counterrevolutionary events in Czechoslovakia!" "cosmopolitan integration!" "defeatism!" "it is significant that Sinyavsky wrote for *Novy Mir!* . . ."

Like an echoing howl! Dementyev, too, had written that Marxism-Leninism, and nothing else, was in danger. Don't call in a wolf when dogs attack you.

Then, with another tug on the strings, they contrived to place in *Sotsialisticheskaya Industria* (why there?) a letter from some lathe operator to Tvardovsky: "We want everybody"—steelworkers and writers—"to march in step"; "we want a Communist answer; any other answer the working class"—or anyway lathe operator Zakharov, its spokesman—"will not accept."

This was it—a *diskussia*, a debate Soviet style! Utterly uninspired, bogus, insulting to the reader, altogether typical of a press above criticism and therefore irresponsible. How degrading is his lot, what elephantine patience he needs, the chief editor of an official magazine, who must pay serious attention while an illiterate idiot critically assesses his contribution to literature—and how many years of Tvardovsky's life had been spent in this way! . . . This time he was clever enough to ask *Sotsialisticheskaya Industria* to send him *at least a photocopy* of the fake letter and to give him the *curriculum vitae* of the mysterious

Zakharov. Zakharov, in fact, turned out to be quite real; he was *the* lathe operator, the one who was a deputy to the Supreme Soviet and a member of the Central Committee, and who now went in for prophetic warnings: "He who does not believe in the working class will be denied the confidence of the working class." The newspaper also produced a photocopy, for a wonder—but what a document it was! Observe the confident (and justified) impudence of Soviet newsmen; no Soviet reader would want to compare two issues with ten days between them, so they had not bothered to touch up the single short page they now reproduced, and make it match the original article! Thus we read:

| *(In the photocopy)* | *(In the newspaper ten days previously)* |
|---|---|
| Dear Comrades at *Sotsialisticheskaya Industria*: For some time past I have been thinking of raising in the press . . . | Dear *Aleksandr Trifonovich!* For some time past I have meant to write to *you* . . . |

but have kept putting it off

| (no corresponding passage) | I am so busy at work, and voluntary public service makes constant demands on me . . . [The unmistakable accents, these, of a true working man!] |
|---|---|

But in a conversation that

| recently took place one of my | recently took place *on our shop* |
|---|---|
| comrades asked me [a comrade in the Central Committee? or in the Supreme Soviet?] | *floor* a comrade, one of my workmates, asked me . . . [and lower down he adds] workers like myself |

We were shown only the first page of this fake, and left to imagine the rest.

And there was no one, anywhere, to give them the lie! So much for the incorruptibility of a press independent of moneybags.

(An old dream of mine: Some photographer should put together an album called *Dictatorship of the Proletariat.* There would be no captions, no text, just faces: two or three hundred ugly mugs, self-important, overfed, lethargic, bloody-minded people getting into cars, mounting public platforms, towering over their desks—with no captions, just the words "Dictatorship of the Proletariat"!)

What was life like for Tvardovsky? Or for the other editors of *Novy Mir?* If I have handled them too roughly in this book, put it right for me—make allowances for their torment, their impotence, their defenselessness.

I, however, knew nothing about these attacks. I had read Dementyev's article, very late, in my dacha on the Istya, and groaned, and howled, and been very angry with *Novy Mir.* I had even made a critical synopsis of the article on a scrap of paper. On 2 September I went to the office.

They could think of nothing but this discussion of theirs (and of course, a skirmish in public was more enjoyable than last spring's attempt to smother Tvardovsky behind closed doors) and their brief reply to *Ogonyok,* which—although the reactions of a monthly like *Novy Mir* were inevitably slow, and in spite of the censors' delays—they had nonetheless managed to pop into the last number and release to the world. Tvardovsky was modestly jubilant:

"Is it an adequate answer?"

(There was nothing much to be said about it. It was moderately clever. And, fortunately, free from Dementyev's overpowering smell.)

"Yes; but all in all, A.T., I found Dementyev's article painful. You attack them from the wrong side. This desiccated dogmatism of Dementyev's . . ."

He was suddenly on the defensive.

"I wrote half that article *myself.*" (I didn't believe him. This was an un-Soviet characteristic of Tvardovsky's: not to distance himself from something under attack, but to cherish it more than ever.) "You know what *they* are—a gang of crooks!"

"I'm not denying it. All the same, you're tackling them from the wrong side. . . . Do you remember at Ryazan, when you were reading my novel: 'Go to the stake if you must, but make sure you have a good reason.'"

"I know, I know," he said, smoking furiously, as he warmed to the argument. "You're all for the churches! For the good old days!" (It might have been better for the peasant poet if he had felt the same.) "That's why they don't attack you."

"They can't even mention my name, let alone attack me."

"Still, I can forgive *you.* But we are defending Leninism. In our position, that takes a lot of doing. *Pure* Marxism-Leninism is a very dangerous doctrine [?!] and is not tolerated. Very well, then, write us an article and tell us where you disagree."

I hadn't an article, but I already had the preceding pages in outline form, on a sheet of paper. I wasn't going to put Samsonov's catastrophe aside to write an article, of course—but perhaps I could at least *say* what I thought? After half a century in which every illuminating word had been suppressed, every thinking head cut off, there was such general confusion that even close friends could not understand one another. These were my friends: could I speak freely on such a subject? I was always made so much at home at *Novy Mir* that I often hadn't the heart to spell out unpleasant things for them.

"Aleksandr Trifonich, have you read *Vekhi?*"

He made me repeat it three times—a short word, but an unfamiliar one.

"No, I haven't."

"Well, has Aleksandr Grigoryich [Dementyev] ever read it? I think not. So why did he aim two quite unnecessary kicks at it?"

A.T. frowned in an effort to remember. "What was it that Lenin wrote about it . . . ?"

"Lenin wrote all sorts of things . . . in the heat of battle," I hastened to add—or it would have sounded too harsh and could have precipitated a split.

Tvardovsky had lost his previous Bolshevik assurance. His new habit of self-questioning showed itself in wrinkles on his face.

"Where can I get it? Is it banned?"

"It isn't banned, but there's a 'hold' on it in the libraries. Your lads can get it for you."

We then went to another office to see the *lads* in question, Khitrov and Lakshin.

Tvardovsky was loud and hearty, though obviously somewhat put out.

"Do you know what? We have here the twelfth man: it's the "letter of the eleven" only because he wasn't in time to sign it!"

When the laughter was over, I said:

"A.T., it won't do. Are you saying that whoever is not one hundred percent for us is against us? . . . Vladimir Yakovlevich! You must find a copy of *Vekhi* for A.T. Have you read it?"

"No."

"Well, you need to read it!"

Lakshin replied quite calmly and coolly: "I—personally—just at present—do not need to."

(I wonder what his private opinion of Dementyev's article is. Those musty cantrips are surely distasteful to him? But if they suit the chief, it's not for him to object.)

I: "Why, then, do you abuse the book?"

Lakshin (with the same deep-voiced, staccato emphasis): "I—personally—do not abuse it."

No, of course he didn't; it was Dementyev.

I: "We always need to read great books."

Suddenly A.T. was standing in the middle of the room, huge and motionless, made even bigger by his outspread arms, and with a smile of disarming candor on his face.

"Well, *emancipate me from Marxism-Leninism,* and things will be different. Till then, it's on Marxism-Leninism that we take our stand."

It tore itself from him, this miraculous cry from the heart! Here at last we saw it—the vector of Tvardovsky's evolution! How far he had traveled in the past year and a half!

If ours were a free country it could be done: we could start another magazine, begin a public discussion with them *from the other flank,* prove to Tvardovsky himself that he was no Dementyev. But our country being what it is, the gray paw had ordered things otherwise: it had descended heavily on me, and on them.

Just as for fifty years now it had crushed and crushed and crushed all growing things.

After the stormy spring of 1968 I had been left in peace, undisturbed, immune from attack, almost too long.

I was awarded a French prize for "best book of the year" (for *Cancer Ward* and *The First Circle* jointly), and on *our side* not a word was said. I was elected to the American Academy of Arts and Letters, and on *our side* not an eyebrow was raised. I was elected to another American academy—that of Arts and Sciences (in Boston), replied accepting this, and on our side there was not so much as an angry flick of the tail. With so much spare time, and so few hindrances, I was able to get into my stride, to pick up speed on *R-17,* and even to work in the Historical Museum, a stone's throw from the Kremlin. (I obtained official permission, and all that happened was that the Chekists came along to see for themselves what I was doing there.) I also traveled about the country unhindered. It was so quiet for so long that I felt short of breath. That summer I did receive information from *my* "agents" (yes, I had as many sympathizers as *they* had paid agents) that preparations for my expulsion from the Writers' Union were afoot, but something had happened to put a stop to them, and a strange telegram had gone out: "Postpone meeting till end October!" Long-term planning, this! The Ryazan branch of the Writers' Union knew so little itself that a week before my expulsion it was issuing the special passes to which membership entitled me. They were given the go-ahead on the fourth Thursday in October, when the name of the Nobel Prize winner for literature was announced, and it was not mine! That was the one thing they had feared. Now their hands were untied. Sobolev pulled his bell rope in Moscow, summoned our Safonov, and the hunt was up.

It so happened that I had been away from Ryazan all through 1969, but had just returned to spend that month of drizzle and slush working at home, with help from the local library, on the most controversial personage in my novel. At that very time a portrait of the Personage had been installed (for all time) in the street right opposite my window. And things went well! Very well. On the night of 3 November I woke up, and my thoughts flowed freely: write them down quickly, you'll never catch them in the morning. In the morning I flung myself on my work with huge enjoyment, and felt that I was getting it right. At last! I had been brooding on it for thirty-three years, a third of a century, and only when . . .

But my Personage is a fighter, and has never been caught napping. At 11 A.M. there was a ring at the door, and a flustered secretary from the Writers' Union rushed in. Taking care not to look me in the eye, she fumblingly thrust a scrap of typewritten paper into my hand, announcing a conference on the *ideological education* of writers at 3 P.M. that same day. She left, and I could put in another three and a half hours' work—but why was it all so sudden? And why ideological education? . . . No, I thought, this has some connection with myself. I tried to carry on, happily working—but no, something was coming unstuck inside me; I felt that I was in danger. I abandoned my novel and took up an old file called "The Writers' Union and Myself," in which there were all sorts of odd bits of paper, records, of the struggle, mutual recriminations, reports to me from various readers on who had said what about me in public and where. It was all in a chaotic state, and I thought that I'd better prepare myself. So I quickly took scissors and paste, and mounted various items just in case. I also had material laid in the year before last for the battle in the secretariat, and not used on that occasion. This, too, I now pasted up or copied out.

In particular, I prepared for them on this subject of *ideological education* a few home truths owing something perhaps to Diderot. "What does it mean when a man takes it on himself to be a writer? He impudently announces that he is undertaking the ideological education of others, with books as his tools. What, then, is meant by the ideological education of writers? This is doubly impudent! So forget about *airing issues,* forget about *organizing meetings,* and write a book instead: if it draws our tears and leaves us wiser, we shall exclaim, 'Aha, that's the way to write, and we, fools that we are, are wandering in the dark! . . .'" I had it ready, but forgot it in my haste. They had left me very short of time.

I arrived at the Writers' Union headquarters in Ryazan five, or perhaps seven, minutes earlier than the appointed time, to grab a seat at the one and only round table and spread myself out with all my colored pens, instead of sitting with my notebook perched on my knee. (I had been expecting to be expelled for some time, and had intended to take a tape recorder to the meeting. I would have done so, but we were supposed to be discussing "ideological education," not my expulsion.) Apparently I needn't have been in so much of a hurry, even with my pens. The Ryazan writers always loafed around for an hour before a meeting—they had nothing to do at home—but lo and behold! the room was empty except for the acting "secretary" of the branch, Vasily Matushkin, who was sitting on a window ledge. (Safonov had suddenly fallen ill, gone in for an operation, taken it into his head to have appendicitis—anything to avoid disgracing himself.) Matushkin was a fine-looking fellow, with a round, good-natured Russian face, a pensioner, and it was he who in the days when Khrushchev had made me the latest sensation located me, hurried me off to fill in forms at the branch headquarters of the Writers' Union and told me how delighted he was with *Ivan Denisovich,* which was for him, he said, "an important lesson in the Russian language." I shook his hand.

"Hello, Vasil Semyonich! Is the meeting off, then?"

He answered solemnly, without getting down from the window ledge:

"No. It's on, all right."

"When will they be here, then?"

"They'll be here, all right."

He seemed depressed, and avoided my eyes. We were alone there, just the two of us: would it have hurt him to whisper in my ear what was going on? But no, the son of a bitch said nothing. I made polite conversation: I hear the oblast theater is putting on another new play of yours. . . . It didn't look as though the table would be of any use to me, but I took my seat there just in case.

And still nobody came. Until the very last minute! Then suddenly they all—and others with them—came in together, in a great hurry, and I didn't notice at first that they had all previously shed their hats and topcoats, which they usually did only in the meeting room.[2] They could easily have avoided me at my table, but one after another the writers went out of their way to shake hands with me, all of them: Rodin (he looked terrible, he was very ill, with a temperature of more than thirty-eight degrees; I asked after his health, and was appalled: "Why ever did you come?"); Baranov, the fox (just recently he was asking, "Can I give them your greetings in Rostov? They envy me the chance to meet you occasionally"); Levchenko (a guileless, simple soul, though a dull one); Zhenya Markin (a young poet, too far to the left and too avant-garde for Ryazan). And there was Taurin, representing the secretariat of the R.S.F.S.R. Writers' Union, respectfully introducing himself to me and respectfully shaking my hand. No, there would be no expulsion. And here was yet another happily beaming overstuffed reptile; he, too, made straight for me and pumped my hand with undisguised joy: this was obviously a red-letter day for him! I pressed his hand in return. But who he was I did not know. The rest did not greet me. They took their seats. Wait a minute—there were twelve altogether, only six of them members of the Writers' Union, the others all outsiders.

I had spread myself out—but evidently I would be doing no writing. One man was scribbling already, notebook on knee—perhaps a KGB man in mufti? Taurin addressed us listlessly, boringly. Anatoly Kuznetsov, he said, had fled the country, a disgraceful occurrence, and the R.S.F.S.R. Writers' Union was putting forward a resolution, they had initiated it through the Tula branch, where everybody was profoundly indignant (his face was utterly expressionless), and they had decided that it ought to be put through all branches. Procedures for checking

---

2. How they were all assembled and processed in advance was described in *Chronicle of Current Events,* no. 12, and I will not repeat it here.

up on writers who went abroad would be tightened and so would indoctrination. . . .

(I had long ceased to be a slavish pygmy, and my heart didn't sink at the thought that somebody might suddenly rap out, "Now let Comrade Solzhenitsyn tell us what he thinks. . . ." I had straightened my back, and would not be made to speak unless I chose. All the same, it was a silly situation to be in. What if they put forward a resolution sternly condemning Kuznetsov? What was I to do—vote for it?) Taurin went on and on:

. . . The branch meeting in Moscow had maintained a satisfactorily high level in its proceedings. Concrete accusations had been made against Lydia Chukovskaya, Lev Kopelev and Bulat Okudzhava. . . .

(It couldn't be avoided. I would have to speak up for them. Still, the cowardly thought flashed through my head that perhaps I need say nothing. After all, this was Ryazan, not Moscow, and it didn't much matter here. . . . If they had been simply liberal writers, and not close friends, I might well have knuckled under for the sake of an easier ride. But for them I firmly resolved to speak out. This was also reason enough not to vote for "the resolution as a whole.")

Taurin played his cards languidly, mournfully, as though none of it meant much:

"Hmm . . . something or other was said about one of your members too, about Comrade Solzhenitsyn."

And that was it. End of report. "Something or other." Obviously nothing serious.

Who would speak next? Matushkin. The old boy climbed down from his window ledge and looked sheepish. He was given a time limit of ten minutes.

I (with my own needs in mind): "Let him have longer; what difference does it make?"

The rest (also foreseeing that I would need longer): "No, no—ten minutes, ten minutes."

Slowly winding into his subject, Matushkin began his attack on me. (The text is well known.) I scribbled and scribbled, wondering all the while how they had brought themselves to it. I had been almost certain that they would not, and this false sense of security had made me impudent. Still, I could see clearly that all this would do them no good, that they were storing up trouble for themselves. Malice had robbed them of their wits.

One after another, with never a pause, my brother writers had their say: courteous Baranov, ingenuous Levchenko, the pure soul Rodin, Markin, hirsute and anxious. Even when he was actually speaking, Markin was obviously undecided: "I don't want to swing with the pendulum —first we expel A.I., then we readmit him, then we expel him again, then we readmit him again . . ." but he still voted for my expulsion. (It might perhaps have helped him if I had spoken sooner. The thing was that Markin had been trying to get a room for the past two years, and had been promised an occupation order for the following day. Levchenko, too, had spent years without an apartment, while Rodin had been begging for a place in Ryazan for years, and still hadn't been given one. Experience shows that this way, you can keep a tighter rein on people.)

I: "Permit me to ask a question."

They wouldn't. Certainly not. Not allowed.

I: "We have no stenographer. There will be no official record."

Never mind; they didn't need one!

The big-bellied man with the air of a victorious Napoleon began holding forth, and I interrupted him:

"Excuse me, who are you, and what are you doing at a meeting of writers?"

He was so taken aback that he burst out laughing.

"Who am I? You mean you don't know? I represent the oblast Party Committee."

"That doesn't answer my question. Who are you exactly?"

"Secretary of the obkom."

I persisted. "In charge of which department?"

All this dimmed his delight in winning: it isn't much of a victory if your opponent doesn't even recognize you.

"Secretary for Agitprop," he said.

"May I ask your name?"

"Humph! Don't you know my name?" He obviously felt insulted, humiliated even. "I'm Kozhevnikov!"

"Well, well, well!" It really was comic. I would have laughed myself if I'd had time. By Soviet standards it was utterly ludicrous: there was he, father to all in Ryazan who worked in the field of ideology, permanently stationed in the town, and I, who had been a Ryazan writer seven years now, asked *who he was!* . . . Anyone would be upset.

"Of course," he said, in headmasterly tones, "you and I have never seen each other."

"Not so," I said. "We've seen each other, but I have a poor visual memory." (There was no end to the jokes it played on me.) "We met when I arrived back from the Kremlin to talk about my meeting with Khrushchev, and you came to hear me."

When I became famous he had telephoned me at school and asked me to go and see him. I answered that I couldn't, I was too tired. So in acknowledgment of my fame under Khrushchev, he had dutifully trudged in and sat quietly in a corner. Later he delivered many sermons for writers—and I was always missing. (They were right to expel me. I was certainly no Soviet writer, no Party stooge!) Then a year ago he had telephoned me at home. "What is your reaction to *Sovetskaya Rossia*'s unfavorable reference to you?" "I haven't read it." He was amazed. "I'll tell you what: I'll read it to you over the phone." "Please don't; I won't be able to follow." "Come in for a chat." "To your private office, for a secret chat? No, I won't! Call a general meeting of writers and we'll have our chat in public." "No, we won't be arranging any meeting."

Well, he had got what he wanted at last. This was his great day. Hence his beaming smiles.

My expulsion had been decided in advance, but how was I to get it all written down? They called on me to speak, but I had nothing ready. My speech was pasted together any old way, and I hadn't read it through once. No sooner had I got going than there were shouts of "Ten minutes! Time's up!"

"What do you mean, ten minutes? It's a matter of life and death! You must give me all the time I need!"

Matushkin (in his unctuous old man's voice): "Give him three minutes more."

I extorted another ten, and rushed through my speech at machinegun speed. Only what I managed to say there could be released to the world at large next day. What went unsaid, however striking it might be, would go nowhere, make no impact. Never mind, I said quite a lot in twenty minutes. I could see that Markin was delighted as he listened to me hammering them, and Rodin, too, enjoyed himself in spite of his illness and his fever. They were both pleased that someone at least was putting up some resistance.

But they voted—obediently.

While I had the pleasure of voting against the resolution "as a whole." (Only one little point in it referred to me.)

The meeting broke up and they chatted cheerfully along the corridors. I collected my pencils and dashed out—but Taurin caught me, all politeness and sympathy.

"I strongly advise you to go up and see the secretariat right away. Tomorrow they have their plenary meeting, and it would be *in your own best interest.*"

I: "Nowhere in the statutes does it say that a member can be expelled within twenty-four hours. I can leave it awhile."

(My unspoken thought was: Just give me time to spread the news, and release my "Record" as quickly as I can, and we'll see what sort of meeting you'll have. I was sure in any case that they could not expel me in absentia. But oh, yes, they could! All things are possible in our country!)

"Listen," said Taurin, clutching at my sleeve. "Nobody wants to see you expelled! Just you write that little bit of paper; that's all that's required of you—a little bit of paper to say how indignant you are about the way people in the West . . ."

Perhaps they were really counting on it? As a present for the October anniversary? Without it, there was certainly no point in expelling me, except as an act of vengeance. As long as they did not expel me, the situation seemed to favor them: the six-thousand-strong Writers' Union hung poised over my head like a great boulder and did not crush me out of compassion, though whenever it wished to it could. But supposing they expelled me and I survived—what then?

Markin also buttonholed me in the corridor and loudly begged forgiveness. (This was pure Dostoyevsky. On a number of other occasions he would express his contrition, weep, go down on his knees, and again forswear himself: he truly suffered, in spirit he was truly on my side, but the flesh was weak.) But I hurried off as fast as I could to a telephone office. Ryazan was a trap; they could easily smother me altogether in Ryazan. I must make sure that the news burst like a bombshell over Moscow: that was my only hope of salvation. We had only one coin-operated telephone for intercity calls in Ryazan, and if that was out of order . . . It wasn't, and there was no queue. . . . I dialed a number. Nobody there. I dialed another. No answer. To whom should I telephone? To *Novy Mir!* It wasn't five o'clock yet, and they wouldn't have left the office. And that is what I did. (Mean-spirited persons would later claim that the *Novy Mir* board was dismissed for this very reason.)

Then, feeling calmer, I returned home and sat down to write my

"Record." I woke at six next morning, switched on the Voice of America as usual, expecting nothing in particular—and jumped as if I had been stung.

"According to private information from Moscow, Aleksandr Solzhenitsyn was yesterday expelled from the writers' organization in his home town, Ryazan."

Well! The age of information! No, I hadn't expected this so extraordinarily soon!

They broadcast it four times in brief news summaries, and four times in extended news programs. Good, good, good. I went out into the public garden to do my morning exercises before there was anyone about, and looked around. There in a snowdrift stood the convertible truck I had noticed once before when I was under surveillance, with a couple of them sitting in the unlit cab. I walked close to the cab as I passed and inspected it: they had no radio and didn't know that they had missed this chance.

All the same, I was worried: they might just *grab* me. As soon as you move away from Moscow you are in a sheer well, and it is the easiest thing in the world to stop up the only air hole.

With many precautions, I posted one copy of the "Record" to safety. [Document 11]

It got light. I pulled back the curtains, and from the billboard across the street the Personage whom I had secretly adopted gave me a bright, bold look from under his cap. But I couldn't manage to write any more about him, and that was the most painful thing of all: to be torn away from such pages! (That was eighteen months ago, and I still can't get back to it. My Personage has shown me that he can look after himself.)

There was a rumpus in the Ryazan obkom! As they saw it: "The BBC is already broadcasting the news of Solzhenitsyn's expulsion. Clearly, they must have agents in Ryazan, observing ideological life and able to report instantly to London." The best they could think of was to plant the same homeless Levchenko by a telephone to tell all callers from Moscow that it had nothing to do with him, that he knew nothing about it, but that no one had been expelled. Western correspondents did call up, pounced on the news, believed it—and *denials* began to be heard from Western stations. But that very same day, 5 November, the secretariat of the R.S.F.S.R. Writers' Union did indeed expel me, managing very well without my assistance!

For another two days I was unaware of this myself and had no thought of writing and disseminating anything except the "Record." Only when I found out did my anger mount, and lines more bitter than any I had earlier hurled at the Union of Writers etched themselves unaided: there was no conscious planning, no calculated maneuver in this; it simply happened. (My only conscious motive was a parallel one: to defend Lydia Chukovskaya and Kopelev, who were under threat. Their names were woven neatly into the text, and I think my defense was a success: the devil's company stumbled and halted.)

I sent the "Record" on ahead to Moscow, and tried to continue work on my Personage in Ryazan, but I had lost my peace of mind and my appetite for it, and the lines of my thunderous letter marched through my head, pounded at the wall of my ribs in their eagerness for battle. When the November holidays were over and there was a little more room in the trains, I went to Moscow. I did not yet realize that I was moving permanently. That I was fated to live in Ryazan no longer, that by expelling me they had closed—locked, bolted and barred—that city to me. (When I was occasionally forced to return I would go over to my desk—and through the window from the billboard over the street the Personage in the flat cap squinted at me as of old. For a whole year, two years, in all weather; there he loomed before my deserted window. Excessive fame is an unenviable thing. I went away again, and he was left behind.)

Meanwhile in Moscow, A.T. could not wait to see me. (Something else had helped to make us still firmer friends. He had read the twelve sample chapters, about the Samsonov catastrophe, in October, had been extremely pleased with them, had praised them greatly, and was already enjoying editorial pleasures to come: I would finish it, and it would all be *viable*, patriotic, and this time no one would stop us, Solzhenitsyn would be published in *Novy Mir,* and life would be marvelous! I didn't tell him how thorny future parts of *August 1914* would be. He would not, could not believe that a discovery and a favorite author of his could be *unviable* forever.) On the eve of my departure Tvardovsky had pressed me to come as soon as possible: he needed to talk, mainly about himself, not me. That motif again! That urge to open old wounds. I had heard the same thing after he had read *The First Circle.*

On 11 November I went straight from the train to *Novy Mir.* The whole editorial board was sitting in A.T.'s office, and some of them had my "Record" before them. They had just had it read out to them, and discussed it. As though at a word of command, they all rose and left the two of us together. (That was normal at *Novy Mir,* a mark of respect for rank. They never waited for A.T. to say, "We want to talk privately.") A.T. ordered tea with biscuits and crackers—the utmost limit of *Novy Mir*'s hospitality.

Wrongly assuming that A.T.'s civic courage was less than full strength, I began to explain why I had not got to the meeting of the secretariat: they had in fact not sent for me, only notified me indirectly, and too late at that. But I found that A.T. needed no convincing. He had thought it too demeaning to go himself. (Oh, those rumors! It was all over Moscow that he had been present and defended me fiercely.)

What he did anxiously inquire about (not for the first time) was money from the West: Could it be true that I was receiving money for Western editions of my novels?

Anathema, anathema, anathema! To the Soviet mind, those who *think otherwise* must certainly have sold themselves for enemy money. If you aren't paid in Soviet coin, die like a patriot, don't take a kopeck from the West!

I: "Not only for the novels. Some has come from the Norwegians for *Ivan Denisovich,* but I'm not picking that up for the time being either. Those tripehounds at the Writers' Union just cannot imagine a man living modestly."

A.T. brightens up. He praises the "Record." But there's another worry: How could it have been possible for my "readers and admirers" to bring him the very same "Record" yesterday?

"Why, because I released it."

He looked almost frightened. How could I? *They* would be furious! (Upstairs, that is.)

My "Open Letter to the Secretariat," all ready for use, is impatiently biding its time in my briefcase. That's an idea! While A.T. is so unbuttoned and responsive, while we are in the same frame of mind, why not . . . ? But no, I dare not show it to him, remembering how often he has held me back and vetoed my plans. All the same, I'll prepare him for it.

"A.T.! You are my friend and well-wisher, but your advice is always grounded in the experience of a bygone age. If, for instance, I had consulted you at the time about sending my letter to the congress, or releasing *Cancer Ward* and *The First Circle,* you would have tried your hardest to dissuade me." (That was putting it mildly! He would have broken his plate-glass desktop over my head.) "But I was right, you know!"

That's an old story, and he can accept it. But I dare not tell him the latest. I can only say:

"Try to understand. It's the only way! Camp experience tells me that the rougher you are with stoolies, the safer you are. You must never appear to acquiesce. If I hold my peace they'll wait a few months and quietly make a meal of me—for having no residence permit, for parasitism, or on some other piffling excuse. But if I make a loud enough noise, their position will be weaker."

Tvardovsky: "Yes, but what are you hoping for? All those 'admiring readers' only play at supporting you. They sigh hypocritically over your expulsion and immediately change the subject. I believe that it's not just a pose when you say you're prepared to die. But what's the use of that; it wouldn't change anything."

If my memory didn't deceive me, it wasn't the first time we had balanced on this seesaw. Only today, instead of bad temper, there was sad solicitude on both sides. And something else. Was it just that we had never felt such warm affection for each other as we did that day? No; there had often been warmth, but there had never been such a sense of equality. For the first time in the eight years since we had known each other I found myself really talking to him as an equal, as a friend.

I: "Let's suppose that it's so. My sacrifice would go for nothing just now. But in the distant future it would have its effect just the same. Though I myself think that it would win support right now."

(I really did think so. I had been spoiled by the support of the hundred writers for my letter to the congress. With my usual overoptimism, my usual premature assumption of success, I expected another mass movement among the writers, a battle, perhaps a mass exodus from the Writers' Union. But none of this was to be. There was no real persecution, there were no arrests, no thunderbolts; still, people were tired and had lost all urge to resist. Seventeen members of the Writers' Union wrote protests varying in volume and vehemence, and eight called on Voronkov in an attempt to frighten him. They were subsequently hauled along to the Central Committee offices, one by one, for chastisement.

A.T.: "At present the waters are receding, leaving shattered stumps and broken reeds exposed. It's a sordid picture."

I: *"Where water has been it will be again."*

What of the talk we were to have about A.T. himself? Here it came at last. To me, losing my membership in the Writers' Union had been a purely formal matter, and in fact a relief, but Tvardovsky was facing a greater tragedy—one that would cut him to the soul. The inevitable day when he would have to abandon his favorite child, *Novy Mir,* was approaching. My expulsion he saw as the last straw. The last but one had been a call from a minor Central Committee official who wanted to come and "do something about" the composition of the editorial board. (Why, when nobody had sent for him? Evidently to oust Lakshin, Khitrov and Kondratovich.)

Religious people of a contemplative disposition never cease to reflect, even at the supreme moments in their lives, on the inevitability of death. In much the same way A.T. had often spoken to me of resigning, even when they had done no more than deny me a Lenin Prize, even when we all seemed to be riding with Khrushchev on the crest of the wave. On each occasion I had tried, and this time (carrying my chair around his big chairman's desk to set it beside his armchair) I tried more strenuously than ever to dissuade him. *Novy Mir* was preserving our cultural tradition; *Novy Mir* was the only honest witness to the times we lived in; there were two or three good articles in every issue, and even one would be enough to redeem all the rest—one like Likhachev's "The Future of Literature," for instance. . . . A.T. cheered up immediately, shook off his depression, and we talked enjoyably for a while about Likhachev's article. And the things he would have to give up! There were, for instance, the memoirs of someone who had taken part in the 1921 peasant rising in Siberia. ("Will you let me read them?" "Of course." We were as thick as thieves again, just as we were at the beginning of the time of *Ivan Denisovich.*)

"But I can't lower myself to the extent of editing Rekemchuk," A.T. kept repeating. "I've stood my ground while I could, but now I'm getting wobbly, I'm cracking, I'm knocked off my pins."

I: "You're not finished yet! Why do you want to hand it to them on a platter? Why leave voluntarily? Let them do their own dirty work."

We agreed that if they didn't touch Lakshin, Khitrov and Kondratovich he would stay, but if they were removed he would go.

I said goodbye. We had talked like bosom friends—and all the time I had had a knife in my boot. I could not possibly have shown it to him; it would have ruined everything.

"Aleksandr Trifonovich," I said cheerfully. "If I should be forced to do something rather drastic, don't take it too much to heart. Just tell them I'm not your son, and you haven't pledged your life for me."

I looked in on Lakshin too. A possible shock-absorber.

"Vladimir Yakovlevich," I said. "Please do your best to mollify A.T., just in case. . . ."

An unwavering stare through his youthful glasses was all I got from Lakshin. And a nod.

No, he wouldn't do it. He had his own problem, and charity begins at home. Why should he cross an irate A.T. at such a moment? My road was not his, and I was not his ally.

Next day, a week late, the blow fell! The secretariat announced its decision.

And without hesitation I struck back! All I had to do was write in the date. And off it would go! [Document 12]

Boris Mozhayev (who behaved splendidly, as he always did when *Novy Mir* was in trouble) was at heart as defiantly free as a river pirate, but he had grown accustomed over the years to looking for compromise solutions. He hung on to me and wouldn't let go:

"You can't possibly send such a letter! Why burn your bridges? Wouldn't it be better to make a formal appeal to the U.S.S.R. secretariat against the decision of the secretariat of the R.S.F.S.R. Writers' Union, and go along to get your case examined?"

"Too late, Borya; you couldn't hold me back with a locomotive."

He laughed. "You're like one of those quick-tempered Polish squires, always spoiling for a fight."

Well, in my opinion it's the most Russian thing imaginable to take a swing and—wham! For one brief moment you feel yourself to be a worthy son of your country. Brave? I'm not brave. There's no one more timid. I have written *Gulag*, but I keep it quiet; I know something about the camps as they now are, but I don't say anything; I kept quiet about Czechoslovakia, and for that alone I must drag myself into action now. What Lydia Chukovskaya once said about political protests was right:

"If I don't do it, I can't write about the things that matter. Until I pull this arrow out of my breast, I can think of nothing else!"

I felt just the same. When all around were so faint-hearted, what sort of man would I be if I left without slamming the door? (Those who needed to justify their own behavior would spread an apologetic rumor: His own high-handedness made it impossible for us to take his part—

we were about to do so when he slammed the door and spoiled every-thing! Once he had mocked "class struggle," you couldn't really stand up for him. . . . This, of course, was just an excuse; those who wanted to help had been quicker about it.)

Once it was sent off, I felt calm and relaxed. That day two flatfooted sleuthhounds were set on my trail around the streets of Moscow, but I did not notice them following me out of town to the blessed asylum that Rostropovich had offered me (right in the heart of the *special zone,* next door to the dachas of all the leaders!). Here (although various "gasmen" and "electricians" turned up from time to time) I felt that no one could see me, no one knew anything about me. I kept out of sight, and made no telephone calls. Back in Moscow my letter would stir up a storm, but here there was healing quiet—and radio reception was so clear that I could pick up the repercussions of my letter, and think hard about what I had done. And also start working.

This refuge, offered by Rostropovich, was the biggest present I remember ever receiving. He had invited me before, in 1968, but I had been rather afraid of inconveniencing him. Anyway, there couldn't have been a more appropriate time than 1969 for me to move and make a new home. What would I have been doing now in a rattrap like Ryazan? Where could I have rested from my wand-erings in the crush and din of Moscow? How long would my resolve have held? But here, in the incomparable peace and quiet of the special zone (where *they* live, there are neither loudspeakers nor tractors to be heard), under the pure trees and the pure stars, it was easy to be firm and keep calm.

This is not the first time that Rostropovich has rapped on these covers for entry. But it's impossible. These sketches are distended to the bursting point already, and Rostropovich has life and color enough for ten. It would be a pity to describe him cursorily.

So carefully did he guard me that autumn, I did not know that the earth was opening, and that hail clouds were creeping close. On one occasion, the order was given for my eviction by a task force of militia-men, but I knew nothing of it as I strolled serenely along his garden paths.

Carefree short-sightedness is sometimes the heart's salvation. God forbid that we should, at certain times, see too sensitively into the future.

I had, however, devised an excellent means of defense in case the militia should come—a rocket so powerful that I was almost sorry not to have to launch it.

I still had some hope that since I had not "appealed to the West," and since A.T. "would not sit in the same field" with the present secretariat, he might react favorably to this latest letter of mine too. The road to a real understanding would then be open!

But this was asking too much of Tvardovsky! In his effort to adjust, to develop, to assimilate, to understand, he had let the swing take him to the highest point of its arc, and now my letter, in which I was so rude about the sacred dogma of class warfare and declared the most advanced society in the world to be "gravely ill," was so much extra weight to jerk him downward and backward all the faster.

There was uproar in the *Novy Mir* office. He threw chairs about, yelled "Traitor!" "He's finished us!" (Finished *Novy Mir,* that is.) "Get him in here"—of course, and of course I wasn't to be found and "nobody knows where he is." It occurred to him to call up Veronica Turkina, and he heaped insults on her, too, while he was at it. She listened quietly and only ventured to say:

"But, A.T.! What A.I. writes is all true."

"No, no, no!" he roared into the telephone. "It's *an anti-Soviet squib!* It's all lies! And *I shall inform the proper authority!"*

This strident voice, these unfortunate words, were not Tvardovsky speaking, but the debased mentality of the thirties, the Russian language trained by tyranny, the loyal patriotic son who "does not answer for his father." I had distributed an *open* letter and he, poor wretch, was going to "inform the proper authorities."

On an unlucky impulse Veronica went to *Novy Mir,* where the dim sycophant Sats saw her, and ran to A.T. with the conclusion he had jumped to—that she had come to "distribute Solzhenitsyn's letter" in the office. They were too obtuse to realize that the "first floor" at *Novy Mir* had always read samizdat before it reached the "second floor." So Tvardovsky vented his rage on Veronica. "Who lets her in? Who gives her reviews?" (She earned a few extra rubles from *Novy Mir.*) "Don't give her any more!"

Then there were parleys with the Writers' Union, in which he disowned me, and others with Demichev (who tried to frighten him, evidently hoping to make him stop me from circulating the letter). Yesterday he had been ready to leave *Novy Mir,* but now he was not ready; he was ruffling up his feathers again like a hen trying to save its chick from kites. A telephone call from a third party found me at Rostropovich's dacha. A.T. was in a terrible state! He was asking for me! He was prepared to wait all day!

But could I really make things easier for him? If I went and we quarreled again, who would be any the better for it? In any case, the letter had already gone out. And I would not retract it. I wasn't a first-aid team. I was a man hiding from the KGB. I didn't want to be seen all over Moscow, and come back with a tail.

I didn't go.

A few days later, when his anger had cooled, I sent him a soothing letter:

> . . . This is a different age—not that in which you had the misfortune to live the greater part of your literary life—and *different* skills are needed. Mine are those of *katorga* and the camps. I can say without affectation that I belong to the Russian convict world no less, and owe no less to it, than I do to Russian literature. I got my education there, and it will last forever. When I am considering any step of importance to my future, I listen above all to the voices of my comrades in *katorga,* some of them already dead, of disease or a bullet, and I hear clearly how they would behave in my place.
>
> . . . By writing this letter, (1) I have shown that I shall resist to the last, that when I say "I will lay down my life" I am not joking; that I shall continue returning blow for blow, and perhaps hit still harder. So that if they are wise, they will think twice before touching me again. In this stance I shall be able to defend myself irrespective of the attitude of "the literary *community.*" (2) I have used an opportunity that was there for a day and will not recur: I was *already* released from the rules and terminology of the Writers' Union, yet I *still* had the right to appeal to it: and the secretariat was a very convenient addressee. (3) I feel that my whole life is a process of rising gradually from my knees, a gradual transition from enforced dumbness to free speech, so that my letter to the congress, and this present letter, have been moments of high delight, of spiritual emancipation. . . .

Tvardovsky himself gradually softened. The peremptory sweep of the swing had hurled him backward, then released him in a forward rush. "Well," he said with a sigh, "he was entitled to write as he did: after all, he was in a camp while we were sitting around editing magazines." And . . . he kept rereading *Ivan Denisovich.* (He had been writing his memoirs for at least a year, and there was something about me in them. And I was writing about him. It was like a game of hide-and-seek.)

We did not meet for three months, and that meant more childish games. Some of the letters of greeting on my birthday, and then at the New Year, arrived at the *Novy Mir* office. He gave orders that they were not to be sent on, and when I asked Elena Chukovskaya to pick them up, he would not let her have them. "He doesn't necessarily have to see *me*, but he must come and get the letters *in person.*" Why *in person?* Why, because he wanted to make peace. It was a hard time he was having. (My greetings to him and to the magazine were written just outside Moscow, but taken to Ryazan and posted there. Let them think that I was in Ryazan after all, and that this was why I hadn't looked in.)

In the middle of these games, fresh anxieties overtook me. I wasn't allowed a moment's respite before a new danger swooped, perhaps more terrible than any before. In some inexplicable way, a fragment of *Prussian Nights* tore loose and appeared in *Die Zeit* on 5 December, with a promise that the whole poem would follow shortly![3] I succeeded in preventing this only because that autumn I had, thank Heaven, acquired a lawyer in the West. (Even the lawyer had to be explained to Tvardovsky: Why had I hired the man without consulting him? Why a bourgeois lawyer? *It just wasn't done!*)

What with these anxieties, and my absorption in *R-17,* I had no eyes for the distant storm cloud gathering over Tvardovsky and *Novy Mir.* A.T.'s instinct had not deceived him: the attempt to *stifle* him had not been just an episode but part of a carefully planned campaign.

*Posev, Grani*'s sister publication, brought out (although it had had no samizdat circulation) his ill-starred and unfinished poem "Memory gives me the right," the joy and grief of his later years, equally unacceptable to the regime and to the public. A.T. was shocked, dismayed, demoralized. Of course he hadn't wanted this! Of course he hadn't known anything about it! He had certainly not sent it to them; he hadn't even let it out of his hands!

In January 1970 they started hauling him *upstairs,* demanding the explanations, expressions of indignation, disavowals, expected of any honest Soviet writer; and he was not averse, but merely publishing a

---

3. The history of this dangerous printing became known to me some years later: the editors of the West German magazine *Stern* had passed along my poem to *Die Zeit,* fervently avowing that the author's express wish was to have it published in the West as soon as possible [1978 note].

disclaimer would no longer have satisfied the authorities: what they wanted now was to smash that odious magazine. For how many months, and how many years, had their mouths been watering for this victim! How many weeks and how many months had the drones and deadheads of Agitprop wasted on plans of campaign, on maneuvers, attacks and flanking movements. Those dried-up brains did not notice that their epoch, all fifty floors of it, had collapsed like a house of cards; they yearned to seize that one landing on the staircase. Samizdat, free and untrammeled, had flooded the country; Russian novels had gone out to the West, been published there, returned to their homeland by way of radio: and still these fungoids imagined that if they could only seize that one stubbornly resistant landing, the choral unison they had so loved in Stalin's time would again prevail, with no voice left to mock them.

Now that Tvardovsky was enfeebled by guilt—his poem had become a *weapon in enemy hands!*—they began suggesting again, as they had in the spring, that members of the board, one or two, or three, or four of them, should be replaced. To reinforce the pressure, a certain Ovcharenko (a wolf-jawed police spy; there was nothing of the sheep dog about him except his name) stood up at one of those innumerable writers' plenums and called Tvardovsky a *kulak poet.* Then Voronkov, behaving as though the poet were his subordinate, started calling him in for daily discussions—and a depressed and guilt-ridden and docile Tvardovsky would obey the summons. They even suggested that he take *the very same Ovcharenko* onto the board! (A perverse twist typical of the thirties.)

As its end drew near, it was more painfully clear than ever that internally the liberal magazine[4] was just as hierarchically organized as the whole system that was trying to disgorge it: Tvardovsky too, who had always lived among the service hierarchy, felt the need to draw a line between those within his own establishment whose rank entitled them to his confidence and the general run. But the "general run" at *Novy Mir* were anything but ordinary. These were no mere hirelings, working just for their pay checks and uninterested in all else: the maga-

---

4. Lakshin, measuring with the traditional yardstick of the intelligentsia, was offended: "ours is not a *liberal* but a *democratic* magazine," by which he meant much farther to the *left*. However paradoxical it may seem, the magazine was *Oktyabrist* in orientation—not in the same sense as Kochetov's thuggish journal, but in prerevolutionary Russian terminology: like the prerevolutionary *Oktyabristy*, they wanted the existing regime to continue but to observe its own constitution.

zine's cause and its future were vitally important to every last editorial assistant, proofreader and typist in the place. But if the chief editor and his intimates had never shared the credit with their staff in the good days, it would obviously not occur to them, now that times were hard, to be frank about the way things were going, still less to get the whole staff together and say: "Friends! You and I have worked together for twelve years. I won't call for a vote, but I need to know what you think. If several members of the board are taken from us, should we stay on or should we all go? Should we try to stick it out, or shouldn't we? Should I personally resign or wait to be removed?' Oh, no! Absent-mindedly acknowledging their greetings, Tvardovsky passed silently through to the inner office, where the members of the board would assemble, and shut themselves up for hours at a time to discuss news and plans, with everyone present pledged to discretion! While the ordinary editorial assistants, all of them women, whose own future was just as much affected, and who fretted just as much about the future of the magazine, would gather in the secretaries' room to eavesdrop at the door, catching fragments of sentences and trying to interpret them. Tvardovsky was more communicative in the writers' colony around his dacha, and his staff would extract information from some writer who came to the office.

The rumor went around Moscow that *Novy Mir* was being pushed under, and more and more writers flocked to the office; rooms and corridors were packed, "the whole of literature was there" (if there was such a thing as Soviet literature, this was the place to look for it), and the writers, following Mozhayev's lead, began hastily putting together a collective letter to the same old Brezhnev, which was fated, however, like thousands of others, to go unanswered. Yet the editorial board itself held aloof from these efforts on the part of the writers! Honorable servants of the state, they could not join in open mutiny, nor even skip the intermediate powers and appeal directly to the top.

On one such day, 10 February, when the removal of Lakshin, Kondratovich and Vinogradov had already been decided upon, I joined the rest in this Tower of Babel. The chairs were piled high with writers' overcoats, the corridors all blocked by groups of writers. A.T. was sitting in his own office (there had always been *something missing* there; what it was would become clear when Kosolapov nailed a bas-relief of Lenin to the wall), sober, sad and passive—except for his dreadful smoking, one coarse, strong cigarette after another. This was our first meeting since the November storm. We shook hands and embraced. I had come to try and persuade him that as there were still four members of the old board left (including himself), the struggle could be carried on from inside the magazine. The next two or three monthly numbers were planned and ready. Only when he was required to sign an utterly disgusting number would it be time to go.

"I'm tired of being humiliated," A.T. replied. "Just sitting at the same table and trying to talk to them seriously . . . They've brought in people I've never seen before—I don't know whether they're blonds or brunets."

(The worst of it was that they weren't even writers. People who had never held a pen in their hands were being put in charge of a literary magazine. A.T. was right, and in his place I would have taken my leave earlier. My suggestion was made in the spirit of *Novy Mir*'s own behavior over the years: only their long suffering had kept them going.)

"But how can you possibly resign of your own accord, A.T.? Christianity prohibits suicide, and the Party's ideology prohibits resignation!"

"You don't know the Party's ways. They'll say, 'Resign!' and I shall."

I tried with greater conviction and insistence to persuade him not to disown the Western edition of his poem, not to denigrate his own work. I did not know that A.T. had disowned it already, and was hoping that they would charitably, mercifully *not refuse* to publish his disclaimer in their newspaper.

(Poor A.T.! I was not so malicious as to remind him how he had said that it was probably I myself who had handed the "Miniatures" to *Grani*. How else could they have appeared there?) He showed me neither the letter of disavowal nor the letter to Brezhnev (in which he had written: "I'm Tvardovsky, not Solzhenitsyn, and I shall behave differently"; too bad—that's no way to win). "No copies," he said, but of course there were things there he would have been ashamed to show me.

And still he asked, shyly and hopefully, "Have *you* read my poem?"

"You know I have! You made me a present of it, and I read it."

(But I couldn't and wouldn't say anything about it, especially on a day like this.)

He guessed what I was thinking.

"What you read wasn't the final version; it improved later on. . . ."

(Alas, it had indeed been the latest version.)

He started worrying again that I might be dirtying my hands by living on Western money; yet again he offered me money from his own pocket.

I tried to cheer him up: "Never mind. You've done your share of donkey work; now you can rest. Rostropovich and I will call for you and carry you off to his castle and I'll let you read that other book of mine."

(I couldn't say *Gulag* with a ceiling over me.)

He beamed; the idea appealed to him.

Then he made a strange pronouncement.

"You have a good excuse for coming to the office today: to pick up your New Year greetings."

This was not said to reproach me or trip me up. Some shadow cast by 1937 had clouded his mind.

"What on earth do you mean? Do I *need* an excuse? And for whose benefit?"

"Well, you know," A.T. said, looking at the floor. "If somebody should ask why you came on this particular day . . ."

"Ask *me*, Aleksandr Trifonich? I'm in my own country, and I don't have to give an account of myself to anybody!"

Surely he must know that all the corridors on the first floor were chock-full of writers. . . .

I found one thing rather touching.

"Aleksandr Trifonovich, there is something spooky about the date. Yesterday was the anniversary—the twenty-fifth, in fact—of my arrest. Today is the anniversary of Pushkin's death, a century and a third ago." (And also the anniversary of the Sinyavsky-Daniel trial. But he mustn't be told that.) "And this is the time they choose to crush you."

"Do you want to hear another uncanny thing?" he suddenly said, with real feeling. "I couldn't sleep last night. I drank some coffee, then took a sedative, and I fell into a troubled sleep. All at once I heard Sofia Khananovna"—his secretary—"saying faintly, but quite audibly, 'Aleksandr Trifonovich! Aleksandr Isayevich has arrived.' And next day it happened."

I was very touched: obviously, he had come in that day hoping to see me. Yet again he was letting me see how much more unpleasant our disagreements were for him than for me.

That whole day was spent wondering what would be in next day's *Literaturnaya Gazeta,* and agents arrived with varying reports: one minute A.T.'s disclaimer was going in, the next it wasn't. First they were going to fudge the announcement so that he appeared to agree with the changes on the board, then they weren't.

*Literaturnaya Gazeta* would not have been true to itself if it had not cheated. There, next day, was the dishonest cover story (of course), there was the irrevocable statement on the removal of the four board members, and there also was A.T.'s letter, which he had pined to see in print, but which brought him little credit.

"... my poem ... by channels absolutely unknown to me ... needless to say against my will ... in the wretched émigré journal *Posev* ... in a distorted form ... the impudence of this operation ... the brazen mendacity ... under a heading intended to compromise me ... *allegedly* "banned in the Soviet Union." (Is it not banned, then? Don't you go around asking your friends whether they've read it? And do you think that this letter will ease the way to publication in the U.S.S.R.?)

And for what have you paid such a price? For the disbandment of your editorial board, Aleksandr Trifonovich?

They had broken him. . . .

By 11 February Tvardovsky could stand no further humiliation, and he signed the letter they had eagerly expected from him for so many years: "I must ask you to release me . . ."

There was something else, which we learned only later. He was summoned that same day to a "conference of the members of the Presidium of COMES"—our statutory representatives in Vigorelli's bootlicking organization, which, however, was just then kicking up a fuss about me. And Tvardovsky—what was he paying for this time?— signed a dictated announcement of his resignation as vice-president of COMES: in other words, surrendered yet another strong point as important to me as to him; though no harm came of it. He embraced me next day with the sincerest affection, without mentioning what had happened, or seeing why he should. If the Party orders you to sign, you sign.

I was in the office again on the twelfth. Everything had changed. The staff were no longer waiting to learn their fate, writers were no longer planning resistance. Desks were being tidied. A multitude of authors had poured in to retrieve their manuscripts. (Some changed their minds later.) Other manuscripts were being torn up into wastepaper baskets or sacks, and the floors were littered with shredded paper. If the board had been arrested en masse, or if the staff were all being deported or evacuated, it would have looked much the same. People had brought in vodka, and editorial assistants and writers were holding wakes in odd corners. Tvardovsky's office, however, was as always out of bounds to the writers. Some of them carried vodka and sausage into Lakshin's office, and asked him to call the chief in, but Lakshin apologized and declined on A.T.'s behalf. It would have been improper even for a discharged chief editor to appear without Party orders among discontented writers.

I found A.T. alone again in his office, but on his feet at the open cupboards, also sorting files and papers. He said that he felt easier now that he had resigned. I agreed that he could not possibly have stayed on. But there had been one sentence in his letter yesterday. . . . (I wish there *had* been only one!) About the poem *allegedly* being banned?

Trifonich began protesting vigorously, aghast to find me so unperceptive (or to think what a blunder he had made).

"You don't understand! It's a *very subtle* sentence. That sentence is the reason they didn't want to publish the letter! This way I've announced to the whole Soviet Union that the poem exists and is being held up."

Not wanting to sharpen the discussion, I didn't try to change his mind.

He mentioned that he would soon be sixty. He had calculated that in his two spells as chief editor he had run *Novy Mir* for sixteen years, and no other Russian journal had ever existed for more than ten.

"You'll be writing just as well at seventy, A.T.," I said to console him.

"Mauriac is eighty-five, and what a writer!" He looked at me coyly. "Bunin never praised anybody in his life except Tvardovsky and Mauriac."

Now we came to the nub.

"A.T.! It's all right for the big boys—jobs have been found for Lakshin and Kondratovich; they'll get paid. But what are your junior colleagues to do?"

"Who—Vinogradov? He'll get an even better job."

"No; the staff."

He hadn't heard. Hadn't understood! Like *Vekhi* when I once mentioned it, the word meant nothing to him: "staff," the other twenty people who . . .

"Our writers, you mean? They won't publish in *Novy Mir* anymore."

True, on the following day, the thirteenth, A.T. did start making the rounds of all the rooms on all three floors, visiting places he had never seen before. He was there to *say goodbye*. He could scarcely hold back his tears, he was so upset, so moved; he had kind words for everybody, he embraced them all . . . but why had he never rallied all two dozen of his staff around him earlier on? And why, instead of fighting back, were they now so movingly, so dismally, so tragically capitulating?[5]

Afterward the members of the board had a drink in Lakshin's room, sat for a while and left. But the small fry were still reluctant to break up the party on this last day. They, and some of the humbler authors, put a ruble apiece in the kitty, fetched more drink and thought they might as well go into Tvardovsky's office! It was dark by now. They turned on the light, set out plates and glasses, made themselves at home in this place to which they had been admitted only rarely, and never all together. "We've been abandoned." No one ventured to sit at Tvardovsky's desk. They put a glass there for him, as if to say, in Pushkin's words about Alexander I: "Let us forgive him his injustice and bullying."*

The new chief was expected next day. Expected in vain—and again for good Soviet reasons. The bit of paper fed into the bureaucratic slot machine somehow did not go through immediately. Hour by hour they had tightened their stranglehold, but suddenly their hands slackened and all was still. All that was necessary was for the secretaries of the Writers' Union to converge at a trot from five adjacent offices and give the order—but evidently telephonic assent from *on high* had not arrived, so the machine stalled, the secretaries sat numb and silent in their offices, and so did Tvardovsky in his office at Pushkin Square, waiting for sentence to be carried out. The days trickled by and a second week began . . . with Tvardovsky arriving at the office sober and anxious, to await the telephone call, the new man's arrival, the order to go. But no one called, no one came. . . . Finally, he himself telephoned, to try and hasten the blow—but once the powers of darkness are blocked, they might as well not exist. Voronkov was in hiding, and would not answer the phone. This is a technique at which the Soviet bureaucrat excels: it is easier to fly over his roof and knock a hole in it with your head than

---

5. I was told about this scene at the time when I was getting ready to describe Samsonov's farewell to his troops—and was immediately struck by the similarity between the two scenes, and the strong resemblance between these two characters. They belonged to the same psychological and national type, they had the same inner greatness, the same bigness, the same purity, the same helplessness in practical matters and the same inability to keep up with the times. And also an aristocratic quality natural in Samsonov, paradoxical in Tvardovsky. I began to explain Samsonov to myself in terms of Tvardovsky, and vice versa—and understood them both better as a result.

to discover from his secretary whether he's still extant, when he will be in, when you can phone him again. Then one evening, when Tvardovsky had already left and while his secretary was still there, Voronkov himself (probably timing it precisely) phoned and said in a mock-dramatic voice: "What, left already? Dear me, what a pity. He's probably offended with me. . . . But it doesn't depend on me, you know. I've passed all the papers to the Central Committee. What can *I* do? Till the Central Committee tells me, I shan't know a thing."

They knew well enough what to think at *Novy Mir.* Voronkov's position was getting shaky. He might even *take a dive.* He'd *fumbled* it.

The decision was in the balance. Perhaps it would never be taken. Although such moments of agonizing suspense under the headsman's ax are not the best time for reflection, they all had the same thought. If Tvardovsky isn't sacked, maybe the magazine is safe? We still have Tvardovsky, so perhaps we have a magazine too? Perhaps we can stay and fight? Since, however, the dismissal of Lakshin, Kondratovich and Vinogradov had already been reported in the press, it was to the Soviet way of thinking irreversible, irreparable, for even the flimsiest browny-yellowy rag of a Soviet newspaper can never make a mistake. Tvardovsky's former deputies had started going to their new jobs, but they also visited *Novy Mir* daily. In these new circumstances, it became clear that A.T.'s darling deputies did not want him to stay on without them. They could not conceive of *Novy Mir* without themselves.

There are many different ways to die. In my view, *Novy Mir* died an unlovely death, without even uncurling its spine. There was not the slightest move to make the struggle public, though this had been tried before and had been seen to work. Need I say that never once while the magazine lived had they dared to put out through samizdat an article or a few paragraphs suppressed by the censor, as Bulgakov's widow, Elena, did with *The Master and Margarita.* I shall be told that this would have destroyed the magazine. They did that anyway. It had been coming for some time. You could hear the death rattle. But why did it have to die on its knees! In those February days they published not a single open letter in samizdat (because it would have put the Party cards and future appointments of the dismissed editors at risk?), they were timid even in petitions submitted by order, and Tvardovsky wrote two degrading letters to *Literaturnaya Gazeta.* Worse still, Tvardovsky and Lakshin were not too squeamish to attend that nonevent the Congress of the R.S.F.S.R. Writers' Union, held shortly afterward. Tvardovsky went and sat in the presidium, and smilingly posed for group photographs with scoundrels, as though deliberately trying to show the world that he was not being persecuted or ill used in any way. (If you had to attend, why couldn't you speak out!) Lakshin, for his part, while making this outward display of loyalty, buttonholed *Novy Mir* writers in the corridors and urged them to withdraw their manuscripts.

Their efforts to this end showed the old editors in an ignoble light. It is always wrong to *demand* sacrifices from others: we may *ask* for them, but only when we have set an example ourselves. Instead of resisting and fighting back, the retiring members of the board, except Tvardovsky, had tamely surrendered; they were going to comfortable posts and were sacrificing nothing—but they ruthlessly demanded sacrifices from all except themselves. *We* have retreated; now scorch the earth behind us! *We* have fallen; none of you must live! That the world may the more surely and suddenly quake to see our beacon extinguished, all writers must leave *Novy Mir* immediately and without fail, taking their manuscripts with them! He who does otherwise is a traitor! (Where were they to publish, though?) If any single member of the staff, any editorial assistant, any secretary, makes any attempt to do anything worthwhile once we are gone, he is a traitor! *A fortiori,* any member of the board who has not yet been ousted must resign immediately, leave at any cost! (At the cost of also leaving the Writers' Union? Of ceasing to exist as a publishable writer? In obedience to that policy, Dorosh, aged sixty and seriously ill, handed in his resignation. It was not accepted—and he became a traitor!)

If *Novy Mir*'s whole existence had consisted of constant compromises with the censorship and with Party policy, why should its writers and its junior staff be denied the right to follow the same line and stretch it as far as they could? Why behave as though the newly dirtied *Novy Mir* was more repulsive than magazines made dirty long ago? They hadn't had the wit to avert defeat, to defend the vessel and keep it whole; why couldn't they let every man scramble onto the floating wreckage as best he could? But no! In this they were implacable.

And this was because, as is so often the case, they saw their conduct over the years quite differently; they did not see that they had acquired a permanent stoop from endless compromise. (What magazine would not under such a regime?) No, they saw it quite differently, as something fine and purposeful. This emerged very clearly when they finally nerved themselves to try samizdat, and put out two anonymous—and exceptionally *orthodox*—panegyrics on the defunct journal. Why such a half-hearted gesture? There was no danger in it, so why the anonymity? (Probably because the authors had to conceal how close they were to the old editors. As it was, they were suspiciously well informed about what had been left in the portfolio of the old magazine and about the day-to-day affairs of the new one. So that it would not have been difficult to identify them anyway.)

There was a bad smell even about the signatures: "Man of Letters," "A Reader"—copying a very bad habit of the Soviet press. "A Reader" begins with an elaborate, slowly unwinding quotation of the sort so dear to *Novy Mir*. From where, do you think? Why, from Marx! In 1970! For samizdat! Later on Lenin, too, is quoted: oh, how transparent are your thought processes, you who write for the censor! . . . In that same February in which *Novy Mir* was disbanded, a nauseating judicial process condemned the first honorable Soviet general, Grigorenko, to a lunatic asylum. In a dozen issues on its faintly printed, well-thumbed cigarette paper, the *Chronicle of Current Events* had by then named hundreds of heroes who had chosen freedom of thought and exchanged bodily freedom for it, paid with loss of employment, imprisonment, banishment, internment in asylums—and our anonymous authors declared the rout of *Novy Mir* "a most important event in our national life," which "will have significant political consequences" (for it to have had consequences, you yourselves should have spoken out more boldly). They grossly flattered themselves: "ours are *the most* honest mouths" (more honest than the mouths of others, locked away in jail?); "the invincibility of Truth in *Novy Mir*" (even in Marshal Konev's memoirs, and in those of the Comintern hacks?); "a most important factor in the restoration of Soviet society to health"; "the voice of the nation's conscience" (as when it endorsed the occupation of Czechoslovakia?). "It alone held out to the end in defense of the purifying process started by the Twentieth Congress." (In what sense was it a purifying process? In heaping all the regime's evil deeds on Stalin's head?) The policy of "loyalty to the Twentieth Congress" is sincerely seen by our authors as the "key to the fundamental problems in which our whole historical destiny resides." We only have to overcome the "positive fanaticism" of the "Stalinist extremists," and of course "the negative fanaticism . . . the nihilistic criticism for the sake of criticism, the embitterment . . ." Well, now, chums, you could have submitted every word of this to *Pravda,* so why the anonymity? This show of loyalty is all the more startling because it is anonymous even in samizdat. If it had appeared in *Novy Mir,* it could at least have made the censorship its excuse. . . . What, then, was the greatest damage done by the disband-ment of *Novy Mir?* "It will now be much easier for *our enemies* to combat the ideological influence of the Communist movement throughout the world." The most important thing of all, needless to say, is *socialism!* Only socialism "is capable of being the progressive histori-cal alternative to the world of capital" (it might have been written specially for the censor); there is "among the people an unimpaired will to fight for genuine socialism." (Where? Scour the earth for it; you may find some lingering remnant, but not in our country.) Well, who is to blame for socialism's failures? Who do you think! Russia, as always: "these perversions of socialism have their roots in the centuries-long heritage of Russian feudalism"—for surely we cannot suppose, com-rades, that socialism is inherently flawed, that it is altogether unrealiza-ble in a pure form!

They could not have written a meaner epitaph for *Novy Mir,* or made it clearer how shallow was their own understanding of what was truly a matter of great moment.

Samizdat, though, is no fool: it knows what is what. These panegyrics were unacceptable to it, did not circulate widely, and soon sank from view. They reached me only through circles close to the editors. And vexed me no less than Dementyev's article.

I did not conceal from the dismissed editors my disapproval of their whole policy at the time of crisis and final collapse. The same message was conveyed to Tvardovsky, though without the detailed reasons given here.

So that once again the frail craft of our friendship was plunged into the dark abyss. Smothered under the same jackboot, we both fell silent —but we were separated. For me, however, solitude meant not just loneliness, but intensive work on *August 1914.* I was no weaker outside the Writers' Union, no weaker without the magazine, but on the con-trary, only more independent and stronger, since I no longer had to account to anyone, and was not tied by any secondary considerations. *"Der Starke ist am mächtigsten allein"*—a man has a freer hand with-out weak allies.

But A.T.'s loneliness was embittered by what he felt as a general betrayal. For years he had sacrificed himself for all the others, and now not one of them wanted to make sacrifices for him: his staff were not leaving *Novy Mir,* and only a few authors had recoiled from it. All the fuss and bother with the "shadow" editorial board, and the incessant discussion of what was happening on the real board, could only exhaust him even further and accelerate the stealthy progress of the disease that his depression had set in motion.

At this point, the defense of Zhores Medvedev, who had been seized, brought us together again, though not face to face. I, as usual, wrote something for samizdat, while A.T. visited the psychiatric hospital at Kaluga (passing the gate of my Rozhdestvo home, which he had never discovered, never seen), and his appearance had a stupefying effect on all the medical torturers.

Then the approach of A.T.'s sixtieth birthday gave us another opportunity to exchange messages. I sent a telegram:

"Dear A.T.! I wish you spacious days, precious discoveries, a happy creative life in your ripe years! Through all our constant quarrels and disagreements I remain immutably your deeply affectionate and ever grateful Solzhenitzyn."

I am told that he was very glad to receive my telegram, and shut himself up in his study with it. He need not have replied—acknowledging anniversary greetings is a chore—but he did:

"Thank you, dear Aleksandr Isayevich, for your kind words on the occasion of my sixtieth birthday. Though I often differ from you in my views, I never falter in my esteem and love for you as an artist. Yours, Tvardovsky."

At this rate, we might have met in a few months' time. I wrote *asking for permission* to show him my completed novel in October. I knew that this would give him pleasure.

But no answer came. Instead we heard that he had cancer (and that this was being kept from him). Cancer is the fate of all who give themselves up to moods of bilious, corrosive resentment and depression. People can live through hardship, but from hard feelings they perish. Many in our land have perished like this: a man is savagely attacked in public—and suddenly he is dead. Some oncologists take the view that cancer cells are present in all of us throughout our lives, and begin proliferating as soon as something upsets the equilibrium of—let's call it the *spirit.* Thanks only to his extraordinary constitution, and in spite of the mistakes made by the Kremlin horse doctors, Tvardovsky still had many months to live, though on his deathbed.

There are many ways of killing a poet.

They killed Tvardovsky by taking *Novy Mir* from him.

*Zhukovka*
*February 1971*

# THIRD SUPPLEMENT

( December 1973 )

# Nobeliana

"Nobeliana" is not an invention of mine. It is the telegraphic address of the Nobel Foundation (Nobelianum), and also the accepted designation of its protracted ceremonies and pompous orchestral extravaganzas. For me, there was no ceremonial to get through, no torture to bear, but the chaotic procedure dragged on for two whole years.

What does the award of a Nobel Prize in Literature mean to an unfettered country? A national triumph. And to the writer himself? The crossing of a ridge, a great divide in his life. Camus said that he was unworthy, Steinbeck that he was so proud he could roar like a lion. (Hemingway, though, could not find time for such frivolities and replied that writing his next book was more interesting—which was no less true, if rather conceited of him.)

And what does a Nobel Prize mean to a writer from a Communist country? Somebody's bungled! Sorry—wrong address! Too hot to handle! Or else, get ready to be tarred and feathered! Because in our country the regime itself, from its bloodthirsty youth up, has forced all imaginative literature into a narrow political channel—a rough-hewn runnel like those they used to hack out of raw tree trunks on the White Sea Canal. The regime itself has drilled it into writers that literature is part of politics, the regime itself (beginning with Trotsky and Bukharin) has called out the official literary placings in its hoarse politician's croak and declared any other standard of judgment quite impossible. So that whenever a Nobel Prize is awarded to one of our fellow countrymen it is interpreted as first and foremost a political event.

The real writers we had in the twenties, thirties and forties could not possibly be distinguished from Stockholm through the howling blizzard. The first Russian to receive the prize was the émigré Bunin, who published his works abroad free from censorship and brutal pressures, just as he wrote them. Obviously, such an award, and the Nobel Prize as an institution, could evoke nothing but contemptuous abuse from the U.S.S.R. It was decided once and for all that these prizes were utterly unimportant, not worth even a couple of lines in small print. Whereas the announcement of Stalin Prize awards was splashed over a whole sheet. We all almost stopped thinking about Nobel Prizes. Until suddenly after twenty-five years the Swedish Academy descried Pasternak and awarded one to him. Everyone knows how this aroused the wrath of the Communist Party (Khrushchev), the Komsomol (Semichastny) and the *whole* Soviet people. The shock waves of their anger hit the foundations of the Swedish Academy so hard that it was obliged to rehabilitate itself in the eyes of *progressive mankind* as quickly as possible. So after a decent interval of seven years, they awarded the prize to a third compatriot of ours, for a book whose authorship has never been established beyond doubt, a book that had been published a third of a century earlier and had received its critical due even before the prize had gone to Bunin. But the award to Sholokhov was gratifying to the Soviet regime and they hastened to applaud it. The Academy's long delay, its subsequent haste, this whole ritual of expiation, and the satisfaction that it gave Soviet officialdom combined to stamp the word "politics" in bold letters all over the third award too.

The Swedish Academy had always been accused of playing politics, but it was *our* whining and yapping that made any other judgment impossible. The same thing happened on the fourth occasion, and unless Russia comes to its senses, it will happen yet again on the fifth.

Since our scientists have never been overwhelmed with them either, these prizes were hardly ever mentioned in the U.S.S.R., and until the storm over Pasternak, few of us knew that such things existed. I had heard of them from someone, I forget who it was, in the camps. And at once drew a conclusion in the spirit of our country—a thoroughly political conclusion—that this was just what I needed to make my great breakthrough when the time came.

My great breakthrough—though for the time being I was in no position to make even a small one. No one, of course, wants to be the author only of "posthumous works"; live just long enough to see yourself in print and you can die happy. But seen from a prison camp, this was an unrealizable dream. *Where* would any such thing be possible in my lifetime? Only abroad. But after the camp came exile in perpetuity:

there would be no getting abroad myself or sending my writings out to safety.

In exile I did, however, manage to reduce all that I had written in the camps to something small enough to be stuffed inside the boards of a book (a volume of Shaw's plays in English). Now, if only somebody would undertake the journey to Moscow, he could thrust the book into the hands of a foreign tourist encountered in the street, who would of course accept it, take it out of the country without difficulty, slit open the covers, and take it along to a publisher, who in turn would joyfully publish the unknown Stepan Khlynov (my pen name), and . . . The world, of course, would not remain indifferent! The world would be horrified. The world would be enraged, and *our masters* would take fright—and dissolve the Archipelago.

Only there wasn't even anyone I could ask to take it to Moscow. I was all on my own during those years, and our Kok-Terek was not a place where Muscovites came to stay with friends.

When I went to Moscow myself in 1956 and looked around for a Western tourist to whom I could pass my book, I saw that there was a KGB interpreter attached to every one of them and—to the utter amazement of a former zek—these tourists were all so sleek and glossy, all so much enjoying their jaunt to the Soviet Union. Why should they want to make trouble for themselves?

So off I went to Torfoprodukt, and then to Ryazan to get on with my work. My time would come—and the more I wrote, the more vigorously I would be able to shake them. But there would also be more and more to fear: an increasingly greater volume of work was in danger of perishing without ever being shown to anyone. One mishap and all would be lost. Live with a secret like this for ten years, twenty years—and it is sure to leak, sure to come to light, and your life is forfeit and with it all the secrets, all those other lives, entrusted to you.

In 1958 I was a Ryazan schoolteacher—and how I envied Pasternak! To him had fallen the destiny that I had dreamed up for myself! He would act it out from beginning to end! He would go abroad at once, he would make *such* a speech, publish so boldly the secret remnant of his work, which he had not dared to publish while he lived here. Obviously, it would be no three-day trip. Obviously, they would not let him back in again. But in the interval he would change the whole world, change us, and return after all, in triumph!

After my camp training I was genuinely incapable of foreseeing that

Pasternak might have other aims and choose another course of action. I measured him against my own intentions, by my own standards—and writhed with shame for him as though for myself. How could he let himself be frightened by mere newspaper abuse, how could he weaken when faced with the threat of exile from the U.S.S.R., demean himself by pleading with the government, mumble about his "mistakes and aberrations," about the novel's "embodying his own guilt," repudiate his own thoughts, his innermost self—all just to escape exile? Then there were such phrases as "our glorious present," "I am proud of the times in which I live" and, inevitably, "shining faith in our common future"—and this was not some professor in a provincial university whimpering under the lash, but our Nobel Prize winner addressing the world! But no—we are incorrigible! No, oh no—if you are challenged to fight, and in such superb conditions, pick up the gage, fight for Russia! I was full of harsh reproaches. I condemned him, I could find no excuse for him. Never, not even in my young days, let alone as a hard-bitten zek, have I been able to understand those who allow attachments to prevail over duty. (No one could have made me understand at the time that Pasternak had already published and said what he had to say, and that the missing Stockholm speech might have turned out to be no more awe-inspiring than his apologias in the newspapers.)

All the more vividly did I see it, all the more eagerly did I brood on it, demand it from the future! I had to have that prize! As a position to be won, a vantage point on the battlefield! And the earlier I got it, the firmer I should stand, the harder I should hit! My behavior then would be the opposite in every way of Pasternak's. I should resolutely *accept* the prize, resolutely go to Stockholm, make a very resolute speech. Obviously, the road back would be closed to me. But I would be able to publish everything! Tell all I knew! Touch off the explosive charge that had been piling up since I first saw the box cells of the Lubyanka, through all those winter work parades in Steplag; speak for all those who had been stifled, shot, starved or frozen to death! Drag it all to the platform of the Nobel Prize ceremony and hurl it like a thunderbolt! For all this, the lot of an outcast was not too high a price to pay. (And in any case, I could picture myself returning before many years were out.)

However, *Ivan Denisovich*, which was seized on all over the world as a Khrushchevite political sensation, and nothing more (it had been mauled into English in Moscow by the potboiling parasite R. Parker, and matters have not improved since), had not brought me much closer to the Nobel Prize. Simply because I had set my mind on it, and mistook a fixed idea for a presentiment, I looked forward to it as something inevitable. Even though Pasternak, by renouncing it and dying so soon after, seemed to have closed the road to Russian prizewinners for the future. How could the prize be given to Russians if it was fatal to them?

The years went by, more and more works were written. I could not publish—they would have my head—and it was more and more difficult to conceal all these things and more and more galling to have them uselessly on my hands. What escape was there, for an underground writer?

Through the years I had never changed in one thing—the conviction forged in me by the camps, the thought I shared with my comrades there: that our zombies must be struck down by our knowledge of the camps, but *from outside.* There I should have all my weapons ready to hand; not a single word need ever again be suppressed, or distorted, or blunted. So thoroughly had I digested this lesson that in 1968, when Alya (Natalya Svetlova), shocked by my attitude, fervently tried to persuade me that it was just the opposite—that if I were *outside* my words would bounce off the iron integument around our country, whereas while I was inside the porously receptive mass would absorb them, fill in the gaps, supply what was left unsaid or merely hinted at—I was shocked in my turn. I decided that she thought this way only because she had never been in a camp.

It was not by chance, nor just once, that she and I discussed the matter. By 1969 I had decided to hand over my literary estate to her —all that I had written, final drafts, preliminary drafts, notes, discarded pieces, reference material, all that I was reluctant to burn, but no longer had wit, strength, time and room to go on preserving: moving it around, remembering where it all was, observing the necessary precautions. I had just passed my fiftieth birthday, and this coincided with a new departure in my work. I was no longer writing about the camps. I had finished all my other work, and an enormous and completely new task stood before me—my novel about 1917 (which I originally thought would take me ten years). This seemed a good time to make provision for all my past work, to make a will and ensure that it would all be preserved and given to the world when I was gone by the firm and faithful hands of my heir, and a head whose thoughts were like mine. I was happy and relieved when I found all this in one person, and all through 1969 we were busy transferring my affairs. It was then, too, that we found, between us, ways of giving Dr. Heeb power of attorney to defend my interests in the West and create an outpost abroad, a branch to continue our work if we both perished in the Soviet Union. We found, too, a reliable two-way channel of communication. Inaudibly and invisibly, ramparts and bulwarks were rising around my literary work.

With all this work to do, where I should be and how I should be placed next year and the year after was a question of more than theoretical significance. At every step, I had to take decisions that depended on this. Besides, I had other active plans: ever since 1965 I had been obsessed with the notion of starting a journal, either in the free Russia of the future, or here and now in samizdat. In summer 1969, Alya and I sat by the Red Brook on the banks of the Pinega and worked out a complicated procedure for publishing a journal: it would be published in samizdat at home (there would be a distribution department, a more deeply hidden operative editorial staff, and a still more deeply hidden shadow staff to take over if the original team came to grief, and set up a second shadow staff). I might be here in the Soviet Union or I might be *over there,* but in any case I should put my signature to the magazine and take part in producing it. In all our planning we could not agree on the fundamental question. Alya thought that everyone should live and die in his homeland whatever turn things took, and I thought, camp fashion, let those who are stupid enough die; I'd sooner live to see my work published. (To live in Russia and hope to publish it all there still seemed, at that time, a gamble that could not possibly pay off.)

As though to taunt me, it was at this very time that A. Kuznetsov *defected* to the West, and by the river Pinega we listened to the news on a transistor radio. There was panic *on high*—and he was triumphant, probably thinking that he was about to change the whole course of history. A typical runaway's error, this failure to see things in proportion. At home here in the U.S.S.R. the educated class disapproved of him almost to a man, and not only because of his earlier compliance with the KGB, not only because he had played the informer, but for his flight itself, for taking the easy way out. An unknown person who has suffered some unpleasantness may be forgiven—but a writer? If you do that—they'll say—how can you call yourself a Russian writer? We are irrational people. We wallow and flounder in liquid dung for decades, and grumble that things are bad. Yet we make no effort to struggle out of it. And if someone does scramble clear and runs away, we yell: "Traitor! Renegade!"

And what of the government? I am sure they thought just as I did. While I'm here in a cage they're only half afraid of me, they can polish me off at any time. But from *outside* I would fill them with dread, I would have time (before they stuck a knife between my ribs, or poisoned me, or shot me, or threw me from a train) to bring into the open all that they had kept hidden for half a century! And after that overwhelming blow, if they lived at all they would hobble to their graves on crutches. (Or so I thought.)

In Stalin's time they had understood that all who disagree must be tied up tightly. But it seems that in recent years new notions had forced their way even into the dim recesses behind those bony brows. They had jailed Sinyavsky and Daniel, and the international outcry had taken them by surprise. They had dispatched Tarsis abroad, and at once all was quiet. There were no unpleasant consequences. (That there was something of a difference between me and Tarsis was too difficult a thought for them.) Demichev, in his heart-to-heart talks with this or that writer, began to give the show away.

"We'll banish Solzhenitsyn, send him abroad to his *masters;* he'll take a look at the capitalist paradise and come crawling back to us on his belly."

People passed this on to me, but I attached no importance to it—just Agitprop up to its usual tricks. Then, on the evening of 25 November 1969, ten days after I had boxed the ears of the secretariat of the Writers' Union, I switched on the Voice of America and heard: "The writer Solzhenitsyn is to be expelled from the Soviet Union." (They had broadcast an incorrect version of an announcement due to appear in *Litgazeta* the following day.)

This was at Rostropovich's dacha, during my first few months there. I had just settled in. I got up. I felt my scalp tingling. They might be coming for me in an hour or so. There was a great deal, far too much, to think about in a hurry—manuscripts, raw materials, books. You can be preparing for it all your life and still it catches you on one foot. I went for a stroll along the paths through the trees. It was a dark, damp evening, unseasonably warm, windy and thundery. I wandered around, gulping fresh air. I found in myself neither protest nor doubt: everything was going as it was meant to go.

One of my favorite images is that of Prince Guidon in Pushkin's *Tsar Saltan.* To make sure of destroying him, they put the infant with his mother in a caulked barrel and launched it on the open sea. But the barrel did not sink, and the yard-long infant grew by the hour, straightened his limbs, exerted his strength, "kicked out the bottom and stepped forth free"—though onto a foreign shore. Stepped out himself and—remember—released his mother too.

The image did not have to agree in every detail; never mind the foreign shore, and to set free my mother country was an honor beyond my deserts. But the barrel ends cracking underfoot and overhead, the staves falling out: that was something I had been aware of for years, though I might just have missed the precise moment at which I had shoved out the barrel ends—if I had yet done so. Was it at the very moment when my expulsion from the Writers' Union had turned into a defeat for my—for our—persecutors? When thirty-one Western writers had formed a solid wall, demonstrating the unity of world literature, and declared in a letter to the *New York Times* that they would not see me harmed? Or was my escape still in the future? Is it still in the future as I now write?

Some echo of the splintering noise reached the ears of the high and mighty conclave that had dared to crush Czechoslovakia, but not to crush me. Some of the jagged, shivered timbers had landed at their feet —for they were not *banishing* me from the country, only *inviting* me, only *authorizing* me to leave. (This I learned an hour later from a copy of the next day's *Litgazeta,* which someone had spirited away from the editorial offices for me.)

This was quite a different hand of cards. A zek buried in Ekibastuz would not have hesitated a minute, given the chance. But what did I, as I now was, want with their offer? By way of answer I launched a mot which went by oral samizdat all around Moscow: "I have the permission of my benefactors to abandon my home. And they have mine to go to China."

Their reply was a warning hint in another newspaper. Then in yet another. These statements awakened loud echoes in the West, and the stout-hearted Norwegians, the only ones in Europe who never for a minute forgot or forgave the invasion of Czechoslovakia, offered me asylum—one of the residences assigned to distinguished artists and writers in Norway. "Let Solzhenitsyn set up his desk in Norway!" I could think of nothing else for days. A second homeland had offered itself to me, opened its arms to me, a northern country. With a winter like ours in Russia. With peasant utensils, wooden cups and dishes, just like those in Russia.

There was a lull. The *top people* subsided. And I was silent too.

A zek's burning ambition is not easily abandoned. My unpublished works cried out that they wanted to live. But another thought, like a silhouetted figure with a reproachful prison stoop, loomed larger in my mind. Were we frogs, or hares, to flee from everyone? This was our land —why should we surrender it to them so readily? Ever since 1917, we had always, all of us, surrendered everything; it seemed to make life easier. So many had succumbed to this error—of overestimating the *other side's* strength and underestimating their own. Yet there have been people, like Akhmatova or Palchinsky, who would not leave, who refused to apply for exit visas in 1923, when they would have been readily granted.

Surely we are not too weak to put up a fight *here?*

The authorities obviously had it firmly fixed in their minds from of old that banishment abroad was the way to rid themselves of nuisances: from this idea of Dzerzhinsky and Lenin came the plan, in 1969–1970, for a new, a "third" emigration, of which we could have no conception at that time. In various closed seminars the full-throated cry went up: "Let Solzhenitsyn clear off abroad!" Louis the First-Informed darted from one embassy party to another, dropping hints to important Westerners: "Why not invite Solzhenitsyn to your country to give a lecture or something?" "Would he be allowed out, though?" they would ask in surprise. "Why, of course he would!"

But no further public statement was made. The autumn crisis seemed to be passing, though very slowly. I was living in Rostropovich's dacha, quite illegitimately, without a residence permit, and what is more in a residential zone for government officials from which anyone can be evicted at the shake of a little finger—yet they didn't evict me, didn't check up on me, didn't come near me. Gradually, a steady rhythm began to prevail in my daily routine and in my mental life. I pushed on fast with my *August 1914,* and for the rest of that year (1970) I would have sat quieter than any mouse, never letting out a squeak—would have, but for the misfortune that befell Zhores Medvedev in early summer. These were the very months, as I finished the first draft and began the second, that might determine the success or failure of the whole structure of *R-17,* and I so much needed to succeed! Nothing called more urgently for a systematic and extended account of itself than the Revolution: the story would soon be so hopelessly tangled by Soviet and by foreign writers that there would be no hope of getting at the truth. Friends, too, advanced prudent arguments about the writer's lot to dissuade me from intervening.

But there is no weighing these things in the scales of reason: If you find something scorching your soles—find the ground like a frying pan under your feet—you'll dance, all right! You feel ashamed to be a mere historical novelist when people are being strangled before your eyes. I should not think much of the author of *Gulag* if he preserved a diplomatic silence about its continuation into the present. For our intelligentsia the internment of Zhores Medvedev in a loony bin held greater dangers and raised larger issues than what had happened to Czechoslovakia. It was a noose around our own throats. So I decided to write something. I began my first drafts very menacingly:

### "WARNING!"

(To *all of them*, all the torturers. I am very apt to be carried away at first, but then I recover my self-control.) During my time in the camps I had got to know the enemies of the human race quite well: they respect the *big fist* and nothing else; the harder you slug them, the safer you will be. (People in the West simply will not understand this, and are forever hoping to mollify them with concessions.) As soon as I rubbed the sleep out of my eyes in the morning I longed to get to my novel, but the urge to rewrite my Warning just once more would be too strong for me, I was so worked up about it. By the fifth draft it had become rather milder: "THE WAY WE LIVE" [Document 13].

In November 1969 some people had rebuked me for rushing so rashly to answer the Writers' Union and so *preventing* my brother writers, and public opinion, from taking my part, frightening them off with my belligerence. This time, to make sure that my pugnacity would not sink Medvedev, I reined myself in, I held back, let the academics have their say, and did not release my letter till Whit Monday, in the middle of June. As far as Zhores was concerned, it was probably superfluous by then: the authorities had lost their nerve anyway. Still, I had spoken out loudly about psychiatric hospitals, and perhaps scared a few of those people—not "Doctor" Lunts, perhaps, but other hearts would quail next time.

For this letter they could not forgive me. Such reliable information as there is suggests that the decision to expel me from the country was taken during those days in June. Certain leading socialist realists (to the apostolic number of twelve, I believe) petitioned the government to banish the miscreant Solzhenitsyn from our holy motherland. There was nothing new in this idea, but a formal beginning had now been made. Markov and Voronkov, that mettlesome pair, passed the thing to *Litgazeta,* and with it, I am told, a decision of the Presidium of the Supreme Soviet, which had also been drafted beforehand, depriving me of Soviet citizenship.

But once again, some gear failed to mesh and the machine went wrong. My belief is that there was too close and conspicuous a connection with the Medvedev affair, and that it would have been embarrassing to expel me for that, so they postponed it for two or three months, thinking that I was bound to commit some other offense.

But then Mauriac, God rest his soul, started his dogged campaign to obtain a Nobel Prize for me, and spoiled the game for *our masters* once again: if they exiled me now it would look like a riposte to Mauriac, and a stupid one. If I should be given the prize, expelling me for that would look no less stupid. The design they cherished was to block the award first, and expel me afterward.

(And this was the autumn in which I thought of nothing but finishing *August 1914* as fast as I could.)

Block the prize? Yes, we can find ways: a high-powered commission of writers (headed by Konstantin Simonov, Simonov the man of many faces, Simonov simultaneously the noble liberal martyr and the esteemed conservative with access to all official quarters).

The commission was to go to Stockholm and as fellow socialists shame the Swedish public into refusing to serve the dark forces of reaction. (No one in the West is proof against such appeals.) However, to keep travel expenses down, the commission's departure was set for 10 October, the very eve of the awards. And what did the Swedish Academy do but announce its decisions two weeks early, on the second Thursday instead of the fourth! How *our masters* howled and gnawed their paws!

For me, 1970 was the last year in which the Nobel Prize could still be of any use to me. After 1970, I would have begun my battle without it.

The award was a shock—a hilarious shock. It had come as it had come to Hemingway in that anecdote, distracting me from my novel, which I was within two short weeks of finishing. . . . After this, I had the greatest difficulty in keeping on.

It had come! And the lucky thing was that it had actually come very early. I had received it without really showing the world anything of my writing, except *Ivan Denisovich, Cancer Ward* and the "lightened" *First Circle;* the rest I had kept in reserve. From my new height I could bowl book after book downhill, helped by the pull of gravity: the three volumes of *Gulag,* the ninety-six-chapter *First Circle, Decembrists Without December, Tanks Know the Truth,* my camp poem. . . .

It had come, and canceled all the mistakes of 1962, mistakes due to dilatoriness and excessive secrecy. All gone and forgotten.

It had come—bursting in on Rostropovich's dacha in a flurry of telephone calls. No one had phoned me there for ages, and suddenly there were several calls in a few minutes. The simple-minded, indeed slightly crazy, woman who then lived in the main dacha ran after me every time—she knew me by the sobriquet "neighbor"—tugged at my sleeve, tried to wrest the telephone from me.

"Is that a *correspondent* you're talking to? I want to tell him about them not giving me an apartment!"

She thought I was talking to a *Pravda* reporter, never imagining that there were others.

It was in fact the Norwegian Per-Egil Hegge, who spoke excellent Russian, a rare thing among Western correspondents in Moscow. He had obtained the number from somewhere and asked me two questions: Would I accept the prize? Would I go to Stockholm?

I thought awhile, then went to fetch pencil and paper, leaving him to suppose, if he liked, that I was disconcerted. My intention had been to make no statement at all for a week, and see what sort of bark *our masters* would let out, how they would tackle the problem. But Hegge's call threatened to wreck my plan. To be silent and evasive now was to set one foot on the path to destruction. If I stuck to my old intention to do everything differently from Pasternak, to do just the opposite, I had no choice but to declare roundly: Yes, I accept! Yes, I certainly shall go, *if the decision is left to me!* (But in this country the handcuffs can be clapped on at any minute.) And I should add that *my health is excellent,* and will not prevent me from making the journey! (All undesirables in our country are of course sick people, which is why they do not travel.)

At that moment I had no doubt at all that I would be going.

Then, in my telegram replying to the Swedish Academy, I said that "I regard the Nobel Prize as a tribute to Russian"—not, of course, to Soviet—"literature, *and to our troubled history.*"

A number of surprises now came my way. Frayed though they are, the connecting threads between the West and ourselves still vibrate. Murmurs began to reach me by indirect routes, reproaching me with those words *"our troubled history":* people might say that I had been given the prize for political reasons. (But for *our troubled history,* I would not have needed the prize. If our history had been easier, we could have managed without help from you!) Then, by two separate indirect channels, came one and the same inquiry: Wouldn't I like to avoid the sensation that my arrival in Stockholm might cause? In particular, the Academy and the Nobel Foundation were worried about demonstrations against me by students with Maoist leanings. So shouldn't I perhaps say no to the Grand Hotel, where Nobel laureates always stayed, and let them hide me away in a quiet apartment?

Fine! The very reason why I trudged my way from camp work parades to the Nobel Prize—to hide in a quiet apartment in Stockholm, and flee with a carload of detectives from a lot of pampered young ne'er-do-wells.

I sent no answer by bush telegraph, but then similar messages started arriving by ordinary post: a telegram from the Nobel Foundation to the same effect—"We shall try to find a quieter and more secluded spot for your stay in Stockholm"—and a letter in which the Academy assumed "that you yourself will wish to spend your time in Stockholm as quietly as possible" and itself undertook to "do everything possible to provide you with a secure apartment. May we add that a laureate is under no obligation to have any dealings whatsoever with the press, radio, etc."

"As quietly as possible"? The last thing I wanted! "No dealings with the press or radio"? Then why the hell go at all?

The courage of the Swedes had come to an abrupt end the moment they decided to give me the prize. (For that decision I owe them a thank-you as high as a seven-story house!) From then on, they had begun to fear some sort of brawl, to fear that politics would come into it.

In their position, it was the right thing to do, perfectly respectable. But my incorrigible zek brain had expected nothing like it. You shuffle and stumble along in column-of-fives, with your hands behind your back, and you think: They can't wait to hear from us *out there.* But in truth they aren't the least bit interested.

The prize they're giving you is for literature. Naturally they want no politics. Only for us, what they call "politics" is a matter of life and death.

That was the situation on the Western front. As for the Eastern, a few days after the award was announced an idea flashed into my head: This was my first chance to talk to the government on equal terms. There was nothing disgraceful in it: I had attained a position of strength, and I would speak to them from it. I wouldn't give an inch, but I would suggest concessions they could make to escape from their present position with some decorum.

To whom should I write? I didn't think twice. To Suslov! For the following reason. When Tvardovsky introduced me to Khrushchev at the Kremlin meeting in December 1962, there was no other member of the Politburo near us and none of them came over. But during the next intermission, when Tvardovsky took me around the foyer and introduced me to such writers, film-makers and artists as he chose, a tall, lean man with an elongated, by no means stupid face came up to us in the cinema annex, took me firmly by the hand and shook it vigorously as he told me how very much he had enjoyed *Ivan Denisovich,* shook it as though from now on I would never have a closer friend. All the others had told me their names, but he did not. I inquired, "Whom have I the honor to . . . ?" and even then the stranger did not declare himself, but Tvardovsky said in a reproachful whisper, "Mikhail Andreyevich." I shrugged as much as to say "What Mikhail Andreyevich?" "Su-u-uslov, who else!" said Tvardovsky, doubly reproachful. We are of course supposed to carry their two dozen portraits at all times on our retinas and in our hearts! But my visual memory quite often lets me down, and I just didn't recognize him. Nor indeed did Suslov seem to mind my failure to do so. But here was the puzzle: Why had he greeted me so warmly? Khrushchev was nowhere near at the time, and no other Politburo member could see him, so it wasn't to ingratiate himself with anybody. What was it, then? An expression of genuine feeling? To show that there was one vacuum-packed, garden-fresh freedom-lover in the Politburo? The chief ideologist of the Party, no less . . . ! Could it be?[1]

This riddle lingered in my mind for many years, and nothing happened to resolve it. Still, I thought: Whatever uncanny influence was at

---

1. Incidentally, it was none other than Suslov who had called V. Grossman in five months earlier, in July 1962, to talk about his confiscated novel: there was too much politics in it, and what he said about the camps was all hearsay. That was no way of writing; it couldn't be taken seriously. Set hard in his desk chair, he felt sure that nothing that wasn't hearsay would ever come to light, that it had all been snuffed out. Then, suddenly, such a pleasant surprise for him—*Ivan Denisovich!*

work will show itself again someday; our paths will cross again. They had not, however, crossed so far. But now, in October 1970, I felt impelled to address—no one but him! [Document 14]

If I could have set in train just the things suggested there (an amnesty for those caught reading me, the quick publication and unrestricted sale of *Cancer Ward,* the lifting of the ban on my previous works, followed by the publication of *August 1914*), it would have meant a change not only for me but in the whole literary situation, and in time not merely the literary situation. And although my heart yearned for something more, something decisive, still, those who change the course of history are the gradualists, in whose hands the fabric of events does not tear. If there were any possibility of changing the situation in our country smoothly, we ought to reconcile ourselves to it and do just that. That would be far more worthwhile than going to *explain* things to the West.

But that was where it ended. I never received an answer. In this instance, as in all others, their arrogance and their pessimism caused *them* to miss every chance of mending matters.

Meanwhile the Swedes kept sending me programs for the celebrations: which banquet I should attend on which day, where to appear in dinner jacket and black tie, and where in tails. The laureate's speech is delivered at a banquet (was I to talk about our Russian tragedy while all around were merrily eating and drinking?), is expected to take no more than three minutes, and preferably contains only words of gratitude.

The album *Les Prix Nobel* revealed to me the pathetic sight of a bunch of uniformly packaged laureates with sheepish smiles and jumbo folders containing their diplomas.

Yet again my expectations lay in ruins and all my resolute intentions had proved futile. I had lived to see an incredible miracle, but how to make use of it I did not know. Courtesy to those who had awarded me the prize meant, I found, not making resounding speeches, but keeping quiet, observing the decencies, smiling by numbers, and having woolly-lambkin curls. True, a Nobel lecture could be composed and delivered. But if there, too, you had to beware of expressing yourself trenchantly, then what was the point of going at all?

During those winter months my firstborn was expected and now the prize threatened to separate us, since we had agreed beforehand that

I should go. With no hope of ever seeing the son who might be born to me.

I was going away to clear my lungs and take in breath for my next work. Going away to—persuade? shake? set in motion?—the West.

But here in my homeland? Who would ever read it all, and when? Who would ever understand that for the sake of my *books* it was better this way?

At the age of fifty I had made a solemn vow: "My only dream is to live up to the hopes that reading Russia places in me." But now a chance to leave had presented itself and I was running away. Was that it?

What, then, should I do? Stay on and fight to the last? Come what may?

Those woolly-lambkin curls, that white bow tie again.

By way of mocking reproof, to teach me not to judge my predecessors too hastily, I was left teetering paralytically on the knife edge of decision.

What I now wanted to do was to record my Nobel lecture, and send the tape *over there* so that they could listen to it in Stockholm. While I stayed here! That would have some effect! A more powerful effect than anything else could!

But in the tense month and a half that followed (on top of everything else I had many family preoccupations) I was in no state to compose a lecture.

Perhaps in Saratov or Irkutsk our next Nobel Prize winner was writhing with shame for that wretched Solzhenitsyn: Why doesn't he bellow like a calving cow? Why doesn't he get out there and do a bit of tub thumping?

Our masters were eagerly watching and waiting for my departure. It would come under the rules of throwaway checkers: on the face of it, I would have *marched* right across the board, taking pieces all the way—but that would make me the loser! I have it on reliable information that a decree depriving me of Soviet citizenship was ready for use. All that remained was to trundle me over the frontier. There is a closing date for handing in a visa application form, after which you are too late. Nobody knows it, but the Visa and Registration Department thinks that everyone does, and they were surprised to see me letting it pass me by. For those few weeks the newspaper campaign against me was muted, then it was silenced altogether. There were only sporadic outbursts in briefing sessions—not everyone could stand the strain of silence. The secretary of the Moscow obkom, echoed by yapping "specialists on international affairs" (for some time no lecture on "international affairs" had been complete without a mention of me), said that "for some reason Mr. Solzhenitsyn has so far not applied for an exit visa."

Tvardovsky too, so I was told, was worrying about me in the Kremlin clinic, and wondering whether there was some way for me to receive the prize without going.

He was lying there with his speech impaired, and a useless right arm, but he could listen to the radio and read, and he followed the story of my Nobel Prize closely, and when his speech began to return said, or rather shouted, to the nurses and attendants: "Bravo! Bravo! Victory!"

On my desk, meanwhile, lay a letter in which I declined to go, and every morning, here a letter, there a comma, was amended. I was trying to choose the best day: perhaps two weeks before the prize-giving ceremony would do. In spite of the granite façade that our government showed the world outside, *internally* the initiative was always in my hands. From first to last, I behaved as though *they* simply did not exist. I ignored *them:* I had decided for myself, and I had announced that *I would go,* and they had not interfered to try and change my mind; now I myself had decided, and was about to announce, that *I would not go,* exposing at the same time the shameful secrets of our police—and once again they would swallow it, and not barge in with unwanted advice.

But how was I to send it? The post would delay it. I would have to take it to the Swedish Embassy myself, and arrange through them for the medal and the diploma to be presented to me in Moscow. Here's an idea: we'll get fifty or so prominent Moscow intellectuals together, and I'll *thump my tub,* all right! If I speak from here the effect will be more powerful, very much more!

But how was I to break through into the embassy? What luck: the Swedes had no militiamen standing outside! It was a snug little detached building in Borisoglebsky Lane. An overfed cat completely filled an armchair. Relays of Swedes escorted me through one door after another (they had been alerted). Gunnar Jarring had just returned to Moscow. He was Swedish ambassador to the U.S.S.R., and what was more, conciliator in the Arab-Israeli conflict, and what was even more, so I had been warned, a contender for the post from which U Thant was retiring, and therefore assiduous in his efforts to oblige the Soviet government. He had been ambassador in Moscow for seven years, during which time the prize had gone to Sholokhov. Jarring had become a close friend of Sholokhov's and made a great fuss over him.

He was dour, hard, tall, dark (not much like a Swede?), and he received me with a certain reserve. I made myself comfortable in an ambassadorial armchair, waved my letter at him, but did not give it to him to read, and said:

"This is a letter I've written to the Swedish Academy about my visit [Document 15], but I'm afraid it may be delayed in the post and it is important for them to know my decision right away. Would you be prepared to send it?"

He understood Russian, but chose to answer me through an interpreter—his cultural attaché, Lundström.

"What have you decided?"

"Not to go."

A twitch of satisfaction. This would save him trouble.

"It will be in Stockholm tomorrow morning."

In other words, he would put it in the diplomatic bag. "Good. I'll send my curriculum vitae with it. But what about the medal and the diploma? Would it be possible to hold a reception in your embassy?"

"Quite impossible. It's never been done that way."

"Yes, but there's never been a case like mine. Don't prejudge the issue, Mr. Jarring. Let the Academy think about it."

Jarring was confident that either the medal and the diploma would be sent to me by post or "we shall present them to you here in my study, just as we are now, without an audience."

And without a lecture? That was no good to me. The Academy could keep it all.

I didn't give him a chance to read the letter in my presence, but left it all with him and took my leave. He had given his word.

I gave the Academy three days to receive my letter and act upon it. I intended to release it through samizdat at the end of the third day. But the Academy sent a telegram saying that it wanted to make the letter public only at the banquet. That would be too late for me. I needed to make it clear *immediately* that I was not going. But the Swedes were not to experience the explosive power of Russian samizdat: the contents of the letter trickled through their own fingers, probably while it was being translated into Swedish, and they sent me a second telegram in hot pursuit of the first: they apologized, deplored the leak, and asked me to send something else for the banquet.

I had not been intending to. I had said the little I wanted to say for the time being, measuring my words, and all that really mattered would go into my lecture. But the telegram set me off again.

It had not been part of my plan, but why not take a paragraph that had dropped out of my Nobel lecture and use it here, making the coincidence in dates my excuse.

"Your Majesty! Ladies and gentlemen! I cannot overlook the remarkable fact that the day on which the Nobel Prizes are being presented coincides with International Human Rights Day. . . ."

(Gentlemen—your Scythian guest is disappointed in you: Why all those lambs-wool hairdos under the arc lights? Why is a white tie *de rigueur* and a camp jerkin not allowed? And what strange custom is this —to listen to the speech in which a laureate sums up his work, his whole life, with food before you? How abundantly the tables are laden, how sumptuous are the dishes, how casually you pass them, as though you saw them every day. Serve yourselves, chew your food, wash it down . . . but what of the writing on the wall, in letters of fire:—"Mene, mene, tekel, upharsin." Do you not see it . . . ?)

"Well, then, let us not forget at this festive table that this very day, political prisoners are holding a hunger strike in defense of rights curtailed or trampled under foot."

I did not say whose prisoners, or where, but it was obvious that I meant in the Soviet Union. Nor was I inventing it, or relying on coincidence. I knew that on 10 December Soviet zeks in Vladimir Central Jail, some of those at Potma and some in the *loony bins* would be on hunger strike. The news would come too late—but I would be just in time.

(Among the messages of congratulation on the award of the Nobel Prize was a collective letter from the Potma camps. It was easier to collect signatures there, but how did the prisoners at Vladimir conjure nineteen signatures onto the same piece of paper through the stone walls of their cells? In a day or two I would receive this most precious of congratulatory messages:

"We hotly dispute the Swedish Academy's claim to have been first to appreciate your valor as a writer and as a citizen at its true worth. We jealously cherish our friend, our cellmate, our comrade of the prison trains. . . .")

Send it off—without hesitation! I was soaring so lightly, why deny myself this piece of mischief? How should I send it? Through the embassy again, of course.

The pitcher had learned its way to the well.

Last time, fearing obstruction, I had gone without telephoning. This time I had the number ready.

"Mr. Lundström . . . ? I've received two telegrams from the Swedish Academy and I should be glad of your *advice*. . . ."

(I couldn't very well say, "I want to dump something in your lap.")

Poor Lundström. His hands were trembling violently, and he couldn't disguise it. He didn't want to insult the laureate with a rough refusal, but Ambassador Jarring was away, and had (as I learned later) forbidden anyone to take anything from me after the impertinent letter which he had not read in time. "Mediating between Israel and the Arabs is quite enough for me, without having to mediate between Solzhenitsyn and the Academy." Lundström had served in Moscow for fourteen years, evidently without trouble, and was strongly attached to it; now he was jeopardizing his career because an ex-zek was being importunate, and he didn't know how to refuse. He mopped his brow, smoked nervously, and his whole figure, his voice, his diction, were apologetic as he said:

"Mr. Solzhenitsyn . . . if you will allow me to give you my frank opinion . . . I must speak as a diplomat. . . . Your message of greeting [Document 16] does, you know, contain political motifs. . . ."

"Political?" I was quite astonished. "Where? Show me!"

"Here, right here." He was pointing at the last sentence as he spoke.

"But that isn't aimed at any particular country or group of countries. International Human Rights Day is a purely moral, not a political occasion."

"Yes, but language of that sort is not in the tradition of the Nobel ceremony."

"If I were there I would be saying it."

"If you were there yourself, of course. But in your absence, the organizers may object. They will probably want to consult the King."

"Let them consult him!"

"Yes, but send it by post."

"It's too late; it may not arrive in time for the banquet."

"Wire it, then."

"I can't. The contents would be *known in advance*. And I have been asked to keep them secret."

I gave him a difficult quarter of an hour. He took from me, with further apologies, a written request to the embassy (to forward my letter). . . . He warned me that it might not be granted. He warned me, too, that this was the last time, and that in no circumstances would he accept my Nobel lecture. . . .

Mercilessly, I left my harangue with him, and went away.

It turned out later that he had spent his own money and sacrificed his weekend on a private trip to Finland, and sent the speech from there.

That's your true European: he had made no promises, but had performed more than he could promise.

All the same, I felt no remorse. The prisoners on hunger strike at Vladimir were worth this outlay of time and money on the part of a diplomat.

One thing upset me: a sentence was omitted from my speech and not read out at the banquet. Perhaps because they were overawed by the occasion, or perhaps because, as some say, they were afraid for me. (Yes, they were all so full of compassion for me. As Academician Lundkvist, a Communist and a Lenin Prize winner, put it: "The Nobel Prize can only harm Solzhenitsyn. Writers such as he are used to living in poverty; they need to live in poverty.")

That very special evening in my life (the evening of the Nobel ceremony), we celebrated with a few close friends in Rostropovich's attic "tavern," sitting at an ancient unpainted table, and drinking from equally outlandish glasses, with candles in several branched candlesticks to light us, listening from time to time to reports of the Nobel ceremony from various radio stations. They got around to relaying the banquet speeches. The jammer badly blurred one broadcast, but I got the impression that my final sentence was missing. We waited for the repetition of the speech in the late news program. I was right; it wasn't there.

(They have a lot to learn about our Russian samizdat! Early tomorrow morning, leaflets carrying my banquet speech will be scattered far and wide.)

More of the same at briefing sessions: "He was given the opportunity to leave, but wouldn't! He has stayed on to continue his wrecking activities here! He does all he can to harm the Soviet state!" But this time (and it is always the same when you show your strength) no newspaper campaign against me materialized. One article turned up in *Pravda,* saying that I was an "internal émigré"—now that I had refused to emigrate!—"alien and hostile to the whole life of our people," that

I had "slid down into the cesspit," and that my novels were "lampoons." The signature under the article was the same as that which had appeared under anti-Czechoslovak articles, which had helped to instigate the occupation, and we naturally expected a blowing of whistles and pounding of feet. But it did not come. In addition, the generals' press, which is more faithful to the ideas of the Party than the Party itself, explained (in *Kommunist Vooruzrennykh Sil*) for the benefit of political officers in the army that "the Nobel Prize is the mark of Cain for betraying his people." Party instructors, at a tug on their leading strings, also produced this one: "*Incidentally,* his name is not Solzhenitsyn, but Solzhenitser. . . ."* And then in *Litgazeta* there was some fugitive American popular singer giving me lessons in Russian patriotism. . . .

Like all they handled, the campaign against me fell flat, and the letter of mine which Suslov had was embedded in a mass of inert dough that refused to rise. No movement anywhere. General paralysis.

My scheme for finding some peaceful solution had come to nothing. But still, the Nobel crisis, which had threatened for a while to tear me up by the roots, to carry me beyond the sea, or to bury me several layers deep, had also petered out after these minor tremors.

Nothing had happened; things were just where they had been before.

How often now I had come to the very edge of the abyss, and found a gentle hollow. The high pass that I must cross, or perhaps the precipice over which I must fall, was ahead, far ahead of me still.

\*          \*

\*

Although I was very far from inactive in the following year (1971), I felt myself passing through a twilight zone, in which resolution and the will to act were dimmed.

I felt this way largely because that side of my life which tension and ceaseless motion had caused me to disregard, to let slip, to leave out of account, came to the fore, painfully forced itself upon me, left me more exhausted than another man would have been in my place, drained more of my strength perhaps than all the potholes on the highway of my life. For the preceding five years I had put up with a deep, an abysmal marital rift, and had continually postponed any decisive action: I was invariably short of time to finish some work, or some part of a work, and every time I backed down, coaxed, wheedled, just to gain another three months, one month, two weeks of precious working time, not to be torn away from what mattered most to me. There is a law that crises never come singly, and the problems I had postponed broke in with a bang on the months immediately before the Nobel award, and then dragged on for a year, two years, and beyond. . . .

(The state was quick to sink its talons into the protracted divorce proceedings, and I found myself vulnerable in the following way: Whatever happened to me, the companion of my labors and mother of my children could neither go with me, nor visit me in prison, nor defend me and my books. All this would strengthen the hands of my enemies.)

Another reason for my apathy, no doubt, was that no spring is endlessly resilient and all resistance is doomed sooner or later to fatigue.

I had so longed for this great event—winning the Nobel Prize—longed to occupy this vantage point for attack; could it be that I had achieved nothing after all, that the whole thing was a fiasco? I hadn't even sent my lecture.

I had thought of my Nobel lecture beforehand as a scouring peal of bells. This, more than anything else, made winning the prize worthwhile. I sat down to it, I even wrote it—but it came out in a form difficult to digest.

I should have liked to talk only about the social and political life of the East, and of the West too, insofar as the West was accessible to my prison-sharpened mother wit. Looking over the lectures given by my predecessors, however, I saw that this would cut across the whole tradition, tear a hole in it: it would never occur to any writer from the free world to talk about such things—they have other platforms, other places, other occasions for it. Those Western writers who had given lectures had spoken on the nature of art, of beauty, of literature. Camus had done it with all the brilliance of French eloquence at its finest. Obviously I ought to talk about the same sort of thing. But any discussion of the nature of literature or its capabilities was for me a boring and distasteful rehash: what *I* am capable of, I can show better by writing; what is beyond my powers I do not discuss. And if I did give such a lecture, what would former zeks think when they read it? Why, they would wonder, had I been given a voice and a platform? Had I taken fright? Gone soft with fame? And betrayed the dead?

I made an effort to *combine* the two themes—society and art. It didn't come off. The two overstrained shafts sprang apart again and would not be bent into line. Friends on whom I tried it confirmed that it was not what was needed. So I wrote to the Swedes telling them honestly just how things were, that for reasons which I gave I wanted to cry off the lecture.

They were perfectly happy. "What seems natural to a scholar may not come naturally at all to a writer—yours is a case in point. . . . You must not feel that it is a breach of tradition."

And with that we buried the lecture. This, however, gave rise to another misunderstanding. The director of the Nobel Foundation had to make a public announcement about my withdrawal. But evidently fearing that he might do me some harm, instead of publishing the real reason he made up one of his own, little thinking—oh, that fatal gulf between the minds of East and West!—that an excuse which looked entirely respectable in the West might bring shame on me in the East. According to him, I had not sent a lecture because I did not know how to transmit it: if it went by a legal route, the censorship would hold it up; if by an illegal route, the authorities in my country would regard that as a crime. In other words, after winning the Nobel Prize I had become a loyal slave? This caught me on the raw. I had to write denying it, but my letter got stuck on the way. You can wave as frantically as you like, at the bottom of the hole we're in. We have no voice and no rights; they can bend us into any shape they like.

(Eighteen months later, after I had given my lecture, the story would surface in the *New York Times* with a different twist: I was supposed originally to have composed a feeble and purely literary version of my lecture, but my friends had cried shame—I must write something more pointed.)

There was a grain of truth in this wild rubbish: the steel-hard resolve with which I had hacked my way through the years since my arrest, and without which I would never reach my goal, had softened somewhat.

I had not stood up for Bukovsky when he was arrested that spring. I had not stood up for Grigorenko. Nor for anyone else. I was busy planning and timing actions far ahead.

My conscience ached, above all, for *Gulag*. In 1969 I had put off publishing it till Christmas 1970. The time had come and gone, and I had deferred it again. Why, then, had we taken such fearful risks to finish it in a hurry? Now that I had the Nobel Prize—how could I keep putting it off? Whatever comfortable excuses I reclined on, to those who had been taken four to a sled and tipped like frozen logs into camp burial pits, my reasons would look most unreasonable. Could it still, in 1971, be untimely to speak of what had happened in 1918, 1930, 1945? To redeem the sacrifice of their lives at least by telling the story? Was it still too soon?

If I had *gone* when I could, I would have been sitting over the proofs of *Gulag* by now. In fact, I would have had it in print in spring 1971. As it was, I was trying to think up an excuse for deferring it, for delaying the cup that I could not in the end put from me.

No, it was not just an excuse, though if I am to be strict with myself, I shall do better to acknowledge it as such. Not just an excuse, because not just I, but many of the 227 zeks who had provided information for my book, might suffer cruelly should it be published. For them, too, it would be better if the book came out later. Whereas for those who were in their graves it could not be soon enough.

Not just an excuse, because the Gulag was only the offspring of the Revolution and heir to it: if I had had to write about Gulag in secrecy, writing about the Revolution required even greater secrecy, deeper burrowing, stranger contortions. To make haste with the Revolution was even more important, certainly no less urgent. And as things had happened, it was I who must do it. How could I ever get through it all unaided?

In the placid literary life of placid countries, what determines the order in which an author publishes his books? His maturity. The order in which they reach completion. The chronological sequence—either that in which he wrote them or that of their subject matter.

But in our country, it is not at all a literary decision, but a matter of anxious strategic planning. Books are like divisions or army corps: at times they must dig themselves in, hold their fire, lie low; at times they must cross bridges in the dark and noiselessly; at times, concealing their preparations to the last dribble of loose earth, they must rush into a concerted offensive from the least expected quarter at the least expected moment. While the author is like a commander in chief, here throwing in a unit, there moving up another to wait its turn.

Once *Gulag* appeared, they would not let me write *R-17*, so I must get through most of it beforehand.

But still, it seemed a senseless undertaking: twenty "Knots,"* each taking a year, meant twenty years. But *August 1914* had been two years in the writing. At that rate, might it take forty? Or fifty?

At last my mind was made up. The critical point would be reached when Lenin appeared openly. As long as he came into only one chapter in each "Knot" and was not directly involved in the action, those chapters could be hidden away, the places they would later occupy left vacant, and the "Knots" could be released without them. This was possible with the first three, but in Knot IV Lenin is already in Petrograd and playing a conspicuous part. Revealing the author's attitude to him would be just as bad as publishing *Gulag*. So then, I must first write and put out Knots I–III, and then throw all my remaining forces into the final offensive.

According to my calculations, this would be in spring 1975.

Man proposes. . . .

This final decision, this final dateline, brought light and ease into my life. For the time being, postpone everything else, and work, work, work. But afterward, a head-on clash was inevitable; there would be no more loopholes. It brought me happiness even. Is it inevitable? Then it's so much the simpler!

For the present, I must publish *August 1914,* which was finished. This was a novel step: openly publishing a book in a Western edition, acknowledging it as my own, no longer disingenuously pleading that someone had made use of my manuscript for his own purposes and circulated it without my knowledge, and that I had been powerless to prevent it. At any rate, I had happily straightened out a sharp bend in my route, and could move straight ahead. Something, too, would be said directly about the God defiled by chewing and spitting atheists.* Nor, with future publications in mind, could I be uninterested in Western reactions to *August 1914.*

With the Lenin chapter removed, there was hardly anything in the novel that could reasonably have prevented our leaders from publishing it in its homeland. But (not without reason) I was an object of such loathing, fear and suspicion that they would never consent to strengthen my position here by publishing me. I understood this, and did not bother sending it to a Soviet publishing house (besides, that would have meant stepping down from my demand in the letter to Suslov: let them publish *Cancer Ward* first). There was no *Novy Mir* now, and I was free of special obligations. I had already sent the manuscript to Paris in March and they had promised to set it in type in three months. At this point Rostropovich made a suggestion reminiscent of his brilliant chess moves: that I should nevertheless send it to a Soviet publisher, "just to show up their unwillingness to publish."

"Not a single copy! They'll never get their paws on it! There's only one batch—and that's for samizdat."

"You needn't give it to them. Just send a bit of a note *informing them* that you've finished a novel. Let *them* ask *you* for it." That I liked. I typed out not one but seven slips for seven publishing houses, varying the wording, but all informing them herewith that I had completed a novel on such and such a theme, and of so many words. I sent them on their way. It was a risky game, all the same. What if someone *did* ask for it? Should I have to give them the manuscript and stop work on it in Paris? They still wouldn't publish it, but they could very easily rob me of a whole year. But there is such a tight traffic jam in the Soviet official world that they did not take advantage of this opening either: not a single publisher responded or showed a flicker of interest. They did, however, procure a manuscript from elsewhere and give it to Langen-Müller in West Germany to bring out a pirated edition before the original appeared in Paris. Where on earth had they got the text? I hadn't given it to samizdat. I can only think that they must have taped it in the apartment where we had collated copies by reading aloud: they have bugging devices everywhere.

Or possibly one of my "first readers" had *leaked*. (In the winter of 1970–1971 I had some thirty of them. Because the historical novel was something new to me, I had asked them to complete a sort of author's questionnaire to help me settle certain questions.) Nor could I quite exclude the possibility that a further copy had been taken from the photocopy that had been with Tvardovsky from February to May and that several readers unknown to me had been allowed to carry home.

Tvardovsky! How eager he had once been to have it for his magazine. He must at least read it before he died.

In February 1971, exactly a year after the rout of *Novy Mir,* he was discharged from the Kremlin hospital, crippled by incorrect treatment and suffering from radiation disease. Rostropovich and I went to see him.

We expected to find him in bed, but—perhaps making a special effort for us—he was sitting in an armchair wearing a hospital pajama top with green and mauve stripes, and hospital bottoms, and wrapped in a traveling rug for good measure. I bent down to embrace him, but he insisted on standing up for this, and as his daughter and son-in-law, one on either side, lifted him I could see that his right side was paralyzed and his right hand badly swollen.

"Get-ting ol-d-der." He brought the words out with difficulty, but clearly. A smile that his lips could not quite complete expressed regret, perhaps a great sadness.

Because of the brevity of the sentence (though it was to be almost the longest and most informative of the whole conversation!), the flatness of his voice and the absence of any accompanying gesture, I wasn't sure whether he was apologizing for getting old himself or was shocked to see how I had aged.

They lowered him into his chair, and we sat facing him. We were in the well-remembered baronial hall again, a yard or two from the fireplace, and indeed on the very spot where I had first been startled by the brisk words and movements in which he had revealed his partiality to samizdat and the BBC. He sat now facing the picture window, almost motionless, almost speechless, and his light-blue eyes seemed at once quite aware of his surroundings and yet unfocused, as though he was losing his ability to organize what he saw around some central point. It was difficult to know whether they were expressing understanding or intermittent failure to understand, but they were all the time fuller of life than his speech.

It soon became evident that he could no longer form connected sentences at all. Straining to find words, he would begin speaking—come on, come on, you're nearly there—but no, what came out was a string of interjections and particles with nothing more coherent in between.

"What about the . . . just the . . . you know . . . one that . . ."

But with his good hand, his left, he smoked and smoked, incorrigibly.

A. T.'s wife brought us the fifth, and last, volume of his collected works. I remembered, out loud, that this was the very volume that had been delayed by his obstinate refusal to omit some paragraphs about me. (But I didn't ask whether they were there now; they had probably been sacrificed.) A. T. nodded. He had understood, he confirmed what I had said. Then I got out the typescript of *August 1914,* bound as two separate volumes, and automatically speaking more slowly and choosing simple words, I showed it to A. T. and explained as though he were a child that it was part of a much larger whole, which part it was, and why there was a map affixed to it. He nodded over and over again. He seemed just as attentive and interested as before, perhaps more so, although his concentration was fitful.

He found his voice: "How many . . . ?"

He couldn't produce the next word, but it was the obvious question for an editor to ask: how many pages of type? (For how many months would it run in *Novy Mir?*)

I also read my Suslov letter to him, pausing between words, and explained my moves and the obstacles I had faced during the "Nobeliana," my dealings with Jarring, the business of the prize money. He took it all in eagerly and sympathetically, and with movements of the head and inhibited gestures showed his far from inhibited feelings. He nodded vigorously, ironically, when I recalled that he had introduced me to Suslov. At times it even looked as though he was laughing, laughing heartily, but only with his eyes and his busily nodding head, not out loud. When he saw the map accompanying *August 1914,* he moaned his surprise, as deaf-mutes do, and moaned again when he learned of my unannounced exclusion from *Litfond.* You would start thinking that he understood everything—and a minute later that he understood only intermittently, when he concentrated.

I have sometimes tried to converse with people suffering from partial aphasia, and know that to do so is to share their torment. You are on the rack yourself. With A.T. it was not so. He realized the impossibility of expressing himself, but when he heard no one prompting him with the word he needed, instead of losing his temper to no purpose, he showed by the unchanging look of kindly acquiescence in his eyes his submissiveness to a higher power above us all which we, his companions, also recognized, but which did not in the least prevent us from understanding one another and being of one mind. A.T.'s powers of active response were paralyzed, but kindly feeling streamed from his eyes unstemmed, and his face, exhausted as it was by illness, still retained its old, childlike expression.

When A.T. was particularly anxious to finish saying something and could not manage it, I helped him out by taking his left hand—which was warm, and free and alive. He squeezed my hand in reply, and in this way we understood each other well enough. . . . Understood that all was forgiven between us. That all the bad things, the hurts, the troubles, might never have been.

I suggested to his family that perhaps he could write with his left hand. Anyone can do it, even without training. At school I used to write fluently with my left hand when my right ached. They found a sheet of cardboard and pinned the paper to it so that it would not slip off. I wrote "Aleksandr Trifonovich" in big letters, and said, "Now you put Tvardovsky." The cardboard was placed on his lap. He took the ball-point pen, and seemed to be holding it easily enough, but his feeble, scratchy strokes would not form themselves into letters, and although there was plenty of room on the sheet, they would straggle off toward my writing and superimpose themselves on it. Worse still, what he wrote was not a complete word; the meaning had disappeared through the gaps: "T-R-S-Y . . ."

How could he let me know what he thought of my novel? What could he get out of reading it? I suggested markers of two different colors, for the passages he liked and those he didn't. (This, too, came to nothing.)

So many other things he would never see, never know! All that was most interesting in twentieth-century Russia.

He had had a presentiment:

> Death is never in short supply,
> Life's stocks are always running low.

He had no idea what he was suffering from. The pain in his chest, and his cough, he put down to smoking. And his head? "I've got the same complaint as Lenin," he told his family.

Later on they got tea ready, put A.T.'s trousers on him, and led him to the table. On a carpet it was more difficult than ever for him to move his useless leg; it dragged heavily behind him, and his escorts had to lift it along for him. They sat their father on a chair, then heaved the chair and his bulk with it up to the table.

Rostropovich talked a lot at the tea table, and as merrily as tact allowed. A.T. listened more and more absently, and stopped responding altogether. He had withdrawn into himself. Perhaps he already had one foot in another place.

Afterward we took him back in his armchair to the window, so that he could see the yard where three years ago he had composed his letter to Fedin while clearing the snow, and the path which someone else had now cleared to the gate, and along which Rostropovich and I were about to take our leave.

Alas, Aleksandr Trifonich! Do you remember our discussion of "Matryona's Home"? . . . How you dreaded to think what would have become of you if the October Revolution had never taken place?

I will tell you what you would have become: the poet of the people, greater than Koltsov or Nikitin. You would have written as freely as a man breathes, you would not have sat through four hundred loathsome meetings, you would not have needed to seek relief in vodka, you would not have contracted cancer as a result of injustice and persecution.

Yet when I went to see him again three months later, at the end of May, to my surprise I found A.T. considerably better. He was sitting in the same hall, in the same armchair, still with his face toward the path by which people from the outside world came and went, while he himself could not struggle as far as the gate. But he had the use of his left leg, and of his left hand (which kept reaching for and lighting cigarettes), and his facial movements were almost as expressive as of old, but best of all, his speech was easier, so that he could say quite lucidly that my book (he'd read it! he'd understood it!) was "marvelous" and reinforce it by movements of his head and eyes, and by moaning.

Cheerful late afternoon light lingered in the hall, and the twittering of birds came from the garden. A.T. was very much more like his old self; he understood everything that he was told, and it was possible to imagine that he was recovering. . . . But he still could not write with his left hand, and he uttered no more articulate sentences.

Alas, even at this last meeting I had to hide things from him, as so often before. I could not confide that the book would be coming out in Paris in two weeks' time.

Still less could I reveal to him (I couldn't mention it in his family's hearing) what I was so busy with that spring. (In the intervals between "Knots," the pauses in my main work, projects proliferated. I had been discussing with a number of people a samizdat magazine for "matters of social concern and for literature," with the authors' names given. The "editor's portfolio" already contained a thing or two.)

On the face of it, there was only one big event in my life that spring —the appearance of *August 1914* with my explicit approval. (I had thought of publishing my letter to Suslov at the same time, to show that I had made them an offer, and that *they* were the ones who had rejected any idea of a peaceful solution. But then I thought again: publication of the book would in itself have a more powerful effect than any letter. That I could publish if they attacked. They did not.)

In reality, as often happens when there is a lull in open hostilities, the subterranean war of sapping and minelaying continued uninterruptedly. A war full of toil, anxieties, high excitements. Will it work, won't it work, is it a fiasco or is it a success? Yet from the outside the war was quite invisible; an outsider would see me leading an inactive, dreamy, solitary country-house life. But we were making photocopies of all those works of mine that were not to be found in the West: there were still many lacunae. Using a channel which I will describe someday, we sent all these things out to the West, and created a safe repository beyond the enemy's reach. This was a major victory, and it determined the whole subsequent course of events. (We had to send a duplicate copy of *Gulag*. The copy dispatched with such risk at the Feast of the Trinity had been reduced to a shapeless mess, I had ceased to have full control over it, and I had to provide my lawyer with an independent copy. This story, too, I must tell another time.[1]) From that moment, in June 1971, I was really ready at last to do battle and to perish.

No, I wasn't quite ready even then. The main clauses of my will (which it was quite impossible to deposit with a Soviet law office) had been sent to Dr. Heeb in 1971, but had not been duly witnessed. Only

---

1. I did not expect to divulge any names, but Olga Carlisle has hastened to do this herself. That's the way it always happens: those who perform the main task are not the ones who seek glory. The selfless Western people who aided me in substantial ways in my struggle, who assured the steady flow of my publications in the West, and who secretly brought out my large archive after my expulsion from the country—they are all modestly silent to this day. A large and completed section of this book is dedicated to them, but the time has not yet come for it to appear in print. I see Olga Carlisle's role in the fate of my works consistently negative. Due to a combination of circumstances—owing to my confidence in the Andreyev family from which she stems, rather than to any close knowledge of Olga Carlisle or the kind of person she is—she was entrusted with the manuscript texts of *The First Circle* and *The Gulag Archipelago,* both of which had already been brought out of the U.S.S.R. At no point did she herself risk anything whatever. The American translation of *The First Circle* was peremptorily edited by her husband Henry Carlisle, who knows no Russian, with the result that considerable further editorial work was necessary. The translation was rejected by the British publisher. She permitted other translations of *The First Circle* to be produced in perfunctory ways: many are inferior in quality, the French especially so. This was the extent of Olga Carlisle's labors, labors that she now claims took six years of her life, involved "huge risks," disrupted her journalistic career, the life of a free painter. On these grounds, probably, she appraised her own services, expenses, sacrifices, losses, sleepless nights, and those of her husband and their lawyer to be worth about half the royalties from the worldwide sale of the novel during the time that she directed it. The struggle described in these pages she characterizes as "Italian opera" and a world of petty intrigue. Her attitude and manner of dealing with people were sharply at odds with all our conceptions during these years of struggle. In the spring of 1970 a message was delivered to me in the U.S.S.R. from Olga Carlisle through an intermediary that the American translation of *Gulag* was finished and ready for the press. This gave me the false assurance that at a critical moment *Gulag* could quickly be published in the most widely read language in the world. But in fact, this translation was not ready even in 1973, when the blow fell on the Russian manuscript. The result was that the English-language edition appeared later than all the other translations. [1979 note]

when Heinrich Böll, on a visit to Moscow in February 1972, had countersigned every page with his own incontestable signature, and I had sent the will to the West in this form, could I rest assured that the future of my books was in the hands of my most faithful friends.

The will began with a program to be published separately:

This present will takes effect in one of three cases:
either—if my death is established beyond doubt
or—if I should disappear without trace from the public eye in Russia (for a period of two weeks)
or—if I should be interned in a prison, or a psychiatric hospital, or a camp, or should be exiled within the U.S.S.R. In any one of these cases, my lawyer, Dr. Heeb, will publish my will simultaneously in a number of major newspapers throughout the world. The will becomes valid as soon as it is so published. In such circumstances, no protest from me, in writing or by word of mouth, from prison or any other place in which my freedom is restricted, can cancel or modify a single point or a single word in this will. Some confidential details in the will, and the names of legatees, executors and those entrusted with various arrangements, will be made public by my lawyer only after the long-awaited day when elementary political rights come into existence in my country, so that the persons named are no longer exposed to any danger by publicity, and it becomes legally possible to execute the will without fear of punishment.

I then dealt with distribution of the Fund for Social Purposes (mentioning not figures but particular causes with which I should like to be associated in the hope that this would attract others eager to help, and that any shortfall in the funds would be made good as a result).

Publication of this program would be a powerful blow in itself.

It takes so long—so very long—to make your armies combat-ready, equip them to the last cartridge, and march them up to their forward positions.

The enemy, meantime, was carrying on sapping operations of his own, about which we, naturally, knew nothing. Pirated editions of *August 1914* were in preparation in England and Germany in 1971, to undermine my lawyer's rights, and to destroy *at that end* the possibility of publishing my work in the West. In the U.S.S.R. the text of *August 1914* was the starting point for investigation of my *social origins.* Nearly all my relatives were dead and buried, but they tracked down my old aunt, and a party of three KGB men was dispatched to pump her for "incriminating" information about me.

Deprived of my Rozhdestvo that summer, I had found writing difficult for the first time in years: I was too nervous. At the height of the summer, when I could stand it no more, I decided to go south, to the scenes of my childhood, to collect material, and to begin by visiting that very same aunt, whom I had not been to see for eight years.

It can easily happen in a war of mines and countermines that the tunnelers collide head on. If I had got as far as my aunt's, the KGB party would have arrived while I was with her. But I got too much sun on the way, and when I was nearly there, at Tikhoretskaya, I turned back, severely sunburned. My KGB "admirers" made a rewarding call on my aunt, obtained from her family records and stories, and departed rejoicing. By the standards of the twenties and thirties, the accusations were lethal—all the things that my mother and I had always concealed, when we had spent our lives cowering and trembling in half-flattened hovels. Another of their sapping operations, however, was thwarted. Because of my sudden return—again we see the rules of subterranean warfare in operation—I had asked a friend of mine (Gorlov) to fetch a spare part for my car from Rozhdestvo. He might have gone any other day, but he had a chance to go as soon as I got back from the south, on 11 August, and was just in time to discover nine KGB men behaving as though they owned my little dacha. If I hadn't come back from the south, their operation would have gone off without a hitch. Who lost and who gained by my return? My former wife was living at Rozhdestvo that summer, under the surveillance of someone she knew, one of *their* people, and the GB boys had been assured that she had gone to Moscow and would not be back that day. And I was down south. They had relaxed discipline to such an extent that they did not post a lookout, and Gorlov caught them in the heat of their labors. Or were they just beginning? Had they installed some complicated apparatus? They had certainly not had time to carry out a thorough search, or else they had never learned to do it properly. I am judging by the fact that much later, in 1972, when I was living in Rozhdestvo again, I discovered a full set of carbons of the very book you are now reading (including the preceding chapter), which I had brought along *a year earlier* and carelessly forgotten to burn, and a similar set from the screenplay *Tanks Know the Truth*. Every carbon had been reused, but much of what was on them could easily be read, and *they* could long ago have had almost complete texts—but no, the Geebees had fumbled it. (I learned later that at 4 A.M. on the following morning, another ten or so had appeared through the mist, to the accompaniment of barking, to finish some part of the job or cover their traces. Frightened neighbors had watched from behind their curtains, but no one had gone outside.) Because of Gorlov they had had to drop everything and run—drop everything except Gorlov, whom they took prisoner and dragged face to the ground behind them. They would undoubtedly have killed him, had he not thought quickly even in those minutes of great danger and pretended to be a citizen of a foreign country. As such, he could not be murdered without instructions from higher authority. Soon afterward some of the neighbors had rushed to the spot, there was the usual questioning at the police station, and so he had escaped with his life. He could have kept silent, as he was told to, and I would have known nothing about it. But his own honesty, and the fresh breezes blowing, would not allow him to keep it from me. True, he did not expect me to act as I did [Document 17]. It took his breath away—but it was also his only hope of safety. I was lying helplessly in bed, swathed in bandages, but my rage would have done credit to the fittest of men. Once more I was tempted to go too far—in my letter to Kosygin [Document 18] I at first demanded the resignation of Andropov, and my friends had great difficulty in talking, and laughing, me out of it.

So one mine had been sprung, and gone off with a bang, singeing the whiskers of Andropov himself. The insignificant zek was rung up (!) and informed on behalf of the minister personally (!) that it wasn't the KGB —oh, dear, no; it must be the militia. . . . (Those who know anything about our system will appreciate the absurdity of this.) It was an apology of sorts. . . .

They sprang other mines in the autumn: the two pirated editions of *August 1914* and then the article in *Stern.* These were, in my view, much feebler explosions. Largely because of the wisdom of an English judge, who established a legal precedent, they lost a whole year of lawsuits, and my lawyer's rights were put on a firmer basis than ever. While the article in *Stern,* instead of creating in the Soviet Union the oppressive atmosphere of a witch hunt, as it would have done in the glorious early years, set off an explosion of mirth: you mean to say he comes of a good, hard-working family? (What's more, they themselves had demolished the "Zionist" interpretation of my career.)[2]

---

2. The fact that it all ended well was no fault of *Stern*'s, for the journal once again did what it could to jeopardize my existence. With great boldness (and poor literary taste),

324 / THE OAK AND THE CALF

What times we lived in! There were only a few of us, a tiny handful, and *they* had the biggest secret police force in the history of the world, so much experience, so many numskulls with far too little to do, such highly mechanized sapping techniques, so much dynamite—yet they could not win the war of mines and countermines.

I say so because this was not the only occasion: there were many others. If I recalled and described them all in detail, you would see that throughout those years most of our effort and anxiety were expended not on major operations with worthwhile results, but on alarms and excursions, reconnaissance raids, anticipatory moves and precautions (all under conditions in which *they* had men for surveillance, *they* had telephonic and postal communications, while we could neither phone nor write nor even meet at times)—in short, on saving the situation by whatever means we could. There were a couple of dozen moments of acute danger—I must not understate it. Someday I will describe them in detail.

Here I shall recall just two or three occasions. One was in the provincial town to which *The First Circle* (the ninety-six-chapter version) had been sent for safekeeping. Not as the result of surveillance, nor on suspicion, but because of some unforeseeable circumstance, the Geebees turned up in the room in which *Circle 96* was kept. They obviously meant to search it, and there was no escape. But instead of searching, they took it into their heads to demand from the man concerned an admission that he had a copy of "Readers on *Ivan Denisovich.*" He confessed and handed it over. But he did not destroy *Circle 96;* he had, after all, been told to keep it, and there was a slow exchange of letters, which had to wait for safe carriers, with us knowing about the KGB visit, fearing that it might be repeated and *The First Circle* seized, urging him to burn it quickly, waiting ages for an answer—before we finally knew that it had been burned.

Another shock: *The Oak and the Calf,* the book you have in your hands, was *going around Moscow!* I was flabbergasted! Because, of course, in this book everything is wide open, people and things are given their own names: what could possibly be more dangerous? We had kept it safe and secret; how had it broken loose? Where? Through

---

it asserted that the action of *August 1914* is only ostensibly set in prerevolutionary times, and that the book is in fact an examination of contemporary problems. By implying that Solzhenitsyn was in reality expressing his hatred for the current leaders of the U.S.S.R., the journal was making a direct and very grave accusation against me.

whom? Why? We mounted an investigation, checked all our copies: we had to go outside Moscow and physically verify that all copies were in place, had not been moved and could not have been photographed. There was suspicion and doubt all around, all was chaos and confusion.

Then we took up the search from the other end of the trail. Who had heard of the book being read? Who had been told that some particular person had read it? Who had read it for himself? What did the copy look like? At whose apartment had people read it? Address and telephone number? (There was no avoiding the excited mentioning of titles over the telephone—the Lubyanka had no doubt noticed and their posse would sweep out to head us off at any minute!) Let's get there fast! Right, then. Give it to me straight—better come clean before the KGB roll up. They come clean, they name names, they put a typed copy in front of me. But it's not one of ours! Ours, of course, had all turned out to be in place. Not one of ours—so it was a copy of a copy! What if there were four or five like it? But it was not even a photocopy of one of ours. Someone had typed an accurate copy, and it even had my latest amendments written in by hand. Obviously someone close to me, someone in the know, had cribbed from me as I went along, looked over my shoulder. But who? Better phone the man who brought it here. Not at home. We sat and waited, to keep out of sight a bit. A few hours later our man came along and sheepishly named his source. One of those we trusted most! We had only lent it to her to read herself. But she had surreptitiously copied it. (For history's sake? To make sure it survived? Or simply because she had a mania for copying things?) She had lent it only to him (he was an intimate friend). But he had brought it to these *other* people, by way of thanks for some small favor. And *they* had called in a very dear lady friend to share their happiness. And *she* had gushed over the telephone to *her* bosom friend. At this fourth remove we had got wind of it. Moscow is big, but no one is far away. We called up the culprit. We arranged to meet her. Sobbing, she confessed. She was struck off our list for the future. I confiscated the booty. In the few hours all this took, there were signs that the Geebees were getting excited. KGB cars with four toughs in each darkened interior went out on the prowl. Lick your chops, comrades! You're just half an hour late! (They had no idea what all the fuss was about. What had we been looking for? What had they missed?)

In December 1969 something very similar happened with *Prussian Nights*. Again the rumor was all over Moscow: it was going the rounds.

Impossible—but there it was. On that occasion, too, I rushed from one apartment to another, tracked down the copy and seized it. Again, it was not one of our own copies! But an exact reproduction! Cribbed! By someone close to us! By whom? I uncovered the trail. A friend had had it for a few days, and *lent it out.* And the other people had tapped out a copy. And kept it secret for four years! But once I had been expelled from the Writers' Union, why not let samizdat have it? I stamped it out in Moscow by one means or another. The manuscript ceased to circulate.

Such are the *quiet* weeks that make up our *quiet* years, the peaceful times in which there are no events of note, while the main forces are stationary, and "nothing happens."

For how many years can I go on like this? So far there have been twenty-seven of them, since my first poems in the *sharashka,* when I first started hiding and burning.

High above this field of petty, furtive skirmishes, the cloud rack of history sails by, the great events that all can see, summoning us in turn to action, extorting a response. Some of it memory retains, some is lost forever.

In December 1971 we buried A.T. Long stretches of the adjoining streets were cordoned off—they had been lavish with policemen—and at the cemetery there were troops too (for a poet's funeral!), and hideously barking megaphones directed buses and lorries. The entrance hall of the Central Writers' Club was also cordoned off, but even so they dared not bar my way. (They regretted this afterward.) Against the incongruous crimson silk on which the dead man's head rested (his look of good-natured, childlike resignation, his best expression, had returned soon after his death) and in which the whole coffin was swathed, against the truculent robot faces of the Writers' Club secretaries, against the grating insincerity of the speakers, I had no way of defending him except to make the sign of the cross after each round of speeches, once at the Writers' Club and once at the cemetery. But that, I think, was plenty for the powers of darkness. I was allowed to join the mourners only on his widow's insistence (she risked making trouble for herself because she knew she was doing what her husband would have wanted), and out of consideration for the family I decided not to put out my farewell speech through samizdat that evening, but held on to it for nine days, so that I was able to read and recite it daily, to immerse myself in that elegiac mood in which the events of our lives are measured by a different scale from that of every day and seen in a different perspective. [Document 19]

I had said my say. It would have been natural to hold my peace now; my very throat needed a rest. But just a week later, on Christmas Eve, I heard a Christmas service from a Western radio station, during which a pastoral letter from Patriarch Pimen was read—and at once I was fired with a desire to write to him! I had no choice but to write! And this meant new troubles, new burdens, new complicating factors.

(It is not from this letter, but earlier, from the appearance of *August 1914,* that we must date the schism among my readers, the steady loss of supporters, with more leaving me than remained behind. I was received with "hurrahs" as long as I appeared to be against Stalinist abuses only; thus far the entire Soviet public was with me. In my first works I was concealing my features from the police censorship—but, by the same token, from the public at large. With each subsequent step I inevitably revealed more and more of myself: the time had come to speak more precisely, to go even deeper. And in doing so I should inevitably lose the reading public, lose my contemporaries in the hope of winning posterity. It was painful, though, to lose support even among those closest to me.)

But why am I saying all this here? And what of the promised "Nobeliana"?

The Nobeliana followed its appointed course. Per-Egil Hegge was very angry with Jarring for his shabby role in the Nobel affair and promised to expose him whatever happened. But Hegge was expelled from the U.S.S.R. and I forgot his threat. He did, however, carry it out, and hit on the best possible time to do so—in September, a month before the new prizes were awarded, and as the United Nations began the session during which it was to elect a new Secretary General, a post that Jarring coveted. At this point Hegge published a book of reminiscences in which he described in detail how Jarring had sided with the Soviet government against me. He created such a scandal in Sweden that even Prime Minister Palme, himself a fleet-winged and nimble-witted socialist, cordially disposed to the land of the victorious proletariat, had to make excuses both on Swedish television and in a letter to the *New York Times.* He began by saying that he, Palme, had known nothing about Jarring's handling of the matter. Then he grew bolder and asked what else Jarring could have done. An embassy was not the place for a political demonstration! (He took it for granted that a purely literary occasion was unthinkable.) Once again, the Swedish Academy was rudely disturbed. It had no peace at all with me. Had there ever been such a troublesome prizewinner before? Karl Ragnar Gierow, the Academy's secretary, announced that he would write to Solzhenitsyn on Monday to ask whether he would receive the Nobel insignia in the embassy. The joke was that the announcement was made on Saturday and broadcast the same day. As it happened, I had an opportunity to send something to the West on Sunday, and was staying up late on Saturday to write a letter. I wrote a "reply" to Gierow at the same time and sent it off on Sunday. It turned out that Gierow did not send me a letter either on Monday or indeed for the next three weeks. Yet he had received my "reply." This was that surely the Nobel Prize ought not to be handed over without witnesses, behind closed doors, as though we were thieves dividing our booty. By the time they sent me the Academy's communiqué, I had heard that, too, on the radio (by the open post, letters took three weeks in each direction) and answered it immediately.

After a long illness I had just plunged into my work on *October 1916* —which turned out to be a vast subject, a double "Knot," if not a treble one: this because I had omitted, for the sake of "economy," the undoubtedly necessary *August 1915*, and skirted around the whole political and spiritual history of Russia from the beginning of the century in Knot I. The arrears had mounted up and now threatened to burst the bounds of the story, to overwhelm it. I wanted only to work—but no, the hubbub of the Nobeliana began all over again. As though having a medal and a diploma would make it any easier for me to stand up against the KGB. But if that was how it was, I must give up the "Knot," I must resuscitate and recast my lecture, and once I had written it—I must deliver it. So much would be said in it that my fragile little existence might be shattered, and my precious quiet haven with Rostropovich lost. Oh, how reluctant I was to give up Knot II. How happy I had been with my plan to work on quietly until 1975!

Man proposes. . . .

This time I somehow succeeded in ridding the lecture of any otiose propaganda or political content, drawing it more tightly together around the theme of art, and perhaps coming close to that genre which no one had yet defined, and of which no one had any clear conception: the Nobel lecture on literature. In the meantime, my correspondence with Karl Gierow, Secretary of the Swedish Academy, went on [Document 20]. The Swedish Ministry of Foreign Affairs again refused to make the embassy available for the ceremony, and I suggested my wife's apartment, where I myself still had no right to live [Document 21]. There was, it seemed, no precedent for this, but Gierow agreed. During those months I came to appreciate greatly his tact and his sensitivity. He behaved less and less like a man merely discharging the duties of an honorary post, and more and more like a man of warm feelings, determination and courage (it took courage to deal with many of his fellow countrymen too). We began trying to fix a date. He could not do it in February or March. This delay also suited me. The delivery of my lecture seemed likely to be an explosive event, and before the explosion I must put my affairs in order (however often I tried to do it, they were always in disarray). I must reduce at least part of Knot II to a readable state; sort out the copious materials that I had accumulated for *R-17,* in anticipation of a possible raid; make another trip to Petersburg to look at places I needed, scenes I might never be allowed to visit again. (How I penetrated into one particular institution is a short story on its own. . . . I'll tell it some other time.)

The novel task of writing to the Patriarch absorbed a good deal of my strength. I had to consult people who knew about such things, and to avoid premature publicity. Just at that moment, *Litgazeta* took a swipe at my ancestry, and at me personally. Reluctantly, I had to defend myself. I still did not know the ways of Western newsmen very well, and I replied through the correspondent of the Hamburg newspaper *Die Welt,* but he passed it on to someone else, and fudged it so that it was no reply at all. It was a small but annoying disappointment. I felt it necessary to reply (not only to this, but to an accumulation of annoyances borne in silence). And the natural thought occurred to me that I could string together several overdue statements, let them cascade out in rapid succession, and afterward answer for all my sins at once. Events crowd in thick and fast at moments of crisis, as in April 1968 when *Cancer Ward* came out, but you can also increase their density deliberately by exploiting the unique characteristics of our Soviet *high-ups:* their obtuseness, their slow-wittedness, their inability to keep two concerns in mind at once. When he put in his visa application on—I think—24 March, Gierow gave the date of the Nobel ceremony as 9 April, the first day of the Orthodox Easter. I had sent my letter to the Patriarch on 17 March, assuming that it would not be published before the end of the month. A few days after, I would make a statement to the press, my first in nine years—they no longer expected me to make statements in this form—and it would be a hefty one. Then, before they had time to digest that, I would go through with the Nobel ceremony and read my lecture, which I considered the most dangerous of all these actions. After which I could sit peacefully and await all the punishments to come.

It went rather differently. My letter to the Patriarch had been put out only on the narrow ecclesiastical samizdat network, with the idea that it would gradually find its way to all those whom it really concerned, but it immediately broke through into the Western press. I learned later that it had left the KGB spluttering with rage—a rage more violent than that excited by most of my moves before or since. (There is no mystery here. Atheism is the core of the whole Communist system.) But paradoxically, this move aroused disapproval and even disgust among the intelligentsia too. How narrow, blind and limited I must be, thought some, to concern myself with such problems as that of the Church. Others argued differently: why bring the clergy into it? They are powerless, just like the intelligentsia—seeking to exculpate themselves by analogy. Let Solzhenitsyn address himself to our rulers. (Well, I'll get at them in due course too.) Though many people condemned me, I have never regretted this step: if our spiritual fathers need not be the first to set us an example of spiritual freedom from the lie, where are we to look for it? Alas, our Orthodox hierarchy has simply left us to free ourselves. Then (according to my subsequent reconstruction), sometime between 20 March and the end of the month, the government took a long-deferred decision: to blacken me publicly and expel me from the country. To this end, the newspaper campaign against me was broadened and intensified. With their usual lack of imagination, they chose a battlefield on which they were at a very great disadvantage. They chose to snipe at *August 1914*, which had not been blocked by the pirated editions, and which they therefore now called my most savagely antipatriotic and indeed anti-Soviet book. For this purpose, they mobilized the Western Communist press (for who could read *August* in the U.S.S.R.?) and reprinted every nugatory scrawl—for the most part in *Litgazeta*, but later in other metropolitan newspapers too. Some articles aimed accusations at me in terminology taken straight from the Criminal Code, while the obedient "Soviet public," from writers to steelworkers, sent in angry "comments on the reviews."

This time, the decision taken was sufficiently firm for them to begin considering practical procedures for deporting me, the first stage being detention by the police, i.e., provisional arrest. (This idea, which replaced the motorcar accident plan, the "Yves Farge version," also filtered through to us.) So firm was the decision that Chakovsky made a solemn public declaration at a *Litgazeta* "planning session" attended by some thirty people: "We shall deport him!" This operation was evidently timed for the middle of April, when the newspaper campaign was due to reach its climax.

But in my timetable events moved more swiftly. Two American correspondents came to see me without the conventional agreement by telephone. Their papers were the two most powerful in their country and this was six weeks before the President of the U.S.A. was due to arrive in the U.S.S.R. The interview had no social significance. I said nothing either about prisoners or about the injustices rife throughout the country. I had kept silent about these things for almost two years, hiding from the world behind my "blackout" shutters, sacrificing all else to *R-17*, and even now I gauged it so as not to go beyond the unavoidable level of conflict, and not to overshadow my lecture. My statement to the press was largely in the form of a wide-ranging apologia. I took a brisk broom to the rubbish showered upon me for years past —though the mere sight of this trash through the bright halo around our "advanced social order" had created quite an impression in the West.

The interview [Document 22] appeared in print so unexpectedly, and its revelations were so sordid, that it left my adversaries dazed, which was what I had been counting on. Rather more dazed, indeed, than I had expected. It was published on 4 April, and instead of pausing to think, the authorities, normally so dilatory, responded less than twenty-four hours later with the most elementary of defensive reflexes: they brought ridicule and disgrace upon themselves by denying the Secretary of the Swedish Academy the right to come and present the Nobel insignia to me. Nothing had been said in letters, or aloud indoors, about a lecture being delivered. The authorities could only have had some vague inkling of it. All that had been said in public was that the Nobel insignia would be presented in a private apartment in Moscow in the presence of the author's friends from the world of literature and the arts. And even this was enough to frighten a government whose might was felt throughout the world. If the Western left were not so ready with excuses for us, this self-inflicted humiliation would have sufficed for some time to show the Soviet cultural rapprochement game for what it is. But under the laws of leftist topsy-turvydom, *red* sinners are always forgiven, *red* sins are soon forgotten. As Orwell writes, those very same Western public figures who were outraged by individual executions anywhere else on earth applauded when Stalin shot hundreds of thousands; they grieved for starving India, but the devastating famine in the Ukraine went unnoticed.

With the usual Soviet skill in blurring the issue, our embassy in Stockholm nonetheless qualified its refusal: it "did not exclude the possibility that Gierow would be given a visa at some other, more convenient time"—this to soothe the irritated, to encourage self-delusion, and to smooth the road to oblivion. The Swedish Ministry of Foreign Affairs followed suit. But we in the Soviet Union understand that sort of game only too well, and I hastened to break it up with a special statement [Document 23]. Forbidding Gierow to come had put the lid on the ceremony, robbed it of all sense. It had also come as a relief—both to the organizers and to those who had agreed to attend.

The preparations for this ceremony, even apart from such domestic problems as whether sixty guests, all either persons of note or else Western newspapermen, could be decently entertained in a very ordinary apartment, were complicated and unusual in other respects too. To begin with, we had to draw up the guest list so as to invite no one whose civic behavior was in any way questionable, to omit no one whose standing in the artistic or scientific world entitled him to an invitation, and at the same time to invite guests who really would come and not funk it. Furthermore, we had to keep the invitation cards hidden until the day on which Gierow announced the date of the ceremony, then ride around delivering them, or else send them, accompanied by letters that argued persuasively that this public-spirited act would be well worth the harassment inevitable from superiors. The number of writers, producers and actors who accepted surprised me: to think that such courage, such a longing to stand upright, such a feeling of shame to be slaves forever, still survived in so many people. The consequences could have been extremely unpleasant for all of them, but now the government had relieved both those invited and itself of unnecessary perturbations. There were of course refusals too, sickeningly in character, from people of international reputation who had nothing to fear.

Preparations for the ceremony had included the choice of Sunday, so that nobody would be detained at work, and daytime, so that the

KGB, the militia and the volunteer auxiliary police could not discreetly bar the way under cover of darkness. In the daytime such maneuvers could be photographed. We also had to find fearless doorkeepers to prevent any irruption of overenthusiastic KGB men. And to take precautions against other forms of interference: interruption of the electricity supply, a continuous ringing of the telephone, stones thrown through the window—gangland methods which have become more and more popular with the KGB in recent years.

Of all these cares the government had relieved us.

By way of a joke I sent invitations to the Minister of Culture, Furtseva, and to two Soviet journalists on newspapers that had not so far attacked me: *Selskaya Zhizn (Rural Life)* and *Trud (Labor)*. *Selskaya Zhizn* did in fact send someone to the ceremony that never took place —my one and only guest, a KGB man, there to see whether there would be some sort of gathering in spite of everything. While *Trud*, the organ of that well-known pillar of the faith Shelepin, hastened to make up for its rotten neutralism, and attacked me a day or two later.

But their campaign was lost and in its dying throes: having panicked, and disgraced themselves over the Nobel ceremony, the authorities stopped hounding me publicly and, circumstances having conspired so unhappily against them, were forced yet again to leave me in my native land and at large.

After eighteen months of it there should have been nothing more to say about the Nobeliana, but there remained what to me was the most important thing—the lecture, now ready. If it was to be included in the Nobel yearbook, it must be dispatched to Sweden as soon as possible. This was difficult, but we managed it (clandestinely, of course, as before—and at great risk). It was due to appear at the beginning of June. Still expecting an explosion, I went off to Tambov oblast, to get my fill of that too, perhaps for the last time.

June went by, and July went by, in that enervatingly hot summer, but still no lecture appeared. Could it possibly have passed completely unnoticed? It was August before I learned that much of Swedish industry, including the printers, had been on holiday during those summer months. The yearbook was not published until the end of August.

The press made quite a fuss about it, for over a week. But there were two surprises in store for me, to show how deficient in foresight I had been: the lecture raised not an eyebrow among our masters, and it produced no big shift of opinion, no shock of realization, in the West.

It seemed to me that I had said a *very* great deal, said all that really mattered. Had it gone in one ear and out the other? Well—the lecture, though crystal clear, was written in general terms, without a single proper name. *Over there,* and *here,* people preferred not to understand.

The Nobeliana was over, and the explosion, the main battle, was still indefinitely postponed.

# Encounter Battle

"Encounter battle" is the name given by military tacticians to a form of warfare distinct from ordinary offensive and defensive engagements: the two sides, each ignorant of the other's intentions, simultaneously decide to attack and unexpectedly collide. This kind of unplanned battle is considered the most complicated of all: it demands very great speed of action, resourcefulness and determination on the part of a commander, and also the possession of adequate reserves.

Such was the battle that took place in the Soviet public arena in late August and September 1973, a battle so little expected that not only did the opposing sides have no knowledge of each other, but on one side there were two columns (Sakharov's and mine), neither of which knew anything of the other's movements and plans.

Although 1971 and 1972, which we have glanced at in the previous chapter, were not such very quiet years for me, they contained fewer shocks than others—or perhaps I had just acquired a tolerance for them. I never forgot for a moment that I had gone to earth, that I was lying low, playing a waiting game, to gain time for *R-17,* but I ceased, as it were, to see contemporary events in sharp focus. And whenever I refused to involve myself, I could explain to no one, least of all to the activists of the "democratic movement" (who were very quick to disseminate information), why I chose silence, why I held myself so aloof, although it might seem that "nothing would happen" to me if I did intervene. Moreover, while fate was dozing, my life at Rostropovich's dacha, in blissful conditions such as I had never had in my life (quiet, country air and urban comfort), also threatened to demagnetize my will. I had not blown myself sky-high with my letter to the head of the KGB, nor with my letter to the Patriarch, nor with my Nobel lecture

—so I could just sit and write. Especially as Knot II had proved so difficult, and the transition to Knot III promised no relief. Then again, I kept putting off the crucial decision that would always hang over me until I stopped avoiding it. So that when at the end of 1972 I finally decided that *Gulag* would appear in 1975, even that seemed to me a sacrifice, a voluntary *speeding up* of events.

The rationale for my life at Rostropovich's dacha was gradually being eroded. He had got to know me accidentally, almost immediately offered me shelter on a magnanimous impulse, when he was still quite unable to imagine, for lack of experience, the prolonged and stupid pressures that he would bring upon his own head; he had even rushed out an open letter after my Nobel Prize; for another year he had gone on defending himself ingeniously against the government's efforts to cramp and thwart him. But Rostropovich had begun to grow weary and to weaken under protracted siege with no hope of relief, with the loss of the post he loved best, his conductorship at the Bolshoi, the banning of his best Moscow concerts, the termination of those trips abroad which had become a habit and which used to occupy half his life. The question grew bigger all the time: Was it right for one artist to wither so that another might flourish? (Alas, even after I had removed myself from his dacha, a vengeful regime did not forgive him for the four-winter-long hospitality he had shown me.)

The police, too, had a hand in slowly sapping the foundations of my existence. It was no longer only the Ministry of Culture that longed to cleanse itself of such a blot. I was an irritating splinter under the skin of all the *top people*, living as I did in their forbidden and privileged *special zone*, their delectable Barvikha. Yet under Soviet law, evicting me would have been a very small matter: twenty-four hours was enough in such a special ministerial zone. But the combination of the two names—Rostropovich's and mine—held them back. Not that no attempts were made. A militia captain had paid a flying visit before I got the Nobel Prize. "I'm a guest here," I told him. He had left me alone.

In March 1971 I had one of my "landslides"—one of those rare and happy days when thoughts crowd in uncontrollably, ranging over the most various themes and in unauthorized directions, tearing at you, sweeping you away with them, so that you can only hope to jot down snatches on any old scrap of paper: work it up later; just catch what you can for now. In this happy state, I went skiing, pausing even out in the snow to add to the notes on my scribbling pad, and returned to hear old Anichkova calling me to the upper story of the big dacha:

"Come back, A.I. The militia's here to evict you."

I had expected it for so long that I had stopped expecting it, though I had a piece of paper ready for such an eventuality—in a blue envelope in a fireproof safe. Surely they wouldn't dare immediately before their Twenty-fourth Congress (may they never see their twenty-fifth!), or didn't they understand what a scandal there would be?

There are three of them, the most junior a captain. It gradually emerges that the most important of them, a certain Anosov, is the head of the Passport Office for Moscow oblast! Quite a big cheese, and an intelligent man with a sense of humor—you do find a few such people among them. In my happy, buoyant mood I slip lightly and easily into conversation with them, adopting my best tone of offhanded superiority which I once used on the customs officers.

Let me just pop over to my own little house for my piece of paper; give me three minutes and I'll lay it before you, or read it out dramatically, standing on my feet, and lift you out of your seats. No. Not this time. They weren't evicting me today. They weren't even drawing up their first report, and the second is the one they refer to the courts. They were only pressing me to do something about a residence permit in the next few days, or else move on. To Ryazan. Into the trap.

Naturally. What can any Soviet citizen, without protection from *on high,* do in such a situation? Quietly submit. There is no way out of it. But thank God, I have already straightened my back and stepped out of the ranks.

I begin by showing great solicitude for them personally:

"Comrades, by all means draw up your report—but take care! I beg you not to make a *personal* error, for which you could suffer. I beg you to check first, *at the very highest level,* whether they have really decided to have me evicted. Otherwise you may be blamed for it later on."

The obtuse major: "When I am acting in accordance with the law and in my own district, I don't have to ask permission from anyone."

I: "Ah, me, Comrade Major, you haven't seen enough service! . . . You don't want to take the law into your own hands. My case is a very *delicate* one."

The Oblast Passport Office: "Yes, but I am not using force."

I: "Why, of course you aren't! But however gently you treat me, there may be a big row."

I speak as confidently as though I can go into the next room and ring Brezhnev at any minute. The experienced courtier understands: Step carefully here; it's a minefield! I must have some grounds for my self-assurance. He hesitates.

But what good will it do me to gain a few days? I must, through them, convey to those *upstairs* how serious the matter is, and *how far I am ready to go.* My life and work are bounded by Rostropovich's dacha. They must be shown that I won't let them do it quietly.

The conversation takes a new turn, when I announce, with a defiant prisoner's glare and with steel in my voice:

"I won't do it! Make my own way to Ryazan? Neither on foot nor on wheels! And if the court issues an order? I won't obey it! If I go, it will be in chains!"

I feel much better now. Fine, in fact. You shan't drown me in a puddle—you'll need a whole ocean! I feel young and strong, a warrior again.

Dismayed, but still polite, they take their leave. They hadn't expected this.

"There'll be a glorious row!" I call after them, by way of encouragement.

Because next time, when they fill out their charge sheet, I shall play the role of an obedient Soviet citizen with them, examining every loop and pothook in the document, demanding a second copy for myself, and when the time comes to sign the thing, suddenly pull out my own piece of paper, sign it and substitute it for their document.

> To the militia, which is forcing me to move from the home of Mstislav Rostropovich, near Moscow, to Ryazan, where I am "registered" with the militia,
>
> MY ANSWER is as follows:
>
> Serfdom was abolished in our country in 1861. The October Revolution is said to have swept away the last remnants of it. I am therefore a free citizen of this country, not a serf, not a slave, and . . .

In all your dealings with *them* you must always try pitching your voice an octave higher. Generalize as long as the words last. Don't just defend yourself, your own narrow little sector; set out to shatter their whole system!

But perhaps the hour has not come for this? How long are we to wait, then?

The wind of battle had blown in my face—and at once I felt merry, I even regretted that they were going and that the marvelous piece of paper I had ready was left lying idle.

Six months later they came again. The same Anosov, with some one-eyed man in plain clothes. This time I took my blue envelope along when I went to meet them. I put it on the table between us. But Anosov was politeness itself. This was just a reminder. Had I, or had I not, done anything about registering? It really was *very awkward*. I had been there two years now (in a place where no one was allowed to stay for two days, and even a Moscow residence permit counted for nothing!). Well, since he was taking such a mild tone . . . I would do it as soon as I got my family affairs straightened out. "You do that, then." He wanted me to hope—and to hurry up. "Ah, but even when I'm legally married they still won't give me a Moscow permit, will they?" . . . "What do you mean? They're obliged to, by law."

To make doubly sure, he pulled out a different stop. "We can, you know, take action against Rostropovich too, as the householder here. He might even have his dacha taken away from him."

"Look," I said. "The situation is bad enough already. No need to pour oil on the fire."

All this time the blue envelope lay between us—innocent, unopened and idle. I spoke again. "If they put too much pressure on you, don't trouble to visit me; just give the local militia their orders —they were so anxious to file a charge. Of course, I shall see that they get publicity. . . ."

The one-eyed man: "What do you mean, publicity? The law is the law."

I: "What do I mean? This sort of thing: I shall refuse to leave if the police order me to, and I shall refuse to attend the court, so you'll have to sentence me to internal exile."

"Now, now! It won't come to that," they said reassuringly.

So my piece of paper stayed where it was. And I went on living illegally at Rostropovich's place for another eighteen months.

When my divorce came through, and I registered my marriage to my second wife, who lived in Moscow, I applied in proper legal form for a Moscow residence permit, whereupon the new head of the Moscow City Passport Office, recently transferred from the oblast office— in fact, the very same Anosov ("They're obliged by law to give you one") —informed me with the same polite smile, *on behalf of the minister personally,* that "the militia in any case does not decide on" questions of registration, but that these were the business of a "council of honored pensioners" (old Stalinists) attached to the Moscow City Soviet, who scrutinized the political features of each candidate to see whether he was fit to live in Moscow. And *these* were the people to whom I should have to submit my request.

I, too, smiled most politely (my blue envelope was ready to go; it was only awaiting the appointed date), and asked him to supply me with a written refusal. He was pleasanter than ever, like an old acquaintance:

"Come, now, Aleksandr Isayevich—do you really need a miserable piece of paper?"

I had expected them to say nothing and keep me dangling, but a straight refusal like this—no, I hadn't. Shameless wretches. They were quite frankly egging me on to get out of Russia of my own accord.

(Their vexation is perhaps understandable: perhaps the authorities were influenced by the rumor, which was spread to my great annoyance by self-styled "close friends" of mine—there were quite a number of them, who presumed to interpret my life and my intentions—that "he only wants to be united with his family, and he will leave immediately, he won't stay a minute longer!" Well, they'd given me my divorce, and now they were "within their rights" in expecting me to leave. Why, they must wonder, was I not going?)

From June 1973 they began using another method to push me out: anonymous letters from pseudogangsters. By post, giving themselves away in their careless haste by gumming a post office receipt over the stamp (on one occasion, to make me nervous, they gummed in an ambiguous kinky hair) and by the swift delivery of their letters (when all other correspondence was held up). The messages were made up of printed letters in various colors; the style was that of Benya Krik,* but in much poorer taste. The first went like this: "We are not gangsters, if you will give us $100,000 we guarantee in return the tranquillity and physical safety of your family"—and to signify my agreement I had to let myself be seen on the steps of the Central Post Office. Next time, no demands, just naked threats: "There will be no third warning, we are not Chinese. Once we lose confidence in you we shall be unable to guarantee anything." They hoped to frighten me into fleeing the country to escape from these "gangsters."

After the second such letter I tried a new tack: a frank "inside" letter to the KGB, an impersonal warning [Document 24]. The letter got through, an acknowledgment slip came back, from KGB registry clerk so-and-so (the name was quite legible). They took three weeks to think about it. Then I got another telephone call from the same colonel who had phoned on behalf of Andropov in 1971. The same phonograph record all over again: "Your declaration [?] has been passed to the militia." As if they would let such a document out of their hands . . . The message was that of the anonymous letters—a hint, a dig in the ribs: "Appeal to the militia for protection." (And on the pretense that they were supplying protection, *they* would be all over me.) There were no more anonymous letters for over a month. At the end of July, however, the third arrived: "Well, bitch, you never came! Now you've only got yourself to blame. We'll *straighten you out.* Just you wait!" They made no demands, they only wanted to frighten me: Go away, you rat!

We had a hard summer of it. Our losses were heavy. Important matters were neglected, sometimes fatally. For weeks on end I had to leave my little boys and my wife, who was near her time, in an unprotected dacha at Firsanovka, where I could not work for the noise of low-flying aircraft, while I went off to Rozhdestvo to write. Whether the thugs were bogus or genuine, whether they really attacked or only made a show of it, my wife and I were prepared for any ordeal. We had known what we might bring on ourselves.

In retrospect, almost all my life since the day I was first arrested had been the same: just for *that* particular week, *that* month, *that* season, *that* year, there had always been some reason for not writing—it was inconvenient or dangerous or I was too busy—always some need to postpone it. If I had given in to common sense, once, twice, ten times, my achievement as a writer would have been incomparably smaller. But I had gone on writing—as a bricklayer, in overcrowded prison huts, in transit jails without so much as a pencil, when I was dying of cancer, in an exile's hovel after a double teaching shift. I had let nothing—dangers, hindrances, the need for rest—interrupt my writing, and only because of that could I say at fifty-five that I now had no more than twenty years of work to get through, and had put the rest behind me.

I know how strong the force of inertia is in me: when I immerse myself in work it is difficult for anyone to disturb me or tear me away from it with news, however sensational. But even in the deepest current of work you are never completely protected from the modern world: it seeps into your consciousness from day to day through radio (Western radio, of course—but from what it says you can always piece together the whole situation in the Soviet Union), and in the form of vague stirrings in the air which cannot be explained or put into words but only sensed. These currents play upon the mind, mingle with your work without hindering it (they are not foreign to it, as are the distracting banalities of everyday life), they create the ambience in which you live, an ambience of calm, or trepidation, or triumph. Sometimes these vague influences impinge on one another so that they acquire the solidity of an insight, an instinctive resolve: you somehow see (sometimes the reason is clear, sometimes it is not) that the time has come to *act!*

I cannot put it in terms of cause and effect. It is not always easy to draw the line between wishful thinking and presentiment. But I have had such intuitions often enough, and they have always proved right.

So it was that summer. Unmoved by all the misfortunes and threats that hemmed us in, I knew that it was time: time to find some way of shocking the West into the realization that it could not look after its own interests, that while it raged implacably against the weak, it invariably lost, invariably surrendered to rock-hard tyrants ("Peace and Violence"). And then, for some reason, came my purely impulsive, quite unpremeditated *Letter to the Leaders*. This suddenly began to exercise such a pull on me, I was so overwhelmed by the crush of ideas and phrases, that for two days at the beginning of August I had to abandon my main work, let the spate expend itself, write it all down, and order it in sections.

All these articles were written easily and quickly, because it was simply a matter of getting the harvest in, of using up underexpended running reserves. Just a natural stretching of cramped limbs.

These vague promptings are sometimes traceable to actual events, though we cannot always make the connection at the time. We felt that we had reached a new low, sunk to new, suffocating depths of civic failure: more people were arrested, others were threatened, and yet others were renouncing all and leaving the country. Sinyavsky came to say goodbye (and to introduce himself at the same time), and I was chilled and saddened to think that fewer and fewer were willing to endure Russia's destiny with her, lead where it might. The authorities had calculated that this "third emigration" would "ease the pressure on the boiler," and they were proved right. (I would have cut a poor figure if I had joined it, even with the Nobel insignia in my possession.) There were fewer and fewer voices capable of protest left in the land. Early in summer Maksimov was expelled from the Writers' Union, and in July he wrote me a justifiably bitter letter: Where was the "solidarity of writers the world over" which I had so extolled in my Nobel lecture, and why did he, Maksimov, not see me among his defenders?

I did not defend him for the same reason that I had not defended all the others: licensing myself to work on the history of the Revolution, I had absolved myself of all other duties. To this day I am not ashamed of such periods of deliberate silence: an artist has no other recourse if he does not want to overheat himself with ephemeral concerns and boil dry.

But there are days when the ground seems to give under you, you plunge to the nadir of your existence, and all your forgotten duties press in on you like the walls of a pit. I needed only a very little more time for Knot II—only four months, the last four months of 1973. But I was denied them. (I had time only to duplicate the novel on film, hastily, just as it was, so that this at least would not perish in the debacle.) So that the third Knot, which had so long lured me into the leaping flames of the Revolution, receded into the mist. All my neatly drawn datelines were buckling and breaking; nothing was clear anymore except that I must speak out!

And obviously, using the "cascade" technique I had made my own, I must inflict five or six blows in quick succession. I must begin defensively, take measures for my own safety in my sunken position, try to get onto firm ground—and then attack.

When you write looking back at the past, you wonder what you were so afraid of, whether you were perhaps exaggerating. It had happened so often before. Why panic? You had always come through safely.

True—and every time I might not have come through (and one of these days I shall not). Besides, each blow I swung at them was more powerful than the last, the shock of impact was greater, the danger was greater—and with that danger to face, it was as well to be ready for the abrupt termination of my precarious but more or less snug existence.

Apart from my manuscripts, what other material possessions of value had I? Only the twelve one-hundredths of a hectare which was my "estate" at Rozhdestvo, and where I had so immersed myself in my work for half of that summer, my last, as I thought. Only half, because my former wife and I had agreed to take turns living here. She was determined to take it over completely, and before striking the blow I had planned, it seemed only sensible to sign the property over to her. In the middle of August, as I left for battle, I made a tour of the familiar places roundabout, and of every yard of the property, saying goodbye to Rozhdestvo forever. I will not deny that I wept. Nowhere is Russia so real, so solidly present to me as in this patch of land on a bend of the Istya, the familiar woods, and the long clearing nearby. Never, and nowhere, have I written so easily, and perhaps I never shall again. However exhausted, disgruntled, distracted, absent-minded I might be when I arrived, some soothing influence emanated from the grass, the water, the birches and the willows, the oaken bench, the table on the brink of the little river—and in two hours' time I was able to write again. It was a miracle. Nowhere else was it the same.

The last week, the last few nights before the offensive, were quite sleepless. Aircraft roared incessantly over the very roofs of Firsanovka, like black hedgehoppers coming home after shedding their bombs. We were afraid that we might have let slip some incautious phrase in the grounds of the dacha, and that the microphones scattered around had picked it up. Perhaps the enemy could already surmise that I was preparing something, and my only hope of success lay in the element of surprise. Before I began the offensive, I must appear more carefree, and dreamier than ever, there must be no superfluous dashing about, no superfluous visitors or appointments, and our conversations, which were probably monitored, must be leisurely and casual.

The one worrying thing was that I might not be given time to carry out the whole scheme. I felt as though I was about to fill a space in the world that was meant for me and had long awaited me, a mold, as it were, made for me alone, but discerned by me only this very moment. I was a molten substance, impatient, unendurably impatient, to pour into my mold, to fill it full, without air bubbles or cracks, before I cooled and stiffened.

It had happened so often: before the next step, next breakthrough, assault, "cascade," I concentrate *solely* on the affair in hand, on these last brief moments; and the rest of my life, the time that lies beyond these critical moments, is completely forgotten, it ceases to exist. All I want is to come through this next crisis, to survive . . . and the future will look after itself.

The first blow I had planned was my letter to the Minister of the Interior, in which I flung the word "serfdom" in their faces [Document 25]. (This was not mere rhetoric—serfdom is the only word for it. But the contrast I drew between the right of millions to freedom in their own country and the right of some hundreds of thousands to emigrate jarred upon the "public.")

I had dated the letter 21 August (the fifth anniversary of the occupation of Czechoslovakia), but because it might have serious consequences I held it back till the twenty-third, so that I could strike my second blow —speak to the press—unhindered. Interviews with the press are a poor genre for writers: you lose control of your pen, the shape of your sentences, your diction; you fall into the hands of reporters with no feel for the things that move you. They had made a hash of my interview eighteen months earlier, but once again I was forced to choose this unrewarding medium because I needed to defend myself on a number of unconnected minor points. (*Le Monde* shredded and garbled this interview too, and even secreted the full text in the French Ministry of Foreign Affairs, so that to restore it to its original size and meaning we had to publish the full Russian text many months later in an émigré journal.) But in this interview, I managed to get onto firm ground—on my knees at first, then on both feet—and to go over from humble self-defense to furious attack [Document 26].

Immediately after the interview I emerged into the sunshine on Gorky Street (which has been so thoroughly ruined that I no longer feel like calling it Tverskaya) and walked quickly toward the Central Post Office to send my registered letter to the Minister, amusing myself by mumbling over and over, "Let's weigh in and weigh into them." The two blows together, I thought, should be pretty weighty.

Moreover, I had learned the day before from the radio that quite independently (though from afar it looked like a concerted movement, and the authorities were sure that there was cunning collusion) and on the same day, 21 August (Coincidence No. 1), another column had gone over to the attack: Sakharov had given a breath-takingly candid and hard-hitting press conference on international problems. "The U.S.S.R. is one great concentration camp, one great restricted area." (That's the way to talk! The thought was mine, and that of every zek, but he had voiced it before me! *Gulag* had lain idle too long.) "How silly of the West to agree not to beam television programs to the territory of the Soviet Union!" "Moscow resorts to downright swindling."

What I did not know was that within hours of these events, on 23 August, in the dark "Dostoyevskian" communal apartment on Romenskaya Street in Leningrad, the unfortunate Elizaveta Denisovna Voronyanskaya was being murdered after having revealed to the KGB where *Gulag* was buried.* The adversary had begun his own offensive.

(Knowing nothing of this, I was feeling merry, in the mood for pranks, and on 31 August I sent a cheeky note to the KGB [Document 27], addressed to the registry clerk who had signed her name so legibly on the acknowledgment I had received. This time there was no acknowledgment. General Abramov saw no advantage in crossing swords openly. Or perhaps he was already leafing through the copy of *Gulag* unearthed near Luga on 30 August?)

As the press began baying, Sakharov, who expected no positive sequel, went off for a holiday in Armenia, and had to follow part of what happened from down there, because he could not get on a train (in the late summer peak period).

The authorities were more puzzled about our plans than ever. They had a plan of their own: to demolish the opposition finally that autumn. The way to do it (they stupidly thought) was to go through with the show trial of Yakir and Krasin, who would repent and "confess" that the whole "democratic movement" was a fake financed by Western subversive agencies—whereupon the Soviet intelligentsia and the Western public would turn away in disgust from these obscenities, and the last dissidents would be gagged. Their defeat, of course, was implicit in the idiotic idea itself: these were the seventies, and it was too late for a hackneyed stunt from the thirties. All the same, they would have succeeded in depressing and demoralizing the Soviet public even more if this trial of theirs had not blundered into the encounter battle. In the past fourteen months they had postponed their inept trial over and over again, intending to make it more terrifying, to give us all the biggest fright they could—and the opening date they hit on was 27 August!

None of us, of course, knew that this would be the date. But I had realized that for all their delays, they would be ready sometime, and had set myself to anticipate their move, to show them up before their show began. So I said in my interview that the trial would be a dismal affair (in the West the word was translated as "deplorable," which conveys something quite different), a rehash of the uninspired farces put on by Stalin and Vyshinsky—even if Western reporters were allowed in. The day I had chosen for publication of the interview was 28 August, Assumption Day.

On the twenty-seventh, then, they began an even shoddier trial, with no foreign reporters, but they were only just settling down to enjoy their five days of excruciating cat-and-mouse play when the Associated

Press (28 August) carried my contemptuous verdict on it all over the world. (Coincidence No. 2. They did, however, introduce my name into the trial, impromptu: I turned out to be the inspiration and the guiding spirit of the *Chronicle of Current Events!*)

Encounter warfare! In places they had us trapped—elsewhere they were trapped by us. On 29, 30, 31 August I heard my press statement broadcast by all the radio stations, and jubilantly finished writing—I could not help myself—my *Letter to the Leaders.* Meanwhile *Gulag* had been dug up. Bad news travels fast, and on 1 September someone came to warn me, although he was rather vague about it. On the third we knew for certain.

We did not learn then, and we have not found out to this day, what exactly happened in Leningrad. All those who were in any way affected by this affair were surrounded by KGB spies, and if I had traveled openly to Leningrad while the trail was still warm, I would only have made things worse. Voronyanskaya was over sixty, her health was poor, she had a bad leg, and the "Big House" in Leningrad had come down on her as heavily as it could. There had been an exhaustive search to begin with, then five days and nights of interrogation, then day after day of unwinking surveillance. All this time, no one had succeeded in getting in touch with us. Our only information on what happened to Voronyanskaya at the last comes from her neighbor, who does not inspire confidence. In some versions of her story, there were bloodstains or even knife wounds on the hanging body, which contradicts the allegation that she committed suicide by hanging herself. There are substantial grounds for suspecting murder—perhaps they were afraid that she would tell me what had happened, perhaps she was trying to do so. The medical certificate recorded "death by asphyxiation," but her relatives were not allowed to see the body. In the two weeks following the interrogation, other feelings had prevailed in the unhappy woman's mind over her old dread of brother wolf—the pain of whose claws and teeth she had always suffered in anticipation more vividly than any of us, although she never mentioned it except in what seemed like a jest or a gibe. She had rushed wildly about the apartment, apparently in search of a means to warn us of the danger.

From what quarter suspicion had fallen on Voronyanskaya, and why the search, are questions that we shall someday clear up completely, together with the whole story of her death. It was three years since she had done any work worth mentioning for me, and we had hardly seen each other in that time. But the most galling thing about it is that there need have been no disaster at all: nothing had been left with her for safekeeping, but because she had a passion for the book and was afraid that the other copies might be lost, she had deceived me, swearing that she had acted on my insistent demand at the third time of asking, and eloquently describing how she had burned *Gulag*. She had done nothing of the kind. And it was only this deception of hers that enabled the KGB to seize the book.

They had not picked it up immediately. It was as good as in their hands anyway, so they took their time. They were obviously afraid, and with good cause, that I might find out. It was even more important to prevent that than to grab the book. Voronyanskaya had kept her treasure at the dacha of a former zek she knew, Leonid Samutin. Under interrogation she now told them this. (In my experience, they have never found anything hidden in the ground just by digging for it, but only as a result of information volunteered under interrogation. The earth is a more reliable custodian of secrets than man.) She told them —and still they did not come and take it. But when, after the funeral, I received a telephone call in Moscow telling me that she was dead, the KGB evidently decided not to wait any longer: I might go to fetch *Gulag* within the next few hours. They picked it up. I learned about this, too, by one of those quite accidental, fantastic wire crossings with which cities holding millions sometimes astonish us. The KGB was hoping to crunch and munch its prey without my knowing, but although I had scarcely stirred in the meantime, I was able to let the world press have my comments by the evening of 5 September [Document 28]. Not everything there is correct: I had been told that Elizaveta Denisovna had gone home from the KGB on the twenty-eighth and died on the twenty-ninth. But in encounter warfare, blows cannot be carefully weighed, nor their effects measured: they are delivered on the move.

So fate hung one more corpse before the covers of this book of martyrs, which holds millions like it.

The disaster seemed bottomless, irreparable. My most dangerously outspoken work—I had always known that I was "putting my head on the block" in writing it, even if it was made known to all the world and so helped to protect me—was now in *their* hands before it had even come in sight of publication, was about to be smothered before it could cry out, and I with it. It was a much greater disaster than that of 1965, when *The First Circle, The Feast of the Victors* and *The Republic of Labor* had all been seized.

But my mood, my feelings, were quite different: not only was it not the end, the ruin of my life; it was not even a defeat. Why? To begin with, there was my *safe* in the West. Nothing would be lost, everything would be published even if I fell at that very minute. And secondly, all around me was the clash and flash of battle, and the battle was going our way, we were crushing the enemy.

The battle was raging in view of the whole planet, its sympathies were on our side: what if our best regiment was surrounded—that wasn't fatal! It was only for a time! We would rescue it! A merry mood, a martial mood—and I remembered that it was on 4–5 September 1944, on the River Narew near Dlugosiedlo, that we had flung ourselves forward without due precautions, and the narrow neck of ground between us and the main body was caught in a vise so that we and the handkerchief-sized patch we stood on were about to be pinched off. But although we were just a handful, we were somehow not at all down-hearted, because the whole trend of the battle was in our favor, our forces were advancing all along a broad front, and by tomorrow we should not only be liberated, but should cross the river on rafts and establish a bridgehead.

Not for a single hour, not for a minute, was I downhearted on this occasion. I was sorry for the poor, rash woman whose impulse—to preserve the book in case I could not—had brought disaster upon it, upon herself and upon many others. But I had enough experience of such sharp bends in the road to know from the prickling of my scalp that God's hand was in it! It is Thy will! Would I, at any time during the battles of August and September, and for all our resounding victories, ever have brought myself to it? Would I have realized that the time had come to throw in *Gulag?* It is certain that I would not. I would have gone on postponing it until the spring of 1975, sitting with feigned composure on the powder barrels. But I had glimpsed the finger of God: Sleepest thou, idle servant? The time has long since come and gone; reveal it to the world!

I had been fortunate: I had come unscathed from the brink of disaster many times—the problem with *Circle 96* a year earlier, the unauthorized distribution of *The Oak and the Calf* six months before that, when I had been denied light and air and the free use of my limbs, when I could not rise quickly to my feet. But now I was in the saddle, at full gallop, the moment was of my own choosing (some premonition had made me begin my campaign while all was quiet and there was no apparent need for it) and others were galloping furiously beside me; all we need do was turn aside slightly and have at them! This latest upset had come while a great historic upheaval was in progress: Europe was for the first time seriously alarmed and the hands of our masters were tied by their hope of an improvement in terms of trade with the Americans, and by the European Conference, so that before me there was a smooth expanse of several months, begging me to act! Whereas only a month ago I seemed to be "putting my head on the block," I could now raise a defiant battle cry: Victory is ours! With God's aid we shall yet prevail!

The position, as I saw it, was just the opposite of that in 1965. Who had been hurt more by the seizure of my archive? They or I? In 1965, winded and expecting to be arrested at any moment, I had seen no way, even in my dreams, to tell the world about it. It was reported two months later, but the West discerned me only dimly through the fog. This time I had broken the news myself, two days after the event, to the whole world, and people everywhere had recoiled in horror: how could anyone live in a country where death by hanging may be the price paid for having a book?

Why, though, did the police hunt down and confiscate hidden manuscripts with such fanatical avidity? *The First Circle* could have lain still indefinitely—but no, they had to nose it out and pounce on it, whooping with joy: so I had decided to *let it loose*, and three years later it was in print. *Gulag* would have stayed put much, much longer—but no, that, too, they nosed out and pounced on, whooping with joy. That, too, I would now let loose. Reader, it's yours three months from now! For the second time, they have sanctioned action against themselves!

If I look back, it has been the same all these years, the same in all things. All the blows they have rained on me have only helped to break my chains, to set me free! This is our assurance that *they* are doomed.

I heard the news on the evening of the third, and on the evening of the fifth I sent off not only an announcement that *Gulag* had been seized, but orders to *publish it immediately!*

On the same day I posted my *Letter to the Leaders.* It could not have been more timely: they had realized at last that we were a force to be reckoned with. (I get carried away at such moments, as I have said before. I wanted to make *Letter to the Leaders* a deafening thunderclap, but my wife stayed my hand: it was pointless, and would destroy the infinitesimal hope that they would heed it instead of instantly dismissing it as propaganda; let them think quietly! I did, and the *Letter* got stuck like a hook cast too far out and snagged on the muddy bottom. I had overcast, but I would reel it in yet.)

There was an uproar in the press. Blows fell thicker on Sakharov, but I got my share. East and West, our names were coupled, and everything that he said was attributed to me too (though some of it I would not have dared to say then: "a country wearing a mask . . . cunning partner of a totalitarian regime . . . they take economic aid where they cannot cope [they are very much behind with computer technology], and divert the resources thus saved to war.") They aimed blows at him, but the flat of the blade sometimes glanced off and hit me. Looked at another way, it was "follow my leader": I left it to him to overcome the main forces of resistance around us, while I husbanded my strength. Nor am I ashamed of it: my battle was ahead, my strength, every ounce of it, would yet be needed. (Yet the Western radio droned away ten times daily about the persecution of Solzhenitsyn, but—touch wood—I had noticed no persecution so far. Persecution—this? Compared with my life in the camps? Our newspapers, of course, yapped on, but I didn't read the stuff. A zek's nerves can stand more than that. As for other forms of harassment, I had never known any respite in the past: I was inured to them.)

This was the first time in fifty-five years, I think, that people hounded by the Soviet press had dared to bark back. Our little group of "dissidents" (Turchin and Shafarevich also spoke out) could act and act boldly that autumn because they were behaving naturally, straightening cramped spines weary of bending. And because we were rising up from the very nadir, when it was no longer possible to endure in silence. When things were so bad that there was no safety in merely holding out—we had to hold forward to victory.

During that same feverish week I dispatched "Peace and Violence" for publication. I had written this article as a concrete illustration of my Nobel lecture—against Western illusions and distortions of perspective. Its object was not to influence the award of Nobel Peace Prizes, although it had something to say about them. But when I heard on 31 August, while the battle was at its hottest, that the Nobel Peace Prize Committee had selected forty-seven candidates, including Nixon and Tito (I didn't yet know about Kissinger and Le Duc Tho), I decided to recast my article so as to obstruct these candidates and put forward Sakharov's candidacy, which fitted in very well with my argument. The article was finished by the fourth of September and sent off on the fifth. On the sixth, a few days before it was due to be published, I showed Sakharov a copy. This was in fact the only occasion on which we met or consulted each other during the encounter battle. We could dimly discern victory ahead. But no one could have supposed that it was so close; that the hounds would be called off on the following day, and the jamming of Western broadcasts would end four days later.

When we entered the fight, neither he nor I could count on help from the West more ample than that we had received over the years: palpable enough to protect us from arrest and destruction, but insufficient to influence the course of events in our own country or abroad. But as though to remind us that the human mind rarely foresees great historical changes, Western sympathy began to grow warmer and warmer until it reached an undreamed-of temperature. (Facts and statements cited below were jotted down in a hurry as I heard them in Russian-language broadcasts from Western stations. This was before the end of jamming. I could not catch everything, there were days when I did not listen in, and all this time I saw not a single newspaper. I may have got some of the dates wrong by a day or two: sometimes the day mentioned is that of the event, sometimes that on which I heard of it by radio.)

Throughout the first week (from 24 August till the end of the month) "dissidents in the U.S.S.R." was the main topic in the whole European press. The Yakir-Krasin trial of course obtruded at this stage. What we had not expected was that the temperature would rise still higher in the following week (beginning 1 September), as the fires of Western indignation were fanned by the hate campaign in the Soviet press.

"We are being asked to pay too high a price for détente—to bolster up tyranny." "The Soviet regime is trying yet again to pull the wool over the eyes of Western intellectuals. Perhaps that is why Sakharov and Solzhenitsyn have decided to warn the West of its danger." (BBC)

"In a grim situation Solzhenitsyn and Sakharov have issued their challenge to the leaders of the Soviet Union and the West. If they are forcibly silenced it will only show that they are speaking the truth." "It is impossible to work for détente with a dictatorial regime." (W. Hayter, former British ambassador to the U.S.S.R.)

Further support for Soviet dissidents came on 3 September from the Austrian Chancellor; on 6 September from the Swedish Minister of Foreign Affairs (in Palme's government, which had hitherto been so considerate of Soviet susceptibilities)—his was "the strongest statement made in Sweden on the U.S.S.R. since the occupation of Czechoslovakia"; in Germany not only from the Christian Democrats but from the Presidium of the Social Democratic Party (only Brandt the peacemaker chose silence). Günter Grass made the first of several statements on 7 September and at once created a furor: previously one of the staunchest supporters of Brandt's *Ostpolitik*, he now called it (in *Stern*) "political insanity"; economic détente should not be pursued at the expense of culture. Interviewed on German television, he repeated his challenge.

By 8 September, enough evidence had accumulated to convince our rulers that their vicious press campaign was a failure and must be terminated. On 8 September *Pravda* "summed up," and this was the signal for everyone to stop. Conditioned by decades of experience, Staraya Ploshchad supposed that the whole thing would end abruptly there: once the pack stopped baying, its terror-stricken quarry would heave a sigh of gratitude and the West would naturally fall silent. How wrong they were! This was just the beginning!

On 8 September Sakharov gave another press conference, on the heinous abuse of psychiatry and the use of the tranquilizer haloperidol in our country, and fighting back against accusations in the press, he said that Soviet newspapers shamelessly play on our people's hatred of war. ("Challenge to the KGB," said the *Daily Telegraph*. Only two days earlier that newspaper had believed that "the ring is steadily tightening around them," but now "the whole purpose of the campaign is to silence them, but they are both determined to hold out to the end.") On 9 September, in an interview for a Dutch radio station, he called for the inspection of our mental hospitals by representatives of the Red Cross! On the ninth, the president of the American Academy of Sciences said that "we were overcome by indignation and shame when we learned that forty academicians had joined in this witch hunt. Breaches of scientific ethics have prevented the Russian people from fully revealing its scientific genius. If Sakharov is deprived of freedom, it will be *difficult* for American scientists to fulfill their obligations to the government under the agreement on scientific collaboration with the U.S.S.R." (No blow could have hurt *our masters* more. And how frustrating it was for them! Nixon had signed, but if the scientists said no, they wouldn't get a thing out of it!) Others who joined in defending us were the (very left-wing) socialist youth organization in West Germany ("We cannot expand trade relations at the expense of such people as Sakharov and Solzhenitsyn"); the youth organization of the Christian Democratic Union; the Norwegian Minister of Foreign Affairs; the Bavarian Academy of Sciences ("Send a Nobel Prize winner to Siberia? That would be a fascist act comparable with the Ossietzky affair"). "This is the touchstone," said the *Observer,* "by which we can judge what sort of society the U.S.S.R. has to offer us." On the tenth, the voice of Wilbur Mills, chairman of the House Ways and Means Committee, was heard from his farm, where he was recovering from an illness. He was against any increase in trade with the U.S.S.R. until the persecution of people like Solzhenitsyn and Sakharov ceased. In other words, the Jackson amendment was being broadened to include human rights in the U.S.S.R. as well as emigration! And the discussion in Mills's committee was approaching the decisive stage at that very moment!

All in all, the force of the West's angry reaction was a surprise to everyone: to the West itself, which had not put up such staunch and massive opposition to the land of communism for a long time past, and even more of a surprise to our rulers, who lost their heads completely. Commentators summed it up by saying that "the Soviet government is now in much the same position as in August 1968." On 13 September the government tried to escape from this situation by putting a stop to jamming, which it had introduced under cover of the clanking of tanks in Czechoslovakia! Now, this was a stupefying victory, quite unexpected (like all victories wrested from *our masters*), and truly historic, since only the Twentieth Congress had previously lifted jamming.

How it cheered our *public,* who just a little while ago had been so demoralized that they had even given up samizdat.

On the tenth, *Aftenposten* published "Peace and Violence." (*Le Monde,* for which the article was meant, had shied away from it: such straight speaking from the Soviet Union offended its sense of leftist decorum. This made it all the more fitting that a Norwegian paper should be the one to take over the article.) It was originally interpreted as no more than an attempt to promote Sakharov's candidacy for a Nobel Peace Prize, and on the tenth he himself replied to the reporters who eagerly telephoned and knocked at his door from day to day (no one ever met with a refusal) that he would gladly accept it, that "my nomination for the Nobel Prize will have a positive effect on the position of the persecuted in our country. It is the best answer" to the witch hunt. Another worldwide campaign was set in motion, to support Sakharov's candidacy. The Nobel Peace Prize Committee (in which the shameful idea of dividing the prize between the occupier and the capitulator was perhaps already ripening) rejected my proposal as both incompetent and ill-timed. Nominations from other sources flooded in at once to take its place: on 11 September certain British MPs adopted the cause. On the twelfth the whole Liberal group in the Danish parliament, then a group of Munich physicists, and still others followed, all urging that Sakharov should be given the prize in 1974 if not in 1973! (It was 12 September before the article was translated in full from Norwegian. People then realized that it did not confine itself to the nomination of Sakharov, and conflicting comments on its central argument began to be heard. It went against the grain with those very circles in the West that had given us all the most support.)

But the campaign in the West gained speed like a racing flywheel. Among the telegrams published in support of Sakharov was one from a hundred British psychiatrists, one from three hundred French doctors ("Send an international commission to determine what goes on in mental hospitals in the U.S.S.R."). Those who spoke out in our defense included the Prime Minister of Denmark, the Burgomaster of West Berlin, the Italian Social Democrats ("can we trust a country which persecutes its own citizens for their opinions?"), the Committee of Concerned Scholars (U.S.A.), the Committee for Intellectual Freedom (also U.S.A.), the Italian Chamber of Deputies, the Consultative Assembly of the European Community, Norwegian writers, scholars and actors, Swiss writers and artists, 188 Canadian intellectuals. The signatures of eighty-nine Nobel Prize winners throughout the world were being collected (this was held up and then the organizers themselves delayed it because of the Middle Eastern war). At a conference of writers, philosophers, editors, journalists and churchmen convened in Paris, the French public was rebuked for its connivance at the denial of freedom in the U.S.S.R. The U.S. Senate published a declaration (which did not commit the government) in defense of freedom in the U.S.S.R., and on the same day the House of Representatives proposed granting Sakharov and Solzhenitsyn the title "honorary citizens of the United States." On 12 September West German Radio said that "people in the West feel more secure if men like Sakharov and Solzhenitsyn are free to move about and to speak their minds in their own country." On 19 September the BBC said that "the West itself will be in danger of infection by tyranny if we ignore the persecution of dissidents in the

U.S.S.R." And it summed up, on the twenty-second, the results of our four-week battle: "All the evidence shows that the Soviet authorities have not succeeded in frightening the dissidents." The *Christian Science Monitor* said that "the Sakharov-Solzhenitsyn affair has become a major international event. It has rapidly become an influence on American political life."

That same week Grigorenko was transferred to an ordinary hospital. Within days of that, Yevgeny Barabanov passed through the firing line. On 15 September he came to me (I knew beforehand that the KGB had repeatedly hauled him in and tried to shut him up), and in my apartment made his quite historic statement to a reporter. A slave like so many others, hitherto unknown to anyone, he soared at once from nonentity to world fame, rose to his full height by throwing off the burden that had bowed all backs for half a century. He declared that sending a manuscript abroad was no crime, but an honorable act, because it saved the manuscript's life.

Then a miracle occurred! Barabanov had already been told to report to the KGB for a final interrogation, from which he would not be going home—he had been promised seven years' imprisonment—and suddenly the unclean power fell back from him, as though its hand had withered: the record of the menacing investigation, laid before the eyes of the world, became a certificate of merit. Barabanov was only dismissed from his job.

Just one such refusal to grovel, one such show of moral courage from all the slaves among us, is all that is needed: we could take a single breath and be free. But we dare not.

The Western reaction to Barabanov's declaration was one of the many things in those months that exceeded our expectations. Priests in Italy were encouraged to refer to his bravery in their sermons. Academicians came to his defense in France.

After the Western world had remained apathetically silent about the annihilation of whole peoples in our country, about events involving millions, its current reaction to such an insignificant event in the East as the public vilification of a little group of dissidents amazed us. We could not believe our ears as we switched over from one radio station to another, every morning and every evening The ink of my interview, and my article bitterly rebuking the West for its weakness and callousness, was scarcely dry, but they were already out of date; the West was in a state of high excitement, had been stirred more deeply than ever before, so that one could succumb to the illusion that the spirit of freedom was reborn in the great and ancient continent. In fact, several ephemeral reasons, indiscernible from where we were, had combined to produce this result (one of them, probably, was distrust of the U.S.S.R. exacerbated by the obstacles it put in the way of emigration). This sudden blaze of feeling, which reminded us of Europe in the years of its glory, could not have happened a month later: the same Europe, craven and disunited, would bow to the threats of Arab oil producers.

But in September—the flames crackled merrily! And dazzled our owlish master. The Yakir trial, a crass idea fumblingly executed, was a shot from a stage pistol, which hit no one, frightened no one, and merely brought disgrace on the KGB. They had put themselves in a worse position than they would have been in without a trial. They hastily cobbled up a lying statement by Soviet psychiatrists that *loony bins* in the Soviet Union were not used as places of internment (3 September), to which, quick as a flash, the Western press published an answer from Sakharov and Shafarevich (4 September). For seven months they had been straining every muscle: they had to have someone to suppress the publication of Soviet manuscripts abroad. On September 21 two announcements were made: in the morning, that VAAP, the Soviet copyright agency, had been set up; in the evening, that I had "thrown down the gauntlet" and was handing over some chapters of *Circle 96* for publication as samizdat to test the strength of their legal position. (The third fortunate coincidence for us. This was merely the next in order of the offensive acts on my timetable [Document 29].) It looked as though we were acting with a speed beyond that of tanks, with highly efficient weapons such as we had never had before. We scoured the battlefield as though we had ten times our numbers.

Seen from the West—with the errors of vision inevitable at a distance—it looked like this: At the end of August, before battle was joined, the *Daily Telegraph* had thought that "In the U.S.S.R. everyone else has been suppressed—only the voice of Sakharov remains, but soon even he will fall silent." At the end of September, the *Deutsche Allgemeine Zeitung* said that "from Magdeburg to Moscow the security services no longer enjoy their former power, they are no longer feared, people no longer worry much about them."

All this time the most trenchant statements came from left-wing and liberal circles—all of them former friends of the U.S.S.R., with more influence than anyone else on Western public opinion, people who had spent decades creating the leftward bias general in the West. Now the American intelligentsia had become hostile to Soviet-American rapprochement. Caught in an impossible situation, the Communists in all Western countries hypocritically squirmed and wriggled: complete refusal to support freedom of speech in the "society of the future" was impossible, but they tried to belittle and discredit us while they were at it. The governments of Nixon and Brandt were in exactly the same predicament, because their whole game was threatened with disruption by the stand we had taken. Kissinger was evasive and noncommittal. The American Secretary of the Treasury and the Secretary of Health, Education and Welfare were visiting the U.S.S.R. while all this was going on. The first promised credits and the second insisted when he got home that American-Soviet cooperation in the field of medicine (cooperation with our psychiatrists!) mattered more than the persecution of dissidents. Brandt's own party wrested from him a reluctant profession of "spiritual affinity with the Soviet dissidents" (9 September) but three days later, to save his *Ostpolitik,* he "would be trying to improve relations with the U.S.S.R., even if Stalin were at its head." ("Improve relations" with the murderer of millions? Why not with his little brother, then, with Hitler? With this needless overemphasis Brandt insulted us all—all the living, and all the prisoners who had perished in the camps.) At the end of September he retreated a little, with another prevarication. In short, he succeeded in facing both ways throughout.

In these weeks of battle for the freedom of the mind, Eastern tyranny found even stauncher supporters in Western businessmen: in other words, the most loyal supporters of the "dictatorship of the proletariat" were the capitalists. They tried to persuade the U.S. Congress that *trade* was the very thing to reinforce the rights of man in the U.S.S.R.! There was one man of rare insight among them, Samuel Pisar, an enthusiast for closer trade relations with the U.S.S.R. for many years, who published on 3 October an open letter to Sakharov: *"The freedom of a single individual is more important than the whole of world trade put together."* The Vatican too, paralyzed by this same rapprochement with the East, preserved its silence throughout the month, although the Pope was criticized for this by ordinary priests. The Pope had not a word to say for himself. There was only a grudging statement from the head of his press department in October, when the battle was over: "The rights of man in the U.S.S.R. are not merely its internal affair."

For me, world support on this scale—out of proportion to anything we could have expected, and decisive—made further participation in the battle, and the completion of my "cascade" plan, superfluous from the middle of September on. The battle was going well without my help. And I needed to husband my working time, my strength, my reserves, for the next, the crueler battle soon to come, a battle that there was no avoiding now that they had seized *Gulag*.

On 21 September, exactly a month after it had begun, I decided that the campaign was won and, as far as I was concerned, over for the time being (with the release that day of the chapter from *Circle 96*). *As far as I was concerned.* Because we had not coordinated our operations, I was, alas, quite unable to make Sakharov feel the same.

It took him another month to extricate himself gradually from the battle and in that time he suffered grievous and damaging losses. Andrei Dimitrievich was so slow in withdrawing because he was unable to say no to importunate, ambitious or merely frivolous newspapermen, who sometimes could not even be bothered to make the trip to Moscow, but lifted a receiver somewhere in Europe and helped themselves to a piece of Sakharov's soul by telephone. The purport of Sakharov's actions was much less clear than it should have been, because he was so painfully divided in his own mind about his future: should he stay on in this land of ours to the end or risk leaving it? (A scheme for him to seek an invitation to the U.S.A. on a lecture tour was under constant consideration.) Less clear, too, because he was only too easily persuaded by people who were only too ready to advise. They inveigled him, for instance, into the unfortunate Neruda episode (21 September), intended to show the world, at home and abroad, that we were objective, that we stood for freedom everywhere, that (who knows what may happen!) we were just as concerned for Neruda (who was in no danger at all) as others were for us. He did not, of course, write it with the unmannerliness that is normal in our country, but qualified his letter in defense of Neruda with the polite assumption that the Chilean government perhaps cherished the noble aim of regenerating its country—and so we exposed our flank to attack by our own and by Western Communists. Sakharov's enemies flung themselves on him ferociously, and positions won earlier were weakened.

By giving an interview to the correspondent (genuine or bogus) for a Lebanese newspaper, Sakharov again exposed himself to attack by both the Communist and the Arab world, when the Arab-Israeli war had already set a natural limit to our fight or marked an interval in it. This interview provoked a raid, supposedly by Arab terrorists: Sakharov was in danger again, and must be rescued if the KGB meant to play such sinister tricks. I wrote Sakharov a letter and made it public [Document 30].

As I retired from the battle, I had as usual surveyed the scene with the enemy's eyes: what measures against me would they think of next? For them, the greatest danger was not in what had already happened but in what might and must happen: the landslide publication of all I had written. *They* had always underestimated me. Till very recently, when they had seized *Gulag,* they cannot, I think, in their gloomiest flights of fantasy, have imagined anything like it: so how can anything he writes be as dangerous or damaging as all that? A couple of *Feast of the Victors* more or less doesn't matter. But now, with *Gulag* in their claws, as they carried it from desk to desk (and hid it in safes, I daresay, to keep it from their own colleagues), passing it directly from the experts to the top bosses, right up to Andropov himself, the blood must have turned to ice in their veins: such a publication might be fatal to the system. (To hell with the system: their soft jobs were in danger!) They had to think of ways not just to wreak their vengeance on me at some future date, but to prevent the book's appearing. They might not believe that I would dare. But if they did believe it? I could see several possibilities open to them.

1. They could take my children hostage—posing as "gangsters," of course. (They did not know that we had thought of this and made a superhuman decision: our children were no dearer to us than the memory of the millions done to death, and nothing could make us stop that book.)

2. They could intercept the manuscripts there in the West—break in and steal them while they were being prepared for publication. (But how could they be sure that they had seized all copies and made publication impossible?)

3. They could bring legal pressures to bear, insist that publication of the work would be illegal and suppress it. (In anticipation of some such onslaught, my lawyer, Dr. Heeb, was already drafting for me a "Confirmation of Power of Attorney," with special reference to *Gulag* and the situation created by Soviet adherence to the Copyright Convention.)

4. Or they could . . . (But that would take time, and would not prevent publication anyway. On the contrary, it would make it doubly

sure, because there would be nothing more to lose.)

5. They could try to blacken me personally (by accusing me of crime or immorality) and so discredit my testimony.

6. They could try to frighten me—with 1 or 4 above.

7. Negotiations?

Against this last I put a large question mark: their arrogance would not let them descend to negotiation at anything lower than intergovernmental level. Demichev had declared furiously: "Negotiate? With Solzhenitsyn? He won't live to see the day!"

(Ah, but I shall, I think. Though it may well be too late—too late to do any good, too late for them and for me.)

When I ended these jottings with the word *"Negotiations?"* I did not really believe in them, did not want them, for myself, could not visualize them. What was there to discuss now, except the contents of my *Letter to the Soviet Leaders?* I had no bargaining counters left, no favors to ask, no concessions to make.

How, in any case, could they make an approach to me? I had long ago cut off all suspicious persons, all hybrids, all peddlers of news and services. *They* and I had no common acquaintance.

I had drawn up my list of possibilities on the twenty-third, and on the twenty-fourth my former wife, Natalya Reshetovskaya, rang up in some excitement and asked me to meet her. On a matter of great moment, to judge from her voice, but I failed to guess what.

I had seen her two days before, and she had been word perfect—it was as though she had memorized a feuilleton from *Komsomolskaya Pravda:* according to her, I was behaving hysterically, shouting about nonexistent threats, slandering the state security organs. Alas, she had already behaved like a common informer, deposited important letters from me with the court, and handed over all my other letters to the KGB. The article that she had written jointly with them had already appeared, bearing the Novosti trademark, in the *New York Times.* Still, she had wavered at times, had sometimes seemed to relent, and I wanted to believe the best of her. I could not identify her with *them* completely.

At the Kazan Station I saw pride in the eyes that had for so many years been steely and spiteful.

"That was a call from Innokenti Volodin.* The matter is very serious, more serious than anything we've discussed before. But don't get upset; from your point of view it's *all to the good.*"

I could see what was coming, and turned cold. I instantly assumed my mask of world-weary apathy, and wore it until we parted.

I had made my years of exile miserable—years of furious longing for a woman—because I was afraid for my books, afraid that some Komsomol girl would betray me. After four years of war and eight years of imprisonment, my first three years as a free man were years of misery, repression and frustration, years of longing for a woman whom I could trust with my manuscripts, with all the names I knew, with my own head. When I came back from exile I had given up and gone back to my former wife.

Now, seventeen years later, this woman had come to me making no attempt to hide the fact that she was an emissary of the KGB, walking sure-footedly along the platform to step as if by right out of the private and into the public reaches of my life, into the battle for *Gulag*. (My record of the meeting was made less than an hour afterward, while I still felt scalded all over.)

"Are you willing to meet *some people* to talk things over?"

"What for?"

"Well, the immediate purpose would be to discuss the possibilities of publishing *Cancer Ward*."

(*Cancer Ward?* I thought of the proverb about the little boy under the ice, and the stepmother who goes looking for him as soon as the thaw comes.)

"You surprise me. There's no need for me to meet anybody. It's quite natural for Russian books to be published by Russian publishers."

(All the same, this meant that *they* wanted to negotiate! We had slugged them good and hard! Harder than we had thought.)

"But you will go to the publishers and sign a contract? They never know what to expect from you. They're afraid you may . . . Anyway, you need to discuss conditions of publication. . . ."

(Playing for time! One whiff of *Gulag* has made them eager to slow me down, to lull me to sleep. Still, I need three months' breathing space. I, too, can gain from lulling their suspicions.)

"No conditions. The full text, exactly as it is."

"Well, after you've been to the publishers, are you willing to meet someone else?"

"That someone else will be on hand anyway—in mufti, sitting to one side of the chief editor's desk."

They were there now—plainclothesmen taking photographs of us and listening in, from platforms parallel with ours. Every inch of my spine registered their presence: no one who has experienced the feeling could mistake it for anything else. It showed in her manner too—she was a woman performing a duty, not just being herself.

"What about somebody *a bit higher up?*"

"Only if it's the Politburo. To talk about the nation's destiny, not my own."

"As it happens, they're the ones who have been persecuting you—the Central Committee, not the KGB. It was they who published *The Feast of the Victors*—and *what a mistake that was!*" (And how outspoken this private citizen was in her criticism of the Central Committee!) "You must realize that the others are quite different these days; they're not responsible for the horrors of the past."

"If so, they should publicly dissociate themselves from the past, condemn it, tell us all about it—then they won't be held responsible. Who *did* kill sixty million people?"

She didn't query the sixty, although she didn't know who they might be, but said quickly and confidently:

"*They* weren't the ones! My circle has become much wider nowadays, and I've been meeting such clever people! Not like those you know—you're surrounded by fools. . . . Why do you keep blaming Andropov for everything? He doesn't come into it at all.[!] It's a different set of people." She looked deep into my eyes, as though I were a black sheep, a lost soul, a half-wit. "All I know is that somebody is deceiving you, inflaming your suspicions, practicing some terrible emotional blackmail on you. Inventing imaginary threats."

"Like the 'gangsters' letters,' for instance."

Heatedly: "The KGB had nothing to do with them!"

"How do you know?"

I speak lazily, a man who could be wrong. She is militantly sure of herself and her new friends.

"You must show me one of those letters sometime. *They* aren't out to attack you. They aren't doing a thing to you!"

"What about when they shoved me out of Rostropovich's dacha and wouldn't give me a residence permit?"

"Stop harping on your permit! They can't give you one just like that. It takes time."

"They're trying to get their hands on my archive again. . . ."

"That's what they're there for—to look for things!"

"For works of literature?"

(I'm surprised, yes, but too weary to argue, weary of the struggle—it has been a long one—with this KGB of yours, longing for a rest. That's the part I'm playing, and I shan't move a hair's breadth from it.)

"You tell the world that your most important works are still to come, that the flow will continue even if you should die—and that way you *force* them to come looking. In your letter to the congress, for instance, you mentioned *Tanks Know the Truth,* and now they're looking for that too. . . ."

(Yes, but how do you know they're looking, and what they're looking for? What titles have you added to the list? Is this book, *The Oak and the Calf,* one of them?)

"You've forced them to make searches, ———'s place, for instance." (She mentioned the woman's name.)

So she had named names already? . . . I spoke, for the first time, with the full power of my voice.

"Nobody could have given her name except you! And if . . ."

"Getting divorced was your idea; you should have thought of all the consequences."

(I had. Long, long ago. There were many people and many things *you* weren't told about. But what of the others, earlier on?)

"I didn't think there'd be any dirty tricks."

"Don't worry. I know what I'm doing."

(Right, good! I shall publish *Gulag* as quickly as I can. So that no one can swipe it and swallow it in the dark. They need darkness—but I'll let some light in on them!)

"Why don't you just make a declaration that all your works are in your exclusive possession, and that you won't publish anything for twenty years?"

(This was it! What she most urgently wanted from me! Wanted for *them!* It was what *they* needed! . . . But how little *you* know me, after all the time we lived together, if you think that a month would leave something to be said, that an hour would pass without a decision, and the day end without it being implemented.)

There's something else I want to make clear: "If they touch any one of the two hundred and twenty, or anybody like Barabanov, I shall immediately come to the defense of those who are ill-treated."

Two deft strokes of the broom. She knew just what to say.

"Those who only talked about the camps have nothing to fear. But those who helped you to *do* things . . ."

(Remember 1968, how we spent the whole spring typing in Rozhd-estvo? You've already told the clever, clever people all about it, I'm sure, in those intimate little chats you have.)

"I shall come to the defense of every single one of them at once and with all the strength I have."

(Once, long ago, we were so straightforward with each other. But long ago I began to catch you at your playacting, or rather caught myself failing to recognize in time what an actress you are. Today, though, on this firm ridge road, this main highway of my existence, you will not get around me with acting, however well rehearsed you are.)

"In general, if you just keep quiet a bit, it will be *better for every-body.*"

"Yes, but I'm not the aggressor; *they* are forcing me to it. . . ."

"You're a fanatic; you have no thought for your own children. . . ."

She mentioned them again later.

"If something happens to one of your children, I suppose you'll say that's the KGB too. . . ."

(This was how their minds worked: no one would suspect them of harming a child.)

"Of course, you have just won a victory. But if *Cancer Ward* is published now, you won't say so in public, will you?"

"Never. Indeed, I'm surprised that you should ask. At most I shall say that this was a sensible decision, for the benefit of the Russian reading public. For me *personally* the publication of *Cancer Ward* hardly matters anymore."

(Indeed: does it matter or doesn't it? How can I help longing, help fighting for the publication of my works in my homeland, more than for anything in the world? The grotesque feature of the situation is that publication has been delayed too long to be worth sacrifices. A token printing, just to make the gullible talk about our freedom? To sell to Moscow intellectuals who have the samizdat version on their shelves anyway? Or to let it be seen briefly in the shops, and then pulp the whole edition? It's come to this—I no longer want the book published myself. Moscow has read it, and Russia at large needs the whole truth more than it needs the long superseded *Cancer Ward.* Put obstacles in its way? I won't do that, I dare not. But still, it's no longer something I need.)

"It was your fault they didn't publish *Cancer Ward* in December 1967!"

"What *do* you mean?"

"You must remember: you pretended to be ill, refused to go, and sent me instead. Tvardovsky only wanted to ask you to sign quite a *mild* letter to the press."

Mild enough, to be sure—just a letter dissociating myself from all the fuss in the West . . . That was all they were concerned with in the secretariat that time too. This was how they would turn my story inside out: The regime hadn't driven me (and all those others before me) into a blind alley; it was I myself (we ourselves). . . .

"If they publish the book, you'll be paid something. . . . But you must give certain undertakings. You won't make any statement to reporters about this proposition, will you? Or about our conversation? It must remain a complete secret."

Surpassing *their,* and her, utmost desires, I replied: "Our conversation will not go beyond the confines of the platform we're standing on."

(The long, narrow platform between the two approach lines for Ryazan trains, which had seen all our arrivals and departures, with groceries, news, fresh hopes, for some twelve years. A long platform, on a sunny September morning, where we strolled in sight of movie cameras and within earshot of tape recorders. And it is within the confines of this platform that I am describing the conversation.)

I still have to learn how hard she tries for me:

"I believe that in discussions I have had, and in particular chapters of my memoirs which I have sent to *certain people,* I have succeeded in explaining your character, defending you, and making your lot easier."

She had taken it upon herself to explain me! She who had never understood me, never never read my heart, never anticipated a single action of mine (any more than she did now), had presumed to explain me to the secret police! And in partnership with them, to the whole world. . . .

Perhaps it is always like that: wounded vanity demands satisfaction, and the more witnesses there are, the greater it will be. Probably so. But to follow where the secret police lead . . . ? Not every woman would.

(When you and I were copying things from one notebook to another, wasn't there a proverb among the things you dictated: "Whoever runs with the wolf is no sheep"?)

"Take care—don't be too ready to accept the services of those birds of darkness. . . . They may suddenly pick you up and carry you off."

"Don't let it worry you. I know what I'm doing."

Whatever she might do on her new path, and for her new masters (she had not managed today's conversation at all well: she should have induced me to meet the Geebees privately, and, instead, we were "awaiting" a publisher's offer; still, she had certain proof that I was not on the offensive, that I wasn't publishing *Gulag,* that I was pacifically disposed)—whatever she might do in the future, I should not be able to isolate myself from it, to fling at her: "That's all your doing!" Whatever she did, I should be doing it with her. . . . Whatever evils poisoned the future, their roots were in the past. I had myself to blame. In jail I could see right through a man as soon as he entered a cell; yet never once had I looked into the heart of the woman at my side. I had allowed the evil to fester and flare up.

This is how we pay for mistakes in the neglected secondary sphere, that sphere which local Party Committees, in their holiday greetings to us, refer to as our "private lives."

Alas, no channels for consultation had been established, no joint operations arranged, between ourselves and the allied column alongside.

I shall venture to speak of Sakharov here only insofar as it is necessary to explain actions of his that have had or seem likely to have important consequences for Russia.

When Lenin conceived and initiated, and Stalin developed and made safe, their inspired scheme for a totalitarian state, they thought of everything, did everything to ensure that the system would stand firm to all eternity, changing only when the leader waved his wand; to ensure that the voice of freedom would never ring out, or any movement against the current ever set in. They foresaw all eventualities but one—a *miracle,* an irrational phenomenon, the causes of which could not be divined, detected and cut short beforehand.

Just such a miracle occurred when Andrei Dmitrievich Sakharov emerged in the Soviet state, among the swarms of corrupt, venal, unprincipled scientists, and what is more, in one of their most important, most secret and most lavishly favored nests—in the neighborhood of the hydrogen bomb. (If he had appeared in some obscure back room, they would have snuffed him out smartly.)

Creator of the twentieth century's most terrible weapon, Hero of Socialist Labor three times over (just like the general secretaries of Communist Parties whom he sat beside at meetings), enjoying the entrée to that narrow circle in which, whatever a man's requirements, the word "impossible" does not exist—Sakharov, like Prince Nekhlyudov in Tolstoy's *Resurrection*, woke up one morning feeling—or, more probably, he had always felt, all his life—that the abundance that threatened to overwhelm him was dust and ashes, that his soul yearned for truth, and that there was no obvious justification for the work he was carrying out. Up to a point, he could quiet his misgivings with the thought that it was for the defense and salvation of our people. But beyond that point, it became only too evident that it served aggressive purposes, and that the tests that were being carried out were ruinous to the environment.

For decades, the creators of all terrible weapons in our country had obeyed without a murmur not just Stalin or Beria but any little colonel in charge of a research establishment or a *sharashka* (in whichever of the two the authorities had been pleased to place them). They had been infinitely grateful for a little Gold Star, a dacha near Moscow, a glass of sour cream for breakfast, and if ever they answered back their superiors, it was only to make sure that the wishes of those superiors were carried out by the best available techniques. (I have seen no evidence that P. Kapitsa's "rebellion"* was aimed at anything higher than his incompetent Beria-ite supervisors.) Then suddenly, braving the raised fist of capricious Nikita, who had already assumed sole command, Andrei Sakharov was brave enough to demand an end to atomic tests, not just those in testing areas that nobody knows about, but the multimegaton tests that shake the whole earth and raise mushroom clouds over it. As early as that he had incurred the wrath and disfavor of authority, become the odd man out in the world of science—unknown, invisible as yet to Russia at large. Sakharov became an avid reader of samizdat and one of the first to intercede for arrested dissidents (Galanskov and Ginzburg), but this, too, went unnoticed at first. What did attract the public eye was his memorandum in summer 1968.

In this episode we can recognize the dominant characteristic of the man: the serene trustfulness which comes from his own purity. To get his memorandum typed, he distributed it a few pages at a time to typists in the Institute (he had no others to turn to, he knew no other way of doing it), supposing (he who had worked in Soviet institutions—or should we say floated through them on a cloud) that these confidential typists would not be clever enough to fathom its meaning, or piece separate parts together. They were, however, clever enough for each to take her own batch of copies to the Special Section, which was reading the memorandum before he had the pages laid out on his table to sort them for samizdat. Sakharov was particularly ill equipped (and therefore readier than anyone!) for single combat with a heartless, ea-gle-eyed, sharp-clawed, unerringly pouncing totalitarian state! At the very last minute the Minister for the Nuclear Industry tried to dissuade Sakharov, warning him of the consequences, but in vain. Like a child to whom the sign "Epidemic Zone" means nothing, Sakharov wan-dered, unprotected, away from his own caste—the well-fed, heavy-jowled and happy—to join the insulted and injured. And—who but a child would do it?—by way of farewell left on the threshold he was abandoning the "surplus money" the state had paid him "for nothing": 150,000 in Khrushchev's new money, a million and a half in Stalin's money.

Before Sakharov knew anything about the liberal samizdat world, he had found support in a fearless young historian (with grandiose theories that the legitimate course of world history had been distorted merely by an unfortunate national character trait). Inevitably, he rejoiced in this ally! And, inevitably, was influenced by him! Read Sakharov's first memorandum, and see what obeisances he makes to Roy Medvedev, how he looks up to him. Suspended weights hold down an air balloon. Presumably the delay in Sakharov's ascent is largely explained by this influence of Roy Medvedev. A certain narrowness of vision is stamped all over the documents that they produced together, and when Sa-kharov struggled free of Marxist trammels, their collaboration was ter-minated by a ground-to-air shot in that aeronaut's back.[1]

I first met Sakharov at the end of August 1968, immediately after our

---

1. In our besieged circumstances it was difficult to avoid some missteps. At one point I, too, allowed my name to be exploited by a person alien to my world view. This was the other Medvedev brother, Zhores, who seized his chance to publish his vapid *Ten Years After Ivan Denisovich* (an example of a book useful for its author but of no use to its readers), as well as the floor plan of my beleaguered Moscow apartment, to say nothing of photographs of me (which he should not have treated as a salable commodity). In the course of his years in the West, Zhores Medvedev has exhibited his true worth clearly enough in the diverse support he has given to Soviet policy. He has even made excuses for the compulsory psychiatric treatment to which he had himself been subjected. In Norway he set about sowing doubts as to whether Sakharov was worthy of the Nobel Peace Prize. His brother Roy has long played the role of "oppositionist" in the U.S.S.R. Ostensibly expressing a point of view that was independent and more intelligent than that of the paid bureaucrats of the Central Committee, he has nevertheless always been able to divine with astonishing accuracy just what was useful or necessary for the Soviet regime, as for instance in his recent attack on Aleksandr Ginzburg, the imprisoned distributor of the Russian Social Fund. His political stance has been of great use to the "Eurocommunists" and to all those in the West who seek to paint a picture of the "freedom of opinion" in the U.S.S.R.[1979 note]

occupation of Czechoslovakia and shortly after the appearance of his memorandum. He had not yet been released from his status as a specially secret and specially guarded personage: he did not have the right to use public telephones (it's not always easy to listen in), only those at his place of work and his home; he could not visit any house or place he pleased, only those previously specified and checked, which he was known to be in the habit of visiting. His bodyguards sometimes followed him, and sometimes did not—he had no way of knowing beforehand. For this reason it was very difficult to arrange my meeting with him. Fortunately, we found that there was a house in which I had been once before, and which he was in the habit of visiting. So we met.

Merely to see him, to hear his first words, is to be charmed by his tall figure, his look of absolute candor, his warm gentle smile, his bright glance, his pleasantly throaty voice, the thick blurring of the *r*'s to which you soon grow accustomed. In spite of the stuffy heat, he was dressed with old-fashioned meticulousness—a carefully knotted tie, a tight collar, a jacket which he unbuttoned only in the course of our conversation—a style apparently inherited from his family, Moscow intellectuals of the old school. We sat together for four hours that evening, although it was already rather late for me, so that I could not think too clearly or express myself as well as I wished. There were, besides, occasional interruptions, so that we were not alone for the whole time. And I could not at first get used to the feeling that I could reach out and touch, through that dark-blue sleeve, the arm that had given the world the hydrogen bomb.

I was, no doubt, insufficiently polite, and too insistently critical, although I was not aware of it at the time. I didn't thank him, didn't congratulate him, did nothing but criticize and dispute and pull to pieces what he had said in his memorandum, and all this with no plan or system. I had somehow not realized that I would need one. It was then, in the two hours during which I made such a bad job of criticizing him, that he conquered me! He was not in the least offended, although I gave him reason enough; he answered mildly, tried to explain himself with an embarrassed little smile, but refused to be the least bit offended —the mark of a large and generous nature. (Among other things, he told me his reason for concentrating mainly on other people's and not on our own Soviet problems: it was painful to him to inflict any hurt on his own country! It was not a logical chain of reasoning, but filial love, anxious and timid affection, that had drawn him off course. I did not make allowances for this at the time, driven as I was by my labor-camp past, and kept pointing out flaws in his reasoning and in the ordering of his facts.)

We then tried to see whether there was something we could do in support of Czechoslovakia—but we couldn't see how we could collect enough signatures for a strong protest: the eminent had refused to a man.

This meeting of ours apparently escaped the notice of the authorities and, cautious as ever, I concealed for some time afterward the fact that we knew each other: such a combination was bound to seem very dangerous to them. A year later, however, when I moved to Rostropovich's place at Zhukovka, I found myself, as fate would have it, living one hundred meters from Sakharov's dacha. Neighbors will be neighbors. We began meeting occasionally. At the end of 1969 I sent him my article on his memorandum ("As Breathing and Consciousness Return"), containing the same criticisms as before, but systematized and in a form intended for samizdat. I had not yet made up my mind to release it. Sakharov was almost its only reader at that time, and although (as he admitted) he had read it, and reread it more than once, with some distress, it left no trace of ill feeling in his attitude to me.

He, too, had a period of apathy: when his wife died after a long illness. For a time no one saw him at all, then he began appearing on Sundays with his favorite son, some twelve years old. At that time we talked sometimes about possible joint action, but it was all left vague.

Even for the zone of the insulted and injured, Sakharov was too pure. He never supposed that here, too, men might be moved by something other than novel impulses and the quest for truth, that they might be selfish and greedy: instead of making your name in the generally accepted way, by serving, or by standing in the production line, why not do it by contact with a miracle, by hitching yourself to this strange, huge, conspicuous balloon, which was soaring to the heights without engine or petrol.

Another of those who gained height with the help of the balloon was V. Chalidze. He began by putting out a very boring samizdat law journal. Then he invented the Committee for the Defense of the Human Rights of Man, with Sakharov's participation an essential ingredient, and with cunningly contrived rules that enabled Chalidze to thwart the will of any other member. Sakharov came to consult me about the proposed Committee in October 1970, but all that he brought with him was a declaration that it had been established. Nothing was said about the rules, and the structure of the Committee remained a mystery. A strange committee it was, of course: set up to advise the cannibals (when requested) on the rights of those they were eating alive. Still, it was, on principle, a non-Party organization, and in our country, where no one has rights, that was something. I saw no reason to object. On 10 December, the very day on which the Nobel Prizes were presented, Sakharov arrived from town in a taxi, just for five minutes—he was in a great hurry—to see whether I would join the Committee as a corresponding member. I need not play any active part, need not attend meetings, and so on. Well . . . I didn't quite see how I fitted in, but why cold-shoulder them? Why shouldn't I support them? I agreed "in principle"—meaning I daresay I will join, one of these days. I couldn't see why there was thought to be any urgency about it. Sakharov didn't know either. He was an innocent messenger. But we soon discovered why Chalidze had rushed him off to see me thirty kilometers away: as soon as he returned, a five-minute meeting was held and the Committee co-opted me (and Galich) *in absentia;* Chalidze immediately informed the Western newspapermen and, to plump out reports of the Nobel Prize ceremonies, an important news item winged its way to the Western press: on the very day and the very hour when he should have been in Stockholm, the prizewinner had turned a decisive corner in his career; he had joined the Committee, which (the reporters were further apprised) marked the beginning of "an important new period in the life of the writer"—utter poppycock.

Sakharov allowed this Committee to absorb much of his time and energy, spreading them thinly over pedantic debates, fruitless inquiries, and Chalidze's prevarications, when what was needed was action. (Thus, when political prisoners were in question: "We must define what we mean by a political prisoner," as though this were not clear enough in the U.S.S.R.; if the internment of dissidents in loony bins came up, the Committee had to broaden its study to include the whole area of the rights of mental patients, up to and including "the possibility of removing controls over their sexual lives.") By his coldly rational braking actions Chalidze stopped or ruined quite a few of the Committee's initiatives, though it could have played a considerably greater role in the evolution of our society. (At a certain point, "exhausted" by his work in defense of the rights of man, the moving spirit of the Committee decided to cross the ocean. The greatest of simpletons will agree that before you get a visa to go and *lecture foreigners on the rights of man in the U.S.S.R.* you will need to talk things over with the KGB. And this Chalidze did while still a member of the Committee!) Once Igor Shafarevich joined, the balance gradually tipped in favor of action, and the Committee made its most important statements: its appeal to the International Congress of Psychiatrists, its protests against the persecution of religion, and so on.

In his many attempts to help individual victims of persecution, his vigils at court buildings into which he was usually not admitted, his pleas for acquittal, reprieve, reduction of sentence, parole, Sakharov was often acting formally in the name of the Committee, but in reality they were his own actions, the result of his constant, his incorrigible urge to champion the persecuted.

The Soviet public (or all those who knew about it, even if only from the radio in some remote province) quite rightly saw in this form of activity—this defense not of "mankind" or "the people" at large but of each individual victim of oppression—a devotion to truth and a love of humanity with miraculous power to heal our ills. But this activity (because of the spiteful resistance and the deafness of our authorities) was also exhausting, and took a toll of Sakharov's health and strength out of all proportion to its results (which were almost nil). What is more, as innumerable appeals appeared over his signature, reports of his efforts in the world press became like ever more minute and dizzying spots before the readers' eyes, especially as he was often coaxed or bullied into an effort out of all proportion to the wrong to be righted, so that when Sakharov wrote the most outspoken of his general declarations in spring 1972—the "Afterword" to his Memorandum to the Central Committee, in which he has gone forward boldly, and a long way, from his first "Meditation," utters many truths about the state of our country which make unpleasant hearing for our rulers, and proposes his wise statute for an "International Council of Experts"—this document came and went, attracting much less attention than it deserved, probably because the author had used his signature too often and too wastefully.

Although Sakharov and I continued to meet in Zhukovka in 1972, no joint projects or actions resulted. This was largely because we were no longer left alone for the space of a single conversation, and I was afraid that anything we said would be passed around the "democratic movement" in a jumbled version. This is part of the reason for our failure to enlist Sakharov's collaboration in *From*

*Under the Rubble,* which was already in preparation. (I can recall nothing in my own activities over the years of which I would ever have spoken in advance except in strict confidence. Whatever effect they had was the result of secrecy and suddenness. Even if I was merely going into town for a day, I would not talk about it indoors or over the telephone, except in hints or some prearranged code, in case the KGB contrived to raid my lair, as had happened at Rozhdestvo, and gut my manuscripts.) But another reason was that Sakharov found this project uninspiring.

So we condemned ourselves to separate action, and when we met we merely exchanged news and opinions on events already in the past. His visits, moreover, became less and less frequent.

The winter of 1972–1973 saw a deterioration in relations between Sakharov and the "democratic movement" (half of which in any case had already gone abroad). The "movement" even took Sakharov to task in an "open letter"—helped by a routine puff of poisoned breath from officialdom alleging that Sakharov was to blame for the death of Petrovsky,* rector of Moscow University. It can happen in the greatest causes, the greatest lives—and a set of baleful circumstances, trivial and even sordid, cast shadows on this great life, blurred its noble lineaments. The cumulative effect of these petty disturbances was aggravated by the general hopelessness with which Sakharov now looked upon our country's future: we would never succeed in any of our endeavors, and they made sense only insofar as they satisfied a moral need. (I had no very substantial arguments against this; it was just that against all reason I had never in my life experienced this hopelessness, but on the contrary had always had a sort of stupid faith in victory.) The Sakharovs visited me at Zhukovka for the last time in spring 1973. They were in this gloomy frame of mind and talked about their plans: his wife's children had been invited to study in one American university, and A.D. himself would shortly be invited to lecture at another. They would make the attempt to leave. The same forked choice that had faced us all was now Sakharov's fate: not a fork in the road at which he could choose his way freely, but a forked branch which had him by the neck.

Even his posture had changed. Instead of sitting straight and tall on his chair as he used to when we first met, when he was first entering the unknown region of public life with a cheerful good-natured smile on his face, he slumped against the back of the chair so that his baldish head was pulled tightly downward and his shoulders were up around his ears.

When I left Rostropovich's place the semblance of neighborliness between Sakharov and me ceased to exist and we saw each other again only in the thick of the encounter battle of August–September, which we entered separately. In the militant interviews he gave in August, the damaging emigration motif is never absent. We hear that "it would be pleasant to visit Princeton." On 4 September the final opinion of the Western press was that "Solzhenitsyn and Sakharov have declared their firm intention of remaining in their homeland whatever happens." But on 5 September Chalidze announced from New York that he had spoken to Sakharov by telephone, and that Sakharov was *considering the invitation* from Princeton. On 6 September Sakharov confirmed this information. On 12 September (in a statement for German television) Sakharov "was afraid that he might not be allowed back." On 15 September (he told *Spiegel*) he was prepared in principle to take a chair at Princeton. (And the Western press said that "Sakharov is prepared to leave the U.S.S.R. This is a new *challenge* [?] to the Soviet government.")

The emigration tune will always be played in countries where society is used to losing all its battles. We need not blame anyone for this weakness, and after the vacillations I have described in the last chapter I certainly do not intend to. But there are private persons, all of whose decisions are a private matter. And there are persons who occupy positions in society too important and conspicuous for their decisions to be private except in "quiet" times: while the public is watching them in tense expectancy, they forfeit all such rights. This was the law that Andrei Dmitrievich broke, observed and broke by fits and starts, and what is most vexatious, he broke it not because he himself believed he should (never for one moment was he tempted to evade responsibility, to set at naught the fate of Russia), but in deference to those close to him, to ideas not his own.

Such was the inspiration of Sakharov's efforts, prolonged over many months, specifically in support of the right to emigrate, which seemed to take precedence over all other problems. In the middle of September Sakharov performed just such another erratic maneuver, of which observers of the battle took little notice, but which in fact disrupted our battle line and robbed us of decisive success. This was just a day or two after the end of jamming, when our own initial impetus was carrying us forward. A group of some ninety Jews had addressed a written appeal to the U.S. Congress—as usual, on behalf of the Jews: Congress should not accord most-favored-nation status to the U.S.S.R. unless Jews were permitted to emigrate. The ninety, who did not feel that Russia was their own country and wanted only to break out of it, naturally gave no thought to further consequences. But to lend weight to their appeal they approached Sakharov with a request to sign a similar text in his own name and send it separately. It had become traditional by now to turn to Sakharov in this way, in the assurance that he would not refuse. And indeed, following both the tradition and his own inclination in the matter, Sakharov gave them his signature—two or three days after the Mills amendment!—without stopping to think that he was making a breach in the front, surrendering positions already in our hands, narrowing down the Mills amendment to the Jackson amendment, and trading the universal rights of man for mere freedom to emigrate. The letter of the ninety Jews was not taken up, passed unnoticed, but the *Washington Post* for 18 September set up Sakharov's letter *in capitals,* and Congress returned to the Jackson amendment. . . . If all we were asking for was emigration, why should the American Senate bother about anything more?

This shift in the fortunes of battle, this vacillation in the column alongside us, was noticed by no one whose pulse did not beat, whose mind did not move, to the rhythm of these events. But I was startled and shocked. On 16 September I wrote to Sakharov about it from out of town, and that was the second and last time our columns made contact during the encounter battle.

In November Sakharov spent days on end in prison waiting rooms while his wife was being interrogated, and on the twenty-ninth of that month we heard over the radio that "Sakharov has applied for permission to visit Princeton." The general feeling was expressed by the *Daily Mail:* "The resistance of a tiny group of people to the totalitarian state looked like a miracle. Sadly, we must recognize that no miracle has happened. Tyranny has triumphed once more."

Can this be a property of all miracles—that they stop short of completeness?

Yet when jamming stopped in Moscow even schoolboys began putting their ears to their radios to follow the ups and downs in our fight. In one school, a pupil in the eighth grade interrupted his history teacher (a woman): "If you speak of Sakharov in this way [in newspaper language], we cannot learn anything worthwhile from you." Whereupon the class disrupted the lesson with whistles and catcalls, and the two adjoining classes, warned in advance, did the same. Must they now learn that Sakharov had had enough and was abandoning them? Letters arrived from the provinces, the telephone kept ringing: "Tell Sakharov not to leave at any price!"

On 1 December the Sakharovs arrived at our home together, as always. His wife was ill, exhausted by interrogation and by chronic anxiety: "I shall be put inside in two weeks' time, my son is a candidate for Potma, my son-in-law will be banished as a parasite within a month, my daughter is out of a job." "Still, we'd better think about it?" Sakharov cautiously ventured. "No; *you* think about it."

We ourselves were expecting *Gulag* to come out in a month—and with it the fate that we were already firmly resolved to meet. *Here.* We tried to persuade them to do the same.

A.D., flushed to his bald crown as he wrestled with this unbearable problem, was deep in thought, and sinking deeper than ever into the uncomfortable armchair, with his head between his shoulders. It was easy to believe that things had never been harder for him in his life, that expulsion from his own caste had been an enjoyable experience by comparison. He had not yet, as it turned out, applied for an exit visa, but had *asked for a character reference* from his Institute—the usual Soviet procedure in cases more ordinary than his. He, Sakharov! In September he had sat in judgment on the governments of Europe, and emerged victorious over the most dreadful of them, but now he stood at the humblest of bureaucratic windows begging the defeated and vengeful to give him a character reference!

"I should come straight back. I just want to take them"—his wife's children—"out of the country. . . . I'm not thinking of leaving myself."

"But they won't let you in again, Andrei Dmitrievich!"

"How can they refuse to let me in if I present myself at the frontier?" (He quite genuinely did not see how they could.)

This scheme had done so much damage already, yet in his heart there was no urge to leave at all. They wouldn't have let him go anyway —but if they had, I believe that he would have faltered at the last minute and not picked up his visa. He and I might have become geographical concepts rather than people, so closely tied to our portion of the earth's surface that we could no longer be shifted laterally but only downward, six feet downward.

For me, the purpose of the whole fight so far—I could see it now—
was to secure a defensible base for attack in readiness for the next, the
main battle, with flashing helms and clashing swords. I could see where
battle would be joined, sketch out some of my tactical moves and how
I must deploy my forces: form a preliminary plan of operations.

But had *they,* the enemy, learned anything in the encounter battle?
From the way they began, it seemed that they had not. Pride in their
conquests throughout the world clouds their minds. They threatened
to wash their dirty linen in public, beat the children out on the street
instead of in the closet—to take legal action abroad against *Gulag.* It
would be difficult to think of anything more foolish. Only blind conceit
could have brought them to it. But put yourself in their place: what else
could they do?

More anonymous letters were aimed at us. "You will find peace in
death! Soon!" Just recently, in December, important officials at strictly
private lectures were being told, *"We shan't let Solzhenitsyn walk
around much longer."*

I could hear the dragon's teeth grating on the stone. Oh, how he
thirsted for my blood! Yes, but have you thought, you villains, how hard
I would be to digest? I would not envy you.

I finished the main body of this book in spring 1967 under circumstances and in a mood rather like those in which I am bringing it to an
end once again—perhaps forever this time. Enough is enough. No pen
can keep up with the events of a lifetime. Then, as now, I was unravel-
ing the threads of memory, so that I would feel easier when the next
blow fell, the next assault came.

I was more frightened then, and with reason: my position was
weaker, I was less sure of myself. This time many blows will be struck
by both sides, but I am standing so much more firmly, and for the first
time, *for the very first time,* I can walk upright and shout aloud as I go
out to do battle.

I had ended my biographical sketch for the Nobel Yearbook with the
suggestion that even events that are already behind us can hardly ever
be weighed and judged accurately while they are still fresh, and that
the course of future events is still less easy to foretell, still more certain
to surprise.

In *my* life, this is the great moment, this struggle, perhaps the reason why I have lived at all. (But when will the din of battle cease? If only I could go away from it all, go away for many years to the back of beyond with nothing but fields and open skies and woods and horses in sight, nothing to do but write my novel at my own pace . . .)

But what does it mean to *them?* Is the time, perhaps, at hand when Russia will at last begin to wake up? Is this the moment foretold by the foul midnight hags, when Birnam Wood shall walk?

Once again, my vision and my calculations are probably faulty. There are many things which I cannot see even at close quarters, many things in which the Hand of the Highest will correct me. But this casts no cloud over my feelings. It makes me happier, more secure, to think that I do not have to plan and manage everything for myself, that I am only a sword made sharp to smite the unclean forces, an enchanted sword to cleave and disperse them.

Grant, O Lord, that I may not break as I strike! Let me not fall from Thy hand!

*Peredelkino*
*December 1973*

# FOURTH SUPPLEMENT

( June 1974 )

# End of the Road

The foregoing Third Supplement was finished, but we still had to retype it, make photocopies, send some to the West, and conceal the remainder. In the autumn I had moved to my new winter hermitage, the Chukovskys' dacha at Peredelkino, and there, on 28 December, listening as usual to the BBC while I had my afternoon snack, I heard the unexpected news that the first volume of *Gulag* had come out in Russian in Paris. Unexpected only because of the date. I was expecting it to be published as I had asked on 7 January, the Orthodox Christmas, but our communications were subject to interruption and my request had arrived too late, so that our selfless publishers had given up their Sundays and their leisure in the evenings and—although people will be surprised to learn someday how weak their forces were—finished their work earlier than I had anticipated. Only ten days earlier, but that is enough to decide the fate of a work of underground literature: you need a few fine days for the harvest, or the crop that has taken months to grow is lost.

I heard the news calmly, and continued forking cabbage into my mouth. I had taken so many steps in those last few years which had looked desperately dangerous, and none of which had brought any response from the government: it was astounding to find that wall (no, that outsize oaken cudgel which I have called an oak tree not because it deserves the name but for the sake of the proverb) so weak and inelastic. The danger had passed me by so often before, why should it not pass again?

An hour later I burned my hand on a gas boiler, and had to go to Moscow for treatment. Was this, I wondered, an omen? But my friends and I were in holiday mood, and we spent the evening celebrating.

What a burden I had shed: secretly, surreptitiously I had carried it, and had brought it safely to its destination! And now it was no longer on my back, but set where all could see it—that unwieldy stone, that great petrified tear. We had not even dared to keep it in the house, but now anyone who felt like it was welcome to come and read it.

For many years I had told myself: Publish *Gulag* and you'll pay with your life. Not to chop off my head will be something they cannot do: if they are untrue to themselves, their empire cannot survive. If you want to keep your head, leave for the West first. While you're here—well, naturally, it's only human, you keep putting it off: look, let's just get Knot I written . . . now let's just write Knot II . . . well, it wouldn't be a bad idea to go as far as Knot IV, because that's when Lenin reaches Petrograd and what began as a historical novel about the war changes explosively into a novel about revolution—may as well perish with the blazing beams falling about us. While you wait, there are always things to do—checking and improving earlier drafts of other works, adding a stroke or two to *The Oak and the Calf.* (I've only taken it this far because I got on with the First, Second and Third Supplements promptly: if I hadn't, it wouldn't have been worth my while now, now that the tension of life underground has snapped, now that I have been hurled into a new and different life, in a little house looking down into a bowl of sunlight ringed by Swiss mountains, now that manuscripts no longer have to be guarded and we can speak openly with a ceiling over our heads. Life has changed too much for me to do it.)

*Gulag* had been postponed again and again—from January 1970, the date at which it was originally intended to appear, and repeatedly thereafter, all the way to May 1975, which was to be absolutely the final date—but it had broken surface now, at Christmas 1973.

How feeble they have become! It is glaringly obvious if you have eyes to see. In adhering to the Copyright Convention they were erecting a flimsy barricade against a charging bull: they thought they could stop *Gulag* with it. As recently as 23 December, Pankin, the head (head jailer) of VAAP (the All-Union Copyright Agency), had uttered threats: "the deal will be declared void . . . and there will be other things to answer for" under the new legislation—but with swords swinging and swishing around him, who is afraid of a cat scratch? VAAP's declaration, immediately before *Gulag* came out, perhaps expressed their considered view that it would be easier for our masters to gag a few publishers abroad than to smother me at home. Yet another miscalculation. *Gulag* was more than a commercial "deal." They could try to stop any novel, even my *October 1916*, and their claims would give the lawyers something to think about: there might be some grounds for them, and there might not. But trying to strangle *Gulag* with fine legal threads would reveal their impotence only too plainly. The American publishers announced that they would welcome a trial of strength, would like the Soviet authorities to take legal action. (That was six months ago; just recently Pankin announced that the grapes had been sour anyway: the West had very much wanted us to take legal action against *Gulag*, but we had denied them that satisfaction.)

It was amazing: they had seized the book and perused it back in August. When they saw this white-hot molten mass, did they still think that the temperature was too low for the metal to flow? They had no gutters, no casting boxes, no dies ready, nothing into which they could channel it. I had lulled their suspicions at the Kazan Station; I had fooled my favorite ministry. They had slept all through October and November. It was December before they roused themselves, and started sending letters with skull and crossbones, obituary notices from *Russkaya Mysl* (who else in the Soviet Union receives it regularly?), promises to do away with me before the year was out, but before that I had stolen a march on them. They had shown the carelessness characteristic of all overgrown bureaucratic systems. What good had it been to create the greatest counterespionage service in the world, only to see it fumble and let slip a book that might be lethal to them; no, worse—drag it into view with their own hands? What good had it been to set up the greatest propaganda machine ever if it had not a single argument to put in the way of this devastating book?

For the first week they were dumfounded. Then from 4 January there was a spluttering flurry of Tass communiqués—only for foreign consumption, though, none of them translated into Russian and published here: "He has spoiled the New Year celebrations . . . an attempt to sow distrust between nations . . . to smear *the people* of the Soviet Union. Everyone who is not rabidly anti-Soviet will reject this book . . . an excuse for attributing to Soviet society the evils of capitalism . . . a lampoon paid for in foreign currency. . . ."

The threadbareness of their arguments betrayed their perplexity and terror. Was this all they had to say? After half a century, after murdering millions—was this the best defense they could put up? Still, the French Communist Laroche outdid the lot of them (on Moscow television, 7 January): Solzhenitsyn's work does not *reflect* (*Gulag* does not reflect!) last year's record harvest, and in general (with all those graves before his eyes) he does not give the U.S.S.R. credit for its economic achievements. A rapid succession of puny blows that did not hurt.

At the New Year I wrote out another forecast of "things they can do." Here it is:

1. Murder. (Out for the present)
2. Arrest and imprisonment. (Not very likely)
3. Banishment without arrest. (Possible)
4. Expatriation. (Possible)
5. Legal action against publishers. (The policy most to be desired from my point of view, the silliest from theirs)
6. Press campaign to cast doubt on the book's credentials. (Most likely)
7. Efforts to discredit the author (with the help of my ex-wife). (Most likely)
8. Negotiations. (Not excluded, but too early)
9. Retreat. Efforts to dissociate themselves from the past: anything that happened before 1956 was "not our doing." (I had added the subtitle 1918–1956). (Not excluded)

In the last two points I was overrating them. These were ideas too large for their stunted minds. My *Letter to the Leaders* had of course been with them since September; they could have looked at it in conjunction with *Gulag* and drawn their conclusions. (Had any of them read it, though?) This had in fact been part of my intention: while striking a direct shattering blow with *Gulag,* to confuse them with the distracting prospect opened up by the *Letter,* to lure them along the path marked Point 9. According to the timetable I had sent my lawyer and my publishers in December, they were automatically to publish the *Letter* twenty-five days after the first volume of *Gulag.* In other words, they should give the leaders twenty-five days to think it over, and if nothing happened they should bring this crux, this painful choice, to the notice of the world outside, of society at large: it should not be merely something hovering over the Politburo's meeting room; they should know that all eyes were watching to see how they would choose.

I believed that they might feel drawn in different directions. It was unimaginable that not one of those at the top would find something to think about in the *Letter.* (At the very least, *new men* on their way to the top might see in it a possible path for themselves, a way out of the impasse.)

Now that *Gulag* had come out early, the publication date for the *Letter* had been brought forward from 31 to 22 January. But once Tass had raised its voice so angrily and abusively, the conciliatory tone of the *Letter* might be taken to mean that I was giving way, that I was scared. They might not notice the date: 5 September. My idea, that I could go straight on from *Gulag* to try and shift the great inert mass of the Soviet state, now looked empty and misconceived. Oh, yes, *Gulag* was destined to affect the course of history, I was sure of that, but not quite so quickly, and evidently the change would not start in Moscow. So when on 10 January a chance presented itself, I hastened to stop publication of the *Letter.* My message got through by telephone at the last moment: the *Letter* was quite long, and was already being set up in type. Work on it was halted.

A different combination, which I had had in mind earlier, would be more logical: *Letter to the Leaders* could be paired with *Live Not by Lies,* which had lain idle for four years—the leaders and the people, two sides of the whole, could be addressed simultaneously, government and people could recoil together from the same abominations.

But now that publication of this crucial book was beginning, and all the works that had accumulated would follow it without a break, was there any need at all for tactical moves and "cascade" effects? Wasn't the steady flow of books enough? (To live like that is still a dream. Withdrawal from a protracted battle is no easy matter. I have been in Western Europe four months now, and for many months ahead I shall have to go on explaining, filling gaps, repelling blows from my pursuers, when all I really want to do is to retire into complete silence, to write —and let my books appear in an uninterrupted stream. A man's social behavior is usually said to be explained by his social circumstances, but the imperatives of age and of change within ourselves go far to determine the choices we make.)

After canceling the *Letter,* I made up my mind to it: however they howled and whistled, I had done all I needed to do for the present. You'll come and *take me in,* will you? Come on, then, I'm ready for jail too. I was in a passively defensive state of mind. However, my wife and I did not seriously expect swift reprisals. Time and time again, we had got away with it. You begin to delude yourself that your impunity will continue indefinitely. On this occasion it was my wife who felt certain that there would be nothing more than vituperative articles, that they would swallow the affront. I did not think so, but I behaved as though I did: instead of locking myself in our Moscow apartment, where there was no daylight (our curtains were kept drawn round the clock, against watchers and photographers), no air, no room to move, I went off quietly to Peredelkino, to take my ease, breathe deeply under the pines and work at a pace unusually slow for me (I would wonder later on where so many good working days had gone) to complete my article for the symposium, *From Under the Rubble.* It is hard to believe now that only last January life was gliding by so steadily, so smoothly, so uneventfully. (Friends who called while the newspapers were busy baiting us would say, "Your house is the one place where there's peace and quiet.") Alya was retyping the final chapters of *The Oak and the Calf,* and we were making photocopies of them ready for dispatch. Outside Moscow, I listened to the radio a great deal: my own *Gulag* came to me from the ether—a thing with a life of its own, full of its own pain, not something that I had ever fashioned, not something that could ever have been created by me—and brought tears to my eyes. Reactions to the Russian-language edition throughout the world surpassed in vehemence and in volume anything I would have thought possible. They alternated, of course, with the West's own concerns, matters more readily understood there: the dread tidings of the barbarous Archipelago with the lifting of the ban on Sunday motoring in West Germany; the inconceivable life of the Archipelago with reports on the three-day work week in Great Britain. The inordinately prosperous West had felt the chilling breath of the energy crisis, and these first, light restrictions had hurt its susceptibilities. It is to the credit of the West, however, that its sufferings from the petrol shortage did not dull it to the sufferings of the Archipelago's dead inhabitants.

Only now, only today, can I see by what surprising ways God brought this enterprise to fulfillment. In 1962, when *Ivan Denisovich,* in samizdat, frisked off to Kiev and Odessa, without a single copy—what miracle can explain it?—escaping abroad (Tvardovsky was so afraid, but I was not—my blood was up and I wanted *Denisovich* to break out in an ungarbled form), I had utterly failed at the time to see that *in no other way* could I have become a prop irremovably wedged into the Kremlin wall, part of Khrushchev's legacy. And when the Leningrad copy of *Gulag,* instead of being burned as I had urged, and as I felt sure it had been, fell into the hands of the Geebees so that the book had to be published in a hurry, while they raged like wild beasts—*this* was how *Gulag* came to be raised up as an unimpeachable monument to the truth. For I have learned, here in the West, that books about Gulag, from its Solovki days onward, have been appearing since the twenties, that as many as forty of them have been published, translated, publicized—and have vanished into the void, leaving no echo behind them, influencing no one, troubling no one's repose. The West had behaved as well-fed and complacent humanity characteristically does: everything had been said, and none of it had sunk in. Besides, the Soviet Gulag was to the leeward of a spanking socialist breeze: the land of socialism can be forgiven for atrocities immeasurably greater than those of Hitler, for its victims are offered up on a resplendent altar. If I had not published *Gulag* till I got to the West, its destructive force would not have been half so great.

As it is, I am astonished to see how clearly its significance was realized:

"A burning question mark over fifty years of Soviet power, over the whole Soviet experiment from 1918 on . . ." *(Vorwärts)*

"Solzhenitsyn tells the world the truth about the cowardice of the Communist Party . . ." *(Guardian)*

"The time may come when we date the beginning of the collapse of the Soviet system from the appearance of *Gulag* . . ." *(Frankfurter Allgemeine)*

"Solzhenitsyn calls for repentance. This book can become the seminal work of a national renaissance if the men in the Kremlin know how to read it . . ." (Deutsche Welle)

The Association of American Publishers expressed its readiness to publish any historical materials that the Soviet government might wish to produce in refutation of *Gulag.* But there were no such materials. In fifty years, the hangmen had not managed to provide themselves with a neat set of excuses. Even in the last six months, with the book in the hands of the KGB, they had not got around to it.

They published Bondarev's feeble article in the *New York Times* (suggesting that Gulag was about the Second World War rather than about Soviet camps and prisons: he kept talking about Stalingrad and General Vlasov). Then came an *Izvestia* article, once again about General Vlasov, and as I opened the paper and saw the size of it, I thought: Now they'll try to deny that Vlasov liberated Prague from the Germans; they have documents, and what's missing they can fake, but how am I to summon my cellmates after all this time? But no! They hadn't the gall. They didn't dare dispute the main point: that the only military operation carried out by Vlasov's divisions was against the Germans—to free Prague!

Without becoming any more sensible in the past half century, the Soviet press had lost something of the verve it possessed in the twenties, in its Comintern days, and all it was now capable of was vulgar abuse, a campaign of crude vilification. *Pravda* began it on 14 January with an article called "The Path of Betrayal." Its contents served as a directive: it was reproduced next day by all the other main and local newspapers, so that it circulated in some fifty million copies all told. On the following day *Litgazeta* recommended a specific designation for me: "literary Vlasovite." For several days I was bombarded with it from every printing shop and every reading stand in the country. The most serious distortion consisted in ignoring completely the theme of camps and prisons; the condemned book was presented as from start to finish an insult to the memory of our war dead. Worse still, there was an exquisitely vague innuendo: the wretch seems to have three cars. (This formulation left retreat open.) No more tantalizing morsel could be thrown to the crowd: "The louse! How greedy can you get!"

*Pravda* had given the signal for the telephonic onslaught on our apartment which began a day later and lasted two weeks. This is one of the twentieth century's new weapons: with an anonymous tinkle you can penetrate locked rooms and sting the startled occupant to the heart, without rising from your office desk or the armchair in which you sit sipping a cocktail.

It began with some thug bellowing, "Get Solzhenitsyn on the line!" "Who are you?" "Just get him; I'm a friend of his!" My wife hung up. There was another ring. She lifted the receiver without a "Hello" or "Who's speaking?" and heard the same loud, hoarse roughneck: "Some of us have done time without betraying our country—get it? We won't leave that son of a bitch above ground much longer! He's had it!" (The Central Committee lecturer had said the same in December, word for word except for the "son of a bitch.") This telephone offensive was something we hadn't expected, something strange to us, and it took strong nerves, quick thinking, a ready tongue and a steady voice to show them they couldn't rile us and might as well not try. Alya quickly mastered the knack and held her own with ease. She would listen patiently to all the abuse, then say quietly: "Tell me, do you get paid fortnightly in the KGB, or monthly like in the army?" Whoever was at the other end was always put off his stroke. Sometimes she would even interpolate a few encouraging remarks, let the man speak his lines, and then say, "Is that all? Right—tell Yuri Vladimirovich [Andropov, head of the KGB] from me that he's heading for trouble with dunces like you on his staff." The calls were regulated so that there was never a break: the idea was that friends would not have a chance to get through to us, but we would lift the receiver every time just in case a friend was calling. Still, we managed to let the outside world know that we were caught in this storm (and that very evening Western radio stations, God bless them, broadcast the news of the telephone offensive). There were voices male and female, abuse, threats, obscenities—on and on until one in the morning, when there was a break until six. They made a few calls to the Chukovskys at Peredelkino too, insulting Lydia Korneyevna, asking to speak to me ("His wife's not well"). Fortunately, we had provided ourselves with a gadget that enabled us to get down telephone conversations on a tape recorder. I gave Alya instructions by telephone —with the KGB on the line—how to switch it on, and she played back, still over the telephone, a sample of the reproduction: i.e., "We shall put some of the choicest passages together on a cassette. Whenever civilization produces a weapon, it also produces the counterweapon." Our trick had its effect. They became more cautious, moderated their language, passed themselves off as well-wishers ("We're afraid they may arrest him!").

That first evening they had been planning something more than mere telephone calls—probably an *outburst of public anger.* A number of persons were summoned to our yard, a few dozen militiamen were also assembled to *protect us*—but neither window-breaking nor "protective action" followed. Obviously the order had been canceled; someday we may know why.

The bombardment of telephone calls continued for two weeks. They became less frequent than on the first day, but more varied.

"Is the Vlasovite still living?"

"I've read all his works, I've worshiped him, but now I can see that my idol is the scum of the earth."

Another time it was a cry of despair (after my latest statement to the press):

"What does he think he's doing, the louse! Why doesn't he get off our backs?"

The themes were not a random sequence: they seemed to succeed one another at a word of command. For a day or two there would be nothing but threats to murder us, then nothing but "disillusioned admirers," then nothing but "friends from the camps," then well-wishers with good advice: not to go out in the street, to take good care of the children, not to buy groceries in shops—poisoned goods were to be put in our way. But the surprising thing is that among all those hundreds of calls, not one showed any skill or artistry, their spuriousness was obvious from the first word, the first sound, whatever their content. These callers were always confounded by a sarcastic retort. Moreover, to avoid waste of leisure time, all the calls were soon fitted into office hours.

This was how they tried to break my family's spirit—and through them mine. But the KGB were unlucky in my second wife. Alya not only withstood their attack; she did not let it divert her from the normal course of her duties. Work went on, our family life continued, and it will be quite a while before our little ones learn that their infancy was in any way out of the ordinary.

Parallel with the telephone attacks (and of course the newspaper campaign) there was also a postal offensive. The hostile letters always bore full and precise addresses, but no signatures. A few friendly ones also got through (a mistake on the part of the censorship: Deutsche Welle had given our address minus apartment number—letters without it went into a different sorting box and were not detained). There was one from "workers in the Urals," and there were others from children of zeks who had died in the camps.

The Soviet newspaper campaign—strident, hysterical, incoherent— was so stupid that it had defeated itself in the international arena within a few days. The *New York Times* uttered a warning: "This campaign may do the U.S.S.R. more harm than the publication of the book itself." And the *Washington Post* wrote that "if they touch a single hair of Solzhenitsyn's head it will put a stop to cultural exchanges and to trade." An exaggeration, of course, it wouldn't quite come to that— nothing must get in the way of détente—but as they read the Western newspapers at Staraya Ploshchad they might find something to ponder: The devil's in this Solzhenitsyn. Is it worth ruining our whole international game for him? The Western press had struck up such a mighty chorus in my defense that murder and imprisonment were both out of the question.

That being so, what was the point of all this barking? Where were the newspapers aimlessly drifting under their dingy gray sails? (For my own part, I saw the very existence of the newspaper campaign as a victory for me: in their eagerness to deafen the world, *they* had forfeited the chance to do what they would once have done—quietly take my throat in their teeth, and sling me in the jug.) There it was: they had started it on an unthinking impulse, out of blind malice: without fully intending to, they had started it, they had disturbed millions of ill-informed minds in their own country and the struggle now beginning would be for them above all, for my fellow countrymen. Though the West, too, must find it hard to understand why I was so slow to say a single word in my own defense, must wonder whether there was something in the malicious gossip about me after all.

You may promise yourself a quiet doze while battle rages. But you will need a different temperament from mine.

I answered with two blows—my statement of 18 January [Document 31] and the brief interview I gave to *Time* magazine on the nineteenth [Document 32]. In my statement, I dealt with the most galling and offensive accusations in the Soviet press, reducing my reply to two short pages. In the interview, I set out my position more fully: I gave the Medvedevs the answer that I had failed to give in November; I reminded myself and Sakharov, and all those who had lost their sense of proportion in the midst of all the din and excitement, that however hard the West worked to defend us, and however grateful for it we were, we must make haste to stand on our own feet; and finally, since no one had yet shut my mouth, and since I did not know yet how I would publish *Live Not by Lies*, I included this most important piece of advice that I had for the young, my one and only real hope; I ended with a sigh of relief, at ease in the knowledge that "I have fulfilled my duty to those who perished. . . .

"We need groan no more, our bones can rest from aching: the word has been spoken, and heard. . . ."

The message was broadcast on many radio and television networks —and in many of the newspapers it appeared on 21 January, the fiftieth anniversary of Lenin's death—a fact that was not remarked on at the time. How many tussles he had won in his lifetime with his oblique pounce and his lightning-swift bite, and how badly he was losing half a century later, though no one yet used the word or seemed to see it.

BBC: "The two-week campaign against Solzhenitsyn has not succeeded in intimidating and silencing him." *Die Welt:* "If Moscow puts him away, it will have to pay as dearly as it did for Budapest and Prague."

So we stood firm for a whole week after *Pravda* had given the signal for all-out attack. Stood firm, so that even Tass had to take notice—but how could it respond to my exhortation to the young not to lie, but to stand up for the truth courageously? This was how: "Solzhenitsyn slings mud at the young Soviet generation, accuses them of lacking courage." But by now it was 22 January—the day of the demonstration by American intellectuals of various persuasions outside the National Press Club building in Washington, which greatly encouraged me: excerpts from *Gulag* were read, and the crowd shouted, "Hands off Solzhenitsyn! The world is watching!"; the day when *Gulag* came out in German and the first printing was sold out in a few hours. We had stood our ground for a week, had got through almost a full month since *Gulag* had been published, that most difficult first month, when our bridgehead was still very small, when the world had still not *read* the book—and yet had understood so much! Now the bridgehead was broadening, the book was winning a mass readership in the West, and such was the impetus of events that it was difficult to see where it would carry us. On the twenty-third I had written down these words: "What if the enemy falters and gives ground (begins to acknowledge the past)? I would not be surprised." (The American edition was supposed to appear still earlier, immediately after the Russian, and I had done all I could to ensure this, but two or three soulless, mercenary products of a Western upbringing made a mess of everything that I had sent out at the Feast of the Trinity in 1968. The American edition would be six months late, and would not help me to hoist myself over the abyss. But for this, I believe, the outcome might have been different. What could have happened, what might have happened instead, was something very like a retreat on the part of our leaders, if at New Year 1974 the whole of America could have read the book for itself, and the best the Kremlin could manage was the calumny that it glorified the Hitlerites.)

The way I saw it was this: In the first month, the question at issue had been what would become of me, but from now on the battle would open out and become more complicated; the issue now was whether the propaganda machine could ingurgitate Russia once more, or whether it would choke in the attempt. Would newspaper lies again and again swamp the country, with nothing to hinder them, or would they meet some resistance at last? I believed that a sharp change for the better was possible, and saw more clearly still the logical thing to do in my position: address my next statements not to the West, but to audiences at home.

At the end of January, the invective in the newspapers grew harsher still, signatures—some famous names among them now—were collected in bigger and bigger bunches, a poster was put up in Gorky Street for the benefit of the multitude: my book with a yellow skull and black crossbones. But at the same time, intrepid young people came forward shyly to fight to the death, stepped out of the ranks tall, erect, unarmored, into the hail of lead: Boris Mikhailov, Vadim Borisov, Yevgeny Barabanov, each of whom, as it happened, had a nonworking wife and two young children. And Lydia Chukovskaya told us who the traitors were [Document 33]. The newspapers kept up their stage thunder, but sensitive ears in the West could tell from afar that in my statements I was "clearly on the offensive," whereas the authorities seemed to be retreating, expending a great deal of effort to no avail. The whole mad menagerie joined in the fun. While the newspapers showered abuse, the KGB fitted Vitkevich out for an interview with somebody from the West. This twist astounded me: The KGB was now accusing me of half-heartedness in my opposition to it, of failure to push in that ugly mug when first we met, instead of leaving it till now. I had been expecting, as the most likely thing for them to do, an attempt to discredit me personally, but had thought that it would be made through my first wife, and had not supposed that it would be through the friend of my youth. They had made me out to be all sorts of things before this —a member of the *Polizei,* a Gestapo agent—and now I was a KGB informer. I would have preferred not to answer at all; it was becoming rather too frequent. But then: If it comes to blows, better keep on your toes. If answer I must, I'd make their ears tingle! [Document 34]

Once again, the world press and radio took up the theme: "You can send in tanks against armed insurgents—but what weapon is there against a book?" *(Kölnische Rundschau)* "The firing squad, Siberia, the madhouse, would only confirm that Solzhenitsyn is right." *(Monitor)* "Their propaganda has boomeranged. . . ." And this was not the first time that Günter Grass had raised his powerful voice in my support.

I began to think that I had won yet another stage in the battle. I had let off another salvo, and *their* attacks seemed to be losing impetus, or to have petered out (a repetition of September?). Was I in a stronger position? On 7 February I made this note: "Forecast for February: Apart from attempts to discredit me, they aren't likely to do anything, and there will probably be a breathing space." It was an unreasonable thing to say, the more so since I had not forgotten for a moment that all my life, the end of January and beginning of February had been a fateful time for me, that great danger had often darkened those few days in the year: capture by the Germans, my arrest, my transfer from jail to camp, my operation, besides many minor troubles—but once I was through them there had always been an easier time ahead. A breathing space was what I wanted, rather than what I expected—to be silent, to withdraw into my lair, as so often before: there had been so many earlier clashes from which I had emerged safe and sound—and chosen silence.

It is one of man's peculiarities that he lives through the menacing, the catastrophic times in his life, and through the more normal periods, in much the same way, preoccupied with simple everyday matters, and it is only later, only in distant retrospect, that he is amazed to see that the earth was once crumbling beneath his feet, the lightning playing about his head.

I myself had noticed no great change. But at the beginning of February my wife sensed that a sinister shift had occurred. Signs of it were that the telephonic offensive against our apartment had come to an end, and even the newspaper campaign seemed to have flagged—the very things with which the authorities had until then camouflaged their irresolution. (Brezhnev had returned from Cuba. I attached no significance to this. But they had been waiting for him to decide what to do about me.)

During that month there were prophetic notes to be heard among all the clamor, though these as always passed unnoticed and had no relevance until a possibility was translated into a decision. Looking back recently over the summary of broadcasts for that month, I was surprised myself to find the BBC correspondent reporting from Moscow on 18 January "hints that they are beginning to favor forcible expatriation." On 20 January, an émigré, G. Svirsky, said: "Solzhenitsyn will be forcibly put aboard a plane." There it is, in black and white! While I had not excluded this possibility, I had somehow never envisaged it in this simplest of forms, failed to see that they could just force me onto a plane, all by myself, without my family. (But wait a minute! Looking through this book just now, sending it off to be printed, I had a shock:

We had been warned directly in March 1972 that this was just what would happen—expatriation by means of temporary arrest. We had quite forgotten it, never given it another thought!) Least of all did I think that Chancellor Brandt had put a sticky label on me when, on 1 February, he told his young socialists (who weren't a bit pleased and wouldn't have cared if I had sunk into the ground) that "Solzhenitsyn could live and work without hindrance in Western Germany." He had said it and that was that.

Expatriation was a possibility, but so it had been more than once in the past, and it had never come very close. If it did happen, my wife and I imagined it like this: They would cordon off our apartment while we were all there together, cut off the telephone and order us to get ready—in a hurry, or at our leisure. If we had taken time to think about it, we might have guessed that this way of doing things would not suit the authorities. But we never had a chance to think unhurriedly; we were always racing to keep up with what was happening right then. For over two years now we had kept by us a piece of paper setting out different versions of the "Earthquake"—we might be overtaken by it when we were together, when we were apart, when we were traveling —yet we had never got around to detailed planning. But then, if I review those years week by week, each week was as crowded as though it had been the most crucial of all; there was always something to be written, something to be finished in a hurry, an old draft to be amended, typing or photocopying to be done, copies to be distributed in different caches (and there were always so many changes of mind: this particular thing, now—shall we keep it at home, or somewhere else? We would try one way, then the other), material to be sent abroad, covering letters to be drafted. These preoccupations, and the running fight with my enemies, prevented us from looking more closely at the problem and turning the "Earthquake" into a plan of action.

On 8 February *Gulag* appeared in Sweden, and our support began to grow. In Norway too, after speeches had been made in the Storting, the Minister of Foreign Affairs conveyed the concern of the public to the Soviet ambassador. Then the Danish Social Democratic Party also came to my defense. I was working away quietly at Peredelkino. Suddenly there was an unscheduled call from Alya. They had tried to deliver a summons from the Public Prosecutor's Office [Document 35]. I was to report without delay, before the end of the working day. (It was impossible, from Peredelkino, even at breakneck speed. Why hadn't they taken this into account? Why had they put it like that?) My wife had picked holes in the summons: it was not properly drawn up; no reasons for summoning me were given; it had no reference number. She did just what she should have done—devoured it with her eyes, pulled it to pieces. And refused to accept it.

The telephone in the Chukovskys' dining room had stood in the same place for many years—on a small, carved oval table, across the room from the window, so that on a dull day, and toward evening, it was in semi-darkness. When I picked up the receiver and heard about the Public Prosecutor's Office I remembered immediately: I was pricked by the recollection of standing in that very place in September 1965 in just such a dim light and hearing Lev Kopelev's voice from the same receiver: "Your case has been passed to the Public Prosecutor." My "case," that time, meant my confiscated archive, together with *The Feast of the Victors* and *The First Circle,* and "passed to the Public Prosecutor" appeared to mean that there would be a trial. (Why they decided against it then is an enigma. They would have done well to try me.) At that time my *First Circle* had simply been put to bed in the Procurator General's safe. But there had been something prophetic in it: a warning that on that very spot in eight years' time the same torpid snake would sting me again.

Still, I had been thundering against them for seven years now. They were bound to give the *word of command* sooner or later.

Over the telephone, my wife and I always conversed in code, putting on an act for the benefit of the Lubyanka. On this occasion, too, we pretended that a summons from the Prosecutor's Office was a fleabite. (She had not even hurried to call me.) But we both realized that it was serious. Serious enough, but we were still misled by the fact that Sakharov had been summoned to the same place in the summer, for nothing more than an exhortation to stop his unseemly activities. True—and this should not be played down—the authorities had always regarded Sakharov and myself differently. He belonged to the establishment: he had three Gold Stars, and who could say that he had done no service to the state? Even *they* couldn't easily cross him off. Whereas I, for as long as they had known me, had been a whiff of ammonia in their nostrils. That was all they had to thank me for. To summon me for a "talking to" was something they just couldn't do. What, then, was it for? What did they want me for? And why must it be before the end of the working day—the last in the week? This should have given me a clue. But no, I was misled by the analogy. (Perhaps they had been counting on this, to lure me in?) Clearly, I shouldn't go of my own free will; and just as clearly—so I thought—I had time to spare, and space to turn around in.

Less than two hours later, there was a tramping of men's feet on the veranda, and a menacingly loud knock on the windowpanes: that *special* Cheka-KGB knock ("Open up, your masters are here!"), that *final* knock. Lydia Chukovskaya knew nothing. Not wanting to interrupt her work, I had not yet told her about the Public Prosecutor, and there was no time for hasty explanations now. We had been caught unprepared, and they were let in. In any case, I could hardly have demurred in someone else's home.

There were three of them. With the silliest of excuses: "come about the repairs" (there would never be any), "been twice before" (to look me and my room over), and two months ago they'd "left the notebook with their estimates behind in the house," so now they'd "come to look for it." They devoured me with their eyes, and went around the rooms with the half-blind Chukovskaya. Suddenly the telephone rang, and one of the "repairmen" (a stranger, in someone else's house!) grabbed the receiver, listened, grunted—and immediately abandoning the search for the lost book, they all left together. Chukovskaya went out after them and was in time to see a car and two or three other men at the gate.

It should have been obvious: they were after me. But no, the fact that I had emerged unscathed on so many previous occasions, and even more, the initial impetus of my work, which had saved me for so many years from sticking in the mud, sinking in the bog, stagnating, this same impetus now prevented me from dropping my work there and then, preparing myself carefully and rolling off to Moscow in the morning. Friday was nearly over, and we could have spent two whole days, Saturday and Sunday, on urgent matters—making our arrangements, and taking thought for the future in the knowledge that the Earthquake had already begun! But no, I stayed on in Peredelkino for three more nights and two more days, half-heartedly continuing my work, finishing nothing, already, as it were, weightlessly suspended yet still on earth, and even on Monday morning I didn't hurry off to Moscow too early, and left behind my traveling kit as well as the things on my desk, and my books.

As I traveled to Moscow on the morning of the eleventh, I already knew what I would say at the Prosecutor's Office. But it was not so very early in the day when I arrived, and it *was* very early in *his* working day that the Prosecutor's messenger (an officer, of course, but with a bashful smile) brought a fresh summons, so that my wife and I didn't have time to discuss things properly, but sat the messenger down in the hall. With him on the premises, I typed out my answer [Document 36] and stuck it on the summons where I should have signed my name. All this took a long time, and the messenger got nervous out in the hall (did he think we were arranging an ambush?), and jumped up and stood to attention for some reason whenever I passed through. When he got the answer, he thanked me and was in such a hurry to leave that he didn't fold the sheet, until I said, "Put it in the envelope; it's raining." He crammed it in clumsily.

Once the fight is on—strike quickly and often! While the messenger was still there we started telephoning Western correspondents and asking them around. At first I meant only to inform them of my answer. But then my feelings ran away with me, my hands started itching: once those words had been spoken, what prohibitions were left? Once I had found my tongue—why not pour out all that was in my heart? So we seized the third volume of *Gulag* and copied out a passage from Part VII, about the Brezhnev period: "There Is No Law." Representatives of the *New York Times* and the BBC arrived, and I read the passage aloud into a microphone. These two replies, disseminated within a few hours, made the whole situation worthwhile.

But we had still not so much as begun to get ourselves ready, to make our farewells. It was just a fight, of the sort we'd often been in before, no more alarming than all the others.

To this day I cannot quite understand why they didn't take me at the dacha in Peredelkino, why they slept on the job through Saturday and Sunday. Then again, why hadn't they come for me immediately after my insolent answer on the morning of the eleventh, if the whole thing had already been decided? They began by hoping that I would come to the Prosecutor's Office myself. (It would have been quite in character for me to dash straight there: the office was nearby, on Push-kin Street, just two minutes' walk away, and it wasn't one of the KGB's haunted houses.) I would have walked right into the trap like an idiot. They could have taken me in, there and then, with no one to hear or see. But why didn't they take me on Monday or Tuesday, instead of letting me trumpet the news to the whole world? Perhaps they had taken fright because I put up such a noisy resistance. If I had reported to the Prosecutor's Office, it would have meant that I still recognized their authority, that there was still some hope of putting pressure on me, of reaching a compromise.

Early in the evening my wife and I went for a stroll and a chat on Strastnoy Boulevard. This was our favorite spot if we wanted a long talk —and I would be surprised to learn that *they* had never eavesdropped on us there (we did, however, turn our heads in different directions while we talked). Strastnoy Boulevard widens at the end until it is like a little park, which we loved both for its own sake and because it was close to *Novy Mir.* It was the site of countless meetings with friends from *Novy Mir!* This time *they* were right on our heels, making themselves conspicuous. But when had they not followed at all? This didn't make the day unusual.

We went over the ground and decided that in a general way we were better prepared than ever. All the most important books were safe, where the KGB could not get at them. Getting ready to be arrested meant collecting a few simple things. But we were tired, and our brains were not working freely. Now that the Earthquake had come—if this was it—we could only discuss it vaguely and half-heartedly. I repeated what I had said before: that I could hold out for two years in jail— survive until all my works were in print—but couldn't be sure of enduring it any longer. That I wouldn't do a single day's work in a camp, though in prison conditions I might even write. Write what? A history of Russia for children, in short narrative episodes, presenting the facts unadorned, in crystal-clear language. (I have had this in mind ever since I had sons of my own, but shall I ever get around to it?) We discussed how to pass important written messages on visiting days. And how I should behave under interrogation and in court. (We had decided long ago that I should not recognize *them* or take part in any dialogue.)

It was a sunless, half-snowy day (the ground was covered with white, the trees and benches were black), and as dusk closed in, hostile lights were burning in the Novosti building, and car headlights swept by on both sides of the boulevard. The day was ending, and they still hadn't taken me.

A peaceful working evening. We made our last microfilm, with my piece on *Quiet Flows the Don.* We listened to the radio, and heard the answer I had given that morning thundering round the world. We put together a rudimentary prison kit, but couldn't find a bag for it. We were getting comfortable and careless! No prison sack ready! In the night, suffering from my usual insomnia, I worked again, correcting *Letter to the Leaders:* my analysis and my suggestions remained as before, but I had to change its original tone; an appeal to reason would look like a confession of weakness now.

I felt quite calm, I had no forebodings, I was not in the least depressed. I didn't rush to examine my papers, burn some of them, hide others more carefully: what was the point when I would be needing it all for my work next day, and next week? Early the following morning we were at work again, at our separate desks. An accumulation of dangerous material still lay openly on my wife's desk. Ten A.M.—the time mentioned in yesterday's summons. Eleven o'clock. Twelve o'-clock. No one came. We worked on quietly. We were working so well, the last trace of worry was erased from our minds. *They had retreated!* Life would go on! When I had answered them with "Bring the Genocides to Trial," there had been peace and quiet. They had licked their chops and retreated. They would have to be patient a while longer. There were no telephone calls from *patriots,* no one tried to burst into the apartment, no suspicious character made sure that he was seen hanging around the front entrance. Perhaps they were staying away because foreign newspapermen were keeping watch near the house?

I did not even check the great untidy heap on my desktop, did not see the microfilm that I had meant to burn long ago. Worse still, there were letters from abroad on my desk—from my confidential agents, from publishers—which I ought to have dealt with quickly and burned, but I couldn't make time for this either. Oh, yes—I remember why I couldn't: I was to meet someone from the West on the evening of the fourteenth, and I ignored everything else in the rush to get ready the things I considered it essential to send off.

I can now reveal something that may seem almost incredible, which is why the KGB never believed, never entertained the idea for a moment: everything I sent to the West was handed over for dispatch not by intermediaries, not through a chain of people, but by me personally, with my own hands! The KGB kept track of all who went into or came out of my apartment, and of their subsequent contacts—but not even the majors, let alone the major generals, with their mandarin mentality and their habit of judging others by themselves, could imagine the Nobel Prize winner flitting like a schoolboy through unlit streets at unearthly hours, with his everyday cap in a rucksack and a different one on his head, hiding in lampless recesses and handing over his manuscripts in person. *Not once did they succeed in trailing me, not once did they catch me in the act!* What a triumph for them it would have been, what a harvest they would have reaped! It helped, of course, that I lived outside Moscow—at Rozhdestvo, at Zhukovka, at Peredelkino: it was usually from there that I went to my *assignations*. At Rozhdestvo I could dress as though I were going for a walk in the neighborhood, stroll idly into the woods, make a detour, and take off for a train stop down the line, five versts away over the open fields. At Zhukovka, instead of traveling by the usual suburban train (there were sometimes flatfoots on duty at the station), I could set off in the opposite direction, then take a roundabout bus ride to Odintsovo. From Peredelkino, instead of going out through the front gate as usual, I could go by way of the backyard, where no one set foot in winter, into the next street and, by snow-covered ways deserted at night, to another little station, called Michurinets. Before doing so I would phone my wife to put her mind at rest, and say that I was just going to bed. I would leave a night light burning in the window. If I had to go to Moscow itself for my rendezvous, I would either leave the city by a suburban train, wander around aimlessly in the dark and then start over for Moscow, or else, or else . . . No, we'll keep the Moscow formulae to ourselves for the present: others may need them. . . . And there was always fast walking. At fifty-five, I didn't think myself too old for such work. In fact, it made me feel younger and kept my spirits up. The flabby Geebees never guessed that I was capable of such things. If they read about it now they'll be surprised.

I did without lunch, and at three in the afternoon took my five-month-old son, Stepan, down to the yard for an airing, carrying his stroller under my arm. In full sight of all those windows, all the passers-by and all the yardmen, I began walking back and forth with my papers, as usual, reading and thinking. I was having a quiet day of it, after all. I hadn't been able to do it earlier, but now the time had come to read those letters from abroad; I must have answers ready by the following day. So, quite openly, where all the world could see, I walked back and forth past the sleeping baby, reading my clandestine letters. . . . But I was fated not to finish reading them: Igor Rostislavich Shafarevich arrived and joined me.

Perhaps the time has come for me to write about him without concealment? Before this book is published, he will make his own dangerous stand and accept his fate, or else God will spare him. I have said a great deal in this book about Tvardovsky—how he helped to open up a path for me, and how I then chose my own way, went forward beside him but hardly together with him. And about Sakharov too: it only looked from a distance as though we were together, but never once did we concert our plans, never once did we so much as put our names to the same statement, strangely enough. Nor did I warn him in advance that *Gulag* was to be published. But Igor Shafarevich and I really had been comrades, marching shoulder to shoulder, for three years now, while we had been working on *From Under the Rubble.* We were tied together not by memories of the past (we shared none), nor even by our present stand against the Dragon, but by a firmer bond: our common views on Russia's future. (This future was soon to be perceived in very different ways in our country.)

We had met at the beginning of 1968. Since I attached some value to my time, and none at all to guffawing table talk, I had side-stepped a number of would-be acquaintances. I was particularly disappointed with those I had met in Academy circles. I was dubious about this new contact, too, and went to see him just for half an hour. The ruggedness, the solidity of the man—not only in his appearance but in his whole personality—were obvious and likable from the start. But our first conversation never became serious: an absurd chance prevented it. On his desk he had some colored photographs of Adriatic scenery. He had been there on scientific business, and for some reason he decided to show them to me. It wasn't at all his style; in fact, it would be hard to think of anything more unlike him. But I jumped to the conclusion that he was one of the pampered few who are always going abroad (nothing could have been further from the truth!) and are always quite useless in practical matters. I told him that all the academicians I had ever seen enjoyed an interesting and indeed a daring conversation, but that when the time came to act, to take a stand, they were always missing. And with that I went away. It was not instantly obvious that anything could bring us together. It became so later. The third time we met, we began to see the outline of the work we would do together. That year was, I think, the noisiest in the history of the "democratic movement," and began to look dangerously like the early 1900s. There was nothing but negation, nothing but demands for freedom with never a thought as to what would come afterward. There was no one with a sense of responsibility toward our unhappy country, no one concerned to save her from a second vainglorious experiment, a second evisceration, at the hands of people who would just as soon see her dead.

We are all creatures of flesh and blood, none of us is made of iron, none finds it easy to set foot on the path of dangerous resistance, perhaps of self-destruction. Some two thousand people in our country are world famous, many of them much more loudly acclaimed than Shafarevich (mathematicians are a small and inconspicuous group among the earth's inhabitants), but in the civic sense they are more ciphers because of their cowardice. Only a dozen or so have raised themselves up from nothingness to stand straight and strong as trees. Of these Shafarevich was one. I had the opportunity to observe, though not often or closely, how civic courage became in him a hardy growth. One thing that Shafarevich did as he rose from the normal servile posture was to join Sakharov's Committee for the Defense of Human Rights, not because he had any faith in its effectiveness, but because he thought it shameful that people were no longer joining, felt it would be unforgivable if he did not lend his own strength to it.

It is harder for a man whose education has not been in the humanities to dedicate himself to civic responsibilities: it requires not just an access of courage, but a redirection of his consciousness, a change in his habits of thought, the acquisition of new specialist skills in maturity, the application of his mind to a field neglected by others (whether he himself now begins to neglect his original profession, as some do, or refuses to do so, like the doubly strong Shafarevich, who remains to this day an active and productive mathematician of international caliber.) When such conversions are superficial, we get dilettantism; when they are more serious, we see the strong and vigorous grip of an independent mind uncluttered with stereotyped preconceptions, capable of sifting the wheat from the chaff. Shafarevich began this second part of his work quite privately, entirely on his own, and in the most natural way possible—from the study of that tragic genius, that pitiful wreck Shostakovich, who had always fascinated him. He tried to understand how Shostakovich steals into our souls and what it is he promises them—a task that cried out to be done, but that no Soviet musicologist had carried out. There was, of course—and still is—nowhere to publish an article on the subject. His study of Shostakovich led Shafarevich to a wider general conclusion about the spiritual condition of the world: that it had reached the climactic point of irreligion, and was on the threshold of a new spiritual era.

These, then, are the three great names that have appeared in these *literary notes*—names of people who have helped to make or still are making our civic history. Let us note that among them only Tvardovsky belongs completely to the humanities. Sakharov is a physicist, Shafarevich a mathematician, and both occupied themselves with what might seem to be none of their business, because there was no one else in Russia to do it. (Note that my education, too, was mathematical, not literary, and that I survived my tribulations thanks only to mathematics, without which I would never have come through. That is how things are in the Soviet Union.)

Besides, Shafarevich was from birth inseparably tied to Russia, the land and its history: they are one flesh, with a common bloodstream, a single heartbeat. His love of Russia is a jealous love—to make up for the past carelessness of our generation? He looks insistently for ways to use his head and his hands so as to requite his country for the love it inspires in him. Among the Soviet intelligentsia of today I have hardly met anyone like him in his readiness to die in and for his homeland rather than seek safety in the West, in the strength and consistency of his preference for unhappiness here at home rather than happiness among strangers beyond the sea.

During the two years when we were continually discussing our symposium, *From Under the Rubble,* and the materials that flowed in to him, Shafarevich and I had to do all our talking, Soviet fashion, out in the open. For this purpose we used to take long walks—near Zhukovka, or among the incomparable hills near Rozhdestvo (on the border of the Moscow and Kaluga oblasts), and just once (at the height of the "encounter battle," on 31 August 1973, before I learned about the seizure of *Gulag*) near the village of Serednikovo, with its gaps where cottages had once been, and its patches of dreary wasteland (it had been ruined by collectivization, then burned down during the war, and never restored afterward), with its marvelous church from the time of Tsar Aleksei, and its cemetery. In the gently meandering valley between Ligachev and Serednikovo we crossed the bright stream, paused on the tiny, timeworn wooden bridge over which women worshipers go every day to the gentle rise, then up the sheer hill to church, and watched the water running clear between grassy and bushy banks. I said:

"How vividly we shall remember all this if . . . ever we are somewhere else, not in Russia."

Shafarevich, who is always so restrained, and avoids any strong expression of feeling in case it seems excessive, answered as though his insides were being drawn out of him, as a fish's insides are drawn out by a hook.

"Life would be impossible anywhere but in Russia."

"Impossible" was a stifled gasp: elsewhere there would be neither air nor water.

With the fresh vision of a detached, unprejudiced and precise mind, Shafarevich also tackled the problem of socialism—tackled it with a freedom and humor of which the Western world, hypnotized as it is from the left, is today incapable. In the symposium there was room only for an article of modest length, but Shafarevich had begun by writing a whole book, a detailed historical survey from Babylon, Plato and the Inca state to Saint-Simon and Marx, because he had little hope that sources would be accessible to him after the publication of *From Under the Rubble.*

The most recent draft of Shafarevich's book had been with me for some weeks. I should have read it, but could never find time. Moreover, I found that I had been given a very faint carbon copy, and I was hoping to get a clearer one. This was what he had brought me at four o'clock on the afternoon of 12 February. He had left his briefcase in my apartment before joining me in the yard. There, in broad daylight, with our every move observed, and probably with every word overheard (though we had had several important conversations in the yard of an evening, and if the KGB drones had eavesdropped just once, surely they would have taken steps to seize and block our symposium), we continued discussing the progress of our volume, speaking tight-lipped and turning our heads from side to side to baffle the listening devices. We finished our discussion without hindrance. It only remained to exchange the unreadable carbon for the new one. To do this I had to go up to the apartment. I left the baby in my older son's care for a minute and went upstairs with Shafarevich. In addition to *The Socialist Phenomenon,* he had just stuffed my two articles for the symposium into a bulging satchel, when there was a ring at the door. My wife opened it but left the chain on while she came to tell me that it was "the Prosecutor's Office again—two of them this time. They've brought the summons again. They say there's something that needs clearing up." It was nearly five, the end of the working day. Something to clear up? The day had passed so reassuringly that my anxiety was dormant. Right, we would go together and let them in. So I simply tossed my unread letters from abroad on the desk and went to the front door, along the short passageway from my study and through the entrance hall, where the pram stood. Nothing in my heart warned me; I had lost my tense alertness. To open the door, we had first to shut it and take the chain off: my wife started pushing it to and found something hindering her. The usual dodge—a foot in the door to keep it open. "Up to their old tricks," I grumbled loudly. But what had become of my old zek reflexes? How could I fail to understand and still open up, after this foot in the door? If I was unperturbed, it was because I had grown unused to them. Now, Alya and I had agreed on a plan of action in case they came to search. We would take care not to let them outnumber us, not let in more of them than there were adults in the flat, or they might plant all sorts of false evidence without our spotting it, and we would try, if the telephone was not yet cut off, to phone as many friends as we could with the news. Still, there were only two of them, and all they wanted was to clear up that little matter. So instead of creating delays and giving ourselves time to think, we meekly played the game according to their rules: this was something I had described in *Gulag,* yet here I was, doing it again. How long must we ordinary human beings be thrashed and beaten before we learn to think? But then, in the last few days we had let in their messengers and nothing had happened.

Of course, if I *had* thought quickly and refused to open the door, they would have broken it down. Wouldn't they have gone on ringing and knocking for a while? They would also have gone to fetch crowbars. And with all that walking up and down stairs, they would either be seen and the news would get around, or they would stop people from using the stairway and so draw attention to themselves. We might only have held out for fifteen minutes, but as the situation grew clearer we would have managed to burn a thing or two, to exchange promises and instructions. . . . This was a very feeble beginning: we simply opened up. (Alas, I still haven't got it right. After I had gone, and not immediately afterward, it was found that when my wife had gone to call me, the KGB boys had jammed the Yale lock so that the door would no longer shut properly! If we didn't mean to open up, we should have refused to do so in the first place, but how could we know who was there? We hadn't even a peephole in the door. . . . And we had thought that we might try to hold out under siege.)

The first and the second of them were still advancing in the normal way when others came pouring out of the dark corner at the head of the stairs, those in the rear jostling those in front, and before we knew what was happening (is that all eight years of prison training has done for you, you dummy?), a whole phalanx of them had pushed their way in between the pram, the coat pegs and the telephone table, forcing my wife and me farther and farther back—some of them in plain clothes, some in police uniform, none of them undersized or narrow-chested, eight of them altogether.

I started shouting the same senseless words over and over again: "So that's your game, is it . . . so that's your game!" It must have sounded like a cry of helpless rage. A hefty dark fellow in a luxurious fur coat, trying to look like a respectable citizen, opened a stiff folder, of the sort in which they keep diplomas awarded for successes in socialist competition, and inside it there was a large uncrumpled sheet of crested white paper. "I'm Senior Counselor Zverev. . . . You must come along with me!" And he thrust his pen at me, for me to sign. I refused, of course.

I was in a state of witless shock, as though flames had suddenly enwrapped and paralyzed me, so that for a moment I had no mind, no memory. Dolt! Is this all the good your training has done you? What's become of your much vaunted wolfish prison ways? I must come along? In this state of shock it all seemed very simple. They had summoned me, I had not gone, so of course they had sent a posse to bring me in. At a lawful hour, in a perfectly legal way. I must come along? "I shall comply." I said so out loud, as they boxed me in and squeezed me toward the door. I wasn't going to fight eight of them.

I must come along? A simple enough concept, easily taken in; I would just pop down there and be back—the Public Prosecutor's Office was nearby. But I was really doing two different things at once: I was also setting off as if to prison, in the way we had planned. "No need for that farce," they yelled, "he'll be right back," but I had to go to my study to collect my prison kit, so off I went, with two of them treading on my wife's toes to push in after me, and me vainly ordering them to stand back. (I caught a glimpse of Shafarevich, black as a cloud, still as a statue, a satchel replete with socialism and algebra in his hand.) Now we were in the study, with me looking for the sack, those people hot on my heels, and a burly captain in a militia greatcoat insolently invading the place of sacred privacy, which only those closest to me ever entered, but— in my state of shock!—I had lost my memory, had no thought, no eyes, for all the confidential papers scattered untidily about the desk, so that he had only to reach out and . . . I ought to have shut him out, but he stuck too close to his prisoner. (His job, however, was to see that I did not leap out of the window, or slash my wrist, or run headfirst at the wall, or hang myself, and he had as little thought for my desk as I had.) "What are you doing?" I said, waking up suddenly. "Have you got a search warrant?" "No," they replied. "You haven't? Out you go, then," my wife shouted. It was like talking to stones. They wouldn't budge. Oh, no—my prison sack wasn't in its place! Here's another—a bag for a schoolchild's galoshes, containing papers of the sort that I regularly took out of town to burn—in other words, the most sensitive papers of all. There they were, unburned, and as if that was not enough, I gutted the bag and left them on a chair, so that my wife could put the prison things we had ready in their place. But the KGB boys were just as dazed by the suddenness of it (or by doubts about their rights?). They did not so much as look at the papers—all they wanted was to keep me in one piece and prevent my escaping. I took the bag and back I went, back we all went, elbowing each other along the corridor, and instead of dawdling, I was actually hurrying. Now, that's strange; why am I hurrying? Why don't I have a bit of fun with them, sit down to a meal for half an hour, discuss domestic matters with my family? I could certainly put on a show—I'm good at that sort of thing! Why had I let the Geebees set the pace? Well, the reason was this—to get them out of there as quickly as possible. (In my state of shock, I thought: Once I go, they'll go, and the apartment will be clean.) The one thing I remembered to do was to dress prison fashion, shabbily—as I had intended all along. I put on an old cap and a sheepskin coat which I had worn in exile. The Geebees thrust my fur jacket at me: "Look what you've got here: why don't you put it on?" No, thank you, I'm not that stupid, you won't catch me that way: something to lie around on cement floors in, that's what I need! I said no goodbyes—I was in too much of a hurry! (how soon would I be back?)—except to my wife, right by the door: with all those Geebees around us, it was like being in a crowded trolley bus. We kissed each other goodbye, unhurriedly, and with the realization returning that it might be forever. Ought I, then, to go back in? Complete our arrangements? Hang back, drag my heels for all I was worth? No; I was galvanized by shock. (All because of my first false step, all because I had so stupidly let them in—and now I would be on hot bricks until I had cleared the apartment and taken them off with me. In my state of shock I was in some confusion as to who was taking whom.)

I made the sign of the cross slowly over my wife. And she blessed me. The Geebees were flummoxed.

"Look after the children."

Then, without a backward glance, down the stairs, not noticing the steps. Just as you would expect: a car had mounted the pavement to hug the main doorway (so that I would have less than one step to take over open ground—the foreign correspondents had only just left), and of course they had its door open and ready, as they always do. No point in resisting. I was well away now. I took the middle seat in the rear. One of them jumped in on each side of me, they slammed the doors, the driver and his navigator were in place already—and we moved off. I could see in the driver's mirror that another car, also full, was following us. Four with me, four behind—so I had drawn all eight off, right? (In my feverish state I couldn't think straight: the driver, the navigator and, I think, the two watchdogs beside me were all new. Where were my original eight?) It wasn't much of a ride. There was no point in riding at all; it would have been quicker by the back gate on foot. Now we were turning onto Pushkin Street. Cars cannot turn down Pushkin Street, so we would have to go the other way and round by the Petrovka. Ah, here's Strastnoy Boulevard. We had been here yesterday discussing what to do if anything happened. Yesterday the slight frost had still not quite yielded, but now the roads were slushy, the windshield wiper swished busily over the window, and I saw that we were entering the left-hand lane: turning, then, not down toward the Prosecutor's Office, but up toward the Sadovoye Ring Road.

"Ah, so that's it, then," I said to myself. (As though I had expected something different. If you're going to jail, does it matter which one? Feverish, I had miscalculated. But now, this left turn at the Petrovsky Gate sufficed to cool me down.) Hat off (the two beside me started), I put it on my knees. Peace descended on me. As I had written about my last arrest:

> Through my body, through my limbs,
> The peace of resignation swims
> The peace of one who sees
> the gallows near.

Suddenly I simply had to rub my throat near my windpipe with two fingers, to massage it as best I could. My escort on the right said quickly, nervously:

"Keep your hands down!"

I answered slowly, calmly, now that my serenity had come back to me:

"I know the rules. I have nothing to stab or cut myself with."

I continue rubbing. It seems to do me good, for some reason. Once again the man on the right speaks up (the one on the left keeps silent; of two thugs on either side, one is always nastier):

"Put your hands down."

I rub on. "I know my rights."

Along the Sadovoye. Turn right. Probably to Lefortovo. Might as well complete the collection. I've been there as a visitor, but never in the cells.

How simply it is all ending. The calf has butted and butted the oak. The pygmy would stand up to Leviathan. Till the world press fulminated: ". . .the only Russian whom the regime fears! He is undermining Marxism—and he walks around central Moscow a free man!"

And all it needed was two cars, and eight men—and that only to make assurance trebly sure.

My serenity had returned to me—and now I made my second mistake: I believed unquestioningly that this was a perfectly ordinary arrest. I had not expected them to behave so resolutely, to take such a risk; I had thought more poorly of them. So? So they were strong, after all; I had to admit it. I had always been prepared for arrest someday. There was nothing to be surprised at. Let's get on with the showdown.

*My wife, as soon as she had torn herself away from me, and without waiting for all the Chekists who thronged the entrance hall to leave, rushed to the study and scooped up all the most dangerous papers from her desk and from mine. Irreplaceable things she hid on her person. Other, less sensitive things she set fire to on the metal tray that always stood ready in the study for the burning of "written conversations." She rushed to the telephone, but it was disconnected; they had expected this, of course. But why had none of our friends or family come to see her? She could hear neither voices nor footsteps; there was not a sound in the apartment—what could have happened there? Patting herself to make sure that the papers she was concealing were secure, she went out into the entrance hall, and this is what she found there: two of the eight had stayed behind, the bruiser of a "militia" captain and the original bashful messenger. So-o: they were waiting for another bunch; they meant to search the place. Meanwhile the two children were still outside—but not for anything in the world could a woman go and fetch them: there could be no question of abandoning the front line. So back she went to the study, signaling Shafarevich to stand guard at the door. He stood there to bar the way, hanging on to his bulky briefcase. Next—a second sorting of papers, more systematic this time, but still at lightning speed. She was reluctant to burn things: at moments like this you may burn anything and everything and curse yourself for it afterward. Where she could, she hid single papers between the pages of books: if they did find them, they would never put them together. The study was full of fumes from the charred paper; the ventilator wasn't taking them away. They drifted, of course, into the entrance hall; the KGB men smelled them but stayed where they were. She felt neither grief, nor excitement, nor dismay; her eyes were dry; she felt nothing but cool rage: my wife sorted through the papers, put some aside, burned others with a speed ordinarily impossible. There were still so many documents handwritten by different people! Still a whole novel! Still all that raw material—mountains of files and envelopes; there was no hope of dealing with them, however long delayed the search was! She went out into the hall—and they were no longer there. They had kept glancing at their watches. Twenty minutes after I had been taken away, one of them had said, "Shall we go?" "Another couple of minutes," said the other. They had left without a word. Twenty-two minutes? It couldn't be the Prosecutor's Office then, nor the Lubyanka. . . . Lefortovo, perhaps? Only then was it discovered that the door could not be shut behind them. The lock was broken, and eighteen-month-old Ignat tried to crawl out onto the landing. Someone went to fetch the other children—and found the yard full of militiamen. What sort of resistance had they expected? Who did they think might interfere? . . . My wife dialed number after number, though she knew it was hopeless. The line wasn't dead: someone was listening in! (To see what numbers they would try to call?) There was a buzz—then the normal dial tone—then an interruption—then a prolonged buzz again. But she couldn't give up. They had taken me away—and no one knew about it! So my wife kept dialing. Stepka was brought home. Now it was time to fetch Yermolai from the kindergarten. Perhaps there would be a public telephone from which they could call the reporters. Then suddenly—inexplicably—the connection was no longer broken, and Alya was able to speak to Irina Zholkovskaya at machine-gun speed: "Listen carefully. Half an hour ago A.I.*

*was removed from the house. There were eight Geebees with orders to*
*bring him in by force if necessary. Hurry it up!" She hung up first, and*
*quickly called the next one! Somehow or other she succeeded in making*
*two more calls. Then the routine of interruptions was resumed for*
*another hour and a half. But three calls were enough: phones began*
*ringing all over Moscow.*

Here were the familiar approaches to Lefortovo. (When I was soaring aloft, and a candidate for a Lenin Prize, I had come here to study
Lefortovo from outside. You never know when it may be useful!) The
familiar sliding gates, the yard, the suite of offices where we had visited
people. By the time we arrived it was already rather dark, and there
were not enough lamps in the yard, where some officers were already
standing and waiting for me. I need not be unduly modest about it: this
was a not altogether ordinary moment in the history of Lefortovo, and
it would not surprise me to learn that someone from the Party high
command had been posted there as an observer. There we are, then:
after all his barking, all his threats—we've nabbed him! Like Pugachev,
in Catherine's day. Here he is, in our hands at last.

They directed the operation as though it was a battle: The car will
stop precisely there—a cordon of ten men will be thrown around it at
the double—this door will be opened and that one will not be—they will
leave the car in the following order. I sat there quietly; I was warm and
comfortable for the time being, and what came next might be worse.
"Out you get!"—on the side facing the prison steps.

I had given it no thought before, the idea suddenly sprang into my
head: as I got out I would do my best to show my disrespect, to annoy
them. I took my galoshes bag—it was made of dark cloth, and had long
strings by which to hang it on a cloakroom peg—and I slung it over my
shoulder so that it looked like a beggar's bundle. Then I clambered out
of the car without hurrying and went into the prison—a few yards to
the steps, then up the steps, then across the entrance hall, in my shabby
flat fur cap, my Kazakh sheepskin coat as worn by Kazakh herdsmen.

"Dressed to go fishing," as Malyarov aptly remarked later, behaving
as though none of them was there, I ambled with a proprietorial air into
my beggar's hovel, weighed down with the alms I had gathered.

The interrogators' offices had been moved elsewhere, and here they
now had their "boxes" for body searches: bare stone everywhere, a bare
table, two bare benches, a miserly light bulb overhead. Two shabby,

seedy little men were sitting on one of the benches—zeks, I thought at first, but it turned out that they had been brought in from the Housing Office next door as witnesses! (See how carefully we observe the law.) I, too, sat down, on the other bench, putting my sack down beside me.

No, I had never thought it would happen. Honestly, I had never expected it.

They had brought themselves to it. . . .

"It's a bit early," said the fox in the trap, "but it looks like my bedtime."

The usual businesslike and faceless body-searcher now came in and cheerfully invited me to empty my things onto the table. And this item of ordinary prison procedure was so simple and reasonable, so honest, even, so free from guile, that I obeyed without fuss. Order is order, we were brought up with it, and how can a jail admit a prisoner without a body search on entry; it would be like sitting down to dinner without a spoon or without washing your hands. So I surrendered my hat, my sheepskin coat, my shirt, my trousers, fully expecting to get them back just as I had given them. Another stout fellow arrived to help him feel the seams of my garments, but I can't say that they were very thorough about it. The searcher didn't tell me to finish undressing in a hurry— I could sit there as I was for a while. Then a highly polished, slack-bellied, gray-headed colonel came in.

When I used to picture what my next spell in jail would be like, I —my present self, with all the strength and importance I had acquired —knew for certain that not only would the interrogators get nothing at all out of me (I would die first), not only would I refuse to recognize the court, ignore it from the start, remain silent throughout (except for the curse I would put on them in my concluding statement)—I was quite sure, too, that in jail I would not accept the humiliations to which Soviet political prisoners are subjected. I myself had written so much in *Gulag* about the way in which even in the twenties our young people had upheld the proud traditions of earlier Russian political prisoners: not standing up when prison officers came into the room, etc., etc. . . . And I—at this stage, what had I to lose? If I couldn't dig in my heels, who could? Who was in a better position to do it than I was?

But as I went through that first bright, clean (glaringly, painfully clean) prison corridor, sat on that first bench in that first frisking box, and unresistingly submitted to being searched—out of habit, like a cow standing stock-still to be milked—I was already wondering what had

happened to my resolve. The wheels went on spinning without knowing or caring (or anyway pretending not to know) whether their victim
was famous or not. As for me, I was strong, all right, as long as I was
eating my fill, walking wherever the whim took me, having my sleep
out, and as long as I had various little accessories to hand—the thing to
put under my head, the other thing to shade my eyes, a third thing to
protect my ears. But now that I had been deprived of nearly all of this,
my blood pressure had risen so that part of my head seemed to be on
fire, and if I started standing on trivial matters of principle with the
prison authorities, it would be the easiest thing in the world to land
myself in the hole, plagued by cold, and hunger, and damp, and
radiculitis, and who knows what besides. I was fifty-five, and not the
twenty-seven-year-old straight from the front and bursting with health,
who had been asked in the first cell he saw, "What holiday resort have
you just come from?" I had the feeling now that my strength might not
be enough for a fight on *two* fronts—against the interrogators and
against the prison officers. And that it might be more sensible to husband my strength for the first front, and give in right away on the
second: what the hell did it matter anyway?

This was the point I had reached when the glossy, sly-looking, gray-
headed colonel came in, with others in attendance. And asked me, very
sure of himself, but not aggressively:

"Why aren't you on your feet? I'm Colonel Komarov, commandant
of the Lefortovo Maximum Security Prison."

I had previously imagined this scene in many different ways, but
always in a cell. (Indeed, a senior prison officer never visits a prisoner
before he is put in a cell.) I would be sitting on my bed, and invite him
to "come and sit by me." Or briefly summarize my reasons: "Political
prisoners did not stand up for prison officers in old Russia. I don't see
why they should in Soviet Russia." Or I would say something about the
inflexibility of my intentions. Or I would innocently stand up when the
key rattled in the lock and pretend that I had been on my feet before
they came.

But now, in the frisking box, almost naked and taken by surprise,
when I saw this suite of officers before me, and heard the formal order
to stand, which all here had to obey, and since I had already calculated
that I ought to save my strength for the main struggle, slowly, awkwardly, reluctantly doing my duty—I stood.

But did this not mean in reality that I had started making concessions? Was this the beginning of total collapse? How would it sound when they reported *up top* that I had submitted to prison rules? Would someone there see the significance of it and gloat? They might think it well worth their while to break me that first evening; they ought at least to try.

Then came further encroachments, and my further retreats. An officer with a registration card asked me my full name and place of birth. Should I laugh at him? Refuse to answer? Well, I knew that they asked everybody these things, that this was just routine. I answered. (The collapse continues?) Here was the doctor, a typical jailer in skirts. What complaints do you suffer from? None at all. (I'm not going to tell you that I have high blood pressure!) Still, we'll just run the stethoscope over you: breathe—stop breathing—turn around—arms open wide. Should I refuse to submit to medical examination? It seemed rather silly. . . . And meanwhile the body-searcher—"arms open wide" again —had nearly finished. (I had submitted to the search at the beginning, so why worry now?) "Turn around—squat—" It's true what they say: Surrender one hair, and you'll end up beardless. But now for something strange—something outside the usual routine: a second doctor creeps up on me, a man this time, not what you'd call an intellectual, a jailhouse ferret but with a perfect bedside manner: "Excuse me, may I take a look at you too?" Sounds my pulse, stethoscope again. (Carry on, I think. You won't hear anything much. My heart's steady, nobody could feel better. I'm amazingly cool and collected—on my home ground here, you know. It's all so familiar to me, nothing to cause me the slightest uneasiness.) Ah, but the wretch gets out his apparatus for measuring blood pressure: May I, please? This is the one I should say no to. My weakness is discovered. I squint at the gauge: I can tell from the pulsations anyway—it's 160/170 and that's just the beginning. I haven't spent a single night in jail yet. No, I shan't last long. "Do you suffer from high blood pressure?" he asks. We had talked about it often enough, with the KGB somewhere along the line, and openly enough. What else would we be talking about over the phone? "No," I said, "I don't."

Well, I'd complied with the rules, but what about *them?* They were hanging on to my gear! For my watch and the cross I wore around my neck I got a receipt, as was usual. Though I had had an argument—my first with them—about the cross: "I need it in my cell!" They wouldn't give it back to me—it was made of metal! But nonmetal things, once they had kneaded the seams thoroughly to make sure there was no blade and no iron hook hidden there—why not return them? Answer: They must go to be disinfected. An inventory? By all means. Right down to the homemade eyeshade. It's all listed. It never used to be like that. But perhaps my knowledge of prison methods was behind the times: what reason was there to think that they didn't disinfect nowadays? I pointed to my sheepskin: "That won't stand oven heat!" "Yes, we know; we won't put it in the oven." This surprised me, but I put it down to a change of customs. In return, they gave me an unbelievably rough undershirt, with hairs that raked my body like corn husks—that was normal. And a black prison or workhouse type of tunic: you couldn't buy one like it if you tried. But to wear on top, a real suit—whether it was a good one or not I don't know, I never could tell—and low shoes (without laces): so this is how they dress them nowadays? In the *sharashka*, too, they had given us suits to wear—at times it was like being at a fancy-dress party. I would get all my own things back in an hour or two, they said. Off we went. A screw in front, a screw behind, rattling their keys through corridors, past intersections and transfer points—all just as it used to be. I gazed around with interest, looking for the American system of iron landings and staircases, of which I had heard so much in stories about Lefortovo. Now I would see it for myself. Up to the second level. There wasn't a lot to be seen. They had had a new idea and covered the gratings on the different landings with dingy canvas sheets so that you could not see from one level to the next. It was rather like a circus by night, hushed and gloomy between shows.

*In response to the telephone calls, five people assembled, led by Sakharov, and picketed the Public Prosecutor's Office on Pushkin Street. It was partly intended as a demonstration, but they were also keeping watch to see if I would emerge. At home, normal rules were suspended during this emergency. A steady procession of visitors passed through the apartment, friends and strangers, in twos or threes or fives, and the door was put on the chain after each new arrival, and remained ajar, gaping ominously. My wife told the first arrivals what had happened and they passed it on to the others, while she got back to all that paper. We had never realized till now how much of it there was; we had lived among it without noticing. Her state was still the same: cold fury went with self-controlled efficiency. What will they do to him? Kill him? Impossible! But arrest had seemed impossible once. She might have despaired, but these thoughts drifted through her mind as though they belonged to someone else. And there were other, more precise thoughts: about what to do, and what should be put where.*

I didn't want to miss the number on the cell door. But I didn't spot it, and thought perhaps there wasn't one. I had felt sure that I was marching to solitary confinement, but as I went in I saw that although it was a one-man cell in size, there were three beds in it, and two young men were lying there smoking: the place was full of smoke. I hadn't expected this for a moment: why hadn't they put me in a one-man cell? And this smoking: at one time I used to enjoy a drag myself, but now my head won't take ten minutes of it. If I had stuck to my firm line, I would have said nothing. I took the weaker line and said, "Please put me in a single cell. Smoking bothers me." The lieutenant colonel accompanying me said politely that he would report my request. In general, they were all very polite: perhaps this, too, was part of the new style (in spite of the fact that the same lieutenant colonel had barked abuse at my two cellmates as we came in). But my composure would be a match for their politeness: I would behave as though I had not been trying to escape them for a quarter of a century, as though we were blood brothers. The thing is that I succeeded in maintaining my composure without difficulty because I had submitted to prison rules. Otherwise I would have worn my nerves to shreds in petty squabbles. I was being cleverer than I knew, saying: Here's my body, do what you will with it, and burst with frustration when you see how unperturbed I am. If somebody with a watching brief from the Central Committee hopefully inquired whether I was furious? fighting mad? in hysterics? he wouldn't get a crumb of satisfaction. I moved no more quickly than usual, when I sat on the bed I pretended to be dozing, when I walked about the cell it was with a measured tread. If they still cherished the hope that I might suddenly weaken, start pleading with them, lose heart and make a deal, it was precisely my calmness that played havoc with their calculations.

They locked the door. My pals looked a bit embarrassed. Right—what are we going to do about this smoking? Why have you got the ventilator closed? Well, it's cold, see—they keep the heat down. We have to put our overcoats over us and it's still cold. All the same, after you've had your smoke we'd better let a little air in.

Yes, yes. It was all just as I had been told, the cells hadn't changed: the revolting gray lavatory pan (at least it wasn't a night bucket); the mugs on the table (at least they didn't keep hopping toward each other because of the roar and shuddering of wind tunnels nearby, as they did that first time: silence is a great blessing in itself); the bright light set in the ceiling, with a wire cage around it; the black bread on the shelf —scarcely touched, although it was evening. The cover over the judas window swished open from time to time, which meant that there wasn't just one of them goggling at me, but several of them were taking turns. Come on, take a look, we've pulled him in! And I hope it chokes you.

I observe myself carefully, and am delighted to find that I have none of the sensations of a novice. I study my cellmates closely (whereas novices are exclusively preoccupied with their own distress). They are both young fellows, one of them dark, fidgety, full of life, as restless as a scalded cat: he was pulled in only twenty-four hours ago, and he's still dazed. The second is fair and it's still apparently less than three days since they, well, didn't arrest him, he says, but detained him—but unless his sluggishness, his puffiness, his pallor, are due to some illness, he has many of the marks of someone who has spent a lot of time inside: stoolies often look like that. The two are on very easy terms with each other, and no doubt the first has told the second his whole story. . . . I ask them not "What are you in for?" but "What are they charging you with?" They are currency speculators.[1]

One of the delights of jail they hadn't yet discovered—pacing the cell. It was only four short steps, but still . . . Walking was something I had never in my life wearied of—and now it stood me in good stead again. Slowly does it. I am wearing somebody else's shoes, and try as I may to step quietly, they clomp like wooden clogs. The shutter over the judas window swishes open again and again. They look and can't get their fill of looking.

Yes, they had found their nerve.

*From time to time, Sakharov's group called from a public telephone near the Prosecutor's Office to say that nothing was happening, and that they had been told "there's no Solzhenitsyn here." At home, the influx of friends into the long, roomy kitchen grew steadily, and by now there were some foreign newspapermen present, but still no one*

---

1. This is hard to explain to the West. They were guilty of currency trading based on the real rate of exchange rather than on the arbitrary Soviet rate.

*came to search. How long must they wait? My wife seethed with impatience for action: why not distribute the archive to these friends and acquaintances, let them stuff parts of it under their coats, into their briefcases or their handbags? But perhaps that's just what they are waiting for? They might grab the visitors one by one, bundle them into cars, take them off and search them without a warrant or without making out a report, so that there would be no proof later on that it had ever happened. . . . No, mustn't do anything rash. Innocent people would suffer. (Anyway, perhaps he hadn't been arrested? Perhaps he would be back yet? They had said "he'll be back in an hour." That was three hours ago. Of course he was under arrest.) Somebody suggested taking three-year-old Yermolai away from that depressing atmosphere. "No—let him get used to it. He's a Solzhenitsyn."*

They had nerved themselves to do it. But had they really failed to understand that I am like one of those booby-trapped bicycles the Germans used to leave in the middle of the road for us: there it lies, yours for the taking, nothing to stop you; but let yourself be tempted, move it an inch—and you and several of your comrades are no more. All my work is long since in the West; it's all ready to be released. The program will take its course automatically now with no help from me: first my will, then the other two volumes of *Gulag,* then this book, *The Oak and the Calf,* including the Third Supplement, the screenplay, *Prussian Nights, The Feast of the Victors, Decembrists, Highway of Enthusiasts,* the ninety-six-chapter *First Circle,* the Lenin chapters, Knot II . . . They don't realize, of course, the full strength of the charge. Right—let's see how you like it. If it weren't for all that, I would be squirming and writhing more miserably than my unhappy cellmate. As it is, I am quite calm. If this is the end—it's the end. I hope *you* perish with me.

The lads offered me some bread and rusks from the shelf. Well, I *am* rather hungry. I remembered being offered lunch at home at three o'clock, and saying no, I'll take Stepan for an airing. So that I'd eaten nothing since morning, had arrived in the cell hungry, and would be given nothing till next morning—the food wagon had gone by for the last time. This was a bad start for a prisoner, with his first day of interrogation ahead of him. And as it happened, I had no purse in my pocket, not a single ruble, not a kopeck for the prison shop, I had been in such a hurry! Bread? But what about yourselves? Oh, we don't want it. You get a bellyful here. Get a bellyful? Wonders will never cease. Nothing like the prisons I used to know. I began pinching morsels from the lump. After the average Moscow black loaf, it's pretty foul bread—like clay, baked badly on purpose. Never mind; I shall get to like it.

But what is all this? I've been waiting two hours, and still haven't got my clothes. I "vote" (raise my finger). They open the serving hatch with alacrity: there's a bustling throng of them out there, including one—no, two officers. I speak quietly, without raising my voice the least bit, not resoundingly "airing my rights" as I would have at one time (because then the only strength I had was a powerful voice, but now I had another source of strength—the steady, inexorable advance of my books), and say almost lazily: "It's time you brought my things back. It can't possibly take so long to disinfect them." "We're looking into it. Looking into the matter." What the blazes is there to look into? Perhaps everything *is* done differently now. (I didn't think in time of asking the lads how long it had taken to toast their clothes.) The lads say, "You'll be done for without an overcoat; it's cold at night with just a blanket." Suddenly the door opens wide, the lieutenant colonel inspects the troops, and another officer brings me a second blanket, a new, unused one straight from the storeroom. The lads are flabbergasted: why this VIP treatment? . . . You mean the disinfecting won't be finished till morning? Strange. All right, then. There's only one more thing I want now: to get to sleep quickly. I'm used to going to bed at nine, and I see nothing wrong with eight, but here the official bedtime isn't till ten, and then it won't be easy to sleep. How tomorrow's tussle goes depends entirely on this first night. I have my usual evening feeling of pleasant lassitude, my mind is slowing down; just the time to snatch an extra hour or two, or three. I have no sedative, so the night will be sleepless—but just now I could fall asleep. Quite impossible: you are allowed only to lie on top of the blanket without undressing or covering yourself up. I lie down, but the blood rushes to my head. It's so low! (How am I to conceal the fact that a low pillow is bad for me nowadays?) As for the lads, they smoke another cigarette, then another, but they air the cell each time. The dark one is fidgeting about behind my head somewhere: "Who could have told on me, though? Who? That's all I want to know." He and his wife, of whom he is obviously very fond, had been trying to brighten their lives as best they could—buying some sticks of furniture, and even a car, things that in a normal country a worker can simply earn, but in our country he must acquire by ingenious lawbreaking.

Some coins were taken from him when he was searched, and now he has to explain them. "Listen, lad, don't do so much of that in the cell. There are microphones here, never fear. Behave as though there's nothing to it. Try keeping it under your hat." That makes him think. I tell them another item or two of prison lore, to pass the time till I can sleep. Suddenly the key rattles in the lock. This is just like the Lubyanka used to be—they wait till nearly bedtime to call you for interrogation. I thought they didn't question people at night nowadays. (Not that I shall have anything to say to them in the daytime either.)

The lieutenant colonel, though, without once mentioning or asking my name, invites me to *come along.* After bedtime I wouldn't have gone for anything. But now—well, all right, maybe they'll give me my sheepskin back; it would be so nice to snuggle up in it—even sitting on a railway track, or in a prisoner transport, or on the bed platform in a camp. It turns out that I have no distance at all to go—they have chosen my cell so that I shall not—and I scarcely have time to run my eyes over those canvas sheets, with an officer in front of me and an officer to the rear, when a colonel, the commandant of Lefortovo, stands in my path and says: Please take the side way. There is a little lobby, another, the door to an office. Bright light. We go around a row of chairs. There are two already sitting there (I can't get a look at their faces. Who are they? Where from? Are they in disguise?), and with those who brought me, that makes five. The gleaming bald head belongs to a small, sharp-featured man crouched over the bigger desk, and there is also a white glare of documents under the desk lamp. In an empty space in the middle of the room, where no one would normally sit, there is a chair right under the lights, facing the sharp-featured one, to which the colonel and the lieutenant colonel direct me. All right—I'd sooner sit than stand. I sit down. And I sense that the rear row is now seated in a semicircle behind my back. No one speaks.

The sharp-featured head man probes and probes me with his eyes, as though he has never seen a human being before.

Help yourself, do. Probe away.

In a voice that is meant to be piercing, and is certainly quite sharp, he says:

"Solzhenitsyn?"

His mistake. He should have said, "Name . . . ?" You've caught me; let's see if you can keep me.

"The same," I tell him.

As sharply as before: "Aleksandr Isayevich?"

(Let's put his mind at rest.)

"Quite so."

Whereupon he informs me in his most bell-like and portentous tones that he is:

"Malyarov, Deputy Prosecutor General of the U.S.S.R.!"

"Ah . . . I've heard of you."

I've read what Sakharov says about him. But Sakharov doesn't mention that he is so tiny. From Sakharov's record you might suppose that he was a great lump of bureaucratic self-importance, an Oskolupov.

He doesn't beat about the bush, though. He is businesslike. Or perhaps he is in a hurry because he can't bear to be in the same room with me and breathe the same air:

"I shall now read you the order. . . ."

I don't remember who had "confirmed" it, whether it was he or the Public Prosecutor himself, but the "order" had been given by a mere Senior Counselor, in fact Zverev of the luxurious fur-coat, who had come to my apartment almost like a militiaman, but was now—can you beat it?—acting on behalf of the whole Politburo.

"For . . . and for . . . you are charged under Article 64." (Like that? Which subsection? Which part?)

I spoke lethargically, and tried to sound like an ignorant yokel.

"That new Code, eh?" (Well, it was only thirteen years old.) "I don't know a thing about it. Article 64—what's that, then?"

A bit different from the good old days when Daddy Stalin was on the throne. If you got a tenner then, you'd soon be reeling off every subsection, word perfect in the dark.

Said Malyarov, bug-eyed:

"Treason!"

I didn't move a muscle.

(Those five sitting in a row behind my back—were they waiting for me to fling myself upon the prosecutor?)

"Sign here!" He turned the sheet of paper around toward me and beckoned me over to the desk.

Without turning a hair, weighing every word, I made the statement I had planned long ago:

"I shall take no part either in your investigation or in your trial. You must carry on without me."

He had probably expected as much. He didn't look particularly surprised.

"Just sign to show that you have been informed."

"I have no more to say."

He didn't argue. He turned the page around again and signed himself.

How hard the interrogator had pressed my young, inexperienced self twenty-nine years ago, knowing as he did that there is something to be squeezed out of every man. And how good it feels to show them that you are of solid rock, so that they don't even try, don't even lift a finger to press you and probe you.

The interrogation will not be so difficult: no need for great mental effort. I have told absolutely everybody, in advance, to speak freely, pour it all out, say what they like: I shan't be contradicting any of it, because I shan't answer a single question.

This is the way to do it. These are the best tactics.

It's over. We reverse the former procedure. Those behind me stand, I stand, and with an officer in front and an officer to the rear, I go through the two lobbies. Hands behind you now! (Not harshly, though: just a reminder.) I needn't do it, of course. But I do. Did you but know it, having my hands behind my back makes me feel surer of myself. It's the undisciplined free workers in a camp who let them dangle untidily. Hands behind for me means that I instantaneously become an iron-hard zek, close ranks with all those millions. You do not know how even a trivial little stroll under escort like this reinforces a zek's confidence in himself.

It doesn't take long; here I am back in my cell.

"What are you going to get?" the lads ask.

Shall I tell them, or not?

I really don't remember, anyway. Up to fifteen years, that's definite. But of course, there's also death by shooting.

No question about it, they've regained their courage. I hadn't expected it of them. So much for the "courses of action open to them." There's no fool like a clever fool.

*It is no longer possible to establish the sequence of events to the minute. But it was not yet 9 P.M. when I was taken to see Malyarov, and they phoned my wife to say that "your husband is being held" at nine-fifteen. It was evidently later still—quite late in the evening by European time—when our ambassador notified the foreign ministry of West Germany that he would call on them in the morning with an important statement. This chronology does not exclude the possibility that during my first hours in prison, and when Malyarov sent for me, they had still not finally and irrevocably decided to expatriate me. (If they had, what was the point of Article 64?) Were they still hedging their bets, hoping that I would be terrified, so that they could start wringing concessions from me? If that was their scheme, my stony apathy had quashed it.*

*A semi-educated voice over the telephone invited my wife to address her inquiries next morning to interrogating officer Balashov, the same Balashov whom I had been asked to go and see in the first place. That was it, then. I was under arrest. She hung up, and as before, the others began dialing, and spreading the news around Moscow.*

At long last a voice through the hatch announced bedtime. Right—quick now; you used to be clever at it once upon a time: blankets unrolled, jacket off, never mind the rest. It's cold, all right; those bastards, pinching my sheepskin! and my woolen socks! Hurry it up, then. If they were in such a hurry to inform you of the charge, you can expect them to get the interrogation rolling first thing tomorrow morning. In the hurly-burly, while we're all moving about, I slip my shoes under the pillow! It's an old zek's trick, for safety, but this time it's also to raise my head higher. The light beats down; let me cover my eyes with the towel —it wasn't forbidden in the Lubyanka. Will they want my hands outside the bedclothes? Maybe not. Let's sleep. A deep breath, now, deep . . . deep . . . (Breathe what, though? It isn't air we have in this cell— I'd forgotten there was anything like it.)

Oh, no! The son of a bitch had noticed the empty space under my bed and flipped the hatch open.

"Get your shoes down on the floor!"

I worked hard building up my pillow without them. Then I began breathing deeply. And fell asleep.

*The children couldn't get to sleep; they were frightened by the noise, the light, all those voices. New visitors kept arriving, Sakharov's group from the Prosecutor's Office among them. (However you look at it, this spate of sympathizers fearlessly visiting the apartment of a man under arrest shows how times have changed! You Bolsheviks are finished— there are no two ways about it.) Sakharov answered a Canadian radio station from our flat:*

*"Solzhenitsyn's arrest is an act of revenge for his book. This is an*

*insult not only to Russian literature but to the memory of those who have perished." There were telephone calls from Stockholm, Amsterdam, Hamburg, Paris, New York, and our visitors took the receiver to confirm the details. Some of them were thinking: "Now that they've pulled in the untouchable Solzhenitsyn, is there anyone they dare not take? Who'll be tidied away tomorrow?"*

*If you have never engaged in clandestine activities yourself, you cannot imagine those tormenting anxieties. Where should the archive be kept? Should it be taken away or left where it is? While we have so many visitors, shall we divide it among them? Surely not all of them will be picked up. If we let this opportunity slip, they may make a lightning raid and seize everything tomorrow! But to divide it up will bring disaster upon some of the helpers. And will it be possible to reassemble the whole thing later on? No, till things became a little clearer, we shall have to rely on hiding places in the house.*

It's easy enough going to sleep in the evening, but not to get back to sleep after you wake up for the first time. All the troubles of the day force their way in at your first awakening, you feel a burning pain in the chest, in the heart; how can you possibly sleep? It wasn't the currency speculator somewhere behind me, sighing, tossing and turning, smoking through the night, it wasn't the light from that diabolical bulb clawing at my eyes—it was my own miscalculations, my own false moves: how they flood into the brain at night, wave after relentless wave.

What tormented me most was the thought of the apartment being searched with Alya there. In the evening, whether because I had had too much to think about and do, or because my mind was winding down, I hadn't worked myself into a state of anxiety about the search. But now everything centered on it, and it was all because of my mistakes. Why had I opened the door? We could have had a half hour for burning, preparing, planning. Why had I been in such a hurry to get out? Nearly all of *them* had stayed behind. I had not seen those eight men again. The same Zverev would be in charge of the search. It *would* have to happen when there were two copies of *The Socialist Phenomenon* there at once, and Shafarevich on the spot with them. Perhaps he wouldn't surrender his briefcase, but he had taken one copy out and put it on my desk, and he wouldn't have a chance to hide it! It was a good thing that he had taken my articles for the symposium, but there were other copies right there on my desk, together with incomplete drafts from other contributors. Oh dear, oh dear—*From Under the Rubble* was done for. For three years we'd been preparing it—for the bottomless pit. Then there were letters from the West lying openly on my desk: no need to search for them, just help yourselves. Not a single one had fallen into their hands before, but if they read these we would have shown all our cards! . . . There might be all sorts of other things there. . . . Oh, yes—the corrections to *Letter to the Leaders,* made on my last night at home. Worse! The final appendix to the book on *Quiet Flows the Don!* It grieved me that we wouldn't be sending it, but still more that they would find out all about it! And oh, yes—there was another microfilm too, a half-spoiled one, a duplicate of the last one we had dispatched. I should have burned it, but had forgotten to take it out of town, and it was difficult to do it in the house: putting a prize like that in their hands was quite senseless and quite disgraceful. And then again —there was a complete typed copy of *The Calf* in the safe. I wanted to deafen the cell with my howling, go into a tailspin, take off at a run. For years it had been a gamble: sometimes we thought everything would be safer with me, and gathered it all in; sometimes we thought that I was getting too hot, and we lugged a whole sackload downstairs and drove off to bury it somewhere. Wasn't there a copy of *Decembrists* there too? And—needless to say—Knot II, and the Lenin chapters. All this was now in their hands. Oh God, oh God—I had stood firm as a rock through twenty-five years of clandestine activity, had known only success, and now this terrible debacle. And all they had had to do was what in their cowardice they had never previously brought themselves to: come straight to me. Nothing more.

The miserable currency speculator was sighing and tossing and fretting and lighting cigarettes somewhere behind my pillow. "Go to sleep," I kept telling him. "It's very important to save your strength; nothing else will help." But no, he kept fretting: "Who can have given me away?" Apart from your own mistakes, the treachery of friends is always the most vexatious of things. Our other cellmate meanwhile slept peacefully.

*By midnight, her feet, head and eyes were throbbing, and she could not think clearly. Her thoughts were not just disconnected; they were a formless jumble, but Alya had no desire at all for sleep. She thought of going into the study for a third time and looking through papers, but her strength failed her. This was when she remembered that she had eaten nothing since breakfast and that her husband had had no lunch when he was taken. The tray previously used for burning paper was no longer big enough, and a bowl that would hold a bonfire was placed on the kitchen floor, where it would stand for the next six weeks.*

*There was a search that night—carried out by fourteen Geebees in Ryazan, at the home of my acquaintances the Radugins. I had never kept anything there in my life, but they came looking for something tremendous, something worse than* Gulag. *It must in fact have been this book* (The Oak and the Calf) *they were looking for—the only thing they still lacked. But they found nothing.*

I was fretting, but not all the time. Why was I so much better off than when I was first jailed? Because my head was untroubled by exhausting calculations: If he asks this, I shall answer thus, and if he asks that, I must answer the other. What a feeling of freedom! I would not give a single answer. Go fly your kites! . . . I breathed deeply to keep calm, I prayed —and healing ripples of sleep rolled over me. After them, I saw everything with painful clarity again. My head was hot and congested, I had both fists under my pillow now, but still it was too low. I had promised my wife that whatever happened, I would stick it out in jail or in a camp for two years. Just till I knew that all my work had been published and I could die content, knowing I had hit them where it hurt. But now I saw that I had promised more than I could deliver. I could have held out for years, adapting myself to any angle from the vertical so long as I had air and silence and a chance to write. But here I would surely be done for in two months.

Two months—the minimum duration of an investigation. I wasn't frightened, and I wouldn't give way an inch, but—surely I would perish?

Even now I found myself reviewing my life with detachment, as though it were already finished. I was content. It had been worthwhile. Neither the present leaders nor those who came after would free themselves from the trouble I had brought crashing down on them—not in fifty years. I wished—oh, how I wished—that I could have finished the "Knots" too. That was what I wanted more than anything. But I praised God for what I had been able to achieve. Look up, lift your eyes above such minor setbacks as this search and you will see that everything you have attempted has been a success. Your books have been sent to the publishers, and all your unfinished work—preliminary sketches, intermediate drafts, projects—is in Alya's firm and dependable hands. It is good to depart this life leaving a worthy successor. Besides, my three sons will grow up and in one way or another carry on their father's cause.

*There was no sleep that night. They were busy scanning papers and burning—but they hadn't the heart to burn much; none of it could ever be reconstituted. Would they come tomorrow? If they meant to, why not immediately, that evening? Suddenly she remembered something, and started searching for the declaration written last summer, before the encounter battle, and abandoned in rough draft, that the courts had no jurisdiction over Russian literature. He had said again last night, on Strastnoy Boulevard, that he would ignore any interrogation, investigation or trial. She suddenly knew just where to look! She found it! [Document 37] Out with it! In the middle of the night? . . . Her hands were hot with impatience! She must not leave it too late! Early in the morning, the "law" would allow them to "call," to discover it, suppress it, consign it to oblivion. It must go out at once, during the night! Call up a reporter, perhaps? Which one? For various reasons she decided on Lacontre of Le Figaro. "Can you come over ? I want to ask you a favor." "Be there in five minutes!" (What's this? A foreign correspondent summoned by telephone, at night, to the home of an arrested man, and not detained? Sure enough, they had lost their nerve, these one-time Bolsheviks. Where are you, fire-eating Dzerzhinsky?) Alya sat at the typewriter and tapped out ten copies at once on thin paper. Lacontre was a reporter: why shouldn't he accept an item of news? It was quite legitimate. He rolled up the copies neatly, assured her that he would distribute them to all the agencies, and left. The sorting of papers continued. There were so many letters from other people to be burned, so many unsafe handwritten documents. Here was something horrible! Two whole microfilms. They had to be pulled slowly through the scanner to make sure that they were unwanted duplicates and could be burned. They would not burn easily. Stacks of paper stood around the bowl, awaiting their turn. On the whole, they made quite a good job of these preparations for the search. And if it came—they wouldn't open up (the lock had been mended by now): "I consider Solzhenitsyn's arrest illegal, and a house search in his absence still more so. You will*

*have to break the door down!" Six A.M. No visitors. Then it was seven,*
*the children were awake, and the grownups had no time for sleep.*

Strangely enough, it wasn't cold in the cell that night, although the ventilator was opened frequently. Surely my breath had not made it warmer. I couldn't touch the radiator, because it was boxed in, and regulated, of course, by the screws—probably for each cell independently, or how could the required conditions be created? (Looking back, I think that they had turned the heat up specially for me.)

Reveille was just the way it always is: we woke, while the night bulb was still burning, to the rattle of the feeding hatch. Getting-up time, of course, was just when everybody was asleep. Not for long: Look lively there—out of bed quickly. They banged all the doors once, then a second time: Who's cell orderly? Here's a brush; get sweeping. But how lenient they had become: once you were dressed and had made your bed, you could lie down on top of it again. (Lint from the blankets clung to your clothes.) There's nothing drearier than early morning in jail; a lot has been written about it, but then, there have been so many such mornings! With the night bulb still glaring down from the ceiling, and the window still dark, you await the usual prison happenings: bread, hot water, the morning head count. It would be at least nine-thirty before they hauled anybody out for interrogation.

But wait a bit—there was a rattle at the lock, and the lieutenant colonel came in again, with the captain in the background (incongruously high ranks at that hour in the morning, but of course I didn't know how things were done now, and what sort of officer might be in charge of a block), and without asking, "Anybody here beginning with S?" without the slightest hesitation over my name, they let me know by word and gesture that I was to *come along.*

You'd think the place was on fire! In a proper prison it takes you twelve hours to get through the bathhouse and into a cell (incidentally, why hadn't I been made to bathe?), but in this place I'd already been charged, and was off for my first interrogation! They *were* in a hurry.

We set off the same way as yesterday, but when we reached the "Malyarov" office we went in the other direction. Here you are—the medical unit. The same two doctors as yesterday. The officers backed out of the room. The female remained in the background, assumed the role of a nurse. The man was full of concern: how did I feel?

Oh, you brutes, there's still something holding you back, some instruction or other. But I must not give myself away before the interrogation. Strip to the waist. Lie down. Where was your tumor? He knows all about me, this shit, and he palpates me quite skillfully, running his hands exactly around the edge of the scar. Obviously a bona fide doctor. He measures my blood pressure again, and yes, it is rather high for the morning. "What do you generally take for your blood pressure?" No good trying to hide it, and anyway they've heard it over the telephone a hundred times. "Herbs." "Which herbs?" What are they going to do —make me a tincture here? What have I to lose, though? If I can reduce my blood pressure for the interrogation, I shall get through it so much more easily. "Some of them are sold in ready-made infusions," I say cheekily. "Crataegus, for instance, or Leonurus." He glances at the nurse, who dives into the cupboard and is back in a second with the familiar vial of Leonurus. (Hardly surprising, though: eight out of ten prisoners in this place end up with abnormally high blood pressure.) They poured some out, and I drank it. How good it was, on an empty stomach! Nothing could be better!

Back to my cell. The lads couldn't get over it: I was certainly some sort of privileged person, not one of them. I was amused myself; I had heard legends about eminent prisoners, had seen for myself how they had treated MVD Colonel Vorobyov; could I expect something along those lines?

Ah, here was the bread ration. No, ration is wrong: on a tray, through the serving hatch, came some notched loaves—you could break off all you wanted. This was the life! The lads had no appetite at all, and took only half a loaf each. I jumped up from my bed in alarm. "Here, hold on!" I said, and breaking all rules of decorum for privileged prisoners, tarnishing all the legends that might grow up about me, I plunged into the feeding hatch and seized two whole loaves. Then I thought again and put one third of a loaf back.

"What's the idea! We shall chew our way through that batch by this evening."

I made a start there and then. But you can't get used to Lefortovo bread in a day; you can't masticate it just because you know you should. When you're some way down the road to nowhere, you'll manage it.

Look—there was sugar, too, and hot water, which was indeed slightly colored with something or other. The same amount of sugar as in 1945—the motherland had grown no richer—and it wasn't even white lump sugar, but some of Fidel's dark granulated stuff. If you kept it on a bit of paper for a day, the draft would blow it away. Pop it in the hot water and be done with it.

No! I didn't believe it! They had brought some gruel! Gruel too—in the morning? Incredible. And so much of it. Almost a mess tin full—six or seven times the Lubyanka lunchtime portion in the old days. Fattening us up for the slaughter . . . !

Not quite, though. There was no fat with it, of course, but there was salt enough to make your eyes water. Conscientious prisoner though I was, I could not eat that mush. They could break a man that way, quite easily, making everything too salty.

Then came the morning rounds. I was getting bolder all the time, and I took it into my head to make a formal statement—just for laughs, really—that I must have a salt-free diet. (They'd tipped their hand anyway; they couldn't bring anything saltier than that gruel.)

*My wife could not call the Prosecutor's Office till nine, and the wait seemed endless. When the shop opened they bought groceries enough to stand a siege. In the night the world outside seemed to have come to a standstill, but as morning came, hearts sank and energies flagged. What would they learn when the phone rang? What shocks were on the way? Her arms hung limply, as though it were late evening, not early morning. Nine o'clock at last. She calls the man called Balashov. No answer, of course. Calls again and again, every ten minutes. No answer . . . no answer . . . What can it mean? What have they done with him? Nothing but the intermittent buzz of an unanswered phone. This was when everything went dark and she almost fainted: perhaps they've killed him. A nonexistent telephone number, a nonexistent Balashov, nobody will ever lift the receiver, nobody will ever answer. Because they've killed him. Why hadn't she realized it last night? When she was rushing around, finding safer hiding places, burning papers. Wherever she turned in desperation she would come up against a blank wall. Some neighbor advised her to call Andropov. To Soviet minds that was the logical course. But—ask a murderer for information? Not for the world. They would still be around later, and would inform her themselves. But could she stand the wait? . . . And then again, no one had come to search the apartment. Why haven't they come? We can hide everything safely in twenty-four hours. Do they think that they needn't hurry, because we're in their hands anyway? Or perhaps there's nothing to be afraid of at all? If they had killed him, surely they would have rushed to seize everything, down to the last line? She went to do some washing—a lot of children's clothes had accumulated.*

Interrogation time came around, and they sent for the lads one after the other, but not for me. Somewhere out there, dawn was breaking; indeed, it would soon be broad daylight—not in the Lefortovo prison yard, of course, but somewhere up above it. In the yard itself there was a lingering gloom and through the cell window came a yellowish half-light. The infernal lamp in the ceiling would keep up its dreary glare all through the day, as it had through the night.

You couldn't help remembering the luxurious cells in the Lubyanka, especially those on the upper levels. The ministry had been demoted to a "Committee under the Council of Ministers," but its personnel had no doubt expanded, and converted the glorious, the eternally memorable cells of the Inner Prison into offices for themselves.

The restless currency speculator was brought back from his first interrogation, and the puffy one taken off to have a tooth pulled. (Perhaps that was the only reason he had been so withdrawn and preoccupied.) My lad had been formally charged. But he had calmed down a bit after his first interrogation (it often has that effect, the first one: "You deny everything, do you?" "Yes, I do." "Right, then—just sign here and go and think it over." The interrogator only wants to record the point at which his expert labors begin.) I warned the lad of the course that the interrogation might take, how he should set himself precise limits, stick to them as though his life depended on it, have ready respectable excuses wherever retreat was unavoidable. I told him about the methods particularly favored by interrogators. (Why had they pushed me in with him, not into a one-man cell? In the hope that I should confide in him . . . ?) After two nights, when he realized that they were his inevitable destination, he started asking about the camps. So much has changed, but I can tell you about the old ones. . . . I did. His horizon was broadening rapidly. (The immortal soul of a zek was being implanted in a frightened rabbit.) The first sign of it was his curiosity about me: when had I been inside, and what for? I didn't tell him much to begin with, but then I thought: Why not leave a living trace of myself? They may swallow me, and no one will ever see me alive anymore, but this man will tell my story in the camp and his hearers will pass it on.

"Did you ever read something called *Ivan Denisovich?*"

"N-no. But I remember some talk about it. Is that you, then—Ivan Denisovich?"

"No, I'm not the man. . . . But did you ever hear the name Solzhenitsyn?"

"Oh, I know—wasn't there something in *Pravda?*" he said more readily, but in some embarrassment: after all, I had been called a traitor, and I must be upset about it. His curiosity was aroused, he began to remember, he asked questions: Had I capital abroad, then? Couldn't I have got permission to go there?

"I could have."

"So what happened?"

"I didn't go."

"Wh-a-a-t? Wha-a-at??" He was so astounded that he put his feet up on the bed. I told him that the Nobel Prize alone came to seventy thousand rubles. He clutched his head and groaned. The pain he felt was for me: How could I have done it? Think of the cars you could buy with all that money! Think of all the . . . In his expressions of amazement and regret there was no trace of covetousness; he was suffering for me, not for himself! In this typical Soviet citizen's philosophy there was no room for the weird idea that a man might have an opportunity to leave the country with seventy thousand gold rubles waiting for him—and not go. (To understand our *top people,* you need look no higher: what else ever occupies their thoughts except ways and means of building country homes at the state's expense, first for themselves and then for their children? Wasn't that why they had got so furious with me—because they couldn't understand why I wouldn't go voluntarily?)

He sat on the bed with his legs tucked under him, while I paced slowly back and forth, the whole length of the cell, in someone else's stiff shoes, in the dull yellow daylight from the window, and listening to that voice full of keen regret, I began to feel that he was right, that coming here of my own sweet will was suicide. In 1970 the road had been open to me through Stockholm to the idyllic life that some of my literary predecessors had enjoyed in the old days: I could have settled on a secluded estate somewhere, with horses, a stream, wooded walks, rocks, a library, and nothing to do but write for ten or twenty years. But I had decreed otherwise: that whole way of life, now lost in the mists, was not to become a reality, none of the most important works in my life were to be written, and I myself after three more years of homelessness had come to die miserably in jail.

Now I felt sorry. Sorry that I had not gone in 1970 . . .

Not once in three years had I regretted it: I had given them hell! The things I had said to them! Nothing like it had ever been uttered under that regime. And now I had published *Gulag,* from the very best vantage point—from *here!*

I had done my duty. What was there to regret? But still, it's easy enough to accept inevitable death, hard to accept death when you might have chosen to live.

The door. The lieutenant colonel again. For me, then. He beckoned me to follow. Now for my interrogation. I was led downstairs to where the interrogators' offices used to be. And where the admissions "boxes" were now. In the box next to the one in which they had frisked me the night before I saw some togs lying on the table. These were as follows: a cap of sealskin or some damned thing, an overcoat made of—who knows what, a spotless white shirt, a tie, shoelaces—too short and thin for a sparrow to hang himself, but still part of the markings of a *free* man —and instead of my rough, prickly undershirt, the underwear traditional in Russian armies and prisons through the ages. The lieutenant colonel appeared rather embarrassed as he said:

"There you are. Put it all on."

I could see that they meant to pinch my sheepskin and my favorite camel's-hair cardigan.

"What do I want all this for? Just give me *my own* things back! How long can you go on sterilizing them?"

The lieutenant colonel was still more ill at ease.

"Later, later . . . Right now it's quite impossible. . . . Right now you're taking a journey. . . ."

*Taking a journey!* Just what Brigade Commander Travkin* told me when I was first arrested. My *journey* then had been from Germany to a Moscow jail.

"But keep the suit on. . . . What on earth . . . !"

Help! Something had happened to that suit. It hadn't been noticeable in the cell, but here in broad daylight . . . ! You couldn't raise a nap like that if you tried! Where I had been lying on the blanket, both jacket and trousers were covered all over not with fluff or feathers, but with hundreds or rather thousands of tiny white things like dog hairs! The lieutenant colonel sprang into action, summoned a lieutenant with a clothes brush, and as there was a tap handy, ordered him to clean my jacket—no, not like that! Shake off the water first, then brush it! No, brush one way only, can't you! As for me, I did nothing at all to help them. What did I care? I just wanted my sheepskin back, and my camel's-hair cardigan, and my own trousers. . . . They made the jacket look a bit cleaner, and then dealt with the trousers on my person: squatting now in front and now behind, the lieutenant and the lieutenant colonel took turns brushing me down, which was no light work, because the hairs had eaten into the cloth. The best thing would have been to remove each one separately, with the fingernails, but evidently time was desperately short.

Where was I going? I had no doubt about it. To see the government, that very Politburo of theirs, of which Mayakovsky had once dreamed.* At long last we would have our first—and last—discussion. I had at times found myself looking forward to the moment when light would break in on them, when they would suddenly be interested in talking to me —and surely it would be in their interest? I had written *Letter to the Leaders* as a substitute for such a conversation—and with an eye to the next one, I was reluctant to abandon all hope: if the fathers had been ordinary Russians, many of them peasants, surely the children could not all be beyond the pale? Intent only on grabbing, thinking only of themselves, not giving a damn for their country? We cannot give up all hope of converting them: we would be less than men if we did. Surely they are not bereft of every last trace of humanity.

The conversation would be a serious one, perhaps the most important in my life. There was no need to plan it: I had carried a plan in my heart and in my head for a long time. Arguments would suggest themselves; I would be utterly unconstrained, and talk to them as their subordinates never do. . . . The necktie? No, keep it; I won't wear it.

I was dressed. They were in a hurry now: to get me out? They ran off, and didn't return for some time. Were the cars waiting, to take us to Staraya Ploshchad? Nobody came. Nobody came. The lieutenant colonel was back again. Apologizing once more.

"You will have to wait a bit longer. . . ." Though he didn't like saying the horrid, dirty words "in your cell," I saw from his gestures, and our route, that we were on our way back there.

The same landings all over again. I was beginning to know them by heart. No, what they reminded me of was not a circus, but rather a ship beached for repair, with its sails spread flat on deck.

My currency speculators were startled: the white shirt lit up the whole cell. I would have sat down on the blanket, but I couldn't see the lieutenant colonel's work wasted, so I walked the floor instead.

As I paced, I was mentally in conversation with the Politburo. Something told me that given two or three hours, I could budge them, shake their certainty. There would have been no getting through to the fanatics in Lenin's Politburo, or the sheep in Stalin's. But these people I (foolishly?) thought could be reached. Why, even Khrush had shown some signs of understanding.

*The laundry could not occupy her for long; questions began forcing themselves on her clouded mind. What is to be done with the Testament and Program? And with* Live Not by Lies? *They have been deposited at a number of launch pads, ready for lift-off if one of the following things befalls the author: death, arrest, expulsion from Moscow. But what has happened? Is it still in the balance? Still unsettled? Has he been formally arrested yet? Perhaps he is no longer alive? No, they would not have come calling if they had not made up their minds. The only thing to do is to attack!* Launch it! *With yesterday's date. (It was airborne in a matter of hours.) Then Heeb the lawyer rings from Zurich: "How can I be of service to Madame Solzhenitsyn?" She is amused at first, as well as touched: how indeed can he "be of service"? Then the thought flashes through her mind. Of course! She speaks solemnly into the telephone: "I must ask Dr. Heeb to arrange for the immediate publication of all those works of Solzhenitsyn's which have hitherto been kept in reserve." For KGB ears, this. The telephone rings and rings, but she tells herself that the ringing is in someone else's apartment. There can be nothing for her in all these calls. Several of them are from foreign capitals; she can learn nothing from them and has nothing to tell them.*

They come for me. They lead me out. Goodbye now! I set off quickly through the hushed "circus by night," thinking we have some way to go. Not at all; we take the nearby turning again, past the doctor's office, and here are Colonel Komarov and another colonel. I go with them into the office in which I was charged with treason yesterday—only now it is brightly lit against the gloomy day outside—and there at yesterday's desk is yesterday's Malyarov: yes, Malyarov; merely Malyarov. Why, then, have they dressed me up? Once again the same chair is waiting for me in the middle of the room. Once again the senior officers take their seats behind me, in case I fling myself on Malyarov.

In the same sharp voice as yesterday, intoning each word distinctly, and endowing it with the same overstrung emphasis, he reads:

"Decree of the Presidium of the Supreme . . ."

Those few words tell me everything, and I listen to the rest with half an ear, just to make sure.

Oh, how often have they varied the load in the past eighteen hours, trying now to crush me, now to stretch me to the snapping point. But I am thankful to find that I am not losing my normal shape. I was not crushed yesterday, and I shall not break now.

So they had no wish to talk to me. They know it all themselves. Yes, but if you know it all, why are your rockets, your motorized infantry, your KGB saboteurs and extortionists, everywhere in retreat —because they are in retreat, aren't they? The calf butted the oak: a futile enterprise, you might think. The oak has not fallen—but isn't it beginning to give just a little? As for the calf, his forehead is intact, as are his budding horns. He has been bounced back—but bounced who knows where.

But the seconds are running by; I must think carefully.

"I can only go with my family. I must return to my family now."

Malyarov stands up, in the black suit he wears on special occasions and a shirt whiter than mine, moves across the room like an actor taking the center of the stage, and says with his head thrown back:

"Your family will follow you."

"We must all go together."

"That's impossible."

That's it, then. Expatriation—in a way I had never expected. But now that I thought about it, this was the only way for them to be rid of me quickly.

"But what guarantee have I?"

"Who would want to keep you apart?"

True, the outcry would be more than you could stand.

"In that case, I must"—they don't give you a second to think; you're bound to overlook something; it's always the same with them—"I must submit a written statement."

Why I said it I still don't know. It wasn't as though a statement from me would carry any weight if they didn't like it. It was just a bit of old zek's cussedness, just playing for time.

Malyarov thought a bit. "To the Visa and Registration Department? Write away."

"Visa and Registration Department, nothing. The decree is signed by Podgorny. He's the one I must write to."

He thought a bit more. Called me over to his desk, put me at one end of it. Gave me paper.

I write busily, listing my family with their dates of birth. Why I am doing it I just don't know. (Somebody had made a mistake: they had been afraid that I would start breaking the windows, and instead I sat peacefully, writing my application.) What else can I think of?

"I can't go by air."

"Why not?"

"My health won't allow it."

He is grave and still. (It's practically a military operation, this; there might even be a medal in it for him.) Did he just nod? Anyway, he'll think about that too.

Given more time to assess the situation, I would have seen that they couldn't risk a train journey: what if there were demonstrations en route or other undesirable incidents?

Back to the cell. I deliberately kept my hands behind my back; it gave me confidence. When I went in, the light was off. The day was at its peak and they give the electricity a rest between noon and one o'clock. Dear God—the gloom, the stuffiness, the air of death about the place. Yet my steps seemed lighter all the time, my feet touched the floor more lightly. I was soaring, floating up from this tomb. By this morning, I had reconciled myself to the idea that I had two months to live, and even *that* two months under interrogation, with intervals in punishment cells. And suddenly I was not ill at all. I was guilty of nothing, I was bound neither for the operating table nor for the scaffold. I could go on living!

The second lad is missing again, but my sympathizer is agog, and eager to hear my story. But I feel ashamed to tell it. When I had been seen off from the Butyrki prison cells* to freedom (by mistake), I had been in a triumphant mood, and shouted my farewells, but now I felt somehow ashamed. Besides, yet another of the latter-day miracles was the daily appearance of a newspaper in the cell. He knew my name, and tomorrow he would read the decree for himself. He would be even more startled than he had been today: Boy-oh-boy! What lovely punishment!

The flap of the feeding hatch falls open. Lunchtime. We go to get it. Cabbage soup and oatmeal gruel. But the dishes I find in my hands are not the ordinary ones. I can't understand it at first. The lad carries his food to his bed and I take the only chair at the little table. I try my first spoonful of soup. What's this? This soup has never seen salt; it's just as I like it, just as they never could make it in jail. Evidently, they had made it to order for me. I spooned up and slurped every last drop of it; prison soup, yes, but still ordinary thin Russian cabbage soup, not any old dishwater. Next came the oatmeal, with nothing to flavor it, but still by Lubyanka standards it was a quintuple helping, and a great deal thicker at that! In my *Decembrists Without December*, a young Russian kidnapped from Europe recognizes the harsh homeland that has been restored to him in the unpalatable soldiers' gruel at the airdrome in Berlin. In much the same way, I say farewell to Russia in this gruel, this Lefortovo gruel, my last food on Russian soil.

I wasn't given time to finish before the key ground in the lock and I was ordered out. At least I'd bolted every last drop of the soup. The bread I flipped onto the shelf. Who would wrestle with it next? One piece I shoved into my jacket pocket. I might need another chunk before I reached those far-off Western horizons! I shook the lad's hand, wished him the best, and was off. I hadn't, after all, had time to memorize all Lefortovo's corridors thoroughly. There was one place in which they warned me every time not to bump my head.

In the admissions "box" I was given back my watch and my cross, which I signed for. The lieutenant colonel was worried by the bulge in my pocket. I showed him the bread. He hesitated, but let it go.

More waiting. And the sly-looking commandant of Lefortovo jail came in to pass the time with me. He wasn't trying to overawe me with his high gloss this time. In fact, he seemed to be curious about me, strangely drawn to me. As he might be to anything mysterious, inexplicable, exempt from life's normal rules—a transient meteorite, for instance. He even gave me what was apparently meant to be a pleasant smile. He looked me over carefully with his head on one side.

"Which artillery school did you go to?"

"Leningrad, Number Three."

"I was at Number Two. And we're contemporaries."

I thought it funny. At one and the same time, we had been officer trainees running about with empty bellies and dreaming of crossed guns on our collars. But now he wore the MVD insignia.

"Yes . . . We fought on the same side, and now you're on the opposite side of the barricades."

Ugh—that nasty Leninist-Trotskyist cant. Barricades: a blister on the tongues of three generations. The world is covered with barricades, according to them. They cannot even see a dog rose in bloom. Barricades are all very well, but rather a lot of the comfortable furniture seems to have been dragged around to your side. On our side it's "Hands behind your backs!"

We go outside. Once more part of the yard is cordoned off. Once more I take the back seat, squeezed between two of them. And here's the same navigator who came from the house with me yesterday—same cap, same collar. . . . Come to think of it, haven't I seen his face too often before? What a dimwit I am! It's my friend the doctor! The one I saw yesterday and first thing this morning. If I'd used my eyes I would have understood more: the doctor had been my inseparable companion from the moment I had walked through the front door, just one step away with his attaché case. They meant to take good care of me.

The accursed gates opened wide and we were off. Two cars, with four men in the other too: once more there were eight of us. I felt my throat again, experimentally—and they looked apprehensive.

This was the second day of a thaw: the streets were slushy and cars splashed each other. Past the Kursk Station. Past the Three Stations. We turned and turned again—onto the Leningrad Prospect. To the Belorussian Station—through which I had been brought back from Europe under arrest. No, past that too. Along the dirty, slushy prospect into the dirty, cheerless afternoon—it could only be to Sheremetevo. The road I had hated since last summer, since our nightmarish time in Firsanovka.

"I can't go by air," I told the doctor.

He turned around to reply in a perfectly human, unprisonlike voice.

"It's too late to make any changes. The plane's waiting."

(If only I had known, it had been waiting three hours. Passengers, some of them with children, were exhausted by the delay and nobody knew why it was. Two inspection teams, one after another, had checked every bit of the plane. Inquiries had been made from Europe; our people had lied, said there was fog.)

"But I shall be with you, and I have all the necessary medicines."

Another half-circle, around the steps this time—in case I dive off and make a run for it. The steps leading to the forward passenger cabin; with me in the cabin are seven men in plain clothes, eight including the doctor. A complete change of guard, except for the doctor. (They had

had to make their security arrangements, familiarize themselves with the plane.) They showed me exactly where to sit: Here, look, middle row on the aisle. There was a neighbor between me and the window, two of them behind us, and one in front. Two more across the aisle. And another two behind them. So that I was encircled. Here comes the doctor bending over me solicitously and explaining which medicine he advises me to take now, which in half an hour's time, and which in two hours, taking each of the tablets out of its factory wrapping while I watch, to show me it's not poison. One of them, however, looks like a sedative to me. I shan't take that. (Is it to calm my nerves for the journey or to stupefy me?) "Is it such a long flight, then?" I ask him innocently. "How many hours will it be?" He is even more disingenuously at a loss: "I don't know exactly. . . ." No more waiting. The hatches are slammed shut, the seat-belt light is on. My neighbor, too, is most attentive. "Haven't you flown before? It fastens like this; look. . . . Have a sweet or two—they really help at takeoff." From the stewardess, in dark blue. She's as innocent as can be. No idea who her customers are. Ordinary Soviet citizens, what else?

The aircraft taxis through the gloom and the slushy snow. Past other aircraft, or are they buildings—I don't try to distinguish. I loathe every one of them, as I loathe everything to do with airports. But all this together is my last sight of Russia.

I am leaving Russia for the second time. The first time was with our advancing army, in a front-line truck:

> Make way, make way, you alien millions!
> Throw wide your gates, O alien land!*

And just once, I had returned: from Germany, all the way to Moscow, with three Geebees for companions. And now I was leaving Moscow with others of their kind, eight of them this time. It was like my arrest in reverse.

As the aircraft took off with a shudder, I crossed myself and bowed to the receding land.

The Geebees goggled.

*There could be nothing of importance in all those telephone calls. . . . Suddenly the apartment rang with shrill cries: "He's flying! They've expelled him! To West Germany!" There were calls to say that these rumors came from friends of Böll—he was expecting his guest in Frank-*

*furt. Was it likely? Could it be believed? Maybe* they *had started the rumor themselves, to divert attention from their dungeons. "I'll believe it only when I hear A.I.'s voice." How had "Böll's friends" come into it? This was a stunt of some sort. If that was what they meant to do, why come for him like that—eight to one? Why disgrace themselves in the whole world's eyes by arresting him, just to deport him? But the agencies kept ringing, one after another, to say that the Ministry of the Interior in North Rhine–Westphalia had confirmed the news: "He is expected in West Germany . . ." or rather, "He's already arrived and is on his way to Böll's residence!" Was it true, then? . . . But why was everybody so happy? This was a misfortune, an act no less brutally arbitrary than imprisonment in a camp. . . . Expatriation: a nasty, hissing, alien word . . . Now that he was expatriated, what next? Confiscation? Oh, dear, I should have distributed it all when I could; I've missed my chance! It rankles. How it rankles. More calls, more congratulations. On our misfortune . . . ?*

What followed is all more familiar to my readers than to me—our passage now through the clouds, now over the clouds, the sunlight on what looks like a snowbound plain. Once we are set on course, I do some thinking: What time is it? About 2 P.M., 15 degrees past high noon. What is our course in relation to the sun? I find that we are on a line between Minsk and Kiev. This means that we can hardly land anywhere in the U.S.S.R., and that means, that means . . . Vienna? I can't imagine where else. I know nothing about airline routes or airports.

We might be hanging motionless in the air. Ahead of us, to the left, there is dazzling sunlight on fields of snowy cloud. Whereas cells for those who think differently are so constructed that by now the night bulbs in the ceiling are burning again, and will burn on till noon tomorrow.

O Lord, if Thou restorest my life to me, how can I reduce those cells to ruins?

I have moved around rather more than I care to in something under twenty-four hours. Now I have a comfortable seat. Sweets to suck. And in my pocket, a piece of Lefortovo bread. I am like someone in a fairy tale, escaping from some wicked enchantment, tearing off and carrying away a lump of something solid to show that it *did really happen* and wasn't a dream.

Not that I would have needed this hunk of bread to remind me.

The flight seemed symbolic: a clean break with the fifty-five years behind me, in transition to whatever number of years, somewhere or other, awaited me. Suspended there. While you ask yourself: Have I lived as I should? I have. Then make no mistake now: this is a new world, with new difficulties.

So I hung in the air thinking, and had neither the time to spare, nor even the wish, to study my escorts. One of them pulled out a radio, grinning all over his ugly mug—great fun, this job. He was dying to switch it on, and asked one of the others. (I don't know which of them was senior; no one was obviously in charge.) Ostentatiously I frowned and shook my head, as much as to say, "It disturbs me" (stops me from thinking). Hands were waved at him, and he put it away. The two behind somehow didn't look the *right sort*. They were reading German newspapers: *Frankfurter Allgemeine*. What were they, diplomats? The Geebees meanwhile were expiring with boredom, reading the advertising material scattered around, brochures and . . . timetables. Aeroflot timetables? Idly, as though I, too, was as bored as I could be, I picked up a timetable and just as indolently looked through it. I don't know one plane from another, but there were lots of flights listed here, Vienna among them, and Zurich too, but the time . . . not one of them would fit. Not a single plane left for any suitable destination in Europe between one-thirty and two o'clock. So they must have laid on a special plane for me. Why not? Soviet coffers are full, and we Russian revolutionaries do things in style.

You needn't even think. Perfect equilibrium. Hang there, and realize that life holds few such hours. However you look at it, it's a victory. The calf has proved no weaker than the oak. However I tried, I couldn't collect my thoughts. At home . . . what sort of haul had the searchers had? (It didn't disturb me to think of it, as it had in the night.) And what was happening to my dear ones now?

*By now all radio stations had repeated it ten times over: He's flying —he's landed—he's on his way to Böll. Then, when no one any longer doubted it: "The plane will arrive in an hour and a half." Why, then, had the minister announced, "He landed some time ago"? And what about all those reporters? Did it mean no one had yet seen him in the flesh? Was it just a stunt? Wasn't he flying at all? Was the real misfortune yet to come? Here it came! A rush of reports, one canceling another. Still in flight. Already landed. Hasn't yet left Moscow. Flight postponed. At last everything was clear. They were taking him somewhere.*

*They'd take him to Egypt or Cuba, throw him out, and disclaim all responsibility. But I'll stick in your throats and choke you, you scoundrels! I'll raise a racket such as you never heard before.*

The stewardess comes around with coffee and biscuits. I'll drink the stuff. It all helps. I can save my bit of bread for later. The doctor leans over again: How am I? Any funny feelings? Would I like this other tablet? He really has been nice, ever since reveille in Lefortovo—and he's probably spent the night in the jail too. "Do you mind if I ask your name and patronymic?" He turns to stone at once and says in a stony voice, "Ivan Ivanych." I have made myself cheap! . . .

Wait a minute. I've been deprived of my precious citizenship. So now I'm a free man. So why don't I go to the lavatory? Where is it? Probably in the tail. Without a word to anyone, I stand up like a free agent and hurry off to the rear. So quickly that the commotion begins two seconds late, but is none the smaller for that. I open the door and there behind is another passenger compartment with room for twenty —completely empty! Never mind; socialism can afford such luxuries. I continue on my way, but three men, "Ivan Ivanych" among them, overtake me. What's this? he asks. What do you think? I'm going to the lavatory. Well, you're going the wrong way; it isn't there, it's in the nose. In the nose, is it? Right, then. I turn back. This I can still just about interpret as exaggerated courtesy. But when we reach the nose I can't shut the door after me: two Geebees barge in, without, however, challenging my priority. I remember my prison manners. Want to watch, do you? All right, then, this is how men do it. Like this, see—nothing to it. Excuse me, please. Of course. They step aside. But when I get back, I find a different one sitting between me and the window, savager-looking. The first had fallen down on the job.

I look my new neighbor over carefully. What a thug! Then I look closely at the others. Three or four of them there have almost certainly killed before now, and if any of them has missed that experience he will be ready to distinguish himself this very day. Yes, this very day . . . What a clod I am, sitting here taking life easy. How could I have believed them? Malyarov! Podgorny! An old zek like me—I've done nothing but make mistakes for the past two days. I must be out of practice. What real zek—"thin, ringing and transparent"—would dare to trust a Soviet procurator, or a Soviet president, for just one minute, trust him an inch? I, of all people—surely I've heard stories enough about our bully boys, just after the war, in every capital of Europe, bundling their victims into cars in the street, in broad daylight, and carrying them off to an embassy basement. Then exporting them wherever they pleased. There are plenty of them in every Soviet embassy—subterranean rooms with stout stone walls. It didn't have to be a cell in Lefortovo.

In Vienna shortly, in nervous neutral Austria, an embassy car will pull up right to the steps of the empty plane, these eight will manhandle me into it without really exerting themselves (or, for that matter, make a bundle of me here in the plane and carry me out that way; how often I've heard such stories!). They'll keep me in the embassy a few days. The decree has been promulgated, I have been expelled, and they are under no obligation to notify reporters when and where to. In a few days' time I shall be found dead beside an Austrian highway—and why should the Soviet government be held responsible for that? For so many years they were, alas, responsible for me, and in that lay my safety. But now?

This whole plan, which had suddenly become clear in my mind, was so true to the style of the KGB that I saw no need to verify my idea or explore it further. Why hadn't I seen through it at once? And what now? This is what: I must be as casual as possible, relaxed and limp and smiling; must even exchange a word or two with one of them to show how completely I trust them. (Just as long as I'm not bundled up, just as long as I get out of here on my own two legs. I know nothing at all about airport regulations, but I cannot believe that a plane can land without a single policeman on hand. And if there is just one, I shall manage a loud shout. This is where my German, learned at school and long neglected, must come to my rescue. I struggle to form a few sentences in my mind: *"Herr Polizei! Achtung! Ich bin Schriftsteller Solschenizyn! Ich bitte um Ihre Hilfe und Verteidigung!"* Shall I have time to get all that out? If I shout even half of it before they gag me, he will understand!)

For the present I just observe them. Half-doze and observe them. What can I read in their faces? What do they seem to be saying to each other? Does it look as though they are actively preparing for something? What objects have they brought along? Most of them have their hands empty; in other words, free. . . . We've been flying nearly three hours now. A longish time. How long does it take to this blessed Vienna? I have no idea; I have never felt the need to know. Ah, now we're beginning our descent. I can't resist one more little test: I amble along the now familiar path to the forward lavatory. Within ten minutes of the airport, am I still a zek, or a zek no longer? Two of them follow me, rather reproachfully; why didn't I wait? (So that one of my escorts would have a chance to take up his position in front of me.) "Does it really matter anymore?" I ask with a smile.

"Anyway, let me open the door for you." Once again, they stand together in the doorway, so that I cannot shut myself in. A chill runs down my spine. They have something up their sleeves, all right. (I understand it now, of course: they had instructions not to let me commit suicide, or cut myself, or injure myself in some other way, as jailbirds sometimes will to avoid being transferred. They would look pretty silly bringing me out of the plane bleeding from my wounds.)

Right. I sit in my old seat and gaze about me, looking limp and apathetic. We are going down. Down, down. I can make out a big city. On a river. Not such a wide river, but not a small one. The Danube? How do I know? We describe a circle. I don't seem to see Vienna's parks and suburbs, there's more industry than I thought, but where won't you find it nowadays? . . . Here's the airport. We taxi along the approaches. One building, looming above the others, bears the legend "Frankfurt am Main." Well, I'm . . . We taxi, and turn. . . . Yes, there are policemen, and quite a few of them, if I am right about their uniform. In general, there seem to be a fair number of people about, a couple of hundred perhaps, so that there will be somebody to shout to.

We come to a stop. The steps are towed up outside. Some of *our* party run into the pilot's compartment and back. I can't wait, though —and anyway, any passenger automatically looks around for his overcoat (in my case, a Lefortovo overcoat, of fraternal Czechoslovak cut), wondering whether to put it on. They block my way immediately, and quite peremptorily order me to sit down. I don't like this. I sit. Three or four of them bustle about, while the rest sit around me like tigers. I sit unconcernedly: you're right, what's the use of stewing in that overcoat? Suddenly an order, loud and harsh, reaches the passenger compartment from the entrance to the pilot's cabin:

"Put his hat and coat on him! Get him out!"

Just as I feared. You can only shout orders like that about a zek. Right —I'm silently rehearsing my German sentences. However, I put my coat on with my own hands. Then my hat. At least I'm not being done up in a bundle. Suddenly, by the entrance to the pilot's cabin, one of the eight rushes at me, stands face to face, chest to chest, and in the space between belly and belly hands me five pieces of paper—five hundred German marks.

Well, I'll be . . . ! As I'm still a zek, I might as well take it. I accept their bread and their cabbage soup, don't I? Still, I make a show of politeness:

"May I inquire to whom I owe this money?"

(They've drunk enough of our blood in their time. When, since 1918, did they ever earn a single Russian ruble with their own hands?)

"You don't, you don't. . . ."

He vanished from my path before I could get a good look at his features.

In fact, my path was quite clear. The Geebees stood aside, the pilot got out.

A voice says, "Go on."

On I go. Down the ramp. Where are the two companions who should be boxing me in? I step over one, two, three cleats. I can't help looking around, in bewilderment. They are not coming! The forces of darkness stay put in the plane, all of them.

No one else is following me. There are two passenger compartments, but I turn out to be the only passenger.

Now I must watch where I put my feet, so as not to stumble. But I take a quick look in front of me too. A couple of hundred people are standing in a wide circle, obviously around the safety barrier, applauding, taking photographs, some turning the handles of motion picture cameras. Have they been expecting me? Do they know all about it? It's the obvious thing to happen, but I wasn't expecting to be met. (I had quite forgotten that a man cannot be brought into a country without its consent. In the Communist code of behavior, no one need be asked: no one, for instance, was asked if we could land in Prague on the night of 20–21 August.)

At the foot of the steps stands a very pleasant-looking man, with a smile on his face, who says in quite good Russian:

"I'm Peter Dingens, representing the Ministry of Foreign Affairs of the Federal Republic."

A woman comes up and presents me with some flowers.

It is 5:05 P.M., Moscow time, exactly twenty-four hours since they shoved their way into my apartment, falling over each other and giving me no time to get ready. . . . No day, of course, should be quite so full.

But now a second, equally eventful, twenty-four hours is beginning.

I am driven from the airport in a police car, by the emergency exit. My companions suggest that we go to Böll's place, and at once we are speeding along the autobahn, talking about this *new* life of mine: it has already begun.

We are speeding along at 75 mph, but another, even faster police car overtakes us and orders us to turn off the road. A red-haired young man jumps out and presents me with a huge bouquet, explaining that it is "from the Minister of the Interior for North Rhine–Westphalia. The Minister believes that this is the first time you have been given a bouquet by a Minister of the Interior."

I should say so! It is indeed! From *our* ministers of the interior I might get a pair of handcuffs. They had even refused to let me live with my family.

*The foreign correspondents in Moscow had been informed of the decree depriving me of citizenship. "His family can join him whenever he wishes": "I shan't believe it until I hear his voice." Now there was a broadcast from West Germany: details of the reception at the airport. This couldn't be pure invention—it couldn't have been an actor, could it? But the* New York Times *correspondent phoned: "I've just called Böll and spoken to Solzhenitsyn. . . ." And at last, he was on the phone himself. To watch her talking to him, some forty people, friends and acquaintances, crowded into the study with the two desks, the room in which only yesterday she and he had been finishing their work in tense silence, into which the Geebees had irrupted later on, and in which, still later, so much paper had been burned. He told her that he had been charged with* treason . . . *dressed from head to foot in Geebee clothes . . . told her about Colonel Komarov. . . . In Moscow there was a rumor, launched in haste, before they could tidy up the loose ends, that he had voluntarily chosen expatriation rather than imprisonment. "You didn't sign any undertakings, did you?" "Certainly not; I never even thought of it." Now he would pitch into them! Now that he was out, he would let them have it! . . .*

That evening, in Böll's little village, we threaded our way between two rows of reporters' cars, already parked along the narrow lanes. We fled from the photographers' flashes into the house, and we could hear noisy reporters outside until late at night and again from early morning. Dear Heinrich let his work slide, poor fellow, while he lavished hospitality on me. In the morning I was told that I could not avoid going outside, should not deny the photographers their prey, must not refuse to say something.

Say what, though? All my life I had been tortured by the impossibility of speaking the truth aloud. My whole life had been spent in hacking my way to an open space where I could tell the truth in public. Now, at last, I was free, as I had never been before, no ax was poised above my head, and dozens of microphones belonging to the world's most important press agencies were held out toward my lips. Say something! It would indeed be unnatural not to say something! Now I could make the weightiest pronouncements, and they would be carried far and wide, to the ends of the earth. . . . But inside me something had snapped. Perhaps because I had been transplanted so quickly that I hadn't even had time to decide how I felt about it, let alone to prepare a speech. That was part of it. But there was something more. I suddenly felt that I would demean myself if I indulged in abuse from a distance, if I spoke out where everyone speaks out, where speaking out is permitted. The words came of their own accord:

"I said quite enough while I was in the Soviet Union. Now I shall be silent for a while."

Today, from this distance, I believe that I did right, that my instinct did not let me down. (When my family arrived in Zurich later on, the reporters were once again dying to hear something from me, assuming that I would let fly now that I had nothing at all to fear. But once again, nothing crystallized, I had no statement to make.)

*"I shall be silent for a while."* I meant, of course, silent before the microphones, but from my very first hours, my very first minutes there, I have seen my existence in Europe as one of purposeful activity, free at last of all restraint: for twenty-seven years I had been writing for the desk drawer, and however much you publish at a distance, you cannot do it as it should be done. Only now can I bring in my harvest like a good husbandman. For me the main thing was and is this: I have been released from Lefortovo, and sure death, to publish my books.

Back home, in Russia, my statement was an enigma and open to misinterpretation. What did I mean by saying, "I shall be silent"? I had to speak for all those who were gripped by the windpipe—how could I be silent? For them, back home, the important thing was the violence that had been done to me and was still being done to them. How could

I be silent? They heard their feelings best expressed in Regelson's letter [Document 38], which echoed the thunderclap of Lermontov's "Death of a Poet." For one moment of mental aberration, they thought: "Better a Soviet camp than live out your days abroad."

Life has so many different jolts and jars—and when the closest of friends are jolted apart even for a day, they cease to think alike.

*Made him wear Geebee clothes! Revolting! What about his own clothes, from his days of exile, the clothes in which the writer Solzhenitsyn seemed to have been born? Were they to be left there? The dirt of the place would stick to them. It was as though they still had his body. She must recover them. But how could she get into Lefortovo? There was no entry. Telephone? One of those numbers you won't find in the book. Call one of the interrogators? Yes; some of our friends knew their tormentors' names. But the interrogator they phoned gave a further number, from which there was no reply. The Public Prosecutor's Office? "We have no telephone number for the Lefortovo prison." "But it's you who took Solzhenitsyn there." "We can tell you nothing." Somebody remembered that Thursday was the day for handing in parcels at Lefortovo. She went straight there, and thumped on the closed window: "Somebody call Colonel Komarov." There was an elaborate rattling of locks somewhere in the wall and out jumped two adjutants to stand to attention on either side of the corpulent, hoary-headed, pompous—*

*"Commandant of the Lefortovo Isolation Prison, Colonel Petrenko."*

*From this side of the barricade it's pretty hopeless trying to track down names, let alone things. They've been burned. Burned the very same day, he says. Or shared out, perhaps, among friends and colleagues? Or kept as disguises for undercover men?*

There were heavier tasks ahead! She now had to begin, and carry through, the most important thing of all: transfer to Switzerland by land, sea or air my whole enormous archive, including twelve years of preparatory materials for several "Knots" to come, without losing a single piece of paper, not even an ordinary file folder, and put it all in the same drawers of the same desk when it arrived. On the way, she must not fail to carry every single page of importance (and I had few that were unimportant) through the steel ring of controls at the frontier, must give them no chance to use the dozen photocopying machines kept ready in the customs sheds, must above all not let them take anything *away* from her, because it is impossible, physically impossible, for the Soviet regime to release so much as a single sheet of paper that is not to its liking.

My wife succeeded in this task. Otherwise, here in exile I would have been a helpless cripple, lamenting my plight, not a writer.

How she did it is yet another story, which I ought to include in this very book. But enough is enough. . . .

*Sternenberg, Zurich Plateau*
*June 1974*

# APPENDIXES

Related
Documentary
Materials

1    Letter to Komoto Sedze
     Moscow, 15 November 1966

I am very touched by your kind invitation to give Japanese newspaper readers a New Year's message. I have copies of all three Japanese editions of *One Day in the Life of Ivan Denisovich*. Although I cannot form any judgment of the translations, I am delighted with the handsome appearance of these books.

Hitherto I have always refused to give interviews or to address messages to newspaper readers. I have, however, recently reconsidered this decision. You will be the first to be granted such an interview.

Let me answer your questions.

1. How do I feel about the reactions of readers and critics to my works?

The avalanche of readers' letters when my works were first published was for me one of the most moving and powerful experiences of my life. I spent many years as a working writer with no readers at all, or fewer than you could count on your fingers. This made my awareness of being read by the whole country an even more vivid sensation.

2. What can I tell you about *Cancer Ward?*

*Cancer Ward* is a long story, twenty-five signatures in length and consisting of two parts. Part One I completed in spring 1966, but I have still not been able to find a publisher. Part Two I hope to complete shortly. The action takes place in 1955 in the oncological clinic of a major Soviet hospital in the south. I was a patient there myself, not expected to live, and I make use of my personal impressions. The story, however, is not only about a hospital, because approached by art, every individual phenomenon becomes a "bundle of intersecting planes," to use a mathematical analogy: several planes of reality are unexpectedly seen to intersect at the chosen point.

3. My literary plans for the future.

Answering a question like this makes sense for a writer who has already published, or presented on the stage, his previous works. But that is not the case with me. My major novel *(The First Circle)* has not yet been published, nor have some of my shorter stories, and my plays *(The Love Girl and the Innocent* and

457

*The Light That Is in You)* have not been performed. In these circumstances I have no particular desire to speak about "literary plans," because they have no practical significance.

The literary form that attracts me most is that of the "polyphonic" novel (with no main hero, the most important character in any chapter being the one whom the narrative "catches up with" at that point), which accurately portrays the time and place of the action.

4. My attitude to Japan, its people and its culture.

It is always my endeavor to write compactly, that is, to pack a great deal into a small space. To me, as a layman and at a distance, this appears to be one of the most important traits in the Japanese national character—the geography of the country has itself helped to develop this trait in the Japanese. This gives me a feeling of "kinship" with the Japanese character, although the feeling has never been accompanied by any special study of Japanese culture on my part. (An exception is the philosophy of Yamaga Soko, even a superficial acquaintance with which has made an indelible impression on me.) For a large part of my life I have been either deprived of freedom or preoccupied with mathematics and physics, which alone gave me the means of existence, and the rest of my time I have devoted to my own literary work, so that I am not very well informed about cultural events in the modern world, and know little about contemporary foreign writers, artists, theater and cinema. This applies to Japan as to other countries. I have had a chance to see only one Japanese theatrical presentation—the Kabuki theater—and three Japanese films, but that is all. Of these, *Naked Island* made a particularly strong impression.

I have a deep respect for the extraordinary talents and capacity for work that the Japanese people demonstrate under permanently difficult natural conditions.

5. What view do I take of the writer's duties in defense of peace?

I shall broaden the scope of this question. The fight for peace is only part of the writer's duties to society. Not one little bit less important is the fight for social justice and for the strengthening of spiritual values in his contemporaries. This, and nowhere else, is where the effective defense of peace must begin— with the defense of spiritual values in the soul of every human being.

I was brought up in the traditions of Russian literature, and I cannot imagine myself working as a writer without such aims.

I wish my Japanese readers a happy New Year!

A. Solzhenitsyn

2    Letter to the Fourth Congress of the Union of Soviet Writers
       (in lieu of a speech)

To the Presidium and Delegates/Members of the U.S.W./Editors of Literary Newspapers and Magazines

Not having access to the platform, I ask the congress to discuss:

I. The no longer tolerable oppression to which our literature has been subjected for decades by the censorship, and to which the Writers' Union can no longer submit.

The censorship, which is not provided for in the constitution and is therefore illegal—a fact that is never publicly mentioned—broods over our literature, using the name of Glavlit as its smoke screen, and gives people completely ignorant of literature arbitrary powers over writers. A survival of the Middle Ages, censorship has managed, Methuselah-like, to drag out its existence almost to the twenty-first century. Perishable, it attempts to arrogate to itself the prerogative of imperishable time—that of separating good books from bad.

Our writers are not supposed to have the right, are not allowed the right, to express their cautionary judgments about the moral life of man and society, or to expound in their own way our social problems, or the historical experience that our country has acquired at the cost of so much suffering. Works that might express what the people urgently need to express, writers who might have a timely and salutary influence in the realm of the spirit or on the development of a social awareness, are banned or mutilated by the censorship on the basis of considerations that are petty, egotistical and—from the national point of view—short-sighted.

Excellent manuscripts by young authors, as yet entirely unknown, are nowadays rejected by editors solely on the ground that they "won't get through." Many members of the Union, even some who are delegates at this congress, know how they themselves have bowed to the pressures of the censorship and made concessions affecting the structure and message of their books—changing chapters, pages, paragraphs or sentences, giving them innocuous titles—just for the sake of seeing them finally in print, and by doing so have done irreparable damage to the content and to their artistic procedures. It is an understood quality of literature that talented works suffer most disastrously from all these distortions, while untalented works are not affected by them. Indeed, it is the best of our literature that is published in mutilated form.

Meanwhile, the censor's labels—"ideologically harmful," "corrupt," and so forth—are proving ephemeral and unstable; in fact, are changing before our very eyes. Even Dostoyevsky, the pride of world literature, was at one time not published in our country (and his works are still not published in full); he was excluded from the school curriculum, made inaccessible to readers and reviled. For how many years was Yesenin considered "counterrevolutionary"? People were even sent to jail for reading his books. Wasn't Mayakovsky called "an anarchistic political hooligan"? For decades the imperishable poetry of Akhmatova was considered anti-Soviet. The first timid printing of the dazzling Tsvetayeva ten years ago was declared a "gross political error." Only after a delay of twenty to thirty years were Bunin, Bulgakov and Platonov returned to us. Inevitably, Mandelstam, Voloshin, Gumilev and Klyuyev will follow in their turn, and at some time or other we shall be forced to "recognize" even Zamyatin and Remizov. The decisive moment in this process comes with the death of a troublesome writer, after which he is sooner or later returned to us with an "explanation of errors." It is not so very long since the name of Pasternak could not be spoken aloud; but then he died, and ever since, his books have been published and poems by him are quoted even at ceremonial occasions.

Pushkin's words proved truly prophetic: *"They are capable of loving only the dead."*

But the belated publication of books and "authorization" of names does not make up for either the social or the artistic losses suffered by our people as a consequence of these monstrous delays and the suppression of artistic consciousness. (In fact, there were writers in the 1920s—Pilnyak, Platonov, Mandelstam—who called attention at a very early stage both to the beginnings of the "personality cult" and to the peculiar traits of Stalin's character; but these writers were silenced and destroyed instead of being listened to.) Literature cannot develop in the categories of "permitted" and "not permitted," "this you can write about, that you can't." A literature that is not the breath of life for the society of its time, that dares not communicate its own pain and its own fears to society, that does not warn in time against threatening moral and social dangers, does not deserve the name of literature; it is only a façade. Such a literature loses the confidence of its own people, and its published works are pulped instead of read.

Our literature has lost the leading position it occupied at the end of the last century and the beginning of this one, and it has lost the brilliance of experimentation that distinguished it in the 1920s. To the entire world the literary life of our country now appears immeasurably more colorless, trivial and inferior than it actually is—than it would be if it were not confined and hemmed in. Not only does our country lose by this—in world opinion—but world literature is the poorer for it too. If the world had unrestricted access to all the fruits of our literature, if it were enriched by our spiritual experience, the whole artistic evolution of the world would move in a different way, acquiring a new stability and rising indeed to new artistic heights.

*I propose that the congress demand and ensure the abolition of all censorship, open or hidden, of imaginative literature and release publishing houses from the obligation to obtain clearance for every printed page.*

II. The duties of the Union toward its members.

These duties are not clearly formulated in the statutes of the Soviet Writers' Union (under "Protection of Copyrights" and "Measures for the Protection of Other Rights of Writers"), and at the same time, in the course of a third of a century it has become lamentably clear that the Union has not defended either the "other" rights or even the copyrights of persecuted writers.

Many writers have been subjected during their lifetime to abuse and slander in the press and from the platform without being afforded the physical possibility of replying. More than that, they have been exposed to violence and personal persecution (Bulgakov, Akhmatova, Tsvetayeva, Pasternak, Zoshchenko, Andrei Platonov, Aleksandr Grin, Vasily Grossman). Not only did the Writers' Union not make its own publications available to these writers for purposes of reply and justification, not only did it not spring to their defense, but its leaders were always first among the persecutors. Names that will be the glory of our twentieth-century poetry found themselves on the list of those expelled from the Union or not even admitted to it in the first place. *A fortiori,* the leadership of the Union cravenly abandoned to their distress those for whom persecution ended in exile, labor camps and death (Pavel Vasilyev, Mandelstam, Artem Vesely, Pilnyak, Babel, Tabidze, Zabolotsky, and others). The list must be curtailed at "and others." We learned after the Twentieth Congress of the Party that there were more than six hundred completely innocent writers whom the Union had obediently handed over to their fate in prisons and camps. However, the roll is even longer, and its curled-up end cannot be and will never be read by our eyes. It contains the names of young prose writers and poets whom we may have known only accidentally through personal encounters, whose talents were destroyed in camps before they could blossom, whose writings never got further than the offices of the state security service in the days of Yagoda, Yezhov, Beria and Abakumov.

There is no historical necessity for the newly elected leadership of the Union to share responsibility for the past with its predecessors.

*I propose that all guarantees provided by the Union for the defense of members subjected to slander and unjust persecutions be clearly formulated in Paragraph 22 of the Union statutes, so that past illegalities will not be repeated.*

If the congress does not remain indifferent to what I have said, I also ask that it consider the interdictions and persecution which I myself have endured.

1. It will soon be two years since the state security authorities took from me my novel *The First Circle* (comprising thirty-five signatures), which has held up its submission to publishers. Instead, in my own lifetime, against my will and even without my knowledge, this novel has been "published" in an unnatural "closed" edition for reading in an unidentified select circle. I have been unable to obtain a public reading and open discussion of the novel, or to prevent misuse and plagiarism. My novel is shown to literary bureaucrats, but concealed from most writers.

2. Together with this novel, my literary archive dating back fifteen to twenty years, and containing things that were not intended for publication, was taken from me. Now, heavily slanted excerpts from these papers have also been covertly "published" and are being disseminated within the same circles. The play *The Feast of the Victors,* which I wrote in verse and memorized in a prison camp (where I wore a four-digit number, and where, condemned to die by starvation, we were forgotten by society, while *no one* outside the camps spoke out against repressions)—this long-abandoned play is being ascribed to me as my very latest work.

3. For three years now, an irresponsible campaign of slander has been conducted against one who fought all through the war as a battery commander and received military decorations. It is being said that I served time as a criminal, or surrendered to the enemy (I was never a prisoner of war), that I "betrayed" my country and "served the Germans." That is the interpretation being put now on the eleven years I spent in camps and in exile for having criticized Stalin. This slander is being spread in secret briefing sessions and meetings by people holding official positions. I have tried in vain to stop the slander by appealing to the board of the Writers' Union of the R.S.F.S.R. and to the press.

The board did not even reply, and not a single paper printed my answer to the slanderers. On the contrary, slander against me from official platforms has intensified and become more vicious within the last year, making use of distorted material from my confiscated archive, while I have no way of replying.

4. My novel *Cancer Ward* (comprising twenty-five signatures), the first part of which was approved for publication by the Prose Section of the Moscow writers' organization, cannot be published by chapters (rejected by five magazines), still less in its entirety (rejected by *Novy Mir, Prostor* and *Zvezda*).

5. The play *The Love Girl and the Innocent,* accepted in 1962 by the "Sovremennik" Theater, has so far not been approved for performance.

6. The screenplay *Tanks Know the Truth,* the stage play *The Light That Is in You,* the short stories "Right Hand," "What a Pity" and my series of "Miniatures" cannot find a producer or a publisher.

7. My stories published in *Novy Mir* have never been reprinted in book form, having been rejected everywhere (by the Sovetski Pisatel and the State Literary Publishing Houses, and by Biblioteka Ogonka). They thus remain inaccessible to the general reading public.

8. I have also been prevented from having any other contacts with readers, through public readings of my works (in November 1966, nine out of eleven scheduled meetings were canceled at the last moment), or through readings over the radio. Even the simple act of giving someone a manuscript for "reading and copying" has now become a criminal act (ancient Russian scribes were permitted to do this five centuries ago).

Thus my work has been completely suppressed, locked away and slanderously misrepresented.

Faced with these flagrant infringements of my copyright and "other" rights, will the Fourth Congress defend me or will it not? It seems to me that the choice is not without importance to the literary future of some of the delegates themselves.

I am of course confident that I shall fulfill my duty as a writer in all circumstances—from the grave even more successfully and incontrovertibly than in my lifetime. No one can bar the road to truth, and to advance its cause I am prepared to accept even death. But may it be that repeated lessons will finally teach us not to stay the writer's pen during his lifetime?

This has never yet added luster to our history.

16 May 1967                                                          A. Solzhenitsyn


3     To the Secretariat of the Board of the Union of Writers of the U.S.S.R.

To all Secretaries of the Board

Although it had the support of more than a hundred writers, my letter to the Fourth Writers' Congress has been neither published nor answered. All that has happened is that rumors—all along the same lines and evidently from a single source—have been spread to pacify public opinion: rumors that my archives and my novel have been returned to me and that *Cancer Ward* and a book of stories are on press. But this, as you know, is all lies.

In an exchange of views with me on 12 June 1967, Secretaries of the Board of the Union of Writers of the U.S.S.R. G. Markov, K. Voronkov, S. Sartakov and L. Sobolev declared that the board of the Union of Writers considered it a duty to refute publicly the base slander that has been spread about me and my military record. However, not only has no refutation followed, but the slanders continue; at confidential briefing sessions, at meetings of activists and at seminars for agitators, more fantastic nonsense is being disseminated about me— that I have defected to the U.A.R., for instance, or to England. (I would like to assure the slanderers that I am less likely to run away than they are). Prominent persons persistently express their regret that I did not die in the camp, that I was ever liberated. (However, the same regret was voiced by some people as soon as *One Day* was published. This book is now being secretly withdrawn from circulation by public libraries.)

These same secretaries of the board promised at least to "look into the question" of publishing my latest long story, *Cancer Ward*. But in the space of three months—a quarter of a year—no progress has been made in this direction either. During these three months, the forty-two secretaries of the board have been unable to make an evaluation of the story or to make a recommendation as to whether it should be published. The story has been in this same strange and equivocal state—no direct prohibition, no direct permission—for over a year, since the summer of 1966. While the journal *Novy Mir* would now like to publish the story, it still awaits permission to do so.

Does the secretariat believe that my story will silently disappear as a result of these endless delays, that it will cease to exist, so that the secretariat will not have to take a vote as to whether to include it in or exclude it from the literature of this country? While this is going on, the book is being read avidly, especially by writers. On the initiative of readers, it has already been circulated in hundreds of typewritten copies. At the 12 June meeting I warned the secretariat that we must make haste to publish the story if we wished to see it appear first in Russian, that under the circumstances we could not prevent its unauthorized appearance in the West.

After the senseless delay of many months, the time has come to state that if this does happen, it will clearly be the fault (or perhaps at the secret wish?) of the secretariat of the board of the Union of Writers of the U.S.S.R.

I insist that my story be published without delay!

12 September 1967                                             Solzhenitsyn


4    Record of the Meeting of the Secretariat of the Union of Soviet Writers, 22 September 1967

[Some thirty secretaries of the Writers' Union were present, together with Comrade Melentyev of the Cultural Department of the Central Committee. K. A. Fedin was in the chair. The meeting, held to discuss letters from the writer Solzhenitsyn, began at 1300 hours, and ended after 1800.]

FEDIN: I found Solzhenitsyn's second letter most distasteful. His excuse for writing it—that his case has come to a standstill—seems to me ill-founded. In my view, this is an insult to our collective. Three and a half months is not at all a long time to spend on examining his manuscripts. I thought I detected something in the nature of a threat. His attempt to justify himself in this way struck me as offensive. Solzhenitsyn's second letter looks like an attempt to force our hand, and make us publish his manuscripts in a hurry. The second letter continues the argument of the first, but whereas the first spoke both more concretely and with greater feeling about the writer's lot, the second I found merely offensive. What is being done to solve the complex problem of publishing Solzhenitsyn's work? None of us denies his talent. But his tone gives all that he writes an unacceptable twist. His letter is like a slap in the face—we are made to appear scoundrels, rather than representatives of the creative intelligentsia. In the final analysis, he himself is slowing down examination of the question with his demands. I did not find the theme of literary comradeship in his letters. Whether we like it or not, we shall have to talk about Solzhenitsyn's works today, but in my view we should confine our discussion mainly to the letters.

SOLZHENITSYN [requests permission to say a few words about the subject under discussion. He reads a written statement]:

It has become known to me that in preparation for the discussion of *Cancer Ward,* the secretaries of the board were invited to read the play *The Feast of the Victors,* which I myself have long since disowned; I have not reread it for ten years. I destroyed all copies of it except the one that was confiscated and has now been reproduced. More than once, I have explained that this play was written not by Solzhenitsyn, member of the Writers' Union, but by nameless prisoner Shch-232 in those distant years when there was no return to freedom for those arrested on political charges, at a time when no one in the community, including the writers' community, in either word or deed protested against repression, even when such repression was directed against entire peoples. I now bear as little responsibility for this play as many other authors would wish to bear for speeches and books that *they* wrote in 1949 but would not write again today. This play bears the stamp of the desperation of the camps in those years when man's consciousness was determined by his being and when there were certainly no prayers raised for the persecutors. This play bears no relation whatsoever to my present work, and examination of it is a deliberate attempt to divert us from businesslike discussion of the novel *Cancer Ward.*

Moreover, it is unworthy of self-respecting writers to discuss a work snatched, as this was, from a private apartment.

As to critical discussion of my novel *The First Circle,* this is a separate matter and should not become a substitute for discussion of *Cancer Ward.*

KORNEICHUK: I have a question to put to Solzhenitsyn. How does he regard the wanton bourgeois propaganda that his letter evoked? Why doesn't he dissociate himself from it? Why does he endure it in silence? How is it that his letter was broadcast over the radio in the West even before the congress started?

FEDIN calls upon Solzhenitsyn to reply.

SOLZHENITSYN replies that he is not a schoolboy and will not jump up to answer every question, but will speak when his turn comes, like the others.

FEDIN says that Solzhenitsyn can wait until there are several questions and then answer them all at the same time.

BARUZDIN: Even though Solzhenitsyn protests against the discussion of *The Feast of the Victors*, we shall have to talk about that play whether we want to or not. One question: why was it necessary for Solzhenitsyn to mention this play at all in his letter to the congress?

SALYNSKY: I would like Solzhenitsyn to tell us by whom, when and under what circumstances these materials were removed. Has the author asked for their return? To whom did he address his request?

FEDIN asks Solzhenitsyn to answer all these questions.

SOLZHENITSYN repeats that he will answer them when making his statement.

FEDIN [with support from others]: But the secretariat cannot begin the discussion until it has the answers to these questions.

MUTTERING VOICES: Solzhenitsyn can refuse to talk to the secretariat at all: If that's what he wants, let him say so.

SOLZHENITSYN: Very well, I shall answer these questions. It is not true that the letter was broadcast by Western radio before the congress; it was broadcast *after* the congress closed, and then not right away. [What follows is quoted verbatim.] "Very suggestive and effective use is made here of the word 'abroad,' as if it referred to some high authority whose opinion is greatly respected. Perhaps this is understandable to those who spend much of their writing time traveling abroad, to those who flood our literature with light-weight sketches about life abroad. But this is alien to me. I have never been abroad. I do not know other countries and have too little time left to learn about them. I do not understand how one can be so sensitive to opinion abroad and so much less sensitive to live public opinion here in one's own country. Throughout my life, I have had the soil of my homeland under my feet; only *its* pain do I feel, only about *it* do I write."

Why was the play *The Feast of the Victors* mentioned in the letter to the congress? This is apparent from the letter itself: in order to protest against the illegal "publication" and dissemination of this play against the will of the author and without his knowledge. Now, concerning the confiscation of my novel and archives. Yes, I did write several times, beginning in 1965, to protest about this matter to the Central Committee. [What follows is quoted verbatim.] "But in recent times, a new version of the confiscation of my archives has been invented. The story is that Teush, the person who was keeping my manuscripts for me, had some tie with another person who is not named, that the latter was arrested while going through customs (no one knows where), and that something or other was found in his possession (we are not told what); what they found was not something of mine, but it was decided to protect me against such an acquaintance. This is all lies. My friend Teush was investigated two years ago, but no such accusation was made against him. The items I had in safekeeping were discovered as a consequence of normal street surveillance, wiretapping, and an indoor eavesdropping device. And here is the remarkable thing: no sooner does the new version appear than it turns up in various parts of the country simultaneously. Lecturer Potemkin has just aired it to a large assemblage in Riga, and one of the secretaries of the Writers' Union has passed it on to writers in Moscow, adding his own invention—that I admitted all these things at the last meeting of the secretariat. But we did not even discuss the matter. I have no doubt that I shall soon start getting letters from all over the country about the dissemination of this version."

VOICE: Has the editorial board of *Novy Mir* rejected or accepted the novel *Cancer Ward?*

ABDUMONUNOV: What kind of authorization does *Novy Mir* require to print the story, and from whom?

TVARDOVSKY: Generally, the decision to print or not to print a particular thing is a matter for the editorial board. But in the situation that has developed around this author's name, the secretariat of the Union must decide.

VORONKOV: Not once has Solzhenitsyn appealed directly to the secretariat of the Writers' Union. After Solzhenitsyn's letter to the congress, some of the comrades in the secretariat expressed the desire to meet him, to answer his questions, to talk things over and to help him. But after the letter had appeared in the filthy bourgeois press and Solzhenitsyn did not react in any way . . .

TVARDOVSKY: Precisely like the Writer's Union!

VORONKOV: . . . this desire died. And now a second letter has come. It is written in the form of an ultimatum; it is offensive and it lowers the dignity of our literary community. Just now Solzhenitsyn referred to "one of the secretaries" who briefed a Party meeting of Moscow writers. I was that secretary. Your informants were quick off the mark, but they made a bad job of it. As to the confiscation of your things, the only thing I mentioned at the last meeting was your admission that the confiscated items were yours and that your *house* had not been searched. Naturally, after your letter to the congress, we ourselves asked to read all your works. But you should not be so rude to your comrades in labor and in literature. As for you, Aleksandr

Trifonovich, if you consider it necessary to print this story, and if the author accepts your corrections, go ahead and print it yourself; why should the secretariat be involved?

TVARDOVSKY: Remember the Bek case? The secretariat also took it up, and made a favorable recommendation—but still he wasn't published.

VORONKOV: But what interests me most of all, now, is Solzhenitsyn's civic conscience. Why doesn't he answer the loathsome bourgeois propaganda? And why does he treat us as he does?

MUSREPOV: I have a question too. How can he write in his letter: "Prominent persons express regret that I did not die in the camp"? What right has he to write such a thing?

SHARIPOV: And by what channels can the letter have reached the West?

FEDIN asks Solzhenitsyn to answer these questions.

SOLZHENITSYN: Worse things than that have been said about me. A person who occupies a very high position to this day has publicly declared that he regrets not having been one of the triumvirate that sentenced me in 1945, that he would have sentenced me to be shot there and then. . . . Here my second letter is interpreted as an ultimatum: either print the story, or it will be printed in the West. But it isn't *I* who present this ultimatum to the secretariat; life presents this ultimatum to you and to me simultaneously. I write that I am disturbed by the distribution of the story in hundreds—this is a rough estimate; I haven't tried to count them—in hundreds of typewritten copies.

VOICE: How did this come about?

SOLZHENITSYN: My works exhibit one strange characteristic: people are forever asking permission to read them, and once they manage to borrow them they spend their own time, or money, on making copies, which they pass on to others. As long as a year ago, the entire Moscow Prose Section read the first part of the story, and I am surprised that Comrade Voronkov said here that they didn't know where to get it and had to ask the KGB. About three years ago, my "Miniatures" or prose poems were disseminated just as rapidly; no sooner had I started letting people read them than they quickly reached several cities in the Soviet Union. And then the editors of *Novy Mir* received a letter from the West from which we learned that these sketches had already been published there. It was to prevent *Cancer Ward* from leaking in this way that I wrote my urgent letter to the secretariat. I am no less astonished that the secretariat failed to react in any way whatever to my letter to the congress before the West did. And how could it fail to react to all the slander that surrounds me? Comrade Voronkov used here the noteworthy expression "comrades in labor and literature." Well, the fact of the matter is that these "comrades" have for two and a half years calmly watched me being oppressed, persecuted and slandered . . .

TVARDOVSKY: Not everyone has been indifferent.

SOLZHENITSYN: . . . and newspaper editors, also comrades, cannot find room for my denials. [What follows is verbatim.] "I shall not speak here about the fact that people in the camps are not allowed to read my book—that it has not been allowed into the camps, that searches for it have been conducted, that it has been confiscated when found, and that people have been put in punishment cells for reading it even during those months when all the newspapers were trumpeting the praises of *One Day in the Life of Ivan Denisovich* and promising that 'this will not happen again.'" But more recently, the book is secretly being withdrawn from public libraries as well. I have received letters from various places telling me that librarians have been forbidden to issue the book; their orders are to tell readers that the book is in the bindery, or on loan, or that there is no access to those particular shelves, and to avoid issuing it. Here is a letter recently received from the Krasnogvardeisky region in the Crimea:

"In the rayon library (of which I am an active member) I was confidentially told of an order that your books should be removed from circulation. A woman on the library staff wanted to present me with *One Day* as a souvenir, since the library no longer needs it, but another woman immediately stopped her rash friend: 'What are you doing, you mustn't! Once the book has been removed to the Special Section, it is dangerous to make a present of it.' "

I am not saying that the book has been removed from *all* libraries; here and there it can still be found. But people coming to visit me in Ryazan were unable to get my book in the Ryazan oblast reading room! They were put off with various excuses, but they did not get the book. . . .

Everybody knows how inexhaustibly inventive, how prolific slander is, but when you run up against it yourself and, what is more, in the completely novel form of slander from a public platform, you are flabbergasted. Nothing has been done to prevent the lie that I was captured by the Germans, and collaborated with them, from spreading in ever wider circles. As if that were not enough, last summer, in the political education network, e.g., in Bolshevo, agitators took down the statement that I had defected to the U.A.R. and changed my citizenship. All this, of course, is written down in notebooks and at every stage in its transmission its audience is multiplied a hundredfold.

And this just outside the capital! Here is another version. In Solikamsk (P.O. Box 389), Major Shestakov declared that I had fled to England on a tourist visa. This is the local deputy commander for political affairs; who dares disbelieve him? Another time, the same man stated: "Solzhenitsyn has been officially *forbidden* to write." Well, here at least he is closer to the truth.

The following is being said about me from the rostrum: "He was wrongly released, before his time was up." Whether I was wrongly released or not can be seen from the court decision of the Military Collegium of the Supreme Court, Rehabilitation Section. It has been presented to the secretariat. . . .

TVARDOVSKY: It also includes Solzhenitsyn's record as a serving officer.

SOLZHENITSYN: And then the phrase "before his time was up" is used with great relish! After completing my eight-year sentence I spent a month in transit prisons—I feel embarrassed even to mention a matter so trivial in our country—then I was exiled in perpetuity without any formal sentence being passed, and I spent three years in exile, believing that I was doomed to be there forever. It was only because of the Twentieth Congress that I was set free—and this is called "ahead of time"! How well this phrase expresses the comfortable philosophy of the 1949–1953 period: If a man did not die beside a camp rubbish heap, if he was able even to crawl out of the camp, this meant that he had been set free "ahead of time"—after all, the sentence was for eternity and anything earlier was "ahead of time."

I was singled out for attention more than once by ex-minister Semichastny, who liked making speeches on literary matters. One of his astonishing, even comical, accusations was the following: "Solzhenitsyn is materially supporting the capitalist world by not picking up his royalties"—for a book the minister did not name, which had appeared he did not say where. Obviously, the reference was to *One Day*, since no other book of mine had yet been published. Now, if any of you knew, if you had read somewhere that it was absolutely necessary for me to wrest the money from the capitalists, then why didn't you inform me about it? I knew nothing about it in Ryazan. What about *Mezhdunarodnaya Kniga* or the Foreign Commission of the Writers' Union? You should have told me: "It's your patriotic duty to pick that money up." This is a farcical situation: whoever collects fees from the West has sold out to the capitalists; whoever does not take the fees is materially supporting them. Is there a third possibility? To fly into the sky, I suppose. Semichastny is no longer a minister, but his idea has not died; lecturers employed by the All-Union Society for the Dissemination of Scientific Information have carried it further. By way of example, the idea was repeated on 16 July of this year by lecturer A. A. Freifeld at the Sverdlovsk Circus. Two thousand persons sat there and marveled: crafty bird, this Solzhenitsyn! Without leaving the Soviet Union, without a single kopeck in his pocket, he has contrived to support world capitalism materially. (The circus was certainly the place for a tale like this.)

That's the sort of rubbish anybody who feels like it can talk about me, with nothing to stop him. On 12 June, we had a discussion here in the secretariat—a quiet and peaceful one. Shortly after we had left this building, rumors were going around Moscow in which all that had happened here was completely distorted. To begin with, Tvardovsky was supposed to have shouted and banged the table at me. But everyone who was present knows that nothing like that took place. Why these lies, then? And right now, each of us hears what everyone else hears, but where is the guarantee that after today's meeting of the secretariat everything will not be turned inside out again? If you really are "comrades in literature and in labor," then my first request is: when you talk about today's session, don't invent things and don't distort things.

I am one person; my slanderers are numbered in hundreds. Naturally I am never able to defend myself, and I never know against what I must defend myself. I wouldn't be surprised if I were declared to be an adherent of the geocentric system, the first to light the pyre of Giordano Bruno.

SALYNSKY: I shall speak of *Cancer Ward*. I believe that it should be printed— it is a vivid and powerful piece of work. To be sure, it contains descriptions of disease in pathological terms, and the reader inevitably succumbs to the dread of cancer—a phobia that is already widespread in our century. This should somehow be eliminated. The sarcastic satirical passages should also be eliminated. Another regrettable feature is that the destinies of almost all the characters are connected with the camp or with camp life in one form or another. This may be all right in the case of Kostoglotov or Rusanov, but why must it necessarily be true of Vadim, Shulubin, and even the soldier?

At the very end, we learn that this is no ordinary soldier from the army, but a camp guard. But the main thrust of the novel is in what it says about the last stages of the difficult past. And now a few words about moral socialism. In my opinion, there is nothing so very terrible about this. It *would* be horrifying if Solzhenitsyn were preaching *im*moral socialism. If he were preaching national socialism, or the Chinese version of national socialism, that would be bad. Each person is free to form his own ideas on socialism and its development. I personally believe that socialism is determined by economic laws. But there is room for argument. Why not print the story, then? [He also calls upon the secretariat to issue a statement decisively refuting the slanders against Solzhenitsyn.]

SIMONOV: I cannot accept *The First Circle* and I oppose its publication. As for *Cancer Ward*, I am in favor of publishing it. Not everything in this story is to my liking, but it does not have to please everyone. Perhaps the author should accept some of the critical remarks that have been made. But naturally he cannot accept all of them. It is also our duty to refute the slander about him. His book of stories should also be published, and the foreword to this book would be a good place in which to publish his biography. In this way, the slander would die out of its own accord. It is we and not he himself who can and must put an end to false accusations. I have not read *The Feast of the Victors*, nor do I desire to do so, since the author doesn't wish it.

TVARDOVSKY: Solzhenitsyn's position is such that he cannot put himself forward to make a statement. It is we ourselves, the Union, who must make a statement refuting the slander. At the same time, we must sternly reprimand Solzhenitsyn for the inadmissible and improper way in which he appealed to the congress and sent the text to so many addresses. The editorial board of *Novy Mir* sees no reason why *Cancer Ward* should not be printed, naturally with certain emendations. We only wish to receive the secretariat's approval or at least word that the secretariat does not object.

[He asks Voronkov to produce the secretariat's draft communiqué, which was prepared back in June.]

VORONKOV indicates that he is in no hurry to produce the communiqué. Meanwhile voices are heard: But we still haven't decided! Some of us are against it!

FEDIN: No, you're wrong. It isn't for the secretariat to print or reject anything. Are we really in any way to blame? Surely you don't blame yourself, Aleksandr Trifonovich?

TVARDOVSKY [quickly, with heavy emphasis]: I? No.

FEDIN: We shouldn't look for specious excuses to make a statement. Mere rumors are not good enough reason. It would be another matter if Solzhenitsyn himself were to find a way to resolve the situation which has arisen. What is needed is a public statement by Solzhenitsyn himself. [To Solzhenitsyn] But think it over, Aleksandr Isayevich—what would be the point of our publishing your protests? You must begin by protesting against the vile ends for which your name is used by our enemies in the West. In the process, you will of course also have the opportunity to voice some of the complaints you've uttered here today. If this proves to be a satisfactory and tactful document, we will print it and help you. That is how you can begin to establish your good intentions, not by discussing your works or haggling over how many months we are entitled to spend examining your manuscript— three months? four months? Is that really so terrible? The terrible thing is this: that your name is exploited there, in the West, for the vilest ends. [Approval is expressed by members of the secretariat.]

KORNEICHUK: We didn't invite you here to cast stones at you. We summoned you in order to help you out of this painful and compromising situation. You were asked questions, but you declined to answer. Do you realize that a colossal, worldwide battle is being fought under very difficult conditions. We cannot stand aloof. With our works, we defend our government, our Party, our people. You have just spoken sarcastically of journeys abroad as if they were enjoyable outings. We travel abroad to carry on the struggle. We return home worn out and exhausted, but with the feeling of having done our duty. Don't think that I personally was offended by the remark about travel sketches. I don't write them. I travel on the business of the World Peace Council. We know that you have suffered a great deal, but you are not the only one. There were many other people in the camps besides you. Some were veteran Communists. From the camps they went to the front. Our past consists not of acts of lawlessness alone; there were also acts of heroism—but for these you had no eyes. You speak only as counsel for the prosecution. *The Feast of the Victors* is malicious, nasty, insulting! And this foul thing is disseminated, and the people read it! When were you imprisoned? Not in

1937. In 1937, *we* went through a great deal, but nothing stopped us! Konstantin Aleksandrovich was right in saying that you must speak up in public and hit out at Western propaganda. Do battle against the foes of our nation! Do you realize that thermonuclear weapons exist in the world and that despite all our efforts for peace, the United States may employ them? How then can we, Soviet writers, not be soldiers?

SOLZHENITSYN: I have repeatedly declared that it is dishonest to discuss *The Feast of the Victors,* and I insist on its exclusion from our discussion.

SURKOV: You can't gag other people.

KOZHEVNIKOV: The long interval between receipt of Solzhenitsyn's letter and today's discussion is in fact evidence of the seriousness with which the secretariat has treated the letter. If we had discussed it at the time, while its impact was still fresh, our words would have been sharper and less carefully weighed. We decided to find out for ourselves just what kind of anti-Soviet manuscripts there were, and we spent a good deal of time reading them. The military service of Solzhenitsyn has seemingly been confirmed by relevant documents; but we are now discussing the writer, not the officer. Today I have heard, for the first time, that Solzhenitsyn renounces the libelous depiction of Soviet reality in *The Feast of the Victors,* but I still cannot get over my first impression of this play. I personally still cannot square the information that Solzhenitsyn disowns *The Feast of the Victors* with my understanding of the play. Perhaps because in both *The First Circle* and *Cancer Ward* I am conscious of the same desire to exact revenge for past sufferings. And if there is any question at all about the fate of those works, the author should remember that he is indebted to the journal that discovered him. Some time ago, I was the first to express apprehension concerning "Matryona's Home." We spent time reading your raw manuscripts, which you could not bring yourself to submit to any editorial board. *Cancer Ward* evokes revulsion with its excessive naturalism, its piling up of all manner of horrors. All the same, its main themes are not medical but social and that is the unacceptable part. . . . And I suppose that the title of the work must be understood accordingly. In your second letter, you demand the publication of your novel, which still requires further work. Is such importunity worthy of a writer? All our Soviet writers willingly listen to the opinions of their editors and do not try to hurry them.

SOLZHENITSYN [verbatim]: "Despite my explanations and objections, despite the utter senselessness of discussing a work written twenty years ago, in another era, in an incomparably different situation, by a different person— a work, moreover, that has never been published or read by anyone, a work stolen from a drawer—some of the speakers have concentrated their attention on this very work. This is much more senseless than, say, at the First Writers' Congress, rebuking Maxim Gorky for his *Untimely Thoughts*\* or Sergeyev-Tsensky for his 'Letters' from Denikin's Information Agency, which after all *had* been published, and only fifteen years earlier. Kornei-chuk has stated here that 'such a thing has never happened and will not happen in the history of Russian literature.' Precisely!"

OZEROV: That letter to the congress was, politically, a terrible thing. First of all, the letter reached our enemies. It contained things that were incorrect. Zamyatin was lumped together with unjustly repressed writers. As regards the publication of *Cancer Ward*, we can make an agreement with *Novy Mir:* the thing may be printed on condition that the manuscript is corrected, and the corrections subsequently discussed. There remains other very important work to be done. The story is uneven in quality. There are good and bad points in it. Most objectionable is the weakness for poster colors, for carica-ture. I would ask that quite a number of things be deleted, things that we simply do not have time to discuss now. The philosophy of moral socialism does not belong merely to the hero. It sounds as though it has the support of the author. This cannot be permitted.

SURKOV: I, too, have read *The Feast of the Victors*. The mood of it is: "Be damned, the lot of you!" The same note is sustained in *Cancer Ward*. Who, of all its characters, becomes a hero? Only that weird Shulubin, who is no more like a Communist than I am like a . . . Shulubin, with his unbelievably antiquated views. I don't mind admitting that I am a well-read man. I know all those economic and social theories quite well. I've even taken a sniff at Mikhailovsky and Vladimir Solovyov, with their naïve notion that economics can be made subordinate to morality. Having suffered so much, you had a right to be angry as a human being, but after all, you are also a writer! I have known Communists who got the "topper," as you put it, but this in no measure affected their world view. No, it is not a physiological but a political story, and its whole thrust is ideological. And then there is that idol on Theater Square—though the monument to Marx had not yet been erected at the time. If *Cancer Ward* were to be published, it could be used against us, and it would be more dangerous than Svetlana's memoirs. Yes, of course, it would be well to forestall its publication in the West, but that is difficult. For example, I was quite close to Anna Andreyevna Akhmatova in recent years. I know she gave [her poem] "Requiem" to several people to read. It was passed around for several weeks, and then suddenly it was printed in the West. Of course, our reader is now so mature and so sophisticated that no silly little book is going to alienate him from communism. All the same, the works of Solzhenitsyn are more dangerous to us than those of Pasternak: Pasternak was a man divorced from life, while Solzhenitsyn has a bold, militant, ideological temperament, is a man with an idea. We represent the first revolution in the history of mankind that has kept unchanged its original slogans and banners. "Moral socialism" is philistine socialism. It is old and primitive, and [speaking in the direction of Salynsky] I don't understand how anyone could fail to understand this, how anyone could find anything in it.

SALYNSKY: I do not defend it in the least.

RYURIKOV: Solzhenitsyn has suffered from those who have slandered him, but he has also suffered from those who have heaped excessive praise on him and ascribed qualities to him that he does not possess. If Solzhenitsyn is renouncing anything, then he should renounce the title of "continuer of Russian realism." The conduct of Marshal Rokossovsky and General Gorbatov is more honest than that of your heroes. The source of this writer's energy lies in his embitterment, in his grudges. As a human being, one can understand this. You write—do you not?—that your things are prohibited. Yet not a single one of your novels has been censored. I marvel that Tvardovsky looks to us for permission. I, for example, have never asked the Writers' Union for permission to publish.

[He asks Solzhenitsyn to trust *Novy Mir* and accept its recommendation and promises to pass on page-by-page comments on *Cancer Ward* from "anyone present."]

BARUZDIN: I happen to be one of those who, from the start, have not been under the spell of Solzhenitsyn's works. "Matryona's Home" was already much weaker than his first thing. And there are many weak passages in *The First Circle*, such as the feeble, naïve and primitive portrayals of Stalin, Abakumov and Poskrebyshev. But *Cancer Ward* is an antihumanitarian work. The end of the story leads to the conclusion that "a different road should have been taken." Did Solzhenitsyn really believe that his letter "instead of a speech" would be read out at the congress, just like that? How many letters did the congress receive?

VORONKOV: About five hundred.

BARUZDIN: There you are, then! How could they possibly be dealt with quickly? I do not agree with Ryurikov: it is proper that the question of permission should be raised in the secretariat. Our secretariat should assume the role of a creative body more frequently, and show itself willing to advise editors.

ABDUMONUNOV: It is a very good thing that Solzhenitsyn has found the courage to repudiate *The Feast of the Victors.* He will also find the courage to think of ways of carrying out the proposal of Konstantin Aleksandrovich [Fedin]. If we publish his *Cancer Ward,* there will be still more commotion and harm than there was after his first letter. Incidentally, what's the meaning of "sprinkled tobacco into the eyes of the rhesus monkey, just for the hell of it"? What do you mean—"just for the hell of it"? This utterance is aimed against our whole social order. In the story, there are the Rusanovs and the great martyrs from the camp—but is that all? And where is Soviet society? One shouldn't lay it on so thick and make the story one of unrelieved gloom. There are many tedious passages, repetitions and naturalistic scenes; all these should be eliminated.

ABASHIDZE: I was able to read only one hundred fifty pages of *Cancer Ward* and therefore can make no thoroughgoing assessment of it. But I didn't get the impression that the novel is unpublishable. But I repeat, I can't make a thorough assessment. Perhaps the most important things are farther on in the book. All of us, honest and talented writers, have fought against embellishers even when we were forbidden to do so. But Solzhenitsyn tends to go to the other extreme: parts of his work are merely denunciatory journalism. The artist is like a child taking a machine apart to see what is inside. But the true test of art lies in putting things together. I have noticed him asking the person sitting next to him the name of each speaker. Why doesn't he know any of us? Because we have never invited him. The proposal of Konstantin Aleksandrovich was correct: Let Solzhenitsyn himself reply to the slanderers, perhaps starting with a statement to a limited audience for further comment.

BROVKA: In Byelorussia there are also many people who were imprisoned. For example, Sergei Grakovsky was also in prison for twenty years. Yet they realized that it was not the people, not the Party and not the Soviet system that were responsible for illegal acts. The people have already seen through the "Notes" of that blithering fishwife Svetlana Stalin—and treat them as a joke. But before us stands a generally acknowledged talent, and therein lies the danger of publication. Yes, you feel the pain of your land, perhaps too keenly. But you don't feel its joys. *Cancer Ward* is too gloomy and should not be printed. [Like all preceding and subsequent speakers, he supports Fedin's proposal that Solzhenitsyn himself speak out against Western slanders concerning his letter.]

YASHEN [lashes out at *The Feast of the Victors*]: The author is not tortured by injustice: he is, rather, poisoned by hatred. People are outraged that there is such a writer in the ranks of the Union of Writers. I should like to propose his expulsion from the Union. He is not the only one who suffered, but others understand the tragedy of the time better. Take the young Ikramov, for example. Of course, the hand of a master is discernible in *Cancer Ward*. The author knows the subject better than any physician or professor. As for the siege of Leningrad, he now blames "others too" besides Hitler. Whom? It's unclear. Is it Beria? Or today's splendid leaders? He should speak out plainly.

[All the same, the speaker supports Tvardovsky's courageous decision to work on the story with the author. After that, it should still be shown to a narrow circle of people first.]

KERBABAYEV: I read *Cancer Ward* with a feeling of great dissatisfaction. Everyone is a former prisoner, everything is gloomy, there is not a single word of warmth. It is utterly nauseating to read. Vera offers the hero her home and her embraces, but he rejects life. And then there is the remark "Ninety-nine weep while one laughs": how are we to understand this? Does this refer to the Soviet Union? I agree with what my friend Korneichuk said. Why does the author see only the dark side? Why don't I write about the dark side?

I always strive to write only about joyful things. It is not enough that he has repudiated *The Feast of the Victors*. I would consider it courageous if he would renounce *Cancer Ward*. Then I would embrace him like a brother.

SHARIPOV: I wouldn't make any allowances for him—I'd expel him from the Union. In his play, not only everything Soviet but even Suvorov is presented negatively. I completely agree: let him repudiate *Cancer Ward*. Our republic has reclaimed virgin and long-fallow lands and is going forward from success to success.

NOVICHENKO: The letter with its inadmissible appeal was sent to the congress over the head of the formal addressee. I approve Tvardovsky's stern words that we should decisively condemn this kind of conduct. I disagree with the principal demands of this letter: it is impossible to let everything be printed. Wouldn't that also mean the publication of *The Feast of the Victors?* Concerning *Cancer Ward*, I have complicated feelings. I am no child; my time will come to die, perhaps in an agony like that of Solzhenitsyn's heroes. But then the crucial issue will be the state of my conscience, my moral reserves. If the novel had been confined to these things, I would have considered its publication necessary. But then there is that deplorable incursion into Soviet literary life—the crudely satirical scene with Rusanov's daughter. The ideological and political message of moral socialism is the negation of Marxism-Leninism. Then there are those lines of Pushkin: "For man in every element/Is tyrant, slave or traitor." This is an insulting theory. All these things are completely unacceptable to us, to our society, and to our people. All who once suffered are now set up in judgment over society, and that is insulting. Rusanov is a loathsome type, accurately portrayed. But it is intolerable that instead of merely representing a particular type he becomes the vehicle and spokesman of Soviet official society at large. I am nauseated by the frequent use of Gorky's name on Rusanov's base and filthy lips. Even if this novel were put into some kind of shape, it would not be a novel of socialist realism. But it would be an event, a work of talent. I have also read *The Feast of the Victors*, and all ties of human sympathy between myself and the author snapped. We must cut off all the roots which this play puts out.

MARKOV: This has been a valuable discussion. [The speaker notes that he has just returned from Siberia, where he spoke before mass audiences five times.] I must say that nowhere did Solzhenitsyn's name create any particular stir. In one place only was a note submitted to me. I ask your forgiveness, but this is exactly the way it was written: "Just when is this Dolzhenitsyn *(sic!)* going to stop reviling Soviet literature?" We await a completely clear answer from Solzhenitsyn to the bourgeois slander; we await his statement in the press. He must defend his honor as a Soviet writer. His declaration with regard to *The Feast of the Victors* has taken a load off my mind. I view *Cancer Ward* in the same light as Surkov does. The thing does have some worth on some kind of practical plane. But the social and political innuendos in it are utterly unacceptable to me. "Somebody"—address unknown—"did it." Given the successful collaboration that has been established between

*Novy Mir* and Aleksandr Isayevich, this story can be put into shape, though it requires very serious work. But of course, it would be impossible to start setting it up today. So what next? A piece of constructive advice: Aleksandr Isayevich should prepare the kind of statement for the press that we talked about. This would be a very good time for it—just on the eve of the holiday. Then it would be possible to issue some kind of communiqué from the secretariat. In spite of everything, I still consider him our comrade. But, Aleksandr Isayevich, it's your fault and no one else's that we find ourselves in this complicated situation. As to the suggestions concerning expulsion from the Union—we should remember the principles of comradeship that are supposed to prevail, and not be unduly hasty.

SOLZHENITSYN: I have already spoken out against discussion of *The Feast of the Victors* several times today, but I must do so yet again. In the final analysis, I can rebuke all of you for not subscribing to the theory of development, if you seriously believe that in twenty years' time and in the face of a complete change in all circumstances, a man does not change. But I have heard an even more serious thing here: Korneichuk, Baruzdin and someone else mentioned that "the people are reading *The Feast of the Victors*," implying that this play is being disseminated. I shall now speak very slowly; let my every word be taken down accurately. If *The Feast of the Victors* is ever widely circulated or printed, I solemnly declare that the full responsibility will fall on the organization that has the only remaining copy—one not read by anyone—and used it for "publication" of the play during my lifetime and against my will; it is this organization that is disseminating the play! For a year and a half, I have repeatedly warned that this is very dangerous. I imagine that there is no reading room there, that one is handed the play and takes it home. But at home there are sons and daughters, and not all desk drawers can be locked. I have issued warnings before, and I am issuing another today!

Now, as to *Cancer Ward*. I am being criticized for the very title on the ground that cancer and cancer wards are not a medical subject but symbols of some sort. I reply that this is a handy symbol indeed, if it can be deciphered only by a person who has himself experienced cancer and all the stages of dying. The texture is too dense, there are too many medical details for it to be a symbol. I have asked some leading cancer specialists for their view of the story, and they have acknowledged that from the medical point of view it is impeccable, and abreast of modern knowledge. Cancer, and nothing else; cancer as writers of light literature avoid showing it, but as it is discovered to be by sick people every day, relatives of yours among them —and some of those present may soon perhaps find themselves in a cancer ward and realize what sort of symbol this is.

I absolutely do not understand why *Cancer Ward* is accused of being antihumanitarian. Quite the reverse is true: life conquers death, the past is conquered by the future. Were this not the case, my character is such that I could never have set out to write it. But I do not believe that it is the task of literature, whether it is concerned with society or with the individual, to conceal the truth from them or to tone it down. Rather, I believe that it is the task of literature to tell people truthfully how things are and what awaits them. We hear the same rule expressed in Russian proverbs: "Love the straight-talker, not the sweet-talker." "Friendship does not speak with a honeyed tongue." In general, the task of the writer cannot be reduced to defense or criticism of this or that mode of distributing the social product, or to defense or criticism of one or another form of government. The tasks of the writer are connected with more general and durable questions, such as the secrets of the human heart and conscience, the confrontation between life and death, the triumph over spiritual sorrow, the laws of humanity over the ages, laws that were born in the depths of time immemorial and will cease to exist only when the sun ceases to shine.

I am disturbed by the fact that some comrades simply did not read certain passages of the story attentively and hence formed the wrong impressions. This is something that should certainly not have happened. For example, "Ninety-nine weep while one laughs" was a popular camp saying addressed to the character who tried to sneak to the head of the line. Kostoglotov comes out with this saying only to let others know what he is, that's all. Yet people draw the conclusion that the phrase somehow refers to the entire Soviet Union. Then there is the case of "the rhesus monkey." It appears twice in the story, and if you compare the two passages, it becomes clear that the spiteful person who spills tobacco in people's eyes for the hell of it is meant to be Stalin specifically. And why the protest over my "just for the hell of it"? If it wasn't "just for the hell of it," was what he did normal and necessary?

Surkov surprised me. At first I couldn't even understand why he was talking about Marx. Where does Marx come into my story? Come now, Aleksei Aleksandrovich! You are a poet, a man with sensitive artistic taste; how can your imagination have failed you so completely that you didn't grasp the meaning of this scene? Shulubin cites Bacon's ideas and employs his terminology. He says "idols of the marketplace," and Kostoglotov tries to imagine a marketplace and in the center a gray idol; Shulubin says "idols of the theater," and Kostoglotov pictures an idol inside a theater—but he can't fit it in, so it must mean on Teatralnaya Ploshchad. How could you imagine that this referred to Moscow and the monument to Marx which had not been erected at the time? . . .

Comrade Surkov has said that once Akhmatova's "Requiem" started going the rounds, it took only a few weeks for it to end up abroad. Well, *Cancer Ward* (Part One) has been in circulation for more than a year. This is what worries me, and this is why I am trying to hurry the secretariat.

One more piece of advice was given to me by Comrade Ryurikov—to give up all idea of continuing the tradition of Russian realism. That I solemnly swear *never* to do.

RYURIKOV: I did not say that you should cease trying to continue Russian realism, but rather that you should repudiate the interpretation that the West puts upon your role.

SOLZHENITSYN: Now, concerning the suggestion of Konstantin Aleksandrovich. Well, of course I welcome it. Publicity is precisely what I am constantly trying to obtain. We have concealed things long enough—we have had enough of hiding our speeches and our transcripts of the discussion of *Cancer Ward*. The Prose Section decided to send a transcript of the discussion to interested editorial boards. And have they, do you think? They have hidden it away, and only very reluctantly agreed to give me, the author, a copy. As for today's transcript, Konstantin Aleksandrovich, may I hope to receive a copy?

Konstantin Aleksandrovich asked: "What interest would be served should your protests be printed?" In my estimation, this is clear: the interest of literature published in this country. Yet strangely, Konstantin Aleksandrovich says it is I who must resolve the situation. I am bound hand and foot and gagged—how am I to resolve the situation? It seems to me that this would be an easier matter for the mighty Union of Writers. My every line is suppressed, while the entire press is in the hands of the Union. I still don't understand and don't see why my letter was not read at the congress. Konstantin Aleksandrovich proposes that the fight be waged not against causes but against effects—against the furor in the West surrounding my letter. You wish me to publish a refutation—of what, precisely? I can make no statement whatsoever concerning an unprinted letter. And most important, my letter contains a general part and a personal part. Should I renounce the general part? Well, the fact is that I am still of the same mind as I was then, and I do not renounce a single word. After all, what is the letter about?

VOICES: About censorship.

SOLZHENITSYN: You can't have understood a thing if you think it is about censorship. This letter is about the fortunes of our great literature, which once conquered and captivated the world but which has now lost its standing. In the West, they say the novel is dead, and we gesticulate and deliver speeches saying that it is not dead. But rather than make speeches, we should publish novels—such novels as would make them blink as if from a brilliant light, and then the "new novel" would sing small and the "neo-avant-gardists" would subside. I have no intention of repudiating the general part of my letter. Presumably, then, I ought to declare that the eight points in the personal part of my letter are unjust and false? But they are all just. Should I say that some of the wrongs mentioned there have already been eliminated or righted? But not one of them has been eliminated or righted. What sort of statement can I make, then? No, it is you who must clear at least a little path for such a statement: first publish my letter, then the Union's communiqué concerning the letter; then indicate on which of the eight complaints corrective action is being taken. Then I shall be able and eager to make my statement. If you wish, you can also publish my statement of today concerning *The Feast of the Victors*, even though I understand neither the discussion of stolen plays nor the need to refute unprinted letters. On 12 June, here at the secretariat, I was assured that the communiqué would be printed unconditionally, and yet, today, conditions are posed. How has the situation changed?

My book *One Day* is banned. Fresh slanders flare up around me all the time. You can refute them, but I cannot. The only comfort I have is that I will never get a heart attack from this slander because I've been hardened in Stalin's camps.

FEDIN: No, that is not the right order in which to do things. The first public statement must come from you. You, who have received so many approving comments on your talent and style, will find the proper form; you can do it. There are no grounds for your riposte that we must act first and you afterward.

TVARDOVSKY: And will the letter itself be published in this process?

FEDIN: No, the letter should have been published right away. Now that foreign countries have beaten us to it, why should we publish it?

SOLZHENITSYN: Better late than never. So nothing will change regarding my eight points?

FEDIN: We'll see about that later.

SOLZHENITSYN: Well, there you have my answer, and I hope that everything has been accurately transcribed.

SURKOV: You should state whether you dissociate yourself from the role ascribed to you in the West—that of leader of a political opposition in the U.S.S.R.

SOLZHENITSYN: Aleksei Aleksandrovich, it makes me quite sick to hear such a thing—and from you of all people. Literary man and leader of the political opposition: are the two compatible? [Several brief statements follow, insisting that Solzhenitsyn must accept what was said by Fedin.]

VOICES: Let him think it over!

SOLZHENITSYN says once again that he is unable to make such a statement first, since the Soviet reader would have no idea what it is all about.

[The proceedings were recorded during the meeting by A. Solzhenitsyn.]

5   Board of the Writers' Union of the U.S.S.R., No. 3142.
    25 November 1967

To Comrade A. I. Solzhenitsyn

Dear Aleksandr Isayevich:

During the meeting of the secretariat of the board of the U.S.S.R. Writers' Union on 22 September this year, at which letters from you were discussed, while sharply critical of your actions, comrades present showed their good will by recognizing that you must be given sufficient time to think over carefully all that was said at the meeting, and only then make a public statement defining your attitude to the anti-Soviet campaign whipped up by hostile propaganda abroad around your name and your letters. That was two months ago.

The secretariat would like to know what decision you have reached.

Respectfully yours,
K. VORONKOV
Secretary of the Board,
U.S.S.R. Writers' Union,
on behalf of the Secretariat


**6** To the Secretariat of the U.S.S.R. Writers' Union Ryazan, 1 December 1967

From your letter No. 3142 of 25 November 1967 I am unable to understand:

1. Whether or not the secretariat intends to protect me from a three-year-old uninterrupted campaign of slander against me in my own country (unfriendly would be too mild a word for it). (New facts: On 5 October 1967, in the House of the Press in Leningrad, the chief editor of *Pravda*, Zimyanin, repeated in the presence of a large audience the tired lie about my having been a prisoner of war, and he also tried out the possibility of using against me a hackneyed recipe for dealing with awkward customers—declaring me a schizophrenic, and my past in the camps an *idée fixe*. While lecturers from the Moscow Party organization have put forward new lying tales of my "trying to knock together" in the army what they sometimes call a "defeatist" and sometimes a "terrorist" organization. It is difficult to understand why the Military Panel of the Supreme Court failed to spot this in the records of my case.)

2. What measures were taken by the secretariat to end the illegal prohibition on the use of my published works in libraries, and the instructions issued by the censorship that any mention of my name must be removed from critical articles. In *Voprosy Literatury* even an article translated from Japanese has been treated in this way. In the University of Perm, disciplinary measures have been taken against a group of students who tried to discuss my published works in one of their academic symposia.

3. Whether the secretariat wants to prevent publication of my book *Cancer Ward* abroad, where we have no control of it, or whether it remains indifferent to this danger. Are any steps being taken to publish excerpts from this novel in *Literaturnaya Gazeta*, and the whole novel in *Novy Mir*?

4. Whether the secretariat intends to petition the government to adhere to the International Copyright Convention. This would provide our authors with an effective means of protecting their works from illegal publication abroad and from the shameless commercial race between rival translations.

5. During the last six months since I wrote my letter to the Congress, has

distribution of the illegal "edition" of excerpts from my archives been stopped and has this "edition" been destroyed?

6. What measures have been taken by the secretariat to get my sequestered archives and my novel *The First Circle* returned to me, apart from public assurances (by Secretary Ozerov, for instance) that they have already been returned?

7. Has the secretariat accepted or rejected K. Simonov's suggestion that a collection of my short stories should be published?

8. Why I have not yet received the verbatim transcript of the meeting of the secretariat on 22 September so that I can study it.

I would be very grateful for clarification of these points.

A. Solzhenitsyn

7   To———, Member of the U.S.S.R. Writers' Union

Almost a year has passed since I sent my unanswered letter to the Writers' Congress. Since that time, I have written two further letters to the secretariat of the Writers' Union and have been there three times in person. Nothing has changed to this very day: my archives have not been returned, my books are not being published, and all mention of my name is forbidden. I have urgently warned the secretariat of the danger of my works finding their way abroad, since they have had a wide hand-to-hand circulation for a long time past. Yet the secretariat not only has not assisted the publication of *Cancer Ward*, already set up in type at *Novy Mir*, but has stubbornly worked to prevent publication, and even hindered the Moscow Prose Section from *discussing* the second part of the story.

A year has passed and the inevitable has happened: recently, chapters from *Cancer Ward* were published in the *Times Literary Supplement*. Nor are further printings precluded—perhaps of inaccurate and incompletely edited versions. What has happened compels me to acquaint our literary community with the contents of the attached letters and statements, so that the position and responsibility of the secretariat of the U.S.S.R. Writers' Union will be clear.

The enclosed transcript of the secretariat's meeting of 22 September 1967, written by me personally, is of course incomplete, but it is absolutely accurate and will provide sufficient information pending the publication of the entire transcript.

16 April 1968                                                    Solzhenitsyn

Enclosures:

1. My letter to all (forty-two) secretaries of the Writers' Union, dated 12 September 1967.

2. Transcript of the session of the secretariat, 22 September 1967

3. Letter from K. Voronkov, 25 November 1967

4. My letter to the secretariat, 1 December 1967

8    To the Secretariat of the U.S.S.R. Writers' Union

(Copies to: *Novy Mir*, *Literaturnaya Gazeta*, Members of the WU)

At the editorial offices of *Novy Mir*, I was shown the following telegram:

NMO177. Frankfurt am Main. Ch2 9 16.20. To Tvardovsky, *Novy Mir*.

We hereby inform you that the Committee for State Security, through the medium of Victor Louis has sent a further copy of *Cancer Ward* to the West, so as to block its publication in *Novy Mir*. We have therefore decided to publish this work immediately.

The Editors of *Grani*

I should like to protest both against the publication of my work in *Grani* and against V. Louis's attempts to have the work published, but the opaque nature of the telegram makes it necessary first of all to clear up the following points:

1. Whether the telegram was actually sent by the editors of the journal *Grani* or whether it was sent by an impostor (this can be established through the international telegraph system; the Moscow telegraph office can wire Frankfurt am Main).

2. Who is Victor Louis, what kind of person is he, of what country is he a citizen? Did he really take a copy of *Cancer Ward* out of the Soviet Union, to whom did he give it, and where else is there a danger of its being published? Furthermore, what does the Committee of State Security [the KGB] have to do with this?

If the secretariat of the Writers' Union has any interest in establishing the truth and stopping the imminent publication of *Cancer Ward* in more than one Russian edition abroad, I believe that it can obtain prompt answers to these questions.

This episode compels us to reflect on the strange dark ways by which the manuscripts of Soviet writers can reach the West. It constitutes a drastic reminder to us that literature must not be put in such a position that literary works become a profitable commodity for any scoundrel who happens to have a visa. The works of our authors must be given the possibility of publication in their own country, and must not become the plunder of foreign publishing houses.

18 April 1968                                                                                          Solzhenitsyn


9    To the Editors of *Le Monde*, *L'Unità*, *Literaturnaya Gazeta*

I have learned from a report in *Le Monde* of 13 April that fragments from my novel *Cancer Ward* are being printed in various places in the West and that the publishers Mondadori (Italy) and The Bodley Head (England) are in litigation for the "copyright" of this novel.

I declare that *no* foreign publisher has received a manuscript of this novel from me, nor any authorization to publish it. Therefore I do not recognize as legal *any* publication of this novel, present or future, carried out without my authorization, and I do not accept that anyone has the right to publish it. All distortions of the text, which are inevitable considering the number of copies involved and their uncontrolled distribution, are harmful to me. I categorically condemn and prohibit all unauthorized adaptations for the screen or the stage.

I already know from experience that *One Day in the Life of Ivan Denisovich* was spoiled by haste, in all the translations. The same fate evidently awaits *Cancer Ward*. But money is one thing, literature another.

25 April 1968                                                                          Solzhenitsyn


10    To the Editorial Board of *Literaturnaya Gazeta* [Copy to the journal *Novy Mir*]

I know that your paper will not publish a single line of mine without distorting or misrepresenting its sense. But there is no way I can answer the many people who have sent me their greetings except through you.

"I thank the readers and writers whose greetings and good wishes on my fiftieth birthday have so moved me. I promise them never to betray the truth. My sole dream is to justify the hopes of the Russian reading public."

Ryazan, 12 December 1968                                                           Solzhenitsyn


11    Record of the Meeting of the Ryazan Writers' Organization, 4 November 1969 [The meeting lasted from 3 P.M. to 4:30 P.M.]

Those present included six of the seven members of the Ryazan writers' organization (Ernst Safonov, secretary of the Ryazan branch, was in hospital for an operation): F. N. Taurin, secretary of the R.S.F.S.R. Union of Writers; Aleksandr Sergeyevich Kozhevnikov, secretary for agitation and propaganda of the Ryazan oblast committee of the CPSU; Povarenkin, publisher's editor, and three other comrades from organizations in the oblast.

The present record was made during the meeting by Solzhenitsyn.

The agenda contained one officially announced item: a statement by Taurin on the resolution of the secretariat of the R.S.F.S.R. Writers' Union concerning "Measures for the Intensification of Ideological-Educational Work Among Writers."

The report itself didn't take up much time. F. Taurin read out the resolution of the R.S.F.S.R. Writers' Union secretariat, occasioned by the defection of A. Kuznetsov, which laid down new measures for tighter control over writers going abroad, and further measures for the ideological indoctrination of writers. He announced that similar meetings had already been held in many oblast writers' organizations and had proceeded on a high level, especially in the Moscow writers' organization, where charges had been laid against Lydia Chukovskaya, Lev Kopelev, Bulat Okudzhava, and also against a member of the Ryazan organization of the WU—Solzhenitsyn.

Discussion (time limit—ten minutes per speaker):

VASILY MATUSHKIN (member of Ryazan WU; after a few general remarks about the condition of the Ryazan organization): I cannot refrain from referring to the attitude of Comrade Solzhenitsyn to literature and to our writers' organization. I bear some share of the responsibility: I once gave him a reference when he was joining the Writers' Union. So that in criticizing him today, I am criticizing myself too. When *One Day* came out, not everything in it was immediately accepted; much of it was distasteful. But after the reviews by Simonov and Tvardovsky, there could be no disagreement. In spite of everything, we cherished hopes that Solzhenitsyn would become an ornament to our organization. Those hopes have not been realized. Take his attitude to our writers' organization. In all these years, he has taken no part at all. He has, it is true, attended election meetings, but he has never spoken. Helping young writers is one of our most important statutory duties: he has ignored it and taken no part in discussing the works of beginners. He has done no *work* whatsoever. Hurtful though it is, we cannot help feeling that he looks down on our writers' organization and our modest achievements in literature. I will honestly and frankly say that all of his recent writing (true, we have no knowledge of it, we haven't read it, we haven't been invited to discuss it) is at cross-purposes with what the rest of us are writing. We acknowledge the existence of our motherland, and nothing else is dearer to us. Solzhenitsyn's work, though, is published abroad and then it all spills over onto our country. When our motherland was besmirched with the help of his writings and Aleksandr Isayevich was told how to reply (an article was even printed in *Literaturnaya Gazeta*), he failed to react: he felt he knew better.

SERGEI BARANOV [chairman]: Your ten-minute time limit is up.

MATUSHKIN: Please, may I continue?

SOLZHENITSYN: Let the comrade have as much time as he likes.
[Extension allowed.]

MATUSHKIN: The Writers' Union is an entirely voluntary organization. There are people who get published though they are not in the Union. The Union's statutes say clearly: the Union brings together persons of like mind who are engaged in building communism, dedicate all their creative work to it, and follow the path of socialist realism. That being so, there is no room for Solzhenitsyn in our writers' organization; let him work on his own. Bitter though it is, I am bound to say: A.I., our paths differ from yours and we shall have to part company.

NIKOLAI RODIN [WU member from Kasimov, hurriedly brought to the meeting, though ill, in order to make up a quorum]: After what Vasily Semyonovich has said, there is nothing to add. If we look at the statutes of the Union and compare with them the civic activities of Aleksandr Isayevich, we shall find great discrepancies. After Vasily Semyonovich's speech I have nothing to add. He has not complied with the statutes, he has by-passed our Union. There have been times when we had no one to whom to pass the manuscript of a budding writer for review, but Solzhenitsyn didn't go in for reading manuscripts. I have serious complaints against him.

BARANOV [WU member, Ryazan]: This is an extremely serious problem and the board of the Writers' Union is raising it just at the right time. In the Union we should be well acquainted with each other's minds and help one another. But what will happen if we skulk each in his own small corner: Who is going to educate the younger people? Who will take charge of the many literary circles that we have in industry and in educational institutions? Vasily Semyonovich was right in raising the question of Aleksandr Isayevich. His work is unknown to us, we do not know his work. At the outset there was a great fuss made about his writings. Personally, I have always seen *One Day* as a work of unrelieved blackness. Or take "Matryona's Home"—wherever did he find a woman so much alone, with her cockroaches and her cat and nobody around to help her? Where could one find such a Matryona? I was still hoping that Aleksandr Isayevich would write things the people needed. But where does he publish his writings and what are they about? We do not know. He must try to respect himself and others more than he does. Solzhenitsyn has broken away from the organization and it seems that we must part company with him.

SOLZHENITSYN asks to be allowed to put one general question to the comrades taking the floor, but the chairman refuses.

EVGENY MARKIN [WU member, Ryazan]: It is especially difficult for me to speak, more so than for any of you. If we are frank with ourselves, we are discussing whether Aleksandr Isayevich should remain in our organization. I wasn't yet a member of the Union when you admitted him. I find myself depressed by the extraordinary swing of the pendulum from one extreme to the other. I was working on the staff of *Literatura i Zhizn* when unprecedented tributes were being paid to Solzhenitsyn. Since then there has been a swing in the opposite direction: never have I heard such harsh views expressed about anyone as about Solzhenitsyn. Such changes, from one extreme to the other, must affect the consciences of those who are trying to make decisions. Let us remember how Yesenin was reviled and then praised to the skies, and that now once again there are people who would like to sink him. Let us recall the harsh judgments uttered after 1946. No one could find it harder to make sense of all that than I do now. If Solzhenitsyn is expelled now and later readmitted, expelled again and again admitted, I don't want to have anything to do with it. Where will those who have avoided the discussion today find another "appendix"?* Our organization has serious defects. Members of the Union aren't given housing. For two years our

Ryazan writers' organization was bossed by the rascally Ivan Abramov, who wasn't even a member of the Union but nonetheless pinned political labels on us. As for Anatoly Kuznetsov, I attended the Literary Institute with him. Our intuition didn't let us down—we disliked him because he was a humbug. As I see it, the relevant article in our statutes can be interpreted in two ways; it's a stick with two ends. Of course, one would like to ask Aleksandr Isayevich why he took no part in public life. Why, in view of the hubbub that the foreign press created about his name, did he say nothing in our press, why didn't he tell us about it? Why did Aleksandr Isayevich not try to explain properly and make his position known to the public at large? I have not read his new works. My view on the continued presence of A.I. in the Writers' Union is that he never has been a member of the *Ryazan* organization. I fully agree with the majority of the writers' organization.

NIKOLAI LEVCHENKO [WU member, Ryazan]: In the main the problem has been clarified by the comrades who spoke earlier. I would like to put myself in the place of Aleksandr Isayevich and try to imagine how I would have behaved. If all my works had become so many weapons in the hands of foreigners, what would I have done? I would have gone along and taken counsel with my comrades. He has isolated himself of his own accord. I side with the majority.

POVARENKIN: Over a number of years, Aleksandr Isayevich has been out of touch with the Writers' Union. Instead of coming to election meetings he has sent telegrams: "I side with the majority"—is that how a man of principle should behave? Gorky used to say that the Writers' Union was a collective body, a social organization. Aleksandr Isayevich evidently joined the Union for other purposes—just to have a writer's card. The ideological qualities of his writings don't help us in building a Communist society. He denigrates our bright future. His own innermost self is black. Only one who is ideologically hostile to us could depict such an uninspiring character as Ivan Denisovich. *He* has put himself outside the writers' organization.

SOLZHENITSYN again asks to be allowed to put a question. Instead he is invited to make his speech now. After some hesitation, the question is allowed. Solzhenitsyn asks the WU members who have reproached him with refusing to review manuscripts or talk to young writers to give specific details of even one such case.

No response from previous speakers.

MATUSHKIN: A member of the Writers' Union should work actively in accordance with the statutes and not wait to be invited.

SOLZHENITSYN: I regret that no shorthand minute is being made of our meeting and that a careful record is not being kept. Yet it may have some interest not just tomorrow or in a week's time, but even later. Incidentally, there were three stenographers working in the secretariat of the U.S.S.R. WU, but the secretariat, while declaring that my record was tendentious, was either unable or unwilling to make available the minutes of that meeting.

First of all, I want to remove a weight from Comrade Matushkin's mind. Let me remind you, Vasily Semyonovich, that you never gave me any recommendation; as WU secretary at the time, you only brought me blank questionnaire forms. At that time, when I was the object of exaggerated praise, the R.S.F.S.R. secretariat was in such a hurry to admit me that it didn't wait for recommendations to be collected, or for the Ryazan primary organization to admit me, but admitted me directly and sent me a congratulatory telegram.

The charges that have been preferred against me here can be divided into two quite different groups. The first concerns the Ryazan organization of the WU; the second concerns my whole future as a writer. In the first group, I would say that there is not a single well-founded charge. Our secretary, Safonov, is not present. But I gave him notice *on the very same day* of every public action taken by me, of every letter I wrote to the congress of the secretariat, and I always asked him to acquaint all the members of the Ryazan WU, and also our younger writers, with those materials. Didn't he show them to you? Was this because he himself didn't want to? Or because he was forbidden to do so by Comrade Kozhevnikov, here present? Not only did I not avoid creative contacts with the Ryazan WU but I requested Safonov, I insisted that my *Cancer Ward*, which had been discussed in the Moscow writers' organization, should without fail be discussed in the Ryazan organization also. I have a copy of my letter to that effect. Yet *Cancer Ward*, too, was for some reason or other kept completely secret from the members of the Ryazan WU. Similarly, I always voiced my willingness to speak in public but I was never allowed to do so, apparently because someone was afraid of something. As regards my alleged "arrogance," that is ridiculous; none of you can recall any occasion, any phrase, any facial expression of the sort; on the contrary, I have always felt that I was on the easiest and most comradely terms with all of you. As to the charge that I did not always put in an attendance at reelections: that is true, but the reason is that most of the time I don't live in Ryazan, I live near Moscow, outside the city. When *One Day* had just been published, I was strongly urged to move to Moscow, but I was afraid of losing my concentration there and I said no. When, several years later, I asked for permission to move, I was refused. I applied to the Moscow organization and asked them to put me on their list; its secretary, V. N. Ilyin, replied that it was impossible, that I should remain a member of the organization where I had my passport registration and that it wasn't important where I actually resided. For that reason it was sometimes difficult for me to come over for elections.

As regards the accusations of a general character, I still fail to understand what kind of "reply" people expect me to make—*what* must I reply to? To the notorious article in *Literaturnaya Gazeta*, where I was contrasted with Anatoly Kuznetsov and it was said that I must reply to the West in his manner and not in my own? I have nothing to say in reply to that anonymous article. It casts doubt on the correctness of the decision to rehabilitate me by using the sly and evasive "he served his sentence"—not a word more, so that you may think that he was rightly punished. The article uttered a falsehood about my novels, alleging that *The First Circle* constitutes a "malicious slander on our social system"—but who has proved or demonstrated or illustrated that allegation? Nobody knows my novels and so anyone can say anything he likes about them. There are also many minor distortions in the article; the whole sense of my letter to the congress has been perverted. Finally, the stale story of *The Feast of the Victors* is chewed over again; it would, incidentally, be legitimate to ask the question: *From what source* did the editors of *Literaturnaya Gazeta* obtain their information about this play, how did they get hold of it for perusal if the *one and only* copy of it was taken from my desk by the KGB?

Generally, what happens with my writings is this: If I myself disown some work or other and wish that it did not exist—as with *The Feast of the Victors—they* make a point of talking about it and "interpreting" it for all they are worth. If, however, I press for my writings to be published, as, for instance, *Cancer Ward* or *The First Circle,* they are hidden away and nothing is said about them.

You say I ought to "reply" to the secretariat? But I have given them a reply already to all the questions put to me, whereas the secretariat has not replied to a single one of mine. I have received no real reply to my letter to the secretariat, in which there was a great deal both on general and on personal matters. It was regarded as of little significance compared with the other business of the congress and swept under the carpet, and I am beginning to think that they deliberately held their hand until it had been circulating widely for two weeks—then, when it was printed in the West, made that a convenient excuse for not publishing it in our country.

Exactly the same procedure was adopted in respect to *Cancer Ward.* As far back as September 1967 I insistently warned the secretariat of the danger that the book might appear in the West because of its wide circulation here. I urged them to give permission for publication here in *Novy Mir.* But the secretariat went on waiting. When, in the spring of 1968, signs began to appear that at any moment now it would be printed in the West, I sent letters to *Literaturnaya Gazeta, Le Monde* and *L'Unità,* in which I forbade the printing of *Cancer Ward* and denied all rights to Western publishers. And what do you think? The letter to *Le Monde,* sent by registered post, was not allowed out. The letter to *L'Unità,* sent with the well-known Communist publicist Vittorio Strada, was taken from him by the customs—and I found myself having to make a fervent appeal to convince the customs officials that, in the interests of our literature, it was essential that the letter should appear in *L'Unità.* Several days after this conversation, early in July, it did after all appear in *L'Unità*—but *Literaturnaya Gazeta* still went on waiting! *What* was it waiting for? Why did it keep my letter secret for a period of *nine* weeks, from 21 April to 26 June? It was waiting for *Cancer Ward* to appear in the West. And when it was issued in the awful Mondadori Russian edition, only *then* did *Litgazeta* publish my protest, in the middle of a long-winded anonymous article of its own in which I was accused of not having protested *energetically or sharply enough* against *Cancer Ward*'s being published. But why did *Litgazeta* hold up the protest for nine weeks? The calculation is obvious: Let *Cancer Ward* appear in the West, then it will be possible to damn it and keep it from the Soviet reader. Yet had it been printed at the right time, my protest could have stopped the publication of *Cancer Ward* in the West: for instance, two American publishers, Dutton and Praeger, as soon as *rumors* reached them that I was protesting against *Cancer Ward*'s being published, in May 1968 dropped their plan to print the book. What would have happened if *Litgazeta* had printed my protest at the time?

CHAIRMAN BARANOV: Your time is up—ten minutes.

SOLZHENITSYN: How can you insist on a time limit in this case? It's a matter of life and death.

BARANOV: But we can't allow you more—there's a time limit.

SOLZHENITSYN insists on his plea. Various members intervene.

BARANOV: How much longer do you want?

SOLZHENITSYN: I have a lot I need to say. Give me another ten minutes at least.

MATUSHKIN: Let him have three minutes.
[After consultations, ten minutes more are granted.]

SOLZHENITSYN [speeding up still further his already fast delivery]: I made an application to the Ministry of Communications asking them to put an end to the postal theft of my correspondence—nondelivery or holdup of letters, telegrams, packets, especially those from abroad, as for instance, when I was replying to congratulations on my fiftieth birthday. But what is one to do if the Soviet WU secretariat itself is abetting these robberies? After all, the secretariat hasn't passed on to me a single letter or telegram from the heap it received addressed to me for my fiftieth birthday. It hangs on to them without saying anything about it.

The whole of my correspondence is closely inspected and, as if that weren't enough, the results of this illegal postal censorship are utilized with brazen cynicism. For example, the secretary of the Frunze region committee, Moscow, summoned the director of the Russian Language Institute of the Academy of Sciences and banned a transcript of a tape recording of my voice in that institute—he had heard about it, you see, from a postal censorship extract supplied to him.

To come now to the accusation that I paint reality too black: Tell me, when and where and in what theory of cognition is the reflection of a thing regarded as more important than the thing itself? Possibly in certain philosophies, but surely not in materialistic dialectics. It works out this way: what matters is not what we do but what people will say about it. And so that they cannot say anything bad, we'll keep our mouths shut about all that goes on. But that isn't a solution. The time to be ashamed of obscenities is not when they are being talked about but when they are being *committed*. The poet Nekrasov said:

He who lives without grief and anger
Cannot love his native land.

The man who is always rosily enraptured is—contrary to appearances—indifferent to his native land.

There has been talk here about the pendulum. Yes, there has certainly been an enormous swing of the pendulum, and not in my case alone but in the whole of our life: people want to conceal, to forget the crimes committed under Stalin, to avoid mentioning them. "Is there any point in recalling the past?" was the question put to Lev Tolstoy by his biographer Biryukov, and Tolstoy replied (I quote from Biryukov's *Biography of Tolstoy*, volume 3/4, page 48) [read at speed]:

If I had a vile disease and I were cured and cleansed of it, I would always be happy to talk about it. I would make no mention of it only if I were still suffering and getting worse and I wanted to deceive myself. We are sick—and always no more and no less sick than before. The form of the sickness has changed but it is still the same disease; only it is called by a different name. . . . The disease that we are suffering from is the disease of killing people. If we recall the past and look it straight in the face, the violence we are now committing will also be revealed.

No! We shall not succeed indefinitely in keeping silent about Stalin's crimes, in going against the truth. The millions of people who suffered from these crimes demand that they be brought to light. It would be a good idea, too, to reflect on the moral effect concealment of these crimes may have on the younger generation. It means the *corruption* of still more millions. The growing generation of young people are no fools; they know full well that millions of crimes were committed and that nobody talks about them—that they are carefully hushed up. What is there, then, to restrain any one of us from taking a hand in other acts of injustice? These, too, will be carefully hushed up.

It only remains for me to say that I retract not one word, not one letter of what I wrote to the Writers' Union. I may conclude with the very words used in that letter [quotes]:

"I am of course confident that I shall fulfill my duty as a writer in all circumstances—from the grave even more successfully and incontrovertibly than in my lifetime. No one can bar the road to truth, and to advance its cause I am prepared to accept even death"—yes, death and not merely expulsion from the Union. "But may it be that repeated lessons will finally teach us not to stay the writer's pen during his lifetime? This has never yet added luster to our history."

Well, then, take the vote—you've got a majority. But remember: the history of literature will someday take an interest in this meeting of ours.

MATUSHKIN: I have got a question to put to Solzhenitsyn. How do you explain the fact that they are so eager to publish your work in the West?

SOLZHENITSYN: And how do you explain the fact that people are so stubbornly unwilling to print me in my own country?

MATUSHKIN: No, you answer my question: it's your turn to answer.

SOLZHENITSYN: I have already answered over and over again. I have asked more questions and asked them earlier: let the secretariat answer me.

KOZHEVNIKOV [interrupting Matushkin]: Never mind—leave it at that. Comrades, I don't want to interfere with your meeting or your decision; you are absolutely independent. But I would like to protest [speaking in a steely voice] against the political tones that Solzhenitsyn wants to impose on our proceedings. We raise one question; he raises another one. He has all the newspapers at his disposal to reply to people abroad but he makes no use of them. He has no desire to reply to our enemies. He has no wish to retort to people abroad; let him reply to our enemies in his own words, without quoting Nekrasov and Tolstoy. The congress turned down your letter as uncalled for and as ideologically incorrect. In that letter you repudiate the guiding role played by the Party—but that is what we take our stand on, the guiding role of the Party. I think your former literary comrades were right in what they said—we cannot be reconciled. We must all toe the line, go forward together, in orderly ranks—all acting as one—not under some kind of lash but following the dictates of our own minds.

FRANZ TAURIN: It will now be for the R.S.F.S.R. secretariat to deal with this matter. It is true to say that the hub of the problem is not failure to review manuscripts or run literary study groups. The main point is that you, Comrade Solzhenitsyn, have not resisted the use made of your name in the West. That might partly be explained by the injustices you have suffered and the wrongs heaped upon you. Sometimes, though, a man must place his country's fortunes above his own. Believe me, no one wants to bring you to your knees. This meeting is an attempt to help you to straighten up, to shake off all that the West has hung on you. The impression that is given over there is that you, with all your native talent, are against your own country. It may be that in this struggle people sometimes go too far, but I am conversant with the minutes of the secretariat meeting. The secretaries, and more especially Comrade Fedin, simply asked you in a fatherly way to make concessions, to give a public rebuff to the clamor aroused in the West. It harms us twice over: we are blackened as a country, and a talented writer is snatched from us. Any decision taken today will be discussed in the R.S.F.S.R. secretariat.

LEVCHENKO [rises to read an already typed draft resolution]: ". . . Paragraph Two: The meeting considers that Solzhenitsyn's conduct is antisocial in character and is radically in conflict with the aims and purposes of the U.S.S.R. Union of Writers.

"In view of his antisocial behavior, which is in contradiction with the aims and objectives of the U.S.S.R. Union of Writers, and of his gross violation of the basic provisions of the Statutes of the U.S.S.R. WU, we resolve that the writer Solzhenitsyn be expelled from the U.S.S.R. Union of Writers.

"We request the secretariat to endorse this decision."

MARKIN: I would like to know the views of our secretary, Comrade Safonov. Has he been notified or not?

BARANOV: He is unwell. Our meeting is properly constituted and within its rights.

[A vote being taken, five were in favor, one (myself) against.]

**12** Open Letter to the Secretariat of the R.S.F.S.R. Writer's Union

Shamelessly trampling under foot your own statutes, you have expelled me in my absence, expelled me precipitately, without even summoning me by telegram, without giving me even the four hours I needed to make my way from Ryazan and be present at the meeting. You have candidly revealed that the *decision* preceded the "discussion." Were you afraid of being obliged to grant me ten minutes for my answer? I am compelled to write this letter as a second best.

Dust off the clock face. You are behind the times. Throw open the sumptuous heavy curtains—you do not even suspect that day is already dawning outside. We are no longer in that muted, that somber, that hopeless age when, just as compliantly, you expelled Akhmatova. We are not even in that timid, shivery period when you expelled Pasternak, howling abuse at him. Is this not disgrace enough for you? Do you want to make it blacker yet? But the time is near when each of you will seek to scratch his signature from today's resolution.

Blind leading the blind! You do not even notice that you are wandering in the opposite direction from the one you yourselves announced. At this time of crisis you are incapable of offering our grievously sick society anything constructive and good, anything but your malevolent vigilance, your "hold tight and don't let go!"

Your overstuffed articles come apart at the seams. No thought takes shape in your enfeebled minds. You are incapable of debate, you can only cast votes and give orders. And that is why neither Sholokhov nor the whole lot of you together had the courage to reply to the famous letter of Lydia Chukovskaya, an essayist of whom Russian literature can be proud. But the administrative pincers are being made ready for her: how could she allow people to read an unpublished book of hers? Once the authorities have made up their minds not to publish you—then stifle yourself, choke yourself, cease to exist, and don't give your stuff to anyone to read!

They are also getting ready to expel Lev Kopelev, a front-line veteran who has already served ten years in prison although he was completely innocent, but who is now guilty of interceding for the persecuted, disclosing the hallowed secrets of his conversation with an influential person, breaking the seal of *official secrecy*. But why do you hold conversations that have to be concealed from the people? Were we not promised fifty years ago that never again would there be any secret diplomacy, secret negotiations, secret and incomprehensible appointments and transfers, that the masses would be informed of all matters and discuss them openly?

"Enemies will overhear"—that is your excuse. These eternal, omnipresent "enemies" are a convenient justification for your functions and your very existence. As if there were no enemies when immediate openness was promised. But what would you do without "enemies"? You could not live without "enemies"; hatred, a hatred no better than racial hatred, has become your sterile atmosphere. But in this way the awareness that mankind is one, and of a piece, is lost, and its doom is accelerated. Should the ice of the Antarctic alone melt tomorrow, we would all become a sea of drowning humanity, and into whose heads would you then be drilling your concepts of "class struggle"? Not to speak of the time when the few surviving bipeds will be wandering over radioactive earth, dying.

It is high time to remember that we belong first and foremost to humanity. And that man has separated himself from the animal world by *thought* and by *speech*. These, naturally, should be *free*. If they are put in chains, we shall return to the state of animals.

*Openness*, honest and complete *openness*—that is the first condition of health in all societies, including our own. And he who does not want this openness for our country cares nothing for his fatherland and thinks only of his own interest. He who does not wish this openness for his fatherland does not want to purify it of its diseases, but only to drive them inward, there to fester.

12 November 1969                                          A. Solzhenitsyn


13    The Way We Live

The way we live, without any warrant for arrest or any medical justification, four militiamen and two doctors come to a healthy man's house, the doctors declare that he is crazy, the militia major shouts, "We are the organs of coercion. Get up!" They twist his arms, handcuff him and drive him off to the madhouse.

This can happen tomorrow to any one of us. It has just happened to Zhores Medvedev, a geneticist and publicist, a man of subtle, precise and brilliant intellect and of warm heart (I know personally of his disinterested help to ordinary citizens in sickness or near death.) It is precisely because of the *diversity* of his gifts that he is charged with abnormality: "a split personality!" It is precisely his sensitivity to injustice, to stupidity, that is presented as a sick deviation: "poor adaptation to the social environment!" Once you think in any but the *approved* way, that means you're abnormal! While well-adjusted people must all think alike. And there is no redress: even the appeals of our best scientists and writers bounce back like peas off a wall.

If only this were the first case! But this devious suppression of people without searching for any guilt, when the real reason is too shameful to state, is becoming a fashion. Some of the victims are widely known, many more are unknown. Servile psychiatrists, breakers of their Hippocratic oath, see social concern, excessive ardor, excessive coolness, brilliant or abundant gifts, as so many symptoms of "mental illness."

Yet elementary prudence ought to act as a restraint. After all, Chaadayev had not a finger laid on him, and even so we have been cursing his persecutors for over a century. It is time to think clearly: the incarceration of free-thinking people in madhouses is *spiritual murder*, it is a variation on the *gas chamber*, but is even more cruel: the torments of those done to death in this way are more heartless and protracted. Like the gas chambers, these crimes will *never* be forgotten, and *all* those involved in them will be condemned in perpetuity, during their lives and after their deaths.

The lawless, the evildoers, must remember that there is a limit beyond which a man becomes a cannibal!

It is short-sighted to think that one can live by constantly relying on force alone, constantly ignoring the protests of conscience.

15 June 1970                                              A. Solzhenitsyn


**14**    To Comrade M. A. Suslov, Secretary of the Central Committee of the Communist Party of the Soviet Union

Mikhail Andreyevich:

I am addressing this letter to you because I recall that we were introduced in December 1962 and that at the time you showed an understanding of my work.

Please give your personal attention to my proposal below, and pass it on to other members of the leadership.

I suggest that you should reexamine the situation created around me and my works by unscrupulous officials of the Writers' Union who have given the government incorrect information.

As you know, I have been awarded the Nobel Prize in Literature. In the course of the eight weeks that remain before it is due to be presented, the leaders of the state have an opportunity to effect a radical change in my literary situation. In that case the presentation will take place in much more favorable circumstances than have been created at present. Because there is so little time left, I confine my proposal to a bare summation:

1. In the shortest possible time my novel *Cancer Ward* should be published in book form (with myself reading the proofs), in a substantial first edition, and put on open sale. (If it is instructed to do so, Goslitizdat has the means of carrying out all this work in two or three weeks.) The banning of this story, which has been approved by the Moscow Prose Section and accepted

for publication by *Novy Mir*, is a pure *misunderstanding*.

2. All punitive measures against persons accused of reading and discussing my books (the expulsion of students from their institutes, etc.) should be canceled. The ban on library use of surviving copies of my previously published works should be lifted. An announcement should be made that a volume of my short stories (they have never before been published in collected form) is being prepared for the press.

If these proposals are accepted and carried out, I can hand over to you for publication my newly completed novel, *August 1914*. This book cannot encounter any difficulties with the censors: it consists of a detailed military analysis of the "Samsonov catastrophe" in 1914, when the selfless heroism and the best endeavors of Russian soldiers and officers were rendered senseless and condemned to failure by the paralysis of the tsarist high command. It would cause general astonishment if this book, too, were banned in our country.

If there is any need for us to meet for a general exchange of views or to discuss this, I am ready to come and see you.

14 October 1970                                                                 Solzhenitsyn


**15    To the Royal Swedish Academy/The Nobel Foundation**

Gentlemen:

In a telegram to the secretary of the Academy I have already expressed, and I now again express, my gratitude for the honor bestowed upon me by the award of a Nobel Prize. In my own mind I share it with those of my predecessors in Russian literature who, because of the difficult conditions of past decades, did not live to receive such a prize or who were little known in their lifetime to the reading world in translation, or even to their countrymen in the original.

In the same telegram, I expressed my intention of accepting your invitation to Stockholm, although I anticipated the humiliating procedure, usual in my country for every trip abroad, of filling out questionnaires, obtaining character references from Party organizations—even nonmembers must have them—and attending briefing sessions on behavior.

However, in recent weeks, the hostile reaction to my prize, manifested in the press of my country, and the fact that my books are still suppressed—for reading them, people are dismissed from work or expelled from higher educational institutions—compel me to assume that my trip to Stockholm would be used to cut me off from my native land, quite simply to prevent me from returning home.

Then again, in the materials you have sent me about the procedure for investiture, I have discovered that the Nobel celebrations have a very significant ceremonial and festive side which would be tiring for me, and for which my character and way of life have not prepared me. The one working occasion, the Nobel lecture, is really not a part of the ceremony. Later, in a telegram and letter, you expressed similar apprehensions about the to-do that might accompany my stay in Stockholm.

Weighing all the foregoing, and taking advantage of your kind explanation that personal presence at the ceremony is not an obligatory condition for receiving the prize, I prefer not to seek permission to travel to Stockholm at the present time.

I could receive the Nobel diploma and medal, if such a procedure would be acceptable to you, in Moscow from your representatives, at a time convenient to you and to me. As provided by the rules of the Nobel Foundation, I am ready to deliver, or present a written text of, my Nobel lecture within six months from 10 December 1970.

This is an open letter, and I do not object to its being published.

With best wishes,

27 November 1970                                          A. Solzhenitsyn


**16**     Your Majesty, Ladies and Gentlemen:

I hope that my involuntary absence will not cast a shadow over today's ceremonies. Among the greetings delivered on this occasion you will expect one from me. I desire even less that my words should cloud this solemn occasion. Yet I cannot pass over the remarkable fact that the day of the Nobel Prize presentation coincides with Human Rights Day. Nobel Prize winners are bound to feel that this coincidence places a responsibility upon them. Everybody present in the Stockholm City Hall must see a symbolic significance in it. So let none at this festive table forget that political prisoners are on hunger strike this very day in defense of the rights that have been curtailed or trampled under foot.

10 December 1970                                  Aleksandr Solzhenitsyn


**17**     Open Letter to Minister of State Security of the U.S.S.R. Andropov

For many years, I have borne in silence the lawlessness of your employees: the inspection of all my correspondence, the confiscation of half of it, the tracking down of my correspondents, their persecution at work and by state agencies, the spying around my house, the shadowing of visitors, the tapping of telephone conversations, the drilling of holes in ceilings, the placing of recording apparatus in my city apartment and at my cottage, and a persistent slander campaign against me from the platforms of lecture halls when they are put at the disposal of officials from your ministry.

But after the raid yesterday, I will no longer be silent. My cottage at Rozhdestvo, in the Naro-Fominsk rayon, was unoccupied, and the eavesdroppers were counting on my absence. I, however, had come back to Moscow after being taken ill suddenly, and had asked my friend Aleksandr Gorlov to get a spare part for the car from my cottage. But it turned out the house was unlocked, and voices could be heard from within. Gorlov stepped inside and demanded the intruders' documents. In that small structure, where three or four can barely turn around, there were about ten of them in plain clothes. At a command from the senior officer—"Take him into the wood and silence him!" —Gorlov was grabbed, knocked to the floor, dragged face down into the woods and beaten viciously. While this was going on, others took a roundabout route through the bushes, carrying parcels, documents and other objects (including perhaps some of the apparatus they had brought before) to their cars. However, Gorlov fought back vigorously and yelled, summoning witnesses. Neighbors from other lots came running in response to his shouts, barred the intruders' way to the highway and demanded their identification documents. Then one of the intruders presented a red identification card and the neighbors let them pass. Gorlov, with a battered face and his suit in ribbons, was taken to a car. "Fine methods you have," he said to his escorts. "We are *on an operation,* and on an operation we can do anything."

The one who, according to papers he had shown the neighbors, was a captain, and according to his own statement called Ivanov, drove Gorlov first to the Naro-Fominsk police station. The local officers greeted "Ivanov" with deference. "Ivanov" then demanded from Gorlov (!) a written explanation of what had happened. Although he had been severely beaten, Gorlov put in writing the purpose of his trip and all the circumstances. After that the senior intruder demanded that Gorlov should sign an undertaking *not to give the matter any publicity.* Gorlov flatly refused. Then they set off for Moscow, and on the road, the senior intruder gave Gorlov, word for word, the following warning: "If Solzhenitsyn finds out what took place at the dacha, you're finished. Your career [Gorlov is a candidate of technical sciences, has presented his doctoral dissertation, and works in the Design and Technical Research Institute of the State Construction Administration] will go no further; you will not be able to defend any dissertation. This will affect your family, your children, and if necessary, we will put you *inside."*

Those who know how we live know the full feasibility of these threats. But Gorlov did not give in to them, refused to sign the pledge, and is now threatened with reprisals.

I demand from you, citizen minister, the public identification of all the intruders, their punishment as criminals and a public explanation of this incident. Otherwise I can only conclude that they were sent by *you.*

13 August 1971                                        A. Solzhenitsyn

**18**   To the Chairman of the Council of Ministers of the U.S.S.R., A. N. Kosygin

I enclose a copy of my letter to the Minister of State Security. I consider him personally responsible for all the illegalities mentioned. If the government of the U.S.S.R. does not approve of these actions of Minister Andropov, I shall expect an investigation into the matter.

13 August 1971                                        A. Solzhenitsyn

**19**     There are many ways of killing a poet.

The method chosen for Tvardovsky was to take away his beloved child—his passion—his journal.

They were not satisfied with sixteen years of insults, meekly endured by this hero so long as his journal survived, so long as literature went on without interruption, so long as people could be printed in it, so long as people could go on reading it. They were not satisfied! So they lit fires around him: scattered his forces, destroyed his journal, dealt with him unjustly. And within six months these fires had consumed him. Within six months he was mortally sick; and only his characteristic fortitude sustained him till now, conscious to the last. Suffering to the last.

Third day. The portrait over the coffin shows the dead man about age forty, his brow unfurrowed by the galling yet cherished burden of his journal, radiant with that childlike bright trustfulness which he carried with him throughout his mortal life and which returned to him even when he was doomed.

To the most beautiful music, wreath after wreath is borne. . . . Here is one "From Soviet soldiers. . . ." With good reason. I remember how soldiers at the front knew to a man the difference between *Tyorkin*, which rang so miraculously true, and all other wartime books. And let us remember, too, how army libraries were forbidden to subscribe to *Novy Mir*, and how not so long ago men in barracks were hauled in for questioning if they read the light-blue journal.

And now the whole awkward squad from the Writers' Union has tumbled onto the stage. In the guard of honor we see the very same seedy deadbeats who once hunted and harassed him with unholy cries. Yes, it's an old, old custom of ours dating from the time of Pushkin: dead poets must fall into the hands of their enemies. The body is speedily disposed of, and the situation saved with a few glib speeches.

They plant themselves around the coffin like a circle of stones, and think that they have isolated it. They break up our one and only journal, and think that they have conquered.

But you know and understand nothing of the last century of Russia's history if you see in this a victory rather than an irreparable blunder.

Madmen! When the voices of the young ring out, harsh and peremptory, how you will miss this patient critic, whose gentle admonitory voice was heeded by all. That is when you will be ready to dig up the earth with your hands to bring back Trifonich. But by then it will be too late.

On the Ninth Day.*

27 December 1971                                                A. Solzhenitsyn


**20**     To Mr. Karl Ragnar Gierow of the Swedish Academy and Mr. Nils K. Stole of the Nobel Foundation
Moscow, 22 October 1971

Gentlemen:

I have received your "statement for the press" dated 7 October 1971, and I thank you.

Ambassador Jarring did indeed suggest last year, among other possibilities, presenting the Nobel medal and diploma to me in the Swedish Embassy in Moscow. I had already realized by the time we had this conversation that I should not be able to go out to Stockholm, and I wanted to accept the alternative suggested to me—supposing that the award would be conferred openly in the presence of a small gathering, and that I should be able to deliver my Nobel lecture to them. However, Ambassador Jarring categorically ruled against this and said that the investiture could only be private—"just as we are now, in this study."

To agree to such a proposal seemed to me an insult to the Nobel Prize itself. It would be as though it were something to be ashamed of, something to be concealed from people. As I understand it, Nobel Prizes are conferred publicly because the ceremony has a public significance.

When I wrote to you on 27 November 1970 that I was prepared to receive the Nobel insignia in Moscow if necessary, I assumed that this obvious and natural interpretation would be given to my words.

Neither my position, nor my viewpoint, has changed since that time. This year, just like last year, I am prepared to receive the Nobel insignia in Moscow, but of course not in private. If, however, the ceremony in this form is considered undesirable or inconvenient, as was the case last year, I shall once more ask you to let my insignia remain in the Nobel Foundation for safekeeping, especially as this does not contravene your rules, as I discovered from the communiqué which you sent me.

If that happens, I shall share with you the patient hope that a year will come at last in which circumstances will be propitious for my participation in the traditional Nobel Prize ceremony in Stockholm.

I offer my profound personal apologies to both of you for having been the unwilling cause of unnecessary work and worry, which you have not experienced with the majority of my predecessors.

With warmest best wishes,

A. Solzhenitsyn


Stockholm, 22 November 1971

Dear Mr. Solzhenitsyn:

Nils Stole and I have now met Gunnar Jarring. Our conversation with him has led to nothing, but we hardly expected positive results. We must conclude that there is no suitable room for a public lecture in the embassy and that the Academy at present has no possibility of arranging accommodation for it elsewhere in Moscow. We must arm ourselves with patience, as you write, and hope that circumstances will permit us later on to realize wishes which for the present we must renounce. The insignia remain here. But I am, naturally, always ready to come to Moscow to hand over the Nobel diploma and medal, if some fitting form can be found, either in the embassy or, as far as possible, in any other place convenient to you. In that case I could perhaps take back with me a copy of your lecture, to be published in *Les Prix Nobel*, in anticipation of the time when you are able to deliver it yourself. This is only a suggestion, which I thought I should mention.

With sincerest good wishes,

Yours,

K. R. Gierow

21   To Mr. Karl Ragnar Gierow, Royal Swedish Academy, Stockholm
     Moscow, 4 December 1971

Dear Mr. Gierow:

Your last four letters (of 7 and 14 October, and 9 and 22 November) throw more and more light on the question as to whether it is feasible for the Nobel insignia to be conferred upon me in Moscow, in, as you put it, fitting surroundings.

Let me say first that although the obstacles appear to be more and more formidable, and my confidence is waning, I appreciate greatly, indeed from the bottom of my heart, the firm intention which you express of coming to Moscow in person at any time and in any circumstances, so that the investiture can take place. I am truly grateful to you for this decision, and I can say quite sincerely that it shines through this obstacle-strewn situation like a shaft of light.

So then, after so many inquiries, newspaper articles, press communiqués, replies from the Swedish Ministry of Foreign Affairs, and even explanations of his personal position from your prime minister, we have arrived back at the offer which Mr. Jarring made with effortless magnanimity a year ago: a secret investiture without publicity behind the doors of his study.

As the proverb says, A lot of baa-ing and not much wool . . .

The whole vexing situation has apparently arisen only because the Swedish Embassy in Moscow simply does not have the *accommodation* for any other procedure. (This unfortunate circumstance probably means that it never holds receptions?)

A suspicion creeps into my mind: is there perhaps a semantic misunderstanding here? Do Mr. Jarring, and his superiors, perhaps think that a "public" or "open" procedure necessarily implies a mass audience? That the only alternative to a *tête-à-tête* is a gathering of a thousand? For that there is indeed no accommodation. But even in Mr. Jarring's study would it not be possible to set out chairs for thirty people? And if these guests were invited by you and me, that would, I think, create entirely fitting conditions for the delivery of a Nobel lecture. This would be the simplest answer.

But alas, alas, I fear that it is not superficial semantics that separate us from the tenants of those premises, but an unexpected discrepancy in our views as to where the frontiers of *culture* run. The Swedish Embassy has a cultural attaché on its staff, and no doubt has within its purview all sorts of cultural questions, transactions and events—but, we may ask, does it regard the presentation of a Nobel Prize (regrettably, on this occasion, to myself) as an event in cultural life that helps to draw our peoples together? If not, if it is seen rather as an incriminating shadow that threatens to blight the whole activity of the embassy—then, however spacious the accommodation, no place can ever be found for the procedure that you and I, Mr. Gierow, have in mind.

But here I derive some comfort from remembering what you said about the Swedish Academy and the Nobel Foundation being independent and free from question in their decisions, and that this position might even be weakened by an official ceremony organized "as it were" by the Swedish government.

Fully understanding and sharing this feeling of yours, and at the same time knowing of no public or cooperative organization in Moscow that would be willing to provide accommodation for our purpose, I venture to suggest another possibility: that the whole ceremony should be performed in a private apartment, in fact, at the address at which you write to me. This apartment is, it is true, certainly no more spacious than the Swedish Embassy, but forty or fifty people can be fitted in quite comfortably by Russian standards. The ceremony may lose something of its official character, but will gain from the warm atmosphere of a home. Besides, can you imagine, Mr. Gierow, what a load we shall be taking off the mind of the Swedish ambassador and indeed off the minds of the Swedish Ministry of Foreign Affairs?!

I am not familiar with the annals of the Nobel Foundation, but I suppose that there may have been a case in the past when a Nobel Prize winner was immobilized—by illness, for example—and a representative of the Foundation or of the Academy made the journey to present the prize at the laureate's home?

What if all these routes are barred to us? Why, we shall submit to fate: let my Nobel insignia remain in the safekeeping of the Nobel Foundation; they will lose none of their value for that. And perhaps someday, even if it is only after my death, your successors will, with a proper sense of the occasion, present the insignia to my son?

However, the Nobel lecture on literature for 1970 has been waiting for a year and is aging fast. What am I to do with it? . . .

I have permitted myself a somewhat flippant tone in this letter, Mr. Gierow, only because unpleasant complications are more easily dealt with in that way. But you will be aware that this flippancy was nowhere directed at you. Your decision is a noble one, and is the limit of what is possible for you, and once again you have my warmest thanks for it.

Give my very best wishes to Mr. Nils Stole, who, as I understand it, fully shares your views and your judgments.

Still trusting that we may yet meet in this life, I firmly shake you by the hand,

Yours sincerely,
A. Solzhenitsyn

**22**     Interview with correspondents of the *New York Times* and the
          *Washington Post*—Moscow, 30 March 1972

[What is he working on now?]

*October 1916*, the second "Knot" of the same book.

[Will he finish it soon?]

No. In the course of work it became clear that this "Knot" was more complicated than I had supposed. It will be necessary to take in the history of social and intellectual currents from the end of the nineteenth century, for they left their impress on the characters. Without the preceding events, there can be no understanding of the people.

[Is he not apprehensive that in delving into the detailed history of Russia, he will isolate himself from universal, timeless subjects?]

On the contrary, I think that new light will be thrown on much that is universal, and even timeless.

[Does this work entail the study of a great deal of source material?]

A very great deal. And in one sense this work is not what I am used to, for until recently I was involved only with the present day and wrote out of live experience. On the other hand, there are so many adverse external circumstances that it was far easier when I was an obscure student in provincial Rostov in 1937–1938 to gather material about the Samsonov disaster (not yet knowing that I was also fated to retrace the same route, only this time it was not we who were going to be surrounded, but we who were to surround the others). And although the hovel where my mother and I lived was demolished by a bomb in '42, and all our effects, books, papers burned, these two notebooks by some miracle were saved, and when I returned from exile they were handed over to me. Now I have made use of them.

Yes, in those days they didn't put special obstacles in my way. But now . . . You Western people can't imagine my situation. I'm living in my native country, writing a novel about Russia, but it is more difficult for me to gather material than if I were writing about Polynesia. For the next "Knot" I need to visit certain historic premises which now house various institutions, but the authorities won't give me a pass. My access to central and provincial archives is blocked. I have to visit the sites of events, and conduct interviews with elderly people, the last witnesses still alive, but for this I need the approval and aid of local authorities, which I cannot get. And without that everybody will shut up, will be too suspicious to tell me anything; without credentials I can be detained whenever I take a step. This has already been put to the test.

[Can others—assistants, secretaries—do this for him?]

They cannot. In the first place, as a nonmember of the Writers' Union, I do not have the right to a secretary or assistant. In the second place, such a secretary, representing my interests, would be as boxed in and restricted as I am. And in the third place, I simply have not the means to pay a secretary. You see, since the royalties from *Ivan Denisovich*, I have had no real earnings, nothing except the money left me by the late K. I. Chukovsky, and now that is running out. I lived for six years on the royalties and three years on the legacy.

I managed because I limited my expenditures and lived at the same level as when I was a teacher. I never spend more on myself than would be necessary to pay a secretary.

[Cannot money be obtained from the West?]

I have made a will, and when the occasion arises to execute it, all the royalties will be channeled by my attorney into social uses in my homeland. (The straight-from-the-heart, never-tell-a-lie *Literaturnaya Gazeta* once announced that "He has given detailed instructions on how the royalties are to be disbursed," but it innocently omitted to mention that they are to be used for social purposes in my homeland.) I myself will use only the Nobel Prize money. However, they have made any attempt on my part to obtain it humiliating, difficult and uncertain of success. The Ministry of Foreign Trade has notified me that for each incoming sum, the collegium must take a special decision as to whether it is to be paid over to me at all, in what form, and at what exchange premium.

[How, then, in spite of everything, does he manage to collect material?]

This brings us to another special feature of Soviet life that Westerners may well find difficult to understand. To the best of my knowledge, though I may be wrong, it is an established practice in the West that any job of work must be paid for, and it is not the normal practice to do work gratis. But in our country, how does samizdat, for instance, support itself, if not by unpaid labor? People expend their labor, their free time, sitting up nights over work for which all they can expect is persecution.

So it is with me. My work and my themes are widely known in the community at large, even beyond the limits of Moscow; well-wishers, often people unknown to me, send me (not by mail, needless to say, for then none of it would reach me) various books, even extremely rare ones, their own reminiscences, etc. Sometimes these things are to the point and very valuable, sometimes they are irrelevant, but it always touches me and strengthens my vivid sense that I am working for Russia, and that Russia is helping me. And another thing: Often I myself ask knowledgeable people, specialists, for advice on sometimes very complex technical matters, or on the selection of materials, which demands time and labor, and not only has no one ever asked for payment; they fall all over themselves to help.

This can, of course, also be very dangerous. A kind of forbidden, contaminated zone has been created around me and my family. To this very day there are people in Ryazan who have been dismissed from work for visiting my home a few years ago. A corresponding member of the Academy of Sciences, T. Timofeyev, director of a Moscow institute, the moment he learned that a mathematician working under him was my wife, was so panic-stricken that he forced through her dismissal with indecent haste, although this was completely against the law, and was almost immediately after she had given birth to a child. A family made a perfectly legal apartment exchange—perfectly legal until it became known that the family was mine. As soon as this was discovered, several officials in the Moscow City Soviet were disciplined: how could they have allowed a Solzhenitsyn, not *the* Solzhenitsyn, it is true, but his infant son, to be registered in the center of Moscow?

So that sometimes one of my informants will meet me for an hour or two to give me the benefit of his knowledge, and immediately comes under close surveillance and personal investigation as though he were a state criminal. Sometimes they go on keeping him under observation, to see whom he meets.

However, it's not always that way. The state security organ has its own schedule and its own deep-laid plans. Some days there is no obvious surveillance, or only the simplest kind. On other days they are all over me, as, for example, before the arrival of Heinrich Böll. They'll park cars at each of the two entries, with three men to a car, and there is more than one shift; they drive off after my visitors, and chase pedestrians as well. If you keep in mind that they are busy round the clock monitoring telephone calls and indoor conversations and analyzing tapes and all my correspondence, and that in some spacious building all the data obtained is assembled and collated (no task for junior personnel), then you cannot help marveling that such a large number of idlers, in the prime of life and at the peak of their powers, who could be employed in productive labor for the good of the homeland, are instead preoccupied with my acquaintances and me and with the invention of enemies for themselves. Then there are others digging into my biography, and sending agents abroad to sow chaos in the publication of my books. It is someone's job to draw up and supervise the general plan for throttling me. That plan has not yet been successful, and has therefore been revised several times in midcourse. But its development through the years can be traced by stages.

It was decided to throttle me in 1965, when they seized my files and were horrified by works from my labor camp years—as if they could choose not to wear the stamp of the perpetually doomed! If this had been in Stalin's time, nothing could have been simpler: I would have disappeared and no one would have asked any questions. But after the Twentieth and Twenty-second Party Congresses it had become more complicated.

First it was decided to make me a nonperson. Not a line would appear anywhere, no one would mention me even to abuse me, and in a few years I would be forgotten. Then I could be tidied away. But by then the era of samizdat had arrived, and my books had spread through the country, then found their way abroad as well. Silence didn't work.

At this point they began (and they have not yet brought to an end) their campaign of *slander at private meetings.*

This, too, is almost impossible for a Westerner to imagine. There exists throughout the country a well-developed network of Party and adult education and a lecture network. There is no institution or military unit, no rayon center or state farm, where lecturers and propagandists do not appear according to a definite schedule, and all of them, in all places, simultaneously say the same thing, on instructions from a single center. There are certain variations—for audiences in the capital, in the provinces, in the armed forces, in the academic world. Thanks to the fact that only personnel of a particular institution or residents in a particular district are admitted, such lectures are in effect, or sometimes by definition, private. Sometimes orders are given, even to the scientific staff, to put away notebooks and pens. Any information, any slogan, can be fed into this network. In 1966 the order went out to say the following about me: first, that under Stalin I was jailed *with reason*, that I was wrongly rehabilitated, that my works are criminal, and so forth. This although the lecturers themselves had never in their lives read these works, because the authorities were afraid to let even these people see them—but still, they ordered them to speak in this way.

The system, the great idea, is to lecture to the staff of only one establishment at a time. Outwardly, all is calm and cozy, no one is being hounded—yet slander spills through the land, and cannot be resisted: you can't travel to every town, they won't let you into those closed auditoriums, there are thousands of lecturers, there is no one to protest, and so the slander takes possession of all minds.

[How does this become known?]

This is a new era, a different era. Quite a lot leaks through to me both from the provinces and through Moscow. The times are such that at all of these lectures, even the most private, I have well-wishers, and they inform me afterward through various channels that on such and such a date in some auditorium or other a lecturer named this or that made such and such a lying and defamatory statement about me. The most lurid stuff I write down; it may come in handy someday, I may confront one of these lecturers with it. Maybe the time will come in our country when they will personally answer for it in court.

[Why don't audiences protest there and then, if they see distortion?]

Well, that's impossible here, even today. No one dares to stand up and contradict a party propagandist, or tomorrow it's goodbye to his job, or even goodbye to his freedom. There have been cases where they have used me like litmus paper to test the loyalty of applicants for graduate school or for a comfortable post: "Have you read Solzhenitsyn: What do you think of him?"—and the fate of the candidate depends on the answer.

They talk a lot of nonsense at these lectures. At one time they were garbling my family history, without really knowing the least thing about it, like the meanest of kitchen gossips. Just think how serious overemployment must be in this country, just think what sort of thing people are paid good wages for, when full-time propagandists in the adult *education* network, not mere fishwives, discuss on public platforms a man's wedding, or the birth and baptism of his son. There was a time when they happily made play with my patronymic, Isayevich. They would say, trying to seem casual: "Incidentally, his real surname is Solzhenit*ser* or Solzhenit*sker;* not, of course, that this is of any importance in our country."

But one charge was taken seriously, one that would always catch the ear of the audience: *Traitor to the motherland.* When someone is hounded in our country, we generally use not reasoned arguments but the most primitive of labels, the grossest and simplest of abusive epithets, in order, as the saying goes, to arouse the "wrath of the masses." In the 1920s it was "counterrevolutionary," in the 1930s "enemy of the people"; from the 1940s onward, "traitor to the motherland." Ah, how eagerly they thumbed through my military records, how they searched, hoping to find that I had been a prisoner of war, if only for two little days, like Ivan Denisovich—that would have been a find! But still, in a closed lecture you can convince a gullible public of any lie. And the word went around for years—*years*—on end, in auditoriums near and far, throughout the whole country: Solzhenitsyn voluntarily surrendered to the Germans! No, he surrendered a whole battery! After that he served as a *Polizei* for the occupiers! No, he was a Vlasovite! No, he served in the Gestapo itself! Outwardly, all is calm, there is no harassment, but under the skin there is this cancer of slander. *Novy Mir* once organized a readers' conference in Novosibirsk, and someone passed Tvardovsky a note: "How could you allow someone who worked for the Gestapo to be printed in your magazine?" Thus public opinion the country over was fully prepared for any reprisal against me. Still, we are no longer in that era when you could crush someone without it becoming known.

True, it had to be admitted publicly that I had been an officer at the front, and that my wartime service was impeccable. The mist hung and hung in the air, but dispersed without rain.

Next there began a new campaign of accusations that I myself had given *Cancer Ward* to the West. What lies did they not tell in those closed lectures: how somewhere on the frontier (where is not known) an acquaintance of an acquaintance of mine (no names) had been detained, and his suitcase had a false bottom, and there were my works (no titles). This drivel was seriously propagated throughout the provinces, and people were horrified to hear what a villain I was, what a traitor to the motherland all over again. Later, with my expulsion from the Writers' Union, there were open hints that I should get out of the country, on the same "treason to the motherland" pretext. Then it started all over again in connection with the Nobel Prize. From public platforms everywhere they harped on the same theme: *The Nobel Prize is Judas's pay for betraying his homeland.* They repeat it even now, without worrying that they may be casting a shadow on Pablo Neruda, for example. They are short-sightedly insulting all Nobel laureates and the Nobel Prize as an institution.

[But after all, you yourself sent *August 1914* abroad—and this has not been treated as a criminal act.]

So far, they have had the good sense not to bring charges. But the honorable *Literaturnaya Gazeta* has been guilty of an abridgment—an innocent one, like all its abridgments: "Solzhenitsyn sent the manuscript of his novel abroad *immediately!*" Oh, no, that's no lie! Just one little thing has been omitted: [immediately] after offering it to seven Soviet publishers: Khudozhestvennaya Literatura, Sovetski Pisatel, *Molodaya Gvardia* and various magazines whom I asked *just to read* my novel, just leaf through it, and not one showed any desire even to take the work into its hands. It was as though they had all come to an agreement. Not one answered my letter, not one asked for the manuscript.

However, the appearance of *August* put a new method into the heads of my persecutors. In this novel I gave detailed information about my maternal and paternal lineage. Although many friends and acquaintances who are alive today knew my relatives, the omniscient state security, absurd though this may seem, learned about them only from the novel. So at that point they rushed to "follow the trail" with the aim of compromising me—by Soviet criteria. Their efforts to this end followed two different lines. First, the *racial* line was again revived. Or more precisely, the Jewish line. A special major of state security named Blagovidov rushed off to check the personal files of all the "Isaakii"s in the archives of Moscow University for 1914 in the hope of proving that I was Jewish. This would open up a very tempting possible "explanation" of my literary position. After all, with the appearance of my historical novel, the task of my pursuers grows complicated: it is not enough to defame the author; it is necessary also to undermine trust in his views of Russian history—those he has already expressed and those he may express in the future.

Alas, the racist researchers were thwarted: I turned out to be a Russian.

Then they abandoned the racial line for a *class* line, which was why they approached my old aunt and pasted together an article out of her stories. This was picked up and printed in *Stern,* the garish magazine.

The editor in chief of *Stern* now insists that it was his own correspondent who visited my aunt. It is of course possible that he was there too, together with the Soviet types. Let us note, however, that the city of Georgievsk, unlike nearby Pyatigorsk, has been completely closed to foreigners for the entire fifty-five years of Soviet rule. A foreigner must have an extraordinary clearance to get into Georgievsk. There were three men altogether, all spoke excellent Russian, and they made five leisurely calls on my aunt. They expressed enthusiastic interest in her life story, asked her if they might read her notes for a few hours, stole them and never returned. Being almost blind, she did not see what they looked like, but in manners and personality they resembled Dickens's Job Trotter. Her guests were from the same stable as Victor Louis, and I don't exclude the possibility that he was among them. *Stern*'s tie with Victor Louis has long been well known. For example, after Louis had visited me to deny that it was he who had sold *Cancer Ward* to the West, the details of our conversation and some photographs (thievishly taken with a telescopic lens from the bushes) appeared in *Stern*—of course—though not under his by-line. Even in my slight experience I have noticed that *Stern* enjoys special privileges in our country. The *Stern* article had scarcely appeared when Verchenko, a secretary of the Writers' Union, said at a party meeting: *"This is a source which we have every reason to believe."*

[The fate of the manuscript of *August 1914.* The publishers, Langen-Müller, maintain that they received the manuscript last spring, via samizdat.]

How could they have received it, when I released only one copy from my desk before June, the one that went to the YMCA Press? Well, let them name the person *from whom* they received it. It would have to be a person very close to me or the sort of thief who comes to a house because he has it on reliable authority that the occupant is absent. The publishers are ignobly trying to hide behind our noble samizdat. They indulge in a logical fallacy: *since* my previous works first appeared in samizdat, it must be so this time too. But this happens to be wrong! I freely gave out my earlier writings to be read. But I wanted to take this book all the way into print myself. Only when the book came out—only then would I begin to give the manuscript to those who wanted to read it.

In the cavalier manner of the *Stern* article, and its offensive insinuations, you can discern the familiar features of its compilers, especially where they hazard an opinion on the nature of literary creation. We learn that Solzhenitsyn has employed a *wily* literary device: he has transferred the action to prerevolutionary times, and to do so has made a profound study of people of another era, read quite a few military and historical works, taken pains to depict not the war he went through himself but another, dissimilar one—all in order to erupt on page 740 with just one phrase, which *Stern* suggests is to be understood in a figurative sense, so that Solzhenitsyn should be put in prison. In just the same way the leaders of the Writers' Union once reproached me for making a detailed study of cancer, for entering a cancer clinic, and for deliberately contracting cancer in order to foist on the reader some kind of symbol. These cowardly mischief-makers venture to discuss the nature of literature. It is impossible for them to get it into their heads that a man may for some time past have had no need for subterfuges, may have been saying openly just what he thinks about the present day.

[How authentic is the information in the *Stern* article?]

Let us speak of the *Literaturnaya Gazeta* article. It is authentic where it coincides with what has already been published in my novel. The rest is part ludicrous rubbish and part carefully contrived and skillfully aimed falsehood. Only, in their zeal they overshoot the mark. For example, they assert that both my grandfathers were *landowners* in the northern Caucasus. It is embarrassing that *Literaturnaya Gazeta* is so ignorant of our country's history. Apart from a few Cossack generals known to everyone, there never were any landowners (no landholding nobles, the progeny of ancient notables who received land for military service) in the northern Caucasus. All the lands belonged to the Terek and Kubna Cossacks. Many of those lands, right up until the twentieth century, were empty and abandoned; there was a shortage of labor. Peasant settlers could purchase only small allotments, but the Cossacks willingly rented out as much land as anyone could want, at fantastically low rents.

My grandfathers were not Cossacks; both of them were peasants. By pure accident, the peasant origin of the Solzhenitsyns is established by documents from as long ago as 1698, when my forebear Filipp suffered the wrath of Peter I (cf. *Voronezhskaya Kommuna*, 9 March 1969, article about the city of Bobrov). And my great-great-grandfather was exiled, for taking part in a rebellion, from the Voronezh province to the lands of the Caucasus military settlements. There, apparently because he was a rebel, he wasn't registered as a Cossack, but was allowed to live on empty land. The Solzhenitsyns were ordinary Stavropol peasants. In Stavropol before the Revolution, a few yoke of oxen and a few horses, a dozen cows or so, and two hundred sheep were by no means regarded as wealth. The whole large family worked with its hands. In the farmstead stood a simple clay hut; I remember it. But to justify the *class* line, in order to demonstrate the truth of the Vanguard Doctrine, it was necessary to invent a bank, to tack zeros onto the sum of our possessions, to dream up fifty farmhands, to call my cousin who works on a collective farm to the administration offices and question her, and to write a caption describing the Shcherbaks'

dacha in Kislovodsk, where I was born, as the Solzhenitsyns' "country manor."[1]
But any fool can see that it is not even a house in a Cossack *stanitsa*. That's the
kind of "landowners" we were. The scum conflated these lies also in order to
impute to my father, a Narodnik and a Tolstoyan, a cowardly suicide "out of fear
of the Reds"—before he had seen the firstborn son he had longed for, and when
he had lived only briefly with his beloved wife! The judgment of a reptile.

[About his mother.]

She raised me in incredibly hard circumstances. Widowed before my birth,
she did not remarry—mainly for fear that a stepfather might be too harsh with
me. We lived in Rostov for nineteen years, until the war. For fifteen of them
we couldn't obtain a room from the state, but rented accommodations in any
old privately owned dilapidated shack at a high price. When we finally did get
a room, it was part of a converted stable. It was always cold and drafty, it was
heated with coal, which was hard to get, and water had to be brought in from
afar. I learned what running water in an apartment means only recently.
Mother knew French and English well, and on top of that learned stenography
and typing, but in the institutions that paid well she was never employed
because of her *social origin:* even in a nonsensitive institution like Melstrio (the
Flour Mill Construction Administration) she was purged—dismissed with restrictions on her future rights. This forced her to look for extra work in the
evenings, and to do her housework late at night, so that she was always short
of sleep. Because of our living conditions she often caught chills, and in the end
she contracted tuberculosis and died at the age of forty-nine. I was at the front
at the time and I did not get to see her grave until twelve years later, after
prison camp and exile.

[Aunt Irina.]

Mama sent me to stay with her two or three times for summer holidays. The
rest is the fruit of her imagination, which is by now pretty hazy. I have never
lived with her.

[How well does he remember his father?]

Only from snapshots, and the accounts of my mother and people who knew
him. From the university he went as a volunteer to the front and served in the
Grenadier Artillery Brigade. Once, there was a fire at the battery and he
himself pulled ammunition boxes away. He had three officers' decorations from
the First World War, but in my childhood they were considered dangerously
incriminating, and I remember my mother and myself burying them in case we
were searched. When almost the whole front had collapsed, the battery in
which my father had served remained in the front lines until the Peace of

---

1. We learned later that this dishonest substitution was made only in the issue of the
paper distributed in the Soviet Union. The caption there read: "The Solzhenitsyn house
in Sabl, which now serves as the hospital of the Kirov collective farm." In the issue of
*Literaturnaya Gazeta* sent abroad (where readers could compare it with the *Stern* article), the caption under the same photograph reads: "The Solzhenitsyn house in Kislovodsk, formerly belonging to Irina Shcherbak. Presently serves as a wing of a sanatorium."

Brest-Litovsk itself. He and Mother were married at the front by the brigade chaplain. Father returned in the spring of 1918 and soon afterward died as the result of an accident and poor medical care. His grave in Georgievsk was leveled by a tractor during the construction of a stadium.

[About the other grandfather.]

My maternal grandfather came from the Crimea as a young boy to herd sheep and work as a farmhand. He started with nothing, then became a tenant farmer, and it is true that by the time he was old he was quite rich. He was a man of rare energy and industry. In his fifty years of work he gave the country more grain and wool than many of today's state farms, and he worked no less hard than their directors. As for his workers, he treated them in such a way that after the Revolution they voluntarily supported the old man for twelve years until he died. Let a state farm director try begging from his workers after his dismissal.

[Is a man's social origin still held against him?]

The habit of judging people by their social origin is not as rampant as it was in the twenties and thirties, but it is firmly implanted in many minds and still quite alive in our country, and it takes very little to fan the fires again at any moment. In fact, quite recently Tvardovsky's enemies were publicly condemning him for his so-called kulak origins. In my case, since the attempt to prove my treason by pretending that I was a prisoner of war has not come off, they hope to get the story across by pointing to my class origin. So the latest articles in *Literaturnaya Gazeta,* for all their illiteracy and stupidity, are by no means random jeering for its own sake.

Incidentally, you notice that *Literaturnaya Gazeta*—which has never debated the *substance* of my works and views, which has never dared to print a single genuine critical review about me, however hostile, for that could uncover a portion of the intolerable *truth*—in its judgments about me seems to have lost its voice altogether, seems to have been separated from its own critics and authors. In its attacks on me it takes cover behind passages reproduced from elsewhere, behind a gutter magazine, behind foreign journalists, even behind music hall singers or jugglers. I do not understand this timidity. Maybe it is because those who, as they say in Finland, are "reared on vinegar from childhood" are nonetheless becoming model socialist realists and even making their way into the management of the Writers' Union and of *Literaturnaya Gazeta* itself?

When, commissioned by *Literaturnaya Gazeta,* the Finnish journalist Larni set out to write and publish an article about me, not at home in Finland, but in a third country, he might as well have undertaken to straighten a steel coil with his teeth. A death-defying act. You know how it is in the circus: a silly-looking clown comes out, everyone laughs at him, he climbs up into the dome where the star performers are, steps onto a wire—and suddenly he is dangling by his teeth, and the whole circus falls silent and sees that he is not a clown at all, that he has risked a death-defying feat. Larni *hints* at certain *hints* of mine. In my novel, the social democrat and defeatist Lenartovich is, in 1914, in favor of a Russian defeat so that the country can then reconstruct its social order. This was precisely what all social democratic defeatists, as distinct from the so-called social patriots, or "defensist" social democrats, did want and count on, and Larni, as a Communist, probably knows it, yet he recklessly stretches out the steel coil with his teeth, not realizing how easily he can come a cropper himself. He stretches the argument to imply that the author himself (myself—by no means a social democrat!) "is not averse to seeing the Germans as victors"—not, apparently, in 1914 but in 1941 (why not transpose the "1" and the "4"—who's to stop you?).

If there is anything that is totally absent in my novel, it is this defeatism. But that doesn't stop them from stretching the point. At all costs they must have a newspaper bridgehead, so that they can subsequently print "angry letters from working people," as they already have more than once. A shameless swindle on the part of a press that is not accustomed to corrections and retractions. Ah, how desperately they require me to have been a prisoner, how desperately their "literary criticism" needs some bit of corroborating evidence from the Gestapo . . . If they stretch things so in front of the whole circus, what wonders can they not perform in their unmonitored closed lectures!

Of course, this is not the last lie, there are probably more ahead than behind, and I cannot defend myself against all of them. Let them hang a few more on me; perhaps someone else will answer for me. Interviews are not the writer's business. I have abstained from interviews for nine years and I am not the least bit sorry.

In general, fame is a heavy burden; it consumes a lot of time to little purpose. At least they do not drag me along to meetings, as they do others; I am thankful that they have expelled me. It was good to work when nobody knew me, nobody exercised his pen making up fairy tales about me, or went around collecting lavatory wall gossip, like those rascals Burg and Feifer.

[What is the Plan?]

The Plan consists in driving me out of this life or out of the country, tossing me into a ditch or sending me to Siberia, or having me "dissolve in an alien fog," as they frankly write. How confident they are that the censor's pets have more right to Russia than others who were also born there. In general, all this harrying shows the stupidity and short-sightedness of those who direct it. They do not want to know the complexity and richness of history in all its diversity. They care only about silencing all voices that are unpleasant to their ears or spoil their peace of mind today, and they do not think about the future. So they have now senselessly silenced *Novy Mir* and Tvardovsky—thus making themselves poorer and even more blind—but they refuse to recognize their loss.

Incidentally, about two weeks ago the *New York Times* published a letter from a certain Soviet poet, Smelyakov, in which he takes issue with my valedictory words on Tvardovsky.

[About access to the Western press.]

No, we don't see it, but sometimes Western radio stations are audible through the grinding noise of the jamming devices. If we learn anything about events in our own country, it is from that source.

This new onslaught against me is striking *in its form:* why, you may wonder, when all the press is in their hands, is there nowhere nearer for answering me than in the *New York Times?* This is what it means to fear the truth: if they answered me in the Soviet press, they would have to quote me at least a little, and that is impossible. But let's take the content: the surprising thing is that Smelyakov criticizes me without, apparently, having read me. I write that they strangled *Novy Mir* and thereby killed Tvardovsky. Smelyakov says evasively that "Tvardovsky had some bad moments." I write that Tvardovsky wrote more candidly about life at the front, and more purely than anyone else. Smelyakov twists it to mean that "Tvardovsky had a negative attitude toward the Soviet army." Where does he get this? I wrote literally about his "gentle, admonitory voice which was heeded by all," and Smelyakov turns it inside out: "Solzhenitsyn ascribes to Tvardovsky his own illusions that someday Soviet rule will crumble and a new generation will build a new Russia." Read my eulogy: where is there anything like that?

That last paragraph is indeed filled with meaning, but what can you do if they refuse, or if they are unable, to read it? The study of Russian history, which has now taken me back to the last years of the last century, has shown me how precious *peaceful* solutions are for our country, how important it is that authority, however autocratic and unlimited it may be, should listen benevolently to society, and that society should understand the real position of the authorities; how important it is that the country be led not by *force* and *coercion*, but by *righteousness.* I think that these studies of mine helped me to recognize in Tvardovsky's activity precisely that conciliatory line. Alas, even the gentlest admonitory voice is intolerable, and to be silenced. How reasonably, with what good will, did Sakharov and Grigorenko speak out here recently: neither of them was given a hearing—they were told to get lost, to shut up. . . .

There we see the pettiness, the ignoble narrow-mindedness of those who are leading the campaign against me. It honestly does not enter their heads that a writer who thinks differently from the majority of his society is an enrichment to that society, not the shame and ruination of it.

[The ninth of April is the day of the Nobel Prize ceremony. Where will it take place?]

So far neither the Swedish Embassy nor our own Ministry of Culture has agreed to give us facilities. It is surprising to a comic degree: why are people so angry about the Nobel Prize? In a few years' time this event will inevitably have to be seen in a different light, and they will feel ashamed.

[On those invited.]

I do not know whom Mr. Karl Gierow will wish to invite. On my side, apart from my close friends, it will be the most eminent representatives of the artistic and scientific intelligentsia—some writers, the chief producers at the leading theaters, important musicians, actors, certain academicians. I shall not name them for the time being, because I do not know whether they will want to come or think it possible to come, or what obstacles they may encounter. In any case, I shall invite those whom I know and whose work I respect, and see what happens.

I should also like to invite my lawyer, Dr. Heeb, to the ceremony, but as a private person I have no official right to invite anyone from abroad.

In addition, I am inviting the Minister of Culture of the U.S.S.R., and correspondents of *Selskaya Zhizn* and *Trud,* the two metropolitan newspapers that have so far not libeled me.

[Can the ceremony be obstructed in any way?]

Theoretically, that is not excluded, and in practice it would be easy, requiring neither a large force nor much intelligence. But I do not anticipate it: it would be a disgraceful act of barbarity.

[What if Mr. Gierow is refused a visa?]

In that case the ceremony will not take place, and my insignia will remain in Stockholm for another ten or twenty years.

[There is a rumor, so far unconfirmed, that the writer Maksimov is to be tried on criminal charges, for his novel *The Seven Days of Creation.*]

Artistic literature is one of man's highest gifts, one of his subtlest and most perfect instruments. Criminal charges can be brought against it only by those who are criminals themselves, who have resolved to put themselves beyond the pale of humanity and of human nature.


## 23

Mr. Gierow and I have made every concession possible: his visit was described as a *private* one, to a *private* apartment, to carry out what was practically a *private* ceremony. Prohibition of the ceremony even in this form is a final and irrevocable prohibition of the conferment of the Nobel Prize upon me on the territory of my native land in any form whatsoever. Therefore the belated concession made by the Swedish Ministry of Foreign Affairs is no longer relevant.

But it is also insulting: the Swedish Ministry of Foreign Affairs stubbornly persists in regarding the conferment of the Nobel Prize upon me not as an event in cultural life but as a political event, which is why it makes conditions that would lead yet again either to the "closed" variant of the ceremony, or to a special screening of those present and the prohibition of any expression by them of their attitude to what was going on, since anything of the kind might be interpreted by somebody as a "political demonstration."

Apart from this, now that Mr. Gierow has been refused a visa, I would consider it humiliating for him and for me if I received the Nobel insignia from any other hands than those of the Permanent Secretary of the Swedish Academy.

Finally, we had already completed the far from easy preparations with our own modest forces: invitations had been sent out (not only within Moscow) to about twenty writers, those whom I consider the fine flower and creative strength of our contemporary literature, and to roughly as many artists, musicians and academicians; many of them had timed or canceled trips, rehearsals and other commitments to fit in with this. Now all these forty guests have been insulted by the refusal of the visa; notes canceling the invitations have been sent out. Both they and I are far too busy to go through the whole procedure a second time.

Under the rules of the Swedish Academy, as they have been explained to me, it can keep the Nobel insignia for an indefinite period. If I do not live long enough myself, I bequeath the task of receiving them to my son.

8 April 1972                                                                 A. Solzhenitsyn


**24**    To the State Security Committee of the U.S.S.R. [KGB].

I am sending you copies of two inept anonymous letters, although you already have other copies in your file.

I have no spare time to play detective with you. If this story has any sequel, I shall publicize it, together with other methods by which your department has persistently interfered with my private life.

2 July 1973                                                                 Solzhenitsyn


**25**    To the U.S.S.R. Minister of the Interior, N. A. Shchelokov

Four months ago I applied for a residence permit so that I might live with my family. After your lengthy meditation on a matter which might seem to need none, I have now been informed that my request has been *rejected* by the militia and by you personally. I would express my inability to understand what human or legal considerations could induce you to prevent a husband from living with his wife, or a father with his two small sons, if I did not know from long experience that neither human nor legal considerations have any existence in our political system.

The demeaning, compulsory "passport system," in which his place of residence may not be chosen by the individual but is chosen for him by the authorities, in which the right to move from city to city, and especially from the country to the city, must be earned as a favor, probably does not exist even in the colonial countries of the world today. And yet for the last forty-two years, millions of my compatriots have suffered and are still suffering daily under that system. With the present wide-ranging discussion about the freedom of emigration for thousands, one cannot but be struck by the fact that millions lack the right to pick their place of residence and occupation even within their own country! That lack of rights has been further aggravated by a law passed in 1973 (Council of Ministers, 19 June) that prevents a peasant from leaving his collective farm even temporarily for seasonal work without permission.

However, I take this opportunity to remind you that serfdom in our country was abolished 112 years ago. And we are told that the October Revolution wiped out its last remnants.

Presumably I, like any other citizen of this country, am neither a serf nor a slave and should be free to live wherever I find it necessary, and no one, not even the highest *leadership*, has a serf owner's right to separate me from my family.

21 August 1973                                                            Solzhenitsyn


**26**     Interview with Associated Press news agency and *Le Monde*—Moscow, 23 August 1973

[Is it true that you receive letters containing threats and demands from gangsters?]

I have received letters with threats rather than demands, threats to make short work of me and my family. This summer such threats have come to me through the mail. Not to mention the psychological mistakes, the many technical mistakes made by the authors have convinced me that these letters were sent by officials of the KGB. For example, the incredible speed of delivery of these bandits' letters—less than twenty-four hours. Only letters from the most important government organs go that fast. Letters mailed to me in Moscow usually take three to five days, but letters of any importance, urgency and usefulness are never delivered to me at all. Then again, they were in such a hurry that the envelopes were sealed only after the post office had stamped them. Yet again, there are terminological errors. Take, for example, the last letter, of 30 July: "Well, bitch, you never came! Now you've only got yourself to blame. We'll *straighten you out.* Just you wait!"

The authors had tried to use thieves' jargon, but were not sufficiently familiar with it, and had used the expression "straighten out," which refers to trial and punishment by the thieves of those among themselves who offend against their code, or betray, but never means punishment of a free man from the despicable outside world—these people are not worthy of a "straightening out," in the opinion of thieves; they are just done away with.

This kind of bandit masquerade is not altogether a novelty to KGB personnel. There are cases of hooligans going unpunished, hooligans who have beaten up undesirable dissidents in the streets, who have snatched briefcases from Western correspondents, who have broken windows of foreign cars. After the failure of the campaign to slander me behind my back, a bandits' masquerade was just what you would expect.

And then there was the case of the respected Michael Scammell, editor of the journal *Index*, who reported the following episode to me after he had left the Soviet Union. At Sheremetyevo Airport he was subjected to a three-hour search, and they found notes on him relating to his trip. To make such notes is considered natural by ordinary human standards everywhere, but by Soviet standards it is criminal. When they made this discovery, the so-called customs officers put pressure on him and proposed that he buy a manuscript about Solzhenitsyn (without naming the author beforehand or showing him the manuscript) and thereby settle the incident. Scammell refused.

This may have been an attempt to compromise Scammell or preparation for a routine provocation against me. But judge for yourself what a wide choice of instruments the KGB has: from "gangsters" and street hooligans to "customs officers" and brokers in literature. And the question arises: if our State Security Committee—the KGB—is there to protect the world's most advanced state order, which according to the One True Doctrine is guaranteed universal historical victory anyway, why all this fuss and why such low methods?

During the winter of 1971–1972, I was warned through several channels (within the KGB apparatus there are also people who are utterly weary of their lot) that they were preparing to kill me in a "car accident." I gave a hint of this in my last interview.

But here is the peculiarity or, I might almost say, the advantage of our social structure: not a single hair falls or will fall from my head or from the heads of members of my family without the knowledge and approval of the KGB, such is the extent to which we are observed, shadowed, spied upon and listened to. And if, for example, today's letter-writing gangsters had happened to be real ones, then after the very first letter they would have come under the full control of the KGB. If, for example, a letter that reaches me by post blows up, it will be impossible to explain why it didn't explode before that in the hands of the censors. And since for a long time I have not suffered from serious diseases, and since I don't drive a car, and since my beliefs would not allow me to commit suicide in any circumstances, if it is announced that I have been killed, or have suddenly met a mysterious end, you can infallibly conclude, with one hundred percent certainty, that I have been killed by the KGB or with its approval.

But I must say that my death will bring no joy to those people who count on it to stop my literary activities. Immediately after my death or immediately after I have disappeared, or have been deprived of my liberty by whatever means, my literary last will and testament will irrevocably come into force (even if there should appear in my name a false and contradictory declaration, like Traicho Kostov's "letter" from the death chamber),* and then the main part of my works will start being published, works I have refrained from publishing all these years.

If the officers of the KGB track down and confiscate copies of the harmless *Cancer Ward* in all provincial cities (and dismiss the holders of these copies from their jobs or expel them from higher educational establishments), what will they do when my posthumous and most important books stream out all over Russia?

[In your last interview, one and a half years ago, you told of restrictions and persecutions in connection with your literary activity, in the gathering of material and in your daily life. Has anything changed for the better?]

Vaganov, the head of the regional archives in Tambov, has refused to let me have a look even at newspapers fifty-five years old, although the whole of the history of Tambov is rotting and feeding the mice on the floor of a damp, disused church. In the Central Archives of Military History, a rigorous investigation was recently made in order to find out who—in 1963!—made available to me mate-

rial about the First World War, and how this happened. A young literary specialist, Gabriel Superfin, who has helped me a lot and who has a remarkable talent,
a remarkably keen eye for archive material, was arrested on 3 July on the basis
of statements made by Yakir and Krasin, and taken to the town of Oryol, where
his trial would be much less visible and audible. He has been accused under
Article 72, which provides for a sentence of up to fifteen years. With his fragile
health, this would mean murder by imprisonment. Of course, he has not been
openly accused of helping me, but that help will make his fate a heavier one.
Aleksandr Gorlov, who in 1971 would not agree to KGB demands that he keep
silent about the raid on my country cottage, has for the three years since then
been denied any opportunity to defend the doctoral thesis which he had already submitted at that time, just as they threatened that he would be. The
thesis has won twenty-five positive assessments, including those of all the official
opponents, and not a single negative assessment. It would be impossible to
reject it on scholarly grounds. But all the same, he will not be able to defend
his thesis (on the mechanics of foundations!) successfully, because "lack of political confidence" has been expressed regarding Gorlov. Preliminary steps have
been taken to dismiss Gorlov from his work. Mstislav Rostropovich has been
persecuted all these years with the tireless and ingenious pettiness that is so
typical of the state machine of a great power. He has been confronted with a
long succession of nagging, needling attacks, hindrances and humiliations at
every step in his daily life, in the hope that they will compel him to deny me
hospitality. Madame Furtseva and her deputies have in fact made this demand
openly and uninhibitedly. For some time they took him, and even Galina
Vishnevskaya, off radio and television, and newspaper reports about them were
distorted. Quite a number of his concerts in the Soviet Union were canceled for
no apparent reason, sometimes when he was on the way to the town where the
concert was to be held.

They have methodically deprived him of professional contact with the
greatest musicians of the world. And because of this—just one example—the
first performance of Lutoslawski's cello concerto in Poland, the composer's
homeland, has been postponed for several years—they won't let Rostropovich
go there—as has the first performance of the concerto by Britten dedicated to
Rostropovich. Finally, he has been prevented from conducting at the Bolshoi
Theater, something that he considers both interesting and important to his
development as a musician. Last spring I felt duty bound to move from his
dacha in order to deliver him from persecution. But the persecutions continue
vindictively to this very day. Nor can they forgive him for the letter he wrote
about the state of the arts in the Soviet Union.

For several years now every single telephone call or indoor conversation
involving me or members of my family, even on the most trivial everyday
matter, has been bugged and (there are clear indications of this) thoroughly
analyzed. By now we are used to the situation that day and night we are always
talking in the presence of the KGB. When their tapes run out they unceremoni-
ously break the telephone conversation to reload the machine while we dial
again. The same is happening to Rostropovich, Sakharov, Shafarevich, to the

Chukovsky family and many other families known to me, and even more who are unknown.

It is strange to hear that elsewhere people are arguing about whether the President has the right to order the installation of electronic bugging equipment for the defense of his country's military secrets. Indeed, a man who had divulged such secrets has even been acquitted by a court! But in our country a person has only once to voice an opinion contrary to the official view and he is considered *guilty* even without a trial. And electronic bugging equipment is installed at his place not by the leader of the country but by an ordinary officer of the KGB. Such electronic bugging, not to mention all the other kinds of surveillance, enmeshes thousands upon thousands of intellectuals and responsible civil servants in the major cities of the Soviet Union. A vast number of parasites in uniform sit and analyze the tapes. And this is not even kept very secret. A minister thinks it permissible to announce to one of his underlings: "I was allowed to listen to one of your telephone conversations the other day," and then to rebuke him for it. And surveillance reaches the point that even for the people who come into contact with me the Fifth Bureau of the KGB (Major General Nikishkin) and its First Department (Shironin) issue written instructions: "Find out what addresses *they* visit." That starts a spiral of the second order.

In our courtyard stands the shabby Moskvich car belonging to our family. Incomparably better cars are parked alongside it during the night, but there are some strange "thieves" who never make an attempt on any but ours. Twice they were unsuccessful, once they damaged it purposely, on a third occasion they drove it off to Georgia. And although the police found the car and the presumed thieves, they were never brought to trial. Not only I, but my friends too, are deluged with offensive anonymous letters. Before the recent municipal elections, an *agitator* ("from the bloc of Communists and non-Party people") stated quite unashamedly about my wife: "Such people ought to be gagged." The editor of the magazine *Oktyabr,* Zverev, has stated in public lectures at the Institute of Virology and Immunology of the Academy of Sciences that I am "a member of the Zionist Executive Committee." Someone naïvely pointed out to him that "in the paper they said Solzhenitsyn is from a landowning family." The resourceful gentleman from *Oktyabr* replied for all to hear: *"At the time* we had to write like that. But *now* we have to consider Solzhenitsyn a Jew." Postal censorship has not let through a *single* newspaper review published in the West about my book *August 1914,* not a single one of the many which my lawyer, Dr. Heeb, has sent me. Therefore I have no way of knowing how my book has been received in the West. The Minister of Foreign Trade, Patolichev, has refused to recognize my right to receive installments of the Nobel Prize money, and they force me to devalue this money by acknowledging that it is "a gift from a private individual" (which, moreover, gives the state the right to confiscate one third of the prize it so angrily condemns). The KGB now and then sends its agents to me in the guise of "young authors" who bring along their literary efforts.

A prominent KGB general has delivered a direct ultimatum through a third person: either I leave the country or they will see me rot in a camp, more specifically, on the Kolyma (in other words, on the model of the Amalrik case, by using an article of the Penal Code normally applied to common criminals).

[You have been refused a permit to live in Moscow with your family. Where do you live now?]

I don't live anywhere anymore. In winter I have no other place to live than the apartment of my family, a natural place for any human being. And I'm going to live here regardless of whether they give me a permit or not. Let them shamelessly come and evict me. That will be a fitting advertisement for our advanced social system.

[How do you evaluate your own position, and the situation of other writers, now that the Soviet Union has joined the World Copyright Convention? There have been semi-official reports that from now on the export of literary works—even works not classified as in any way "anti-Soviet"—will be viewed as a criminal act in itself, a violation of the state monopoly on foreign trade.]

Tsar Nicholas I never pronounced himself proprietor of Pushkin's poetry. Nor, under Alexander II, were the novels of Tolstoy, Turgenev or Goncharov state property. Alexander II never told Chekhov where to publish his works. The merchants and financiers of so-called capitalism have never seen any chance of trading in creations of the intellect or works of art unless the author himself has given them such rights. And if, under the first socialist state, mean mercantile brains think that a product of spiritual creativity, a product newly sprung from the soul or mind of its creator, automatically becomes a commodity and the property of the Ministry of Foreign Trade, then such notions can provoke nothing but utter contempt.

As long as all roads to publication in my own country are closed, I shall go on printing my books with Western publishing houses, completely ignoring all such stunts, which are at once commercial ventures and police measures, and the mediocrities responsible for them. I declare incompetent in advance any criminal proceedings against Russian literature, or any of its books, or any Russian writer.

But I don't think it will go that far. On the other hand, I foresee that our country's adherence to the Convention even increases in one particular sense the freedom of our writers. For example, I have not given any of my works to samizdat recently because I feared that they would be reprinted in pirate editions abroad. But now, so we are told, the rights of Soviet writers are firmly protected, and therefore they can give their works to samizdat without fear, and our readers can get to know works that have not yet been accorded official publication.

[When do you plan to publish the second "Knot" of your series?]

I shall probably not release *October 1916* before the third volume, *March 1917,* is ready. These volumes are too closely knit, and only together do they explain the course of events as I see it.

[Is it true that the original version of your Nobel lecture was purely literary, and that it was given a sharper edge on the advice of your friends?]

I don't know where the *New York Times* correspondent got that story. Not only does it not correspond to the truth; it is also inconsistent with my temperament. On the contrary, the lecture was *toned down* and kept within a literary frame of reference. That was why its publication was delayed a year.

[Would you like to comment on contemporary Soviet literature?]

I can talk about contemporary Russian prose. Some of it should be taken very seriously. And if you take into consideration the incredible mincing machine of censorship through which writers have to pass their works, then you cannot but marvel at their growing skill in preserving and passing on to us by means of minute artistic details an enormous area of life that it is forbidden to portray. I will mention a few names, but it's difficult, and there will probably be some omissions. Some authors, like Yuri Kazakov, suddenly and inexplicably abandon large-scale work and deprive us of the chance to enjoy their prose. My attitude toward others, like Zalygin—whose novel about Stepan Chauzov is one of the finest works of Soviet literature in fifty years—may seem unobjective. I feel that they are alien to me because they and I have different conceptions of the ways in which our contemporary literature can serve today's society. A third category undoubtedly have brilliant gifts, but their creative works are superficial or not relevant enough to the mainstream of our life. But with all these reservations, I will give you the names who represent the core of contemporary Russian prose as I view it: Abramov, Astafyev, Belov, Bykov, Vladimov, Voinovich, Maksimov, Mozhayev, Nosov, Okudzhava, Soloukhin, Tendryakov, Trifonov, Shukshin.

[What have you to say about Vladimir Maksimov's expulsion from the Writers' Union?]

I have no desire to talk seriously about the Writers' Union: what kind of writers' union is it with KGB generals like Viktor Ilyin in charge?
As for Vladimir Maksimov, he is an honest, courageous writer with a disinterested and self-sacrificing devotion to truth, and he has had great successes in his quest for it. So his expulsion from the lying Writers' Union is perfectly normal.

[What have you to say about the decision to deprive Zhores Medvedev of Soviet citizenship?]

This is not a unique case, and a pattern is beginning to emerge.

1. Citizenship in our country is not a natural inalienable right of every human being born on its soil, but a kind of coupon which is held by an exclusive clique of people who have done nothing at all to prove that they have more right than others to the Russian soil. And this clique, if it doesn't approve of some citizen's convictions, can by a simple declaration deprive him of his homeland. I leave it to you to find a word for such a social system.

2. In cases when they've missed their chance to get rid of a person with behind-the-scenes methods (as they would with someone less well known), they find that the least painful thing is to fling him out to the West, preferably with his voluntary consent to what is represented as a temporary assignment abroad or a departure with no arrangements for return.

3. We must, alas, admit that they are not mistaken in their calculations. The environment in our country resembles a dense and viscous medium: it is incredibly difficult to make even the smallest movements because it immediately draws some part of the environment after it. In the democratic West the atmosphere is like a rarefied gas, almost a vacuum: there it is easy to wave one's arms, jump, run, turn somersaults—but none of this has any effect on anybody; everyone else is doing exactly the same, in a chaotic manner.

[What do you think about the expected trial of Yakir and Krasin?]

Even if they admit Western correspondents to this trial, it looks as though it will be just a dismal repetition of the clumsy Stalin-Vyshinsky farces. In the thirties, though, these farces, in spite of the primitive stagecraft, the smeared grease paint, the loudness of the prompter, were still a great success with *thinking people* among Western intellectuals: so great was their *yearning to believe* in our advanced social system. Such *thinking people* can also be found in today's generation.

But if no correspondents are admitted to the trial, it means that it has been pitched two grades lower still.

Since, as far as I know, nobody has said just this when brought face to face with Yakir and Krasin, let me, as an old zek, tell them here and now that they have conducted themselves faint-heartedly, basely and even ludicrously, by repeating forty years later, and in incongruous circumstances, the inglorious experience of a bewildered generation, those inflated historical personages, the capitulators of the thirties.

[What have you to say about the latest attacks on Sakharov in the Soviet press?]

Let me mention at the same time Sakharov's colleague on the Human Rights Committee, my friend Igor Rostislavich Shafarevich. Shafarevich, president of the Moscow Mathematical Society, is well known in mathematical circles all over the world as a distinguished algebraist. But by turning to public activities, he has cut himself off from scientific contacts all over the world and forfeited full membership of the Academy of Sciences. Harassment and surveillance were intensified after his report on religious persecution in our country, and after his vigorous representations to psychiatric congresses on the inhuman use of psychiatry in our country. A congress of psychiatrists diplomatically preferred not to defend those who suffer. At the present time, not only is Shafarevich being forced out of Moscow University, where he has been teaching for thirty years, but even his postgraduate students and his former pupils (doctors of science) all find themselves barred from scientific work.

Until recently our press ignored the tireless public activities of Andrei D. Sakharov, but now it has begun to peddle lies about them. For example, he is declared a "purveyor of slander," an "ignoramus" (all the greatest scientific brains in our country have invariably been put on the level of the most ignorant as soon as they have refused to parrot the general line), a "naïve fantasist," and above all, a "malevolent critic who hates his own country and is . . . unconstructive."

It would be difficult to think up a less plausible string of lies: every single one of these accusations is wide of the mark. Those who have followed Sakharov's articles for some years, his proposals on social problems, his efforts to find ways to save our planet, his letters to the government, his friendly admonitions, cannot fail to see how very well informed he is on the processes of Soviet life, how he suffers for his country, the torments he endures because of mistakes made by others, his good will and his conciliatory position, which make him acceptable to quite incompatible groups (in this he recalls Tvardovsky). I myself find much that I cannot support in Sakharov's concrete proposals for our country, but their *constructiveness* is indisputable. None of his proposals is a chimerical daydream: "Oh, how nice it would be—if only we knew how to bring it about." No, every proposal is skillfully geared to what exists today, and offers the possibility of a smooth transition, with no explosions.

Tass in its reply to Sakharov says that "even the sharpest criticism in our country is regarded as something useful." This is a blatant lie. No serious criticism whatever, on any level whatever, however constructive it may be, is permitted in our country from *anybody,* except a small circle of people who have reached their positions by obediently taking orders for years, which of course has done little to develop their critical faculties. Sakharov, alas, is too well known, and therefore has to be crushed publicly (just as *Novy Mir* was crushed, because it promoted the same conciliatory constitutional line). But unknown critics are soundlessly crushed in great numbers, in the provinces, in the backwoods, and how many people never mentioned by anybody are now languishing and perishing in provincial psychiatric hospitals?

Check for yourselves: during the last ten, twenty or thirty years, has rational *argument* ever been used against any dissident? No, never, because no such arguments exist. They always reply with curses and slander. Such was the "answer" to Sakharov. And just as empty was the "answer" to Heinrich Böll. But most often total silence has been the answer—to Sakharov's petitions and appeals, my open letters, Rostropovich's, Vladimov's and Maksimov's letters, the heaps of collective petitions for an amnesty, to all attempts to save innocent people, to save the ancient Russian visage of Moscow, to save the Russian countryside, to prevent the closing of churches. The answer is always: summary judicial sanctions, abuse or silence—the three ways out for those who have *no real answer* to give.

And here they go again, whipping out that well-thumbed and beslobbered trump card of the thirties—aid to foreign intelligence services—for use against Sakharov. What an absurdity! Would a man who has armed them with their most terrible weapon, the weapon on which their power has rested for decades, and still rests, provide help to foreign intelligence services? The suggestion must verge on the utmost limit of shameless ingratitude.

And yet there is in his behavior a profound significance, a lofty symbol, a logical working-out of his own destiny: the inventor of the most destructive weapon of our age has submitted to the overpowering pull of the World's Conscience, and the eternally afflicted conscience of Russia; weighed down by our common sins, and the sins of each and every one of us, he has abandoned the abundantly good life of which he was assured and which destroys so many people in the world today, and has stepped out in front of the jaws of all-powerful violence.

[How would you assess the social situation in the U.S.S.R. today? Do the statements and attitudes of cultural personalities in the West have any influence on its development?]

For a long time the true history of our country has not been recorded, has not been written, has not been exhibited. And when, among a whole army of historians—the laureates, the eminent, the average and the young—just one is found (I'm thinking of Andrei Amalrik) who doesn't chew the common cud, who doesn't wrap himself in quotations from the Founding Fathers of the Vanguard Doctrine, but who dares to give an independent analysis of today's social structure and predict the future, predict things that may indeed befall our country, then instead of analyzing his works and taking from them what is true and practically useful, they simply put him in jail.

And when from the ranks of our dazzlingly bemedaled generals a single Grigorenko turns up and dares to express his nonconformist opinions on the course of the last war and on today's Soviet society, opinions which incidentally are consistently Marxist-Leninist, this is declared clinical madness.

For several years the selfless *Chronicle* quenched a general and natural human thirst to know what was going on. It reported, though in a very incomplete manner, names, dates, places, prison terms, forms of persecution. It brought to the surface from the abyss of ignorance just a tiny, tiny part of our terrible history—and for that it has been destroyed and crushed with a systematic thoroughness far beyond that with which (to take the favorite Western example) plotters against the state are persecuted in Greece.

Now, without the *Chronicle*, we shall perhaps not be informed immediately of the latest victims of a prison-camp regime which kills by cruel treatment over a protracted period, as it killed the sick Yuri Galanskov, the elderly Talantov and the aged Yakov Odobesku (who went on hunger strike against the oppressive regime in the camp). And maybe we won't be informed about people who while serving one sentence are sentenced for a second and third time: how for example, Svyatoslav Karavansky and Stepan Soroka (who got twenty-five years for reading a few nationalist brochures when he was a tenth-grade pupil) and the Latvian pastor Iona Shtagers were put back inside to complete the twenty-five-year sentences from which they had once been let off; or how Yuri Shukhevich, in the place at which he was released, got another ten years because of evidence given by a man who had not known him twenty-four hours—and just recently has been taken in for a third ten years; or how, because of his religious beliefs, Boris Zkorovets was sentenced for a third time; how Pyotr Tokar got twenty-five years all at once (and is now serving his twenty-fourth year!); or how some people, after serving their sentences in Vladimir Prison, will be transferred to the Smolensk Psychiatric Hospital for an indefinite term, as were Zynovi Krasivsky and Yuri Belov.

And the fate that awaits the already sentenced Svetlychny, Sverstyuk, Ogurtsov, Boris Bykov (of the "Young Workers" group in Alma-Ata), Oleg Vorbyov (samizdat in Perm), Gershuni, Vyacheslav Platonov, Yevgeny Vagin, Nina Strokata, Stefaniya Shabatura, Irina Stasiv, and many, many others unknown except to their families, colleagues and neighbors will be hidden from our eyes and our knowledge.

And thanks solely to the complete secrecy that surrounds practically everything that happens in our country, when Marchenko's *My Testimony* surfaced in the West it was regarded there as an "exaggeration." Few people gave much thought, for instance, to his testimony that in the tsarist Vladimir Prison the lighting—to mention only this—has become four times worse under Soviet power: there are only a quarter as many windows. And it has become more than four times colder and more brutal.

The world, used by now to the idea that nothing can ever be discovered about us anyway, overlooks even the most obvious and open piece of information: that in this impressive country with its most advanced socialist structure *there has been not a single amnesty for political prisoners for half a century!* When our prison terms were twenty-five years and ten years, when eight years in our country was seriously thought of as "a child's term," we had the famous Stalin amnesty (7 July 1945), which released political prisoners sentenced to three years or less—that is, nobody. Prisoners who had a bit more (up to five years) were released under the "Voroshilov" amnesty of March 1953, the sole achievement of which was to flood the country with criminals. In September 1955 Khrushchev, releasing to Adenauer the Germans who were serving terms in the Soviet Union, also had to give amnesty to those who had collaborated with the Germans. But for *dissidents* there has *never* been a single amnesty in half a century. Who would be able to point to another example on our planet of a social structure or state system so confident of its stability? Those who like to indulge in comparisons with Greece are free to do so.

When at the end of the forties we were overwhelmed with twenty-five-year terms, there was nothing in the newspapers except the unheard-of reprisals in Greece. And today the many statements made by the Western press and Western public men, even those who are most aware of oppression and persecution in the East, always end with the qualification "just as in Greece, Spain, Turkey," to create an artificial balance for the sake of left-wing circles. And as long as this artificial phrase—"just as in . . ."—is added, sympathy for us loses its significance, its depth, even offends us. And our sympathizers don't see the danger signal themselves.

I shall be so bold as to state that it is *not* "just as in . . ." I shall be so bold as to observe that in all these countries, violence does not reach the level of today's gas chambers, that is, the prison psychiatric clinics, that Greece is not surrounded by a concrete wall with electronic killing devices at the border, and that young Greeks don't pass in hundreds over the lethal line in the faint hope of breaking out to freedom. And nowhere east of Greece is it possible for an exiled minister (Karamanlis) to have his antigovernment program printed in the papers. Even in Turkey they cannot (as they did in Albania) shoot a priest because he baptized a child. Even in Turkey a hundred people a day do not throw themselves into the sea (as the Chinese do around Hong Kong) in order to take a chance on "freedom or death" among the sharks. Even in Spain they do not jam radio broadcasts either from Cuba or from Chile. Even Portugal has admitted foreign reporters to investigate suspicions that had arisen. These correspondents would never have received such an invitation to the other end of Europe. They never will receive it, yet they will *remain quite happy;* they won't even dare to protest! That is the most typical feature of the situation.

The first line drawn on one scale may mean 10, the first on another, $10^6$— i.e., 1 million. And would illiteracy or wrong-headedness on the part of observers be sufficient to explain their conclusion that "the first line has been passed on both scales"?

In my Nobel Prize lecture a year ago I vainly tried to draw attention in a restrained way to these two noncomparable scales by which the size and moral significance of events are gauged. And to make the point that what happens in countries that decide the fate of the world cannot be considered entirely their own affair.

I pointed there, also in vain, to the fact that jamming of Western radio broadcasts in the East creates a situation comparable to that on the eve of a universal catastrophe, that it robs international agreements and guarantees of all meaning because they cease to exist in the minds of half of mankind. Their superficial traces are easily expunged in a matter of days or even hours. I assumed at the time that the precarious position of the author when the lecture was delivered—not from a fortified rostrum but from those high rocks in which glaciers are born to creep out over the earth—would make a distracted world pay rather more attention to his warnings.

I was wrong. It is as if what I said had never been said. And maybe it is as useless to repeat it now.

What jamming of radio broadcasts means is impossible to explain to those who haven't experienced it themselves, who haven't lived under it for years. Every day they spit into your eyes and ears. It is an insult to human beings, it degrades them to the level of robots, no matter whether they jam with a "total blackout" of the wave band, or with the "rusty saw," or with vulgar music. It means that grown persons are reduced to infants: swallow what mother has chewed up for you. Even the most benevolent broadcasts during the most friendly visits are jammed just as uncompromisingly; there must not be the slightest deviation in the evaluation of events, in the nuances, in the accents. Everybody has to assimilate and remember an event in precisely the same way. And many facts about the world must not be made known to our population at all. Moscow and Leningrad have paradoxically become the most uninformed metropolises in the world: their inhabitants ask people who come in from the countryside what news there is. Out in the country—for financial reasons (our population has to pay very dearly for these jamming *services*)—jamming is weaker. But according to the observations of people from various places, jamming has been extended during the last few months, has conquered new areas, has been intensified. (I recall the fate of Sergei Khanzhenkov, who had by 1973 served seven years for attempting—or rather, for merely intending—to blow up the jamming station in Minsk. And yet if you look at it from the viewpoint of general human concern, it is impossible to see this "criminal" as anything other than a fighter for universal peace.)

The general aim of the suppression of thought in our country today might be called "Sinification," an effort to realize Chinese ideals—except that these ideals existed in our country before, in the thirties, and were then lost sight of. How much did people in the West, in the thirties, know about Mikhail Bulgakov, Platonov or Florensky, for instance? In the same way, there are thousands of dissidents, there are underground writers and philosophers in China today, but the world will know about them only an epoch later, in fifty or a hundred years' time, and then only about those few who manage to preserve their works while they pass between inexorable millstones. And these are the ideals to which they now want us to return.

But I declare confidently that it is no longer possible in our country to return to such a regime.

The first reason is the flow of information between countries, the ideas, facts and human protests that filter through in spite of everything and have an influence. It is important to understand that the East is not at all indifferent to protests from public opinion in the West. On the contrary, it goes in *deadly fear* of them—and them *alone*—but only when it is a matter of the united, mighty voice of hundreds of prominent personalities, the opinion of a whole continent which might shake the authority of our *advanced* society. But when timid, isolated protests are heard, without any faith in their success, and accompanied by the inevitable lip service—"just as, of course, in Greece, Turkey and Spain" —then they evoke only the laughter of the aggressors.

When the racial composition of a basketball team becomes a bigger world event than the daily injections given to prisoners in psychiatric prisons, brain-destroying injections, then what can you feel but contempt toward an egoistic, short-sighted and defenseless civilization?

Our prisons retreat and hide from the light of world publicity. A lengthy settling of accounts with Amalrik was planned as early as 1970, but they were forced to try him as a "common criminal" and give him three years to begin with, in order to cut him off from the political camps in Mordovia and push him out to the Kolyma. And now, because of renewed world publicity, they have been forced to limit themselves to "only" three years more. Otherwise it would have been longer.

The Western world has already helped a lot through its publicity, and saved many of our persecuted. But the lesson the Western world has drawn from this is an incomplete one; it has not felt strongly enough to realize that our persecuted are not only grateful for protection, but also provide a lofty example of spiritual endurance and readiness for sacrifice, at the very point of death and under the syringe of the murderer-psychiatrists.

And this is the second and most important reason why I am sure that the Chinese ideal is no longer attainable in our country.

The unyielding General Grigorenko requires incomparably more courage than is demanded on the battlefield, to spurn daily, after four years in the hell of a prison psychiatric hospital, the temptation to buy freedom from torment at the price of his convictions, pretending to see wrong as right.

Vladimir Bukovsky, who throughout his young life has been ground by the alternating mincing knives of psychiatric prisons, ordinary prisons and camps, did not break down and choose a free existence when it was open to him, but was ready to lay down his life as a deliberate sacrifice for others. This year he was brought to Moscow and this offer was made to him: he could be set free and he could leave the country so long as he did not indulge in political activities before his departure. That was all they wanted—and he was quite free to go abroad for his health. By present Western standards of courage, one can pay much more for freedom and for release from torment: some American prisoners of war felt themselves able to sign any documents against their own country, obviously setting greater store by their lives than by their convictions. But Bukovsky considered his convictions more precious than his life. He is a striking example to his contemporaries in the West, though, most probably, a useless one. Bukovsky's reply was the following condition: that all those about whom he had written be released from prison psychiatric hospitals. It was not enough for him to be released without having committed any base act himself: he did not want to run away, leaving others in misery. So he was sent off to a camp to serve his twelve years to the end.

A similar choice was offered to Amalrik this spring: he could confirm the testimony of Krasin and Yakir, in return for which he was offered his freedom. But he, too, refused and was sent to the Kolyma for a second term. And of all the cases about which we still lack the details, in which torture and torment are hidden from us as jealously guarded "state secrets," we can say with no doubt at all, judging merely by the fact that a man is *not* let out, that his conditions are *not* made easier, that "this man remains staunchly true to his convictions."

A similar choice is also often put before people who lead a more normal life. They are not prisoners, but that does not make their choice much easier. Take Gorlov, for example, who surprised the burglars from the KGB at my country cottage two years ago. The only reason they didn't kill him at the time was his active resistance, which attracted a crowd. But in return they demanded that he keep silent and threatened to cut short his professional and scientific career. And it was made clear that this was no empty threat, and that he would also sacrifice the well-being of his family—and still he did not succumb to the temptation to keep silent. Yet keep silent was all he had to do.

This series of sacrificial decisions by single individuals is a beacon to our future.

There is one psychological peculiarity in human beings that always surprises me. In times of prosperity and ease, a man will shy from the least little worry on the periphery of his existence, try not to know about the sufferings of others (and his own in the future), make many concessions even in matters of central, of intimate importance to him, just to prolong his present well-being. Yet a man who is approaching the last frontier, who is already a naked beggar deprived of all that may be thought to beautify life, can suddenly find in himself the strength to dig in his heels and refuse to take the final step, can surrender his life but not his principles!

Because of the first quality, man has never been able to hold on to one single plateau he has attained. Thanks to the second quality, mankind has pulled itself out of all kinds of bottomless pits.

Of course, it wouldn't be a bad thing to foresee your future downfall and the size of the reckoning to come while you are still on the plateau, to show yourself steadfast and brave a little before the critical hour—to sacrifice less, but a little earlier.

We must not accept that the disastrous course of history cannot be corrected, that the Spirit, if it has confidence in itself, cannot influence the mightiest Power in the world.

The experience of the last few generations has, I think, fully demonstrated that only the unbending strength of the human spirit firmly taking its stand on the shifting frontier of encroaching violence, and declaring "not one step further," though death may be the end of it—only this unwavering firmness offers any genuine defense of peace for the individual, of general peace for mankind at large.


**27**  To the KGB
For the attention of Registry Clerk Polyakova

In my earlier letter, which you received on 3 July, I warned you that the farce of the gangsters was only too transparent, and that it would be more sensible to stop it. By its third, extremely unpleasant letter, your department has compelled me to give an interview to the press.

If you see Ivan Pavlovich Abramov, please pass this on to him.

31 August 1973                                                                 Solzhenitsyn

**28**    According to a statement made by Solzhenitsyn in Leningrad at the end of August, the KGB confiscated a typewritten copy of his book *The Gulag Archipelago,* an investigation in several volumes of Soviet prison camps from 1918 to 1956, containing only authentic facts, the names of real places and the names of persons still living (more than two hundred of them). The author fears that they will all now be persecuted for their testimony, given ten years ago, to the torments that they suffered in Stalin's camps.

Information as to the place in which the book was concealed was given by Elizaveta Voronyanskaya, who was interrogated by the KGB for five days and nights without a break. When she got home she hanged herself.

5 September 1973

**29**    On the title page of a samizdat publication

From the Author
The adherence of the U.S.S.R. to the World Copyright Convention permits us to assume that Soviet authors will now be defended against unauthorized publication of their works abroad. On that assumption, the author releases this excerpt as samizdat.

21 September 1973

**30**    Letter to A. D. Sakharov
          28 October 1973

Dear Andrei Dmitrievich:
I was away when news of the attack on you came, which is why I am writing only now.

Our country is in a humiliating position vis-à-vis the Arabs if they see no reason to respect our national honor. That's all we needed—Arab terrorists helping to "correct" the course of Russian history.

However, I am bound to assert that given the continuous surveillance and aural monitoring of which you are the object, such an attack is impossible in our native land without the knowledge and encouragement of the authorities. If it had been independent of and unwelcome to the authorities, the numerous members of the security organs would have had no difficulty in preventing it, or stopping it in the hour and a half for which it lasted, or apprehending the criminals immediately afterward. They would never have dared to stir without having received permission! Anyone familiar with Soviet conditions would find this absurd.

This is only the latest method. What can answer the free words of a free man? Arguments do not exist. Rockets are irrelevant. Iron bars would damage their reputation. Only hired killers remain.

If they should ever succeed in such an attack on you while I remain alive, you may be certain that I shall dedicate what remains of my literary powers and of my life to ensuring that the murderers will not win but lose.

With warmest personal regards,

A. Solzhenitsyn

## 31    Statement by A. Solzhenitsyn
18 January 1974

The furious press campaign conceals the main thing from the Soviet reader: What is this book about? What is this strange word "Gulag" in its title? *Pravda* lies when it says that the author "sees with the eyes of those who hanged revolutionary workers and peasants." No! with the eyes of those who were shot and tortured by the NKVD. *Pravda* asserts that in our country there is "unqualified criticism" of the pre-1956 period. So let them just give us a sample of their unqualified criticism. I have provided them with the richest factual material for it.

Even today—even today—this path is not closed. And what a cleansing that would be for the country!

While publishing *The Gulag Archipelago,* I still did not expect they would disavow to such an extent even their own former weak confessions. The way in which our propaganda organs choose to behave is dictated by their animal fear of exposure. It demonstrates how grimly they cling to the bloody past and shows they want to drag it with them, like an unopened bag, into the future —rather than speak a word even of moral censure, let alone pass sentence on a single one of the hangmen, the investigators and informers. Typically, as soon as Deutsche Welle announced half-hour readings from *Gulag* every day, they rushed to jam it: not a single word of this must break through into our country.

As if it could be for long! I am certain that the time will soon come when this book will be read widely and even freely in our country. And there will be people with memories and with curiosity who will be eager to check: What did the Soviet press write when this book appeared? and who signed it?

And in the murky torrent of abuse, they will not find the names of those responsible. Everywhere there will be cowardly anonymity and pseudonymity.

That is why it is so easy for them to talk any lying nonsense they please: to assert that, according to my book: "the Hitlerites were lenient and merciful to enslaved people," and "the battle of Stalingrad was won by penal battalions." All lies, Comrade *Pravda* Writers. I ask you to cite the exact pages. (You will find that they will not cite them.)

Or here is Tass: "In his autobiography, Solzhenitsyn himself confesses his hatred for the Soviet system and the Soviet people." My autobiography is printed in the Nobel yearbook of 1970. It is open to the whole world. See for yourselves how impudently the Telegraph Agency of the Soviet Union lies. But why talk about Tass now that it has had the shamelessness to spit in the closed eyes of all those who were killed, claiming that I wrote about these sufferings and deaths only for the sake of hard currency. This was what Kiril Andreyev [a Tass commentator] said. Is *his* father alive? Or was he also shot there?

Yet here, too, Tass is wide of the mark: the sale price of the book, in all languages, will be extremely low so that the widest possible number of persons may read it. The price is such as to cover only the work of the translators, the printing houses and the materials consumed. And if royalties are left over, they will be spent to commemorate those who perished and to assist families of political prisoners in the Soviet Union. And I will appeal to the publishers to donate their profits to the same purposes.

Next, the lies of *Literaturnaya Gazeta:* in my book, they say, "Soviet people are fiends" and the essence of the Russian soul is such "that a Russian is prepared to sell his father and mother for a ration of bread." Name pages, liars! The purpose of writing like this is to incite my uninformed compatriots against me: Solzhenitsyn "equates Soviet people with fascist murderers." The facts have been shuffled a little: I do indeed equate fascist murderers and murderers from the Cheka, the GPU, the NKVD. But *Literaturnaya Gazeta* drags in "all Soviet people" so that our hangmen may hide more conveniently among them.

But what pages will they cite? From what book? *Literaturnaya Gazeta* has been caught pillaging, stripping a corpse: it is quoting from a confiscated copy, the fourth and fifth parts of *The Gulag Archipelago*, which haven't yet been printed anywhere—which is to say that the suspicious "literator" compiled his notes in the offices of State Security and nowhere else. When the fourth part is published, you will read this quotation at the end of Chapter 1: "I have come to understand the falsehood of all the revolutions in history." And this judgment, not on Russian man but on Soviet life outside prison, in Chapter 3 (with the following section headings): "Constant Fear," "Secrecy and Mistrust," "Betrayal as a Form of Existence" and "Corruption [of the Soul]."

They also dare to allege that the publication date of *The Gulag Archipelago* was determined by world reaction, to wreck détente. But the date was in fact determined by our State Security, the main worldwide reactionary force today in its lust for seizing manuscripts. If it sets any store by relaxation of tension, why did it last August spend five days coercing and tormenting an unfortunate woman to get the manuscript out of her? In this seizure I was the hand of God, and realized the time had come. As Macbeth was told: Birnam Wood will come . . .

## 32    Interview with *Time* Magazine, 19 January 1974

[The Medvedev brothers express the belief that reforms in the U.S.S.R. can come about only from within, and what is more, from above, and that Western public opinion can give little real help. Sakharov expresses the opinion that only pressure from below and from outside can be effective. You and he have been reproached with appealing to Western governments and reactionary circles in the West. What have you to say to this?]

I have never personally appealed to foreign governments or parliaments or to foreign political circles. As for Sakharov, as far as I know, only once has he appealed to the American Senate and once, with indirect advice, to the governments of Western Europe. It is true that this is not the quarter to which we should address ourselves, neither is it the path we should be taking. We have been appealing to world public opinion, to cultural figures. Their support for us is priceless, has always been effective, always helps. We are both still alive and well thanks only to this. However, it cannot be endless and we dare not abuse appeals for support: all countries have their own worries and they are not obliged to concern themselves with ours all the time.

But Roy Medvedev's proposal—made in his woolly article which is almost dull enough to be officially approved—is quite laughable. He suggests we appeal for help to Western Communist circles—to those people who did not even have the desire and the energy to defend the Communist cause itself in Czechoslovakia—so are they likely to defend us? (Khrushchev was rebuked by Gomulka and Ulbricht for publishing *Ivan Denisovich*.)

The Medvedev brothers suggest that we should wait patiently, on our knees, until somewhere "at the top" some mythical "leftists," whom no one knows or names, defeat the so-called right-wingers, or until a "new generation of leaders" emerges. But what are we, the living, supposed to do? "Develop Marxism," although in the meantime we may be jailed, and although repression may be stepped up "temporarily." This is pure nonsense.

It might seem natural for us to appeal to our government and our leaders, on the assumption that they are not completely indifferent to the fate of the people from which they themselves have come. Such letters have in fact been written many times—by Grigorenko, by Sakharov, by me, and by hundreds of people, with constructive suggestions on the way out of the difficulties and dangers facing our country. But they have never been taken up for discussion, and there has never been any response but a punitive one.

All that remains is our right, and our direct course, to appeal to our readers, to our compatriots and especially to our young people. And if our young people, once they have learned everything and understood everything, do not support us, it will only be because they lack courage. And then both they and we will have deserved our sad fate; we shall have no one and nothing to blame except our own inner slavishness.

[How can your compatriots and Soviet youth show their support for you?]

Not with physical acts but merely by rejecting the lie, by *refusing to participate personally in the lie*. Everyone must stop cooperating with the lie absolutely everywhere that he sees it himself: whether they are trying to force him to speak, write, quote or sign, or simply to vote or even to read. In our country the lie has become not just a moral category, but a pillar of the state. In recoiling from the lie we are performing a moral act, not a political act; and not one that can be punished by criminal law, but an act that would have an immediate effect on our whole life.

[Tass says that the publication of your book *The Gulag Archipelago* creates the danger of a return to the atmosphere of the "cold war" and harms détente between East and West.]

It is not those who talk about crimes that have been committed who harm peace and good relations between people and nations, but those who committed, or are committing, these crimes.

Personal, public and national repentance can only purify the atmosphere. If we openly admit our terrifying past and sternly condemn it, not just in empty words, then this can only strengthen trust in our country throughout the whole world.

[Your new book will not be published here, but many Russians will hear it by radio. What do you think their reaction will be—especially that of the younger generation, which knows little about the events you describe?]

It is not clear whether they will hear it by radio. *The Gulag Archipelago* is already being jammed on Deutsche Welle. But all the same, the truth will get through and will become known.

It was so carefully hidden for decades that its appearance in all its enormity will shock anyone who does not know—but it will broaden his mind and give him light and strength for the future.

[What do you think the authorities are going to do to you?]

I will not risk any forecast. My family and I are ready for anything. I have fulfilled my duty to those who perished, and this gives me relief and peace of mind. The truth about all this was doomed to perish—*they* had tried to stifle it, drown it, burn it and grind it to powder. But here it is, whole once more, living and in print. And no one can ever wipe it out again.

## 33   Breaking the Barrier of Silence

I believe that the appearance in 1973 of Solzhenitsyn's new book, *The Gulag Archipelago,* is a tremendous event. In the immeasurability of its consequences it can only be compared with an event that occurred in 1953: the death of Stalin.

Our papers have declared Solzhenitsyn a traitor.

What he has in fact betrayed is not, of course, his native land, for which he fought with honor, nor the people, on whom he confers honor by his life and writings, but the Chief Administration of Corrective Labor Camps, GULAG: he has *betrayed to the public* the story of how millions perished; has told, with concrete facts, testimonies and biographies at his fingertips, a story that everyone ought to know by heart, but their knowledge of which the authorities, for incomprehensible reasons, are trying not to betray but to bury.

Who, here, is the traitor?

The Twentieth Congress lifted the bloodstained edge of the matting that covered those stacked corpses. This alone in the fifties saved millions from destruction: the living, the half-dead, and those in whom life still flickered faintly. Praise be to the Twentieth Congress. The Twenty-second Congress took a decision on the erection of a memorial to those who had perished. But what happened was just the opposite: after a few brief years assiduous efforts began to be made to extirpate from the people's memory the crimes perpetrated in our country, which were on a scale unprecedented in history. Millions of people had perished, all in identical fashion, but weren't they all, every one of them, not flies but human beings, each with his own individual fate, his own individual death? "Posthumously rehabilitated." "The consequences of the Stalin personality cult." But what has become of the personality, not the one at the center of the cult, but the personality—every one of those personalities—of which all that remains is a certificate of posthumous rehabilitation? Where has it disappeared, where is it buried, that personality? What happened to the person, what did he live through from the moment he was taken from his home to the moment he was restored to his family in the form of a certificate?

What lies behind the words "posthumously rehabilitated"? What sort of life? What punishment, what death? From about 1965 onward, silence has been the order of the day.

Solzhenitsyn, a living tradition, a living legend, has once more run the blockade of muteness; he has reinvested the deeds of the past with reality, restored names to a multitude of victims and sufferers, and most important, he has re-endowed events with their true weight and instructive meaning.

We have discovered it all anew, we hear and see what it was all like: search, arrest, interrogation, prison, deportation, transit camp, prison camp. Hunger, beatings, labor, corpses.

*The Gulag Archipelago.*

Moscow, 4 February 1974                                                    Lydia Chukovskaya

## 34    Statement by A. Solzhenitsyn, 2 February 1974

In December, before *The Gulag Archipelago* was published, lecturers in the Moscow City network of the CPSU (Kapitsa at Gosplan, for instance) were stating in so many words that "we shan't let Solzhenitsyn walk around much longer." These promises from the authorities were in close agreement with the spurious gangster letters, which added only the skull and crossbones. *The Gulag Archipelago* came out—and the gangsters' favorite device was transferred from their anonymous letters to the display window of the Artists' Union, and the threats to kill now became the theme of attacks by telephone. ("We will carry out the sentence!") This telephonic onslaught on my family (two women and four children) was conducted in hooligan fashion by State Security agents working two shifts, from 8 A.M. to 12 midnight, except on Saturdays and Sundays, when they took their statutory holidays.

In reality, the shrill press campaign was not directed against me: they could fill whole columns with their abuse and the lot of it would not ruin a single working day for me. The press campaign was directed against our people, against our public life: intended to deafen and daze my compatriots, cause them to recoil in horror from my book, stamp out the spark of *knowledge* in Soviet people, should it somehow penetrate the barrier of jamming. It played on low instincts: Solzhenitsyn has three cars, the bourgeois! Who, and what way, was there to refute the omnipotent liars, tell the world that the three cars did not exist and never had existed, that I moved around on my own two legs and by trolley bus, something to which the lowliest of Tass correspondents would not stoop. It harped, too, on the note of lofty indignation: he is defiling the graves of those who fell in the Fatherland war! Who could see beyond these towering newspaper lies to the fact that my book was not about that war at all, and not about the twenty million of our war dead, but about the other *sixty* million destroyed by internal warfare over the last forty years, those secretly done to death by exhaustion, those frozen to death in uninhabited wastes; about whole republics decimated by famine?

A few weeks back there was still an honorable way out: to acknowledge the truth about the past and so purge the guilt for old crimes. But convulsively, in animal terror, they decided to stand up for the lie to the end, secure behind their newspaper bastions.

World public opinion, rallying to the author's defense, makes it impossible at present to kill or even arrest him: that would be the best confirmation of what the book says. But there remains the method of slander of efforts to discredit me personally, and to this they are now unanimously resorting. Thus Vitkevich, once my codefendant, was called in from the provinces, and to save his academic career he made APN, that tried and trusted affiliate of the KGB (after they had "kindly shown him" the record of the investigation in 1945—I should like to see anyone else get hold of such records), his medium for praise of the investigating procedures at that time: "the investigator had no need to distort the truth." In twenty-nine years he had never found fault with my behavior during the investigation—but now he could not have chosen a better time to join in the general chorus. He knew very well that no one had suffered as a result of my testimony, and that his case and mine had been decided independently of the investigation, and indeed before we were arrested: the accusations were based on our censored correspondence (it was a whole year being photographed) in which abuse was aimed at Stalin, and later still on "Resolution No. 1," taken from our map cases, which we had drawn up together there in the front line, and which censured our system of government. He referred to my "testimony at the trial," although I was never, in fact, formally tried, but was sentenced *in absentia* by a Special Tribunal. He writes quite correctly that we "belong to different categories of people": he was insisting that we should forget all the deaths and all the suffering—our own and that of other people. But this was only the beginning. They ferret out people with whom I shared some part of the journey, or merely met, in my half century of life, and force them to bear false witness. There are even former zeks, not too seriously damaged, not totally exhausted, from whom statements are squeezed that they have never suffered, have never been tortured, that there was no Archipelago.

The Central Committee, the KGB and the editorial staffs of our newspapers, who in secret are eagerly reading *The Gulag Archipelago*, are not intelligent enough to realize that in this book I have told the reader intimate truths about myself that are much worse than all the bad things their time servers can fabricate. That is the point of my book: it is a call to repentance, not a pamphlet.

All this present song and dance in the press, with people prominent in the world of the arts joining in the whirl (though others have refused to do so, and their courage is on all lips)—this whole campaign is a battle against the people's conscience, against the people's right to the truth. Barring the way to the truth with the black folds of its cloak, the great sweep of its wings, the hornèd force of evil has resolved upon this hopeless battle to extend its power over men's souls before the matins bell rings. But the more desperately they daub the truth black, the more thorough will be the retribution when the truth becomes known.

For half a century now our people has been able to get at the truth only by digging it out from the lie. People have learned their lesson and know now when and why these inordinate howls are raised. Assurances of support flow in to me, in telephone calls, in letters and notes from people named or unknown, which somehow reach me:

"From the people of the Urals. We understand completely. Keep it up, friend! A group of workers." People write individual protests to the newspapers, although they foresee all the disastrous consequences for themselves. And now three fearless young men—*Boris Mikhailov, Vadim Borisov, Yevgeny Baraba-nov* (each of whom has small children)—have come to my defense in public, armed only with the knowledge that they are right. Perhaps they and I alike will be crushed, but the truth cannot be crushed, however many pathetic notables are made to join hands in the witches' dance.

I have never doubted that the truth would be restored to my people. I believe that we shall repent, that we shall be spiritually cleansed, that the Russian nation will be reborn.


35    Office of the Public Prosecutor of the U.S.S.R. 103793.
      15-a Pushkin Street, Moscow k-9, 8 February 1974. No. ———
      To Citizen Solzhenitsyn A. I. Apartment 169, 12 Gorky Street, Moscow

Citizen Solzhenitsyn A. I.
      You are required to report to the office of the Public Prosecutor of the U.S.S.R., 15-a Pushkin Street at 1700 hrs on 8 February 1974, 5th floor, Room No. 513.
A. Balashov
Procurator in the Investigations Administration
Public Prosecutor's Office


36    To the Office of the Public Prosecutor of the U.S.S.R. in reply to
      its repeated summons

In the circumstances created by the universal and unrelieved illegality enthroned for many years past in our country (and in my particular case also by an eight-year campaign of slander and persecution), I refuse to acknowledge the legality of your summons and shall not report for questioning to any government agency.

Before requiring citizens to observe the law you must learn to carry it out yourselves. Set free the innocent people now imprisoned. Punish those responsible for mass extermination, and the false informers. Punish the administrators and the special squads who carried out the policy of genocide (the deportation of *whole peoples*). *This very day,* deprive the local and departmental satraps of their unlimited power over citizens, their arbitrary use of courts and psychiatrists. Satisfy the *millions* of lawful but suppressed complaints.

11 February 1974                                                    A. Solzhenitsyn

**37**   I declare in advance that any criminal proceedings against Russian literature, against any single book in Russian literature, or against any Russian author are improper and invalid. If such proceedings are taken against me, I will not go to the court on my own two legs. I shall have to be delivered with my hands bound and in a Black Maria. I shall not answer a single question put by such a court. If I am sentenced to imprisonment, I shall only submit to the sentence in handcuffs. In confinement, I who have already given the eight best years of my life to forced labor for the state, and by way of wages contracted cancer, will never do another half hour's work for the oppressors.

In this way I leave them the simple recourse open to all arrant bullies: to kill me quickly for writing the truth about Russia's history.

A. Solzhenitsyn

**38**   From a Letter to the Government of the U.S.S.R. concerning the Expatriation of Solzhenitsyn

Irresponsible rulers of a great country!

. . . You have, it seems, gradually begun to understand that in a spiritual battle an opponent slain is more dangerous than an opponent still living. . . . But . . . you have still not realized that with the appearance of *The Gulag Archipelago,* that hour in history has struck which will be fatal to you. . . . You have still not realized that *Birnam Wood is already on the march* . . . that tens of murdered millions have risen up against you. . . . They have long been knocking for entrance into our lives, but there was no one to open the door. . . . *The Gulag Archipelago* is the indictment with which your trial at the hands of the human race begins. . . . May the paralysis with which God punished your first leader serve as a prophetic prefiguring of the spiritual paralysis which is now inexorably advancing upon you.

. . . Perhaps some of you may begin to ask yourselves: And is there not One over us all who will demand a full reckoning?

Never doubt it—there is.

He will demand a reckoning. And you will answer.

. . . Take Russia out of the hands of Cain, and give her back to God.

Moscow, 17 February 1974                                          L. L. Regelson

# Publisher's Notes

177 **Bunin:** Ivan Bunin, the first Russian writer to win a Nobel Prize in Literature (1933), became an émigré in 1920. His abhorrence of the Revolution and its consequences finds expression in *Accursed Days,* an account of Bunin's experiences in revolutionary Moscow and Odessa. Despite this open hostility to the Soviet system, Bunin's other works have been extensively published in the U.S.S.R. in the post-Stalin era; a nine-volume *Collected Works,* coedited and introduced by Tvardovsky, appeared in 1965–1967.

180 **Shevardino:** The Shevardino redoubt was the site of a brief but significant clash between Russian and French forces on the eve of the battle of Borodino in 1812.

192 **friend Mack:** Presumably a reference to the Austrian general Karl Mack, overwhelmingly defeated by Napoleon in October 1805.

199 **his very name:** The name Tvardovsky is derived from a Slavic root meaning "hard" or "firm."

206 **thinking people:** *Grani,* the name of the émigré journal, means "aspects," or "facets."

210 **propaganda:** The translations of *Ivan Denisovich* into the principal Western languages were for the most part done in great haste, evidently in an attempt to benefit from the political sensation caused by the book's appearance in the U.S.S.R. Predictably enough, several translations are unacceptable in quality.

213 **Ruslan:** Among the fantastic adventures described in Pushkin's *Ruslan and Lyudmila* is an encounter with a giant severed head that lives on in an old battlefield.

218 **eighty-seven-chapter version:** YMCA Press (Paris) published the full ninety-six-chapter version of *The First Circle* in 1978.

218 **wooden dacha:** In the Russian Orthodox tradition, houses and especially churches are decorated with green branches and flowers on the Feast of the Trinity (Pentecost).

220 **a first time:** In November 1920, winds caused the shallow waters of Sivash Bay in the Crimea to recede, thereby opening an attack route for the Red Army and decisively affecting the course of the Russian Civil War. This event symbolizes the good fortune which, the author believes, has all too often been with the Bolsheviks.

220 **ashamed to be Soviet:** Alexander Herzen (1812–1870), a political émigré who published an oppositionist Russian-language newspaper abroad, reacted with particular anguish and dismay to the suppression of the 1863 Polish revolt by the Russian army. "Lament" ("Plach"), one of Herzen's essays on the subject, ends with the following words: "As I walk along the street, I want no one to recognize me as a Russian."

228 **good job there:** Lydia Chukovskaya's essay in defense of Solzhenitsyn is entitled "The Responsibility of the Writer and the Irresponsibility of *Literaturnaya Gazeta.*"

235 **ignore them:** The gem-covered fur headdress of Vladimir Monomakh, twelfth-century prince of Kiev, was used in the coronation ceremonies of Muscovite tsars. "Heavy thou art, crown of Monomakh!" exclaims Tsar Boris in Pushkin's *Boris*

*Godunov,* and this phrase has become a proverbial complaint of the burdens that go with responsibility.

236  **Uritsky:** Head of the Petrograd Cheka.

237  **Novocherkassk revolt:** The fullest available account of the 1962 disturbances in Novocherkassk is contained in *The Gulag Archipelago,* Volume III, pages 507–514.

246  **Iz Glubiny:** *Iz Glubiny (De Profundis)* is a collection of essays critical of the Russian Revolution. Suppressed immediately after its publication in Moscow in 1921, the book contains contributions by Berdyaev, S. Bulgakov, Pyotr Struve and other major thinkers.

246  **aluminum palaces:** "Aluminum palaces" figure in a vision of the ideal future in Chernyshevsky's programmatic 1863 novel *What Is to Be Done?*

246  **Peredvizhniki:** A group of Russian painters formed in 1870, who emphasized the social role of art. Although the movement included several outstanding realist painters, it tended to politicize art and is justifiably seen as the forerunner of "socialist realism." Mikhail Nesterov and Mikhail Vrubel were among the artists who turned away from this mode, primarily to religious and mystical themes.

250  **Vekhi:** A seminal collection of essays published in 1909 and directed against the mystique of revolution that had typified the Russian intelligentsia.

251  **Morlock:** The Morlocks are a race of subhuman slaves depicted in H. G. Wells's *The Time Machine.*

280  **Pushkin's words:** The words are drawn from a stanza in "19 October" (1825) where the poet, celebrating the anniversary of his old school, proposes a toast to the tsar who had founded it. This was the same tsar who had sent Pushkin into exile.

310  **Solzhenitser:** A name like Solzhenitser would suggest a Jewish origin.

313  **"Knots":** The term "Knot" is derived from the mathematical concept of "nodal point." It suggests a point in history where the complex and interrelated issues of the time find their sharpest focus and where the essential (and otherwise frequently hidden) forces of the historical process are revealed. *August 1914* is subtitled "Knot I"; the following two "Knots" will be *October 1916* and *March 1917.*

314  **atheists:** In the afterword to the Russian edition of *August 1914,* omitted in the English translation, the author condemns the ideologically inspired Soviet custom of writing "God" with a lower-case *g.*

340  **Benya Krik:** A colorful and swaggering gangster in Isaak Babel's *Odessa Stories.*

346  **buried:** The author has new information to refute the official verdict of suicide.

361  **Volodin:** In the opening chapter of *The First Circle,* the Soviet diplomat Innokenti Volodin telephones a friend to warn him of a trap set by the secret police. (In the ninety-six-chapter version of the novel, Volodin instead tries to alert the American Embassy to the existence of a spy ring.) Reshetovskaya is ascribing an equally momentous role to her conversation with the author.

368 **P. Kapitsa's "rebellion":** In 1946 the physicist Pyotr Kapitsa lost the directorship of Moscow's Institute of Physical Problems and rumor had it that he had refused to work on the development of nuclear weapons. He returned to head the Institute after Stalin's death.

374 **Petrovsky:** I. G. Petrovsky had promised Sakharov to look into the case of the imprisoned psychiatrist Semyon Gluzman. It was insinuated that Petrovsky had committed suicide as a result of becoming embroiled in this affair.

436 **Travkin:** Reference to Solzhenitsyn's arrest in 1945 in the presence of Travkin, his brigade commander, who remained favorably disposed to Solzhenitsyn in spite of the arrest. See *The Gulag Archipelago*, Volume I, pages 19–20.

437 **Mayakovsky had once dreamed:** See, for example, Mayakovsky's "Homeward Bound" (1925).

440 **Butyrki prison cells:** On this episode see *The Gulag Archipelago*, Volume I, pages 274–276.

443 **"alien land":** Opening lines of Solzhenitsyn's *Prussian Nights.*

472 **Untimely Thoughts:** Gorky's initial hostility to the Bolshevik regime found expression in a series of articles published in 1917 and 1918, most of which bore the title *Untimely Thoughts.* Sergei Sergeyev-Tsensky, the author of numerous works glorifying the "transfiguration" of Russia under the Communists, had at one point collaborated with the Whites during the Russian Civil War.

486 **appendix:** Reference to Safonov's diplomatic illness. See page 258 above.

499 **On the Ninth Day:** The Eastern Orthodox tradition calls for a special memorial service to be performed on the ninth day after a person's death.

517 **"letter" from the death chamber:** Traicho Kostov, a Bulgarian Communist leader, was arrested in Stalin's purge of high-ranking Party members in Eastern Europe. At his public trial in 1949, he unexpectedly repudiated his earlier confession and refused to admit any guilt. But shortly before his execution, a letter purportedly written by Kostov was released in which he acknowledged "Titoist machinations."

# Glossary

This glossary provides brief biographical information on individuals mentioned in the text who are not readily recognizable to the nonspecialist reader. Also glossed are a number of literary and historical allusions, institutions, terms and places.

*Abakumov, Viktor Semyonovich* (1897–1954). High government official; Minister of State Security 1946–1952; executed under Khrushchev.

*Abalkin, Nikolai Aleksandrovich* (b. 1906). Drama critic.

*Abashidze, Irakly Vissarionovich* (b. 1909). Georgian poet, literary bureaucrat.

*Abdumonunov, Toktobolot* (b. 1922). Kirghiz playwright.

*Abramov, Fyodor Aleksandrovich* (b. 1920). Literary critic and novelist of village life.

*Adzhubei, Aleksei Ivanovich* (b. 1924). Khrushchev's son-in-law; editor in chief of *Izvestia* during Khrushchev's years in power.

*Agitprop.* Agitation and propaganda; an important function carried out by professionals at all levels of Soviet society and coordinated at the highest levels of the Party.

*Aitmatov, Chingiz* (b. 1928). Kirghiz author; writes in his native language and in Russian.

*Akhmatova (Gorenko), Anna Andreyevna* (1889–1966). Poet, one of the greatest in Russia's "Silver Age." Denounced by Zhdanov in 1946.

*Aksakov, Ivan Sergeyevich* (1823–1886). Poet and Slavophile essayist.

*Aleksei Mikhailovich* (1629–1676). Became Tsar of Moscow in 1645.

*Alekseyev, Mikhail Nikolayevich* (b. 1918). Editor of the journal *Moskva,* official of the Writers' Union.

*Alexander II* (1818–1881). Tsar 1855–1881; his reign was notable for the emancipation of the serfs (1861) and other important reforms. Assassinated by terrorists.

*Alliluyeva, Svetlana.* Stalin's daughter; escaped to the West in 1967.

*Alya. See* Svetlova.

543

*Amalrik, Andrei Alekseyevich* (b. 1938). Dissident historian and writer, author of *Will the Soviet Union Survive Till 1984?* Imprisoned and exiled to Siberia. Emigrated in 1976.

*Andropov, Yuri Vladimirovich* (b. 1914). Head of the KGB since 1967.

*APN. See* Novosti.

*apparatchik.* A functionary of the Party or government. The word suggests a cog in a machine or "apparatus."

*Asanov, Nikolai Aleksandrovich* (b. 1906). Poet and prose writer.

*Astafyev, Viktor Petrovich* (b. 1924). Writer especially concerned with rural life.

*Babel, Isaak Emmanuilovich* (1894–1941). Major short story writer; died during the purge.

*Bandera, Stepan* (1902–1959). Leader of militant Ukrainian nationalist movement. Assassinated in Munich by a Soviet agent.

*Barabanov, Yevgeny Viktorovich* (b. 1944). Art historian; contributor to the collection *From Under the Rubble.*

*Baruzdin, Sergei Alekseyevich* (b. 1926). Author of children's books.

*Barvikha.* Resort and rest home near Moscow set aside for high government and Party officials.

*Bazhan, Mikola* (b. 1904). Ukrainian poet and government official.

*Bek, Aleksandr Alfredovich* (b. 1902). Writer. His novel about high-level Soviet bureaucrats, *The New Appointment,* was announced for publication in *Novy Mir* in 1965 but banned by the censors.

*Belov, Vasily Ivanovich* (b. 1933). Writer particularly interested in village life.

*Belov, Yuri Sergeyevich* (b. 1941). After a term in camp, Belov described his experience in *Report from Darkness.* The manuscript was seized and Belov was rearrested in 1968 and sent to a strict regime camp, then to a psychiatric institution to be "cured" of his religious convictions.

*Benckendorff, Count Aleksandr Khristoforovich* (1781–1844). Chief of the secret police (the so-called Third Department) under Tsar Nicholas I.

*Berdyaev, Nikolai Aleksandrovich* (1874–1948). Philosopher and religious thinker, exiled to the West in 1922. His works have been very influential among Soviet dissidents.

*Beria, Lavrenti Pavlovich* (1899–1953). Head of Stalin's internal security agencies from 1938 until Stalin's death. Executed.

*Big House.* KGB headquarters in Leningrad.

*Bogoraz, Larissa* (b. 1929). Arrested with six others for demonstrating against the 1968 Soviet invasion of Czechoslovakia. Sentenced to four years in corrective labor camp.

*Böll, Heinrich* (b. 1917). German novelist; winner of 1972 Nobel Prize in Literature.

*Bondarev, Yuri Vasilyevich* (b. 1924). Official of the Writers' Union. The *New York Times* published his comment on *The Gulag Archipelago* on January 24, 1974.

*Borisov, Vadim* (b. 1945). Dissident Church historian, contributor to the collection *From Under the Rubble.*

*Brooke, Gerald.* British lecturer arrested and tried in the Soviet Union in 1965 for bringing in anti-Soviet materials. Cooperated with the prosecution.

*Brovka, Petrus* (b. 1905). Byelorussian poet and government official.

*Bukharin, Nikolai Ivanovich* (1888–1938). Prominent Party official and economic theorist. Executed after 1938 show trial.

*Bukovsky, Vladimir Konstantinovich* (b. 1942). Celebrated dissident and veteran of prisons, camps and special psychiatric hospitals. In 1971 sent to the West detailed forensic case reports on several dissenters being held in psychiatric institutions. Arrested and sentenced to twelve years, but in 1976 exchanged for a Chilean Communist.

*Bulgakov, Mikhail Afanasyevich* (1891–1940). Satirical novelist. Author of *The Master and Margarita.*

*Bulgakov, Father Sergius* (Sergei Nikolayevich; 1871–1944). Philosopher, controversial theologian and ordained priest; exiled to the West in 1922.

*Bunin, Ivan Alekseyevich* (1870–1953). Winner of 1933 Nobel Prize in Literature. Lived in France after 1920.

*Burg, David.* British journalist born in the Soviet Union. Coauthor, with George Feifer, of a 1972 biography of Solzhenitsyn, which the subject has denounced as unreliable.

*Bykov, Vasily Vladimirovich* (b. 1924). Byelorussian writer; principal works deal with the Second World War.

*Chaadayev, Pyotr Yakovlevich* (1794–1856). Philosopher; his 1836 essay argued that Russia had neither past nor future, largely because of the absence of the shaping force of Catholicism. Declared insane, Chaadayev was confined to his home for a year.

*Chakovsky, Aleksandr Borisovich* (b. 1913). Writer; head of *Literaturnaya Gazeta* since 1962.

*Chalidze, Valery Nikolayevich* (b. 1938). Physicist; cofounder (1970) of the Moscow Human Rights Committee. Stripped of Soviet citizenship while on a trip to the West.

*Chalmayev, Viktor Andreyevich* (b. 1932). Critic and journalist who tries to combine traditional Russian nationalism with loyalty to the regime.

*Cheka.* Acronym for Extraordinary Commission, the Soviet internal security agency from 1917 to 1922. The term is often applied informally to the succeeding security agencies (GPU, OGPU, NKVD, MGB, KGB).

*Chernyshevsky, Nikolai Gavrilovich* (1828–1889). Literary critic and radical essayist, author of the novel *What Is to Be Done?* (1863), which influenced revolutionary ideology. Spent nineteen years in Siberian exile.

*CHON.* Acronym for Special Purpose Forces, punitive military units used during the early years of the Soviet regime.

*Chukovskaya, Lydia Korneyevna* (b. 1907). Critic, essayist and novelist. Expelled from the Writers' Union in 1974.

*Chukovsky, Kornei Ivanovich* (1882–1969). Critic, essayist, translator, celebrated author of poems for children and Solzhenitsyn's benefactor.

*COMES.* Acronym for Comunità Europea degli Scrittori, a leftist writers' organization formed in 1958.

*CPSU.* Communist Party of the Soviet Union.

*Daniel, Yuli Markovich* (b. 1925). Writer; arrested and tried with Andrei Sinyavsky in 1965 for having published abroad.

*Decembrists.* The Russian officers who took part in the unsuccessful liberal uprising against Nicholas I on December 14, 1825.

*Dementyev, Aleksandr Grigoryevich* (b. 1904). Critic and journalist; member of editorial board of *Novy Mir* in the 1960s.

*Demichev (Dyomichev), Pyotr Nilovich* (b. 1918). High Party official, specialist in ideology; Secretary of the Central Committee of the CPSU.

*Dobrolyubov, Nikolai Aleksandrovich* (1836–1867). Literary critic and essayist. With Chernyshevsky, he laid the theoretical foundations of the Russian radical movement.

*Dorosh, Yefim Yakovlevich* (1908–73). Writer whose main works are set in the Russian countryside. Best known for *Rural Diary* (1956–67).

*Dyakov, Boris Aleksandrovich* (b. 1902). Writer; arrested in 1949. Two works based on his years in the camps appeared in the early 1960s; both reveal unwavering faith in the Party.

*Dzerzhinsky, Feliks Edmundovich* (1877–1926). First head of the Soviet internal security agencies.

*Ehrenburg, Ilya Grigoryevich* (1891–1967). Novelist and journalist; veteran Soviet representative at various international congresses.

*Eshliman. See* Yakunin.

*Fadeyev, Aleksandr Aleksandrovich* (1901–1956). Novelist and playwright; official of the Writers' Union. Committed suicide after Khrushchev's revelations of the crimes of Stalin.

*Farge, Yves* (1899–1953). President of the peace movement in France. Died in an alleged automobile accident in the Soviet Union.

*FBON.* Acronym for Fundmanetal Library of the Social Sciences, an institution affiliated with the Academy of Sciences.

*Fedin, Konstantin Aleksandrovich* (1892–1977). Novelist, president of the Writers' Union from 1971 till his death.

*Feifer, George.* American writer and journalist. *See* Burg, David.

*Florensky, Pavel Aleksandrovich* (1882–1943). Scientist, philosopher and theologian, later ordained priest. Arrested in the 1920s, he spent the remainder of his life in prisons and camps.

*Frank, Semyon Lyudvigovich* (1877–1950). Philosopher and leading representative of the religious and philosophical renaissance of the early twentieth century. Lived in the West after 1922.

*Furtseva, Yekaterina Alekseyevna* (1910–1974). High Party official; Minister of Culture from 1960 until her death.

*Galanskov, Yuri Timofeyevich* (1939–1972). Dissident poet, essayist and editor. Imprisoned several times in psychiatric institutions. In 1966 ruled "responsible" and sentenced to seven years in strict regime camp, where he died from lack of medical care.

*Galich, Aleksandr Akadyevich* (1919–1978). Poet and "bard" whose songs became widely popular in the Soviet Union. Expelled from the Writers' Union in 1971, emigrated in 1974.

*Gerasimov, Yevgeny Nikolayevich* (b. 1903). Writer and journalist.

*Gershuni, Vladimir Lvovich* (b. 1930). Bricklayer, veteran of the camps.

*Ginzburg, Aleksandr Ilyich* (b. 1937). Dissident writer and journalist; compiler of "White Book" on Sinyavsky-Daniel trial. Rearrested in 1977 for aid to families of political prisoners; deported to the U.S. in 1979.

*Glavlit.* Acronym for Main Administration of Literary and Publishing Affairs, the Soviet censorship agency.

*Gonchar, Oles Terentyevich* (b. 1918). Ukrainian writer and high Party official.

*Goncharov, Ivan Aleksandrovich* (1814–1891). Novelist; best remembered for *Oblomov* (1859).

*Gorbatov, Aleksandr Vasilyevich* (b. 1891). General in the Red Army, spent 1929 to 1941 in Siberian exile, published ideologically orthodox memoirs in the mid 1960s.

*Grani.* Russian émigré literary journal, published in Frankfurt since 1945. Has specialized in printing samizdat materials.

*Granin, Daniil Aleksandrovich* (b. 1918). Novelist.

*Great Break.* Designation for the radical change in Soviet society brought about by the first Five-Year Plan (1928–1933). Its most significant component was the forced collectivization of agriculture, which precipitated a catastrophic famine.

*Grigorenko, Pyotr Grigoryevich* (b. 1907). Retired major general of the Soviet army, first arrested in 1964, rearrested in 1969 for defending the rights of the Crimean Tatars. Confined to a psychiatric institution; released in 1974. Came to U.S. in 1977; stripped of Soviet citizenship in 1978.

*Grin (Grinevsky), Aleksandr Stepanovich* (1880–1932). Popular writer of adventure stories. In the late 1940s subjected to a violent posthumous attack as a purveyor of "cosmopolitanism."

*Grossman, Vasily Semyonovich* (1905–1964). Author of the novel *Forever Flowing,* posthumously published abroad, whose protagonist is a veteran of the camps.

*Gumilev, Nikolai Stepanovich* (1886–1921). Acmeist poet; first husband of Anna Akhmatova. Shot for alleged involvement in a counterrevolutionary conspiracy.

*Henry, Ernst* (pseud.). Soviet journalist frequently sent on missions abroad.

*Hermogen, Patriarch.* Head of the Russian Orthodox Church in the early seventeenth century, influential advocate of Russian resistance to the Poles during the Time of Troubles.

*Ikramov, Kamil Akmalevich* (b. 1927). Writer and playwright.

*Ilyichev, Leonid Fyodorovich* (b. 1906). Member of the Central Committee of the CPSU; chief of the Agitprop department of the Central Committee 1958–1965.

*Isakovsky, Mikhail Vasilyevich* (1900–1973). Poet; a number of his poems have become popular songs.

*Ivanov, Vyacheslav Vsevolodovich* (b. 1929). Linguist, literary scholar, specialist in poetics.

*John of Kronstadt.* Popular appellation of Father John Sergiev (1829–1908), parish priest in the naval fortress of Kronstadt. Regarded by his many admirers as a living saint, he was detested in left-wing circles for his conservative political views. Canonized by the Russian Orthodox Church Abroad in 1964.

*Kapitsa, Pyotr Leonidovich* (b. 1894). Physicist; ranking member of the Academy of Sciences.

*Karavansky, Svyatoslav* (b. 1920). Ukrainian nationalist; imprisoned for some 30 years. Emigrated in 1979.

*Karyakin, Yuri Fyodorovich* (b. 1920). Philosopher and literary critic.

*katorga.* Word used in tsarist era for "forced labor," reintroduced by Stalin in 1943 to designate the harshest labor camps.

*Kaverin (Silber), Veniamin Aleksandrovich* (b. 1902). Liberal novelist.

*Kazakevich, Emmanuil Genrikhovich* (1913–62). Writer and journalist.

*Kazakov, Yuri Pavlovich* (b. 1927). Writer prominent in the 1960s.

*Kedrina, Zoya Sergeyevna* (b. 1904). "Public prosecutor" at the trial of Sinyavsky and Daniel.

*Kerbabayev, Berdy* (b. 1894). Turkmenian writer and literary official.

*Kerensky, Aleksandr Fyodorovich* (1881–1970). Socialist Revolutionary politician, head of provisional government July–November 1917. Fled to France; died in the U.S.

*Khrennikov, Tikhon Nikolayevich* (b. 1913). Long-term head of the Union of Soviet Composers.

*Kirov (Kostrikov), Sergei Mironovich* (1886–1934). High Party official in Leningrad whose assassination (allegedly inspired by Stalin) was a pretext for Stalin's great purge.

*Klychkov (Leshenkov), Sergei Antonovich* (1889–1940). Poet and prose writer, with particular interest in the peasant tradition. Arrested in 1937 and died in camp.

*Klyuchevsky, Vasily Osipovich* (1841–1911). Russian historian.

*Klyuyev, Nikolai Alekseyevich* (1887–1937). Peasant poet who at first welcomed the Revolution. Arrested in 1933 for "kulak sympathies"; died in Siberia.

*Kochetov, Vsevolod Anisimovich* (1912–1973). Prolific novelist; editor of *Oktyabr* from 1961 until his death.

*Kohout, Pavel* (b. 1928). Czech novelist, playwright and leading dissident. Stripped of Czech citizenship in 1979 while abroad.

*Koltsov, Aleksei Vasilyevich* (1809–1842). Poet of country life.

*Konev (Koniev), Ivan Stepanovich* (1897–1973). Marshal of the Soviet Union in World War II; Commander in Chief of the Warsaw Pact 1955–1960.

*Kopelev, Lev Zinovyevich* (b. 1912). Critic and essayist, specialist in German literature. Solzhenitsyn's fellow prisoner in the Marfino *sharashka*.

*Korin, Pavel Dmitriyevich* (1892–1967). Painter whose portraits of priests, monks and nuns (studies for a projected large-scale painting), first exhibited in 1963, are known collectively as "Vanishing Russia."

*Korneichuk, Aleksandr Yevdokimovich* (1905–1972). Ukrainian playwright and public official.

*Kosolapov, Valery Aleksandrovich* (b. 1910). Writer and journalist; Tvardovsky's successor as editor in chief of *Novy Mir* 1970–1974.

*Kosygin, Aleksei Nikolayevich* (b. 1904). Chairman of the Council of Ministers of the U.S.S.R.; member of Politburo.

*Kozhevnikov, Vadim Mikhailovich* (b. 1909). Ideologically orthodox novelist.

*Krasin, Viktor* (b. 1929). Economist; veteran of Stalin's camps. Defendant with Pyotr Yakir in a 1973 trial designed to stop publication of *Chronicle of Current Events*. Received a light sentence in return for cooperating with the prosecution. Emigrated.

*Krasivsky, Zynovi.* Imprisoned Ukrainian nationalist.

*kuluk.* In Soviet times, the designation of any prosperous peasant, all of whom were considered "class enemies."

*Kurchatov Institute.* Nuclear physics research institute in Moscow.

*Kuznetsov, Anatoly Vasilyevich* (1929–1979). Writer; best known for his novel *Babi Yar* (1966), which describes the mass atrocities in World War II in German-occupied Kiev. Defected in 1969.

*Lakshin, Vladimir Yakovlevich* (b. 1933). Literary critic.

*Larni, Martti* (b. 1909). Finnish Communist writer and journalist.

*Lebedev, Vladimir Semyonovich.* Ex-journalist; Khrushchev's adviser and personal secretary.

*Leonov, Leonid Maksimovich* (b. 1899). Novelist and playwright.

*Leontiev (Leontyev), Konstantin Nikolayevich* (1831–1891). Writer, critic, philosophical opponent of Western democratic tradition.

*Leontovich, Mikhail Aleksandrovich* (b. 1903). Theoretical physicist.

*Lermontov, Mikhail Yuryevich* (1814–1841). Romantic poet and novelist, first famous for his bitter poem on Pushkin's death ("Death of a Poet," 1837). Killed in a duel.

*Lifshitz, Mikhail Aleksandrovich* (b. 1905). Marxist philosopher and literary critic.

*Likhachev, Dmitri Sergeyevich* (b. 1906). Literary scholar and medievalist.

*Literaturnaya Gazeta.* Literary weekly, published in Moscow by the Writers' Union. Commonly referred to as *Litgazeta.*

*Litfond.* Founded in 1934 and affiliated with the Writers' Union; gives financial assistance to writers, controls vacation retreats, clinics, clubs and bookstores reserved for members of the union.

*Litfrontovtsy.* Adherents of "Litfront," a superorthodox Marxist group which split with RAPP (q.v.) over ideology in 1930.

*Litvinov, Pavel Mikhailovich.* (b. 1940). Physicist; spent five years in exile for participating in 1968 demonstration against the invasion of Czechoslovakia. Emigrated in 1974.

*Lubyanka.* Chief prison in Moscow and headquarters of the KGB.

*Lundkvist, Arthur* (b. 1906). Swedish poet; Lenin Prize winner in 1957.

*Lunts, Daniil* (b. 1911). Psychiatrist; head of the diagnostic section of Moscow's Serbsky Institute, notorious for diagnosing "schizophrenia" in political dissidents and religious believers.

*Maksimov, Vladimir Yemelyanovich* (b. 1932). Writer; expelled from the Writers' Union in 1973; emigrated in 1974.

*Mandelstam, Osip Emilyevich* (1891–1938). Major poet; arrested for anti-Stalin epigram, he died in a camp. A collection of his poems was finally published in the Soviet Union in 1973.

*Marchenko, Anatoly Tikhonovich* (b. 1938). Working-class dissident; in *My Testimony,* described his seven years in prison. Rearrested several times since 1967.

*Markov, Georgi Mokeyevich* (b. 1911). Official in the Writers' Union.

*Marshak, Samuil Yakovlevich* (1887–1964). Poet, translator, editor; best known for his poems for children.

*Maryamov, Aleksandr Moiseyevich* (b. 1909). Writer and critic.

*Matushkin, Vasily Semyonovich* (b. 1906). Minor writer.

*Mayakovsky, Vladimir Vladimirovich* (1893–1930). Called the "poet of the Russian Revolution," he was nevertheless attacked by the ideologues of RAPP (q.v.). Committed suicide.

*Medvedev, Roy Aleksandrovich* (b. 1925). Historian who argues that the offenses of the Stalin era are accidental deformations in the fundamentally sound Marxist-Leninist system.

*Medvedev, Zhores Aleksandrovich* (b. 1925). Biologist; twin brother of Roy. Opposed Lysenko's genetics. Arrested and confined in a psychiatric institution (1970) for criticizing the regime. Released after international protests; stripped of his Soviet citizenship while in England.

*Mezhelaitis, Eduardas* (b. 1919). Lithuanian poet and Party official.

*Mikhailov, Boris.* Defended Solzhenitsyn during violent 1974 Soviet campaign against *The Gulag Archipelago.*

*Mikhailovsky, Nikolai Konstantinovich* (1842–1904). Literary critic and essayist; chief ideologist of Russian populism.

*Mikhalkov, Sergei Vladimirovich* (b. 1913). Conformist poet and prose writer, best known for his children's books.

*Mikoyan, Anastas Ivanovich* (1895–1978). High Party official, famous for his flexibility in adapting to changes in the Party line.

*Molodaya Gvardia.* Conservative political and literary journal with nationalist tendencies.

*Moskva.* Literary monthly. Despite its generally conservative editorial policy, some important works have appeared in its pages (Bulgakov's *The Master and Margarita,* Bunin's *Life of Arsenyev,* etc.).

*Mozhayev, Boris Andreyevich* (b. 1923). Writer about village life.

*Musrepov, Gabid Makhmudovich* (b. 1902). Kazakh writer and Party functionary.

*Napostovtsy.* Writers connected with the journal *Na postu* (On Guard), later *Na literaturnom postu,* devoted to "pure" proletarian literature.

*Nekrasov, Nikolai Alekseyevich* (1821–1877). Poet, essayist and editor; radical sympathizer, remembered for his poetic descriptions of peasant and lower-class life.

*Nekrasov, Viktor Platonovich* (b. 1911). Novelist, best known for his war novel *In the Trenches of Stalingrad* (1946). Emigrated in 1974.

*Nicholas I* (1796–1855). Tsar 1825–1855.

*Nikitin, Ivan Savvich* (1829–1861). Poet of rural life.

*Nosov, Yevgeny Ivanovich* (b. 1925). Writer about rural life.

*Novichenko, Leonid Nikolayevich* (b. 1914). Ukrainian literary critic.

*Novosti.* Soviet press agency (abbreviated as APN), formed in 1961. Publishes books, magazines, newspapers, bulletins and brochures in over fifty languages to "aid friendship among peoples."

*Novy Mir.* Literary and political monthly, published in Moscow since 1925. The leading voice of liberalism in the 1950s and '60s.

*obkom.* Acronym for *oblastnoy komitet,* a governing body of the Party at the oblast, or district, level.

*Ogonyok.* Illustrated large-circulation weekly with regular literary supplements.

*Ogurtsov, Igor Vyacheslavovich* (b. 1937). Leader of the All-Russian Social-Christian Union for the Liberation of the People. Arrested in 1967, sentenced to twenty years of prison and exile.

*Oktyabr.* Politically orthodox literary monthly, founded in 1924 as a "proletarian" journal. The only major periodical that did not praise *One Day in the Life of Ivan Denisovich.*

*Okudzhava, Bulat Shalvovich* (b. 1924). Novelist, poet, popular song writer and singer.

*Old Believers.* Long persecuted (until mid nineteenth century) members of the Russian Orthodox Church who refused to accept seventeenth-century reforms.

*oprichniki.* In the sixteenth century, the special corps created by Ivan the Terrible to suppress opposition; used by extension to designate a police force characterized by extreme cruelty.

*Ossietzky, Carl von* (1889–1938). German journalist imprisoned 1933–1936 for criticizing Hitler and Nazis. Released from prison after receiving 1935 Nobel Peace Prize. His last two years were spent in semi-captivity in a hospital.

*Ozerov, Vitaly Mikhailovich* (b. 1917). Literary critic and journalist; secretary of the board of the Writers' Union.

*Pakhra (Krasnaya Pakhra).* A settlement of summer homes for the Soviet elite in the vicinity of Moscow.

*Palchinsky, Pyotr Akimovich* (1878–1929). High-level technical expert and former politician, shot in purge of the old intelligentsia.

*Pankin, Boris D.* (b. 1931). Head of VAAP, the Soviet copyright agency.

*Pankov, Viktor Ksenofontovich* (b. 1920). Critic and literary historian.

*Paustovsky, Konstantin Georgiyevich* (1892–1968). Writer. Six volumes of his memoirs appeared between 1945 and 1963.

*Peredelkino.* Settlement near Moscow restricted to the Soviet elite; includes a large proportion of writers.

*Petrovsky, Ivan Georgiyevich* (1901–1973). Mathematician; rector of Moscow University from 1951 until his death.

*Pilnyak (Vogau), Boris Andreyevich* (1894–1937). Writer who welcomed the Revolution but recoiled from its excesses. Shot during purge.

*Pimen.* Patriarch of Moscow and of All Russia (ecclesiastical name of Sergei Mikhailovich Izvekov, b. 1910). Elected head of the Russian Church in 1971.

*Pitsunda.* Resort on the Black Sea, used as a holiday retreat by Khrushchev.

*Platonov, Andrei Platonovich* (1899–1951). Novelist criticized in the 1930s for "kulak sympathies," whose work is widely admired in the Soviet Union today.

*pochvenniki.* Adherents to the concept of *pochvennichestvo* ("closeness to the soil"), which maintained that the nineteenth-century intelligentsia must return to the traditional values of the Russian people. Dostoyevsky was the best known of the *pochvenniki.*

*Podgorny, Nikolai Viktorovich* (b. 1903). High Party official; Chairman of the Presidium of the Supreme Soviet 1965–1977.

*Polikarpov, Dmitri Aleksandrovich* (b. 1905). Veteran of Agitprop; since 1962 chief of the Cultural Department of the Central Committee.

*Polizei.* A Soviet citizen in German-occupied territory who agreed to serve in a police unit under German control during World War II.

*Pomerantsev, Vladimir Mikhailovich* (b. 1907). Writer and literary critic. His article "On Sincerity in Literature" (*Novy Mir* 1953, No. 12) attacked the deadening conformity and didacticism of Stalinist literature. Tvardovsky first lost his job as editor of *Novy Mir* for publishing it.

*Posev.* Anti-Communist Russian political journal, published in Frankfurt since 1945.

*Pospelov, Gennady Nikolayevich* (b. 1899). Literary historian.

*Pozdnyayev, K. M.* Critic and journalist; editor of the weekly *Literaturnaya Rossia.*

*Pugachev, Yemelyan Ivanovich* (c. 1742–1775). Head of a large-scale uprising of Cossacks and peasants in the reign of Catherine II. Captured and executed.

*Pushkin House.* Major literary research institute in Leningrad, affiliated with the Academy of Sciences.

*Radishchev, Aleksandr Nikolayevich* (1742–1802). Generally regarded as the founder of the Russian revolutionary tradition. In his *Journey from St. Petersburg to Moscow* (1790) he attacked serfdom and called for the extermination of the nobles. Charged with treason and banished to Siberia. After returning, as member of a commission to draw up a new legal code, he tried to ease the lot of the serfs; committed suicide when his efforts were opposed.

*RAPP.* Russian Association of Proletarian Writers, an organization active 1925–1932 and noted for intolerance. Its members were known as *Rappovtsy.*

*Regelson, Lev Lvovich.* Physicist, dissident church historian. Arrested in 1979.

*Rekemchuk, Aleksandr Yevseyevich* (b. 1927). Journalist.

*Remizov, Aleksei Mikhailovich* (1877–1957). Novelist and dramatist. Emigrated to France in 1921.

*Reshetovskaya, Natalya Alekseyevna* (b. 1920). Chemist; married Solzhenitsyn in 1940, divorced him in 1949 while he was a prisoner. Remarried him in

1956, separated in late 1960s, final divorce in 1973.

*Rokossovski, Konstantin Konstantinovich* (1896–1968). Marshal of the Soviet Union. Military commander in World War II.

*Rostropovich, Mstislav Leopoldovich* (b. 1927). Cellist and conductor. After increasing harassment for having sheltered Solzhenitsyn, went abroad in 1974 with his wife, the soprano Galina Vishnevskaya; stripped of Soviet citizenship in 1978.

*Rublev (Rublyov), Andrei* (c. 1360–1430). Celebrated icon painter.

*Rudenko, Roman Andreyevich* (b. 1904). Attorney General of the U.S.S.R. since 1953.

*Rumyantsev, Aleksei Matveyevich* (b. 1905). Editor in chief of *Pravda* after Khrushchev's fall from power.

*Ryurikov, Boris Sergeyevich* (1909–1969). Literary critic, essayist, Party official in charge of Agitprop. Editor of *Inostrannaya Literatura* 1963–1969.

*Safonov, Ernst.* Chairman of the Ryazan branch of the Writers' Union.

*Sakharov, Andrei Dmitrievich* (b. 1921). Nuclear physicist; central figure in the dissident movement. Winner of 1975 Nobel Peace Prize.

*Salynsky, Afanasy Dmitrievich* (b. 1920). Writer.

*samizdat.* Material reproduced and circulated in unofficial or clandestine manner.

*Samsonov, Aleksandr Vasilyevich* (1859–1914). World War I general of the Imperial Russian Army; committed suicide after Russian defeat at the Battle of Tannenberg.

*Sartakov, Sergei Venediktovich* (b. 1908). Writer; official of the Writers' Union.

*Sats, Igor Aleksandrovich* (b. 1903). Literary critic and translator.

*Semichastny, Vladimir Yefimovich* (b. 1914). Head of the KGB 1961–1967; member of Central Committee of the CPSU 1964–1971.

*Serafim of Sarov, Saint* (1759–1833). A monk of the Sarov monastery who revived the tradition of the *starets* (spiritual adviser). Canonized in 1903.

*Sergius of Radonezh, Saint* (1314–1392). The most popular Russian saint, who combined mysticism with a practical concern for the Russian nation.

*Shafarevich, Igor Rostislavovich* (b. 1923). Mathematician of worldwide repute; winner of Lenin Prize in 1959; corresponding member of the Academy of Sciences. Contributor to *From Under the Rubble* and author of *The Socialist Phenomenon.*

*Shakhovskoy, D. I.* Literary critic, specialist on Chaadayev. Disappeared during purge.

*Shalamov, Varlam Tikhonovich* (b. 1907). Poet and prose writer. Arrested in 1937 and spent some twenty years in the camps, including seventeen in the Kolyma complex. His *Kolyma Stories,* based on this experience, are unpublished in the U.S.S.R., but his less controversial work appears regularly.

*sharashka.* Prison slang for a research institute staffed by prisoners, such as the one in *The First Circle.*

*Sharipov, Ady Sharipovich* (b. 1912). High government official and literary bureaucrat from Kazakhstan.

*Shcheglov, Mark Aleksandrovich* (1925–1956). Literary scholar and critic.

*Shelepin, Aleksandr Nikolayevich* (b. 1918). Head of the KGB 1958–1961; Secretary of the Central Committee 1961–1967. Dropped from C.C. in 1967; stripped of power in 1975. Nicknamed "Iron Shurik" for his hard-line views.

*Shelest, Georgi Ivanovich* (b. 1903). Minor prose writer.

*Shevchenko, Taras Grigoryevich* (1814–1861). Greatest Ukrainian poet. Spent ten years in exile for nationalist activities.

*Sholokhov, Mikhail Aleksandrovich* (b. 1905). Novelist notorious for excessive ideological orthodoxy. Winner of 1965 Nobel Prize in Literature. His authorship of the novel *Quiet Flows the Don* (1928–1940) is disputed.

*Shostakovich, Dmitri Dmitrievich* (1906–1975). Composer accused of "formalism" in 1936–1937 and again in 1948, but generally considered loyal to the regime. His *Testimony,* posthumously published abroad (1979), contradicts this assumption.

*Shukhevych, Yuri.* Ukrainian nationalist, imprisoned since the age of fourteen.

*Shukshin, Vasily Makarovich* (1929–1974). Writer about village life, film director, actor, and a cult figure since his death.

*Simonov, Konstantin Mikhailovich* (1915–1979). Poet, novelist, journalist and Party official. Editor in chief of *Novy Mir* 1946–1950 and 1954–1958.

*Sinyavsky, Andrei Donatovich* (b. 1925). Literary scholar and prose writer. Published his fictional works abroad under the pseudonym Abram Terz. Codefendant with Yuli Daniel in 1965; sentenced to seven years in camp. Emigrated to France in 1973.

*Smelyakov, Yaroslav Vasilyevich* (1913–72). Poet; imprisoned for several years in the 1930s.

*Smoktunovsky, Innokenty Mikhailovich* (b. 1925). Leading Soviet stage and film actor.

*Sobolev, Leonid Sergeyevich* (1898–1971). Novelist; official in Writers' Union.

*Sofronov, Anatoly Vladimirovich* (b. 1911). Poet and playwright; editor of *Ogonyok* since 1953.

*Soloukhin, Vladimir Alekseyevich* (b. 1924). Poet and prose writer.

*Solovyov, Vladimir Sergeyevich* (1853–1900). Philosopher and poet; influential figure in the turn-of-the-century religious and philosophical renaissance.

*Sovremennik.* Journal founded by Pushkin in 1836; one of the chief organs of the liberal and radical intelligentsia after 1847.

*"Sovremennik."* Theater in Moscow with liberal reputation.

*Strada, Vittorio.* Italian liberal Communist, specialist in Soviet literature.

*Struve, Pyotr Berngardovich* (1870–1944). Economist and political writer. Starting as a theorist of Marxism, he became a leading member of the *Vekhi* movement.

*Surkov, Aleksei Aleksandrovich* (b. 1899). Ideologically orthodox poet and editor; first secretary of the Writers' Union during the Pasternak affair.

*Suslov, Mikhail Andreyevich* (b. 1902). Politburo's ideological specialist, instrumental in ousting Khrushchev.

*Suvorov, Aleksandr Vasilyevich* (1730–1800). Outstanding military commander.

*Sverstyuk, Yevhen.* Ukrainian nationalist literary critic.

*Svetlova, Natalya Dmitrievna (Alya).* Mathematician; second wife of Solzhenitsyn.

*Svetlychny, Ivan.* Ukrainian literary critic and dissident.

*Svirsky, Grigory Tsezarovich.* Writer; expelled from Writers' Union in 1968 for criticizing inadequate opposition to anti-Semitism. Emigrated to Israel in 1971.

*Sytin, Ivan Dmitrievich* (1851–1934). Prominent pre-Revolutionary book publisher.

*Tabidze, Titsian Yustinovich* (1895–1937). Georgian poet; died in purge.

*Talantov, Boris Vladimirovich* (1903–1971). Mathematics teacher, essayist on church affairs and religious persecution. Arrested in 1969; died in camp.

*Tambov.* Town some 250 miles SE of Moscow, center of a massive anti-Bolshevik peasant uprising in 1920–1921.

*Tarsis, Valery Yakovlevich* (b. 1906). Writer arrested in 1962 after two stories were published abroad; interned in a psychiatric institution, released after Western protests. His *Ward No. 7* was the first detailed exposition of Soviet abuse of psychiatry. Emigrated in 1966.

*Taurin, Franz Nikolayevich* (b. 1911). Writer and literary bureaucrat. After Tvardovsky's removal in 1970, became editor of prose department of *Novy Mir.*

*Tendryakov, Vladimir Fyodorovich* (b. 1923). Popular novelist.

*Tolstoy, Aleksandra Lvovna* (1884–1979). Youngest daughter of Lev Tolstoy; his secretary in his last years. Arrested several times after the Revolution, emigrated in 1929, eventually to U.S. In 1939 she established the Tolstoy Foundation, a refugee resettlement agency.

*Trifonov, Yuri Valentinovich* (b. 1925). Novelist.

*TsAGI.* Acronym for Central Aero-Hydrodynamics Institute (Moscow).

*TsGALI.* Acronym for Central State Archive of Literature and Art (Moscow).

*Tsvetayeva, Marina Ivanovna* (1892–1941). Poet and essayist; emigrated in 1922. Returned to the U.S.S.R. in 1939 and committed suicide.

*Turchin, Valentin F.* Physicist (b. 1931). Prominent member of the Democratic Movement. Emigrated in 1977.

*Tvardovsky, Aleksandr Trifonovich* (1910–71). Poet, journalist, high Party official. Editor in chief of *Novy Mir* 1950–54 and 1958–70.

*Twentieth Congress of the Communist Party.* February 1956, scene of Khrushchev's famous speech on Stalin's "cult of personality" and its dire consequences.

*Twenty-second Congress of the Communist Party.* October 1961, the high point of Khrushchev's de-Stalinization campaign. Voted to remove Stalin's body from the Lenin-Stalin mausoleum. Tvardovsky called on writers to abandon Stalinist portrayal of Soviet life.

*Tychina, Pavlo Grigoryevich* (1891–1967). Ukrainian poet and Party official.

*VAAP.* Soviet agency formed in 1973, after the U.S.S.R. became a signatory to the International Copyright Convention, to handle all dealings of Soviet authors with foreign publishers.

*Vagin, Yevgeny Aleksandrovich* (b. 1938). Literary scholar; spent eight years in the camps for his role in the All-Russian Social-Christian Union for the Liberation of the People (*see* Ogurtsov). Emigrated in 1976.

*Vasilyev, Pavel Nikolayevich* (1910–1937). Poet; shot during purge.

*Vertinsky, Aleksandr Nikolayevich* (1889–1957). Poet, composer; popular performer of his own works. Emigrated in 1919, returned to the Soviet Union in 1943.

*Vesely, Artem* (*Kochkurov, Nikolai Ivanovich;* 1899–1939). Writer; disappeared during purge.

*Vigorelli, Giancarlo* (b. 1913). Italian journalist; secretary general of the European Community of Writers (COMES).

*Vinogradov, Viktor Vladimirovich* (1895–1969). Philologist; head of the Institute of Russian Language at the Academy of Sciences.

*Vitkevich, Nikolai.* Solzhenitsyn's codefendant in 1945. Joined the attack on Solzhenitsyn after publication of *The Gulag Archipelago.*

*Vladimir Prison.* High-security prison complex in the city of Vladimir.

*Vladimov, Georgi Nikolayevich* (b. 1931). Writer. Resigned from the Writers' Union in 1977 in protest against expulsion of nonconformist writers.

*Vlasov, Andrei Andreyevich* (1900–1946). General of the Soviet Army, captured by the Germans in 1942; leader of Russian prisoner-of-war units within German army. Surrendered to U.S. forces in 1945 and was turned over to the Soviets. Executed.

*Voinovich, Vladimir* (b. 1932). Satirist; expelled from the Writers' Union in 1974; author of *The Life and Extraordinary Adventures of Private Ivan Chonkin.*

*Voloshin, Maksimilian Aleksandrovich* (1878–1932). Symbolist poet, essayist and painter, champion of universal human values against political ones.

*Vorobyov, I. Y.* Former colonel of the MVD, accorded special privileges in the Marfino *sharashka* in Solzhenitsyn's time.

*Vorobyov, Oleg.* Dissident.

*Voronkov, Konstantin V.* Minor writer; official in the Writers' Union.

*Voroshilov Amnesty.* March 1953 decree releasing many thousands of nonpolitical prisoners from the camps. Klimenty Voroshilov was Soviet President 1953–1960.

*Voznesensky, Andrei Andreyevich* (b. 1933). Poet.

*Vyshinsky, Andrei Yanuaryevich* (1883–1955). High Party official, lawyer, close associate of Stalin. Chief state prosecutor in the show trials of the 1930s.

*Writers' Union.* Professional organization formed by Party decree in 1932 (all other literary organizations were simultaneously dissolved).

*Yagoda, Genrikh Grigoryevich* (1891–1938). Head of NKVD in 1934; conducted the early phase of Stalin's great purge. Replaced by Yezhov in 1936, accused of treason and shot.

*Yakir, Pyotr Ionovich* (b. 1923). Dissident historian. Codefendant with Victor Krasin (q.v.) in 1973 trial.

*Yakubovich-Melshin, Pyotr Filippovich* (1860–1911). Revolutionary poet. Arrested for terrorist activity, served eighteen years at hard labor. Author of *In the World of Outcasts* (1895–1898).

GLOSSARY / 557

*Yakunin, Father Gleb* (b. 1934). Activist dissident priest. Author, with Fr. Nikolai Eshliman, of "An Open Letter to His Holiness the Patriarch" (1965). Arrested in 1979.

*Yamaga Soko* (1622–1685). Japanese Confucian philosopher, formulated Samurai code.

*Yashen, Kamil* (b. 1909). Uzbek poet and high Party official.

*Yesenin, Sergei Aleksandrovich* (1895–1925). Lyric poet, vilified in the 1930s for alleged "kulak sympathies." Committed suicide.

*Yevtushenko, Yevgeny Aleksandrovich* (b. 1933). Poet.

*Yezhov, Nikolai Ivanovich* (1895–1939). Head of the NKVD in 1936, responsible for carrying out the great purge of 1936–1938. Succeeded by Beria.

*Yunost.* Literary monthly. Under the editorship of Katayev (1955–1962), acquired a liberal reputation.

*Zaks, Boris Germanovich.* Managing Secretary of *Novy Mir* in the 1950s and 1960s. Emigrated in 1979.

*Zabolotsky, Nikolai Alekseyevich* (1903–1958). Major poet; spent several years in camps and exile.

*Zalygin, Sergei Pavlovich* (b. 1913). Writer about village life.

*Zamyatin, Yevgeny Ivanovich* (1884–1937). Novelist, naval engineer, master stylist. Author of anti-utopian novel *We* (1921). Emigrated in 1931.

*Zdorovets, Boris.* Baptist dissident.

*zek.* Camp slang for "prisoner."

*Zhdanov, Andrei Andreyevich* (1896–1948). High Party functionary, Stalin's overseer of the arts. In charge of campaigns against "formalism" and other Western influences; denounced Akhmatova and Zoshchenko.

*Zholkovskaya, Irina.* Dissident; wife of Aleksandr Ginzburg.

*Zhukov, Georgi Konstantinovich* (1896–1974). Marshal of the Soviet Union; planned and carried out final Soviet assault on the German armies in World War II.

*Znamya.* Conservative literary monthly published by the Writers' Union.

*Zoshchenko, Mikhail Mikhailovich* (1895–1958). Satirist, enormously popular in the 1920s. Denounced by Zhdanov in 1946.

Glossary and Publisher's Notes compiled by Alexis Klimoff.

# Index